# THE UNDERGROUND RAILROAD

# THE UNDERGROUND RAILROAD

WILLIAM STILL

**Disclaimer**
Throughout the text, readers may find language and sentiments that appear both offensive and unacceptable. These words were duly reported by the former slave who wrote this book, and was forced to endure such dehumanizing attitudes on a daily basis. To better serve the author's original intentions and to ensure that the full impact of the writing is retained, we have decided to keep the original language in its entirety, though many segments may prove uncomfortable for the modern reader.

This edition published in 2020 by Arcturus Publishing Limited
26/27 Bickels Yard, 151–153 Bermondsey Street,
London SE1 3HA



Cover design: Peter Ridley
Cover illustration: Peter Gray

AD005695US

Printed in the UK

FSC www.fsc.org
MIX
Paper from responsible sources
FSC® C018072

# Contents

# *Introduction*

William Still's landmark *The Underground Railroad* was first published in 1872. Its emotive accounts of runaway black slaves were the product of the turbulent decade of the 1850s, as the country tumbled towards Civil War and the status of African-Americans, free and enslaved, reached its nadir. That war did not break out earlier was the result of a deal brokered between politicians from North and South that seemed to secure the future of slavery. The so-called Compromise of 1850 consisted of a clutch of new laws that sought to meet the challenges posed by the vast territories acquired by the United States at the end of the Mexican-American War of 1846–8.

At their heart lay the passing of the Fugitive Slave Act of 1850. This law strengthened the original 1793 act which had criminalized those assisting runaway slaves but had been weakly enforced. The deal benefitted the South, enraged Northerners, and undermined the security of the thousands of African-Americans living in non-slave states. The new law increased the punishment for those involved. Penalties were to be strictly enforced by federal officers across the Union committed to the recapture of fugitive slaves, even those who had been living in freedom for decades.

Unsurprisingly, the law also endangered the lives of freeborn African-Americans who, with little or no legal protection, became potential victims of ruthless Southern slave catchers supported by the might of the federal government. Reaction to the law, passed in September 1850, was immediate as anti-slavery societies across the Northern states asserted their opposition. In Philadelphia, few were more active than William Still.

Still was born in New Jersey in 1821, the son of a free black father and a fugitive slave mother who, in her escape from her owner in Maryland, had been forced to abandon two of her four children. The rescue of William's brother Peter from slavery by white abolitionist Seth Conklin more than forty years later forms the centerpiece of *The Underground Railroad*'s first gripping narrative. In 1844, Still left the family farm and moved to Philadelphia where he taught himself to read and write. By 1847, he was clerk of the city's Anti-Slavery Society, and in 1851, such were his talents that he was appointed Chairman of the society's most politicized branch, the Philadelphia Vigilance Committee. It aimed to oppose and subvert the new Fugitive Slave Law by aiding runaways in transit along the Underground Railroad to safe locations in the far North and Canada.

The rail road was, in fact, no rail road at all in the literal sense. However, whilst some historians of the mid-twentieth century argued that the term had no relevance beyond the realm of legend, it is now accepted that the concept of a rail road was very real for those involved. For William Still and others, the term "rail road" described a complex series of networks scattered across the states, North and South. This was no cohesive unified system. Instead, they operated at a local level and were linked by groups and individual agents. Together, they provided interconnected routes along which fugitives were transported via a series of safe houses to freedom. Common rail road terminology of the time was used to describe the various elements. Financial supporters were "stockholders," those who transported escapees were "conductors," the escapees themselves were "passengers," and they travelled from "station" to "station." These are all terms that resonate throughout Still's narratives. The term "underground railroad" emerged in the 1830s, though its exact origin is unclear. However, it undoubtedly reflected the transport revolution taking place across America. As rail road construction boomed, resulting in almost 30,000 miles of track by 1860, the country promoted the technological realization of its "Manifest Destiny" to span the continent. In response, African-Americans trumpeted their own aspirations for the future in the form of a railroad that led them to freedom.

Still's remit was broad. Philadelphia lay at the center of networks that extended along the east coast as far south as Georgia and as far north as Massachusetts. Throughout the 1850s, the Vigilance Committee supported the needs of hundreds of fugitives, providing medical and financial support, and assistance in securing the freedom of family members left behind. It also functioned as a communications hub for the broader African-American community, within and without the borders of the United States. Those who passed through Philadelphia were interviewed and it was Still who recorded their testimonies. Many remained in contact with him once they had reached freedom, soliciting his support and expressing their thanks.

The greatest irony, however, was that freedom for most was not to be found in the "land of liberty" itself. Some settled in the western part of New York State, but as Still's testimonies make clear, the majority opted for the neighboring province of Canada West, today's Ontario. As early as 1793, the Act Against Slavery had been passed in what was then Upper Canada, prohibiting the further importation of slaves and freeing the children of female slaves born after the passage of the act at the age of 25. In 1834, slavery was banned across the British Empire. The black population of the British colonies continued to battle prejudice and carry out most of the menial tasks, but they could run their own businesses, they had the right to vote, and, as British subjects, they received legal protection equal to whites. Many African-Americans, therefore, were more than happy to abandon the struggle for US citizenship and embrace that the protection being a British subject offered. Indeed, in the black imagination, the British provinces attained a status of mythic proportions. Crossing the Ohio River from slave to free state might have been the equivalent of crossing the Jordan. It was to the north that Canaan beckoned, and, to borrow a term coined by the African-Canadian poet Wayde Compton, the fleeing slave would arrive in an imagined "Xanada" (a combination of "Xanadu" and "Canada.")

It was not only fugitives who found succor in Canada. As early as 1829, free blacks in Cincinnati, Ohio, faced with the passing of restrictive anti-black laws, crossed the Detroit River to found the settlement of Wilberforce, named after the leading British abolitionist. Though the settlement was eventually disbanded, other communities such as Dawn and Elgin followed, ensuring that Canada West remained a Promised Land for them and their fugitive siblings. By 1860, approximately 30,000 African-Americans had fled the United States to find protection under the British flag. The letters that Still received from refugees, whose escape he had assisted, resonate with anguish over the wives, husbands, parents, and children left behind, but they also bear witness to the new-found sense of security enjoyed in British America.

Hitherto kept secret, Still's records and correspondence were published in 1872. *The Underground Railroad* was a massive work of several hundred pages, yet it immediately sold out. Such was the prestige of this archive of African-American voices that it was displayed at the Philadelphia Centennial Exhibition in 1876. Two other editions followed, in 1878 and 1883, both of which were avidly consumed by a fascinated public. What follows is a new abridged version of the 1878 edition, highlighting the most dramatic and poignant of the fugitive testimonies. Escape in a wooden crate, pursuit by bloodhounds, women disguised as men and vice versa, the terror of recapture: all are to be found in the accounts which Still entrusted to his diaries over more than a decade. The 1872 Preface was written during the high-tide of optimism that followed the passage of the Thirteenth Amendment abolishing slavery in the United States, and the Radical Reconstruction taking place in the defeated South with its promise of a bright future for the nation's newly enfranchised African-American citizens. Still made it clear that publication had been undertaken at the request of the Pennsylvania Anti-Slavery Society, which asked him to, "compile and publish his reminiscences and experiences relating to the 'Underground Rail Road.'" For him personally, the work freed the voices of those hitherto silent, raising the possibility of reunion for loved ones separated, whether by the auction block or the enforced flight to freedom, both echoing his own painful family experience. He also sought to commemorate a hard fought battle, "to show what efforts were made and what success was gained for Freedom under difficulties."

The tone of the Preface to this edition, however, is very different. By 1878, Reconstruction was on the wane leading to the emergence of a segregated society and the adoption of Jim Crow laws across the South, ghettoizing African-Americans, cheating them of the vote, relegating them to the status of second-class citizens. When Still reminds us that the antebellum South was "the prison-house," he seems to be drawing his readers' attention to both dangers overcome and those that lay ahead. Now, his aim was to reinvigorate the spirits of his fellow freedmen: "I have always cherished that this work would encourage the race in efforts for self-elevation." His testimonies have become reminders of a bitter past and aspirations only partially realized. His voices spoke of "the struggles of men and women to obtain their freedom, education and property," and for him, the future no longer seemed certain: "In the political struggles, the hopes of the race have been sadly disappointed. From this direction no great advantage is likely to arise very soon."

Throughout his life, Still continued to participate in Philadelphia's African-American community. He founded the city's first black YMCA, served as President of the Board of Managers of The Home for Aged and Infirm Colored Persons, and was known for his unstinting charitable donations. But it was for his work on the great rail road that he was remembered. Upon his death in 1902, the *New York Times* obituary of July 15th noted that Still "was known throughout the country as the 'Father of the Underground Railroad.'" This was a tribute not only to the key role he had played in assisting and supporting fellow African-Americans during their darkest hours and placing himself in great danger, but also testimony to the archival monument that he left to posterity in the form of *The Underground Railroad*.

GARETH HALLETT DAVIS
University College London
January 2017

# *Preface to the Revised Edition*

Like millions of my race, my mother and father were born slaves, but were not contented to live and die so. My father purchased himself in early manhood by hard toil. Mother saw no way for herself and children to escape the horrors of bondage but by flight. Bravely, with her four little ones, with firm faith in God and an ardent desire to be free, she forsook the prison house, and succeeded, through the aid of my father, to reach a free State. Here life had to be begun anew. The old familiar slave names had to be changed, and others, for prudential reasons, had to be found. This was not hard work. However, hardly months had passed ere the keen scent of the slave-hunters had trailed them to where they had fancied themselves secure. In those days all power was in the hands of the oppressor, and the capture of a slave mother and her children was attended with no great difficulty other than the crushing of freedom in the breast of the victims. Without judge or jury, all were hurried back to wear the yoke again. But back this mother was resolved never to stay. She only wanted another opportunity to again strike for freedom. In a few months after being carried back, with only two of her little ones, she took her heart in her hand and her babes in her arms, and this trial was a success. Freedom was gained, although not without the sad loss of her two older children, whom she had to leave behind. Mother and father were again reunited in freedom, while two of their little boys were in slavery. What to do for them other than weep and pray, were questions unanswerable. For over forty years the mother's heart never knew what it was to be free from anxiety about her lost boys. But no tidings came in answer to her many prayers, until one of them, to the great astonishment of his relatives, turned up in Philadelphia, nearly fifty years of age, seeking his long-lost parents. Being directed to the Anti-Slavery Office for instructions as to the best plan to adopt to find out the whereabouts of his parents, fortunately he fell into the hands of his own brother, the writer, whom he had never heard of before, much less seen or known. And here began revelations connected with this marvellous coincidence, which influenced me, for years previous to Emancipation, to preserve the matter found in the pages of this humble volume.

And in looking back now over these strange and eventful Providences, in the light of the wonderful changes wrought by Emancipation, I am more and more constrained to believe that the reasons, which years ago led me to aid the bondman and preserve the records of his sufferings, are to-day quite as potent in convincing me that the necessity of the times requires this testimony.

And since the first advent of my book, wherever reviewed or read by leading friends of freedom, the press, or the race more deeply represented by it, the expressions of approval and encouragement have been hearty and unanimous, and the thousands of volumes which have been sold by me, on the subscription plan, with hardly any facilities for the work, makes it obvious that it would, in the hands of a competent publisher, have a wide circulation.

And here I may frankly state, that but for the hope I have always cherished that this work would encourage the race in efforts for self-elevation, its publication never would have been undertaken by me.

I believe no more strongly at this moment than I have believed ever since the Proclamation of Emancipation was made by Abraham Lincoln, that as a class, in this country, no small exertion will have to be put forth before the blessings of freedom and knowledge can be fairly enjoyed by this people; and until colored men manage by dint of hard acquisition to enter the ranks of skilled industry, very little substantial respect will be shown them, even with the ballot-box and musket in their hands.

Well-conducted shops and stores; lands acquired and good farms managed in a manner to compete with any other; valuable books produced and published on interesting and important subjects – these are some of the fruits which the race are expected to exhibit from their newly gained privileges.

If it is asked "how?" I answer, "through extraordinary determination and endeavor," such as are demonstrated in hundreds of cases in the pages of this book, in the struggles of men and women to obtain their freedom, education and property.

These facts must never be lost sight of.

The race must not forget the rock from whence they were hewn, nor the pit from whence they were digged.

Like other races, this newly emancipated people will need all the knowledge of their past condition which they can get.

The bondage and deliverance of the children of Israel will never be allowed to sink into oblivion while the world stands.

Those scenes of suffering and martyrdom millions of

Christians were called upon to pass through in the days of the Inquisition are still subjects of study, and have unabated interest for all enlightened minds.

The same is true of the history of this country. The struggles of the pioneer fathers are preserved, produced and re-produced, and cherished with undying interest by all Americans, and the day will not arrive while the Republic exists, when these histories will not be found in every library.

While the grand little army of abolitionists was waging its untiring warfare for freedom, prior to the rebellion, no agency encouraged them like the heroism of fugitives. The pulse of the four millions of slaves and their desire for freedom, were better felt through "The Underground Railroad" than through any other channel.

Frederick Douglass, Henry Bibb, Wm. Wells Brown, Rev. J.W. Logan, and others, gave unmistakable evidence that the race had no more eloquent advocates than its own self-emancipated champions.

Every step they took to rid themselves of their fetters, or to gain education, or in pleading the cause of their fellow-bondmen in the lecture-room, or with their pens, met with applause on every hand, and the very argument needed was thus furnished in large measure. In those dark days previous to emancipation, such testimony was indispensable.

The free colored men are as imperatively required now to furnish the same manly testimony in support of the ability of the race to surmount the remaining obstacles growing out of oppression, ignorance, and poverty.

In the political struggles, the hopes of the race have been

sadly disappointed. From this direction no great advantage is likely to arise very soon.

Only as desert can be proved by the acquisition of knowledge and the exhibition of high moral character, in examples of economy and a disposition to encourage industrial enterprises, conducted by men of their own ranks, will it be possible to make political progress in the face of the present public sentiment.

Here, therefore, in my judgment is the best possible reason for vigorously pushing the circulation of this humble volume – that it may testify for thousands and tens of thousands, as no other work can do.

WILLIAM STILL, Author.
September, 1878. Philadelphia, Pa.

# SETH CONCKLIN

In the long list of names who have suffered and died in the cause of freedom, not one, perhaps, could be found whose efforts to redeem a poor family of slaves were more Christlike than Seth Concklin's, whose noble and daring spirit has been so long completely shrouded in mystery. Except John Brown, it is a question, whether his rival could be found with respect to boldness, disinterestedness and willingness to be sacrificed for the deliverance of the oppressed.

By chance one day he came across a copy of the *Pennsylvania Freeman*, containing the story of Peter Still, "the Kidnapped and the Ransomed," – how he had been torn away from his mother, when a little boy six years old; how, for forty years and more, he had been compelled to serve under the yoke, totally destitute as to any knowledge of his parents' whereabouts; how the intense love of liberty and desire to get back to his mother had unceasingly absorbed his mind through all these years of bondage; how, amid the most appalling discouragements, prompted alone by his undying determination to be free and be reunited with those from whom he had been sold away, he contrived to buy himself; how, by extreme economy, from doing over-work, he saved up five hundred dollars, the amount of money required for his ransom, which, with his freedom, he, from necessity, placed unreservedly in the confidential keeping of a Jew, named Joseph Friedman, whom he had known for a long time and could venture to trust, – how he had further toiled to save up money to defray his expenses on an expedition in search of his mother and kindred; how, when this end was accomplished, with an earnest purpose he took his carpet-bag in his hand, and his heart throbbing for his old home and people, he turned his mind very privately towards Philadelphia, where he hoped, by having notices read in the colored churches to the effect that "forty-one or forty-two years before two little boys[1] were kidnapped and carried South" – that the memory of some of the older members might recall the circumstances, and in this way he would be aided in his ardent efforts to become restored to them.

And, furthermore, Seth Concklin had read how, on arriving in Philadelphia, after traveling sixteen hundred miles, that almost the first man whom Peter Still sought advice from was his own unknown brother (whom he had never seen or heard of), who made the discovery that he was the long-lost boy, whose history and fate had been enveloped in sadness so long, and for whom his mother had shed so many tears and offered so many prayers, during the long years of their separation; and, finally, how this self-ransomed and restored captive, notwithstanding his great success, was destined to suffer the keenest pangs of sorrow for his wife and children, whom he had left in Alabama bondage.

Seth Concklin was naturally too singularly sympathetic and humane not to feel now for Peter, and especially for his wife and children left in bonds as bound with them. Hence, as Seth was a man who seemed wholly insensible to fear, and to know no other law of humanity and right, than whenever the claims of the suffering and the wronged appealed to him, to respond unreservedly, whether those thus injured were amongst his

1 Sons of Levin and Sidney – the last names of his parents he was too young to remember.

nearest kin or the greatest strangers, – it mattered not to what race or clime they might belong, – he, in the spirit of the good Samaritan, owning all such as his neighbors, volunteered his services, without pay or reward, to go and rescue the wife and three children of Peter Still.

The magnitude of this offer can hardly be appreciated. It was literally laying his life on the altar of freedom for the despised and oppressed whom he had never seen, whose kins-folk even he was not acquainted with. At this juncture even Peter was not prepared to accept this proposal. He wanted to secure the freedom of his wife and children as earnestly as he had ever desired to see his mother, yet he could not, at first, hearken to the idea of having them rescued in the way suggested by Concklin, fearing a failure.

To J.M. McKim and the writer, the bold scheme for the deliverance of Peter's family was alone confided. It was never submitted to the Vigilance Committee, for the reason that it was not considered a matter belonging thereto. On first reflection, the very idea of such an undertaking seemed perfectly appalling. Frankly was he told of the great dangers and difficulties to be encountered through hundreds of miles of slave territory. Seth was told of those who, in attempting to aid slaves to escape, had fallen victims to the relentless Slave Power, and had either lost their lives, or been incarcerated for long years in penitentiaries, where no friendly aid could be afforded them; in short, he was plainly told, that without a very great chance, the undertaking would cost him his life. The occasion of this interview and conversation, the seriousness of Concklin and the utter failure in presenting the various obstacles to his plan, to create the slightest apparent misgiving in his mind, or to produce the slightest sense of fear or hesitancy, can never be effaced from the memory of the writer. The plan was, however, allowed to rest for a time.

In the meanwhile, Peter's mind was continually vacillating between Alabama, with his wife and children, and his new-found relatives in the North. Said a brother, "If you cannot get your family, what will you do? Will you come North and live with your relatives?" "I would as soon go out of the world, as not to go back and do all I can for them," was the prompt reply of Peter.

The problem of buying them was seriously considered, but here obstacles quite formidable lay in the way. Alabama laws utterly denied the right of a slave to buy himself, much less his wife and children. The right of slave masters to free their slaves, either by sale or emancipation, was positively prohibited by law. With these reflections weighing upon his mind, having stayed away from his wife as long as he could content himself to do, he took his carpet-bag in his hand, and turned his face toward Alabama, to embrace his family in the prison house of bondage.

His approach home could only be made stealthily, not daring to breathe to a living soul, save his own family, his nominal Jew master, and one other friend – a slave – where he had been, the prize he had found, or anything in relation to his travels. To his wife and children his return was unspeakably joyous. The situation of his family concerned him with tenfold more weight than ever before,

As the time drew near to make the offer to his wife's master to purchase her with his children, his heart failed him through fear of awakening the ire of slaveholders against him, as he knew that the law and public sentiment were alike deadly opposed to the spirit of freedom in the slave. Indeed, as innocent as a step in this direction might appear, in those days a man would have stood about as good a chance for his life in entering a lair of hungry hyenas, as a slave or free colored man would, in talking about freedom.

He concluded, therefore, to say nothing about buying. The plan proposed by Seth Concklin was told to Vina, his wife; also what he had heard from his brother about the Underground Rail Road, – how, that many who could not get their freedom in any other way, by being aided a little, were daily escaping to Canada. Although the wife and children had never tasted the pleasures of freedom for a single hour in their lives, they hated slavery heartily, and being about to be far separated from husband and father, they were ready to assent to any proposition that looked like deliverance.

So Peter proposed to Vina, that she should give him certain small articles, consisting of a cape, etc., which he would carry with him as memorials, and, in case Concklin or any one else should ever come for her from him, as an unmistakable sign that all was right, he would send back, by whoever was to befriend them, the cape, so that she and the children might not doubt but have faith in the man, when he gave her the sign (cape).

Again Peter returned to Philadelphia, and was now willing to accept the offer of Concklin. Ere long, the opportunity of an interview was had, and Peter gave Seth a very full description of the country and of his family, and made known to him, that he had very carefully gone over with his wife and children the matter of their freedom. This interview interested Concklin most deeply. If his own wife and children had been in bondage, scarcely could he have manifested greater sympathy for them.

For the hazardous work before him he was at once prepared to make a start. True he had two sisters in Philadelphia for whom he had always cherished the warmest affection, but he conferred not with them on this momentous mission. For full well did he know that it was not in human nature for them to acquiesce in this perilous undertaking, though one of these sisters, Mrs. Supplee, was a most faithful abolitionist.

Having once laid his hand to the plough he was not the man to look back, – not even to bid his sisters good-bye, but he actually left them as though he expected to be home to his dinner as usual. What had become of him during those many weeks of his perilous labors in Alabama to rescue this family was to none a greater mystery than to his sisters. On leaving home he simply took two or three small articles in the way of apparel with one hundred dollars to defray his expenses for a time; this sum he considered ample to start with. Of course he had very safely concealed about him Vina's cape and one or two other articles which he was to use for his identification in meeting her and the children on the plantation. His first thought was, on reaching his destination, after becoming acquainted with the family, being familiar with Southern manners, to have them all prepared at a given hour for the starting of the steamboat for Cincinnati, and to join him at the wharf, when he would boldly assume the part of a slaveholder, and the family naturally that of slaves, and in this way he hoped to reach Cincinnati direct, before their owner had fairly discovered their escape.

But alas for Southern irregularity, two or three days' delay after being advertised to start, was no uncommon circumstance with steamers; hence this plan was abandoned. What this heroic man endured from severe struggles and unyielding exertions, in traveling thousands of miles on water and on foot, hungry and fatigued, rowing his living freight for seven days and seven nights in a skiff, is hardly to be paralleled in the annals of the Underground Rail Road.

The following interesting letters penned by the hand of Concklin convey minutely his last struggles and characteristically represent the singleness of heart which impelled him to sacrifice his life for the slave –

EASTPORT, MISS.,
*Feb. 3, 1851.*

To Wm. Still: – Our friends in Cincinnati have failed finding anybody to assist me on my return. Searching the country opposite Paducah, I find that the whole country fifty miles round is inhabited only by Christian wolves. It is customary, when a strange negro is seen, for any white man to seize the negro and convey such negro through and out of the State of Illinois to Paducah, Ky., and lodge such stranger in Paducah jail, and there claim such reward as may be offered by the master.

There is no regularity by the steamboats on the Tennessee River. I was four days getting to Florence from Paducah. Sometimes they are four days starting, from the time appointed, which alone puts to rest the plan for returning by steamboat. The distance from the mouth of the river to Florence, is from between three hundred and five to three hundred and forty-five miles by the river; by land, two hundred and fifty, or more.

I arrived at the shoe shop on the plantation, one o'clock, Tuesday, 28th. William and two boys were making shoes. I immediately gave the first signal, anxiously waiting thirty minutes for an opportunity to give the second and main signal, during which time I was very sociable. It was rainy and muddy – my pants were rolled up to the knees. I was in the character of a man seeking employment in this country. End of thirty minutes gave the second signal.

William appeared unmoved; soon sent out the boys; instantly sociable; Peter and Levin at the Island; one of the young masters with them; not safe to undertake to see them till Saturday night, when they would be at home; appointed a place to see Vina, in an open field, that night; they to bring me something to eat; our interview only four minutes; I left; appeared by night; dark and cloudy; at ten o'clock appeared William; exchanged signals; led me a few rods to where stood Vina; gave her the signal sent by Peter; our interview ten minutes; she did not call me "master," nor did she say "sir," by which I knew she had confidence in me.

Our situation being dangerous, we decided that I meet Peter and Levin on the bank of the river early dawn of day, Sunday, to establish the laws. During our interview, William prostrated on his knees, and face to the ground; arms sprawling; head cocked back, watching for wolves, by which position a man can see better in the dark. No house to go to safely, traveled round till morning, eating hoe cake which William had given me for supper; next day going around to get employment. I thought of William, who is a Christian preacher, and of the Christian preachers in Pennsylvania. One watching for wolves by night, to rescue Vina and her three children from Christian licentiousness; the other standing erect in open day, seeking the praise of men.

During the four days waiting for the important Sunday morning, I thoroughly surveyed the rocks and shoals of the river from Florence seven miles up, where will be my place of departure. General notice was taken of me as being a stranger, lurking around. Fortunately there are several small grist mills within ten miles around. No taverns here, as in the North; any planter's house entertains travelers occasionally.

One night I stayed at a medical gentleman's, who is not a large planter; another night at an ex-magistrate's house in South Florence – a Virginian by birth – one of the late census takers; told me that many more persons cannot read and write than is reported; one fact, amongst many others, that many persons who do not know the letters of the alphabet, have learned to write their own names; such are generally reported readers and writers.

It being customary for a stranger not to leave the house early in the morning where he has lodged, I was under the necessity of staying out all night Saturday, to be able to meet Peter and Levin, which was accomplished in due time. When we approached, I gave my signal first; immediately they gave theirs. I talked freely. Levin's voice, at first, evidently trembled. No wonder, for my presence universally attracted attention by the lords of the land. Our interview was less than one hour; the laws were written. I to go to Cincinnati to get a rowing boat and provisions; a first class clipper boat to go with speed. To depart from the place where the laws were written, on Saturday night of the first of March. I to meet one of them at the same place Thursday night, previous to the fourth Saturday from the night previous to the Sunday when the laws were written. We to go down the Tennessee river to some place up the Ohio, not yet decided on, in our row boat. Peter and Levin are good oarsmen. So am I. Telegraph station at Tuscumbia, twelve miles from the plantation, also at Paducah. Came from Florence to here Sunday night by steamboat. Eastport is in Mississippi. Waiting here for a steamboat to go down; paying one dollar a day for board. Like other taverns here, the wretchedness is indescribable; no pen, ink, paper or newspaper to be had; only one room for everybody, except the gambling rooms. It is difficult for me to write. Vina intends to get a pass for Catharine and herself for the first Sunday in March.

The bank of the river where I met Peter and Levin is two miles from the plantation. I have avoided saying I am from Philadelphia. Also avoided talking about negroes. I never talked so much about milling before. I consider most of the trouble over, till I arrive in a free State with my crew, the first week in March; then will I have to be wiser than Christian serpents, and more cautious than doves. I do not consider it safe to keep this letter in my possession, yet I dare not put it in the post-office here; there is so little business in these post-offices that notice might be taken.

I am evidently watched; everybody knows me to be a miller. I may write again when I get to Cincinnati, if I should have time. The ex-magistrate, with whom I stayed in South Florence, held three hours' talk with me, exclusive of our morning talk. Is a man of good general information; he was exceedingly inquisitive. "I am from Cincinnati, formerly from the *State of New York*." I had no opportunity to get anything to eat from seven o'clock Tuesday morning till six o'clock Wednesday evening, except the hoe cake, and no sleep.

Florence is the head of navigation for small steamboats. Seven miles, all the way up to my place of departure, is swift water, and rocky. Eight hundred miles to Cincinnati. I found all things here as Peter told me, except the distance of the river. South Florence contains twenty white families, three warehouses of considerable business, a post-office, but no school. McKiernon is here waiting for a steamboat to go to New Orleans, so we are in company.

PRINCETON, GIBSON COUNTY, INDIANA,
*Feb. 18, 1851.*

To Wm. Still: – The plan is to go to Canada, on the Wabash, opposite Detroit. There are four routes to Canada. One through Illinois, commencing above and below Alton; one through to North Indiana, and the Cincinnati route, being the largest route in the United States.

I intended to have gone through Pennsylvania, but the risk going up the Ohio river has caused me to go to Canada.

Steamboat traveling is universally condemned, though many go in boats, consequently many get lost. Going in a skiff is new, and is approved of in my case. After I arrive at the mouth of the Tennessee river, I will go up the Ohio seventy-five miles, to the mouth of the Wabash, then up the Wabash, forty-four miles to New Harmony, where I shall go ashore by night, and go thirteen miles east, to Charles Grier, a farmer, (colored man), who will entertain us, and next night convey us sixteen miles to David Stormon, near Princeton, who will take the command, and I be released.

David Stormon estimates the expenses from his house to Canada, at forty dollars, without which, no sure protection will be given. They might be instructed concerning the course, and beg their way through without money. If you wish to do what should be done, you will send me fifty dollars, in a letter, to Princeton, Gibson county, Inda., so as to arrive there by the 8th of March. Eight days should be estimated for a letter to arrive from Philadelphia.

The money to be State Bank of Ohio, or State Bank, or Northern Bank of Kentucky, or any other Eastern bank. Send no notes larger than twenty dollars.

Levi Coffin had no money for me. I paid twenty dollars for the skiff. No money to get back to Philadelphia. It was not understood that I would have to be at any expense seeking aid.

One half of my time has been used in trying to find persons to assist, when I may arrive on the Ohio river, in which I have failed, except Stormon.

Having no letter of introduction to Stormon from any source, on which I could fully rely, I traveled two hundred miles around, to find out his stability. I have found many

Abolitionists, nearly all who have made propositions, which themselves would not comply with, and nobody else would. Already I have traveled over three thousand miles. Two thousand and four hundred by steamboat, two hundred by railroad, one hundred by stage, four hundred on foot, forty-eight in a skiff.

I have yet five hundred miles to go to the plantation, to commence operations. I have been two weeks on the decks of steamboats, three nights out, two of which I got perfectly wet. If I had had paper money, as McKim desired, it would have been destroyed. I have not been entertained gratis at any place except Stormon's. I had one hundred and twenty-six dollars when I left Philadelphia, one hundred from you, twenty-six mine.

Telegraphed to station at Evansville, thirty-three miles from Stormon's, and at Vinclure's, twenty-five miles from Stormon's. The Wabash route is considered the safest route. No one has ever been lost from Stormon's to Canada. Some have been lost between Stormon's and the Ohio. The wolves have never suspected Stormon. Your asking aid in money for a case properly belonging east of Ohio, is detested. If you have sent money to Cincinnati, you should recall it. I will have no opportunity to use it.

Seth Concklin, Princeton, Gibson county, Ind.

P.S. First of April, will be about the time Peter's family will arrive opposite Detroit. You should inform yourself how to find them there. I may have no opportunity.

I will look promptly for your letter at Princeton, till the 10th of March, and longer if there should have been any delay by the mails.

In March, as contemplated, Concklin arrived in Indiana, at the place designated, with Peter's wife and three children, and sent a thrilling letter to the writer, portraying in the most vivid light his adventurous flight from the hour they left Alabama until their arrival in Indiana. In this report he stated, that instead of starting early in the morning, owing to some unforeseen delay on the part of the family, they did not reach the designated place till towards day, which greatly exposed them in passing a certain town which he had hoped to avoid.

But as his brave heart was bent on prosecuting his journey without further delay, he concluded to start at all hazards, notwithstanding the dangers he apprehended from passing said town by daylight. For safety he endeavored to hide his freight by having them all lie flat down on the bottom of the skiff; covered them with blankets, concealing them from the effulgent beams of the early morning sun, or rather from the "Christian Wolves" who might perchance espy him from the shore in passing the town.

The wind blew fearfully. Concklin was rowing heroically when loud voices from the shore hailed him, but he was utterly deaf to the sound. Immediately one or two guns were fired in the direction of the skiff, but he heeded not this significant call; consequently here ended this difficulty. He supposed, as the wind was blowing so hard, those on shore who hailed him must have concluded that he did not hear them and that he meant no disrespect in treating them with seeming indifference. Whilst many straits and great dangers had to be passed, this was the greatest before reaching their destination.

But suffice it to say that the glad tidings which this letter contained filled the breast of Peter with unutterable delight and his friends and relations with wonder beyond degree.[2] No fond wife had ever waited with more longing desire for the return of her husband than Peter had for this blessed news. All doubts had disappeared, and a well grounded hope was cherished that within a few short days Peter and his fond wife and children would be reunited in Freedom on the Canada side, and that Concklin and the friends would be rejoicing with joy unspeakable over this great triumph. But alas, before the few days had expired the subjoined brief paragraph of news was discovered in the morning *Ledger*.

> RUNAWAY NEGROES CAUGHT. – At Vincennes, Indiana, on Saturday last, a white man and four negroes were arrested. The negroes belong to B. McKiernon, of South Florence, Alabama, and the man who was running them off calls himself John H. Miller. The prisoners were taken charge of by the Marshall of Evansville. – *April 9th.*

How suddenly these sad tidings turned into mourning and gloom the hope and joy of Peter and his relatives no pen could possibly describe; at least the writer will not attempt it here, but will at once introduce a witness who met the noble Concklin and the panting fugitives in Indiana and proffered them sympathy and advice. And it may safely be said from a

2 In some unaccountable manner this, the last letter Concklin ever penned, perhaps, has been unfortunately lost.

truer and more devoted friend of the slave they could not have received counsel.

EVANSVILLE, INDIANA,
*March 31st, 1851.*

WM. STILL: *Dear Sir*, – On last Tuesday I mailed a letter to you, written by Seth Concklin. I presume you have received that letter. It gave an account of his rescue of the family of your brother. If that is the last news you have had from them, I have very painful intelligence for you. They passed on from near Princeton, where I saw them and had a lengthy interview with them, up north, I think twenty-three miles above Vincennes, Ind., where they were seized by a party of men, and lodged in jail. Telegraphic dispatches were sent all through the South. I have since learned that the Marshall of Evansville received a dispatch from Tuscumbia, to look out for them. By some means, he and the master, so says report, went to Vincennes and claimed the fugitives, chained Mr. Concklin and hurried all off. Mr. Concklin wrote to Mr. David Stormon, Princeton, as soon as he was cast into prison, to find bail. So soon as we got the letter and could get off, two of us were about setting off to render all possible aid, when we were told they all had passed, a few hours before, through Princeton, Mr. Concklin in chains. What kind of process was had, if any, I know not. I immediately came down to this place, and learned that they had been put on a boat at 3 P.M. I did not arrive until 6. Now all hopes of their recovery are gone. No case ever so enlisted my sympathies. I had seen Mr. Concklin in Cincinnati. I had given him aid and counsel.

I happened to see them after they landed in Indiana. I heard Peter and Levin tell their tale of suffering, shed tears of sorrow for them all; but now, since they have fallen a prey to the unmerciful blood-hounds of this state, and have again been dragged back to unrelenting bondage, I am entirely unmanned. And poor Concklin! I fear for him. When he is dragged back to Alabama, I fear they will go far beyond the utmost rigor of the law, and vent their savage cruelty upon him. It is with pain I have to communicate these things. But you may not hear them from him. I could not get to see him or them, as Vincennes is about thirty miles from Princeton, where I was when I heard of the capture.

I take pleasure in stating that, according to the letter he (Concklin) wrote to Mr. D. Stewart, Mr. Concklin did not abandon them, but risked his own liberty to save them. He was not with them when they were taken; but went afterwards to take them out of jail upon a writ of Habeas Corpus, when they seized him too and lodged him in prison.

I write in much haste. If I can learn any more facts of importance, I may write you. If you desire to hear from me again, or if you should learn any thing specific from Mr. Concklin, be pleased to write me at Cincinnati, where I expect to be in a short time. If curious to know your correspondent, I may say I was formerly Editor of the *New Concord Free Press*, Ohio. I only add that every case of this kind only tends to make me abhor my (no!) *this* country more and more. It is the Devil's Government, and God will destroy it.

Yours for the slave, N.R. JOHNSTON.

P.S. I broke open this letter to write you some more. The foregoing pages were written at night. I expected to mail it next morning before leaving Evansville; but the boat for which I was waiting came down about three in the morning; so I had to hurry on board, bringing the letter along. As it now is I am not sorry, for coming down, on my way to St. Louis, as far as Paducah, there I learned from a colored man at the wharf that, that same day, in the morning, the master and the family of fugitives arrived off the boat, and had then gone on their journey to Tuscumbia, but that the "white man" (Mr. Concklin) had "got away from them," about twelve miles up the river. It seems he got off the boat some way, near or at Smithland, Ky., a town at the mouth of the Cumberland River. I presume the report is true, and hope he will finally escape, though I was also told that they were in pursuit of him. Would that the others had also escaped. Peter and Levin could have done so, I think, if they had had resolution. One of them rode a horse, he not tied either, behind the coach in which the others were. He followed apparently "contented and happy." From report, they told their master, and even their pursuers, before the master came, that Concklin had decoyed them away, they coming unwillingly. I write on a very unsteady boat.

Yours, N.R. JOHNSTON.

A report found its way into the papers to the effect that "Miller," the white man arrested in connection with the capture of the family, was found drowned, with his hands and feet in chains and his skull fractured. It proved, as his friends feared, to be Seth Concklin. And in irons, upon the river bank, there is no doubt he was buried.

In this dreadful hour one sad duty still remained to be performed. Up to this moment the two sisters were totally ignorant of their brother's whereabouts. Not the first whisper of his death had reached them. But they must now be made acquainted with all the facts in the case. Accordingly an interview was arranged for a meeting, and the duty of conveying this painful intelligence to one of the sisters, Mrs. Supplee, devolved upon Mr. McKim. And most tenderly and considerately did he perform his mournful task.

Although a woman of nerve, and a true friend to the slave, an earnest worker and a liberal giver in the Female Anti-Slavery Society, for a time she was overwhelmed by the intelligence of her brother's death. As soon as possible, however, through very great effort, she controlled her emotions, and calmly expressed herself as being fully resigned to the awful event. Not a word of complaint had she to make because she had not been apprised of his movements; but said repeatedly, that, had she known ever so much of his intentions, she would have been totally powerless in opposing him if she had felt so disposed, and as an illustration of the true character of the man, from his boyhood up to the day he died for his fellow-man, she related his eventful career, and recalled a number of instances of his heroic and daring deeds for others, sacrificing his time and often periling his life in the cause of those who he considered were suffering gross wrongs and oppression. Hence, she concluded, that it was only natural for him in this case to have taken the steps he did. Now and then overflowing tears would obstruct this deeply thrilling and most remarkable story she was telling of her brother, but her memory seemed quickened by the sadness of the occasion, and she was enabled to recall vividly the chief events connected with his past history. Thus his agency in this movement, which cost him his life, could readily enough be accounted for, and the individuals who listened attentively to the story were prepared to fully appreciate his character, for, prior to offering his services in this mission, he had been a stranger to them.

The following extract, taken from a letter of a subsequent date, in addition to the above letter, throws still further light upon the heart-rending affair, and shows Mr. Johnston's deep sympathy with the sufferers and the oppressed generally –

## EXTRACT OF A LETTER FROM REV. N.R. JOHNSTON.

My heart bleeds when I think of those poor, hunted and heart-broken fugitives, though a most interesting family, taken back to bondage ten-fold worse than Egyptian. And then poor Concklin! How my heart expanded in love to him, as he told me his adventures, his trials, his toils, his fears and his hopes! After hearing all, and then seeing and communing with the family, now joyful in hopes of soon seeing their husband and father in the land of freedom; now in terror lest the human blood-hounds should be at their heels, I felt as though I could lay down my life in the cause of the oppressed. In that hour or two of intercourse with Peter's family, my heart warmed with love to them. I never saw more interesting young men. They would make Remonds or Douglasses, if they had the same opportunities.

While I was with them, I was elated with joy at their escape, and yet, when I heard their tale of woe, especially that of the mother, I could not suppress tears of deepest emotion.

My joy was short-lived. Soon I heard of their capture. The telegraph had been the means of their being claimed. I could have torn down all the telegraph wires in the land. It was a strange dispensation of Providence.

On Saturday the sad news of their capture came to my ears. We had resolved to go to their aid on Monday, as the trial was set for Thursday. On Sabbath, I spoke from Psalm xii. 5. "For the oppression of the poor, for the sighing of the needy, now will I arise," saith the Lord: "I will set him in safety from him that puffeth at (from them that would enslave) him." When on Monday morning I learned that the fugitives had passed through the place on Sabbath, and Concklin in chains, probably at the very time I was speaking on the subject referred to, my heart sank within me. And even yet, I cannot but exclaim, when I think of it – O, Father! how long ere Thou wilt arise to avenge the wrongs of the poor slave! Indeed, my dear brother, His ways are very mysterious. We have the consolation, however, to know that all is for the best. Our Redeemer does all things well. When He hung upon the cross, His poor broken hearted disciples could not understand the providence; it was a dark time to them; and yet that was an event that was fraught with more joy to the world than any that has occurred or could occur. Let us stand at our post and wait God's time. Let us have on the whole armor of God, and fight for the right, knowing, that though we may fall in battle, the victory will be ours, sooner or later.

May God lead you into all truth, and sustain you in your labors, and fulfill your prayers and hopes. Adieu.

N.R. JOHNSTON.

## LETTERS FROM LEVI COFFIN.

The following letters on the subject were received from the untiring and devoted friend of the slave, Levi Coffin, who for many years had occupied in Cincinnati a similar position to that of Thomas Garrett in Delaware, a sentinel and watchman commissioned of God to succor the fleeing bondman –

CINCINNATI, 4TH MO.,
*10th, 1851.*

FRIEND WM. STILL: – We have sorrowful news from our friend Concklin, through the papers and otherwise. I received a letter a few days ago from a friend near Princeton, Ind., stating that Concklin and the four slaves are in prison in Vincennes, and that their trial would come on in a few days. He states that they rowed seven days and nights in the skiff, and got safe to Harmony, Ind., on the Wabash river, thence to Princeton, and were conveyed to Vincennes by friends, where they were taken. The papers state, that they were all given up to the Marshal of Evansville, Indiana.

We have telegraphed to different points, to try to get some information concerning them, but failed. The last information is published in the *Times* of yesterday, though quite incorrect in the particulars of the case. Inclosed is the slip containing it. I fear all is over in regard to the freedom of the slaves. If the last account be true, we have some hope that Concklin will escape from those bloody tyrants. I cannot describe my feelings on hearing this sad intelligence. I feel ashamed to own my country. Oh! what shall I say. Surely a God of justice will avenge the wrongs of the oppressed.

Thine for the poor slave,
LEVI COFFIN.

N.B. – If thou hast any information, please write me forthwith.

CINCINNATI, 5TH MO.,
*11th, 1851.*

WM. STILL: – *Dear Friend* – Thy letter of 1st inst., came duly to hand, but not being able to give any further information concerning our friend, Concklin, I thought best to wait a little before I wrote, still hoping to learn something more definite concerning him.

We that became acquainted with Seth Concklin and his hazardous enterprises (here at Cincinnati), who were very few, have felt intense and inexpressible anxiety about them. And particularly about poor Seth, since we heard of his falling into the hands of the tyrants. I fear that he has fallen a victim to their inhuman thirst for blood.

I seriously doubt the rumor, that he had made his escape. I fear that he was sacrificed.

Language would fail to express my feelings; the intense and deep anxiety I felt about them for weeks before I heard of their capture in Indiana, and then it seemed too much to bear. O! my heart almost bleeds when I think of it. The hopes of the dear family all blasted by the wretched bloodhounds in human shape. And poor Seth, after all his toil, and dangerous, shrewd and wise management, and almost unheard of adventures, the many narrow and almost miraculous escapes. Then to be given up to Indianians, to these fiendish tyrants, to be sacrificed. O! Shame, Shame!!

My heart aches, my eyes fill with tears, I cannot write more. I cannot dwell longer on this painful subject now. If you get any intelligence, please inform me. Friend N.R. Johnston, who took so much interest in them, and saw them just before they were taken, has just returned to the city. He is a minister of the Covenanter order. He is truly a lovely man, and his heart is full of the milk of humanity; one of our best Anti-Slavery spirits. I spent last evening with him. He related the whole story to me as he had it from friend Concklin and the mother and children, and then the story of their capture. We wept together. He found thy letter when he got here.

He said he would write the whole history to thee in a few days, as far as he could. He can tell it much better than I can.

Concklin left his carpet sack and clothes here with me, except a shirt or two he took with him. What shall I do with them? For if we do not hear from him soon, we must conclude that he is lost, and the report of his escape all a hoax.

Truly thy friend,
LEVI COFFIN.

Stunning and discouraging as this horrible ending was to all concerned, and serious as the matter looked in the eyes of Peter's friends with regard to Peter's family, he could not for a moment abandon the idea of rescuing them from the jaws of the destroyer. But most formidable difficulties stood in the way of opening correspondence with reliable persons in Alabama. Indeed it seemed impossible to find a merchant, lawyer, doctor, planter or minister, who was not too completely interlinked with slavery to be relied upon to manage a negotiation of this nature. Whilst waiting and hoping for something favorable to turn up, the subjoined letter from the owner of Peter's family was received and is here inserted precisely as it was written, spelled and punctuated –

## McKIERNON'S LETTER

*SOUTH FLORENCE ALA*
*6 Augest 1851*

Mr WILLIAM STILL
*No 31 North Fifth street Philadelphia*

Sir a few days sinc mr Lewis Tharenton of Tuscumbia Ala shewed me a letter dated 6 June 51 from Cincinnati signd samuel Lewis in behalf of a Negro man by the name of peter Gist who informed the writer of the Letter that you ware his brother and wished an answer to be directed to you as he peter would be in philadelphi. the object of the letter was to purchis from me 4 Negros that is peters wife & 3 children 2 sons & 1

Girl the Name of said Negres are the woman Viney the (mother) Eldest son peter 21 or 2 years old second son Leven 19 or 20 years 1 Girl about 13 or 14 years old. the Husband & Father of these people once Belonged to a relation of mine by the name of Gist now Decest & some few years since he peter was sold to a man by the Name of Freedman who removed to cincinnati ohio & Tuck peter with him of course peter became free by the volentary act of the master some time last march a white man by the name of Miller apperd in the nabourhood & abducted the bove negroes was caut at vincanes Indi with said negroes & was thare convicted of steling & remanded back to Ala to Abide the penalty of the law & on his return met his Just reward by Getting drownded at the mouth of cumberland River on the ohio in attempting to make his escape I recovered & Braught Back said 4 negroes or as You would say coulard people under the Belief that peter the Husband was accessory to the offence thareby putting me to much Expense & Truble to the amt $1000 which if he gets them he or his Friends must refund these 4 negroes are worth in the market about 4000 for thea are Extraordinary fine & likely & but for the fact of Elopement I would not take 8000 Dollars for them but as the thing now stands you can say to peter & his new discovered Relations in Philadelphia I will take 5000 for the 4 culerd people & if this will suite him & he can raise the money I will delever to him or his agent at paduca at mouth of Tennessee river said negroes but the money must be Deposeted in the Hands of some respectabl person at paduca before I remove the property it wold not be safe for peter to come to this countery write me a line on recpt of this & let me Know peters views on the above

I am Yours &c B. McKIERNON.

N B say to peter to write & let me Know his viewes amediately as I am determined to act in a way if he don't take this offer he will never have an other opportunity

B McKIERNON.

## WM. STILL'S ANSWER

PHILADELPHIA,
*Aug. 16th, 1851.*

To B. McKIERNON, ESQ.: *Sir* – I have received your letter from South Florence, Ala., under date of the 6th inst. To say that it took me by surprise, as well as afforded me pleasure, for which I feel to be very much indebted to you, is no more than true. In regard to your informants of myself – Mr. Thornton, of Ala., and Mr. Samuel Lewis, of Cincinnati – to them both I am a stranger. However, I am the brother of Peter, referred to, and with the fact of his having a wife and three children in your service I am also familiar. This brother, Peter, I have only had the pleasure of knowing for the brief space of one year and thirteen days, although he is now past forty and I twenty-nine years of age. Time will not allow me at present, or I should give you a detailed account of how Peter became a slave, the forty long years which intervened between the time he was kidnapped, when a boy, being only six years of age, and his arrival in this city, from Alabama, one year and fourteen days ago, when he was re-united to his mother, five brothers and three sisters.

None but a father's heart can fathom the anguish and sorrows felt by Peter during the many vicissitudes through which he has passed. He looked back to his boyhood and saw himself snatched from the tender embraces of his parents and home to be made a slave for life. During all his prime days he was in the faithful and constant service of those who had no just claim upon him. In the meanwhile he married a wife, who bore him eleven children, the greater part of whom were emancipated from the troubles of life by death, and three only survived. To them and his wife he was devoted. Indeed I have never seen attachment between parents and children, or husband and wife, more entire than was manifested in the case of Peter.

Through these many years of servitude, Peter was sold and resold, from one State to another, from one owner to another, till he reached the forty-ninth year of his age, when, in a good Providence, through the kindness of a friend and the sweat of his brow, he regained the God-given blessings of liberty. He eagerly sought his parents and home with all possible speed and pains, when, to his heart's joy, he found his relatives.

Your present humble correspondent is the youngest of Peter's brothers, and the first one of the family he saw after arriving in this part of the country. I think you could not fail to be interested in hearing how we became known to each other, and the proof of our being brothers, etc., all of which I should be most glad to relate, but time will not permit me to do so. The news of this wonderful occurrence, of Peter finding his kindred, was published quite extensively, shortly afterwards, in various newspapers, in this quarter, which may account for the fact of "Miller's" knowledge of the whereabouts of the "fugitives." Let me say, it is my firm conviction that no one had any hand in persuading "Miller" to go down from Cincinnati, or any other place, after the family. As glad as I should be, and as much as I would do for the liberation of Peter's family (now no longer young), and his three "likely" children, in whom he prides himself – how much, if you are a father, you can imagine; yet I would not, and could not, think of persuading any friend to peril his life, as would be the case, in an errand of that kind.

As regards the price fixed upon by you for the family, I must say I do not think it possible to raise half that amount, though Peter authorized me to say he would give you twenty-five hundred for them. Probably he is not as well aware as I am, how difficult it is to raise so large a sum of money from the public. The applications for such objects are so frequent among us in the North, and have always been so liberally met, that it is no wonder if many get tired of being called upon. To be sure some of us brothers own some property, but no great amount; certainly not enough to enable us to bear so great a burden. Mother owns a small farm in New Jersey, on which she has lived for nearly forty years, from which she derives her support in her old age. This small farm contains between forty and fifty acres, and is the fruit of my father's toil. Two of my brothers own small places also, but they have young families, and consequently consume nearly as much as they make, with the exception of adding some improvements to their places.

For my own part, I am employed as a clerk for a living, but my salary is quite too limited to enable me to contribute any great amount towards so large a sum as is demanded. Thus you see how we are situated financially. We have plenty of friends, but little money. Now, sir, allow me to make an appeal to your humanity, although we are aware of your power to hold as property those poor slaves, mother, daughter and two sons, – that in no part of the United States could they escape and be secure from your claim – nevertheless, would your understanding, your heart, or your conscience reprove you, should you restore to them, without price, that dear freedom, which is theirs by right of nature, or would you not feel a satisfaction in so doing which all the wealth of the world could not equal? At all events, could you not so reduce the price as to place it in the power of Peter's relatives and friends to raise the means for their purchase? At first, I doubt not, but that you will think my appeal very unreasonable; but, sir, serious reflection will decide, whether the money demanded by you, after all, will be of as great a benefit to you, as the satisfaction you would find in bestowing so great a favor upon those whose entire happiness in this life depends mainly upon your decision in the matter. If the entire family cannot be purchased or freed, what can Vina and her daughter be purchased for? Hoping, sir, to hear from you, at your earliest convenience, I subscribe myself,

Your obedient servant, WM. STILL.

To B. McKiernon, Esq.

No reply to this letter was ever received from McKiernon. The cause of his reticence can be as well conjectured by the reader as the writer.

Time will not admit of further details kindred to this narrative. The life, struggles, and success of Peter and his family were ably brought before the public in the *Kidnapped and the Ransomed*, being the personal recollections of Peter Still and his wife "Vina," after forty years of slavery, by Mrs. Kate E.R. Pickard; with an introduction by Rev. Samuel J. May, and an appendix by William H. Furness, D.D., in 1856. But, of course it was not prudent or safe, in the days of Slavery, to publish such facts as are now brought to light; all such had to be kept concealed in the breasts of the fugitives and their friends.

The following brief sketch, touching the separation of Peter and his mother, will fitly illustrate this point, and at the same time explain certain mysteries which have been hitherto kept hidden –

**THE SEPARATION**

With regard to Peter's separation from his mother, when a little boy, in few words, the facts were these: His parents, Levin and Sidney, were both slaves on the Eastern Shore of Maryland. "I will die before I submit to the yoke," was the declaration of his father to his young master before either was twenty-one years of age. Consequently he was allowed to buy himself at a very low figure, and he paid the required sum and obtained his "free papers" when quite a young man – the young wife and mother remaining in slavery under Saunders Griffin, as also her children, the latter having increased to the number of four, two little boys and two little girls. But to escape from chains, stripes, and bondage, she took her four little children and fled to a place near Greenwich, New Jersey. Not a great while, however, did she remain there in a state of freedom before the slave-hunters pursued her, and one night they pounced upon the whole family, and, without judge or jury, hurried them all back to slavery. Whether this was kidnapping or not is for the reader to decide for himself.

Safe back in the hands of her owner, to prevent her from escaping a second time, every night for about three months she was cautiously "kept locked up in the garret," until, as they supposed, she was fully "cured of the desire to do so again." But she was incurable. She had been a witness to the fact that her own father's brains had been blown out by the discharge of a heavily loaded gun, deliberately aimed at his head by his drunken master. She only needed half a chance to make still greater struggles than ever for freedom.

She had great faith in God, and found much solace in singing some of the good old Methodist tunes, by day and night. Her owner, observing this apparently tranquil state of mind, indicating that she "seemed better contented than ever," concluded that it was safe to let the garret door remain unlocked at night. Not many weeks were allowed to pass before she resolved to again make a bold strike for freedom. This time she had to leave the two little boys, Levin and Peter, behind.

On the night she started she went to the bed where they were sleeping, kissed them, and, consigning them into the hands of God, bade her mother good-bye, and with her two little girls wended her way again to Burlington County, New

Jersey, but to a different neighborhood from that where she had been seized. She changed her name to Charity, and succeeded in again joining her husband, but, alas, with the heart-breaking thought that she had been compelled to leave her two little boys in slavery and one of the little girls on the road for the father to go back after. Thus she began life in freedom anew.

Levin and Peter, eight and six years of age respectively, were now left at the mercy of the enraged owner, and were soon hurried off to a Southern market and sold, while their mother, for whom they were daily weeping, was they knew not where. They were too young to know that they were slaves, or to understand the nature of the afflicting separation. Sixteen years before Peter's return, his older brother (Levin) died a slave in the State of Alabama, and was buried by his surviving brother, Peter.

No idea other than that they had been "kidnapped" from their mother ever entered their minds; nor had they any knowledge of the State from whence they supposed they had been taken, the last names of their mother and father, or where they were born. On the other hand, the mother was aware that the safety of herself and her rescued children depended on keeping the whole transaction a strict family secret. During the forty years of separation, except two or three Quaker friends, including the devoted friend of the slave, Benjamin Lundy, it is doubtful whether any other individuals were let into the secret of her slave life. And when the account given of Peter's return, etc., was published in 1850, it led some of the family to apprehend serious danger from the partial revelation of the early condition of the mother, especially as it was about the time that the Fugitive Slave law was passed.

Hence, the author of *The Kidnapped and the Ransomed* was compelled to omit these dangerous facts, and had to confine herself strictly to the "personal recollections of Peter Still" with regard to his being "kidnapped." Likewise, in the sketch of Seth Concklin's eventful life, written by Dr. W.H. Furness, for similar reasons he felt obliged to make but bare reference to his wonderful agency in relation to Peter's family, although he was fully aware of all the facts in the case.

# WILLIAM PEEL

ALIAS WILLIAM
BOX PEEL JONES

*ARRIVED PER ERRICSON LINE OF STEAMERS, WRAPPED IN STRAW AND BOXED UP.*

**APRIL, 1859.**

William is twenty-five years of age, unmistakably colored, good-looking, rather under the medium size, and of pleasing manners. William had himself boxed up by a near relative and forwarded by the Erricson line of steamers. He gave the slip to Robert H. Carr, his owner (a grocer and commission merchant), after this wise, and for the following reasons: For some time previous his master had been selling off his slaves every now and then, the same as other groceries, and this admonished William that he was liable to be in the market any day; consequently, he preferred the box to the auction-block.

He did not complain of having been treated very badly by Carr, but felt that no man was safe while owned by another. In fact, he "hated the very name of slaveholder." The limit of the box not admitting of straightening himself out he was taken with the cramp on the road, suffered indescribable misery, and had his faith taxed to the utmost, – indeed was brought to the very verge of "screaming aloud" ere relief came. However, he controlled himself, though only for a short season, for before a great while an excessive faintness came over him. Here nature became quite exhausted. He thought he must "die;" but his time had not yet come. After a severe struggle he revived, but only to encounter a third ordeal no less painful than the one through which he had just passed. Next a very "cold chill" came over him, which seemed almost to freeze the very blood in his veins and gave him intense agony, from which he only found relief on awaking, having actually fallen asleep in that condition.

Finally, however, he arrived at Philadelphia, on a steamer, Sabbath morning. A devoted friend of his, expecting him, engaged a carriage and repaired to the wharf for the box. The bill of lading and the receipt he had with him, and likewise knew where the box was located on the boat. Although he well knew freight was not usually delivered on Sunday, yet his deep solicitude for the safety of his friend determined him to do all that lay in his power to rescue him from his perilous situation. Handing his bill of lading to the proper officer of the boat, he asked if he could get the freight that it called for. The officer looked at the bill and said, "No, we do not deliver freight on Sunday;" but, noticing the anxiety of the man, he asked him if he would know it if he were to see it. Slowly – fearing that too much interest manifested might excite suspicion – he replied: "I think I should." Deliberately looking around amongst all the "freight," he discovered the box, and said, "I think that is it there." Said officer stepped to it, looked at the directions on it, then at the bill of lading, and said, "That is right, take it along." Here the interest in these two bosoms was thrilling in the highest degree. But the size of the box was too large for the carriage, and the driver refused to take it. Nearly an hour and a half was spent in looking for a furniture car. Finally one was procured, and again the box was laid hold of by the occupant's particular friend, when, to his dread alarm, the poor fellow within gave a sudden cough. At this startling circumstance he dropped the box; equally as quick, although dreadfully frightened, and, as if helped by some invisible agency, he commenced singing, "Hush, my babe, lie still and slumber," with the most apparent indifference, at the same time slowly making his way from the box. Soon his fears subsided, and it was presumed that no one was any the wiser on account of the accident, or coughing. Thus, after summoning courage, he laid hold of the box a third time, and the Rubicon was passed. The car driver, totally ignorant of the contents of the box, drove to the number to which he was directed to take it – left it and went about his business. Now is a moment of intense interest – now of inexpressible delight. The box is opened, the straw removed, and the poor fellow is loosed; and is rejoicing, I will venture to say, as mortal never did rejoice, who had not been in similar peril. This particular friend was scarcely less overjoyed, however, and their joy did not abate for several hours; nor was it confined to themselves, for two invited members of the Vigilance Committee also partook of a full share. This box man was named Wm. Jones. He was boxed up in Baltimore by the friend who received him at the wharf, who did not come in the boat with him, but came in the cars and met him at the wharf.

The trial in the box lasted just seventeen hours before victory was achieved. Jones was well cared for by the Vigilance Committee and sent on his way rejoicing, feeling that Resolution, Underground Rail Road, and Liberty were invaluable.

On his way to Canada, he stopped at Albany, and the subjoined letter gives his view of things from that stand-point –

MR. STILL: – I take this opportunity of writing a few lines to you hoping that tha may find you in good health and femaly. i am well at present and doing well at present i am now in a store and getting sixteen dollars a month at the present. i feel very much o blige to you and your family for your kindnes to me while i was with you i have got a long without any trub le a tal. i am now in albany City. give my lov to mrs and mr miller and tel them i am very much a blige to them for there kind ns. give my lov to my Brother nore Jones tel him i should like to here from him very much and he must write. tel him to give my love to all of my perticnlar frends and tel them i should like to see them very much. tel him that he must come to see me for i want to see him for sum thing very perticler. please ansure this letter as soon as posabul and excuse me for not writting sooner as i don't write myself. no more at the present.

WILLIAM JONES.

derect to one hundred 125 lydus. Stt

His good friend returned to Baltimore the same day the box man started for the North, and immediately dispatched through the post the following brief letter, worded in Underground Rail Road parables:

BALTIMO
*April 16, 1859.*

W. STILL: – Dear brother i have taken the opportunity of writing you these few lines to inform you that i am well an hoping these few lines may find you enjoying the same good blessing please to write me word at what time was it when isreal went to Jerico i am very anxious to hear for thare is a mighty host will pass over and you and i my brother will sing hally luja i shall notify you when the great catastrophe shal take place No more at the present but remain your brother

N.L.J.

# WESLEY HARRIS

## ALIAS ROBERT JACKSON, AND THE MATTERSON BROTHERS

In setting out for freedom, Wesley was the leader of this party. After two nights of fatiguing travel at a distance of about sixty miles from home, the young aspirants for liberty were betrayed, and in an attempt made to capture them a most bloody conflict ensued. Both fugitives and pursuers were the recipients of severe wounds from gun shots, and other weapons used in the contest.

Wesley bravely used his firearms until almost fatally wounded by one of the pursuers, who with a heavily loaded gun discharged the contents with deadly aim in his left arm, which raked the flesh from the bone for a space of about six inches in length. One of Wesley's companions also fought heroically and only yielded when badly wounded and quite overpowered. The two younger (brothers of C. Matterson) it seemed made no resistance.

In order to recall the adventures of this struggle, and the success of Wesley Harris, it is only necessary to copy the report as then penned from the lips of this young hero, while on the Underground Rail Road, even then in a very critical state. Most fearful indeed was his condition when he was brought to the Vigilance Committee in this City.

## UNDERGROUND RAIL ROAD RECORD

> *November 2d*, 1853. – Arrived: Robert Jackson (shot man), alias Wesley Harris; age twenty-two years; dark color; medium height, and of slender stature.

Robert was born in Martinsburg, Va., and was owned by Philip Pendleton. From a boy he had always been hired out. At the first of this year he commenced services with Mrs. Carroll, proprietress of the United States Hotel at Harper's Ferry. Of Mrs. Carroll he speaks in very grateful terms, saying that she was kind to him and all the servants, and promised them their freedom at her death. She excused herself for not giving them their freedom on the ground that her husband died insolvent, leaving her the responsibility of settling his debts. But while Mrs. Carroll was very kind to her servants, her manager was equally as cruel. About a month before Wesley left, the overseer, for some trifling cause, attempted to flog him, but was resisted, and himself flogged. This resistance of the slave was regarded by the overseer as an unpardonable offence; consequently he communicated the intelligence to his owner, which had the desired effect on his mind as appeared from his answer to the overseer, which was nothing less than instructions that if he should again attempt to correct Wesley and he should repel the wholesome treatment, the overseer was to put him in prison and sell him. Whether he offended again or not, the following Christmas he was to be sold without fail.

Wesley's mistress was kind enough to apprise him of the intention of his owner and the overseer, and told him that if he could help himself he had better do so. So from that time Wesley began to contemplate how he should escape the doom which had been planned for him.

> A friend [says he] by the name of C. Matterson, told me that he was going off. Then I told him of my master's writing to Mrs. Carroll concerning selling, etc., and that I was going off too. We then concluded to go together. There were two others

– brothers of Matterson – who were told of our plan to escape, and readily joined with us in the undertaking. So one Saturday night, at twelve o'clock, we set out for the North. After traveling upwards of two days and over sixty miles, we found ourselves unexpectedly in Terrytown, Md. There we were informed by a friendly colored man of the danger we were in and of the bad character of the place towards colored people, especially those who were escaping to freedom; and he advised us to hide as quickly as we could. We at once went to the woods and hid. Soon after we had secreted ourselves a man came near by and commenced splitting wood, or rails, which alarmed us. We then moved to another hiding-place in a thicket near a farmer's barn, where we were soon startled again by a dog approaching and barking at us. The attention of the owner of the dog was drawn to his barking and to where we were. The owner of the dog was a farmer. He asked us where we were going. We replied to Gettysburg – to visit some relatives, etc. He told us that we were running off. He then offered friendly advice, talked like a Quaker, and urged us to go with him to his barn for protection. After much persuasion, we consented to go with him.

Soon after putting us in his barn, himself and daughter prepared us a nice breakfast, which cheered our spirits, as we were hungry. For this kindness we paid him one dollar. He next told us to hide on the mow till eve, when he would safely direct us on our road to Gettysburg. All, very much fatigued from traveling, fell asleep, excepting myself; I could not sleep; I felt as if all was not right.

About noon men were heard talking around the barn. I woke my companions up and told them that that man had betrayed us. At first they did not believe me. In a moment afterwards the barn door was opened, and in came the men, eight in number. One of the men asked the owner of the barn if he had any long straw. "Yes," was the answer. So up on the mow came three of the men, when, to their great surprise, as they pretended, we were discovered. The question was then asked the owner of the barn by one of the men, if he harbored runaway negroes in his barn? He answered, "No," and pretended to be entirely ignorant of their being in his barn. One of the men replied that four negroes were on the mow, and he knew of it. The men then asked us where we were, going. We told them to Gettysburg, that we had aunts and a mother there. Also we spoke of a Mr. Houghman, a gentleman we happened to have some knowledge of, having seen him in Virginia. We were next asked for our passes. We told them that we hadn't any, that we had not been required to carry them where we came from. They then said that we would have to go before a magistrate, and if he allowed us to go on, well and good. The men all being armed and furnished with ropes, we were ordered to be tied. I told them if they took me they would have to take me dead or crippled. At that instant one of my friends cried out – "Where is the man that betrayed us?" Spying him at the same moment, he shot him (badly wounding him). Then the conflict fairly began. The constable seized me by the collar, or rather behind my shoulder. I at once shot him with my pistol, but in consequence of his throwing up his arm, which hit mine as I fired, the effect of the load of my pistol was much turned aside; his face, however, was badly burned, besides his shoulder being wounded. I again fired on the pursuers, but do not know whether I hit anybody or not. I then drew a sword, I had brought with me, and was about cutting my way to the door, when I was shot by one of the men, receiving the entire contents of one load of a double barreled gun in my left arm, that being the arm with which I was defending myself. The load brought me to the ground, and I was unable to make further struggle for myself. I was then badly beaten with guns, &c. In the meantime, my friend Craven, who was defending himself, was shot badly in the face, and most violently beaten until he was conquered and tied. The two young brothers of Craven stood still, without making the least resistance. After we were fairly captured, we were taken to Terrytown, which was in sight of where we were betrayed. By this time I had lost so much blood from my wounds, that they concluded my situation was too dangerous to admit of being taken further; so I was made a prisoner at a tavern, kept by a man named Fisher. There my wounds were dressed, and thirty-two shot were taken from my arm. For three days I was crazy, and they thought I would die. During the first two weeks, while I was a prisoner at the tavern, I raised a great deal of blood, and was considered in a very dangerous condition – so much so that persons desiring to see me were not permitted. Afterwards I began to get better, and was then kept privately – was strictly watched day and night. Occasionally, however, the cook, a colored woman (Mrs. Smith), would manage to get to see me. Also James Matthews succeeded in getting to see me; consequently, as my wounds healed, and my senses came to me, I began to

> plan how to make another effort to escape. I asked one of the friends, alluded to above, to get me a rope. He got it. I kept it about me four days in my pocket; in the meantime I procured three nails. On Friday night, October 14th, I fastened my nails in under the window sill; tied my rope to the nails, threw my shoes out of the window, put the rope in my mouth, then took hold of it with my well hand, clambered into the window, very weak, but I managed to let myself down to the ground. I was so weak, that I could scarcely walk, but I managed to hobble off to a place three quarters of a mile from the tavern, where a friend had fixed upon for me to go, if I succeeded in making my escape. There I was found by my friend, who kept me secure till Saturday eve, when a swift horse was furnished by James Rogers, and a colored man found to conduct me to Gettysburg. Instead of going direct to Gettysburg, we took a different road, in order to shun our pursuers, as the news of my escape had created general excitement. My three other companions, who were captured, were sent to Westminster jail, where they were kept three weeks, and afterwards sent to Baltimore and sold for twelve hundred dollars a piece, as I was informed while at the tavern in Terrytown.

The Vigilance Committee procured good medical attention and afforded the fugitive time for recuperation, furnished him with clothing and a free ticket, and sent him on his way greatly improved in health, and strong in the faith that, "He who would be free, himself must strike the blow." His safe arrival in Canada, with his thanks, were duly announced. And some time after becoming naturalized, in one of his letters, he wrote that he was a brakesman on the Great Western R.R., (in Canada – promoted from the U.G.R.R.,) the result of being under the protection of the British Lion.

# JAMES MERCER

## WM. H. GILLIAM,
## AND JOHN CLAYTON

*STOWED AWAY IN A HOT BERTH.*

This arrival came by Steamer. But they neither came in Stateroom nor as Cabin, Steerage, or Deck passengers.

A certain space, not far from the boiler, where the heat and coal dust were almost intolerable, – the colored steward on the boat in answer to an appeal from these unhappy bondmen, could point to no other place for concealment but this. Nor was he at all certain that they could endure the intense heat of that place. It admitted of no other posture than lying flat down, wholly shut out from the light, and nearly in the same predicament in regard to the air. Here, however, was a chance of throwing off the yoke, even if it cost them their lives. They considered and resolved to try it at all hazards.

Henry Box Brown's sufferings were nothing, compared to what these men submitted to during the entire journey.

They reached the house of one of the Committee about three o'clock, A.M.

All the way from the wharf the cold rain poured down in torrents and they got completely drenched, but their hearts were swelling with joy and gladness unutterable. From the thick coating of coal dust, and the effect of the rain added thereto, all traces of natural appearance were entirely obliterated, and they looked frightful in the extreme. But they had placed their lives in mortal peril for freedom.

Every step of their critical journey was reviewed and commented on, with matchless natural eloquence, – how, when almost on the eve of suffocating in their warm berths, in order to catch a breath of air, they were compelled to crawl, one at a time, to a small aperture; but scarcely would one poor fellow pass three minutes being thus refreshed, ere the others would insist that he should "go back to his hole." Air was precious, but for the time being they valued their liberty at still greater price.

After they had talked to their hearts' content, and after they had been thoroughly cleansed and changed in apparel, their physical appearance could be easily discerned, which made it less a wonder whence such outbursts of eloquence had emanated. They bore every mark of determined manhood.

The date of this arrival was February 26, 1854, and the following description was then recorded –

> Arrived, by Steamer *Pennsylvania*, James Mercer, William H. Gilliam and John Clayton, from Richmond.

James was owned by the widow, Mrs. T.E. White. He is thirty-two years of age, of dark complexion, well made, good-looking, reads and writes, is very fluent in speech, and remarkably intelligent. From a boy, he had been hired out. The last place he had the honor to fill before escaping, was with Messrs. Williams and Brother, wholesale commission merchants. For his services in this store the widow had been drawing one hundred and twenty-five dollars per annum, clear of all expenses.

He did not complain of bad treatment from his mistress, indeed, he spoke rather favorably of her. But he could not close his eyes to the fact, that at one time Mrs. White had been in possession of thirty head of slaves, although at the time he was counting the cost of escaping, two only remained – himself and William, (save a little boy) and on himself a mortgage for seven hundred and fifty dollars was then resting.

He could, therefore, with his remarkably quick intellect, calculate about how long it would be before he reached the auction block.

He had a wife but no child. She was owned by Mr. Henry W. Quarles. So out of that Sodom he felt he would have to escape, even at the cost of leaving his wife behind. Of course he felt hopeful that the way would open by which she could escape at a future time, and so it did, as will appear by and by. His aged mother he had to leave also.

Wm. Henry Gilliam likewise belonged to the Widow White, and he had been hired to Messrs. White and Brother to drive their bread wagon. William was a baker by trade. For his services his mistress had received one hundred and thirty-five dollars per year. He thought his mistress quite as good, if not a little better than most slave-holders. But he had never felt persuaded to believe that she was good enough for him to remain a slave for her support.

Indeed, he had made several unsuccessful attempts before this time to escape from slavery and its horrors. He was fully posted from A to Z, but in his own person he had been smart enough to escape most of the more brutal outrages. He knew how to read and write, and in readiness of speech and general natural ability was far above the average of slaves.

He was twenty-five years of age, well made, of light complexion, and might be put down as a valuable piece of property.

This loss fell with crushing weight upon the kind-hearted mistress, as will be seen in a letter subjoined which she wrote to the unfaithful William, some time after he had fled.

## LETTER FROM MRS. L.E. WHITE

RICHMOND,
*16th, 1854.*

DEAR HENRY: – Your mother and myself received your letter; she is much distressed at your conduct; she is remaining just as you left her, she says, and she will never be reconciled to your conduct.

I think Henry, you have acted most dishonorably; had you have made a confidant of me I would have been better off; and you as you are. I am badly situated, living with Mrs. Palmer, and having to put up with everything – your mother is also dissatisfied – I am miserably poor, do not get a cent of your hire or James', besides losing you both, but if you can *reconcile* so do. By renting a cheap house, I might have lived, now it seems starvation is before me. Martha and the Doctor are living in Portsmouth, it is not in her power to do much for me. I know you will repent it. I heard six weeks before you went, that you were trying to persuade him off – but we all liked you, and I was unwilling to believe it – however, I leave it in God's hands He will know what to do. Your mother says that I must tell you servant Jones is *dead* and old *Mrs. Galt.* Kit is well, but we are very uneasy, losing your and *James' hire*, I fear poor little fellow, that he will be obliged to go, as I am compelled to live, and it will be your fault. I am quite unwell, but of course, you don't care.

Yours,
L.E. WHITE.

> If you choose to come back you could. I would do a very good part by you, Toler and Cooke has none.

This touching epistle was given by the disobedient William to a member of the Vigilant Committee, when on a visit to Canada, in 1855, and it was thought to be of too much value to be lost. It was put away with other valuable U.G.R.R. documents for future reference. Touching the "rascality" of William and James and the unfortunate predicament in which it placed the kind-hearted widow, Mrs. Louisa White, the following editorial clipped from the wide-awake *Richmond Despatch*, was also highly appreciated, and preserved as conclusive testimony to the successful working of the U.G.R.R. in the Old Dominion. It reads thus –

> RASCALITY SOMEWHERE. – We called attention yesterday to the advertisement of two negroes belonging to Mrs. Louisa White, by Toler & Cook, and in the call we expressed the opinion that they were still lurking about the city, preparatory to going off. Mr. Toler, we find, is of a different opinion. He believes that they have already cleared themselves – have escaped to a Free State, and we think it extremely probable that he is in the right. They were both of them uncommonly intelligent negroes. One of them, the one hired to Mr. White, was a tip-top baker. He had been all about the country, and had been in the habit of supplying the U.S. *Pennsylvania* with bread; Mr. W. having the contract. In his visits for this purpose, of course, he formed acquaintances with all sorts of sea-faring characters; and there is every reason to believe that he has been assisted to get off in that way, along with the other boy,

> hired to the Messrs. Williams. That the two acted in concert, can admit of no doubt. The question is now to find out how they got off. They must undoubtedly have had white men in the secret. Have we then a nest of Abolition scoundrels among us? There ought to be a law to put a police officer on board every vessel as soon as she lands at the wharf. There is one, we believe for inspecting vessels before they leave. If there is not there ought to be one.
>
> These negroes belong to a widow lady and constitute all the property she has on earth. They have both been raised with the greatest indulgence. Had it been otherwise, they would never have had an opportunity to escape, as they have done. Their flight has left her penniless. Either of them would readily have sold for $1,200; and Mr. Toler advised their owner to sell them at the commencement of the year, probably anticipating the very thing that has happened. She refused to do so, because she felt too much attachment to them. They have made a fine return, truly.

No comment is necessary on the above editorial except simply to express the hope that the editor and his friends who seemed to be utterly befogged as to how these "uncommonly intelligent negroes" made their escape, will find the problem satisfactorily solved in this book.

However, in order to do even-handed justice to all concerned, it seems but proper that William and James should be heard from, and hence a letter from each is here appended for what they are worth. True they were intended only for private use, but since the "True light" (Freedom) has come, all things may be made manifest.

## LETTER FROM WILLIAM HENRY GILLIAM

ST. CATHARINES, C.W.,
*May 15th, 1854.*

My Dear Friend: – I receaved yours, Dated the 10th and the papers on the 13th, I also saw the pice that was in Miss Shadd's paper About me. I think Tolar is right About my being in A free State, I am and think A great del of it. Also I have no compassion on the penniless widow lady, I have Served her 25 yers 2 months, I think that is long Enough for me to live A Slave. Dear Sir, I am very sorry to hear of the Accadent that happened to our Friend Mr. Meakins, I have read the letter to all that lives in St. Catharines, that came from old Virginia, and then I Sented to Toronto to Mercer & Clayton to see, and to Farman to read fur themselves. Sir, you must write to me soon and let me know how Meakins gets on with his tryal, and you must pray for him, I have told all here to do the same for him. May God bless and protect him from prison, I have heard A great del of old Richmond and Norfolk. Dear Sir, if you see Mr. or Mrs. Gilbert Give my love to them and tell them to write to me, also give my respect to your Family and A part for yourself, love from the friends to you Soloman Brown, H. Atkins, Was. Johnson, Mrs. Brooks, Mr. Dykes. Mr. Smith is better at presant. And do not forget to write the News of Meakin's tryal. I cannot say any more at this time; but remain yours and A true Friend ontell Death.

W.H. GILLIAM, the widow's Mite.

"Our friend Minkins," in whose behalf William asks the united prayers of his friends, was one of the "scoundrels" who assisted him and his two companions to escape on the steamer. Being suspected of "rascality" in this direction, he was arrested and put in jail, but as no evidence could be found against him he was soon released.

## JAMES MERCER'S LETTER

TORONTO,
*March 17th, 1854.*

My dear friend Still: – I take this method of informing you that I am well, and when this comes to hand it may find you and your family enjoying good health. Sir, my particular for writing is that I wish to hear from you, and to hear all the news from down South. I wish to know if all things are working Right for the Rest of my Brotheran whom in bondage. I will also Say that I am very much please with Toronto, So also the friends that came over with. It is true that we have not been Employed as yet; but we are in hopes of be'en so in a few days. We happen here in good time jest about time the people in this country are going work. I am in good health and good Spirits, and feeles Rejoiced in the Lord for my liberty. I Received cople of paper from you to-day. I wish you see James Morris whom or Abram George the first and second on the Ship *Penn.*, give my respects to them, and ask James if he will call at Henry W. Quarles on May street oppisit the Jews synagogue and call for Marena Mercer, give my love to her ask her of all the times about

Richmond, tell her to Send me all the news. Tell Mr. Morris that there will be no danger in going to that place. You will also tell M. to make himself known to her as she may know who sent him. And I wish to get a letter from you.

JAMES M. MERCER.

## JOHN H. HILL'S LETTER

My friend, I would like to hear from you, I have been looking for a letter from you for Several days as the last was very interesting to me, please to write Right away.

Yours most Respectfully,
JOHN H. HILL.

Instead of weeping over the sad situation of his "penniless" mistress and showing any signs of contrition for having wronged the man who held the mortgage of seven hundred and fifty dollars on him, James actually "feels rejoiced in the Lord for his liberty," and is "very much pleased with Toronto;" but is not satisfied yet, he is even concocting a plan by which his wife might be run off from Richmond, which would be the cause of her owner (Henry W. Quarles, Esq.) losing at least one thousand dollars,

ST. CATHARINE, CANADA,
*June 8th, 1854.*

MR. STILL, DEAR FRIEND: – I received a letter from the poor old widow, Mrs. L.E. White, and she says I may come back if I choose and she will do a good part by me. Yes, yes I am choosing the western side of the South for my home. She is smart, but cannot bung my eye, so she shall have to die in the poor house at last, so she says, and Mercer and myself will be the cause of it. That is all right. I am getting even with her now for I was in the poor house for twenty-five years and have just got out. And she said she knew I was coming away six weeks before I started, so you may know my chance was slim. But Mr. John Wright said I came off like a gentleman and he did not blame me for coming for I was a great boy. Yes I here him enough he is all gas. I am in Canada, and they cannot help themselves.

About that subject I will not say anything more. You must write to me as soon as you can and let me here the news and how the Family is and yourself. Let me know how the times is with the U.G.R.R. Co. Is it doing good business? Mr. Dykes sends his respects to you. Give mine to your family.

Your true friend,
W.H. GILLIAM.

John Clayton, the companion in tribulation of William and James, must not be lost sight of any longer. He was owned by the Widow Clayton, and was white enough to have been nearly related to her, being a mulatto. He was about thirty-five years of age, a man of fine appearance, and quite intelligent. Several years previous he had made an attempt to escape, but failed. Prior to escaping in this instance, he had been laboring in a tobacco factory at $150 a year. It is needless to say that he did not approve of the "peculiar institution." He left a wife and one child behind to mourn after him. Of his views of Canada and Freedom, the following frank and sensible letter, penned shortly after his arrival, speaks for itself –

TORONTO,
*March 6th, 1854.*

DEAR MR. STILL: – I take this method of informing you that I am well both in health and mind. You may rest assured that I fells myself a free man and do not fell as I did when I was in Virginia thanks be to God I have no master into Canada but I am my own man. I arrived safe into Canada on friday last. I must request of you to write a few lines to my wife and jest state to her that her friend arrived safe into this glorious land of liberty and I am well and she will make very short her time in Virginia. tell her that I likes here very well and hopes to like it better when I gets to work I don't meane for you to write the same words that are written above but I wish you give her a clear understanding where I am and Shall Remain here untel She comes or I hears from her.

Nothing more at present but remain yours most respectfully,
JOHN CLAYTON.

You will please to direct the to Petersburg Luenena Johns or Clayton John is best.

# CLARISSA DAVIS

*ARRIVED DRESSED IN MALE ATTIRE.*

Clarissa fled from Portsmouth, Va., in May, 1854, with two of her brothers. Two months and a half before she succeeded in getting off, Clarissa had made a desperate effort, but failed. The brothers succeeded, but she was left. She had not given up all hope of escape, however, and therefore sought "a safe hiding-place until an opportunity might offer," by which she could follow her brothers on the U.G.R.R. Clarissa was owned by Mrs. Brown and Mrs. Burkley, of Portsmouth, under whom she had always served.

Of them she spoke favorably, saying that she "had not been used as hard as many others were." At this period, Clarissa was about twenty-two years of age, of a bright brown complexion, with handsome features, exceedingly respectful and modest, and possessed all the characteristics of a well-bred young lady. For one so little acquainted with books as she was, the correctness of her speech was perfectly astonishing.

For Clarissa and her two brothers a "reward of one thousand dollars" was kept standing in the papers for a length of time, as these (articles) were considered very rare and valuable; the best that could be produced in Virginia.

In the meanwhile the brothers had passed safely on to New Bedford, but Clarissa remained secluded, "waiting for the storm to subside." Keeping up courage day by day, for seventy-five days, with the fear of being detected and severely punished, and then sold, after all her hopes and struggles, required the faith of a martyr. Time after time, when she hoped to succeed in making her escape, ill luck seemed to disappoint her, and nothing but intense suffering appeared to be in store. Like many others, under the crushing weight of oppression, she thought she "should have to die" ere she tasted liberty. In this state of mind, one day, word was conveyed to her that the steamship, *City of Richmond*, had arrived from Philadelphia, and that the steward on board (with whom she was acquainted) had consented to secrete her this trip, if she could manage to reach the ship safely, which was to start the next day. This news to Clarissa was both cheering and painful. She had been "praying all the time while waiting," but now she felt "that if it would only rain right hard the next morning about three o'clock, to drive the police officers off the street, then she could safely make her way to the boat." Therefore she prayed anxiously all that day that it would rain, "but no sign of rain appeared till towards midnight." The prospect looked horribly discouraging; but she prayed on, and at the appointed hour (three o'clock – before day), the rain descended in torrents. Dressed in male attire, Clarissa left the miserable coop where she had been almost without light or air for two and a half months, and unmolested, reached the boat safely, and was secreted in a box by Wm. Bagnal, a clever young man who sincerely sympathized with the slave, having a wife in slavery himself; and by him she was safely delivered into the hands of the Vigilance Committee.

Clarissa Davis here, by advice of the Committee, dropped her old name, and was straightway christened "Mary D. Armstead." Desiring to join her brothers and sister in New Bedford, she was duly furnished with her U.G.R.R. passport and directed thitherward. Her father, who was left behind when she got off, soon after made his way on North, and joined his children. He was too old and infirm probably to be worth anything, and had been allowed to go free, or to purchase himself for a mere nominal sum. Slaveholders would, on some such occasions, show wonderful liberality in letting their old slaves go free, when they could work no more. After reaching New Bedford, Clarissa manifested her gratitude in writing to her friends in Philadelphia repeatedly, and evinced a very lively interest in the U.G.R.R. The appended letter indicates her sincere feelings of gratitude and deep interest in the cause –

NEW BEDFORD,
*August 26, 1855.*

MR. STILL: – I avail my self to write you thes few lines hopeing they may find you and your family well as they leaves me very well and all the family well except my father he seams to be improveing with his shoulder he has been able to work a little I received the papers I was highly delighted to receive them I was very glad to hear from you in the wheler case I was very glad to hear that the persons ware safe I was very sory to hear that mr Williamson was put in prison but I know if the praying part of the people will pray for him and if he will put his trust in the lord he will bring him out more than conquer please remember my Dear old farther and sisters and brothers to your family kiss the children for me I hear that the yellow fever is very bad down south now if the underground railroad could have free course the emergrant would cross the river of gordan rapidly I hope it may continue to run and I hope the wheels of the car may be greesed with more substantial greese so they may run over swiftly I would have wrote before but circumstances would not permit me Miss Sanders and all the friends desired to be remembered to you and your family I shall be pleased to hear from the underground rail road often.

Yours respectfully,

MARY D. ARMSTEAD.

# ANTHONY BLOW
## ALIAS HENRY LEVISON

*SECRETED TEN MONTHS BEFORE STARTING – EIGHT DAYS STOWED AWAY ON A STEAMER BOUND FOR PHILADELPHIA.*

Arrived from Norfolk, about the 1st of November, 1854. Ten months before starting, Anthony had been closely concealed. He belonged to the estate of Mrs. Peters, a widow, who had been dead about one year before his concealment.

On the settlement of his old mistress' estate, which was to take place one year after her death, Anthony was to be transferred to Mrs. Lewis, a daughter of Mrs. Peters (the wife of James Lewis, Esq.). Anthony felt well satisfied that he was not the slave to please the "tyrannical whims" of his anticipated master, young Lewis, and of course he hated the idea of having to come under his yoke. And what made it still more unpleasant for Anthony was that Mr. Lewis would frequently remind him that it was his intention to "sell him as soon as he got possession – the first day of January." "I can get fifteen hundred dollars for you easily, and I will do it." This contemptuous threat had caused Anthony's blood to boil time and again. But Anthony had to take the matter as calmly as possible, which, however, he was not always able to do.

At any rate, Anthony concluded that his "young master had counted the chickens before they were hatched." Indeed here Anthony began to be a deep thinker. He thought, for instance, that he had already been shot three times, at the instance of slave-holders. The first time he was shot was for refusing a flogging when only eighteen years of age. The second time, he was shot in the head with squirrel shot by the sheriff, who was attempting to arrest him for having resisted three "young white ruffians," who wished to have the pleasure of beating him, but got beaten themselves. And in addition to being shot this time, Anthony was still further "broke in" by a terrible flogging from the Sheriff. The third time Anthony was shot he was about twenty-one years of age. In this instance he was punished for his old offence – he "would not be whipped."

This time his injury from being shot was light, compared with the two preceding attacks. Also in connection with these murderous conflicts, he could not forget that he had been sold on the auction block. But he had still deeper thinking to do yet. He determined that his young master should never get "fifteen hundred dollars for him on the 1st of January," unless he got them while he (Anthony) was running. For Anthony had fully made up his mind that when the last day of December ended, his bondage should end also, even if he should have to accept death as a substitute. He then began to think of the Underground Rail Road and of Canada; but who the agents were, or how to find the depot, was a serious puzzle to him. But his time was getting so short he was convinced that whatever he did would have to be done quickly. In this frame of mind he found a man who professed to know something about the Underground Rail Road, and for "thirty dollars" promised to aid him in the matter.

The thirty dollars were raised by the hardest effort and passed over to the pretended friend, with the expectation that it would avail greatly in the emergency. But Anthony found himself sold for thirty dollars, as nothing was done for him. However, the 1st day of January arrived, but Anthony was not to be found to answer to his name at roll call. He had "took out" very early in the morning. Daily he prayed in his place of concealment how to find the U.G.R.R. Ten months passed away, during which time he suffered almost death, but persuaded himself to believe that even that was better than slavery. With Anthony, as it has been with thousands of others similarly situated, just as everything was looking the most hopeless, word came to him in his place of concealment that a friend named Minkins, employed on the steamship *City of Richmond*, would undertake to conceal him on the boat, if he could be crowded in a certain place, which was about the only spot that would be perfectly safe. This was glorious news to Anthony; but it was well for him that he was ignorant of the situation that awaited him on the boat, or his heart might have failed him. He was willing, however, to risk his life for freedom, and, therefore, went joyfully.

The hiding-place was small and he was large. A sitting attitude was the only way he could possibly occupy it. He was contented. This place was "near the range, directly over the boiler," and of course, was very warm. Nevertheless, Anthony felt that he would not murmur, as he knew what suffering was pretty well, and especially as he took it for granted that he would be free in about a day and a half – the usual time it took the steamer to make her trip. At the appointed hour the steamer left Norfolk for Philadelphia, with Anthony sitting flat down in his U.G.R.R. berth, thoughtful and hopeful. But before the steamer had made half her distance the storm was tossing the ship hither and thither fearfully. Head winds blew terribly, and for a number of days the elements seemed perfectly mad. In addition to the extraordinary state of the weather, when the storm subsided the fog took its place and held the mastery of the ship with equal despotism until the end of over seven days, when finally the storm, wind, and fog all disappeared, and on the eighth day of her boisterous passage the steamship *City of Richmond* landed at the wharf of Philadelphia, with this giant and hero on board who had suffered for ten months in his concealment on land and for eight days on the ship.

Anthony was of very powerful physical proportions, being six feet three inches in height, quite black, very intelligent, and of a temperament that would not submit to slavery. For some years his master, Col. Cunnagan, had hired him out in Washington, where he was accused of being in the schooner *Pearl*, with Capt. Drayton's memorable "seventy fugitives on board, bound for Canada." At this time he was stoker in a machine shop, and was at work on an anchor weighing "ten thousand pounds." In the excitement over the attempt to escape in the *Pearl*, many were arrested, and the officers with irons visited Anthony at the machine shop to arrest him, but he declined to let them put the hand-cuffs on him, but consented to go with them, if permitted to do so without being ironed. The officers yielded, and Anthony went willingly to the jail. Passing unnoticed other interesting conflicts in his hard life, suffice it to say, he left his wife, Ann, and three children, Benjamin, John and Alfred, all owned by Col. Cunnagan. In this brave-hearted man, the Committee felt a deep interest, and accorded him their usual hospitalities.

# SHERIDAN FORD

*SECRETED IN THE WOODS –*
*ESCAPES IN A STEAMER.*

About the twenty-ninth of January, 1855, Sheridan arrived from the Old Dominion and a life of bondage, and was welcomed cordially by the Vigilance Committee. Miss Elizabeth Brown of Portsmouth, Va. claimed Sheridan as her property. He spoke rather kindly of her, and felt that he "had not been used very hard" as a general thing, although, he wisely added, "the best usage was bad enough." Sheridan had nearly reached his twenty-eighth year, was tall and well made, and possessed of a considerable share of intelligence.

Not a great while before making up his mind to escape, for some trifling offence he had been "stretched up with a rope by his hands," and "whipped unmercifully." In addition to this he had "got wind of the fact," that he was to be auctioneered off; soon these things brought serious reflections to Sheridan's mind, and among other questions, he began to ponder how he could get a ticket on the U.G.R.R., and get out of this "place of torment," to where he might have the benefit of his own labor. In this state of mind, about the fourteenth day of November, he took his first and daring step. He went not, however, to learned lawyers or able ministers of the Gospel in his distress and trouble, but wended his way "directly to the woods," where he felt that he would be safer with the wild animals and reptiles, in solitude, than with the barbarous civilization that existed in Portsmouth.

The first day in the woods he passed in prayer incessantly, all alone. In this particular place of seclusion he remained "four days and nights," "two days suffered severely from hunger, cold and thirst." However, one who was a "friend" to him, and knew of his whereabouts, managed to get some food to him and consoling words; but at the end of the four days this friend got into some difficulty and thus Sheridan was left to "wade through deep waters and head winds" in an almost hopeless state. There he could not consent to stay and starve to death. Accordingly he left and found another place of seclusion – with a friend in the town – for a pecuniary consideration. A secret passage was procured for him on one of the steamers running between Philadelphia and Richmond, Va. When he left his poor wife, Julia, she was then "lying in prison to be sold," on the simple charge of having been suspected of conniving at her husband's escape. As a woman she had known something of the "barbarism of slavery", from every-day experience, which the large scars about her head indicated – according to Sheridan's testimony. She was the mother of two children, but had never been allowed to have the care of either of them. The husband, utterly powerless to offer her the least sympathy in word or deed, left this dark habitation of cruelty, as above referred to, with no hope of ever seeing wife or child again in this world.

The Committee afforded him the usual aid and comfort, and passed him on to the next station, with his face set towards Boston. He had heard the slaveholders "curse" Boston so much, that he concluded it must be a pretty safe place for the fugitive.

# HENRY PREDO

*BROKE JAIL, JUMPED OUT OF THE WINDOW AND MADE HIS ESCAPE.*

Henry fled from Buckstown, Dorchester Co., Md., March, 1857. Physically he is a giant. About 27 years of age, stout and well-made, quite black, and no fool, as will appear presently. Only a short time before he escaped, his master threatened to sell him south. To avoid that fate, therefore, he concluded to try his luck on the Underground Rail Road, and, in company with seven others – two of them females – he started for Canada. For two or three days and nights they managed to outgeneral all their adversaries, and succeeded bravely in making the best of their way to a Free State.

In the meantime, however, a reward of $3,000 was offered for their arrest. This temptation was too great to be resisted, even by the man who had been intrusted with the care of them, and who had faithfully promised to pilot them to a safe place. One night, through the treachery of their pretended conductor, they were all taken into Dover Jail, where the Sheriff and several others, who had been notified beforehand by the betrayer, were in readiness to receive them. Up stairs they were taken, the betrayer remarking as they were going up, that they were "cold, but would soon have a good warming." On a light being lit they discovered the iron bars and the fact that they had been betrayed. Their liberty-loving spirits and purposes, however, did not quail. Though resisted brutally by the Sheriff with revolver in hand, they made their way down one flight of stairs, and in the moment of excitement, as good luck would have it, plunged into the Sheriff's private apartment, where his wife and children were sleeping. The wife cried murder lustily. A shovel full of fire, to the great danger of burning the premises, was scattered over the room; out of the window jumped two of the female fugitives. Our hero Henry, seizing a heavy andiron, smashed out the window entire, through which the others leaped a distance of twelve feet. The railing or wall around the jail, though at first it looked forbidding, was soon surmounted by a desperate effort.

At this stage of the proceedings, Henry found himself without the walls, and also lost sight of his comrades at the same time. The last enemy he spied was the sheriff in his stockings without his shoes. He snapped his pistol at him, but it did not go off. Six of the others, however, marvellously got off safely together; where the eighth went, or how he got off, was not known.

# MARY EPPS

## ALIAS EMMA BROWN – JOSEPH AND ROBERT ROBINSON

*A SLAVE MOTHER LOSES HER SPEECH AT THE SALE OF HER CHILD – BOB ESCAPES FROM HIS MASTER, A TRADER, WITH $1,500 IN NORTH CAROLINA MONEY.*

Mary fled from Petersburg and the Robinsons from Richmond. A fugitive slave law-breaking captain by the name of B., who owned a schooner, and would bring any kind of freight that would pay the most, was the conductor in this instance. Quite a number of passengers at different times availed themselves of his accommodations and thus succeeded in reaching Canada.

His risk was very great. On this account he claimed, as did certain others, that it was no more than fair to charge for his services – indeed he did not profess to bring persons for nothing, except in rare instances. In this matter the Committee did not feel disposed to interfere directly in any way, further than to suggest that whatever understanding was agreed upon by the parties themselves should be faithfully adhered to.

Many slaves in cities could raise, "by hook or by crook," fifty or one hundred dollars to pay for a passage, providing they could find one who was willing to risk aiding them. Thus, while the Vigilance Committee of Philadelphia especially neither charged nor accepted anything for their services, it was not to be expected that any of the Southern agents could afford to do likewise.

The husband of Mary had for a long time wanted his own freedom, but did not feel that he could go without his wife; in fact, he resolved to get her off first, then to try and escape himself, if possible. The first essential step towards success, he considered, was to save his money and make it an object to the captain to help him. So when he had managed to lay by one hundred dollars, he willingly offered this sum to Captain B., if he would engage to deliver his wife into the hands of the Vigilance Committee of Philadelphia. The captain agreed to the terms and fulfilled his engagement to the letter. About the 1st of March, 1855, Mary was presented to the Vigilance Committee. She was of agreeable manners, about forty-five years of age, dark complexion, round built, and intelligent. She had been the mother of fifteen children, four of whom had been sold away from her; one was still held in slavery in Petersburg; the others were all dead.

At the sale of one of her children she was so affected with grief that she was thrown into violent convulsions, which caused the loss of her speech for one entire month. But this little episode was not a matter to excite sympathy in the breasts of the highly refined and tender-hearted Christian mothers of Petersburg. In the mercy of Providence, however, her reason and strength returned.

She had formerly belonged to the late Littleton Reeves, whom she represented as having been "kind" to her, much more so than her mistress (Mrs. Reeves). Said Mary, "She being of a jealous disposition, caused me to be hired out with a hard family, where I was much abused, frequently flogged, and stinted for food," etc.

But the sweets of freedom in the care of the Vigilance Committee now delighted her mind, and the hope that her husband would soon follow her to Canada, inspired her with expectations that she would one day "sit under her own vine and fig tree where none dared to molest or make her afraid."

The Committee rendered her the usual assistance, and in due time, forwarded her on to Queen Victoria's free land in Canada. On her arrival she wrote back as follows –

TORONTO,
*March 14th, 1855.*

DEAR MR. STILL: – I take this opportunity of addressing you with these few lines to inform you that I arrived here to-day, and hope that this may find yourself and Mrs. Still well, as this leaves me at the present. I will also say to you, that I had no difficulty in getting along. the two young men that was with me left me at Suspension Bridge. they went another way.

I cannot say much about the place as I have ben here but a short time but so far as I have seen I like very well. you will give my Respect to your lady, & Mr & Mrs Brown. If you have not written to Petersburg you will please to write as soon as can I have nothing More to Write at present but yours Respectfully

EMMA BROWN (old name MARY EPPS).

Now, Joseph and Robert (Mary's associate passengers from Richmond) must here be noticed. Joseph was of a dark orange color, medium size, very active and intelligent, and doubtless, well understood the art of behaving himself. He was well acquainted with the auction block – having been sold three times, and had had the misfortune to fall into the hands of a cruel master each time. Under these circumstances he had had but few privileges. Sundays and week days alike he was kept pretty severely bent down to duty. He had been beaten and knocked around shamefully. He had a wife, and spoke of her in most endearing language, although, on leaving, he did not feel at liberty to apprise her of his movements, "fearing that it would not be safe so to do." His four little children, to whom he appeared warmly attached, he left as he did his wife – in Slavery. He declared that he "stuck to them as long as he could." George E. Sadler, the keeper of an oyster house, held the deed for "Joe," and a most heartless wretch he was in Joe's estimation. The truth was, Joe could not stand the burdens and abuses which Sadler was inclined to heap upon him. So he concluded to join his brother and go off on the U.G.R.R.

Robert, his younger brother, was owned by Robert Slater, Esq., a regular negro trader. Eight years this slave's duties had been at the slave prison, and among other daily offices he had to attend to, was to lock up the prison, prepare the slaves for sale, etc. Robert was a very intelligent young man, and from long and daily experience with the customs and usages of the slave prison, he was as familiar with the business as a Pennsylvania farmer with his barn-yard stock. His account of things was too harrowing for detail here, except in the briefest manner, and that only with reference to a few particulars. In order to prepare slaves for the market, it was usual to have them greased and rubbed to make them look bright and shining. And he went on further to state, that "females as well as males were not uncommonly stripped naked, lashed flat to a bench, and then held by two men, sometimes four, while the brutal trader would strap them with a broad leather strap." The strap being preferred to the cow-hide, as it would not break the skin, and damage the sale. "One hundred lashes would only be a common flogging." The separation of families was thought nothing of. "Often I have been flogged for refusing to flog others." While not yet twenty-three years of age, Robert expressed himself as having become so daily sick of the brutality and suffering he could not help witnessing, that he felt he could not possibly stand it any longer, let the cost be what it might. In this state of mind he met with Captain B. Only one obstacle stood in his way – material aid. It occurred to Robert that he had frequent access to the money drawer, and often it contained the proceeds of fresh sales of flesh and blood; and he reasoned that if some of that would help him and his brother to freedom, there could be no harm in helping himself the first opportunity.

The captain was all ready, and provided he could get three passengers at $100 each he would set sail without much other freight. Of course he was too shrewd to get out papers for Philadelphia. That would betray him at once. Washington or Baltimore, or even Wilmington, Del., were names which stood fair in the eyes of Virginia. Consequently, being able to pack the fugitives away in a very private hole of his boat, and being only bound for a Southern port, the captain was willing to risk his share of the danger. "Very well," said Robert, "to-day I will please my master so well, that I will catch him at an unguarded moment, and will ask him for a pass to go to a ball to-night (slave-holders love to see their slaves fiddling and dancing of nights), and as I shall be leaving in a hurry, I will take a grab from the day's sale, and when Slater hears of me again, I will be in Canada." So after having attended to all his disagreeable duties, he made his "grab," and got a hand full. He did not know, however, how it would hold out. That evening, instead of participating with the gay dancers, he was just one degree lower down than the regular bottom of Captain B's. deck, with several hundred dollars in his pocket, after paying the worthy captain one hundred each for himself and his brother, besides making the captain an additional present of nearly one hundred. Wind and tide were now what they prayed for to speed on the U.G.R.R. schooner, until they might reach the depot at Philadelphia.

The Richmond *Dispatch*, an enterprising paper in the interest of slaveholders, which came daily to the Committee, was received in advance of the passengers, when lo! and behold, in turning to the interesting column containing the elegant illustrations of "runaway negroes," it was seen that the unfortunate Slater had "lost $1,500 in North Carolina money, and also his dark orange-colored, intelligent, and good-looking turnkey, Bob." "Served him right, it is no stealing for one piece of property to go off with another piece," reasoned a member of the Committee.

In a couple of days after the *Dispatch* brought the news, the three U.G.R.R. passengers were safely landed at the usual place, and so accurate were the descriptions in the paper, that, on first seeing them, the Committee recognized them instantly, and, without any previous ceremonies, read to them the advertisement relative to the "$1,500 in N.C. money, &c.," and put the question to them direct: "Are you the ones?" "We are," they owned up without hesitation. The Committee did not see a dollar of their money, but understood they had about $900, after paying the captain; while Bob considered he made a "very good grab," he did not admit that the amount advertised was correct. After a reasonable time for recruiting, having been so long in the hole of the vessel, they took their departure for Canada.

From Joseph, the elder brother, is appended a short letter, announcing their arrival and condition under the British Lion –

SAINT CATHARINE,
*April 16, 1855.*

MR. WILLIAM STILL, DEAR SIR: – Your letter of date April 7th I have just got, it had been opened before it came to me. I have not received any other letter from you and can get no account of them in the Post Office in this place. I am well and have got a good situation in this city and intend staying here. I should be very glad to hear from you as soon as convenient and also from all of my friends near you. My Brother is also at work with me and doing well.

There is nothing here that would interest you in the way of news. There is a Masonic Lodge of our people and two churches and societys here and some other institutions for our benefit. Be kind enough to send a few lines to the Lady spoken of for that mocking bird and much oblige me. Write me soon and believe me your obedient Serv't

Love & respects to Lady and daughter

JOSEPH ROBINSON.

As well as writing to a member of the Committee, Joe and Bob had the assurance to write back to the trader and oyster-house keeper. In their letter they stated that they had arrived safely in Canada, and were having good times, – in the eating line had an abundance of the best, – also had very choice wines and brandies, which they supposed that they (trader and oyster-house keeper) would give a great deal to have a "smack at." And then they gave them a very cordial invitation to make them a visit, and suggested that the quickest way they could come would be by telegraph, which they admitted was slightly dangerous, and without first greasing themselves, and then hanging on very fast, the journey might not prove altogether advantageous to them. This was wormwood and gall to the trader and oyster-house man. A most remarkable coincidence was that, about the time this letter was received in Richmond, the captain who brought away the three passengers, made it his business for some reason or other, to call at the oyster-house kept by the owner of Joe, and while there, this letter was read and commented on in torrents of Billingsgate phrases; and the trader told the captain that he would give him "two thousand dollars if he would get them;" finally he told him he would "give every cent they would bring, which would be much over $2,000," as they were "so very likely." How far the captain talked approvingly, he did not exactly tell the Committee, but they guessed he talked strong Democratic doctrine to them under the frightful circumstances. But he was good at concealing his feelings, and obviously managed to avoid suspicion.

# HENRY BOX BROWN

*ARRIVED BY ADAMS' EXPRESS.*

Although the name of Henry Box Brown has been echoed over the land for a number of years, and the simple facts connected with his marvelous escape from slavery in a box published widely through the medium of anti-slavery papers, nevertheless it is not unreasonable to suppose that very little is generally known in relation to this case.

Briefly, the facts are these, which doubtless have never before been fully published –

Brown was a man of invention as well as a hero. In point of interest, however, his case is no more remarkable than many others. Indeed, neither before nor after escaping did he suffer one-half what many others have experienced.

He was decidedly an unhappy piece of property in the city of Richmond, Va. In the condition of a slave he felt that it would be impossible for him to remain. Full well did he know, however, that it was no holiday task to escape the vigilance of Virginia slave-hunters, or the wrath of an enraged master for committing the unpardonable sin of attempting to escape to a land of liberty. So Brown counted well the cost before venturing upon this hazardous undertaking. Ordinary modes of travel he concluded might prove disastrous to his hopes; he, therefore, hit upon a new invention altogether, which was to have himself boxed up and forwarded to Philadelphia direct by express. The size of the box and how it was to be made to fit him most comfortably, was of his own ordering. Two feet eight inches deep, two feet wide, and three feet long were the exact dimensions of the box, lined with baize. His resources with regard to food and water consisted of the following: One bladder of water and a few small biscuits. His mechanical implement to meet the death-struggle for fresh air, all told, was one large gimlet. Satisfied that it would be far better to peril his life for freedom in this way than to remain under the galling yoke of Slavery, he entered his box, which was safely nailed up and hooped with five hickory hoops, and was then addressed by his next friend, James A. Smith, a shoe dealer, to Wm. H. Johnson, Arch street, Philadelphia, marked, "This side up with care." In this condition he was sent to Adams' Express office in a dray, and thence by overland express to Philadelphia. It was twenty-six hours from the time he left Richmond until his arrival in the City of Brotherly Love. The notice, "This side up, &c.," did not avail with the different expressmen, who hesitated not to handle the box in the usual rough manner common to this class of men. For a while they actually had the box upside down, and had him on his head for miles. A few days before he was expected, certain intimation was conveyed to a member of the Vigilance Committee that a box might be expected by the three o'clock morning train from the South, which might contain a man. One of the most serious walks he ever took – and they had not been a few – to meet and accompany passengers, he took at half past two o'clock that morning to the depot. Not once, but for more than a score of times, he fancied the slave would be dead. He anxiously looked while the freight was being unloaded from the cars, to see if he could recognize a box that might contain a man; one alone had that appearance, and he confessed it really seemed as if there was the scent of death about it. But on inquiry, he soon learned that it was not the one he was looking after, and he was free to say he experienced a marked sense of relief. That same afternoon, however, he received from Richmond a telegram, which read thus, "Your case of goods is shipped and will arrive to-morrow morning."

At this exciting juncture of affairs, Mr. McKim, who had been engineering this important undertaking, deemed it expedient to change the programme slightly in one particular at least to insure greater safety. Instead of having a member of the Committee go again to the depot for the box, which might excite suspicion, it was decided that it would be safest to have the express bring it direct to the Anti-Slavery Office.

But all apprehension of danger did not now disappear, for there was no room to suppose that Adams' Express office had any sympathy with the Abolitionist or the fugitive, consequently for Mr. McKim to appear personally at the express office to give directions with reference to the coming of a box from Richmond which would be directed to Arch street, and yet not intended for that street, but for the Anti-Slavery office at 107 North Fifth street, it needed of course no great discernment to foresee that a step of this kind was wholly impracticable and that a more indirect and covert method would have to be adopted. In this dreadful crisis Mr. McKim, with his usual good judgment and remarkably quick, strategical mind, especially in matters pertaining to the U.G.R.R., hit upon the following plan, namely, to go to his friend, E.M. Davis,[3] who was then extensively engaged in mercantile business, and relate

3 E.M. Davis was a member of the Executive Committee of the Pennsylvania Anti-Slavery Society and a long-tried Abolitionist, son-in-law of James and Lucretia Mott.

the circumstances. Having daily intercourse with said Adams' Express office, and being well acquainted with the firm and some of the drivers, Mr. Davis could, as Mr. McKim thought, talk about "boxes, freight, etc.," from any part of the country without risk. Mr. Davis heard Mr. McKim's plan and instantly approved of it, and was heartily at his service.

## RESURRECTION OF HENRY BOX BROWN

"Dan, an Irishman, one of Adams' Express drivers, is just the fellow to go to the depot after the box," said Davis. "He drinks a little too much whiskey sometimes, but he will do anything I ask him to do, promptly and obligingly. I'll trust Dan, for I believe he is the very man." The difficulty which Mr. McKim had been so anxious to overcome was thus pretty well settled. It was agreed that Dan should go after the box next morning before daylight and bring it to the Anti-Slavery office direct, and to make it all the more agreeable for Dan to get up out of his warm bed and go on this errand before day, it was decided that he should have a five dollar gold piece for himself. Thus these preliminaries having been satisfactorily arranged, it only remained for Mr. Davis to see Dan and give him instructions accordingly, etc.

Next morning, according to arrangement, the box was at the Anti-Slavery office in due time. The witnesses present to behold the resurrection were J.M. McKim, Professor C.D. Cleveland, Lewis Thompson, and the writer.

Mr. McKim was deeply interested; but having been long identified with the Anti-Slavery cause as one of its oldest and ablest advocates in the darkest days of slavery and mobs, and always found by the side of the fugitive to counsel and succor, he was on this occasion perfectly composed.

Professor Cleveland, however, was greatly moved. His zeal and earnestness in the cause of freedom, especially in rendering aid to passengers, knew no limit. Ordinarily he could not too often visit these travelers, shake them too warmly by the hand, or impart to them too freely of his substance to aid them on their journey. But now his emotion was overpowering.

Mr. Thompson, of the firm of Merrihew & Thompson – about the only printers in the city who for many years dared to print such incendiary documents as anti-slavery papers and pamphlets – one of the truest friends of the slave, was composed and prepared to witness the scene.

All was quiet. The door had been safely locked. The proceedings commenced. Mr. McKim rapped quietly on the lid of the box and called out, "All right!" Instantly came the answer from within, "All right, sir!"

The witnesses will never forget that moment. Saw and hatchet quickly had the five hickory hoops cut and the lid off, and the marvellous resurrection of Brown ensued. Rising up in his box, he reached out his hand, saying, "How do you do, gentlemen?" The little assemblage hardly knew what to think or do at the moment. He was about as wet as if he had come up out of the Delaware. Very soon he remarked that, before leaving Richmond he had selected for his arrival-hymn (if he lived) the Psalm beginning with these words: "I waited patiently for the Lord, and He heard my prayer." And most touchingly did he sing the psalm, much to his own relief, as well as to the delight of his small audience.

He was then christened Henry Box Brown, and soon afterwards was sent to the hospitable residence of James Mott and E.M. Davis, on Ninth street, where, it is needless to say, he met a most cordial reception from Mrs. Lucretia Mott and her household. Clothing and creature comforts were furnished in abundance, and delight and joy filled all hearts in that stronghold of philanthropy.

As he had been so long doubled up in the box he needed to promenade considerably in the fresh air, so James Mott put one of his broad-brim hats on his head and tendered him the hospitalities of his yard as well as his house, and while Brown promenaded the yard flushed with victory, great was the joy of his friends.

After his visit at Mr. Mott's, he spent two days with the writer, and then took his departure for Boston, evidently feeling quite conscious of the wonderful feat he had performed, and at the same time it may be safely said that those who witnessed this strange resurrection were not only elated at his success, but were made to sympathize more deeply than ever before with the slave. Also the noble-hearted Smith who boxed him up was made to rejoice over Brown's victory, and was thereby encouraged to render similar service to two other young bondmen, who appealed to him for deliverance. But, unfortunately, in this attempt the undertaking proved a failure. Two boxes containing the young men alluded to above, after having been duly expressed and some distance on the road, were, through the agency of the telegraph, betrayed, and the heroic young fugitives were captured in their boxes and dragged back to hopeless bondage. Consequently, through this deplorable failure, Samuel A. Smith was arrested, imprisoned, and was called upon to suffer severely, as may be seen from the subjoined correspondence, taken from the *New York Tribune* soon after his release from the penitentiary.

## THE DELIVERER OF BOX BROWN – MEETING OF THE COLORED CITIZENS OF PHILADELPHIA

[Correspondence of the *N.Y. Tribune*.]

PHILADELPHIA,
*Saturday, July 5, 1856.*

Samuel A. Smith, who boxed up Henry Box Brown in Richmond, Va., and forwarded him by overland express to Philadelphia, and who was arrested and convicted, eight years ago, for boxing up two other slaves, also directed to Philadelphia, having served out his imprisonment in the Penitentiary, was released on the 18th ultimo, and arrived in this city on the 21st.

Though he lost all his property; though he was refused witnesses on his trial (no officer could be found, who would serve a summons on a witness); though for five long months, in hot weather, he was kept heavily chained in a cell four by eight feet in dimensions; though he received five dreadful stabs, aimed at his heart, by a bribed assassin, nevertheless he still rejoices in the motives which prompted him to "undo the heavy burdens, and let the oppressed go free." Having resided nearly all his life in the South, where he had traveled and seen much of the "peculiar institution," and had witnessed the most horrid enormities inflicted upon the slave, whose cries were ever ringing in his ears, and for whom he had the warmest sympathy, Mr. Smith could not refrain from believing that the black man, as well as the white, had God-given rights. Consequently, he was not accustomed to shed tears when a poor creature escaped ftom his "kind master;" nor was he willing to turn a deaf ear to his appeals and groans, when he knew he was thirsting for freedom. From 1828 up to the day he was incarcerated, many had sought his aid and counsel, nor had they sought in vain. In various places he operated with success. In Richmond, however, it seemed expedient to invent a new plan for certain emergencies, hence the Box and Express plan was devised, at the instance of a few heroic slaves, who had manifested their willingness to die in a box, on the road to liberty, rather than continue longer under the yoke. But these heroes fell into the power of their enemies. Mr. Smith had not been long in the Penitentiary before he had fully gained the esteem and confidence of the Superintendent and other officers. Finding him to be humane and generous-hearted – showing kindness toward all, especially in buying bread, &c., for the starving prisoners, and by a timely note of warning, which had saved the life of one of the keepers, for whose destruction a bold plot had been arranged – the officers felt disposed to show him such favors as the law would allow. But their good intentions were soon frustrated. The Inquisition (commonly called the Legislature), being in session in Richmond, hearing that the Superintendent had been speaking well of Smith, and circulating a petition for his pardon, indignantly demanded to know if the rumor was well founded. Two weeks were spent by the Inquisition, and many witnesses were placed upon oath, to solemnly testify in the matter. One of the keepers swore that his life had been saved by Smith. Col. Morgan, the Superintendent, frequently testified in writing and verbally to Smith's good deportment; acknowledging that he had circulated petitions, &c.; and took the position, that he sincerely believed, that it would be to the interest of the institution to pardon him; calling the attention of the Inquisition, at the same time, to the fact, that not unfrequently pardons had been granted to criminals, under sentence of death, for the most cold-blooded murder, to say nothing of other gross crimes. The effort for pardon was soon abandoned, for the following reason given by the Governor: "I can't, and I won't pardon him!"

In view of the unparalleled injustice which Mr. S. had suffered, as well as on account of the aid he had rendered to the slaves, on his arrival in this city the colored citizens of Philadelphia felt that he was entitled to sympathy and aid, and straightway invited him to remain a few days, until arrangements could be made for a mass meeting to receive him. Accordingly, on last Monday evening, a mass meeting convened in the Israel church, and the Rev. Wm. T. Catto was called to the chair, and Wm. Still was appointed secretary. The chairman briefly stated the object of the meeting. Having lived in the South, he claimed to know something of the workings of the oppressive system of slavery generally, and declared that, notwithstanding the many exposures of the evil which came under his own observation, the most vivid descriptions fell far short of the realities his own eyes had witnessed. He then introduced Mr. Smith, who arose and in a plain manner briefly told his story, assuring the audience that he had always hated slavery, and had taken great pleasure in helping many out of it, and though he had suffered much physically and pecuniarily for the cause' sake, yet he murmured not, but rejoiced in what he had done. After taking his seat, addresses were made by the Rev. S. Smith, Messrs. Kinnard, Brunner, Bradway, and others. The following preamble and resolutions were adopted –

WHEREAS, We, the colored citizens of Philadelphia, have among us Samuel A. Smith, who was incarcerated over seven years in the Richmond Penitentiary, for doing an act that was honorable to his feelings and his sense of justice and humanity, therefore,

*Resolved*, That we welcome him to this city as a martyr to the cause of Freedom.

*Resolved*, That we heartily tender him our gratitude for the good he has done to our suffering race.

*Resolved*, That we sympathize with him in his losses and sufferings in the cause of the poor, down-trodden slave.

W.S.

During his stay in Philadelphia, on this occasion, he stopped for about a fortnight with the writer, and it was most gratifying to learn from him that he was no new worker on the U.G.R.R. But that he had long hated slavery thoroughly, and although surrounded with perils on every side, he had not failed to help a poor slave whenever the opportunity was presented.

Pecuniary aid, to some extent, was rendered him in this city, for which he was grateful, and after being united in marriage, by Wm. H. Furness, D.D., to a lady who had remained faithful to him through all his sore trials and sufferings, he took his departure for Western New York, with a good conscience and an unshaken faith in the belief that in aiding his fellow-man to freedom he had but simply obeyed the word of Him who taught man to do unto others as he would be done by.

# A SLAVE GIRL'S NARRATIVE

*CORDELIA LONEY, SLAVE OF MRS. JOSEPH CAHELL (WIDOW OF THE LATE HON. JOSEPH CAHELL, OF VA.), OF FREDERICKSBURG, VA. – CORDELIA'S ESCAPE FROM HER MISTRESS IN PHILADELPHIA.*

Rarely did the peculiar institution present the relations of mistress and maid-servant in a light so apparently favorable as in the case of Mrs. Joseph Cahell (widow of the late Hon. Jos. Cahell, of Va.), and her slave, Cordelia. The Vigilance Committee's first knowledge of either of these memorable personages was brought about in the following manner.

About the 30th of March, in the year 1859, a member of the Vigilance Committee was notified by a colored servant, living at a fashionable boarding-house on Chestnut street that a lady with a slave woman from Fredericksburg, Va., was boarding at said house, and, that said slave woman desired to receive counsel and aid from the Committee, as she was anxious to secure her freedom, before her mistress returned to the South. On further consultation about the matter, a suitable hour was named for the meeting of the Committee and the Slave at the above named boarding-house. Finding that the woman was thoroughly reliable, the Committee told her "that two modes of deliverance were open before her. One was to take her trunk and all her clothing and quietly retire." The other was to "sue out a writ of habeas corpus; and bring the mistress before the Court, where she would be required, under the laws of Pennsylvania, to show cause why she restrained this woman of her freedom." Cordelia concluded to adopt the former expedient, provided the Committee would protect her. Without hesitation the Committee answered her, that to the extent of their ability, she should have their aid with pleasure, without delay. Consequently a member of the Committee was directed to be on hand at a given hour that evening, as Cordelia would certainly be ready to leave her mistress to take care of herself. Thus, at the appointed hour, Cordelia, very deliberately, accompanied the Committee away from her "kind hearted old mistress."

In the quiet and security of the Vigilance Committee Room, Cordelia related substantially the following brief story touching her relationship as a slave to Mrs. Joseph Cahell. In this case, as with thousands and tens of thousands of others, as the old adage fitly expresses it, "All is not gold that glitters." Under this apparently pious and noble-minded lady, it will be seen, that Cordelia had known naught but misery and sorrow.

Mrs. Cahell, having engaged board for a month at a fashionable private boarding-house on Chestnut street, took an early opportunity to caution Cordelia against going into the streets, and against having anything to say or do with "free niggers in particular"; withal, she appeared unusually kind, so much so, that before retiring to bed in the evening, she would call Cordelia to her chamber, and by her side would take her Prayer-book and Bible, and go through the forms of devotional service. She stood very high both as a church communicant and a lady in society.

For a fortnight it seemed as though her prayers were to be answered, for Cordelia apparently bore herself as submissively as ever, and Madame received calls and accepted invitations from some of the *elite* of the city, without suspecting any intention on the part of Cordelia to escape. But Cordelia could not forget how her children had all been sold by her mistress!

Cordelia was about fifty-seven years of age, with about an equal proportion of colored and white blood in her veins; very neat, respectful and prepossessing in manner.

From her birth to the hour of her escape she had worn the yoke under Mrs. C., as her most efficient and reliable maid-servant. She had been at her mistress' beck and call as seamstress, dressing-maid, nurse in the sickroom, etc., etc., under circumstances that might appear to the casual observer uncommonly favorable for a slave. Indeed, on his first interview with her, the Committee man was so forcibly impressed with the belief, that her condition in Virginia had been favorable, that he hesitated to ask her if she did not desire her liberty. A few moments' conversation with her, however, convinced him of her good sense and decision of purpose with regard to this matter. For, in answer to the first question he put to her, she answered, that, "As many creature comforts and religious privileges as she had been the recipient of under her 'kind mistress,' still she 'wanted to be free,' and 'was bound to leave,' that she had been 'treated very cruelly,' that her children had 'all been sold away' from her; that she had been threatened with sale herself 'on the first insult,'" etc.

She was willing to take the entire responsibility of taking care of herself. On the suggestion of a friend, before leaving her mistress, she was disposed to sue for her freedom, but, upon a reconsideration of the matter, she chose rather to accept the hospitality of the Underground Rail Road, and leave in a quiet way and go to Canada, where she would be free indeed. Accordingly she left her mistress and was soon a free woman.

The following sad experience she related calmly, in the presence of several friends, an evening or two after she left her mistress:

Two sons and two daughters had been sold from her by her mistress, within the last three years, since the death of her master. Three of her children had been sold to the Richmond market and the other in Nelson county.

Paulina was the first sold, two years ago last May. Nat was the next; he was sold to Abram Warrick, of Richmond. Paulina was sold before it was named to her mother that it had entered her mistress's mind to dispose of her. Nancy, from infancy, had been in poor health. Nevertheless, she had been obliged to take her place in the field with the rest of the slaves, of more rugged constitution, until she had passed her twentieth year, and had become a mother. Under these circumstances, the overseer and his wife complained to the mistress that her health was really too bad for a field hand and begged that she might be taken where her duties would be less oppressive. Accordingly, she was withdrawn from the field, and was set to spinning and weaving. When too sick to work her mistress invariably took the ground, that "nothing was the matter," notwithstanding the fact, that her family physician, Dr. Ellsom, had pronounced her "quite weakly and sick."

In an angry mood one day, Mrs. Cahell declared she would cure her; and again sent her to the field, "with orders to the overseer, to whip her every day, and make her work or kill her." Again the overseer said it was "no use to try, for her health would not stand it," and she was forthwith returned. The mistress then concluded to sell her.

One Sabbath evening a nephew of hers, who resided in New Orleans, happened to be on a visit to his aunt, when it occurred to her, that she had "better get Nancy off if possible."

Accordingly, Nancy was called in for examination. Being dressed in her "Sunday best" and "before a poor candle-light," she appeared to good advantage; and the nephew concluded to start with her on the following Tuesday morning. However, the next morning, he happened to see her by the light of the sun, and in her working garments, which satisfied him that he had been grossly deceived; that she would barely live to reach New Orleans; he positively refused to carry out the previous evening's contract, thus leaving her in the hands of her mistress, with the advice, that she should "doctor her up."

The mistress, not disposed to be defeated, obviated the difficulty by selecting a little boy, made a lot of the two, and thus made it an inducement to a purchaser to buy the sick woman; the boy and the woman brought $700.

In the sale of her children, Cordelia was as little regarded as if she had been a cow.

"I felt wretched," she said, with emphasis, "when I heard that Nancy had been sold," which was not until after she had been removed. "But," she continued, "I was not at liberty to make my grief known to a single white soul. I wept and couldn't help it." But remembering that she was liable, "on the first insult," to be sold herself, she sought no sympathy from her mistress, whom she describes as "a woman who shows as little kindness towards her servants as any woman in the States of America. She neither likes to feed nor clothe well."

With regard to flogging, however, in days past, she had been up to the mark. "A many a slap and blow" had Cordelia received since she arrived at womanhood, directly from the madam's own hand.

One day smarting under cruel treatment, she appealed to her mistress in the following strain: "I stood by your mother in all her sickness and nursed her till she died!" "I waited on your niece, night and day for months, till she died." "I waited upon your husband all my life – in his sickness especially, and shrouded him in death, etc., yet I am treated cruelly." It was of no avail.

Her mistress, at one time, was the owner of about five hundred slaves, but within the last few years she had greatly lessened the number by sales.

She stood very high as a lady, and was a member of the Episcopal Church.

To punish Cordelia, on several occasions, she had been sent to one of the plantations to work as a field hand. Fortunately, however, she found the overseers more compassionate than her mistress, though she received no particular favors from any of them.

Asking her to name the overseers, etc., she did so. The first was "Marks, a thin-visaged, poor-looking man, great for swearing." The second was "Gilbert Brower, a very rash, portly man." The third was "Buck Young, a stout man, and very sharp." The fourth was "Lynn Powell, a tall man with red whiskers, very contrary and spiteful." There was also a fifth one, but his name was lost.

Thus Cordelia's experience, though chiefly confined to the "great house," extended occasionally over the corn and tobacco fields, among the overseers and field hands generally. But under no circumstances could she find it in her heart to be thankful for the privileges of Slavery.

After leaving her mistress she learned, with no little degree of pleasure, that a perplexed state of things existed at the boarding-house; that her mistress was seriously puzzled to imagine how she would get her shoes and stockings on and off; how she would get her head combed, get dressed, be attended to in sickness, etc., as she (Cordelia), had been compelled to discharge these offices all her life.

Most of the boarders, being slave-holders, naturally sympathized in her affliction; and some of them went so far as to offer a reward to some of the colored servants to gain a knowledge of her whereabouts. Some charged the servants with having a hand in her leaving, but all agreed that "she had left a very kind and indulgent mistress," and had acted very foolishly in running out of Slavery into Freedom.

A certain Doctor of Divinity, the pastor of an Episcopal church in this city and a friend of the mistress, hearing of her distress, by request or voluntarily, undertook to find out Cordelia's place of seclusion. Hailing on the street a certain colored man with a familiar face, who he thought knew nearly all the colored people about town, he related to him the predicament of his lady friend from the South, remarked how kindly she had always treated her servants, signified that Cordelia would rue the change, and be left to suffer among the "miserable blacks down town," that she would not be able to take care of herself; quoted Scripture justifying Slavery, and finally suggested that he (the colored man) would be doing a duty and a kindness to the fugitive by using his influence to "find her and prevail upon her to return."

It so happened that the colored man thus addressed, was Thomas Dorsey, the well-known fashionable caterer of Philadelphia, who had had the experience of quite a number of years as a slave at the South, – had himself once been pursued as a fugitive, and having, by his industry in the condition of Freedom, acquired a handsome estate, he felt entirely qualified to reply to the reverend gentleman, which he did, though in not very respectful phrases, telling him that Cordelia had as good a right to her liberty as he had, or her mistress either; that God had never intended one man to be the slave of another; that it was all false about the slaves being better off than the free colored people; that he would find as many "poor, miserably degraded," of his own color "down-town," as among the "degraded blacks"; and concluded by telling him that he would "rather give her a hundred dollars to help her off, than to do aught to make known her whereabouts, if he knew ever so much about her."

What further steps were taken by the discomfited divine, the mistress, or her boarding-house sympathizers, the Committee was not informed.

But with regard to Cordelia: she took her departure for Canada, in the midst of the Daniel Webster (fugitive) trial, with the hope of being permitted to enjoy the remainder of her life in Freedom and peace. Being a member of the Baptist Church, and professing to be a Christian, she was persuaded that, by industry and assistance of the Lord, a way would be opened to the seeker of Freedom even in a strange land and among strangers.

This story appeared in part in the *N.Y. Evening Post*, having been furnished by the writer, without his name to it. It is certainly none the less interesting now, as it may be read in the light of Universal Emancipation.

# ARRIVAL OF JACKSON, ISAAC, AND EDMONDSON TURNER FROM PETERSBURG

*TOUCHING SCENE ON MEETING THEIR OLD BLIND FATHER AT THE U.G.R.R. DEPOT.*

## LETTERS AND WARNING TO SLAVEHOLDERS.

About the latter part of December, 1857, Isaac and Edmondson, brothers, succeeded in making their escape together from Petersburg, Va. They barely escaped the auction block, as their mistress, Mrs. Ann Colley, a widow, had just completed arrangements for their sale on the coming first day of January. In this kind of property, however, Mrs. Colley had not largely invested. In the days of her prosperity, while all was happy and contented, she could only boast of "four head:" these brothers, Jackson, Isaac and Edmondson and one other. In May, 1857, Jackson had fled and was received by the Vigilance Committee, who placed upon their books briefly in the following light:

> RUNAWAY – *Fifty Dollars Reward,* – Ran away some time in May last, my *Servantman*, who calls himself *Jackson Turner*. He is about 27 years of age, and has one of his front teeth out. He is quite black, with thick lips, a little bow-legged, and looks down when spoken to. I will give a reward of Fifty dollars if taken out of the city, and, twenty five Dollars if taken within the city. I forewarn all masters of vessels from harboring or employing the said slave; all persons who disregard this Notice will be punished as the law directs.
>
> Petersburg, June 8th, 1857
>
> ANN COLLEY.

JACKSON is quite dark, medium size, and well informed for one in his condition. In Slavery, he had been "pressed hard." His hire, "ten dollars per month" he was obliged to produce at the end of each month, no matter how much he had been called upon to expend for "doctor bills, &c." The woman he called mistress went by the name of Ann Colley, a widow, living near Petersburg. "She was very quarrelsome," although a "member of the Methodist Church." Jackson seeing that his mistress was yearly growing "harder and harder," concluded to try and better his condition "if possible." Having a free wife in the North, who was in the habit of communicating with him, he was kept fully awake to the love of Freedom. The Underground Rail Road expense the Committee gladly bore. No further record of Jackson was made. Jackson found his poor old father here, where he had resided for a number of years in a state of almost total blindness, and of course in much parental anxiety about his boys in chains. On the arrival of Jackson, his heart overflowed with joy and gratitude not easily described, as the old man had hardly been able to muster faith enough to believe that he should ever look with his dim eyes upon one of his sons in Freedom. After a day or two's tarrying, Jackson took his departure for safer and more healthful localities, – her "British Majesty's possessions." The old man remained only to feel more keenly than ever, the pang of having sons still toiling in hopeless servitude.

In less than seven months after Jackson had shaken off the yoke, to the unspeakable joy of the father, Isaac and Edmondson succeeded in following their brother's example, and were made happy partakers of the benefits and blessings of the Vigilance Committee of Philadelphia. On first meeting his two boys, at the Underground Rail Road Depot, the old man took each one in his arms, and as looking through a glass darkly, straining every nerve of his almost lost sight, exclaiming, whilst hugging them closer and closer to his bosom for some minutes, in tears of joy and wonder, "My son Isaac, is this you? my son Isaac, is this you, &c.?" The scene was calculated to awaken the deepest emotion and to bring tears to eyes not accustomed to weep. Little had the old man dreamed in his days of sadness, that he should share such a feast of joy over the deliverance of his sons. But it is in vain to attempt to picture the affecting scene at this reunion, for that would be impossible. Of their slave life, the records contain but a short notice, simply as follows:

"Isaac is twenty-eight years of age, hearty-looking, well made, dark color and intelligent. He was owned by Mrs. Ann Colley, a widow, residing near Petersburg, Va. Isaac and Edmondson were to have been sold, on New Year's day; a few days hence. How sad her disappointment must have been on finding them gone, may be more easily imagined than described."

Edmondson is about twenty-five, a brother of Isaac, and a smart, good-looking young man, was owned by Mrs. Colley also. "This is just the class of fugitives to make good subjects for John Bull," thought the Committee, feeling pretty well assured that they would make good reports after having enjoyed free air in Canada for a short time. Of course, the Committee enjoined upon them very earnestly "not to forget their brethren left behind groaning in fetters; but to prove by their industry, uprightness, economy, sobriety and thrift, by the remembrance of their former days of oppression and their obligations to their God, that they were worthy of the country to which they were going, and so to help break the bands of the oppressors, and undo the heavy burdens of the oppressed." Similar advice was impressed upon the minds of all travelers passing over this branch of the Underground Rail Road. From hundreds thus admonished, letters came affording the most gratifying evidence that the counsel of the Committee was not in vain. The appended letter from the youngest brother, written with his own hand, will indicate his feelings and views in Canada:

HAMILTON, CANADA WEST
*Mar. 1, 1858.*

MR. STILL, DEAR SIR: – I have taken the oppertunity to enform you yur letter came to hand 27th I ware glad to hear from you and yer famly i hope this letter May fine you and the famly Well i am Well my self My Brother join me in Love to you and all the frend. I ware sorry to hear of the death of Mrs freaman. We all must die sune or Late this a date we all must pay we must Perpar for the time she ware a nise lady dear sir the all is well and san thar love to you Emerline have Ben sick But is better at this time. I saw the hills the war well and san thar Love to you. I war sory to hear that My brother war sol i am glad that i did come away when i did god works all the things for the Best he is young he may get a long in the wole May god Bless hem ef you have any News from Petersburg Va Plas Rite me a word when you anser this Letter and ef any person came form home Letter Me know. Please sen me one of your Paper that had the under grands R wrod give My Love to Mr Careter and his family I am Seving with a barber at this time he have promust to give me the trad ef i can lane it he is much of a gentman. Mr Still sir i have writing a letter to Mr Brown of Petersburg Va Pleas reed it and ef you think it right Plas sen it by the Mail or by hand you wall see how i have writen it the will know how sent it by the way this writing ef the ancer it you can sen it to Me i have tol them direc to yor care for Ed. t. Smith Philadelphia i hope it may be right i promorst to rite to hear Please rite to me sune and let me know ef you do sen it on write wit you did with that ma a bught the cappet Bage do not fergit to rite tal John he mite rite to Me. I am doing as well is i can at this time but i get no wagges But my Bord but is satfid at that thes hard time and glad that i am Hear and in good helth. Northing More at this time

yor truly

EDMUND TURNER.

# ROBERT BROWN

## ALIAS THOMAS JONES

*CROSSING THE RIVER ON HORSEBACK IN THE NIGHT.*

In very desperate straits many new inventions were sought after by deep-thinking and resolute slaves, determined to be free at any cost. But it must here be admitted, that, in looking carefully over the more perilous methods resorted to, Robert Brown, alias Thomas Jones, stands second to none, with regard to deeds of bold daring. This hero escaped from Martinsburg, Va., in 1856. He was a man of medium size, mulatto, about thirty-eight years of age, could read and write, and was naturally sharp-witted. He had formerly been owned by Col. John F. Franie, whom Robert charged with various offences of a serious domestic character.

Furthermore, he also alleged, that his "mistress was cruel to all the slaves," declaring that "they (the slaves), could not live with her," that "she had to hire servants," etc.

In order to effect his escape, Robert was obliged to swim the Potomac river on horseback, on Christmas night, while the cold, wind, storm, and darkness were indescribably dismal. This daring bondman, rather than submit to his oppressor any longer, perilled his life as above stated. Where he crossed the river was about a half a mile wide. Where could be found in history a more noble and daring struggle for Freedom?

The wife of his bosom and his four children, only five days before he fled, were sold to a trader in Richmond, Va., for no other offence than simply "because she had resisted" the lustful designs of her master, being "true to her own companion." After this poor slave mother and her children were cast into prison for sale, the husband and some of his friends tried hard to find a purchaser in the neighborhood; but the malicious and brutal master refused to sell her – wishing to gratify his malice to the utmost, and to punish his victims all that lay in his power, he sent them to the place above named.

In this trying hour, the severed and bleeding heart of the husband resolved to escape at all hazards, taking with him a daguerreotype likeness of his wife which he happened to have on hand, and a lock of hair from her head, and from each of the children, as mementoes of his unbounded (though sundered) affection for them.

After crossing the river, his wet clothing freezing to him, he rode all night, a distance of about forty miles. In the morning he left his faithful horse tied to a fence, quite broken down. He then commenced his dreary journey on foot – cold and hungry – in a strange place, where it was quite unsafe to make known his condition and wants. Thus for a day or two, without food or shelter, he traveled until his feet were literally worn out, and in this condition he arrived at Harrisburg, where he found friends. Passing over many of the interesting incidents on the road, suffice it to say, he arrived safely in this city, on New Year's night, 1857, about two hours before day break (the telegraph having announced his coming from Harrisburg), having been a week on the way. The night he arrived was very cold; besides, the Underground train, that morning, was about three hours behind time; in waiting for it, entirely out in the cold, a member of the Vigilance Committee thought he was frosted. But when he came to listen to the story of the Fugitive's sufferings, his mind changed.

Scarcely had Robert entered the house of one of the Committee, where he was kindly received, when he took from his pocket his wife's likeness, speaking very touchingly while gazing upon it and showing it. Subsequently, in speaking of his family, he showed the locks of hair referred to, which he had carefully rolled up in paper separately. Unrolling them, he said, "this is my wife's;" "this is from my oldest daughter, eleven years old;" "and this is from my next oldest;" "and this from the next," "and this from my infant, only eight weeks old." These mementoes he cherished with the utmost care as the last remains of his affectionate family. At the sight of these locks of hair so tenderly preserved, the member of the Committee could fully appreciate the resolution of the fugitive in plunging into the Potomac, on the back of a dumb beast, in order to flee from a place and people who had made such barbarous havoc in his household.

His wife, as represented by the likeness, was of fair complexion, prepossessing, and good looking – perhaps not over thirty-three years of age.

# BARNABY GRIGBY

ALIAS JOHN BOYER, AND MARY ELIZABETH, HIS WIFE; FRANK WANZER, ALIAS ROBERT SCOTT; EMILY FOSTER, ALIAS ANN WOOD

*(TWO OTHERS WHO STARTED WITH THEM WERE CAPTURED.)*

All these persons journeyed together from Loudon Co., Va. on horseback and in a carriage for more than one hundred miles. Availing themselves of a holiday and their master's horses and carriage, they as deliberately started for Canada, as though they had never been taught that it was their duty, as servants, to "obey their masters." In this particular showing a most utter disregard of the interest of their "kind-hearted and indulgent owners." They left home on Monday, Christmas Eve, 1855, under the leadership of Frank Wanzer, and arrived in Columbia the following Wednesday at one o'clock. As willfully as they had thus made their way along, they had not found it smooth sailing by any means. The biting frost and snow rendered their travel anything but agreeable. Nor did they escape the gnawings of hunger, traveling day and night. And whilst these "articles" were in the very act of running away with themselves and their kind master's best horses and carriage – when about one hundred miles from home, in the neighborhood of Cheat river, Maryland, they were attacked by "six white men, and a boy," who, doubtless, supposing that their intentions were of a "wicked and unlawful character" felt it to be their duty in kindness to their masters, if not to the travelers to demand of them an account of themselves. In other words, the assailants positively commanded the fugitives to "show what right" they possessed, to be found in a condition apparently so unwarranted.

The *spokesman* amongst the fugitives, affecting no ordinary amount of dignity, told their assailants plainly, that "no gentleman would interfere with persons riding along civilly" – not allowing it to be supposed that they were slaves, of course. These "gentlemen," however, were not willing to accept this account of the travelers, as their very decided steps indicated. Having the law on their side, they were for compelling the fugitives to surrender without further parley.

At this juncture, the fugitives verily believing that the time had arrived for the practical use of their pistols and dirks, pulled them out of their concealment – the young women as well as the young men – and declared they would not be "taken!" One of the white men raised his gun, pointing the muzzle directly towards one of the young women, with the threat that he would "shoot," etc. "Shoot! Shoot!! Shoot!!!" she exclaimed, with a double barrelled pistol in one hand and a long dirk knife in the other, utterly unterrified and fully ready for a death struggle. The male *leader* of the fugitives by this time had "pulled back the hammers" of his "pistols," and was about to fire! Their adversaries seeing the weapons, and the unflinching determination on the part of the *runaways* to stand their ground, "spill blood, kill, or die," rather than be "taken," very prudently "sidled over to the other side of the road," leaving at least four of the victors to travel on their way.

At this moment the four in the carriage lost sight of the two on horseback. Soon after the separation they heard firing, but what the result was, they knew not. They were fearful, however, that their companions had been captured.

The following paragraph, which was shortly afterwards taken from a Southern paper, leaves no room to doubt, as to the fate of the two.

> Six fugitive slaves from Virginia were arrested at the Maryland line, near Hood's Mill, on Christmas day, but, after a severe fight, four of them escaped and have not since been heard of. They came from Loudoun and Fauquier counties.

Though the four who were successful, saw no "severe fight," it is not unreasonable to suppose, that there was a fight, nevertheless; but not till after the number of the fugitives had been reduced to two, instead of six. As chivalrous as slave-holders and slave-catchers were, they knew the value of their precious lives and the fearful risk of attempting a capture, when the numbers were equal.

The party in the carriage, after the conflict, went on their way rejoicing.

The young men, one cold night, when they were compelled to take rest in the woods and snow, in vain strove to keep the feet of their female companions from freezing by lying on them; but the frost was merciless and bit them severely, as their feet very plainly showed. The following disjointed report was cut from the *Frederick (Md.) Examiner*, soon after the occurrence took place:

> Six slaves, four men and two women, fugitives from Virginia, having with them two spring wagons and four horses, came to Hood's Mill, on the Baltimore and Ohio Railroad, near the dividing line between Frederick and Carroll counties, on Christmas day. After feeding their animals, one of them told a Mr. Dixon whence they came; believing them to be fugitives, he spread the alarm, and some eight or ten persons

> gathered round to arrest them; but the negroes drawing revolvers and bowie-knives, kept their assailants at bay, until five of the party succeeded in escaping in one of the wagons, and as the last one jumped on a horse to flee, he was fired at, the load taking effect in the small of the back. The prisoner says he belongs to Charles W. Simpson, Esq., of Fauquier county, Va., and ran away with the others on the preceding evening.

This report from the *Examiner*, while it is not wholly correct, evidently relates to the fugitives above described. Why the reporter made such glaring mistakes, may be accounted for on the ground that the bold stand made by the fugitives was so bewildering and alarming, that the "assailants" were not in a proper condition to make correct statements. Nevertheless the *Examiner's* report was preserved with other records, and is here given for what it is worth.

These victors were individually noted on the Record thus: Barnaby was owned by William Rogers, a farmer, who was considered a "moderate slaveholder," although of late "addicted to intemperance." He was the owner of about one "dozen head of slaves," and had besides a wife and two children.

Barnaby's chances for making extra "change" for himself were never favorable; sometimes of "nights" he would manage to earn a "trifle." He was prompted to escape because he "wanted to live by the sweat of his own brow," believing that all men ought so to live. This was the only reason he gave for fleeing.

Mary Elizabeth had been owned by Townsend McVee (likewise a farmer), and in Mary's judgment, he was "severe," but she added, "his wife made him so." McVee owned about twenty-five slaves; "he hardly allowed them to talk – would not allow them to raise chickens," and "only allowed Mary three dresses a year;" the rest she had to get as she could. Sometimes McVee would sell slaves – last year he sold two. Mary said that she could not say anything good of her mistress. On the contrary, she declared that her mistress "knew no mercy nor showed any favor."

It was on account of this "domineering spirit," that Mary was induced to escape.

Frank was owned by Luther Sullivan, "the meanest man in Virginia," he said; he treated his people just as bad as he could in every respect. "Sullivan," added Frank, "would 'lowance the slaves and stint them to save food and get rich," and "would sell and whip," etc. To Frank's knowledge, he had sold some twenty-five head. "He sold my mother and her two children to Georgia some four years previous." But the motive which hurried Frank to make his flight was his laboring under the apprehension that his master had some "pretty heavy creditors who might come on him at any time." Frank, therefore, wanted to be from home in Canada when these gentry should make their visit. "My poor mother has been often flogged by master," said Frank. As to his mistress, he said she was "tolerably good."

Ann Wood was owned by McVee also, and was own sister to Elizabeth. Ann very fully sustained her sister Elizabeth's statement respecting the character of her master.

The above-mentioned four were all young and likely. Barnaby was twenty-six years of age, mulatto, medium size, and intelligent – his wife was about twenty-four years of age, quite dark, good-looking, and of pleasant appearance. Frank was twenty-five years of age, mulatto, and very smart; Ann was twenty-two, good-looking, and smart. After their pressing wants had been met by the Vigilance Committee, and after partial recuperation from their hard travel, etc., they were forwarded on to the Vigilance Committee in New York. In Syracuse, Frank (the leader), who was engaged to Emily, concluded that the knot might as well be tied on the U.G.R.R., although penniless, as to delay the matter a single day longer. Doubtless, the bravery, struggles, and trials of Emily throughout the journey, had, in his estimation, added not a little to her charms. Thus after consulting with her on the matter, her approval was soon obtained, she being too prudent and wise to refuse the hand of one who had proved himself so true a friend to Freedom, as well as so devoted to her. The twain were accordingly made one at the U.G.R.R. Station, in Syracuse, by Superintendent-Rev. J.W. Loguen. After this joyful event, they proceeded to Toronto, and were there gladly received by the Ladies' Society for aiding colored refugees.

The following letter from Mrs. Agnes Willis, wife of the distinguished Rev. Dr. Willis, brought the gratifying intelligence that these brave young adventurers fell into the hands of distinguished characters and warm friends of Freedom:

TORONTO,
*28th January, Monday evening, 1856.*

MR. STILL, DEAR SIR: – I have very great pleasure in making you aware that the following respectable persons have arrived here in safety without being annoyed in any way after you saw them. The women, two of them, viz: Mrs. Greegsby and Mrs. Graham, have been rather ailing, but we hope they will very soon be well. They have been attended to by the Ladies' Society, and are most grateful for any attention they have received. The solitary person, Mrs. Graves, has also been attended to; also her box will be looked after. She is pretty well, but rather dull; however, she will get friends and feel more at home by and bye. Mrs. Wanzer is quite well; and also young William Henry Sanderson. They are all of them in pretty good spirits, and I have no doubt they will succeed in whatever business they take up. In the mean time the men are chopping wood, and the ladies are getting plenty sewing. We are always glad to see our colored refugees safe here. I remain, dear sir,

yours respectfully,
AGNES WILLIS,

Treasurer to the Ladies' Society to aid colored refugees.

For a time Frank enjoyed his newly won freedom and happy bride with bright prospects all around; but the thought of having left sisters and other relatives in bondage was a source of sadness in the midst of his joy. He was not long, however, in making up his mind that he would deliver them or "die in the attempt." Deliberately forming his plans to go South, he resolved to take upon himself the entire responsibility of all the risks to be encountered. Not a word did he reveal to a living soul of what he was about to undertake. With "twenty-two dollars" in cash and "three pistols" in his pockets, he started in the lightning train from Toronto for Virginia. On reaching Columbia in this State, he deemed it not safe to go any further by public conveyance, consequently he commenced his long journey on foot, and as he neared the slave territory he traveled by night altogether. For two weeks, night and day, he avoided trusting himself in any house, consequently was compelled to lodge in the woods. Nevertheless, during that space of time he succeeded in delivering one of his sisters and her husband, and another friend in the bargain. You can scarcely imagine the Committee's amazement on his return, as they looked upon him and listened to his "noble deeds of daring" and his triumph. A more brave and self-possessed man they had never seen.

He knew what Slavery was and the dangers surrounding him on his mission, but possessing true courage unlike most men, he pictured no alarming difficulties in a distance of nearly one thousand miles by the mail route, through the enemy's country, where he might have in truth said, "I could not pass without running the gauntlet of mobs and assassins, prisons and penitentiaries, bailiffs and constables, &c." If this hero had dwelt upon and magnified the obstacles in his way he would most assuredly have kept off the enemy's country, and his sister and friends would have remained in chains.

The following were the persons delivered by Frank Wanzer. They were his trophies, and this noble act of Frank's should ever be held as a memorial and honor. The Committee's brief record made on their arrival runs thus:

> "August 18, 1856. Frank Wanzer, Robert Stewart, alias Gasberry Robison, Vincent Smith, alias John Jackson, Betsey

Smith, wife of Vincent Smith, alias Fanny Jackson. They all came from Alder, Loudon county, Virginia."

Robert is about thirty years of age, medium size, dark chestnut color, intelligent and resolute. He was held by the widow Hutchinson, who was also the owner of about one hundred others. Robert regarded her as a "very hard mistress" until the death of her husband, which took place the Fall previous to his escape. That sad affliction, he thought, was the cause of a considerable change in her treatment of her slaves. But yet "nothing was said about freedom," on her part. This reticence Robert understood to mean, that she was still unconverted on this great cardinal principle at least. As he could see no prospect of freedom through her agency, when Frank approached him with a good report from Canada and his friends there, he could scarcely wait to listen to the glorious news; he was so willing and anxious to get out of slavery. His dear old mother, Sarah Davis, and four brothers and two sisters, William, Thomas, Frederick and Samuel, Violet and Ellen, were all owned by Mrs. Hutchinson. Dear as they were to him, he saw no way to take them with him, nor was he prepared to remain a day longer under the yoke; so he decided to accompany Frank, let the cost be what it might.

Vincent is about twenty-three years of age, very "likely-looking," dark color, and more than ordinarily intelligent for one having only the common chances of slaves.

He was owned by the estate of Nathan Skinner, who was "looked upon," by those who knew him, "as a good slave-holder." In slave property, however, he was only interested to the number of twelve head. Skinner "neither sold nor emancipated." A year and a half before Vincent escaped, his master was called to give an account of his stewardship, and there in the spirit land Vincent was willing to let him remain, without much more to add about him.

Vincent left his mother, Judah Smith, and brothers and sisters, Edwin, Angeline, Sina Ann, Adaline Susan, George, John and Lewis, all belonging to the estate of Skinner.

Vincent was fortunate enough to bring his wife along with him. She was about twenty-seven years of age, of a brown color, and smart, and was owned by the daughter of the widow Hutchinson. This mistress was said to be a "clever woman."

# WILLIAM JORDAN

## ALIAS WILLIAM PRICE

Under Governor Badger, of North Carolina, William had experienced Slavery in its most hateful form. True, he had only been twelve months under the yoke of this high functionary. But William's experience in this short space of time, was of a nature very painful.

Previous to coming into the governor's hands, William was held as the property of Mrs. Mary Jordon, who owned large numbers of slaves. Whether the governor was moved by this consideration, or by the fascinating charms of Mrs. Jordon, or both, William was not able to decide. But the governor offered her his hand, and they became united in wedlock. By this circumstance, William was brought into his unhappy relations with the Chief Magistrate of the State of North Carolina. This was the third time the governor had been married. Thus it may be seen, that the governor was a firm believer in wives as well as slaves. Commonly he was regarded as a man of wealth. William being an intelligent piece of property, his knowledge of the governor's rules and customs was quite complete, as he readily answered such questions as were propounded to him. In this way a great amount of interesting information was learned from William respecting the governor, slaves, on the plantation, in the swamps, etc. The governor owned large plantations, and was interested in raising cotton, corn, and peas, and was also a practical planter. He was willing to trust neither overseers nor slaves any further than he could help.

The governor and his wife were both equally severe towards them; would stint them shamefully in clothing and food, though they did not get flogged quite as often as some others on neighboring plantations. Frequently, the governor would be out on the plantation from early in the morning till noon, inspecting the operations of the overseers and slaves.

In order to serve the governor, William had been separated from his wife by sale, which was the cause of his escape. He parted not with his companion willingly. At the time, however, he was promised that he should have some favors shown him; – could make over-work, and earn a little money, and once or twice in the year, have the opportunity of making visits to her. Two hundred miles was the distance between them.

He had not been long on the governor's plantation before his honor gave him distinctly to understand that the idea of his going two hundred miles to see his wife was all nonsense, and entirely out of the question. "If I said so, I did not mean it," said his honor, when the slave, on a certain occasion, alluded to the conditions on which he consented to leave home, etc.

Against this cruel decision of the governor, William's heart revolted, for he was warmly attached to his wife, and so he made up his mind, if he could not see her "once or twice a year even," as he had been promised, he had rather "die," or live in a "cave in the wood," than to remain all his life under the governor's yoke. Obeying the dictates of his feelings, he went to the woods. For ten months before he was successful in finding the Underground Road, this brave-hearted young fugitive abode in the swamps – three months in a cave – surrounded with bears, wild cats, rattle-snakes and the like.

While in the swamps and cave, he was not troubled, however, about ferocious animals and venomous reptiles. He feared only man!

From his own story there was no escaping the conclusion, that if the choice had been left to him, he would have preferred at any time to have encountered at the mouth of his cave a ferocious bear than his master, the governor of North Carolina. How he managed to subsist, and ultimately effected his escape, was listened to with the deepest interest, though the recital of these incidents must here be very brief.

After night he would come out of his cave, and, in some instances, would succeed in making his way to a plantation, and if he could get nothing else, he would help himself to a "pig," or anything else he could conveniently convert into food. Also, as opportunity would offer, a friend of his would favor him with some meal, etc. With this mode of living he labored to content himself until he could do better. During these ten months he suffered indescribable hardships, but he felt that his condition in the cave was far preferable to that on the plantation, under the control of his Excellency, the Governor. All this time, however, William had a true friend, with whom he could communicate; one who was wide awake, and was on the alert to find a reliable captain from the North, who would consent to take this "property," or "freight," for a consideration. He heard at last of a certain Captain, who was then doing quite a successful business in an Underground way. This good news was conveyed to William, and afforded him a ray of hope in the wilderness. As Providence would have it, his hope did not meet with disappointment; nor did his ten months' trial, warring against the barbarism of Slavery, seem too great to endure for Freedom. He was about to leave his cave and his animal and reptile neighbors, – his heart swelling with gladness, – but the thought of soon being beyond the reach of his mistress and master thrilled him with inexpressible delight. He was brought away by Captain F., and turned over to the Committee, who were made to rejoice with him over the signal victory he had gained in his martyr-like endeavors to throw off the yoke, and of course they took much pleasure in aiding him. William was of a dark color, stout made physically, and well knew the value of Freedom, and how to hate and combat Slavery. It will be seen by the appended letter of Thomas Garrett, that William had the good luck to fall into the hands of this tried friend, by whom he was aided to Philadelphia:

WILMINGTON,
*12th mo., 19th, 1855.*

DEAR FRIEND, WILLIAM STILL: – The bearer of this is one of the twenty-one that I thought had all gone North; he left home on Christmas day, one year since, wandered about the forests of North Carolina for about ten months, and then came here with those forwarded to New Bedford, where he is anxious to go. I have furnished him with a pretty good pair of boots, and gave him money to pay his passage to Philadelphia. He has been at work in the country near here for some three weeks, till taken sick; he is, by no means, well, but thinks he had better try to get farther North, which I hope his friends in Philadelphia will aid him to do. I handed this morning Captain Lambson's[4] wife twenty dollars to help

4 Captain Lambson had been suspected of having aided in the escape of slaves from the neighborhood of Norfolk, and was in prison awaiting his trial.

fee a lawyer to defend him. She leaves this morning, with her child, for Norfolk, to be at the trial before the Commissioner on the 24th instant. Passmore Williamson agreed to raise fifty dollars for him. As none came to hand, and a good chance to send it by his wife, I thought best to advance that much.

Thy friend,
THOS. GARRETT.

# JOSEPH GRANT AND JOHN SPEAKS

*TWO PASSENGERS ON THE UNDERGROUND RAIL ROAD, VIA LIVERPOOL.*

It is to be regretted that, owing to circumstances, the account of these persons has not been fully preserved. Could justice be done them, probably their narratives would not be surpassed in interest by any other in the history of fugitives. In 1857, when these remarkable travelers came under the notice of the Vigilance Committee, as Slavery seemed likely to last for generations, and there was but little expectation that these records would ever have the historical value which they now possess, care was not always taken to prepare and preserve them. Besides, the cases coming under the notice of the Committee were so numerous and so interesting, that it seemed almost impossible to do them anything like justice. In many instances the rapt attention paid by friends, when listening to the sad recitals of such passengers, would unavoidably consume so much time that but little opportunity was afforded to make any record of them. Particularly was this the case with regard to the above-mentioned individuals. The story of each was so long and sad, that a member of the Committee in attempting to write it out, found that the two narratives would take volumes. That all traces of these heroes might not be lost, a mere fragment is all that was preserved.

The original names of these adventurers were Joseph Grant and John Speaks. Between two and three years before escaping, they were sold from Maryland to John B. Campbell, a negro trader, living in Baltimore, and thence to Campbell's brother, another trader in New Orleans, and subsequently to Daniel McBeans and Mr. Henry, of Harrison county, Mississippi.

Though both had to pass through nearly the same trial, and belonged to the same masters, this recital must be confined chiefly to the incidents in the career of Joseph. He was about twenty-seven years of age, well made, quite black, intelligent and self-possessed in his manner.

He was owned in Maryland by Mrs. Mary Gibson, who resided at St. Michael's on the Eastern Shore. She was a *nice woman* he said, but her property was under mortgage and had to be sold, and he was in danger of sharing the same fate.

Joseph was a married man, and spoke tenderly of his wife. She "promised" him when he was sold that she would "never marry," and earnestly entreated him, if he "ever met with the luck, to come and see her." She was unaware perhaps at that time of the great distance that was to divide them; his feelings on being thus sundered need not be stated. However, he had scarcely been in Mississippi three weeks, ere his desire to return to his wife, and the place of his nativity, constrained him to attempt to return; accordingly he set off, crossing a lake eighty miles wide in a small boat, he reached Kent Island. There he was captured by the watchman on the Island, who with *pistols, dirk and cutlass* in hand, threatened if he resisted that death would be his instant doom. Of course he was returned to his master.

He remained there a few months, but could content himself no longer to endure the ills of his condition. So he again started for home, walked to Mobile, and thence he succeeded in stowing himself away in a steamboat and was thus conveyed to Montgomery, a distance of five hundred and fifty miles through solid slave territory. Again he was captured and returned to his owners; one of whom always went for immediate punishment, the other being mild thought persuasion the better plan in such cases. On the whole, Joseph thus far had been pretty fortunate, considering the magnitude of his offence.

A third time he summoned courage and steered his course homewards towards Maryland, but as in the preceding attempts, he was again unsuccessful.

In this instance Mr. Henry, the harsh owner, was exasperated, and the mild one's patience so exhausted that they concluded that nothing short of stern measures would cause Joe to reform. Said Mr. Henry: "I had rather lose my right arm than for him to get off without being punished, after having put us to so much trouble."

*Joseph* will now speak for himself.

> He (master) sent the overseer to tie me. I told him I would not be tied. I ran and stayed away four days, which made Mr. Henry very anxious. Mr. Beans told the servants if they saw me, to tell me to come back and I should not be hurt. Thinking that Mr. Beans had always stood to his word, I was over persuaded and came back. He sent for me in his parlor, talked the matter over, sent me to the steamboat (perhaps the one he tried to escape on). After getting cleverly on board the captain told me, I am sorry to tell you, you have to be tied. I was tied and Mr. Henry was sent for. He came: "Well, I have got you at last, beg my pardon and promise you will never run away again and I will not be so hard on you." I could not do it. He then gave me three hundred lashes well laid on. I was stripped entirely naked, and my flesh was as raw as a piece of beef. He made John (the companion who escaped with him) hold one of my feet which I broke loose while being whipped, and when done made him bathe me in salt and water.
>
> Then I resolved to 'go or die' in the attempt. Before starting, one week, I could not work. On getting better we

> went to Ship Island; the sailors, who were Englishmen, were very sorry to hear of the treatment we had received, and counselled us how we might get free.

The counsel was heeded, and in due time they found themselves in Liverpool. There their stay was brief. Utterly destitute of money, education, and in a strange land, they very naturally turned their eyes again in the direction of their native land. Accordingly their host, the keeper of a sailor's boarding house, shipped them to Philadelphia.

But to go back, Joseph saw many things in New Orleans and Mississippi of a nature too horrible to relate, among which were the following:

> I have seen Mr. Beans whip one of his slaves to death, at the tree to which he was tied.
>
> Mr. Henry would make them lie down across a log, stripped naked, and with every stroke would lay the flesh open. Being used to it, some would lie on the log without being tied.
>
> In New Orleans, I have seen women stretched out just as naked as my hand, on boxes, and given one hundred and fifty lashes, four men holding them. I have helped hold them myself: when released they could hardly sit or walk. This whipping was at the *Fancy House*.

The "chain-gangs" he also saw in constant operation. Four and five slaves chained together and at work on the streets, cleaning, &c., was a common sight. He could hardly tell Sunday from Monday in New Orleans, the slaves were kept so constantly going.

# ARRIVAL FROM BALTIMORE

*JEFFERSON PIPKINS, ALIAS DAVID JONES; LOUISA PIPKINS; ELIZABETH BRIT; HARRIET BROWN, ALIAS JANE WOOTON; GRACY MURRY, ALIAS SOPHIA SIMS; EDWARD WILLIAMS, ALIAS HENRY JOHNSON; CHAS. LEE, ALIAS THOMAS BUSHIER.*

Six very clever-looking passengers, all in one party from Baltimore, Md., the first Sunday in April, 1853. Baltimore used to be in the days of Slavery one of the most difficult places in the South for even free colored people to get away from, much more for slaves. The rule forbade any colored person leaving there by rail road or steamboat, without such applicant had been weighed, measured, and then given a bond signed by unquestionable signatures, well known. Baltimore was rigid in the extreme, and was a never-failing source of annoyance, trouble and expense to colored people generally, and not unfrequently to slave-holders too, when they were traveling North with "colored servants." Just as they were ready to start, the "Rules" would forbid colored servants until the law was complied with. Parties hurrying on would on account of this obstruction "have to wait until their hurry was over." As this was all done in the interest of Slavery, the matter was not very loudly condemned. But, notwithstanding all this weighing, measuring and requiring of bonds, many travelers by the Underground Rail Road took passage from Baltimore.

The enterprising individual, whose name stands at the head of this narrative, came directly from this stronghold of Slavery. The widow Pipkins held the title deed for Jefferson. She was unfortunate in losing him, as she was living in ease and luxury off of Jefferson's sweat and labor. Louisa, Harriet, and Grace owed service to Geo. Stewart of Baltimore; Edward was owned by Chas. Moondo, and Chas. Lee by the above Stewart.

Those who would have taken this party for stupid, or for know-nothings, would have found themselves very much mistaken. Indeed they were far from being dull or sleepy on the subject of Slavery at any rate. They had considered pretty thoroughly how wrongfully they, with all others in similar circumstances, had been year in and year out subjected to unrequited toil so resolved to leave masters and mistresses to shift for themselves, while they would try their fortunes in Canada.

Four of the party ranged in age from twenty to twenty-eight years of age, and the other two from thirty-seven to forty. The Committee on whom they called, rendered them due aid and advice, and forwarded them to the Committee in New York.

The following letter from Jefferson, appealing for assistance on behalf of his children in Slavery, was peculiarly touching, as were all similar letters. But the mournful thought that these appeals, sighs, tears and prayers would continue in most cases to be made till death, that nothing could be done directly for the deliverance of such sufferers was often as painful as the escape from the auction block was gratifying.

## LETTER FROM JEFFERSON PIPKINS.

*Sept. 28, 1856.*

To WM. STILL. SIR: – I take the liberty of writing to you a few lines concerning my children, for I am very anxious to get them and I wish you to please try what you can do for me. Their names are Charles and Patrick and are living with Mrs. Joseph G. Wray Murphysborough Hartford county, North Carolina; Emma lives with a Lawyer Baker in Gatesville North Carolina and Susan lives in Portsmouth

Virginia and is stopping with Dr. Collins sister a Mrs. Nash you can find her out by enquiring for Dr. Collins at the ferry boat at Portsmouth, and Rose a coloured woman at the Crawford House can tell where she is. And I trust you will try what you think will be the best way. And you will do me a great favour.

Yours Respectfully,
JEFFERSON PIPKINS.

P.S. I am living at Yorkville near Toronto Canada West. My wife sends her best respects to Mrs. Still.

# BLOOD FLOWED FREELY

*ABRAM GALLOWAY AND RICHARD EDEN, TWO PASSENGERS SECRETED IN A VESSEL LOADED WITH SPIRITS OF TURPENTINE. SHROUDS PREPARED TO PREVENT BEING SMOKED TO DEATH.*

The Philadelphia branch of the Underground Rail Road was not fortunate in having very frequent arrivals from North Carolina. Of course such of her slave population as managed to become initiated in the mysteries of traveling North by the Underground Rail Road were sensible enough to find out nearer and safer routes than through Pennsylvania.

Nevertheless the Vigilance Committee of Philadelphia occasionally had the pleasure of receiving some heroes who were worthy to be classed among the bravest of the brave, no matter who they may be who have claims to this distinction.

In proof of this bold assertion the two individuals whose names stand at the beginning of this chapter are presented. Abram was only twenty-one years of age, mulatto, five feet six inches high, intelligent and the picture of good health. "What was your master's name?" inquired a member of the Committee. "Milton Hawkins," answered Abram. "What business did Milton Hawkins follow?" again queried said member. "He was chief engineer on the Wilmington and Manchester Rail Road" (not a branch of the Underground Rail Road), responded Richard. "Describe him," said the member. "He was a slim built, tall man with whiskers. He was a man of very good disposition. I always belonged to him; he owned three. He always said he would sell before he would use a whip. His wife was a very mean woman; she would whip contrary to his orders." "Who was your father?" was further inquired. "John Wesley Galloway," was the prompt response. "Describe your father?" "He was captain of a government vessel; he recognized me as his son, and protected me as far as he was allowed so to do; he lived at Smithfield, North

Carolina. Abram's master, Milton Hawkins, lived at Wilmington, N.C." "What prompted you to escape?" was next asked. "Because times were hard and I could not come up with my wages as I was required to do, so I thought I would try and do better." At this juncture Abram explained substantially in what sense times were hard, &c. In the first place he was not allowed to own himself; he, however, preferred hiring his time to serving in the usual way. This favor was granted Abram; but he was compelled to pay $15 per month for his time, besides finding himself in clothing, food, paying doctor bills, and a head tax of $15 a year.

Even under this master, who was a man of very good disposition, Abram was not contented. In the second place, he "always thought Slavery was wrong," although he had "never suffered any personal abuse." Toiling month after month the year round to support his master and not himself, was the one intolerable thought. Abram and Richard were intimate friends, and lived near each other. Being similarly situated, they could venture to communicate the secret feelings of their hearts to each other. Richard was four years older than Abram, with not quite so much Anglo-Saxon blood in his veins, but was equally as intelligent, and was by trade, a "fashionable barber," well-known to the ladies and gentlemen of Wilmington. Richard owed service to Mrs. Mary Loren, a widow. "She was very kind and tender to all her slaves." "If I was sick," said Richard, "she would treat me the same as a mother would." She was the owner of twenty, men, women and children, who were all hired out, except the children too young for hire. Besides having his food, clothing and doctor's expenses to meet, he had to pay the "very kind and tender-hearted widow" $12.50 per month, and head tax to the State, amounting to twenty-five cents per month. It so happened, that Richard at this time, was involved in a matrimonial difficulty. Contrary to the laws of North Carolina, he had lately married a free girl, which was an indictable offence, and for which the penalty was then in soak for him – said penalty to consist of thirty-nine lashes, and imprisonment at the discretion of the judge.

So Abram and Richard put their heads together, and resolved to try the Underground Rail Road. They concluded that liberty was worth dying for, and that it was their duty to strike for Freedom even if it should cost them their lives. The next thing needed was information about the Underground Rail Road. Before a great while the captain of a schooner turned up, from Wilmington, Delaware. Learning that his voyage extended to Philadelphia, they sought to find out whether this captain was true to Freedom. To ascertain this fact required no little address. It had to be done in such a way, that even the captain would not really understand what they were up to, should he be found untrue. In this instance, however, he was the right man in the right place, and very well understood his business.

Abram and Richard made arrangements with him to bring them away; they learned when the vessel would start, and that she was loaded with tar, rosin, and spirits of turpentine, amongst which the captain was to secrete them. But here came the difficulty. In order that slaves might not be secreted in vessels, the slave-holders of North Carolina had procured the enactment of a law requiring all vessels coming North to be smoked.

To escape this dilemma, the inventive genius of Abram and Richard soon devised a safe-guard against the smoke. This safe-guard consisted in silk oil cloth shrouds, made large, with drawing strings, which, when pulled over their heads, might be drawn very tightly around their waists, whilst the process of smoking might be in operation. A bladder of water and towels were provided, the latter to be wet and held to their nostrils, should there be need. In this manner they had determined to struggle against death for liberty. The hour approached for being at the wharf. At the appointed time they were on hand ready to go on the boat; the captain secreted them, according to agreement. They were ready to run the risk of being smoked to death; but as good luck would have it, the law was not carried into effect in this instance, so that the "smell of smoke was not upon them." The effect of the turpentine, however, of the nature of which they were totally ignorant, was worse, if possible, than the smoke would have been. The blood was literally drawn from them at every pore in frightful quantities. But as heroes of the bravest type they resolved to continue steadfast as long as a pulse continued to beat, and thus they finally conquered.

The invigorating northern air and the kind treatment of the Vigilance Committee acted like a charm upon them, and they improved very rapidly from their exhaustive and heavy loss of blood. Desiring to retain some memorial of them, a member of the Committee begged one of their silk shrouds, and likewise procured an artist to take the photograph of one of them; which keepsakes have been valued very highly. In the regular order of arrangements the wants of Abram and Richard were duly met by the Committee, financially and otherwise, and they were forwarded to Canada. After their safe arrival in Canada, Richard addressed a member of the Committee thus:

KINGSTON,
*July 20, 1857.*

MR. WILLIAM STILL – *Dear Friend*: – I take the opertunity of wrighting a few lines to let you no that we air all in good health hoping thos few lines may find you and your family engoying the same blessing. We arived in King all saft Canada West Abram Galway gos to work this morning at $1.75 per day and John pediford is at work for mr george mink and i will opne a shop for my self in a few days My wif will send a daugretipe to your cair whitch you will pleas to send on to me Richard Edons to the cair of George Mink

Kingston C W
Yours with Respect,

RICHARD EDONS.

Abram, his comrade, allied himself faithfully to John Bull until Uncle Sam became involved in the contest with the rebels. In this hour of need Abram hastened back to North Carolina to help fight the battles of Freedom. How well he acted his part, we are not informed. We only know that, after the war was over, in the reconstruction of North Carolina, Abram was promoted to a seat in its Senate. He died in office only a few months since. The portrait is almost a "fac-simile."

# THE ESCAPE OF A CHILD FOURTEEN MONTHS OLD

There is found the following brief memorandum on the Records of the Underground Rail Road Book, dated July, 1857:

"A little child of fourteen months old was conveyed to its mother, who had been compelled to flee without it nearly nine months ago."

While the circumstances connected with the coming of this slave child were deeply interesting, no further particulars than the simple notice above were at that time recorded. Fortunately, however, letters from the good friends, who plucked this infant from the jaws of Slavery, have been preserved to throw light on this little one, and to show how true-hearted sympathizers with the Slave labored amid dangers and difficulties to save the helpless bondman from oppression. It will be observed, that both these friends wrote from Washington, D.C., the seat of Government, where, if Slavery was not seen in its worst aspects, the Government in its support of Slavery appeared in a most revolting light.

## LETTER FROM "J.B."

WASHINGTON, D.C.,
*July 12, 1857.*

DEAR SIR: – Some of our citizens, I am told, lately left here for Philadelphia, three of whom were arrested and brought back.

I beg you will inform me whether two others – (I., whose wife is in Philadelphia, was one of them), ever reached your city.

To-morrow morning Mrs. Weems, *with her baby*, will start for Philadelphia and see you probably over night.

Yours Truly,
J.B.

"J.B." was not only a trusty and capable conductor of the Underground Rail Road in Washington, but was also a practical lawyer, at the same time. His lawyer-like letter, in view of the critical nature of the case, contained but few words, and those few naturally enough were susceptible of more than one construction.

Doubtless those styled "our citizens," – three of whom were arrested and brought back," – were causing great anxiety to this correspondent, not knowing how soon he might find himself implicated in the "running off," etc. So, while he felt it to be his duty, to still aid the child, he was determined, if the enemy intercepted his letter, he should not find much comfort or information. The cause was safe in such careful hands. The following letters, bearing on the same case, are also from another good conductor, who was then living in Washington.

## LETTERS FROM E.L. STEVENS

WASHINGTON, D.C.,
*July 8,1857.*

MY DEAR SIR: – I write you now to let you know that the children of E. are yet well, and that Mrs. Arrah Weems will start with one of them for Philadelphia to-morrow or next day. She will be with you probably in the day train. She goes for the purpose of making an effort to redeem her last child, now in Slavery. The whole amount necessary is raised, except about $300. She will take her credentials with her, and you can place the most implicit reliance on her statements. The story in regard to the Weems' family was published in Frederick Douglass' paper two years ago. Since then the two middle boys have been redeemed and there is only one left in Slavery, and he is in Alabama. The master has agreed to take for him just what he gave, $1,100. Mr. Lewis Tappan has his letter and the money, except the amount specified. There were about $5,000 raised in England to redeem this family, and they are now all free except this one. And there never was a more excellent and worthy family than the Weems' family. I do hope, that Mrs. W. will find friends who can advance the amount required.

Truly Yours,

E.L. STEVENS.

WASHINGTON, D.C.,
*July 13th, 1857.*

MY FRIEND: – Your kind letter in reply to mine about Arrah was duly received. As she is doubtless with you before this, she will explain all. I propose that a second journey be made by her or some one else, in order to take the other. They have been a great burden to the good folks here and should have been *at home* long ere this. Arrah will explain everything. I want, however, to say a word in her behalf. If there is a person in the world, that deserves the hearty co-operation of every friend of humanity, that person is Arrah Weems, who now, after a long series of self-sacrificing labor to aid others in their struggle for their God-given rights, solicits a small amount to redeem the last one of her own children in Slavery. Never have I had my sympathies so aroused in behalf of any object as in behalf of this most worthy family. She can tell you what I have done. And I do hope, that our friends in Philadelphia and New York will assist her to make up the full amount required for the purchase of the boy.

After she does what she can in P., will you give her the proper direction about getting to New York and to Mr. Tappan's? Inform him of what she has done, &c.

Please write me as soon as you can as to whether she arrived safely, &c. Give me your opinion, also, as to the proposal about the other. Had you not better keep the little one in P. till the other is taken there? Inform me also where E. is, how she is getting along, &c., who living with, &c.

Yours Truly,

E.L.S.

In this instance, also, as in the case of "J.B.," the care and anxiety of other souls, besides this child, crying for deliverance, weighed heavily on the mind of Mr. Stevens, as may be inferred from certain references in his letters. Mr. Stevens' love of humanity, and impartial freedom, even in those dark days of Slavery, when it was both unpopular and unsafe to allow the cries of the bondman to awaken the feeling of humanity to assist the suffering, was constantly leading him to take sides with the oppressed, and as he appears in this correspondence, so it was his wont daily to aid the helpless, who were all around him. Arrah Weems, who had the care of the child, alluded to so touchingly by Mr. Stevens, had known, to her heart's sorrow, how intensely painful it was to a mother's feelings to have her children torn from her by a cruel master and sold. For Arrah had had a number of children sold, and was at that very time striving diligently to raise money to redeem the last one of them. And through such kind-hearted friends as Mr. Stevens, the peculiar hardships of this interesting family of Weems' were brought to the knowledge of thousands of philanthropists in this country and England, and liberal contributions had already been made by friends of the Slave on both sides of the ocean. It may now be seen, that while this child had not been a conscious sufferer from the wicked system of Slavery, it had been the object of very great anxiety and suffering to several persons, who had individually perilled their own freedom for its redemption. This child, however, was safely brought to the Vigilance Committee, in Philadelphia, and was duly forwarded, *via* friends in New York, to its mother, in Syracuse, where she had stopped to work and wait for her little one, left behind at the time she escaped.

# ESCAPE OF A YOUNG SLAVE MOTHER

*LEFT HER LITTLE BABY-BOY, LITTLE GIRL AND HUSBAND BEHIND.*

She anxiously waits their coming in Syracuse, N.Y. Not until after the foregoing story headed, the "Escape of a Child," etc., had been put into the hands of the printer and was in type, was the story of the mother discovered, although it was among the records preserved. Under changed names, in many instances, it has been found to be no easy matter to cull from a great variety of letters, records and advertisements, just when wanted, all the particulars essential to complete many of these narratives. The case of the child, alluded to above, is a case in point. Thus, however, while it is impossible to introduce the mother's story in its proper place, yet, since it has been found, it is too important and interesting to be left out. It is here given as follows:

> $300 REWARD. – RAN AWAY from the subscriber on Saturday, the 30th of August, 1856, my SERVANT WOMAN, named EMELINE CHAPMAN, about 25 years of age; quite dark, slender built, speaks short, and stammers some; with two children, one a female about two and a half years old; the other a male, seven or eight months old, bright color. I will give the above reward if they are delivered to me in Washington.
>
> MRS. EMILY THOMPSON,
> Capitol Hill, Washington, D.C.

Emeline Chapman, so particularly described in the *Baltimore Sun* of the 23d of September, 1856, arrived by the regular Underground Rail Road train from Washington. In order to escape the responsibility attached to her original name, she adopted the name of Susan Bell. Thus for freedom she was willing to forgo her name, her husband, and even her little children. It was a serious sacrifice; but she had been threatened with the auction block, and she well understood what that meant. With regard to usage, having lived away from her owner, Emeline did not complain of any very hard times. True, she had been kept at work very constantly, and her owner had very faithfully received all her hire. Emeline had not even been allowed enough of her hire to find herself in clothing, or anything for the support of her two children – for these non-essentials, her kind mistress allowed her to seek elsewhere, as best she could. Emeline's husband was named John Henry; her little girl she called Margaret Ann, and her babe she had named after its father, all with the brand of Slavery upon them. The love of freedom, in the breast of this spirited young Slave-wife and mother, did not extinguish the love she bore to her husband and children, however otherwise her course, in leaving them, as she did, might appear. For it was just this kind of heroic and self-sacrificing struggle, that appealed to the hearts of men and compelled attention. The letters of Biglow and Stevens, relative to the little child, prove this fact, and additional testimony found in the appended letter from Rev. J.W. Loguen conclusively confirms the same. Indeed, who could close his eyes and ears to the plaintive cries of such a mother? Who could refrain from aiding on to freedom children honored in such a heroic parent?

SYRACUSE,
*Oct. 5, 1856.*

DEAR FRIEND STILL: – I write to you for Mrs. Susan Bell, who was at your city some time in September last. She is from Washington city. She left her dear little children behind (two children). She is stopping in our city, and wants to hear from her children very much indeed. She wishes to know if you have heard from Mr. Biglow, of Washington city. She will remain here until she can hear from you. She feels very anxious about her children, I will assure you. I should have written before this, but I have been from home much of the time since she came to our city. She wants to know if Mr. Biglow has heard anything about her husband. If you have not written to Mr. Biglow, she wishes you would. She sends her love to you and your dear family. She says that you were all kind to her, and she does not forget it. You will direct your letter to me, dear brother, and I will see that she gets it.

Miss F.E. Watkins left our house yesterday for Ithaca, and other places in that part of the State. Frederick Douglass, Wm. J. Watkins and others were with us last week; Gerritt Smith with others. Miss Watkins is doing great good in our part of the State. We think much indeed of her. She is such a good and glorious speaker, that we are all charmed with her. We have had thirty-one fugitives in the last twenty-seven days; but you, no doubt, have had many more than that. I hope the good Lord may bless you and spare you long to do good to the hunted and outraged among our brethren.
Yours truly,

J.W. LOGUEN,

Agent of the Underground Rail Road.

# "FLEEING GIRL OF FIFTEEN" IN MALE ATTIRE

*PROFESSORS H. AND T. OFFER THEIR SERVICES – CAPTAINS B. ALSO ARE ENLISTED – SLAVE-TRADER GRASPING TIGHTLY HIS PREY, BUT SHE IS RESCUED – LONG CONFLICT, BUT GREAT TRIUMPH – ARRIVAL ON THANKSGIVING DAY, NOV. 25, 1855.*

It was the business of the Vigilance Committee, as it was clearly understood by the friends of the Slave, to assist all needy fugitives, who might in any way manage to reach Philadelphia, but, for various reasons, not to send agents South to incite slaves to run away, or to assist them in so doing. Sometimes, however, this rule could not altogether be conformed to. Cases, in some instances, would appeal so loudly and forcibly to humanity, civilization, and Christianity, that it would really seem as if the very stones would cry out, unless something was done. As an illustration of this point, the story of the young girl, which is now to be related, will afford the most striking proof. At the same time it may be seen how much anxiety, care, hazard, delay and material aid, were required in order to effect the deliverance of some who were in close places, and difficult of access. It will be necessary to present a considerable amount of correspondence in this case, to bring to light the hidden mysteries of this narrative. The first letter, in explanation, is the following:

## LETTER FROM J. BIGELOW, ESQ.

WASHINGTON, D.C.,
*June 27, 1854.*

MR. WM. STILL – *Dear Sir*: – I have to thank you for the prompt answer you had the kindness to give to my note of 22d inst. Having found a correspondence so quick and easy, and withal so very flattering, I address you again more fully.

The liberal appropriation for *transportation* has been made chiefly on account of a female child of ten or eleven years old, for whose purchase I have been authorized to offer $700 (refused), and for whose sister I have paid $1,600, and some $1,000 for their mother, &c.

This child sleeps in the same apartment with its master and mistress, which adds to the difficulty of removal. She is some ten or twelve miles from the city, so that really the chief hazard will be in bringing her safely to town, and in secreting her until a few days of *storm* shall have abated. All this, I think, is now provided for with entire safety.

The child has two cousins in the immediate vicinity: a young man of some twenty-two years of age, and his sister, of perhaps seventeen – *both Slaves*, but bright and clear-headed as anybody. The young man I have seen often – the services of *both* seem indispensable to the main object suggested; but having once rendered the service, they cannot, and ought not return to Slavery. They look for *freedom* as the reward of what they shall now do.

Out of the $300, cheerfully offered for the whole enterprise, I must pay some reasonable sum for transportation to the city and sustenance while here. It cannot be much; for the balance, I shall give a draft, which will be *promptly paid* on their arrival in New York.

If I have been understood to offer the whole $300, *it shall be paid*, though I have meant as above stated. Among the various ways that have been suggested, has been that of taking *all of them* into the cars here; that, I think, will be found impracticable. I find so much vigilance at the depot, that I would not deem it safe, though, in any kind of carriage they might leave in safety at any time.

All the rest I leave to the experience and sagacity of the gentleman who maps out the enterprise.

Now I will thank you to reply to this and let me know that it reaches you in safety, and is not put in a careless place, whereby I may be endangered; and state also, whether all my propositions are understood and acceptable, and whether, (pretty quickly after I shall inform you that *all things are ready*), the gentleman will make his appearance?

I live alone. My office and bed-room, &c., are at the corner of E. and 7th streets, opposite the east end of the General Post Office, where any one may call upon me.

It would, of course, be imprudent, that this letter, or any other *written* particulars, be in his pockets for fear of accident.

Yours very respectfully,

J. BIGELOW.

While this letter clearly brought to light the situation of things, its author, however, had scarcely begun to conceive of the numberless difficulties which stood in the way of success before the work could be accomplished. The information which Mr. Bigelow's letter contained of the painful situation of this young girl was submitted to different parties who could be trusted, with a view of finding a person who might possess sufficient courage to undertake to bring her away. Amongst those consulted were two or three captains who had on former occasions done good service in the cause. One of these captains was known in Underground Rail-Road circles as the "powder boy."[5] He was willing to undertake the work, and immediately concluded to make a visit to Washington, to see how the "land lay." Accordingly in company with another Underground Rail Road captain, he reported himself one day to Mr. Bigelow with as much assurance as if he were on an errand for an office under the government. The impression made on Mr. Bigelow's mind may be seen from the following letter; it may also be seen that he was fully alive to the necessity of precautionary measures.

## SECOND LETTER FROM LAWYER BIGELOW

WASHINGTON, D.C.,
*September 9th, 1855.*

MR. WM. STILL, DEAR SIR: – I strongly hope the little matter of business so long pending and about which I have written you so many times, will take a move now. I have the promise that the merchandize shall be delivered in this city to-night. Like so many other promises, this also may prove a failure, though I have reason to believe that it will not. I shall, however, know before I mail this note. In case the goods arrive here I shall hope to see your long-talked of "Professional gentleman" in Washington, as soon as possible. He will find

5 He had been engaged at different times in carrying powder in his boat from a powder magazine, and from this circumstance, was familiarly called the "Powder Boy."

me by the enclosed card, which shall be a satisfactory introduction for him. You have never given me his name, nor am I anxious to know it. But on a pleasant visit made last fall to friend Wm. Wright, in Adams Co., I suppose I accidentally learned it to be a certain Dr. H – – . Well, let him come.

I had an interesting call a week ago from two gentlemen, masters of vessels, and brothers, one of whom, I understand, you know as the "powder boy." I had a little light freight for them; but not finding enough other freight to ballast their craft, they went down the river looking for wheat, and promising to return soon. I hope to see them often.

I hope this may find you returned from your northern trip,[6] as your time proposed was out two or three days ago.

I hope if the whole particulars of Jane Johnson's case[7] are printed, you will send me the copy as proposed.

I forwarded some of her things to Boston a few days ago, and had I known its importance in court, I could have sent you one or two witnesses who would prove that her freedom was intended by her before she left Washington, and that a man was *engaged* here to go on to Philadelphia the same day with her to give notice there of her case, though I think he failed to do so. It was beyond all question her purpose, *before leaving Washington and provable too*, that if Wheeler should make her a free woman by taking her to a free state "*to use it rather.*"

Tuesday, 11th September. The attempt was made on

6 Mr. Bigelow's correspondent had been on a visit to the fugitives to Canada.

7 Jane Johnson of the Passmore Williamson Slave Case.

Sunday to forward the merchandize, but failed through no fault of any of the parties that I now know of. It will be repeated soon, and you shall know the result.

"Whorra for Judge Kane." I feel so indignant at the man, that it is not easy to write the foregoing sentence, and yet who is helping our cause like Kane and Douglas, not forgetting Stringfellow. I hope soon to know that this reaches you in safety.

It often happens that light freight would be offered to Captain B., but the owners cannot by possibility *advance* the amount of freight. I wish it were possible in some such extreme cases, that after advancing *all they have*, some public fund should be found to pay the balance or at least lend it.

[I wish here to caution you against the supposition that I would do any act, or say a word towards helping servants to escape. Although I hate slavery so much, I keep my hands clear of any such wicked or illegal act.]

Yours, very truly,

J.B.

Will you recollect, hereafter, that in any of my future letters, in which I may use [] whatever words may be within the brackets are intended to have no signification whatever to you, only to blind the eyes of the uninitiated. You will find an example at the close of my letter.

Up to this time the chances seemed favorable of procuring the ready services of either of the above mentioned captains who visited Lawyer Bigelow for the removal of the merchandize to Philadelphia, providing the shipping master could have it in readiness to suit their convenience. But as these captains had a number of engagements at Richmond, Petersburg, &c., it was not deemed altogether safe to rely upon either of them, consequently in order to be prepared in case of an emergency, the matter was laid before two professional gentlemen who were each occupying chairs in one of the medical colleges of Philadelphia. They were known to be true friends of the slave, and had possessed withal some experience in Underground Rail Road matters. Either of these professors was willing to undertake the operation, provided arrangements could be completed in time to be carried out during the vacation. In this hopeful, although painfully indefinite position the matter remained for more than a year; but the correspondence and anxiety increased, and with them disappointments and difficulties multiplied. The hope of Freedom, however, buoyed up the heart of the young slave girl during the long months of anxious waiting and daily expectation for the hour of deliverance to come. Equally true and faithful also did Mr. Bigelow prove to the last; but at times he had some painfully dark seasons to encounter, as may be seen from the subjoined letter:

WASHINGTON, D.C.,
*October 6th, 1855.*

MR. STILL, DEAR SIR: – I regret exceedingly to learn by your favor of 4th instant, that all things are not ready. Although I cannot speak of any immediate and positive danger. [*Yet it is well known that the city is full of incendiaries.*]

Perhaps you are aware that any colored citizen is liable at any hour of day or night without any show of authority to have his house ransacked by constables, and if others do it and commit the most outrageous depredations none but white witnesses can convict them. Such outrages are always common here, and no kind of property exposed to colored protection only, can be considered safe. [I don't say that *much liberty* should not be given to constables on account of numerous runaways, but it don't always work for good.] Before advertising they go round and offer rewards to sharp colored men of perhaps *one or two hundred dollars*, to betray runaways, and having discovered their hiding-place, seize them and then cheat their informers out of the money.

[*Although a law-abiding man*,] I am anxious in this case of *innocence* to raise no conflict or suspicion. [*Be sure that the manumission is full and legal*.] And as I am *powerless* without your aid, *I pray you* don't lose a moment in giving me relief. The idea of waiting yet for weeks seems dreadful; do reduce it to days if possible, and give me notice of the *earliest possible time*.

The property is not yet advertised, but will be, [and if we delay too long, may be sold and lost.]

It was a great misunderstanding, though not your fault, that so much delay would be necessary. [I repeat again that I must have the thing done legally, therefore, please get a good lawyer to draw up the deed of manumission.]

Yours Truly,

J. BIGELOW.

Great was the anxiety felt in Washington. It is certainly not too much to say, that an equal amount of anxiety existed in Philadelphia respecting the safety of the merchandise. At this juncture Mr. Bigelow had come to the conclusion that it was no longer safe to write over his own name, but that he would do well to henceforth adopt the name of the renowned Quaker, Wm. Penn, (he was worthy of it) as in the case of the following letter.

WASHINGTON, D.C.,
*November 10th, 1855.*

DEAR SIR: – Doctor T. presented my card last night about half past eight which I instantly recognized. I, however, soon became suspicious, and afterwards confounded, to find the doctor using your name and the well known names of Mr. McK. and Mr. W. and yet, neither he nor I, could conjecture the object of his visit.

The doctor is agreeable and sensible, and doubtless a true-hearted man. He seemed to see the whole matter as I did, and was embarrassed. He had nothing to propose, no information to give of the "P. Boy," or of any substitute, and seemed to want no particular information from me concerning my anxieties and perils, though I stated them to him, but found him as powerless as myself to give me relief. I had an agreeable interview with the doctor till after ten, when he left, intending to take the cars at six, as I suppose he did do, this morning.

This morning after eight, I got your letter of the 9th, but it gives me but little enlightenment or satisfaction. You simply say that the doctor is a *true man*, which I cannot doubt, that you thought it best we should have an interview, and that you supposed I would meet the expenses. You informed me also that the "P. Boy" left for Richmond, on Friday, the 2d, to be gone *the length of time named in your last*, I must infer that to be *ten days* though in your last *you assured me* that the "P. Boy" would certainly start for *this place* (not Richmond) in two or three days, though the difficulty about freight might cause delay, and the whole enterprise might not be accomplished under ten days, &c., &c. That time having elapsed and I having agreed to an extra fifty dollars to ensure promptness. I have scarcely left my office since, except for my hasty meals, awaiting his arrival. You now inform me he has gone to Richmond, to be gone ten days, which will expire tomorrow, but you do not say he will return here or to Phila, or where, at the expiration of that time, and Dr. T. could tell me nothing whatever about him. Had he been able to tell me that this *best plan*, which I have so long rested upon, would fail, or was abandoned, I could then understand it, but he says no such thing, and you say, as you have twice before said, "ten days more."

Now, my dear sir, after this recapitulation, can you not see that I have reason for great embarrassment? I have given assurances, both here and in New York, founded on your assurances to me, and caused my friends in the latter place great anxiety, so much that I have had no way to explain my own letters but by sending your last two to Mr. Tappan.

I cannot doubt, I do not, but that you wish to help me, and the cause too, for which both of us have made many and large sacrifices with no hope of reward in this world. If in this case I have been very urgent since September Dr. T. can give you some of my reasons, they have not been selfish.

The whole matter is in a nutshell. Can I, in your opinion, depend on the "P. Boy," and when?

If he promises to come here next trip, will he come, or go to Richmond? This I think is the best way. Can I depend on it?

Dr. T. promised to write me some explanation and give some advice, and at first I thought to await his letter, but on second thought concluded to tell you how I feel, as I have done.

Will you answer my questions with some explicitness, and without delay?

I forgot to inquire of Dr. T. who is the head of your Vigilance Committee, whom I may address concerning other and further operations?

Yours very truly,

WM. PENN.

P.S. I ought to say, that I have no doubt but there were good reasons for the P. Boy's going to Richmond instead of W.; *but what can they be*?

Whilst there are a score of other interesting letters, bearing on this case, the above must suffice, to give at least, an idea of the perplexities and dangers attending its early history. Having accomplished this end, a more encouraging and pleasant phase of the transaction may now be introduced. Here the difficulties, at least very many of them, vanish, yet in one respect, the danger became most imminent. The following letter shows that the girl had been successfully rescued from her master, and that a reward of five hundred dollars had been offered for her.

WASHINGTON, D.C.,
*October 12, 1855.*

MR. WM. STILL: – AS YOU PICK UP ALL THE NEWS THAT IS STIRRING, I CONTRIBUTE A FEW SCRAPS TO YOUR STOCK, GOING TO SHOW THAT THE POOR SLAVE-HOLDERS HAVE THEIR TROUBLES AS WELL AS OTHER PEOPLE.

FOUR HEAVY LOSSES ON ONE SMALL SCRAP CUT FROM A SINGLE NUMBER OF THE "SUN!" HOW VEXATIOUS! HOW PROVOKING! ON THE OTHER HAND, THINK OF THE POOR, TIMID, BREATHLESS, FLYING CHILD OF FIFTEEN! **FIVE HUNDRED DOLLARS REWARD!** OH, FOR SUCCOR! TO WHOM IN ALL THIS WIDE LAND OF FREEDOM SHALL SHE FLEE AND FIND SAFETY? ALAS! – ALAS! – THE LAW POINTS TO NO ONE!

IS SHE STILL RUNNING WITH BLEEDING FEET?[8]

8 At the time this letter was written, she was then under Mr. B.'s protection in Washington, and had to be so kept for six weeks. His question, therefore, "is she still running with bleeding feet," etc., was simply a precautionary step to blind any who might perchance investigate the matter.

OR HIDES SHE IN SOME COLD CAVE, TO REST AND STARVE? "$500 REWARD." YOURS, FOR THE WEAK AND THE POOR. **PERISH** THE REWARD.

J.B.

Having thus succeeded in getting possession of, and secreting this fleeing child of fifteen, as best they could, in Washington, all concerned were compelled to "possess their souls in patience," until the storm had passed. Meanwhile, the "child of fifteen" was christened "Joe Wright," and dressed in male attire to prepare for traveling as a lad. As no opportunity had hitherto presented itself, whereby to prepare the "package" for shipment, from Washington, neither the "powder boy" nor Dr. T.[9] was prepared to attend to the removal, at this critical moment. The emergency of the case, however, cried loudly for aid. The other professional gentleman (Dr. H.), was now appealed to, but his engagements in the college forbade his absence before about Thanksgiving day, which was then six weeks off. This fact was communicated to Washington, and it being the only resource left, the time named was necessarily acquiesced in. In the interim, "Joe" was to perfect herself in the art of wearing pantaloons, and all other male rig. Soon the days and weeks slid by, although at first the time for waiting seemed long, when, according to promise, Dr. H. was in Washington, with his horse and buggy prepared for duty.

9 Dr. T. was one of the professional gentlemen alluded to above, who had expressed a willingness to act as an agent in the matter.

The impressions made by Dr. H., on William Penn's mind, at his first interview, will doubtless be interesting to all concerned, as may be seen in the following letter:

WASHINGTON, D.C.,
*November 26, 1855.*

MY DEAR SIR: – A recent letter from my friend, probably has led you to expect this from me. He was delighted to receive yours of the 23d, stating that the boy was *all right*. He found the "Prof. gentleman" a *perfect gentleman*; cool, quiet, thoughtful, and *perfectly competent to execute his undertaking*. At the first three minutes of their interview, he felt assured that all would be right. He, and all concerned, give you and that gentleman sincere thanks for what you have done. May the blessings of Him, who cares for the poor, be on your heads.

The especial object of this, is to inform you that there is a half dozen or so of packages here, *pressing for transportation*; twice or thrice that number are also pressing, but less so than the others. Their aggregate means will average, say, $10 each; besides these, we know of a few, say three or four, *able and smart*, but utterly destitute, and kept so purposely by their oppressors. For all these, we feel deeply interested; $10 each would not be enough for the "powder boy." Is there any fund from which a pittance could be spared to help these poor creatures? I don't doubt but that they would honestly repay a small loan as soon as they could earn it. I know full well, that if you begin with such cases, there is no boundary at which you can stop. For years, one half at least, of my friend's time here has been gratuitously given to cases of distress among this class. He never expects or desires to do less; he literally has the *poor always with him.* He knows that it is so with you also, therefore, he only states the case, being especially anxious for at least those to whom I have referred.

I think a small lot of hard coal might always be sold here *from the vessel* at a profit. Would not a like lot of Cumberland coal always sell in Philadelphia?

My friend would be very glad to see the powder boy here again, and if he brings coal, there are those here, who would try to help him sell.

Reply to your regular correspondent as usual.

WM. PENN.

By the presence of the Dr., confidence having been reassured that all would be right, as well as by the "inner light," William Penn experienced a great sense of relief. Everything having been duly arranged, the doctor's horse and carriage stood waiting before the White House (William Penn preferred this place as a starting point, rather than before his own office door). It being understood that "Joe" was to act as coachman in passing out of Washington, at this moment he was called for, and in the most polite and natural manner, with the fleetness of a young deer, he jumped into the carriage, took the reins and whip, whilst the doctor and William Penn were cordially shaking hands and bidding adieu. This done, the order was given to Joe, "drive on." Joe bravely obeyed. The faithful horse trotted off willingly, and the doctor sat in his carriage as composed as though he had succeeded in procuring an honorable and lucrative office from the White House, and was returning home to tell his wife the good news. The doctor had some knowledge of the roads, also some acquaintances in Maryland, through which State he had to travel; therefore, after leaving the suburbs of Washington, the doctor took the reins in his own hands, as he felt that he was more experienced as a driver than his young coachman. He was also mindful of the fact, that, before reaching Pennsylvania, his faithful beast would need feeding several times, and that they consequently would be obliged to pass one or two nights at least in Maryland, either at a tavern or farm-house.

In reflecting upon the matter, it occurred to the doctor, that in earlier days, he had been quite intimately acquainted with a farmer and his family (who were slave-holders), in Maryland, and that he would about reach their house at the end of the first day's journey. He concluded that he could do no better than to renew his acquaintance with his old friends on this occasion. After a very successful day's travel, night came on, and the doctor was safely at the farmer's door with his carriage and waiter boy; the doctor was readily recognized by the farmer and his family, who seemed glad to see him; indeed, they made quite a "fuss" over him. As a matter of strategy, the doctor made quite a "fuss" over them in return; nevertheless, he did not fail to assume airs of importance, which were calculated to lead them to think that he had grown older and wiser than when they knew him in his younger days. In casually referring to the manner of his traveling, he alluded to the fact, that he was not very well, and as it had been a considerable length of time since he had been through that part of the country, he thought that the drive would do him good, and especially the sight of old familiar places and people. The farmer and his family felt themselves exceedingly honored by the visit from the distinguished doctor, and manifested a marked willingness to spare no pains to render his night's lodging in every way comfortable.

The Dr. being an educated and intelligent gentleman, well posted on other questions besides medicine, could freely talk about farming in all its branches, and "niggers" too, in an emergency, so the evening passed off pleasantly with the Dr. in the parlor, and "Joe" in the kitchen. The Dr., however, had given "Joe" precept upon precept, "here a little, and there a little," as to how he should act in the presence of master white people, or slave colored people, and thus he was prepared to act his part with due exactness. Before the evening grew late, the Dr., fearing some accident, intimated that he was feeling a "little languid," and therefore thought that he had better "retire." Furthermore he added, that he was "liable to vertigo," when not quite well, and for this reason he must have his boy "Joe" sleep in the room with him. "Simply give him a bed quilt and he will fare well enough in one corner of the room," said the Dr. The proposal was readily acceded to, and carried into effect by the accommodating host. The Dr. was soon in bed, sleeping soundly, and "Joe," in his new coat and pants, wrapped up in the bed quilt, in a corner of the room quite comfortably.

The next morning the Dr. arose at as early an hour as was prudent for a gentleman of his position, and feeling refreshed, partook of a good breakfast, and was ready, with his boy, "Joe," to prosecute their journey. Face, eyes, hope, and steps, were set as flint, Pennsylvania-ward. What time the following day or night they crossed Mason and Dixon's line is not recorded on the Underground Rail Road books, but at four o'clock on Thanksgiving Day, the Dr. safely landed the "fleeing girl of fifteen" at the residence of the writer in Philadelphia. On delivering up his charge, the Dr. simply remarked to the writer's wife, "I wish to leave this young lad with you a short while, and I will call and see further about him." Without further explanation, he stepped into his carriage and hurried away, evidently anxious to report himself to his wife, in order to relieve her mind of a great weight of anxiety on his account. The writer, who happened to be absent from home when the Dr. called, returned soon afterwards. "The Dr. has been here" (he was the family physician), "and left this 'young lad,' and said, that he would call again and see about him," said Mrs. S. The "young lad" was sitting quite composedly in the dining-room, with his cap on. The writer turned to him and inquired, "I suppose you are the person that the Dr. went to Washington after, are you not?" "No," said "Joe." "Where are you from then?" was the next question. "From York, sir." "From York? Why then did the Dr. bring you here?" was the next query. "The Dr. went expressly to Washington after a young girl, who was to be brought away dressed up as a boy, and I took you to be the person." Without replying "the lad" arose and walked out of the house. The querist, somewhat mystified, followed him, and then when the two were alone, "the lad" said, "I am the one the Dr. went after." After congratulating her, the writer asked why she had said, that she was not from Washington, but from York. She explained, that the Dr. had strictly charged her not to own to any person, except the writer, that she was from Washington, but from York. As there were persons present (wife, hired girl, and a fugitive woman), when the questions were put to her, she felt that it would be a violation of her pledge to answer in the affirmative. Before this examination, neither of the individuals present for a moment entertained the slightest doubt but that she was a "lad," so well had she acted her part in every particular. She was dressed in a new suit, which fitted her quite nicely, and with her unusual amount of common sense, she appeared to be in no respect lacking. To send off a prize so rare and remarkable, as she was, without affording some of the stock-holders and managers of the Road the pleasure of seeing her, was not to be thought of. In addition to the Vigilance Committee, quite a number of persons were invited to see her, and were greatly astonished. Indeed it was difficult to realize, that she was not a boy, even after becoming acquainted with the facts in the case.

The following is an exact account of this case, as taken from the Underground Rail Road records:

THANKSGIVING DAY,
*Nov., 1855.*

Arrived, Ann Maria Weems, alias "Joe Wright," alias "Ellen Capron," from Washington, through the aid of Dr. H. She is about fifteen years of age, bright mulatto, well grown, smart and good-looking. For the last three years, or about that length of time, she has been owned by Charles M. Price, a negro trader, of Rockville, Maryland. Mr. P. was given to "intemperance," to a very great extent, and gross "profanity." He buys and sells many slaves in the course of the year. "His wife is cross and peevish." She used to take great pleasure in "torturing" one "little slave boy." He was the son of his master (and was owned by him); this was the chief cause of the mistress' spite.

Ann Maria had always desired her freedom from childhood, and although not thirteen, when first advised to escape, she received the suggestion without hesitation, and ever after that time waited almost daily, for more than two years, the chance to flee. Her friends were, of course, to aid her, and make arrangements for her escape. Her owner, fearing that she might escape, for a long time compelled her to sleep in the chamber with "her master and mistress;" indeed she was so kept until about three weeks before she fled. She left her parents living in Washington. Three of her brothers had been sold South from their parents. Her mother had been purchased for $1,000, and one of her sisters for $1,600 for freedom. Before Ann Maria was thirteen years of age $700 was offered for her by a friend, who desired to procure her freedom, but the offer was promptly refused, as were succeeding ones repeatedly made. The only chance of procuring her freedom, depended upon getting her away on the Underground Rail Road. She was neatly attired in male habiliments, and in that manner came all the way from Washington. After passing two or three days with her new friends in Philadelphia, she was sent on (in male attire) to Lewis Tappan, of New York, who had likewise been deeply interested in her case from the beginning, and who held himself ready, as was understood, to cash a draft for three hundred dollars to compensate the man who might risk his own liberty in bringing her on from Washington. After having arrived safely in New York, she found a home and kind friends in the family of the Rev. A.N. Freeman, and received quite an ovation characteristic of an Underground Rail Road.

After having received many tokens of esteem and kindness from the friends of the slave in New York and Brooklyn, she was carefully forwarded on to Canada, to be educated at the "Buxton Settlement."

An interesting letter, however, from the mother of Ann Maria, conveying the intelligence of her late great struggle and anxiety in laboring to free her last child from Slavery is too important to be omitted, and hence is inserted in connection with this narrative.

## LETTER FROM THE MOTHER

WASHINGTON, D.C.,
*September 19th, 1857.*

WM. STILL, ESQ., Philadelphia, Pa. SIR: – I have just sent for my son Augustus, in Alabama. I have sent eleven hundred dollars which pays for his body and some thirty dollars to pay his fare to Washington. I borrowed one hundred and eighty dollars to make out the eleven hundred dollars. I was not very successful in Syracuse. I collected only twelve dollars, and in Rochester only two dollars. I did not know that the season was so unpropitious. The wealthy had all gone to the springs. They must have returned by this time. I hope you will exert yourself and help me get a part of the money I owe, at least. I am obliged to pay it by the 12th of next month. I was unwell when I returned through Philadelphia, or I should have called. I had been from home five weeks.

My son Augustus is the last of the family in Slavery. I feel rejoiced that he is soon to be free and with me, and of course feel the greatest solicitude about raising the one hundred and eighty dollars I have borrowed of a kind friend, or who has borrowed it for me at bank. I hope and pray you will help me as far as possible. Tell Mr. Douglass to remember me, and if he can, to interest his friends for me.

You will recollect that five hundred dollars of our money was taken to buy the sister of Henry H. Garnett's wife. Had I been able to command this I should not be necessitated to ask the favors and indulgences I do.

I am expecting daily the return of Augustus, and may Heaven grant him a safe deliverance and smile propitiously upon you and all kind friends who have aided in his return to me.

Be pleased to remember me to friends, and accept yourself the blessing and prayers of your dear friend,

EARRO WEEMS.

P.S. Direct your letter to E.L. Stevens, in Duff Green's Row, Capitol Hill, Washington, D.C.

E.W.

That William Penn who worked so faithfully for two years for the deliverance of Ann Maria may not appear to have been devoting all his time and sympathy towards this single object it seems expedient that two or three additional letters, proposing certain grand Underground Rail Road plans, should have a place here. For this purpose, therefore, the following letters are subjoined.

## LETTERS FROM WILLIAM PENN

WASHINGTON, D.C.,
*Oct. 3, 1854*

DEAR SIR: – I address you to-day chiefly at the suggestion of the Lady who will hand you my letter, and who is a resident of your city.

After stating to you, that the case about which I have previously written, remains just as it was when I wrote last – full of difficulty – I thought I would call your attention to another enterprise; it is this: to find a man with a large heart for doing good to the oppressed, who will come to Washington to live, and who will *walk out to Penn'a., or a part of the way there, once or twice a week*. He will find parties who will *pay him for doing so*. Parties of say, two, three, five or so, who will pay him *at least* \$5 each, for the privilege of following him, but *will never speak to him*; but will keep just in sight of him and obey any sign he may give; say, he takes off his hat and scratches his head as a sign for them to go to some barn or wood to rest, &c. No living being shall be found to say he ever spoke to them. A white man would be best, and then even parties led out by him could not, if they would, testify to any *understanding* or anything else against a white man. I think he might make a good living at it. Can it not be done?

If one or two safe stopping-places could be found on the way – such as a barn or shed, they could walk quite safely all night and then sleep all day – about two, or *easily* three nights would convey them to a place of safety. The traveler might be a peddler or huckster, with an old horse and cart, and bring us in eggs and butter if he pleases.

Let him once plan out his route, and he might then take ten or a dozen at a time, and they are often able and willing to pay $10 a piece.

I have a hard case now on hand; a brother and sister 23 to 25 years old, whose mother lives in your city. They are cruelly treated; they want to go, they *ought* to go; but they are utterly destitute. Can nothing be done for such cases? If you can think of anything let me know it. I suppose you know me?

WASHINGTON, D.C.,
*April 3, 1856.*

DEAR SIR: – I sent you the recent law of Virginia, under which all vessels are to be searched for fugitives within the waters of that State.

It was long ago suggested by a sagacious friend, that the "powder boy" might find a better port in the Chesapeake bay, or in the Patuxent river to communicate with this vicinity, than by entering the Potomac river, even were there no such law.

Suppose he opens a trade with some place south-west of Annapolis, 25 or 30 miles from here, or less. He might carry wood, oysters, &c., and all his customers from this vicinity might travel in *that direction* without any of the suspicions that might attend their journeyings *towards this city*. In this way, doubtless, a good business might be carried on without interruption or competition, and provided the plan was conducted without affecting the inhabitants along that shore, no suspicion would arise as to the manner or magnitude of his business operations. How does this strike you? What does the "powder boy" think of it?

I heretofore intimated a *pressing necessity* on the part of several females – they are variously situated – two have children, say a couple each; some have none – of the latter, one can raise $50, another, say 30 or 40 dollars – another who was gazetted last August (a copy sent you), can raise, through her friends, 20 or 30 dollars, &c., &c. None of these can walk so far or so fast as scores of *men* that are constantly leaving. I cannot shake off my anxiety for these poor creatures. Can you think of anything for any of these? Address your other correspondent in answer to this at your leisure.

Yours,

WM. PENN.

P.S. – April 3d. Since writing the above, I have received yours of 31st. I am rejoiced to hear that business is so successful and prosperous – may it continue till *the article* shall cease to be merchandize.

I spoke in my last letter of the departure of a "few friends." I have since heard of their good health in Penn'a. Probably you may have seen them.

In reference to the expedition of which you think you can "hold out some little encouragement," I will barely remark, that I shall be glad, if it is undertaken, to have all the notice of the *time and manner* that is possible, so as to make ready.

A friend of mine says, anthracite coal will always pay here from Philadelphia, and thinks a small vessel might run often – that she never would be searched in the Potomac, unless she went outside.

You advise caution towards Mr. P. I am precisely of your opinion about him, that he is a "queer stick," and while I advised him carefully in reference to his own undertakings, I took no counsel of him concerning mine.

Yours,

W.P.

# FIVE YEARS AND ONE MONTH SECRETED

*JOHN HENRY, HEZEKIAH, AND JAMES HILL. JOHN MAKES A DESPERATE RESISTANCE AT THE SLAVE AUCTION AND ESCAPES AFTER BEING SECRETED NINE MONTHS. HEZEKIAH ESCAPED FROM A TRADER AND WAS SECRETED THIRTEEN MONTHS BEFORE HIS FINAL DELIVERANCE. JAMES WAS SECRETED THREE YEARS IN A PLACE OF GREAT SUFFERING, AND ESCAPED. IN ALL FIVE YEARS AND ONE MONTH.*

Many letters from John Henry show how incessantly his mind ran out towards the oppressed, and the remarkable intelligence and ability he displayed with the pen, considering that he had no chance to acquire book knowledge. After having fled for refuge to Canada and having become a partaker of impartial freedom under the government of Great Britain, to many it seemed that the fugitive should be perfectly satisfied. Many appeared to think that the fugitive, having secured freedom, had but little occasion for anxiety or care, even for his nearest kin. "Change your name." "Never tell any one how you escaped." "Never let any one know where you came from." "Never think of writing back, not even to your wife; you can do your kin no good, but may do them harm by writing." "Take care of yourself." "You are free, well, be satisfied then." "It will do you no good to fret about your wife and children; that will not get them out of Slavery." Such was the advice often given to the fugitive. Men who had been slaves themselves, and some who had aided in the escape of individuals, sometimes urged these sentiments on men and women whose hearts were almost breaking over the thought that their dearest and best friends were in chains in the prison house. Perhaps it was thoughtlessness on the part of some, and a wish to inspire due cautiousness on the part of others, that prompted this advice. Doubtless some did soon forget their friends. They saw no way by which they could readily communicate with them. Perhaps Slavery had dealt with them so cruelly, that little hope or aspiration was left in them.

It was, however, one of the most gratifying facts connected with the fugitives, the strong love and attachment that they constantly expressed for their relatives left in the South; the undying faith they had in God as evinced by their touching appeals on behalf of their fellow-slaves. But few probably are aware how deeply these feelings were cherished in the breasts of this people. Forty, fifty, or sixty years, in some instances elapsed, but this ardent sympathy and love continued warm and unwavering as ever. Children left to the cruel mercy of slave-holders, could never be forgotten. Brothers and sisters could not refrain from weeping over the remembrance of their separation on the auction block: of having seen innocent children, feeble and defenceless women in the grasp of a merciless tyrant, pleading, groaning, and crying in vain for pity. Not to remember those thus bruised and mangled, it would seem alike unnatural, and impossible. Therefore it is a source of great satisfaction to be able, in relating these heroic escapes, to present the evidences of the strong affections of this greatly oppressed race.

John Henry never forgot those with whom he had been a fellow-sufferer in Slavery; he was always fully awake to their wrongs, and longed to be doing something to aid and encourage such as were striving to get their Freedom. He wrote many letters in behalf of others, as well as for himself, the tone of which was always marked by the most zealous devotion to the slave, a high sense of the value of Freedom, and unshaken confidence that God was on the side of the oppressed, and a strong hope, that the day was not far distant, when the slave power would be "suddenly broken and that without remedy."

Notwithstanding the literary imperfections of these letters, they are deemed well suited to these pages. Of course, slaves were not allowed book learning. Virginia even imprisoned white women for teaching free colored children the alphabet. Who has forgotten the imprisonment of Mrs. Douglass for this offense? In view of these facts, no apology is needed on account of Hill's grammar and spelling.

In these letters, may be seen, how much liberty was valued, how the taste of Freedom moved the pen of the slave; how the thought of fellow-bondmen, under the heel of the slave-holder, aroused the spirit of indignation and wrath; how importunately appeals were made for help from man and from God; how much joy was felt at the arrival of a fugitive, and the intense sadness experienced over the news of a failure or capture of a slave. Not only are the feelings of John Henry Hill represented in these epistles, but the feelings of very many others amongst the intelligent fugitives all over the country are also represented to the letter. It is more with a view of doing justice to a brave, intelligent class, whom the public are ignorant of, than merely to give special prominence to John and his relatives as individuals, that these letters are given.

## ESCAPE OF JOHN HENRY HILL FROM THE SLAVE AUCTION IN RICHMOND, ON THE FIRST DAY OF JANUARY, 1853

JOHN HENRY at that time, was a little turned of twenty-five years of age, full six feet high, and remarkably well proportioned in every respect. He was rather of a brown color, with marked intellectual features. John was by trade, a carpenter, and was considered a competent workman. The year previous to his escape, he hired his time, for which he paid his owner $150. This amount John had fully settled up the last day of the year. As he was a young man of steady habits, a husband and father, and withal an ardent lover of Liberty; his owner, John Mitchell, evidently observed these traits in his character, and concluded that he was a dangerous piece of property to keep; that his worth in money could be more easily managed than the man. Consequently, his master unceremoniously, without intimating in any way to John, that he was to be sold, took him to Richmond, on the first day of January (the great annual sale day), and directly to the slave-auction. Just as John was being taken into the building, he was invited to submit to hand-cuffs. As the thought flashed upon his mind that he was about to be sold on the auction-block, he grew terribly desperate. "Liberty or death" was the watchword of that awful moment. In the twinkling of an eye, he turned on his enemies, with his fist, knife, and feet, so tiger-like, that he actually put four or five men to flight, his master among the number. His enemies thus suddenly baffled, John wheeled, and, as if assisted by an angel, strange as it may appear, was soon out of sight of his pursuers, and securely hid away. This was the last hour of John Henry's slave life, but not, however, of his struggles and sufferings for freedom, for before a final chance to escape presented itself, nine months elapsed. The mystery as to where, and how he fared, the following account, in his own words, must explain –

> Nine months I was trying to get away. I was secreted for a long time in a kitchen of a merchant near the corner of Franklyn and 7th streets, at Richmond, where I was well

taken care of, by a lady friend of my mother. When I got Tired of staying in that place, I wrote myself a pass to pass myself to Petersburg, here I stopped with a very prominent Colored person, who was a friend to Freedom stayed here until two white friends told other friends if I was in the city to tell me to go at once, and stand not upon the order of going, because they had hard a plot. I wrot a pass, started for Richmond, Reached Manchester, got off the Cars walked into Richmond, once more got back into the same old Den, Stayed here from the 16th of Aug. to 12th Sept. On the 11th of Sept. 8 o'clock P.M. a message came to me that there had been a State Room taken on the steamer *City of Richmond* for my benefit, and I assured the party that it would be occupied if God be willing. Before 10 o'clock the next morning, on the 12th, a beautiful Sept. day, I arose early, wrote my pass for Norfolk left my old Den with a many a good bye, turned out the back way to 7th St., thence to Main, down Main behind 4 night waich to old Rockett's and after about 20 minutes of delay I succeed in Reaching the State Room. My Conductor was very much Excited, but I felt as Composed as I do at this moment, for I had started from my Den that morning for Liberty or for Death providing myself with a Brace of Pistels.

Yours truly

J.H. HILL.

A private berth was procured for him on the steamship City of Richmond, for the amount of $125, and thus he was brought on safely to Philadelphia. While in the city, he enjoyed the hospitalities of the Vigilance Committee, and the greetings of a number of friends, during the several days of his sojourn. The thought of his wife, and two children, left in Petersburg, however, naturally caused him much anxiety. Fortunately, they were free, therefore, he was not without hope of getting them; moreover, his wife's father (Jack McCraey), was a free man, well known, and very well to do in the world, and would not be likely to see his daughter and grandchildren suffer. In this particular, Hill's lot was of a favorable character, compared with that of most slaves leaving their wives and children.

## FIRST LETTER
### ON ARRIVING IN CANADA

TORONTO,
*October 4th, 1853.*

DEAR SIR: – I take this method of informing you that I am well, and that I got to this city all safe and sound, though I did not get here as soon as I expect. I left your city on Saterday and I was on the way untel the Friday following. I got to New York the same day that I left Philadelphia, but I had to stay there untel Monday evening. I left that place at six o'clock. I got to Albany next morning in time to take the half past six o'clock train for Rochester, here I stay untel Wensday night. The reason I stay there so long Mr. Gibbs given me a letter to Mr Morris at Rochester. I left that place Wensday, but I only got five miles from that city that night. I got to Lewiston on Thurday afternoon, but too late for the boat to this city. I left Lewiston on Friday at one o'clock, got to this city at five. Sir I found this to be a very handsome city. I like it better than any city I ever saw. It are not as large as the city that you live in, but it is very large place much more so than I expect to find it. I seen the gentleman that you given me letter to. I think him much of a gentleman. I got into work on Monday. The man whom I am working for is name Myers; but I expect to go to work for another man by name of Tinsly, who is a master workman in this city. He says that he will give me work next week and everybody advises me to work for Mr. Tinsly as there more surity in him.

Mr. Still, I have been looking and looking for my friends for several days, but have not seen nor heard of them. I hope and trust in the Lord Almighty that all things are well with them. My dear sir I could feel so much better sattisfied if I could hear from my wife. Since I reached this city I have talagraphed to friend Brown to send my thing to me, but I cannot hear a word from no one at all. I have written to Mr. Brown two or three times since I left the city. I trust that he has gotten my wife's letters, that is if she has written. Please direct your letters to me, near the corner Sarah and Edward street, until I give you further notice. You will tell friend B. how to direct his letters, as I forgotten it when I writt to him, and ask him if he has heard anything from Virginia. Please to let me hear from him without delay for my very soul is trubled about my friends whom I expected to of seen here before this hour. Whatever you do please to write. I shall look for you paper shortly.

Believe me sir to be your well wisher.

JOHN H. HILL.

## SECOND LETTER

*Expressions of gratitude – The Custom House refuses to charge him duty – He is greatly concerned for his wife*

TORONTO,
*October 30th, 1853.*

MY DEAR FRIEND: – I now write to inform you that I have received my things all safe and sound, and also have shuck hand with the friend that you send on to this place one of them is stopping with me. His name is Chas. Stuert, he seemes to be a tolerable smart fellow. I Rec'd my letters. I have taken this friend to see Mr. Smith. However will give him a place to board untell he can get to work. I shall do every thing I can for them all that I see the gentleman wish you to see his wife and let her know that he arrived safe, and present his love to her and to all the friend. Mr. Still, I am under ten thousand obligation to you for your kindness when shall I ever repay? S. speek very highly of you. I will state to you what Custom house master said to me. He ask me when he Presented my efects are these your efects. I answered yes. He then ask me was I going to settle in Canada. I told him I was. He then ask me of my case. I told all about it. He said I am happy to see you and all that will come. He ask me how much I had to pay for my Paper. I told him half dollar. He then told me that I should have my money again. He a Rose from his seat and got my money. So my friend you can see the people and tell them all this is a land of liberty and believe they will find friends here. My best love to all.

My friend I must call upon you once more to do more kindness for me that is to write to my wife as soon as you get this, and tell her when she gets ready to come she will pack and consign her things to you. You will give her some instruction, but not to your expenses but to her own.

When you write direct your letter to Phillip Ubank, Petersburg, Va. My Box arrived here the 27th.

My dear sir I am in a hurry to take this friend to church, so I must close by saying I am your humble servant in the cause of liberty and humanity.

JOHN H. HILL.

## THIRD LETTER

*Canada is highly praised – The Vigilance Committee is implored to send all the Fugitives there – "Farmers and Mechanics wanted" – "No living in Canada for Negroes," as argued by "Masters," flatly denied, &c., &c., &c.*

So I ask you to send the fugitives to Canada. I don't know much of this Province but I beleaves that there is Rome enough for the colored and whites of the United States. We wants farmers mechanic men of all qualification &c., if they are not made we will make them, if we cannot make the old, we will make our children.

Now concerning the city toronto this city is Beautiful and Prosperous Levele city. Great many wooden codages more than what should be but I am in hopes there will be more of the Brick and Stonn. But I am not done about your Republicanism. Our masters have told us that there was no living in Canada for a Negro but if it may Please your gentlemanship to publish these facts that we are here able to earn our bread and money enough to make us comftable. But I say give me freedom, and the United States may have all her money and her Luxtures, yeas give Liberty or Death. I'm in America, but not under Such a Government that I cannot express myself, speak, think or write So as I am able, and if my master had allowed me to have an education I would make them American Slave-holders feel me, Yeas I would make them tremble when I spoke, and when I take my Pen in hand their knees smote together. My Dear Sir suppose I was an educated man. I could write you something worth reading, but you know we poor fugitives whom has just come over from the South are not able to write much on no subject whatever, but I hope by the aid of my God I will try to use my midnight lamp, untel I can have some influence upon the American Slavery. If some one would say to me, that they would give my wife bread untel I could be Educated I would stoop my trade this day and take up my books.

But a crisis is approaching when assential requisite to the American Slaveholders when blood Death or Liberty will be required at their hands. I think our people have depened too long and too much on false legislator let us now look for ourselves. It is true that England however the Englishman is our best friend but we as men ought not to depened upon her Remonstrace with the Americans because she loves her commercial trade as any Nations do. But I must say, while we look up and acknowledge the Power greatness and honor of old England, and believe that while we sit beneath the Silken folds of her flag of Perfect Liberty, we are secure, beyond the reach of the aggressions of the Blood hounds and free from the despotism that would wrap around our limbs by the damable Slaveholder. Yet we would not like spoiled childeren depend upon her, but upon ourselves and as one means of strengthening ourselves, we should agitate the emigration to Canada. I here send you a paragraph which I clipted from the weekly *Glob*. I hope you will publish so that Mr. Williamson may know that men are not chattel here but reather they are men and if he wants his chattle let him come here after it or his thing. I wants you to let the whole United States know we are satisfied here because I have seen more Pleasure since I came here then I saw in the U.S. the 24 years that I served my master. Come Poor distress men women and come to Canada where colored men are free. Oh how sweet the word do sound to me yeas when I contemplate of these things, my very flesh creaps my heart thrub when I think of my beloved friends whom I left in that cursid hole. Oh my God what can I do for them or shall I do for them. Lord help them. Suffer them to be no longer depressed beneath the Bruat Creation but may they be looked upon as men made of the Bone and Blood as the Anglo-Americans. May God in his mercy Give Liberty to all this world. I must close as it am late hour at night. I Remain your friend in the cause of Liberty and humanity,

JOHN H. HILL, a fugitive.

If you know any one who would give me an education write and let me know for I am in want of it very much.

Your with Respect,

J.H.H.

If the sentiments in the above letter do not indicate an uncommon degree of natural intelligence, a clear perception of the wrongs of Slavery, and a just appreciation of freedom, where shall we look for the signs of intellect and manhood?

## FOURTH LETTER

*Longs for his wife – In hearing of the return of a Fugitive from Philadelphia is made sorrowful – His love of Freedom increases, &c., &c.*

TORONTO,
*November 12th, 1853.*

MY DEAR STILL: – Your letter of the 3th came to hand thursday and also three copes all of which I was glad to Received they have taken my attention all together Every Time I got them. I also Rec'd. a letter from my friend Brown. Mr. Brown stated to me that he had heard from my wife but he did not say what way he heard. I am looking for my wife every day. Yes I want her to come then I will be better satisfied. My friend I am a free man and feeles alright about that matter. I am doing tolrable well in my line of business, and think I will do better after little. I hope you all will never stop any of our Brotheran that makes their Escep from the South but send them on to this Place where they can be free man and woman. We want them here and not in your State where they can be taken away at any hour. Nay but let him come here where he can Enjoy the Rights of a human being and not to be trodden under the feet of men like themselves. All the People that comes here does well. Thanks be to God that I came to this place. I would like very well to see you all but never do I expect to see you in the United States. I want you all to come to this land of Liberty where the bondman can be free. Come one come all come to this place, and I hope my dear friend you will send on here. I shall do for them as you all done for me when I came on here however I will do the best I can for them if they can they shall do if they will do, but some comes here that can't do well because they make no efford. I hope my friend you will teach them such lessons as Mrs. Moore Give me before I left your city. I hope she may live a hundred years longer and enjoy good health. May God bless her for the good cause which she are working in. Mr. Still you ask me to remember you to Nelson. I will do so when I see him, he are on the lake so is Stewart. I received a letter to-day for Stewart from your city which letter I will take to him when he comes to the city. He are not stoping with us at this time. I was very sorry a few days ago when I heard that a man was taken from your city.

Send them over here, then let him come here and take them away and I will try to have a finger in the Pie myself. You said that you had written to my wife ten thousand thanks for what you have done and what you are willing to do. My friend whenever you hear from my wife please write to me. Whenever she come to your city please give instruction how to travel. I wants her to come the faster way. I wish she was here now. I wish she could get a ticket through to this place. I have mail a paper for you to day.

We have had snow but not to last long. Let me hear from you. My Respect friend Brown. I will write more when I have the opportunity.

Yours with Respect,

JOHN H. HILL.

P.S. My dear Sir. Last night after I had written the above, and had gone to bed, I heard a strange voice in the house, Saying to Mr. Myers to come quickly to one of our colod Brotheran out of the street. We went and found a man a Carpenter laying on the side walk woltun in his Blood. Done by some unknown Person as yet but if they stay on the earth the law will deteck them. It is said that party of colord people done it, which party was seen to come out an infame house.

Mr. Myers have been down to see him and Brought the Sad news that the Poor fellow was dead. Mr. Scott for Henry Scott was the name, he was a fugitive from Virginia he came here from Pittsburg Pa. Oh, when I went where he laid what a shock, it taken my Sleep altogether night. When I got to

Sopt his Body was surrounded by the Policeman. The law has taken the woman in cusidy. I write and also send you a paper of the case when it comes out.

J.H. HILL.

## FIFTH LETTER

*He rejoices over the arrival of his wife – but at the same time, his heart is bleeding over a dear friend whom he had promised to help before he left Slavery.*

TORONTO,
*December 29th, 1853.*

MY DEAR FRIEND: – It affords me a good deel of Pleasure to say that my wife and the Children have arrived safe in this City. But my wife had very bad luck. She lost her money and the money that was belonging to the children, the whole amount was 35 dollars. She had to go to the Niagara falls and Telegraph to me come after her. She got to the falls on Sat'dy and I went after her on Monday. We saw each other once again after so long an Abstance, you may know what sort of metting it was, joyful times of corst. My wife are well Satisfied here, and she was well Pleased during her stay in your city. My Trip to the falls cost Ten Eighty Seven and half. The things that friend Brown Shiped to me by the Express costed $24¼. So you can see fiting out a house Niagara falls and the cost for bringing my things to this place, have got me out of money, but for all I am a free man.

The weather are very cold at Present, the snow continue to fall though not as deep here as it is in Boston. The people haves their own Amousements, the weather as it is now, they don't care for the snow nor ice, but they are going from Ten A.M. until Twelve P.M., the hous that we have open don't take well because we don't Sell Spirits, which we are trying to avoid if we can.

Mr. Still, I hold in my hand A letter from a friend of South, who calls me to promise that I made to him before I left. My dear Sir, this letter have made my heart Bleed, since I Received it, he also desires of me to remember him to his beloved Brethren and then to Pray for him and his dear friends who are in Slavery. I shall Present his letter to the churches of this city. I forward to your care for Mrs. Moore, a few weeks ago. Mrs. Hill sends her love to your wife and yourself.

Please to write, I Sincerely hope that our friends from Petersburg have reached your city before this letter is dated. I must close by saying, that I Sir, remain humble and obedient Servant,

J.H.H.

## SIXTH LETTER

*He is now earnestly appealing in behalf of a friend in Slavery, with a view to procuring aid and assistance from certain parties, by which this particular friend in bondage might be rescued.*

Toranto,
*March 8th, 1854.*

My Dear Friend Still: – We will once more truble you opon this great cause of freedom, as we know that you are a man, that are never fatuged in Such a glorious cause. Sir, what I wish to Say is this. Mr. Forman has Received a letter from his wife dated the 29th ult. She States to him that She was Ready at any time, and that Everything was Right with her, and she hoped that he would lose no time in sending for her for she was Ready and awaiting for him. Well friend Still, we learnt that Mr. Minkens could not bring her the account of her child. We are very sorry to hear Such News, however, you will please to read this letter with care, as we have learnt that Minkens Cannot do what we wishes to be done; we perpose another way. There is a white man that Sale from Richmond to Boston, that man are very Safe, he will bring F's wife with her child. So you will do us a favour will take it upon yourself to transcribe from this letter what we shall write. I.E. this there is a Colored gen. that workes on the basin in R – – this man's name is Esue Poster, he can tell Mrs. forman all about this Saleor. So you can place the letter in the hands of M. to take to forman's wife, She can read it for herself. She will find Foster at ladlum's warehouse on the Basin, and when you write call my name to him and he will trust it. this foster are a member of the old Baptist Church. When you have done all you can do let us know what you have done, if you hears anything of my uncle let me know.

## SEVENTH LETTER.

*He laments over his uncle's fate, who was suffering in a dungeon-like place of concealment daily waiting for the opportunity to escape.*

Toronto,
*March 18th, 1864.*

My Dear Still: – Yours of the 15th Reached on the 11th, found myself and family very well, and not to delay no time in replying to you, as there was an article in your letter which article Roused me very much when I read it; that was you praying to me to be cautious how I write down South. Be so kind as to tell me in your next letter whether you have at any time apprehended any danger in my letters however, in those bond southward; if there have been, allow me to beg ten thousand pardon before God and man, for I am not design to throw any obstacle in the way of those whom I left in South, but to aide them in every possible way. I have done as you Requested, that to warn the friends of the dager of writing South. I have told all you said in yours that Mr. Minkins would be in your city very soon, and you would see what you could do for me, do you mean or do speak in reference to my dear uncle. I am hopes that you will use every ifford to get him from the position in which he now stand. I know how he feels at this time, for I have felt the same when I was a runway. I was bereft of all participation with my family for nearly nine months, and now that poor fellow are place in same position. Oh God help I pray, what a pitty it is that I cannot do him no good, but I sincerely hope that you will not get fatigued at doing good in such cases, nay, I think other wises of you, however, I Say no more on this subject at present, but leave it for you to judge.

On the 13th inst. you made Some Remarks concerning friend Forman's wife, I am Satisfied that you will do all you can for her Release from Slavery, but as you said you feels for them, so do I, and Mr. Foreman comes to me very often to know if I have heard anything from you concerning his wife, they all comes to for the same.

God Save the Queen. All my letters Southward have passed through your hands with an exception of one.

JOHN H. HILL.

## EIGHTH LETTER.

*Death has snatched away one of his children and he has cause to mourn. In his grief he recounts his struggles for freedom, and his having to leave his wife and children. He acknowledges that he had to "work very hard for comforts," but he declares that he would not "exchange with the comforts of ten thousand slaves."*

TORONTO,
*Sept. 14th, 1854.*

MY DEAR FRIEND STILL: – this are the first oppertunity that I have had to write you since I Reed your letter of the 20th July, there have been sickness and Death in my family since your letter was Reed, our dear little Child have been taken from us one whom we loved so very Dear, but the almighty God knows what are best for us all.

Louis Henry Hill, was born in Petersburg Va May 7th 1852. and Died Toronto August 19th 1854 at five o'clock P.M.

Dear Still I could say much about the times and insidince that have taken place since the coming of that dear little angle jest spoken of. it was 12 months and 3 days from the time that I took departure of my wife and child to proceed to Richmond to awaite a conveyance up to the day of his death.

it was thursday the 13th that I lift Richmond, it was Saturday the 15th that I land to my great joy in the city of Phila. then I put out for Canada. I arrived in this city on Friday the 30th and to my great satisfaction. I found myself upon Briton's free land, not only free for the white man bot for all.

this day 12 months I was not out of the reach the slave-holders, but this 14th day of Sept. I am as Free as your President Pearce. only I have not been free so long However the 30th of the month I will have been free only 12 months.

It is true that I have to work very hard for comfort but I would not exchange with ten thousand slave that are equel with their masters. I am Happy, Happy.

Give love to Mrs. Still. My wife laments her child's death too much, wil you be so kind as to see Mr. Brown and ask him to write to me, and if he have heard from Petersburg Va.

Yours truely

J.H. HILL.

## NINTH LETTER

*He is anxiously waiting for the arrival of friends from the South. Hints that slaveholders would be very unsafe in Canada, should they be foolish enough to visit that country for the purpose of enticing slaves back.*

TORONTO,
*Jan. 19th, 1854.*

MY DEAR STILL: – Your letter of the 16th came to hand just in time for my perpose I perceivs by your statement that the money have not been to Petersburg at all done just what was right and I would of sent the money to you at first, but my dear friend I have called upon you for so many times that I have been ashamed of myself to call any more So you may perceive by the above written my obligations to you, you said that you had written on to Petersburg, you have done Right which I believes is your general way of doing your business, the money are all right I only had to pay a 6d on the Ten dollars. this money was given to by a friend in the city N. york, the friend was from Richmond Virginia (a white man) the amount was fifteen dollars, I forward a letter to you yesterday which letter I forgot to date. my friend I wants to hear from virginia the worst of all things. you know that we expect some freneds on and we cannot hear any thing from them which makes us uneasy for fear that they have attempt to come away and been detected. I have ears open at all times, listen at all hours expecting to hear from them Please to see friend Brown and know from him if he has heard anything from our friends, if he have not. tell him write and inquiare into the matter why it is that they have not come over, then let me hear from you all.

We are going to have a grand concert &c I mean the Abolisnous Socity. I will attend myself and also my wife if the Lord be willing you will perceive in previous letter that I mension something concerning Mr Forman's wife if there be any chance whatever please to proceed, Mr Foreman sends his love to you Requested you to do all you can to get his wife away from Slavery.

Our best respects to your wife. You promisted me that you would write somthing concerning our arrival in Canada but I suppose you have not had the time as yet, I would be very glad to read your opinion on that matter I have notice several articles in the freeman one of the Canada weaklys concerning the Christiana prisoners respecting Castnor Hanway and also Mr. Rauffman. if I had one hundred dollars to day I would give them five each, however I hope that I may be able to subscribe something for their Relefe. in Regards to the letters have been written from Canada to the South the letters was not what they thought them to be and if the slave-holders know when they are doing well they had better keep their side for if they comes over this side of the lake I am under the impression they will not go back with somethin that their mother boned them with whether thiar slaves written for them or not. I know some one here that have written his master to come after him, but not because he expect to go with him home but because he wants to retaleate upon his persecutor, but I would be sorry for man that have written for his master expecting to return with him because the people here would kill them. Sir I cannot write enough to express myself so I must close by saying I Remain yours.

JOHN H. HILL.

## TENTH LETTER

*Great joy over an arrival – Twelve months praying for the deliverance of an Uncle groaning in a hiding-place, while the Slave-hunters are daily expected – Strong appeals for aid, &c., &c.*

TORONTO,
*January 7th, 1855.*

MY DEAR FRIEND: – It is with much pleasure that I take this opportunity of addressing you with these few lines hoping when they reeches you they may find yourself and family enjoying good health as they leaves us at present.

And it is with much happiness that I can say to you that Mrs. Mercer arrived in this city on yesterday. Mr. Mercer was at my house late in the evening, and I told him that when he went home if hear anything from Virginia, that he must let me know as soon as possible. He told me that if he went home and found any news there he would come right back and inform me thereof. But little did he expect to find his dearest there. You may judge what a meeting there was with them, and may God grant that there may be some more meetings with our wives and friends. I had been looking for some one from the old sod for several days, but I was in good hopes that it would be my poor Uncle. But poor fellow he are yet groaning under the sufferings of a horrid sytam, Expecting every day to Receive his Doom. Oh, God, what shall I do, or what can I do for him? I have prayed for him more than 12 months, yet he is in that horrid condition. I can never hear anything Directly from him or any of my people.

Once more I appeal to your Humanity. Will you act for him, as if you was in slavery yourself, and I sincerely believe that he will come out of that condition? Mrs. M. have told me that she given some directions how he could be goten at, but friend Still, if this conductor should not be successfull this time, will you mind him of the Poor Slave again. I hope you will as Mrs. Mercer have told the friend what to do I cannot do more, therefore I must leve it to the Mercy of God and your Exertion.

The weather have been very mile Ever since the 23rd of Dec. I have thought considerable about our condition in this country Seeing that the weather was so very faverable to us. I was thinking a few days ago, that nature had giving us A country & adopted all things Sutable.

You will do me the kindness of telling me in your next whether or not the ten slaves have been Brought out from N.C.

I have not hard from Brown for Nine month he have done some very Bad letting me alone, for what cause I cannot tell. Give my Best Respect to Mr. B. when you see him. I wish very much to hear from himself and family. You will please to let me hear from you. My wife Joines me in love to yourself and family.

Yours most Respectfully,

JOHN H. HILL.

P.S. Every fugitive Regreated to hear of the Death of Mrs. Moore. I myself think that there are no other to take her Place.

yours
J.H.H.

## ELEVENTH LETTER
[Extract]

*Rejoices at hearing of the success of the Underground Rail Road – Inquires particularly after the "fellow" who "cut off the Patrol's head in Maryland."*

HAMILTON,
*August 15th, 1856.*

DEAR FRIEND: – I am very glad to hear that the Underground Rail Road is doing such good business, but tell me in your next letter if you have seen the heroic fellow that cut off the head of the Patrol in Maryland. We wants that fellow here, as John Bull has a great deal of fighting to do, and as there is a colored Captain in this city, I would seek to have that fellow Promoted, Provided he became a soldier.

Great respect,

JOHN H. HILL.

P.S. – Please forward the enclosed to Mr. McCray.

## TWELFTH LETTER

[Extract]

*Believes in praying for the Slave – but thinks "fire and sword" would be more effective with Slave-holders.*

HAMILTON,
*Jan. 5th, 1857.*

MR. STILL: – Our Pappers contains long details of insurrectionary movements among the slaves at the South and one paper adds that a great Nomber of Generals, Captains with other officers had being arrested. At this day four years ago I left Petersburg for Richmond to meet the man whom called himself my master, but he wanted money worser that day than I do this day, he took me to sell me, he could not have done a better thing for me for I intended to leave any how by the first convaiance. I hard some good Prayers put up for the suffers on last Sunday evening in the Baptist Church. Now friend still I beleve that Prayers affects great good, but I beleve that the fire and sword would affect more good in this case. Perhaps this is not your thoughts, but I must acknowledge this to be my Polacy. The world are being turned upside down, and I think we might as well take an active part in it as not. We must have something to do as other people, and I hope this moment among the Slaves are the beginning. I wants to see something go on while I live.

Yours truly,

JOHN H. HILL.

## THIRTEENTH LETTER

*Sad tidings from Richmond – Of the arrest of a Captain with Slaves on board as Underground Rail Road passengers.*

HAMILTON,
*June 5th, 1858.*

DEAR FRIEND STILL: – I have just heard that our friend Capt. B. have being taken Prisoner in Virginia with slaves on board of his vessel. I hard this about an hour ago. the Person told me of this said he read it in the newspaper, if this be so it is awfull. You will be so kind as to send me some information. Send me one of the Virginia Papers. Poor fellow if they have got him, I am sorry, sorry to my heart. I have not heard from my Uncle for a long time if have heard or do hear anything from him at any time you will oblige me by writing. I wish you to inquire of Mr. Anderson's friends (if you know any of them), if they have heard anything from him since he was in your city. I have written to him twice since he was here according to his own directions, but never received an answer. I wants to hear from my mother very much, but cannot hear one word. You will present my best regards to the friend. Mrs. Hill is quite sick.

Yours truly,

J.H. HILL.

P.S. – I have not received the Anti-Slavery Standard for several weeks. Please forward any news relative to the Capt.

J.H.H.

## THE ESCAPE OF HEZEKIAH HILL (UNCLE OF JOHN HENRY HILL)

Impelled by the love of freedom Hezekiah resolved that he would work no longer for nothing; that he would never be sold on the auction block: that he no longer would obey the bidding of a master, and that he would die rather than be a slave. This decision, however, had only been entertained by him a short time prior to his escape. For a number of years Hezekiah had been laboring under the pleasing thought that he should succeed in obtaining freedom through purchase, having had an understanding with his owner with this object in view. At different times he had paid on account for himself nineteen hundred dollars, six hundred dollars more than he was to have paid according to the first agreement. Although so shamefully defrauded in the first instance, he concluded to bear the disappointment as patiently as possible and get out of the lion's mouth as best he could.

He continued to work on and save his money until he had actually come within one hundred dollars of paying two thousand. At this point instead of getting his free papers, as he firmly believed that he should, to his surprise one day he saw a notorious trader approaching the shop where he was at work. The errand of the trader was soon made known. Hezekiah simply requested time to go back to the other end of the shop to get his coat, which he seized and ran. He was pursued but not captured. This occurrence took place in Petersburg, Va., about the first of December, 1854. On the night of the same day of his escape from the trader, Hezekiah walked to Richmond and was there secreted under a floor by a friend. He was a tall man, of powerful muscular strength, about thirty years of age just in the prime of his manhood with enough pluck for two men.

A heavy reward was offered for him, but the hunters failed to find him in this hiding-place under the floor. He strongly hoped to get away soon; on several occasions he made efforts, but only to be disappointed. At different times at least two captains had consented to afford him a private passage to Philadelphia, but like the impotent man at the pool, some one always got ahead of him. Two or three times he even managed to reach the boat upon the river, but had to return to his horrible place under the floor. Some were under the impression that he was an exceedingly unlucky man, and for a time captains feared to bring him. But his courage sustained him unwaveringly.

Finally at the expiration of thirteen months, a private passage was procured for him on the steamship *Pennsylvania*, and with a little slave boy, seven years of age (the son of the man who had secreted him), though placed in a very hard berth, he came safely to Philadelphia, greatly to the astonishment of the Vigilance Committee, who had waited for him so long that they had despaired of his ever coming.

The joy that filled Hezekiah's bosom may be imagined but never described. None but one who had been in similar straits could enter into his feelings.

He had left his wife Louisa, and two little boys, Henry and Manuel. His passage cost one hundred dollars.

Hezekiah being a noted character, a number of the true friends were invited to take him by the hand and to rejoice with him over his noble struggles and his triumph; needing rest and recruiting, he was made welcome to stay, at the expense of the committee, as long as he might feel disposed so to do. He remained several days, and then went on to Canada rejoicing. After arriving there he returned his acknowledgment for favors received, &c., in the following letter:

TORONTO
*Jan 24th 1856.*

MR. STILL: – this is to inform you that Myself and little boy, arrived safely in this city this day the 24th, at ten o'clock after a very long and pleasant trip. I had a great deal of attention paid to me while on the way.

I owes a great deel of thanks to yourself and friends. I will just say hare that when I arrived at New York, I found Mr. Gibbs sick and could not be attended to there. However, I have arrived alright.

You will please to give my respects to your friend that writes in the office with you, and to Mr Smith, also Mr Brown, and the friends, Mrs Still in particular.

Friend Still you will please to send the enclosed to John Hill Petersburg I want him to send some things to me you will be so kind as to send your direction to them, so that the things to your care. if you do not see a convenient way to send it by hands, you will please direct your letter to Phillip Ubank Petersburg.

Yours Respectfully
H HILL.

## JAMES – (BROTHER OF JOHN HENRY HILL)

For three years James suffered in a place of concealment, before he found the way opened to escape. When he resolved on having his freedom he was much under twenty-one years of age, a brave young man, for three years, with unfailing spirit, making resistance in the city of Richmond to the slave Power!

Such heroes in the days of Slavery, did much to make the infernal system insecure, and to keep alive the spirit of freedom in liberty-loving hearts the world over, wherever such deeds of noble daring were made known. But of his heroism, but little can be reported here, from the fact, that such accounts as were in the possession of the Committee, were never transferred from the loose slips of paper on which they were first written, to the regular record book. But an important letter from the friend with whom he was secreted, written a short while before he escaped (on a boat), gives some idea of his condition:

RICHMOND, VA.,
*February 16th, 1861.*

DEAR BROTHER STILL: – I received a message from brother Julius anderson, asking me to send the bundle on but I has no way to send it, I have been waiting and truly hopeing that you would make some arrangement with some person, and send for the parcel. I have no way to send it, and I cannot communicate the subject to a stranger there is a Way by the N.y. line, but they are all strangers to me, and of course I could not approach them With this subject for I would be indangered myself greatly. this business is left to you and to you alone to attend to in providing the way for me to send on the parcel, if you only make an arrangement with some person and let me know the said person and the article which they is to be sent on then I can send the parcel. unless you do make an arrangement with some person, and assure them that they will receive the funs for delivering the parcel this Business cannot be accomplished. it is in your power to try to make some provision for the article to be sent but it is not in my power to do so, the bundle has been on my hands now going on 3 years, and I have suffered a great deal of danger, and is still suffering the same. I have understood Sir that there were no difficul about the mone that you had it in your possession Ready for the bundle whenever it is delivered. But Sir as I have said I can do nothing now. Sir I ask you please through sympathy and feelings on my part & his try to provide a way for the bundle to be sent and relieve me of the danger in which I am in. you might succeed in making an arrangement with those on the New york Steamers for they dose such things but please let me know the man that the arrangement is made with – please give me an answer by the bearer.

yours truly friend

C.A.

At last, the long, dark night passed away, and this young slave safely made his way to freedom, and proceeded to Boston, where he now resides. While the Committee was looked to for aid in the deliverance of this poor fellow, it was painful to feel that it was not in their power to answer his prayers – not until after his escape, was it possible so to do. But his escape to freedom gave them a satisfaction which no words can well express. At present, John Henry Hill is a justice of the peace in Petersburg. Hezekiah resides at West Point, and James in Boston, rejoicing that all men are free in the United States, at last.

# FOUR ARRIVALS

*CHARLOTTE AND HARRIET ESCAPE IN DEEP MOURNING – MASTER IN THE SAME CAR HUNTING FOR THEM, SEES THEM, BUT DOES NOT KNOW THEM – WHITE LADY AND CHILD WITH A COLORED COACHMAN, TRAVELING – AT CHAMBERSBUEG AT A HOTEL, THE PROPRIETOR DETECTS THEM AS U.G.R.R. PASSENGERS – THREE "LIKELY" YOUNG MEN FROM BALTIMORE – "FOUR LARGE AND TWO SMALL HAMS" – POLICE OFFICES IMPARTING INFORMATION AT THE ANTI-SLAVERY OFFICE – U.G.R.R. PASSENGERS TRAVELING WITH THEIR MASTERS' HORSES AND CARRIAGES – "BREAK DOWN" – CONFLICT WITH WHITE MEN – SIX PASSENGERS RIDING TWO HORSES, &c.*

About the 31st of May, 1856, an exceedingly anxious state of feeling existed with the active Committee in Philadelphia. In the course of twenty-four hours four arrivals had come to hand from different localities. The circumstances connected with the escape of each party, being so unusual, there was scarcely ground for any other conclusion than that disaster was imminent, if not impossible to be averted.

It was a day long to be remembered. Aside from the danger, however, a more encouraging hour had never presented itself in the history of the Road. The courage, which had so often been shown in the face of great danger, satisfied the Committee that there were heroes and heroines among these passengers, fully entitled to the applause of the liberty-loving citizens of Brotherly Love. The very idea of having to walk for days and nights in succession, over strange roads, through by-ways, and valleys, over mountains, and marshes, was fitted to appal the bravest hearts, especially where women and children were concerned.

Being familiar with such cases, the Committee was delighted beyond measure to observe how wisely and successfully each of these parties had managed to overcome these difficulties.

Party No. 1 consisted of Charlotte Giles and Harriet Eglin, owned by Capt. Wm. Applegarth and John Delahay. Neither of these girls had any great complaint to make on the score of ill-treatment endured.

So they contrived each to get a suit of mourning, with heavy black veils, and thus dressed, apparently absorbed with grief, with a friend to pass them to the Baltimore depot (hard place to pass, except aided by an individual well known to the R.R. company), they took a direct course for Philadelphia.

While seated in the car, before leaving Baltimore (where slaves and masters both belonged), who should enter but the master of one of the girls! In a very excited manner, he hurriedly approached Charlotte and Harriet, who were apparently weeping. Peeping under their veils, "What is your name," exclaimed the excited gentleman. "Mary, sir," sobbed Charlotte. "What is your name?" (to the other mourner) "Lizzie, sir," was the faint reply. On rushed the excited gentleman as if moved by steam – through the cars, looking for his property; not finding it, he passed out of the cars, and to the delight of Charlotte and Harriet soon disappeared. Fair business men would be likely to look at this conduct on the part of the two girls in the light of a "sharp practice." In military parlance it might be regarded as excellent strategy. Be this as it may, the Underground Rail Road passengers arrived safely at the Philadelphia station and were gladly received.

A brief stay in the city was thought prudent lest the hunters might be on the pursuit. They were, therefore, retained in safe quarters.

In the meantime, Arrival No. 2 reached the Committee. It consisted of a colored man, a white woman and a child, ten years old. This case created no little surprise. Not that quite a number of passengers, fair enough to pass for white, with just a slight tinge of colored blood in their veins, even sons and daughters of some of the F.F.V., had not on various occasions come over the U.G.R.R. But this party was peculiar. An explanation was sought, which resulted in ascertaining that the party was from Leesburg, Virginia; that David, the colored man, was about twenty-seven years of age, intelligent, and was owned, or claimed by Joshua Pusey. David had no taste for Slavery, indeed, felt that it would be impossible for him to adapt himself to a life of servitude for the special benefit of others; he had, already, as he thought, been dealt with very wrongfully by Pusey, who had deprived him of many years of the best part of his life, and would continue thus to wrong him, if he did not make a resolute effort to get away. So after thinking of various plans, he determined not to run off as a slave with his "budget on his back," but to "travel as a coachman," under the "protection of a white lady." In planning this pleasant scheme, David was not blind to the fact that neither himself nor the "white lady," with whom he proposed to travel, possessed either horse or carriage.

But his master happened to have a vehicle that would answer for the occasion. David reasoned that as Joshua, his so called master, had deprived him of his just dues for so many years, he had a right to borrow, or take without borrowing, one of Joshua's horses for the expedition. The plan was submitted to the lady, and was approved, and a mutual understanding here entered into, that she should hire a carriage, and take also her little girl with them. The lady was to assume the proprietorship of the horse, carriage and coachman. In so doing all dangers would be, in their judgment, averted. The scheme being all ready for execution, the time for departure was fixed, the carriage hired, David having secured his master Joshua's horse, and off they started in the direction of Pennsylvania. White people being so accustomed to riding, and colored people to driving, the party looked all right. No one suspected them, that they were aware of, while passing through Virginia.

On reaching Chambersburg, Pa., in the evening, they drove to a hotel, the lady alighted, holding by the hand her well dressed and nice-looking little daughter, bearing herself with as independent an air as if she had owned twenty such boys as accompanied her as coachman. She did not hesitate to enter and request accommodations for the night, for herself, daughter, coachman, and horse. Being politely told that they could be accommodated, all that was necessary was, that the lady should show off to the best advantage possible. The same duty also rested with weight upon the mind of David.

The night passed safely and the morning was ushered in with bright hopes which were overcast but only for a moment, however. Breakfast having been ordered and partaken of, to the lady's surprise, just as she was in the act of paying the bill, the proprietor of the hotel intimated that he thought that matters "looked a little suspicious," in other words, he said plainly, that he "believed that it was an Underground Rail Road movement;" but being an obliging hotel-keeper, he assured her at the same time, that he "would not betray them." Just here it was with them as it would have been on any other rail road when things threaten to come to a stand; they could do nothing more than make their way out of the peril as best they could. One thing they decided to do immediately, namely, to "leave the horse and carriage," and try other modes of travel. They concluded to take the regular passenger cars. In this way they reached Philadelphia. In Harrisburg, they had sought and received instructions how to find the Committee in Philadelphia.

What relations had previously existed between David and this lady in Virginia, the Committee knew not. It looked more like the time spoken of in Isaiah, where it is said, "And a little child shall lead them," than any thing that had ever been previously witnessed on the Underground Rail Road. The Underground Rail Road never practised the proscription governing other roads, on account of race, color, or previous condition. All were welcome to its immunities, white or colored, when the object to be gained favored freedom, or weakened Slavery. As the sole aim apparent in this case was freedom for the slave the Committee received these travellers as Underground Rail Road passengers.

Arrival No. 3. Charles H. Ringold, Robert Smith, and John Henry Richards, all from Baltimore. Their ages ranged from twenty to twenty-four years. They were in appearance of the class most inviting to men who were in the business of buying and selling slaves. Charles and John were owned by James Hodges, and Robert by Wm. H. Normis, living in Baltimore. This is all that the records contain of them. The exciting and hurrying times when they were in charge of the Committee probably forbade the writing out of a more detailed account of them, as was often the case.

With the above three arrivals on hand, it may be seen how great was the danger to which all concerned were exposed on account of the bold and open manner in which these parties had escaped from the land of the peculiar institution. Notwithstanding, a feeling of very great gratification existed in view of the success attending the new and adventurous modes of traveling. Indulging in reflections of this sort, the writer on going from his dinner that day to the anti-slavery office, to his surprise found an officer awaiting his coming. Said officer was of the mayor's police force. Before many moments had been allowed to pass, in which to conjecture his errand, the officer, evidently burdened with the importance of his mission, began to state his business substantially as follows:

"I have just received a telegraphic despatch from a slaveholder living in Maryland, informing me that six slaves had escaped from him, and that he had reason to believe that they were on their way to Philadelphia, and would come in the regular train direct from Harrisburg; furthermore I am requested to be at the depot on the arrival of the train to arrest the whole party, for whom a reward of $1,300 is offered. Now I am not the man for this business. I would have nothing to do with the contemptible work of arresting fugitives. I'd rather help them off. What I am telling you is confidential. My object in coming to the office is simply to notify the Vigilance Committee so that they may be on the look-out for them at the depot this evening and get them out of danger as soon as possible. This is the way I feel about them; but I shall telegraph back that I will be on the look-out."

While the officer was giving this information he was listened to most attentively, and every word he uttered was carefully weighed. An air of truthfulness, however, was apparent; nevertheless he was a stranger and there was cause for great cautiousness. During the interview an unopened telegraphic despatch which had come to hand during the writer's absence, lay on the desk. Impressed with the belief that it might shed light on the officer's story, the first opportunity that offered, it was seized, opened, and it read as follows (copied from the original):

> HARRISBURG,
> *May 31st, 1856.*
>
> WM. STILL, N. 5th St.: – I have sent via at two o'clock four large and two small hams.
>
> JOS. C. BUSTILL.

Here there was no room for further doubt, but much need for vigilance. Although the despatch was not read to the officer, not that his story was doubted, but purely for prudential reasons, he was nevertheless given to understand, that it was about the same party, and that they would be duly looked after. It would hardly have been understood by the officer, had he been permitted to read it so guardedly was it worded, it was indeed dead language to all save the initiated. In one particular especially, relative to the depot where they were expected to arrive, the officer was in the dark, as his despatch pointed to the regular train, and of course to the depot at Eleventh and Market streets. The Underground Rail Road despatch on the contrary pointed to Broad and Callowhill streets "Via," *i.e.* Reading.

As notified, that evening the "four large and two small hams" arrived, and turned out to be of the very finest quality, just such as any trader would have paid the highest market price for. Being mindful of the great danger of the hour, there was felt to be more occasion just then for anxiety and watchfulness, than for cheering and hurrahing over the brave passengers. To provide for them in the usual manner, in view of the threatening aspect of affairs, could not be thought of. In this critical hour it devolved upon a member of the Committee, for the safety of all parties, to find new and separate places of accommodation, especially for the six known to be pursued. To be stored in other than private families would not answer. Three or four such were visited at once; after learning of the danger much sympathy was expressed, but one after another made excuses and refused. This was painful, for the parties had plenty of house room, were identified with the oppressed race, and on public meeting occasions made loud professions of devotion to the cause of the fugitive, &c. The memory of the hour and circumstances is still fresh.

Accommodations were finally procured for a number of the fugitives with a widow woman (Ann Laws), whose opportunities for succor were far less than at the places where refusals had been met with. But Mrs. L. was kind-hearted, and nobly manifested a willingness to do all that she could for their safety. Of course the Committee felt bound to bear whatever expense might necessarily be incurred. Here some of the passengers were kept for several days, strictly private, long enough to give the slave-hunters full opportunity to tire themselves, and give up the chase in despair. Some belonging to the former arrivals had also to be similarly kept for the same reasons. Through careful management all were succored and cared for. Whilst much interesting information was obtained from these several arrivals: the incidents connected with their lives in Slavery, and when escaping were but briefly written out. Of this fourth arrival, however, the following intelligence will doubtless be highly gratifying to the friends of freedom, wherever the labors of the Underground Rail Road may be appreciated. The people round about Hagerstown, Maryland, may like to know how these "articles" got off so successfully, the circumstances of their escape having doubtless created some excitement in that region of the country.

Arrival No. 4. Charles Bird, George Dorsey, Angeline Brown, Albert Brown, Charles Brown and Jane Scott.

Charles was twenty-four years of age, quite dark, of quick motion, and ready speech, and in every way appearing as though he could take care of himself. He had occupied the condition of a farm laborer. This calling he concluded to forsake, not because he disliked farming, but simply to get rid of David Clargart, who professed to own him, and compelled him to work without pay, "for nothing." While Charles spoke favorably of Clargart as a man, to the extent, at all events, of testifying that he was not what was called a hard man, nevertheless Charles was so decidedly opposed to Slavery that he felt compelled to look out for himself. Serving another man on the no pay principle, at the same time liable to be flogged, and sold at the pleasure of another, Charles felt was worse than heathenish viewed in any light whatsoever. He was prepared therefore, to leave without delay. He had four sisters in the hands of Clargart, but what could he do for them but leave them to Providence.

The next on the list was George Dorsey, a comrade of Charles. He was a young man, of medium size, mixed blood, intelligent, and a brave fellow as will appear presently.

This party in order to get over the road as expeditiously as possible, availed themselves of their master's horses and wagon and moved off civilly and respectably. About nine miles from home on the road, a couple of white men, finding their carriage broken down approached them, unceremoniously seized the horses by the reins and were evidently about to assume authority, supposing that the boys would surrender at once. But instead of so doing, the boys struck away at them with all their might, with their large clubs, not even waiting to hear what these superior individuals wanted. The effect of the clubs brought them prostrate in the road, in an attitude resembling two men dreaming (it was in the night). The victorious passengers, seeing that the smashed up carriage could be of no further use to them, quickly conceived the idea of unhitching and attempting further pursuit on horseback. Each horse was required to carry three passengers. So up they mounted and off they galloped with the horses' heads turned directly towards Pennsylvania. No further difficulty presented itself until after they had traveled some forty miles. Here the poor horses broke down, and had to be abandoned. The fugitives were hopeful, but of the difficulties ahead they wot not; surely no flowery beds of ease awaited them. For one whole week they were obliged to fare as they could, out in the woods, over the mountains, &c. How they overcame the trials in this situation we cannot undertake to describe. Suffice it to say, at the end of the time above mentioned they managed to reach Harrisburg and found assistance as already intimated.

George and Angeline (who was his sister) with her two boys had a considerable amount of white blood in their veins, and belonged to a wealthy man by the name of George Schaeffer, who was in the milling business. They were of one mind in representing him as a hard man. "He would often threaten to sell, and was very hard to please." George and Angeline left their mother and ten brothers and sisters.

Jane was a well-grown girl, smart, and not bad-looking, with a fine brown skin, and was also owned by Schaeffer.

Letters from the enterprising Charlotte and Harriet (arrival No. 1), brought the gratifying intelligence, that they had found good homes in Western New York, and valued their freedom highly. Three out of quite a number of letters received from them from time to time are subjoined.

SENNETT,
*June, 1856.*

MR. WILLIAM STILL: – *Dear Sir*: – I am happy to tell you that Charlotte Gildes and myself have got along thus far safely. We have had no trouble and found friends all the way along, for which we feel very thankful to you and to all our friends on the road since we left. We reached Mr. Loguen's in Syracuse, on last Tuesday evening & on Wednesday two gentlemen from this community called and we went with them to work in their families. What I wish you would do is to be so kind as to send our clothes to this place if they should fall into your hands. We hope our uncle in Baltimore will get the letter Charlotte wrote to him last Sabbath, while we were at your house, concerning the clothes. Perhaps the best would be to send them to Syracuse to the *care of Mr. Loguen* and he will send them to us. This will more certainly ensure our getting them. If you hear anything that would be interesting to Charlotte or me from Baltimore, please direct a letter to us to this place, to the care of Revd. Chas. Anderson, Sennett, Cayuga Co., N.Y. Please give my love and Charlotte's to Mrs. Still and thank her for her kindness to us while at your house.

Your affectionate friend,

HARRIET EGLIN.

## SECOND LETTER

SENNETT,
*July 31st, 1856.*

MR. WM. STILL: – *My Dear Friend*: – I have just received your note of 29th inst. and allow me dear sir, to assure you that the only letter I have written, is the one you received, an answer to which you sent me. I never wrote to Baltimore, nor did any person write for me there, and it is with *indescribable grief*, that I hear what your letter communicates to me, of those who you say have gotten into difficulty on my account. My Cousin Charlotte who came with me, got into a good place in this vicinity, but she could not content herself to stay here but just *one week* – she then went to Canada – and she is the one who by writing (if any one), has brought this trouble upon those to whom you refer in Baltimore.

She has written me two letters from Canada, and by neither of them can I ascertain *where she lives* – her letters are mailed at Suspension Bridge, but she does not live there as her letters show. In the first she does not even sign her name. She has evidently employed some person to write, who is nearly as ignorant as herself. If I knew where to find her I would find out *what* she has written.

I don't know but she has told where I live, and may yet get me and my friends here, in trouble too, as she has some in other places. I don't wish to have you trouble yourself about my clothes, I am in a place where I can get all the clothes I want or need. Will you please write me when convenient and tell me what you hear about those who I fear are suffering as the result of their kindness to me? May God, in some way, grant them deliverance. Oh the misery, the sorrow, which this cursed system of Slavery is constantly bringing upon millions in this land of boasted freedom!

Can you tell me where Sarah King is, who was at your house when I was there? She was going to Canada to meet her husband. Give my love to Mrs. Still & accept the same yourself. Your much indebted & obliged friend,

HARRIET EGLIN.

The "difficulty" about which Harriet expressed so much regret in the above letter, had reference to a letter supposed to have been written by her friend Charlotte to Baltimore, about her clothing. It had been intercepted, and in this way, a clue was obtained by one of the owners as to how they escaped, who aided them, etc. On the strength of the information thus obtained, a well-known colored man, named Adams, was straightway arrested and put in prison at the instance of one of the owners, and also a suit was at the same time instituted against the Rail Road Company for damages – by which steps quite a huge excitement was created in Baltimore. As to the colored man Adams, the prospect looked simply hopeless. Many hearts were sad in view of the doom which they feared would fall upon him for obeying a humane impulse (he had put the girls on the cars). But with the Rail Road Company it was a different matter; they had money, power, friends, etc., and could defy the courts. In the course of a few months, when the suit against Adams and the Rail Road Company came up, the Rail Road Company proved in court, in defense, that the prosecutor entered the cars in search of his runaway, and went and spoke to the two young women in "mourning" the day they escaped, looking expressly for the identical parties, for which he was seeking damages before the court, and that he declared to the conductor, on leaving the cars, that the said "two girls in mourning, were not the ones he was looking after," or in other words, that "neither" belonged to him. This positive testimony satisfied the jury, and the Rail Road Company and poor James Adams escaped by the verdict not guilty. The owner of the lost property had the costs to pay of course, but whether he was made a wiser or better man by the operation was never ascertained.

## THIRD LETTER.

SENNETT,
*October 28th, 1856.*

DEAR MR. STILL: – I am happy to tell you that I am well and happy. I still live with Rev. Mr. Anderson in this place, I am learning to read and write. I do not like to trouble you too much, but I would like to know if you have heard anything more about my friends in Baltimore who got into trouble on our account. Do be pleased to write me if you can give me any information about them. I feel bad that they should suffer for me. I wish all my brethren and sisters in bondage, were as well off as I am. The girl that came with me is in Canada, near the Suspension Bridge. I was glad to see Green Murdock, a colored young man, who stopped at your house about six weeks ago, he knew my folks at the South. He has got into a good place to work in this neighborhood. Give my love to Mrs Still, and believe me your obliged friend,

HARRIET EGLIN.

P.S. I would like to know what became of Johnson,[1] the man whose foot was smashed by jumping off the cars, he was at your house when I was there.

H.E.

1 Johnson was an unfortunate young fugitive, who, while escaping, beheld his master or pursuer in the cars, and jumped therefrom, crushing his feet shockingly by the bold act.

# CHARLES GILBERT

*FLEEING FROM DAVIS A NEGRO TRADER, SECRETED UNDER A HOTEL, UP A TREE, UNDER A FLOOR, IN A THICKET, ON A STEAMER.*

In 1854 Charles was owned in the city of Richmond by Benjamin Davis, a notorious negro trader. Charles was quite a "likely-looking article," not too black or too white, but rather of a nice "ginger-bread color." Davis was of opinion that this "article" must bring him a tip-top price. For two or three months the trader advertised Charles for sale in the papers, but for some reason or other Charles did not command the high price demanded.

While Davis was thus daily trying to sell Charles, Charles was contemplating how he might escape. Being uncommonly shrewd he learned something about a captain of a schooner from Boston, and determined to approach him with regard to securing a passage. The captain manifested a disposition to accommodate him for the sum of ten dollars, provided Charles could manage to get to Old Point Comfort, there to embark. The Point was about one hundred and sixty miles distant from Richmond.

A man of ordinary nerve would have declined this condition unhesitatingly. On the other hand it was not Charles' intention to let any offer slide; indeed he felt that he must make an effort, if he failed. He could not see how his lot could be made more miserable by attempting to flee. In full view of all the consequences he ventured to take the hazardous step, and to his great satisfaction he reached Old Point Comfort safely. In that locality he was well known, unfortunately too well known, for he had been raised partly there, and, at the same time, many of his relatives and acquaintances were still living there. These facts were evidently well known to the trader, who unquestionably had snares set in order to entrap

Charles should he seek shelter among his relatives, a reasonable supposition. Charles had scarcely reached his old home before he was apprised of the fact that the hunters and watch dogs of Slavery were eagerly watching for him. Even his nearest relatives, through fear of consequences had to hide their faces as it were from him. None dare offer him a night's lodging, scarcely a cup of water, lest such an act might be discovered by the hunters, whose fiendish hearts would have found pleasure in meting out the most dire punishments to those guilty of thus violating the laws of Slavery. The prospect, if not utterly hopeless, was decidedly discouraging. The way to Boston was entirely closed. A "reward of $200" was advertised for his capture. For the first week after arriving at Old Point he entrusted himself to a young friend by the name of E.S. The fear of the pursuers drove him from his hiding-place at the expiration of the week. Thence he sought shelter neither with kinfolks, Christians, nor infidels, but in this hour of his calamity he made up his mind that he would try living under a large hotel for a while. Having watched his opportunity, he managed to reach Higee hotel, a very large house without a cellar, erected on pillars three or four feet above the ground. One place alone, near the cistern, presented some chance for a hiding-place, sufficient to satisfy him quite well under the circumstances. This dark and gloomy spot he at once willingly occupied rather than return to Slavery. In this refuge he remained four weeks. Of course he could not live without food; but to communicate with man or woman would inevitably subject him to danger. Charles' experience in the neighborhood of his old home left no ground for him to hope that he would be likely to find friendly aid anywhere under the shadow of Slavery. In consequence of these fears he received his food from the "slop tub," securing this diet in the darkness of night after all was still and quiet around the hotel. To use his own language, the meals thus obtained were often "sweet" to his taste.

One evening, however, he was not a little alarmed by the approach of an Irish boy who came under the hotel to hunt chickens. While prowling around in the darkness he appeared to be making his way unconsciously to the very spot where Charles was reposing. How to meet the danger was to Charles' mind at first very puzzling, there was no time now to plan. As quick as thought he feigned the bark of a savage dog accompanied with a furious growl and snarl which he was confident would frighten the boy half out of his senses, and cause him to depart quickly from his private apartment. The trick succeeded admirably, and the emergency was satisfactorily met, so far as the boy was concerned, but the boy's father hearing the attack of the dog, swore that he would kill him. Charles was a silent listener to the threat, and he saw that he could no longer remain in safety in his present quarter. So that night he took his departure for Bay Shore; here he decided to pass a day in the woods, but the privacy of this place was not altogether satisfactory to Charles' mind; but where to find a more secure retreat he could not, – dared not venture to ascertain that day. It occurred to him, however, that he would be much safer up a tree than hid in the bushes and undergrowth. He therefore climbed up a large acorn tree and there passed an entire day in deep meditation. No gleam of hope appeared, yet he would not suffer himself to think of returning to bondage. In this dilemma he remembered a poor washer-woman named Isabella, a slave who had charge of a wash-house. With her he resolved to seek succor. Leaving the woods he proceeded to the wash-house and was kindly received by Isabella, but what to do with him or how to afford him any protection she could see no way whatever. The schooling which Charles had been receiving a number of weeks in connection with the most fearful looking-for of the threatened wrath of the trader made it much easier for him than for her to see how he could be provided for. A room and comforts he was not accustomed to. Of course he could not expect such comforts now. Like many another escaping from the relentless tyrant, Charles could contrive methods which to his venture-some mind would afford hope, however desperate they might appear to others. He thought that he might be safe under the floor. To Isabella the idea was new, but her sympathies were strongly with Charles, and she readily consented to accom-modate him under the floor of the wash-house. Isabella and a friend of Charles, by the name of John Thomas, were the only persons who were cognizant of this arrangement. The kindness of these friends, manifested by their willingness to do anything in their power to add to the comfort of Charles, was proof to him that his efforts and sufferings had not been altogether in vain. He remained under the floor two weeks, accessible to kind voices and friendly ministrations. At the end of this time his repose was again sorely disturbed by reports from without that suspicion had been awakened towards the wash-house. How this happened neither Charles nor his friends could conjecture. But the arrival of six officers whom he could hear talking very plainly in the house, whose errand was actually to search for him, convinced him that he had never for a single moment been in greater danger. The officers not only searched the house, but they offered his friend John Thomas $25 if he would only put them on Charles' track. John professed to know nothing; Isabella was equally ignorant. Discouraged with their efforts on this occasion, the officers gave up the hunt and left the house. Charles, however, had had enough of the floor accommodations. He left that night and returned to his old quarters under the hotel. Here he stayed one week, at the expiration of which time the need of fresh air was so imperative, that he resolved to go out at night to Allen's cottage and spend a day in the woods. He had knowledge of a place where the undergrowth and bushes were almost impenetrable. To rest and refresh himself in this thicket he felt would be a great comfort to him. Without serious difficulty he reached the thicket, and while pondering over the all-absorbing matter as to how he should ever manage to make his escape, an old man approached. Now while Charles had no reason to think that he was sought by the old intruder, his very near approach admonished him that it would neither be safe nor agreeable to allow him to come nearer. Charles remembering that his trick of playing the dog, when previously in danger under the hotel, had served a good end, thought that it would work well in the thicket. So he again tried his power at growling and barking hideously for a moment or two, which at once caused the man to turn his course. Charles could hear him distinctly retreating, and at the same time cursing the dog.

The owner of the place had the reputation of keeping "bad dogs," so the old man poured out a dreadful threat against "Stephens' dogs," and was soon out of the reach of the one in the thicket.

Notwithstanding his success in frightening off the old man, Charles felt that the thicket was by no means a safe place for him. He concluded to make another change. This time he sought a marsh; two hours' stay there was sufficient to satisfy him, that that too was no place to tarry in, even for a single night. He, therefore, left immediately. A third time, he returned to the hotel, where he remained only two days. His appeals had at last reached the heart of his mother – she could no longer bear to see him struggling, and suffering, and not render him aid, whatever the consequences might be. If she at first feared to lend him a helping hand, she now resolutely worked with a view of saving money to succor him. Here the prospect began to brighten.

A passage was secured for him on a steamer bound for Philadelphia. One more day, and night must elapse, ere he could be received on board. The joyful anticipations which now filled his breast left no room for fear; indeed, he could scarcely contain himself; he was drunk with joy. In this state of mind he concluded that nothing would afford him more pleasure before leaving, than to spend his last hours at the wash house, "under the floor." To this place he went with no fear of hunters before his eyes. Charles had scarcely been three hours in this place, however, before three officers came in search of him. Two of them talked with Isabella, asked her about her "boarders," etc.; in the meanwhile, one of them uninvited, made his way up stairs. It so happened, that Charles was in this very portion of the house. His case now seemed more hopeless than ever. The officer up stairs was separated from him simply by a thin curtain. Women's garments hung all around. Instead of fainting or surrendering, in the twinkling of an eye, Charles' inventive intellect, led him to enrobe himself in female attire. Here, to use his own language, a "thousand thoughts" rushed into his mind in a minute. The next instant he was going down stairs in the presence of the officers, his old calico dress, bonnet and rig, attracting no further attention than simply to elicit the following simple questions: "Whose gal are you?" "Mr. Cockling's, sir." "What is your name?" "Delie, sir." "Go on then!" said one of the officers, and on Charles went to avail himself of the passage on the steamer which his mother had procured for him for the sum of thirty dollars.

In due time, he succeeded in getting on the steamer, but he soon learned, that her course was not direct to Philadelphia, but that some stay would be made in Norfolk, Va. Although disappointed, yet this being a step in the right direction, he made up his mind to be patient. He was delayed in Norfolk four weeks. From the time Charles first escaped, his owner (Davis the negro trader) had kept a standing reward of $550 advertised for his recovery. This showed that Davis was willing to risk heavy expenses for Charles as well as gave evidence that he believed him still secreted either about Richmond, Petersburg, or Old Point Comfort. In this belief he was not far from being correct, for Charles spent most of his time in either of these three places, from the day of his escape until the day that he finally embarked. At last, the long looked-for hour arrived to start for Philadelphia.

He was to leave his mother, with no hope of ever seeing her again, but she had purchased herself and was called free. Her name was Margaret Johnson. Three brothers likewise were ever in his thoughts (in chains), "Henry," "Bill," and "Sam," (half brothers). But after all the hope of freedom outweighed every other consideration, and he was prepared to give up all for liberty. To die rather than remain a slave was his resolve.

Charles arrived per steamer, from Norfolk, on the 11th day of November, 1854. The Richmond papers bear witness to the fact, that Benjamin Davis advertised Charles Gilbert, for mouths prior to this date, as has been stated in this narrative. As to the correctness of the story, all that the writer has to say is, that he took it down from the lips of Charles, hurriedly, directly after his arrival, with no thought of magnifying a single incident. On the contrary, much that was of interest in the story had to be omitted. Instead of being overdrawn, not half of the particulars were recorded. Had the idea then been entertained, that the narrative of this young slave-warrior was to be brought to light in the manner and time that it now is, a far more thrilling account of his adventures might have been written. Other colored men who knew both Davis and Charles, as well as one man ordinarily knows another, rejoiced at seeing Charles in Philadelphia, and they listened with perfect faith to his story. So marvellous were the incidents of his escape, that his sufferings in Slavery, previous to his heroic struggles to throw off the yoke, were among the facts omitted from the records. While this may be regretted it is, nevertheless, gratifying on the whole to have so good an account of him as was preserved. It is needless to say, that the Committee took especial pleasure in aiding him, and listening to so remarkable a story narrated so intelligently by one who had been a slave.

# LIBERTY OR DEATH
# JIM BOW-LEGS
## ALIAS BILL PAUL

In 1855 a traveler arrived with the above name, who, on examination, was found to possess very extraordinary characteristics. As a hero and adventurer some passages of his history were most remarkable. His schooling had been such as could only be gathered on plantations under brutal overseers; – or while fleeing, – or in swamps, – in prisons, – or on the auction-block, etc.; in which condition he was often found. Nevertheless in these circumstances his mind got well stored with vigorous thoughts – neither books nor friendly advisers being at his command. Yet his native intelligence as it regarded human nature, was extraordinary. His resolution and perseverance never faltered. In all respects he was a remarkable man. He was a young man, weighing about one hundred and eighty pounds, of uncommon muscular strength. He was born in the State of Georgia, Oglethorpe county, and was owned by Dr. Thomas Stephens, of Lexington. On reaching the Vigilance Committee in Philadelphia, his story was told many times over to one and another. Hour after hour was occupied by friends in listening to the simple narrative of his struggles for freedom. A very full account of "Jim," was forwarded in a letter to M.A. Shadd, the then Editress of the *Provincial Freeman*. Said account has been carefully preserved, and is here annexed as it appeared in the columns of the above named paper:

> I must now pass to a third adventurer. The one to whom I allude, is a young man of twenty-six years of age, by the name of "Jim," who fled from near Charleston, S.C. Taking all the facts and circumstances into consideration respecting the courageous career of this successful adventurer for freedom, his case

is by far more interesting than any I have yet referred to. Indeed, for the good of the cause, and the honor of one who gained his liberty by periling his life so frequently: – shot several times, – making six unsuccessful attempts to escape from the far South, – numberless times chased by bloodhounds, – captured, imprisoned and sold repeatedly, – living for months in the woods, swamps and caves, subsisting mainly on parched corn and berries, &c., &c., his narrative ought, by all means, to be published, though I doubt very much whether many could be found who could persuade themselves to believe one-tenth part of this marvellous story.

Though this poor Fugitive was utterly ignorant of letters, his natural good sense and keen perception qualified him to arrest the attention and interest the heart in a most remarkable degree.

His master finding him not available, on account of his absconding propensities, would gladly have offered him for sale. He was once taken to Florida, for that purpose; but, generally, traders being wide awake, on inspecting him, would almost invariably pronounce him a "d – – n rascal," because he would never fail to eye them sternly, as they inspected him. The obedient and submissive slave is always recognized by hanging his head and looking on the ground, when looked at by a slave-holder. This lesson Jim had never learned, hence he was not to be trusted.

His head and chest, and indeed his entire structure, as solid as a rock, indicated that he was physically no ordinary man; and not being under the influence of the spirit of "non-resistance," he had occasionally been found to be a rather formidable customer.

His father was a full-blooded Indian, brother to the noted Indian Chief, Billy Bowlegs; his mother was quite black and of unmixed blood.

For five or six years, the greater part of Jim's time was occupied in trying to escape, and in being in prison for sale, to punish him for running away.

His mechanical genius was excellent, so were his geographical abilities. He could make shoes or do carpenter's work very handily, though he had never had the chance to learn. As to traveling by night or day, he was always road-ready and having an uncommon memory, could give exceedingly good accounts of what he saw, etc.

When he entered a swamp, and had occasion to take a nap he took care first to decide upon the posture he must take, so that if come upon unexpectedly by the hounds and slave-hunters, he might know in an instant which way to steer to defeat them. He always carried a liquid, which he had prepared, to prevent hounds from scenting him, which he said had never failed. As soon as the hounds came to the place where he had rubbed his legs and feet with said liquid, they could follow him no further, but howled and turned immediately.

Quite a large number of the friends of the slave saw this noble-hearted fugitive, and would sit long and listen with the most undivided attention to his narrative – none doubting for a moment, I think, the entire truthfulness of his story. Strange as his story was, there was so much natural simplicity in his manner and countenance, one could not refrain from believing him.

# AN IRISH GIRL'S DEVOTION TO FREEDOM

*IN LOVE WITH A SLAVE – GETS HIM OFF TO CANADA – FOLLOWS HIM – MARRIAGE, &C.*

Having dwelt on the sad narratives of Samuel Green and his son in the preceding chapter, it is quite a relief to be able to introduce a traveler whose story contains incidents less painful to contemplate. From the record book the following brief account is taken:

"April 27, 1855. John Hall arrived safely from Richmond, Va., per schooner, (Captain B). One hundred dollars were paid for his passage." In Richmond he was owned by James Dunlap, a merchant. John had been sold several times, in consequence of which, he had possessed very good opportunities of experiencing the effect of change of owners. Then, too, the personal examination made before sale, and the gratification afforded his master when he (John), brought a good price – left no very pleasing impressions on his mind.

By one of his owners, named Burke, John alleged that he had been "cruelly used." When quite young, both he and his sister, together with their mother, were sold by Burke. From that time he had seen neither mother nor sister – they were sold separately. For three or four years the desire to seek liberty had been fondly cherished, and nothing but the want of a favorable opportunity had deterred him from carrying out his designs. He considered himself much "imposed upon" by his master, particularly as he was allowed "no choice about living" as he "desired." This was indeed ill-treatment as John viewed the matter. John may have wanted too much. He was about thirty-five years of age, light complexion – tall – rather handsome-looking, intelligent, and of good manners. But notwithstanding these prepossessing features, John's owner valued him at only $1,000. If he had been a few shades darker and only about half as intelligent as he was, he would have been worth at least $500 more. The idea of having had a white father, in many instances, depreciated the pecuniary value of male slaves, if not of the other sex. John emphatically was one of this injured class; he evidently had blood in his veins which decidedly warred against submitting to the yoke. In addition to the influence which such rebellious blood exerted over him, together with a considerable amount of intelligence, he was also under the influence and advice of a daughter of old Ireland. She was heart and soul with John in all his plans which looked Canada-ward. This it was that "sent him away."

It is very certain, that this Irish girl was not annoyed by the kinks in John's hair. Nor was she overly fastidious about the small percentage of colored blood visible in John's complexion. It was, however, a strange occurrence and very hard to understand. Not a stone was left unturned until John was safely on the Underground Rail Road. Doubtless she helped to earn the money which was paid for his passage. And when he was safe off, it is not too much to say, that John was not a whit more delighted than was his intended Irish lassie, Mary Weaver. John had no sooner reached Canada than Mary's heart was there too.

Circumstances, however, required that she should remain in Richmond a number of months for the purpose of winding up some of her affairs. As soon as the way opened for her, she followed him. It was quite manifest, that she had not let a single opportunity slide, but seized the first chance and arrived partly by means of the Underground Rail Road and partly by the regular train. Many difficulties were surmounted before and after leaving Richmond, by which they earned their merited success. From Canada, where they anticipated entering upon the matrimonial career with mutual satisfaction, it seemed to afford them great pleasure to write back frequently, expressing their heartfelt gratitude for assistance, and their happiness in the prospect of being united under the favorable auspices of freedom! At least two or three of these letters, bearing on particular phases of their escape, etc., are too valuable not to be published in this connection:

## FIRST LETTER

HAMILTON,
*March 25th, 1856.*

Mr. Still: – Sir and Friend – I take the liberty of addressing you with these few lines hoping that you will attend to what I shall request of you.

I have written to Virginia and have not received an answer yet. I want to know if you can get any one of your city to go to Richmond for me. If you can, I will pay the expense of the whole. The person that I want the messenger to see is a white girl. I expect you know who I allude to, it is the girl that sent me away. If you can get any one to go, you will please write right away and tell me the cost, &c. I will forward the money and a letter. Please use your endeavors.

Yours Respectfuliy,

JOHN HALL.

Direct yours to Mr. Hill.

## SECOND LETTER

HAMILTON,
*Sept. 15th, 1856.*

To Mr. Still, Dear Sir: – I take this opportunity of addressing these few lines to you hoping to find you in good health I am happy to inform you that Miss Weaver arrived here on Tuesday last, and I can assure you it was indeed a happy day. As for your part that you done I will not attempt to tell you how thankful I am, but I hope that you can imagine what my feelings are to you. I cannot find words sufficient to express my gratitude to you, I think the wedding will take place on Tuesday next, I have seen some of the bread from your house, and she says it is the best bread she has had since she has been in America. Sometimes she has impudence enough to tell me she would rather be where you are in Philadelphia than to be here with me. I hope this will be no admiration to you for no honest hearted person ever saw you that would not desire to be where you are, No flattery, but candidly speaking, you are worthy all the praise of any person who has ever been with you, I am now like a deserted Christian, but yet I have asked so much, and all has been done yet I must ask again, My love to Mrs. Still. Dear Mr.

Still I now ask you please to exercise all your influence to get this young man Willis Johnson from Richmond for me It is the young man that Miss Weaver told you about, he is in Richmond I think he is at the corner of Fushien Street, & Grace in a house of one Mr. Rutherford, there is several Rutherford in the neighborhood, there is a church call'd the third Baptist Church, on the R.H. side going up Grace street, directly opposite the Baptist church at the corner, is Mrs. Meads Old School at one corner, and Mr. Rutherfords is at the other corner. He can be found out by seeing Fountain Tombs who belongs to Mr. Rutherford and if you should not see him, there is James Turner who lives at the Governors, Please to see Captain Bayliss and tell him to take these directions and go to John Hill, in Petersburgh, and he may find him. Tell Captain Bayliss that if he ever did me a friendly thing in his life which he did do one friendly act, if he will take this on himself, and if money should be lacking I will forward any money that he may require, I hope you will sympathize with the poor young fellow, and tell the captain to do all in his power to get him and the costs shall be paid. He lies now between death or victory, for I know the man he belongs to would just as soon kill him as not, if he catches him, I here enclose to you a letter for Mr. Wm. C. Mayo, and please to send it as directed. In this letter I have asked him to send a box to you for me, which you will please pay the fare of the express upon it, when you get it please to let me know, and I will send you the money to pay the expenses of the carriage clear through. Please to let Mr. Mayo know how to direct a box to you, and the best way to send it from Richmond to Philadelphia. You will greatly oblige me by so doing. In this letter I have enclosed a trifle for postage which you will please to keep on account of my letters I hope you wont think hard of me but I simply send it because I know you have done enough, and are now doing more, without imposing in the matter I have done it a great many more of our people who you have done so much fore. No more from your humble and oldest servant.

JOHN HALL, Norton's Hotel, Hamilton.

## THIRD LETTER

MONDAY,
*Sept. 29, 56.*

Sir: – I take this opportunity of informing you that we are in excellent health, and hope you are the same, I wrote a letter to you about 2 weeks ago and have not yet had an answer to it I wish to inform you that the wedding took place on Tuesday last, and Mrs. Hall now sends her best love to you, I enclose a letter which I wish you to forward to Mr. Mayo, you will see in his letter what I have said to him and I wish you would furnish him with such directions as it requires for him to send them things to you. I have told him not to pay for them but to send them to you so when you get them write me word what the cost of them are, and I will send you the money for them. Mary desires you to give her love to Mrs. Still. If any letters come for me please to send to me at Nortons Hotel, Please to let me know if you had a letter from me about 12 days ago. You will please

Direct the enclosed to Mr. W.C. Mayo, Richmond, Va. Let me know if you have heard anything of Willis Johnson Mr. & Mrs. Hill send their kind love to you, they are all well, no more at present from your affect.,

JOHN HALL

Nortons Hotel.

## FOURTH LETTER

HAMILTON,
*December 23d, 1856.*

DEAR SIR: – I am happy to inform you that we are both enjoying good health and hope you are the same. I have been expecting a letter from you for some time but I suppose your business has prevented you from writing. I suppose you have not heard from any of my friends at Richmond. I have been longing to hear some news from that part, you may think "Out of sight and out of mind," but I can assure you, no matter how far I may be, or in what distant land, I shall never forget you, if I can never reach you by letters you may be sure I shall always think of you. I have found a great many friends in my life, but I must say you are the best one I ever met with, except one, you must know who that is, 'tis one who if I did not consider a friend, I could not consider any other person a friend, and that is Mrs. Hall. Please to let me know if the navigation between New York & Richmond is closed. Please to let me know whether it would be convenient to you to go to New York if it is please let me know what is the expense. Tell Mrs Still that my wife would be very happy to receive a letter from her at some moment when she is at leisure, for I know from what little I have seen of domestic affairs it keeps her pretty well employed, And I know she has not much time to write but if it were but two lines, she would be happy to receive it from her, my reason for wanting you to go to New York, there is a young man named Richard Myers and I should like for you to see him. He goes on board the *Orono* to Richmond and is a particular friend of mine and by seeing him I could get my clothes from Richmond, I expect to be out of employ in a few days, as the hotel is about to close on the 1st January and I hope you will write to me soon I want you to send me word how you and all the family are and all the news you can, you must excuse my short letter, as it is now near one o'clock and I must attend to business, but I have not written half what I intended to, as time is short, hoping to hear from you soon I remain yours sincerely,

JOHN HALL.

Mr. and Mrs. Hill desire their best respects to you and Mrs. Still.

It cannot be denied that this is a most extraordinary occurrence. In some respects it is without a parallel. It was, however, no uncommon thing for white men (slave-holders) in the South to have colored wives and children whom they did not hesitate to live with and acknowledge by their actions, with their means, and in their wills as the rightful heirs of their substance. Probably there is not a state in the Union where such relations have not existed. Seeing such usages, Mary might have reasoned that she had as good a right to marry the one she loved most as anybody else, particularly as she was in a "free country."

# "SAM" NIXON

## ALIAS DR. THOMAS BAYNE

*THE ESCAPE OF A DENTIST ON THE U.G.R.R. – HE IS TAKEN FOR AN IMPOSTOR – ELECTED A MEMBER OF CITY COUNCIL IN NEW BEDFORD – STUDYING MEDICINE, ETC.*

But few could be found among the Underground Rail Road passengers who had a stronger repugnance to the unrequited labor system, or the recognized terms of "master and slave," than Dr. Thomas Bayne. Nor were many to be found who were more fearless and independent in uttering their sentiments. His place of bondage was in the city of Norfolk, Va., where he was held to service by Dr. C.F. Martin, a dentist of some celebrity. While with Dr. Martin, "Sam" learned dentistry in all its branches, and was often required by his master, the doctor, to fulfil professional engagements, both at home and at a distance, when it did not suit his pleasure or convenience to appear in person. In the mechanical department, especially, "Sam" was called upon to execute the most difficult tasks. This was not the testimony of "Sam" alone; various individuals who were with him in Norfolk, but had moved to Philadelphia, and were living there at the time of his arrival, being invited to see this distinguished professional piece of property, gave evidence which fully corroborated his. The master's professional practice, according to "Sam's" calculation, was worth $3,000 per annum. Full $1,000 of this amount in the opinion of "Sam" was the result of his own fettered hands. Not only was "Sam" serviceable to the doctor in the mechanical and practical branches of his profession, but as a sort of ready reckoner and an apt penman, he was obviously considered by the doctor, a valuable "article." He would frequently have "Sam" at his books instead of a book-keeper. Of course, "Sam" had never received, from Dr. M., an hour's schooling in his life, but having perceptive faculties naturally very large, combined with much self-esteem, he could hardly help learning readily. Had his master's design to keep him in ignorance been ever so great, he would have found it a labor beyond his power. But there is no reason to suppose that Dr. Martin was opposed to Sam's learning to read and write. We are pleased to note that no charges of ill-treatment are found recorded against Dr. M. in the narrative of "Sam."

True, it appears that he had been sold several times in his younger days, and had consequently been made to feel keenly, the smarts of Slavery, but nothing of this kind was charged against Dr. M., so that he may be set down as a pretty fair man, for aught that is known to the contrary, with the exception of depriving "Sam" of the just reward of his labor, which, according to St. James, is pronounced a "fraud." The doctor did not keep "Sam" so closely confined to dentistry and book-keeping that he had no time to attend occasionally to outside duties. It appears that he was quite active and successful as an Underground Rail Road agent, and rendered important aid in various directions. Indeed, Sam had good reason to suspect that the slave-holders were watching him, and that if he remained, he would most likely find himself in "hot water up to his eyes." Wisdom dictated that he should "pull up stakes" and depart while the way was open. He knew the captains who were then in the habit of taking similar passengers, but he had some fears that they might not be able to pursue the business much longer. In contemplating the change which he was about to make, "Sam" felt it necessary to keep his movements strictly private. Not even was he at liberty to break his mind to his wife and child, fearing that it would do them no good, and might prove his utter failure. His wife's name was

Edna and his daughter was called Elizabeth; both were slaves and owned by E.P. Tabb, Esq., a hardware merchant of Norfolk.

No mention is made on the books, of ill-treatment, in connection with his wife's servitude; it may therefore be inferred, that her situation was not remarkably hard. It must not be supposed that "Sam" was not truly attached to his wife. He gave abundant proof of true matrimonial devotion, notwithstanding the secrecy of his arrangements for flight. Being naturally hopeful, he concluded that he could better succeed in securing his wife after obtaining freedom himself, than in undertaking the task beforehand.

The captain had two or three other Underground Rail Road male passengers to bring with him, besides "Sam," for whom, arrangements had been previously made – no more could be brought that trip. At the appointed time, the passengers were at the disposal of the captain of the schooner which was to bring them out of Slavery into freedom. Fully aware of the dangerous consequences should he be detected, the captain, faithful to his promise, secreted them in the usual manner, and set sail northward. Instead of landing his passengers in Philadelphia, as was his intention, for some reason or other (the schooner may have been disabled), he landed them on the New Jersey coast, not a great distance from Cape Island. He directed them how to reach Philadelphia. Sam knew of friends in the city, and straightway used his ready pen to make known the distress of himself and partners in tribulation. In making their way in the direction of their destined haven, they reached Salem, New Jersey, where they were discovered to be strangers and fugitives, and were directed to Abigail

Goodwin, a Quaker lady, an abolitionist, long noted for her devotion to the cause of freedom, and one of the most liberal and faithful friends of the Vigilance Committee of Philadelphia.

This friend's opportunities of witnessing fresh arrivals had been rare, and perhaps she had never before come in contact with a "chattel" so smart as "Sam." Consequently she was much embarrassed when she heard his story, especially when he talked of his experience as a "Dentist." She was inclined to suspect that he was a "shrewd impostor" that needed "watching" instead of aiding. But her humanity forbade a hasty decision on this point. She was soon persuaded to render him some assistance, notwithstanding her apprehensions. While tarrying a day or two in Salem, "Sam's" letter was received in Philadelphia. Friend Goodwin was written to in the meantime, by a member of the Committee, directly with a view of making inquires concerning the stray fugitives, and at the same time to inform her as to how they happened to be coming in the direction found by her. While the mind of the friend was much relieved by the letter she received, she was still in some doubt, as will be seen by the appended extract from a letter on the subject:

## LETTER FROM A. GOODWIN

SALEM,
*3 mo., 25, '55.*

DEAR FRIEND: – Thine of the 22d came to hand yesterday noon.

I do not believe that any of them are the ones thee wrote about, who wanted Dr. Lundy to come for them, and promised they would pay his expenses. They had no money, the minister said, but were pretty well off for clothes. I gave him all I had and more, but it seemed very little for four travelers – only a dollar for each – but they will meet with friends and helpers on the way. He said they expected to go away to-morrow. I am afraid, it's so cold, and one of them had a sore foot, they will not get away – it's dangerous staying here. There has been a slave-hunter here lately, I was told yesterday, in search of a woman; he tracked her to our Alms-house – she had lately been confined and was not able to go – he will come back for her and his infant – and will not wait long I expect. I want much to get her away first – and if one had a C.C. Torney here no doubt it would be done; but she will be well guarded. How much I wish the poor thing could be secreted in some safe place till she is able to travel Northward; but where that could be it's not easy to see. I presume the Carolina freed people have arrived ere now. I hope they will meet many friends, and be well provided for. Mary Davis will be then paid – her cousins have sent her twenty-four dollars, as it was not wanted for the purchase money – it was to be kept for them when they arrive. I am glad thee did keep the ten for the fugitives.

Samuel Nixon is now here, just come – a smart young man – they will be after him soon. I advise him to hurry on to Canada; he will leave here to-morrow, but don't say that he will go straight to the city. I would send this by him if he did. I am afraid he will loiter about and be taken – do make them go on fast – he has left. I could not hear much he said

– some who did don't like him at all – think him an impostor – a great brag – said he was a dentist ten years. He was asked where he came from, but would not tell till he looked at the letter that lay on the table and that he had just brought back. I don't feel much confidence in him – don't believe he is the one thee alluded to. He was asked his name – he looked at the letter to find it out. Says nobody can make a better set of teeth than he can. He said they will go on to-morrow in the stage – he took down the number and street of the Anti-slavery office – you will be on your guard against imposition – he kept the letter thee sent from Norfolk. I had then no doubt of him, and had no objection to it. I now rather regret it. I would send it to thee if I had it, but perhaps it is of no importance.

He wanted the names taken down of nine more who expected to get off soon and might come here. He told us to send them to him, but did not seem to know where he was going to. He was well dressed in fine broad-cloth coat and overcoat, and has a very active tongue in his head.

But I have said enough – don't want to prejudice thee against him, but only be on thy guard, and do not let him deceive thee, as I fear he has some of us here.

With kind regards,

A. GOODWIN.

In due time Samuel and his companions reached Philadelphia, where a cordial welcome awaited them. The confusion and difficulties into which they had fallen, by having to travel an indirect route, were fully explained, and to the hearty merriment of the Committee and strangers, the dilemma of their good Quaker friend Goodwin at Salem was alluded to. After a sojourn of a day or two in Philadelphia, Samuel and his companions left for New Bedford. Canada was named to them as the safest place for all Refugees; but it was in vain to attempt to convince "Sam" that Canada or any other place on this Continent, was quite equal to New Bedford. His heart was there, and there he was resolved to go – and there he did go too, bearing with him his resolute mind, determined, if possible, to work his way up to an honorable position at his old trade, Dentistry, and that too for his own benefit.

Aided by the Committee, the journey was made safely to the desired haven, where many old friends from Norfolk were found. Here our hero was known by the name of Dr. Thomas Bayne – he was no longer "Sam." In a short time the Dr. commenced his profession in an humble way, while, at the same time, he deeply interested himself in his own improvement, as well as the improvement of others, especially those who had escaped from Slavery as he himself had. Then, too, as colored men were voters and, therefore, eligible to office in New Bedford, the Doctor's naturally ambitious and intelligent turn of mind led him to take an interest in politics, and before he was a citizen of New Bedford four years, he was duly elected a member of the City Council. He was also an outspoken advocate of the cause of temperance, and was likewise a ready speaker at Anti-slavery meetings held by his race. Some idea of his abilities, and the interest he took in the Underground Rail Road, education, etc., may be gathered from the appended letters:

NEW BEDFORD,
*June 23d, 1855.*

W. Still: – Sir – I write you this to inform you that I has received my things and that you need not say any thing to Bagnul about them – I see by the Paper that the under ground Rail Road is in operation. Since 2 weeks a go when Saless Party was betrayed by that Capt whom we in mass. are so anxious to Learn his name – There was others started last Saturday night – They are all my old friends and we are waiting their arrival, we hope you will look out for them they may come by way of Salem, N.J. if they be not overtaken. They are from Norfolk – Times are very hard in Canada 2 of our old friends has left Canada and come to Bedford for a living. Every thing are so high and wages so low They cannot make a living (owing to the War) others are Expected shortly – let me hear from Sales and his Party. Get the Name of the Capt. that betrayed him let me know if Mrs. Goodwin of Salem are at the same place yet – John Austin are with us. C. Lightfoot is well and remembers you and family. My business increases more since I has got an office. Send me a Norfolk Paper or any other to read when convenient.

Let me hear from those People as soon as possible. They consist of woman and child 2 or 3 men belonging to Marsh Bottimore, L. Slosser and Herman & Co – and Turner – all of Norfolk, Va.

Truly yours,

THOS. BAYNE.

Direct to Box No. 516, New Bedford, Mass. Don't direct my letters to my office. Direct them to my Box 516. My office is 66-1/2 William St. The same street the Post office is near the city market.

The Doctor, feeling his educational deficiency in the enlightened city of New Bedford, did just what every uncultivated man should, devoted himself assiduously to study, and even applied himself to abstruse and hard subjects, medicine, etc., as the following letters will show:

NEW BEDFORD,
*Jan., 1860.*

No. 22, Cheapside, opposite City Hall.

My Dear Friend: – Yours of the 3d inst. reached me safely in the midst of my misfortune. I suppose you have learned that my office and other buildings burned down during the recent fire. My loss is $550, insured $350.

I would have written you before, but I have been to R.I. for some time and soon after I returned before I examined the books, the fire took place, and this accounts for my delay. In regard to the books I am under many obligations to you and all others for so great a piece of kindness, and shall ever feel indebted to you for the same. I shall esteem them very highly for two reasons, first, The way in which they come, that is through and by your Vigilance as a colored man helping a colored man to get such knowledge as will give the lie to our enemies. Secondly – their contents being just the thing I needed at this time. My indebtedness to you and all concerned for me in this direction is inexpressible. There are some books the Doctor says I must have, such as the Medical Dictionary, Physician's Dictionary, and a work on Anatomy. These I will have to get, but any work that may be of use to a student of anatomy or medicine will be thankfully received. You shall hear from me again soon.

Truly Yours,

THOS. BAYNE.

NEW BEDFORD,
*March 18th, 1861.*

Mr. Wm. Still: – Dear Sir – Dr. Powell called to see me and informed me that you had a medical lexicon (Dictionary) for me. If you have such a book for me, it will be very thankfully received, and any other book that pertains to the medical or dental profession. I am quite limited in means as yet and in want of books to prosecute my studies. The books I need most at present is such as treat on midwifery, anatomy, &c. But any book or books in either of the above mentioned cases will be of use to me. You can send them by Express, or by any friend that may chance to come this way, but by Express will be the safest way to send them. Times are quite dull. This leaves me well and hope it may find you and family the same. My regards to your wife and all others.

Yours, &c.,

THOMAS BAYNE,

22 Cheapside, opposite City Hall.

Thus the doctor continued to labor and improve his mind until the war removed the hideous institution of Slavery from the nation; but as soon as the way opened for his return to his old home, New Bedford no longer had sufficient attractions to retain him. With all her faults he conceived that "Old Virginia" offered decided inducements for his return. Accordingly he went directly to Norfolk, whence he escaped. Of course every thing was in the utmost confusion and disorder when he returned, save where the military held sway. So as soon as the time drew near for reorganizing, elections, &c., the doctor was found to be an aspirant for a seat in Congress, and in "running" for it, was found to be a very difficult candidate to beat. Indeed in the first reports of the election his name was amongst the elected; but subsequent counts proved him to be among the defeated by only a very slight majority.

At the time of the doctor's escape, in 1855, he was thirty-one years of age, a man of medium size, and about as purely colored, as could readily be found, with a full share of self-esteem and pluck.

# SUNDRY ARRIVALS

*FROM LOUDON CO., VA., NORFOLK, BALTIMORE, MD., PETERSBURG, VA., &C., ABOUT THE MONTH OF JUNE, 1855.*

The first arrival to be here noticed consisted of David Bennett, and his wife Martha, with their two children, a little boy named George, and a nameless babe one month old. This family journeyed from Loudon county, Va. David, the husband, had been in bonds under Captain James Taylor. Martha, the wife, and her two children were owned by George Carter. Martha's master was represented as a very barbarous and cruel man to the slaves. He made a common practice of flogging females when stripped naked. This was the emphatic testimony of Martha. Martha declared that she had been so stripped, and flogged by him after her marriage. The story of this interesting young mother, who was about twenty-seven years of age, was painful to the ear, particularly as the earnestness and intelligence of this poor, bruised, and mangled soul bore such strong evidence to the truthfulness of her statements. During the painful interview the mind would involuntarily picture this demon, only as the representative of thousands in the South using the same relentless sway over men and women; and this fleeing victim and her little ones, before escaping, only as sharers of a common lot with many other mothers and children, whose backs were daily subjected to the lash. If on such an occasion it was hard to find fitting words of sympathy, or adequate expressions of indignation, the pleasure of being permitted to give aid and comfort to such was in part a compensation and a relief. David, the husband of this woman, was about thirty-two years of age. No further notice was made of him.

Arrival No. 2 consisted of Henry Washington, alias Anthony Hanly, and Henry Stewart. Henry left Norfolk and a "very mild master," known by the name of "Seth March," out of sheer disgust for the patriarchal institution. Directly after speaking of his master in such flattering terms he qualified the "mild," &c. by adding that he was excessively close in money matters. In proof of this assertion, Henry declared, that out of his hire he was only allowed $1.50 per week to pay his board, clothe himself, and defray all other expenses; leaving no room whatever for him to provide for his wife. It was, therefore, a never-failing source of unhappiness to be thus debarred, and it was wholly on this account that he "took out," as he did, and at the time that he did. His wife's name was "Sally." She too was a slave, but "had not been treated roughly."

For fifty long years Henry had been in the grasp of this merciless system – constrained to toil for the happiness of others, to make them comfortable, rich, indolent, and tyrannical. To say that he was like a bird out of a cage, conveys in no sense whatever the slightest idea of his delight in escaping from the prison house. And yet, his pleasure was sadly marred by the reflection that his bosom companion was still in bondage in the gloomy prison-house. Henry was a man of dark color, well made, and of a reflective turn of mind. On arriving in Canada, he manifested his gratitude through Rev. H. Wilson, as follows –

ST. CATHARINES,
*Aug. 20th, 1855.*

DEAR BR. STILL: – I am requested by Henry Washington to inform you that he got through safe, and is here in good business. He returns to you his sincere thanks for your attention to him on his way. I had the pleasure of receiving seven fugitives last week. Send them on, and may God speed them in the flight. I would like to have a miracle-working power, that I could give wings to them all so that they could come faster than by Railroads either underground or above.

Yours truly,

HIRAM WILSON.

While he was thus hopefully succeeding in Canada, separated from his companion by many hundreds of miles, death came and liberated her from the yoke, as the subjoined letter indicates –

ST. CATHARINES, C.W.
*Nov. 12, 1855.*

MR. WILLIAM STILL: – *Dear Sir*: – I have received a letter from Joseph G. Selden a friend in Norfolk, Va., informing me of the death of my wife, who deceased since I saw you here; he also informs me that my clothing will be forwarded to you by Jupiter White, who now has it in his charge. You will therefore do me a great favor, if you will be so good as to forward them to me at this place St. Catharines, C.W.

The accompanying letter is the one received from Mr. Selden which I send you, that you may see that it is all right. You will please give my respects to Mrs. Still and family. Most respectfully yours,

HENRY WASHINGTON.

Henry Stewart, who accompanied the above mentioned traveler to Canada, had fled a short while before from Plymouth, North Carolina. James Monroe Woodhouse, a farmer, claimed Stewart as his property, and "hired him out" for $180 per annum. As a master, Woodhouse was considered to be of the "moderate" type, according to Stewart's judgment. But respecting money matters (when his slaves wanted a trifle), "he was very hard. He did not flog, but would not give a slave a cent of money upon any consideration."

It was by procuring a pass to Norfolk, that Henry managed to escape. Although a father and a husband, having a wife (Martha) and two children (Mary Ann and Susan Jane), he felt that his lot as a slave utterly debarred him from discharging his duty to them; that he could exercise no rights or privileges whatever, save as he might obtain permission from his master. In the matter of separation, even although the ties of husband and wife, parents and children were most closely knit, his reason dictated that he would be justified in freeing himself if possible; indeed, he could not endure the pressure of Slavery any longer. Although only twenty-three years of age, the burdens that he had been called upon to bear, made his naturally intelligent mind chafe to an unusual degree, especially when reflecting upon a continued life of Slavery. When the time decided upon for his flight arrived, he said nothing to his wife on the subject, but secured his pass and took his departure for Norfolk. On arriving there, he sought out an Underground Rail Road captain, and arranged with him to bring him to Philadelphia. Whether the sorrow-stricken wife ever afterwards heard of her husband, or the father of his two little children, the writer is unable to say. It is possible that this narrative may reveal to the mother and her offspring (if they are still living), the first ray of light concerning the missing one. Indeed it is not unreasonable to suppose, that thousands of anxious wives, husbands and children, who have been scattered in every direction by Slavery, will never be able to learn as much of their lost ones as is contained in this brief account of Henry Stewart.

Arrival No. 3, brought William Nelson, his wife, Susan, and son, William Thomas, together with Louisa Bell, and Elias Jasper. These travelers availed themselves of the schooner of Captain B. who allowed them to embark at Norfolk, despite the search laws of Virginia. It hardly need be said, however, that it was no trifling matter in those days, to evade the law. Captains and captives, in order to succeed, found that it required more than ordinary intelligence and courage, shrewdness and determination, and at the same time, a very ardent appreciation of liberty, without which, there could be no success. The simple announcement then, that a party of this number had arrived from Norfolk, or Richmond, or Petersburg, gave the Committee unusual satisfaction. It made them quite sure that there was pluck and brain somewhere.

These individuals, in a particularly marked degree, possessed the qualities that greatly encouraged the efforts of the Committee. William Nelson was a man of a dark chestnut color, medium size, with more than an ordinary degree of what might be termed "mother wit." Apparently, William possessed well settled convictions, touching the questions of morals and religion, despite the overflowing tide of corruption and spurious religious teachings consequent on the existing pro-slavery usages all around him. He was a member of the Methodist Church, under the charge of the Rev. Mr. Jones. For twenty years, William had served in the capacity of a "packer" under Messrs. Turner and White, who held a deed for William as their legal property. While he declared that he had been very "tightly worked" he nevertheless admitted that he had been dealt with in a mild manner in some respects. For his board and clothing, William had been allowed $1.50 per week. Truly a small sum for a hard-working man with a family – yet this was far more than many slaves received from their masters. In view of receiving this small pittance, he had toiled hard – doing over-work in order to make "buckle and strap meet." Once he had been sold on the auction-block. A sister of his had also shared the same fate. While seriously contemplating his life as a slave, he was soon led to the conclusion that it was his duty to bend his entire energies towards freeing himself and his family if possible. The idea of not being able to properly provide for his family rendered him quite unhappy; he therefore resolved to seek a passage North, via the Underground Rail Road. To any captain who would aid him in the matter, he resolved to offer a large reward, and determined that the amount should only be limited by his inability to increase it. Finally, after much anxious preparation, agreement was entered into with Captain B., on behalf of himself, wife, child, and Louisa Bell, which was mutually satisfactory to all concerned, and afforded great hope to

William. In due time the agreement was carried into effect, and all arrived safely and were delivered into the hands of the Committee in Philadelphia. The fare of the four cost $240, and William was only too grateful to think, that a Captain could be found who would risk his own liberty in thus aiding a slave to freedom.

The Committee gladly gave them aid and succor, and agreed with William that the Captain deserved all that he received for their deliverance. The arrival of William, wife, and child in Canada was duly announced by the agent at St. Catharines, Rev. H. Wilson, as follows:

ST. CATHARINES, C.W.,
*June 28th, 1855.*

MR. WM. STILL: – *My Dear Friend*: – I am happy to announce the safe arrival of Thomas Russell with his wife and child. They have just arrived. I am much pleased with their appearance. I shall do what I can for their comfort and encouragement. They stopt at Elmira from Monday night till this morning, hoping that Lucy Bell would come up and join them at that place. They are very anxious to hear from her, as they have failed of meeting with her on the way or finding her here in advance of them. They wish to hear from you as soon as you can write, and would like to know if you have forwarded Lucy on, and if so, what route you sent her. They send their kind respects to you and your family and many thanks for your kindness to them.

They wish you to inquire after Lucy if any harm has befallen her after her leaving Philadelphia. Please write promptly in my care.

Yours truly in the love of freedom,

HIRAM WILSON.

The man who came to us as Wm. Nelson, is now known only as "Thomas Russell." It may here be remarked, that, owing to the general custom of changing names, as here instanced, it is found difficult to tell to whom the letters severally refer. Where the old and new names were both carefully entered on the book there is no difficulty, of course, but it was not always thus.

Susan Bell, the wife of William, was about thirty years of age, of a dark color, rather above medium size, well-made, good-looking, and intelligent – quite equal to her husband, and appeared to have his affections undividedly. She was owned by Thomas Baltimore, with whom she had lived for the last seven years. She stated that during a part of her life she had been treated in a "mild manner." She had no complaint to make until after the marriage of her master. Under the new wife and mistress, Susan found a very marked change for the worse. She fared badly enough then. The mistress, on every trifling occasion for complaint, was disposed to hold the auction-block up to Susan, and would likewise influence her husband to do the same. From the fact, that four of Susan's sisters had been sold away to "parts unknown," she was not prepared to relish these almost daily threats from her irritable mistress, so she became as anxious for a trip on the Underground Rail Road as was her husband.

About one hundred miles away in the country, her father, mother, three brothers, and one sister were living; but she felt that she could not remain a slave on their account. Susan's owner had already fixed a price on her and her child, twenty-two months old, which was one thousand dollars. From this fate she was saved only by her firm resolution to seek her freedom.

Louisa Bell was also of Wm. Nelson's party, and a fair specimen of a nice-looking, wide awake woman; of a chestnut color, twenty-eight years of age. She was the wife of a free man, but the slave of L. Stasson, a confectioner. The almost constant ringing in her ears of the auction-block, made her most miserable, especially as she had once suffered terribly by being sold, and had likewise seen her mother, and five sisters placed in the same unhappy situation, the thought of which never ceased to be most painful. In reflecting upon the course which she was about to pursue in order to free herself from the prison-house, she felt more keenly than ever for her little children, and readily imagined how sadly she would mourn while thinking of them hundreds of miles distant, growing up only to be slaves. And particularly would her thoughts dwell upon her boy, six years of age; full old enough to feel deeply the loss of his mother, but without hope of ever seeing her again.

Heart-breaking as were these reflections, she resolved to leave Robert and Mary in the hands of God, and escape, if possible from her terrible thraldom. Her plan was submitted to her husband; he acquiesced fully and promised to follow her as soon as an opportunity might present itself. Although the ordeal that she was called upon to pass through was of the most trying nature she bravely endured the journey through to Canada. On her arrival there the Rev. H. Wilson wrote on behalf of herself, and the cause as follows:

ST. CATHERINES, C.W.
*July 6th, 1855.*

DEAR BR. STILL: – I have just received your letters touching U.G.R.R. operations. All is right. Jasper and Mrs. Bell got here on Saturday last, and I think I dropt you a line announcing the fact. I write again thus soon because two more by name of Smith, John and Wm., have arrived the present week and were anxious to have me inform you that they are safely landed and free in this refuge land. They wish me to communicate their kind regards to you and others who have aided them. They have found employment and are likely to do well. The 5 of last week have gone over to Toronto. I gave them letters to a friend there after furnishing them as well as I could with such clothing as they required. I am afraid that I am burdening you too much with postage, but can't help doing so unless I fail to write at all, as my means are not half equal to the expenses to which I am subject.

Faithfully and truly yours,

HIRAM WILSON.

Elias Jasper, who was also a fellow-passenger with Wm. Nelson and Co., was noticed thus on the Underground Rail Road: Age thirty-two years, color dark, features good, and gifted both with his tongue and hands. He had worked more or less at the following trades: Rope-making, carpentering, engineering, and photographing. It was in this latter calling that he was engaged when the Underground Rail Road movement first arrested his attention, and so continued until his departure.

For several years he had been accustomed to hire his time, for which he had been required to pay $10 per month. In acquiring the above trades he had been at no expense to his master, as he had learned them solely by his own perseverance, endowed as he was with a considerable share of genius. Occasionally he paid for lessons, the money being earned by his over-work. His master, Bayham, was a "retired gentleman."

Elias had been sold once, and had suffered in various other ways, particularly from being flogged. He left his wife, Mary, but no child. Of his intention to leave Elias saw not how to impart to his wife, lest she should in some way let the "cat out of the bag." She was owned by a Miss Portlock, and had been treated "tolerably well," having had the privilege of hiring her time. She had $55 to pay for this favor, which amount she raised by washing, etc. Elias was a member of the Methodist Church, as were all of his comrades, and well did they remember the oft-repeated lesson, "Servants obey your masters," etc. They soon understood this kind of preaching after breathing free air. The market value of Elias was placed at $1,200.

Arrival, No. 4. Maria Joiner. Captain F. arrived, from Norfolk, with the above named passenger, the way not being open to risk any other on that occasion. This seemed rather slow business with this voyager, for he was usually accustomed to bringing more than one. However, as this arrival was only one day later than the preceding one noticed, and came from the same place, the Committee concluded, that they had much reason for rejoicing nevertheless. As in the case of a great number among the oppressed of the South, when simply looking at Maria, no visible marks of ill usage in any way were discernible. Indeed, as she then appeared at the age of thirty-three, a fine, fresh, and healthy-looking mulatto woman, nine out of every ten would have been impressed with the idea, that she had never been subjected to hard treatment; in other words, that she had derived her full share of advantages from the "Patriarchal Institution." The appearance of just such persons in Southern cities had often led Northerners, when traveling in those parts, to regard the lot of slaves as quite comfortable. But the story of Maria, told in an earnest and intelligent manner, was at once calculated to dissipate the idea of a "comfortable" existence in a state of bondage. She frankly admitted, however, that prior to the death of her old master, she was favorably treated, compared with many others; but, unfortunately, after his death, she had fallen into the hands of one of the old man's daughters, from whom, she declared, that she had received continued abuse, especially when said daughter was under the influence of liquor. At such times she was very violent. Being spirited, Maria could not consent to suffer on as a slave in this manner. Consequently she began to cogitate how she might escape from her mistress (Catharine Gordon), and reach a free State. None other than the usual trying and hazardous ways could be devised – which was either to be stowed away in the hold of a schooner, or concealed amongst the rubbish of a steamer, where, for the time being, the extreme suffering was sure to tax every nerve even of the most valiant-hearted men. The daily darkening prospects constrained her to decide, that she was willing to suffer, not only in adopting this mode of travel, but on the other hand, that she had better be dead than remain under so cruel a woman as her mistress. Maria's husband and sister (no other relatives are noticed) were naturally formidable barriers in the way of her escape. Notwithstanding her attachment to them, she fully made up her mind to be free. Immediately she took the first prerequisite step, which was to repair to a place of concealment with a friend in the city, and there, like the man at the pool, wait until her turn came to be conveyed thence to a free State. In this place she was obliged to wait eight long months, enduring daily suffering in various ways, especially during the winter season. But, with martyr-like faith, she endured to the end, and was eventually saved from the hell of Slavery. Maria was appraised at $800.

Arrival No. 5. Richard Green, alias Wm. Smith, and his brother George. These young brothers fled from George Chambers of Baltimore. The elder brother was twenty-five, the younger twenty-three. Both were tall and well made and of a chestnut color, and possessed a good degree of natural ability. When desiring to visit their parents, their request was positively refused by their owner. Taking offence at this step, both mutually resolved to run away at the earliest opportunity. Thus in accordance with well premeditated plans, they set out and unobstructedly arrived in Philadelphia. At first it was simply very pleasant to take them by the hand and welcome them; then to listen for a few moments to their intelligent narration of how they escaped, the motives that prompted them, etc. But further inquiries soon brought out incidents of the most thrilling and touching nature – not with regard to hardships which they had personally experienced, but in relation to outrages which had been perpetrated upon their mother. Such simple facts as were then written are substantially as follows: Nearly thirty years prior to the escape of Richard and his brother their mother was in very bad health, so much so that physicians regarded her incurable. Her owner was evidently fully impressed with the belief that instead of being profitable to him, she might be an expense, which he could not possibly obviate, while he retained her as a slave. Now there was a way to get out of this dilemma. He could emancipate her and throw the responsibility of her support upon herself. Accordingly he drew up papers, called for his wife's mother to witness them, then formally put them into the hands of the invalid slave woman (Dinah), assuring her at the same time, that she was free – being fully released as set forth in her papers. "Take notice I have no more claim on you nor you on me from this time." Marvellous liberality! After working the life out of a woman, in order that he should not have her to bury, he becomes hastily in favor of freedom. He is, however, justified by the laws of Maryland. Complaint, therefore, would simply amount to nothing. In the nature of the case Dinah was now free, but she was not wholly alone in the world. She had a husband, named Jacob Green, who was owned by Nathan Childs for a term of years only, at the expiration of which time he was to be free. All lived then in Talbot county, Md. At the appointed time Jacob's bondage ended, and he concluded that he might succeed better by moving to Baltimore. Indeed the health of his wife was so miserable that nothing in his old home seemed to offer any inducement in the way of a livelihood. So off they moved to Baltimore. After a time, under careful and kind treatment, the faithful Jacob was greatly encouraged by perceiving that the health of his companion was gradually improving – signs indicated, that she might yet become a well woman. The hopes of husband and wife, in this particular, were, in the lapse of time, fully realized. Dinah was as well as ever, and became the mother of another child – a little boy. Everything seemed to be going on happily, and they had no apparent reason to suspect any troubles other than such as might naturally have to be encountered in a state of poverty and toil.

The unfettered boy was healthy, and made rapid advance in a few years. That any one should ever claim him was never for a moment feared.

The old master, however, becoming tired of country life, had also moved to Baltimore. How, they knew not, but he had heard of the existence of this boy.

That he might satisfy himself on this point, he one day very slyly approached the house with George. No sooner was the old man within the enclosures than he asked Dinah, "Whose child is that?" pointing to the boy. "Ask Jacob," was the reply of the mother. The question was then put to Jacob, the father of the boy. "I did not think that you would ask such a question, or that you would request anything like that," Jacob remarked, naturally somewhat nervous, but he added, "I have the privilege of having any one I please in my house." "Where is he from?" again demanded the master. The father repeated, "I have a right to have," etc., "I am my own man," etc. "I have found out whose he is," the hunter said. "I am going presently to take him home with me." At this juncture he seized the little fellow, at the same time calling out, "Dinah, put his clothes on." By this time the father too had seized hold of the child. Mustering courage, the father said, "Take notice that you are not in the country, pulling and hauling people about." "I will have him or I will leave my heart's blood in the house," was the savage declaration of the master. In his rage he threatened to shoot the father. In the midst of the excitement George called in two officers to settle the trouble. "What are you doing here?" said the officers to the slave-holder. "I am after my property – this boy," he exclaimed. "Have you ever seen it before?" they inquired. "No," said the slave-holder. "Then how do you know that he belongs to you?" inquired the officers. "I believe he is mine," replied the slave-holder.

All the parties concerned were then taken by the officers before an Alderman. The father owned the child but the mother denied it. The Alderman then decided that the child should be given to the father.

The slave-holder having thus failed, was unwilling, nevertheless, to relinquish his grasp. Whereupon he at once claimed the mother. Of course he was under the necessity of resorting to the Courts in order to establish his claim. Fortunately the mother had securely preserved the paper given her by her master so many years before, releasing her. Notwithstanding this the suit was pending nearly a year before the case was decided. Everything was so clear the mother finally gained the suit. This decision was rendered only about two months prior to the escape of Richard and George.

Arrival No. 6. Henry Cromwell. This passenger fled from Baltimore county, Md. The man that he escaped from was a farmer by the name of William Roberts, who also owned seven other young slaves. Of his treatment of his slaves nothing was recorded.

Henry was about six feet high, quite black, visage thin, age twenty-five. He left neither wife, parents, brothers nor sisters to grieve after him. In making his way North he walked of nights from his home to Harrisburg, Pa., and there availed himself of a passage on a freight car coming to Philadelphia.

Arrival No. 7. Henry Bohm. Henry came from near Norfolk, Va. He was about twenty-five years of age, and a fair specimen of a stout man, possessed of more than ordinary physical strength. As to whom he fled from, how he had been treated, or how he reached Philadelphia, the record book is silent. Why this is the case cannot now be accounted for, unless the hurry of getting him off forbade sufficient delay to note down more of the particulars.

Arrival No. 8. Ralph Whiting, James H. Forman, Anthony Atkinson, Arthur Jones, Isaiah Nixon, Joseph Harris, John Morris, and Henry Hodges. A numerous party like this had the appearance of business. They were all young and hopeful, and belonged to the more intelligent and promising of their race. They were capable of giving the best of reasons for the endeavors they were making to escape to a free country.

They imparted to the Committee much information respecting their several situations, together with the characters of their masters in relation to domestic matters, and the customs and usages under which they had been severally held to service – all of which was listened to with deep interest. But it was not an easy matter, after having been thus entertained, to write out the narratives of eight such persons. Hundreds of pages would hardly have contained a brief account of the most interesting portion of their histories. It was deemed sufficient to enter their names and their forsaken homes, etc., as follows:

"Ralph was twenty-six years of age, five feet ten inches high, dark, well made, intelligent, and a member of the Methodist Church. He was claimed by Geo. W. Kemp, Esq., cashier of the Exchange Bank of Norfolk, Va. Ralph gave Mr. Kemp the credit of being a 'moderate man' to his slaves. Ralph was compelled to leave his wife, Lydia, and two children, Anna Eliza, and Cornelius."

"James was twenty-three years of age, dark mulatto, nearly six feet high, and of prepossessing appearance. He fled from James Saunders, Esq. Nothing, save the desire to be free, prompted James to leave his old situation and master. His parents and two sisters he was obliged to leave in Norfolk."

Two brief letters from James, one concerning his "sweet-heart," whom he left in Norfolk, the other giving an account of her arrival in Canada and marriage thereafter will, doubtless, be read with interest. They are here given as follows:

NIAGARA FALLS, June 5th, 1856. MR. STILL: – Sir – I take my pen in hand to write you theas few lines to let you know that I am well at present and hope theas few lines may find you the same. Sir my object in writing to you is that I expect a young Lady by the name of Miss Mariah Moore, from Norfolk, Virginia. She will leave Norfolk on the 13th of this month in the Steamship *Virginia* for Philadelphia you will oblige me very much by seeing her safely on the train of cars that leaves Philadelphia for the Suspension Bridge Niagara Falls pleas to tell the Lady to telegraph to me what time she will leave Philadelphia so i may know what time to meet her at the Suspension Bridge my Brother Isaac Porman send his love also his family to you and your family they are all well at present pleas to give my respects to Mr. Harry Londay, also Miss Margaret Cunigan, no more at present.

I remain your friend,

JAMES H. FORMAN.

When you telegraph to me direct to the International Hotel, Niagara Falls, N.Y.

NIAGARA FALLS,
*July 24th, 1856.*

DEAR SIR: – I take this opportunity of writing these few lines to you hoping that they may find you enjoying good health as these few lines leave me at present. I thank you for your kindness. Miss Moore arrived here on the 30th of June and I was down to the cars to receive her. I thought I would have written to you before, but I thought I would wait till I got married. I got married on the 22d of July in the English Church Canada about 11 o'clock my wife sends all her love to you and your wife and all enquiring friends please to kiss your two children for her and she says she is done crying and I am glad to hear she enjoyed herself so well in Philadelphia give my respects to Miss Margaret Cuningham and I am glad to hear her sister arrived my father sends his respects to you no more at present but remain your friend,

JAMES H. FORMAN.

Direct your letter to the International Hotel, Niagara Falls.

Anthony was thirty-six years of age, and by blood, was quite as nearly related to the Anglo-Saxon as the Anglo-African. He was nevertheless, physically a fine specimen of a man. He was about six feet high, and bore evidence of having picked up a considerable amount of intelligence considering his opportunities. He had been sold three times. Anthony was decidedly opposed to having to pass through this ordeal a fourth time, therefore, the more he meditated over his condition, the more determined he became to seek out an Underground Rail Road agent, and make his way to Canada.

Concluding that Josiah Wells, who claimed him, had received a thousand times too much of his labor already, Anthony was in a fit state of mind to make a resolute effort to gain his freedom. He had a wife, but no children. His father, one sister, and two brothers were all dear to him, but all being slaves "one could not help the other," Anthony reasoned, and wisely too. So, at the command of the captain, he was ready to bear his part of the suffering consequent upon being concealed in the hold of a vessel, where but little air could penetrate.

Arthur was forty-one years of age, six feet high – chestnut color, well made, and possessed good native faculties needing cultivation. He escaped from a farmer, by the name of John Jones, who was classed, as to natural temperament, amongst "moderate slave-holders."

"I wanted my liberty," said Arthur promptly and emphatically, and he declared that was the cause of his escape. He left his mother, two sisters, and three brothers in Slavery.

Isaiah was about twenty-two, small of stature, but smart, and of a substantially black complexion. He had been subjected to very hard treatment under Samuel Simmons who claimed him, and on this account he was first prompted to leave. His mother and three brothers he left in bondage.

Joseph was twenty-three years of age, and was, in every way, "likely-looking." According to the laws of Slavery, he was the property of David Morris, who was entitled to be ranked amongst the more compassionate slave-holders of the South. Yet, Joseph was not satisfied, deprived of his freedom. He had not known hardships as many had, but it was not in him notwithstanding, to be contented as a slave. In leaving, he had to "tear himself away" from his parents, three brothers, and two sisters.

Henry escaped from S. Simmons of Plymouth, North Carolina, and was a fellow-servant with Isaiah. Simmons was particularly distinguished for his tyrannical rule and treatment of his slaves – so Henry and Isaiah had the good sense to withdraw from under his yoke, very young in life; Henry being twenty-three.

John was about twenty-one years of age, five feet eight inches high, dark color, and well-grown for his years. Before embarking, he had endured seven months of hard suffering from being secreted, waiting for an opportunity to escape. It was to keep his master from selling him, that he was thus induced to secrete himself. After he had remained away some months, he resolved to suffer on until his friends could manage to procure him a passage on the Underground Rail Road. With this determined spirit he did not wait in vain.

Arrival No. 9. Robert Jones and wife: – In the majority of cases, in order to effect the escape of either, sad separations between husbands and wives were unavoidable. Fortunately, it was not so in this case. In journeying from the house of bondage, Robert and his wife were united both in sympathies and in struggles. Robert had experienced "hard times," just in what way, however, was not recorded; his wife had been differently treated, not being under the same taskmaster as her husband. At the time of their arrival all that was recorded of their bondage is as follows –

August 2d, 1855, Robert Jones and wife, arrived from Petersburg, Va. Robert is about thirty-five, chestnut color, medium size, of good manners, intelligent, had been owned by Thomas N. Lee, "a very hard man." Robert left because he "wanted his liberty – always had from a boy." Eliza, his wife, is about forty years of age, chestnut color, nice-looking, and well-dressed. She belonged to Eliza H. Richie, who was called a "moderate woman" towards her slaves. Notwithstanding the limited space occupied in noting them on the record book, the Committee regarded them as being among the most worthy and brave travelers passing over the Underground Rail Road, and felt well satisfied that such specimens of humanity would do credit in Canada, not only to themselves, but to their race.

Robert had succeeded in learning to read and write tolerably well, and had thought much over the condition and wrongs of the race, and seemed to be eager to be where he could do something to lift his fellow-sufferers up to a higher plane of liberty and manhood. After an interview with Robert and his wife, in every way so agreeable, they were forwarded on in the usual manner, to Canada. While enjoying the sweets of freedom in Canada, he was not the man to keep his light under a bushel. He seemed to have a high appreciation of the potency of the pen, and a decidedly clear idea that colored men needed to lay hold of many enterprises with resolution, in order to prove themselves qualified to rise equally with other branches of the human family. Some of his letters, embracing his views, plans and suggestions, were so encouraging and sensible, that the Committee was in the habit of showing them to friendly persons, and indeed, extracts of some of his letters were deemed of sufficient importance to publish. One alone, taken from many letters received from him, must here suffice to illustrate his intelligence and efforts as a fugitive and citizen in Canada.

Hamilton, C.W.,
*August 9th, 1856.*

MR. WM. STILL; – *Dear Friend*: – I take this opportunity of writing you these few lines to inform you of my health, which is good at present, &c. * * * *

I was talking to you about going to Liberia, when I saw you last, and did intend to start this fall, but I since looked at the condition of the colored people in Canada. I thought I would try to do something for their elevation as a nation, to place them in the proper position to stand where they ought to stand. In order to do this, I have undertaken to get up a military company amongst them. They laughed at me to undertake such a thing; but I did not relax my energies. I went and had an interview with Major J.T. Gilepon, told him what my object was, he encouraged me to go on, saying that he would do all he could for the accomplishment of my object. He referred to *Sir Allan McNab, &c.* * * * * I took with me Mr. J.H. Hill to see him – he told me that it should be done, and required us to write a petition to the *Governor General*, which has been done. * * * * The company is already organized. Mr. Howard was elected Captain; J.H. Hill, 1st Lieutenant; Hezekiah Hill, Ensign; Robert Jones, 1st Sergeant. The company's name is, Queen Victoria's Rifle Guards. You may, by this, see what I have been doing since I have been in Canada. When we receive our appointments by the Government. I will send by express, my daguerreotype in uniform.

My respects, &c. &c., Robert Jones.

# HEAVY REWARD

When this arrival made its appearance, it was at first sight quite evident that one of the company was a man of more than ordinary parts, both physically and mentally. Likewise, taking them individually, their appearance and bearing tended largely to strengthen the idea that the spirit of freedom was rapidly gaining ground in the minds of the slaves, despite the efforts of the slave-holders to keep them in darkness. In company with the three men, for whom the above large reward was offered, came a woman by the name of Eliza Nokey.

As soon as the opportunity presented itself, the Active Committee feeling an unusual desire to hear their story, began the investigation by inquiring as to the cause of their escape, etc., which brought simple and homely but earnest answers from each. These answers afforded the best possible means of seeing Slavery in its natural, practical workings – of obtaining such testimony and representations of the vile system, as the most eloquent orator or able pen might labor in vain to make clear and convincing, although this arrival had obviously been owned by men of high standing. The fugitives themselves innocently stated that one of the masters, who was in the habit of flogging adult females, was a "moderate man." Josiah Bailey was the leader of this party, and he appeared well-qualified for this position. He was about twenty-nine years of age, and in no particular physically, did he seem to be deficient. He was likewise civil and polite in his manners, and a man of good common sense. He was held and oppressed by William H. Hughlett, a farmer and dealer in ship timber, who had besides invested in slaves to the number of forty head. In his habits he was generally taken for a "moderate" and "fair" man, "though he was in the habit of flogging the slaves – females as well as males," after they had arrived at the age of maturity. This was not considered strange or cruel in Maryland. Josiah was the "foreman" on the place, and was entrusted with the management of hauling the ship-timber, and through harvesting and busy seasons was required to lead in the fields. He was regarded as one of the most valuable hands in that part of the country, being valued at $2,000. Three weeks before he escaped, Joe was "stripped naked," and "flogged" very cruelly by his master, simply because he had a dispute with one of the fellow-servants, who had stolen, as Joe alleged, seven dollars of his hard earnings. This flogging produced in Joe's mind, an unswerving determination to leave Slavery or die: to try his luck on the Underground Rail Road at all hazards. The very name of Slavery made the fire fairly burn in his bones. Although a married man, having a wife and three children (owned by Hughlett), he was not prepared to let his affection for them keep him in chains – so Anna Maria, his wife, and his children Ellen, Anna Maria, and Isabella, were shortly widowed and orphaned by the slave lash.

William Bailey was owned by John C. Henry, a large slaveholder, and a very "hard" one, if what William alleged of him was true. His story certainly had every appearance of truthfulness. A recent brutal flogging had "stiffened his back-bone," and furnished him with his excuse for not being willing to continue in Maryland, working his strength away to enrich his master, or the man who claimed to be such. The memorable flogging, however, which caused him to seek flight on the

Underground Rail Road, was not administered by his master or on his master's plantation. He was hired out, and it was in this situation that he was so barbarously treated. Yet he considered his master more in fault than the man to whom he was hired, but redress there was none, save to escape.

The hour for forwarding the party by the Committee, came too soon to allow time for the writing of any account of Peter Pennington and Eliza Nokey. Suffice it to say, that in struggling through their journey, their spirits never flagged; they had determined not to stop short of Canada. They truly had a very high appreciation of freedom, but a very poor opinion of Maryland.

# SLAVE TRADER HALL IS FOILED

ROBERT McCOY
*alias* WILLIAM DONAR

In October, 1854, the Committee received per steamer, directly from Norfolk, Va., Robert McCoy and Elizabeth Saunders. Robert had constantly been in the clutches of the negro-trader Hall, for the last sixteen years, previous to his leaving, being owned by him. He had, therefore, possessed very favorable opportunities for varied observation and experience relative to the trader's conduct in his nefarious business, as well as for witnessing the effects of the auction-block upon all ages – rending asunder the dearest ties, despite the piteous wails of childhood or womanhood, parental or conjugal relations. But no attempt will be made to chronicle the deeds of this dealer in human flesh. Those stories fresh from the lips of one who had just escaped, were painful in the extreme, but in the very nature of things some of the statements are too revolting to be published. In lieu of this fact, except the above allusions to the trader's business, this sketch will only refer to Robert's condition as a slave, and finally as a traveler on the Underground Rail Road.

Robert was a man of medium size, dark mulatto, of more than ordinary intelligence. His duties had been confined to the house, and not to the slave pen. As a general thing, he had managed, doubtless through much shrewdness, to avoid very severe outrages from the trader. On the whole, he had fared "about as well" as the generality of slaves.

Yet, in order to free himself from his "miserable" life, he was willing, as he declared, to suffer almost any sacrifice. Indeed, his conduct proved the sincerity of this declaration, as he had actually been concealed five months in a place in the city, where he could not possibly avoid daily suffering of the most trying kind. His resolve to be free was all this while maturing. The trader had threatened to sell Robert, and to prevent it Robert (thus) "took out." Successfully did he elude the keen scent and grasp of the hunters, who made diligent efforts to recapture him. Although a young man – only about twenty-eight years of age – his health was by no means good. His system had evidently been considerably shattered by Slavery, and symptoms of consumption, together with chronic rheumatism, were making rapid headway against the physical man. Under his various ills, he declared, as did many others from the land of bondage, that his faith in God afforded him comfort and hope. He was obliged to leave his wife, Eliza, in bonds, not knowing whether they should ever meet again on earth, but he was somewhat hopeful that the way would open for her escape also.

After reaching Philadelphia, where his arrival had long been anticipated by the Vigilance Committee, his immediate wants were met, and in due order he was forwarded to New Bedford, where, he was led to feel, he would be happy in freedom.

Scarcely had he been in New Bedford one month, before his prayers and hopes were realized with regard to the deliverance of his wife. On hearing of the good news of her coming he wrote as follows –

NEW BEDFORD,
*Nov. 3, 1859.*

DEAR SIR: – i embrace this opertunity to inform you that i received your letter with pleasure, i am enjoying good health and hope that these few lines will find you enjoying the same blessing. i rejoise to hear from you i feel very much indetted to you for not writing before but i have been so bissy that is the cause, i rejoise to heare of the arrival of my wife, and hope she is not sick from the roling of the sea and if she is not, pleas to send her on here Monday with a six baral warlian and a rifall to gard her up to my residance i thank you kindly for the good that you have don for me. Give my respects to Mrs. Still, tell her i want to see her very bad and you also i would come but i am afraid yet to venture, i received your letter the second, but about the first of spring i hope to pay you a visit or next summer. i am getting something to do every day. i will write on her arrivall and tell you more. Mr. R. White sends his love to you and your famerly and says that he is very much indetted to you for his not writing and all so he desires to know wheather his cloths has arived yet or not, and if they are please to express them on to him or if at preasant by Mrs. Donar. Not any more at preasent. i remain your affectionate brother,

WILLIAM DONAR.

By the same arrival, and similarly secreted, Elizabeth Frances, alias Ellen Saunders, had the good luck to reach Philadelphia. She was a single young woman, about twenty-two, with as pleasant a countenance as one would wish to see. Her manners were equally agreeable. Perhaps her joy over her achieved victory added somewhat to her personal appearance. She had, however, belonged to the more favored class of slaves. She had neither been over-worked nor badly abused. Elizabeth was the property of a lady a few shades lighter than herself (Elizabeth was a mulatto) by the name of Sarah Shephard, of Norfolk. In order the more effectually to profit by Elizabeth's labor, the mistress resorted to the plan of hiring her out for a given sum per month. Against this usage Elizabeth urged no complaint. Indeed the only very serious charge she brought was to the effect, that her mistress sold her mother away from her far South, when she was a child only ten years old. She had also sold a brother and sister to a foreign southern market. The reflections consequent upon the course that her mistress had thus pursued, awakened Elizabeth to much study relative to freedom, and by the time that she had reached womanhood she had very decided convictions touching her duty with regard to escaping. Thus growing to hate slavery in every way and manner, she was prepared to make a desperate effort to be free. Having saved thirty-five dollars by rigid economy, she was willing to give every cent of it (although it was all she possessed), to be aided from Norfolk to Philadelphia. After reaching the city, having suffered severely while coming, she was invited to remain until somewhat recruited. In the healthy air of freedom she was soon fully restored, and ready to take her departure for New Bedford, which place she reached without difficulty and was cordially welcomed. The following letter, expressive of her obligations for aid received, was forwarded soon after her arrival in New Bedford:

NEW BEDFORD, Mass.,
*October 16th, 1854.*

MR. STILL: – Dear Sir – I now take my pen in my hand to inform you of my health which is good at present all except a cold I have got but I hope when these few lines reach you you may be enjoying good health. I arrived in New Bedford Thursday morning safely and what little I have seen of the city I like it very much my friends were very glad to see me. I found my sister very well. Give my love to Mrs. Still and also your dear little children. I am now out at service. I do not think of going to Canada now. I think I shall remain in this city this winter. Please tell Mrs. Still I have not met any person who has treated me any kinder than she did since I left. I consider you both to have been true friends to me. I hope you will think me the same to you. I feel very thankful to you indeed. It might been supposed, out of sight out of mind, but it is not so. I never forget my friends. Give my love to Florence. If you come to this city I would be very happy to see you. Kiss your dear little children for me. Please to answer this as soon as possible, so that I may know you received this. No more at present. I still remain your friend,

ELLEN SAUNDERS.

ELIZA MCCOY – the wife of Robert McCoy, whose narrative has just been given, and who was left to wait in hope when her husband escaped – soon followed him to freedom. It is a source of great satisfaction to be able to present her narrative in so close proximity to her husband's. He arrived about the first of October – she about the first of November, following. From her lips testimony of much weight and interest was listened to by several friends relative to her sufferings as a slave – on the auction-block, and in a place of concealment seven months, waiting and praying for an opportunity to escape. But it was thought sufficient to record merely a very brief outline of her active slave life, which consisted of the following noticeable features.

Eliza had been owned by Andrew Sigany, of Norfolk – age about thirty-eight – mulatto, and a woman whose appearance would readily command attention and respect anywhere outside of the barbarism of Slavery. She stated that her experience as a sufferer in cruel hands had been very trying, and that in fretting under hardships, she had "always wanted to be free." Her language was unmistakable on this point. Neither mistress nor servant was satisfied with each other; the mistress was so "queer" and "hard to please," that Eliza became heartily sick of trying to please her – an angel would have failed with such a woman. So, while matters were getting no better, but, on the contrary, were growing worse and worse, Eliza thought she would seek a more pleasant atmosphere in the North. In fact she felt that it would afford her no little relief to allow her place to be occupied by another. When she went into close quarters of concealment, she fully understood what was meant and all the liabilities thereto. She had pluck enough to endure unto the end without murmuring. The martyrs in olden times who dwelt in "dens and caves of the earth," could hardly have fared worse than some of these way-worn travelers.

After the rest, needed by one who had suffered so severely until her arrival in Philadelphia, she was forwarded to her anxiously waiting husband in New Bedford, where she was gladly received.

# ESCAPING IN A CHEST

$150 REWARD. Ran away from the subscriber, on Sunday night, 27th inst., my NEGRO GIRL, Lear Green, about 18 years of age, black complexion, round-featured, good-looking and ordinary size; she had on and with her when she left, a tan-colored silk bonnet, a dark plaid silk dress, a light mouslin delaine, also one watered silk cape and one tan colored cape. I have reason to be confident that she was persuaded off by a negro man named Wm. Adams, black, quick spoken, 5 feet 10 inches high, a large scar on one side of his face, running down in a ridge by the corner of his mouth, about 4 inches long, barber by trade, but works mostly about taverns, opening oysters, &c. He has been missing about a week; he had been heard to say he was going to marry the above girl and ship to New York, where it is said his mother resides. The above reward will be paid if said girl is taken out of the State of Maryland and delivered to me; or fifty dollars if taken in the State of Maryland.

JAMES NOBLE.

No. 153 Broadway, Baltimore.

Lear Green, so particularly advertised in the *Baltimore Sun* by "James Noble," won for herself a strong claim to a high place among the heroic women of the nineteenth century. In regard to description and age the advertisement is tolerably accurate, although her master might have added, that her countenance was one of peculiar modesty and grace. Instead of being "black," she was of a "dark-brown color." Of her bondage she made the following statement: She was owned by "James Noble, a Butter Dealer" of Baltimore. He fell heir to Lear by the will of his wife's mother, Mrs. Rachel Howard, by whom she had previously been owned. Lear was but a mere child when she came into the hands of Noble's family. She, therefore, remembered but little of her old mistress. Her young mistress, however, had made a lasting impression upon her mind; for she was very exacting and oppressive in regard to the tasks she was daily in the habit of laying upon Lear's shoulders, with no disposition whatever to allow her any liberties. At least Lear was never indulged in this respect. In this situation a young man by the name of William Adams proposed marriage to her. This offer she was inclined to accept, but disliked the idea of being encumbered with the chains of slavery and the duties of a family at the same time.

After a full consultation with her mother and also her intended upon the matter, she decided that she must be free in order to fill the station of a wife and mother. For a time dangers and difficulties in the way of escape seemed utterly to set at defiance all hope of success. Whilst every pulse was beating strong for liberty, only one chance seemed to be left, the trial of which required as much courage as it would to endure the cutting off the right arm or plucking out the right eye. An old chest of substantial make, such as sailors commonly use, was procured. A quilt, a pillow, and a few articles of raiment, with a small quantity of food and a bottle of water were put in it, and Lear placed therein; strong ropes were fastened around the chest and she was safely stowed amongst the ordinary freight on one of the Erricson line of steamers. Her intended's mother, who was a free woman, agreed to come as a passenger on the same boat. How could she refuse? The prescribed rules of the Company assigned colored passengers to the deck. In this instance it was exactly where this guardian and mother desired to be – as near the chest as possible. Once or twice, during the silent watches of the night, she was drawn irresistibly to the chest, and could not refrain from venturing to untie the rope and raise the lid a little, to see if the poor child still lived, and at the same time to give her a breath of fresh air. Without uttering a whisper, that frightful moment, this office was successfully performed. That the silent prayers of this oppressed young woman, together with her faithful protector's, were momentarily ascending to the ear of the good God above, there can be no question. Nor is it to be doubted for a moment but that some ministering angel aided the mother to unfasten the rope, and at the same time nerved the heart of poor Lear to endure the trying ordeal of her perilous situation. She declared that she had no fear.

After she had passed eighteen hours in the chest, the steamer arrived at the wharf in Philadelphia, and in due time the living freight was brought off the boat, and at first was delivered at a house in Barley street, occupied by particular friends of the mother. Subsequently chest and freight were removed to the residence of the writer, in whose family she remained several days under the protection and care of the Vigilance Committee.

Such hungering and thirsting for liberty, as was evinced by Lear Green, made the efforts of the most ardent friends, who were in the habit of aiding fugitives, seem feeble in the extreme. Of all the heroes in Canada, or out of it, who have purchased their liberty by downright bravery, through perils the most hazardous, none deserve more praise than Lear Green.

She remained for a time in this family, and was then forwarded to Elmira. In this place she was married to William Adams, who has been previously alluded to. They never went to Canada, but took up their permanent abode in Elmira. The brief space of about three years only was allotted her in which to enjoy freedom, as death came and terminated her career. About the time of this sad occurrence, her mother-in-law died in this city. The impressions made by both mother and daughter can never be effaced. The chest in which Lear escaped has been preserved by the writer as a rare trophy, and her photograph taken, while in the chest, is an excellent likeness of her and, at the same time, a fitting memorial.

# ISAAC WILLIAMS, HENRY BANKS, AND KIT NICKLESS

*MONTHS IN A CAVE – SHOT BY SLAVE-HUNTERS.*

Rarely were three travelers from the house of bondage received at the Philadelphia station whose narratives were more interesting than those of the above-named individuals. Before escaping they had encountered difficulties of the most trying nature. No better material for dramatic effect could be found than might have been gathered from the incidents of their lives and travels. But all that we can venture to introduce here is the brief account recorded at the time of their sojourn at the Philadelphia station when on their way to Canada in 1854. The three journeyed together. They had been slaves together in the same neighborhood. Two of them had shared the same den and cave in the woods, and had been shot, captured, and confined in the same prison; had broken out of prison and again escaped; consequently their hearts were thoroughly cemented in the hope of reaching freedom together.

Isaac was a stout-made young man, about twenty-six years of age, possessing a good degree of physical and mental ability. Indeed his intelligence forbade his submission to the requirements of Slavery, rendered him unhappy and led him to seek his freedom. He owed services to D. Fitchhugh up to within a short time before he escaped. Against Fitchhugh he made grave charges, said that he was a "hard, bad man." It is but fair to add that Isaac was similarly regarded by his master, so both were dissatisfied with each other. But the master had the advantage of Isaac, he could sell him. Isaac, however, could turn the table on his master, by running off. But the master moved quickly and sold Isaac to Dr. James, a negro trader. The trader designed making a good speculation out of his investment: Isaac determined that he should be disappointed;

indeed that he should lose every dollar that he paid for him. So while the doctor was planning where and how he could get the best price for him, Isaac was planning how and where he might safely get beyond his reach. The time for planning and acting with Isaac was, however, exceedingly short. He was daily expecting to be called upon to take his departure for the South. In this situation he made known his condition to a friend of his who was in a precisely similar situation; had lately been sold just as Isaac had to the same trader James. So no argument was needed to convince his friend and fellow-servant that if they meant to be free they would have to set off immediately.

That night Henry Banks and Isaac Williams started for the woods together, preferring to live among reptiles and wild animals, rather than be any longer at the disposal of Dr. James. For two weeks they successfully escaped their pursuers. The woods, however, were being hunted in every direction, and one day the pursuers came upon them, shot them both, and carried them to King George's Co. jail. The jail being an old building had weak places in it; but the prisoners concluded to make no attempt to break out while suffering badly from their wounds. So they remained one month in confinement. All the while their brave spirits under suffering grew more and more daring. Again they decided to strike for freedom, but where to go, save to the woods, they had not the slightest idea. Of course they had heard, as most slaves had, of cave life, and pretty well understood all the measures which had to be resorted to for security when entering upon so hazardous an undertaking. They concluded, however, that they could not make their condition any worse, let circumstances be what they might in this respect. Having discovered how they could break jail, they were not long in accomplishing their purpose, and were out and off to the woods again. This time they went far into the forest, and there they dug a cave, and with great pains had every thing so completely arranged as to conceal the spot entirely. In this den they stayed three months. Now and then they would manage to secure a pig. A friend also would occasionally serve them with a meal. Their sufferings at best were fearful; but great as they were, the thought of returning to Slavery never occurred to them, and the longer they stayed in the woods, the greater was their determination to be free. In the belief that their owner had about given them up they resolved to take the North Star for a pilot, and try in this way to reach free land.

Kit, an old friend in time of need, having proved true to them in their cave, was consulted. He fully appreciated their heroism, and determined that he would join them in the undertaking, as he was badly treated by his master, who was called General Washington, a common farmer, hard drinker, and brutal fighter, which Kit's poor back fully evinced by the marks it bore. Of course Isaac and Henry were only too willing to have him accompany them.

In leaving their respective homes they broke kindred ties of the tenderest nature. Isaac had a wife, Eliza, and three children, Isaac, Estella, and Ellen, all owned by Fitchhugh. Henry was only nineteen, single, but left parents, brothers, and sisters, all owned by different slave-holders. Kit had a wife, Matilda, and three children, Sarah Ann, Jane Frances, and Ellen, slaves.

# "PETE MATTHEWS," ALIAS SAMUEL SPARROWS

*"I MIGHT AS WELL BE IN THE PENITENTIARY"*

Up to the age of thirty-five "Pete" had worn the yoke steadily, if not patiently under William S. Matthews, of Oak Hall, near Temperanceville, in the State of Virginia. Pete said that his "master was not a hard man," but the man to whom he "was hired, George Matthews, was a very cruel man." "I might as well be in the penitentiary as in his hands," was his declaration.

One day, a short while before Pete "took out," an ox broke into the truck patch, and helped himself to choice delicacies, to the full extent of his capacious stomach, making sad havoc with the vegetables generally. Peter's attention being directed to the ox, he turned him out, and gave him what he considered proper chastisement, according to the mischief he had done. At this liberty taken by Pete, the master became furious. "He got his gun and threatened to shoot him," "Open your mouth if you dare, and I will pat the whole load into you," said the enraged master. "He took out a large dirk-knife, and attempted to stab me, but I kept out of his way," said Pete. Nevertheless the violence of the master did not abate until he had beaten Pete over the head and body till he was weary, inflicting severe injuries. A great change was at once wrought in Pete's mind. He was now ready to adopt any plan that might hold out the least encouragement to escape. Having capital to the amount of four dollars only, he felt that he could not do much towards employing a conductor, but he had a good pair of legs, and a heart stout enough to whip two or three slave-catchers, with the help of a pistol. Happening to know a man who had a pistol for sale, he went to him and told him that he wished to purchase it. For one dollar the pistol became Pete's property. He had but three dollars left, but he was determined to make that amount answer his purposes under the circumstances. The last cruel beating maddened him almost to desperation, especially when he remembered how he had been compelled to work hard night and day, under Matthews. Then, too, Peter had a wife, whom his master prevented him from visiting; this was not among the least offences with which Pete charged his master. Fully bent on leaving, the following Sunday was fixed by him on which to commence his journey.

The time arrived and Pete bade farewell to Slavery, resolved to follow the North Star, with his pistol in hand ready for action. After traveling about two hundred miles from home he unexpectedly had an opportunity of using his pistol. To his astonishment he suddenly came face to face with a former master, whom he had not seen for a long time. Pete desired no friendly intercourse with him whatever; but he perceived that his old master recognized him and was bent upon stopping him. Pete held on to his pistol, but moved as fast as his wearied limbs would allow him, in an opposite direction. As he was running, Pete cautiously cast his eye over his shoulder, to see what had become of his old master, when to his amazement, he found that a regular chase was being made after him. Need of redoubling his pace was quite obvious. In this hour of peril, Pete's legs saved him.

After this signal leg-victory, Pete had more confidence in his "understandings," than he had in his old pistol, although he held on to it until he reached Philadelphia, where he left it in the possession of the Secretary of the Committee. Considering it worth saving simply as a relic of the Underground Rail Road, it was carefully laid aside. Pete was now christened

Samuel Sparrows. Mr. Sparrows had the rust of Slavery washed off as clean as possible and the Committee furnishing him with clean clothes, a ticket, and letters of introduction, started him on Canada-ward, looking quite respectable. And doubtless he felt even more so than he looked; free air had a powerful effect on such passengers as Samuel Sparrows.

The unpleasantness which grew out of the mischief done by the ox on George Matthews' farm took place the first of October, 1855. Pete may be described as a man of unmixed blood, well-made, and intelligent.

# WILLIAM BUTCHER

## ALIAS WILLIAM T. MITCHELL

## "HE WAS ABUSEFUL."

This passenger reported himself from Massey's Cross-Roads, near Georgetown, Maryland. William gave as his reason for being found destitute, and under the necessity of asking aid, that a man by the name of William Boyer, who followed farming, had deprived him of his hard earnings, and also claimed him as his property; and withal that he had abused him for years, and recently had "threatened to sell" him. This threat made his yoke too intolerable to be borne.

He here began to think and plan for the future as he had never done before. Fortunately he was possessed with more than an average amount of mother wit, and he soon comprehended the requirements of the Underground Rail Road. He saw exactly that he must have resolution and self-dependence, very decided, in order to gain the victory over Boyer. In his hour of trial his wife, Phillis, and child, John Wesley, who were free, caused him much anxiety; but his reason taught him that it was his duty to throw off the yoke at all hazards, and he acted accordingly. Of course he left behind his wife and child. The interview which the Committee held with William was quite satisfactory, and he was duly aided and regularly despatched by the name of William T. Mitchell. He was about twenty-eight years of age, of medium size, and of quite a dark hue.

## "WHITE ENOUGH TO PASS."

John Wesley Gibson represented himself to be not only the slave, but also the son of William Y. Day, of Taylor's Mount, Maryland. The faintest shade of colored blood was hardly discernible in this passenger. He relied wholly on his father's white blood to secure him freedom. Having resolved to serve no longer as a slave, he concluded to "hold up his head and put on airs." He reached Baltimore safely without being discovered or suspected of being on the Underground Rail Road, as far as he was aware of. Here he tried for the first time to pass for white; the attempt proved a success beyond his expectation. Indeed he could but wonder how it was that he had never before hit upon such an expedient to rid himself of his unhappy lot. Although a man of only twenty-eight years of age, he was foreman of his master's farm, but he was not particularly favored in any way on this account. His master and father endeavored to hold the reins very tightly upon him. Not even allowing him the privilege of visiting around on neighboring plantations. Perhaps the master thought the family likeness was rather too discernible. John believed that on this account all privileges were denied him, and he resolved to escape. His mother, Harriet, and sister, Frances, were named as near kin whom he had left behind. John was quite smart, and looked none the worse for having so much of his master's blood in his veins. The master was alone to blame for John's escape, as he passed on his (the master's) color.

# ESCAPING WITH MASTER'S CARRIAGES AND HORSES

*HARRIET SHEPHARD, AND HER FIVE CHILDREN, WITH FIVE OTHER PASSENGERS.*

One morning about the first of November, in 1855, the sleepy, slave-holding neighborhood of Chestertown, Maryland, was doubtless deeply excited on learning that eleven head of slaves, four head of horses, and two carriages were missing. It is but reasonable to suppose that the first report must have produced a shock, scarcely less stunning than an earthquake. Abolitionists, emissaries, and incendiaries were farther below par than ever. It may be supposed that cursings and threatenings were breathed out by a deeply agitated community for days in succession.

Harriet Shephard, the mother of five children, for whom she felt of course a mother's love, could not bear the thought of having her offspring compelled to wear the miserable yoke of Slavery, as she had been compelled to do. By her own personal experience, Harriet could very well judge what their fate would be when reaching man and womanhood. She declared that she had never received "kind treatment." It was not on this account, however, that she was prompted to escape. She was actuated by a more disinterested motive than this. She was chiefly induced to make the bold effort to save her children from having to drag the chains of Slavery as she herself had done.

Anna Maria, Edwin, Eliza Jane, Mary Ann, and John Henry were the names of the children for whom she was willing to make any sacrifice. They were young; and unable to walk, and she was penniless, and unable to hire a conveyance, even if she had known any one who would have been willing to risk the law in taking them a night's journey. So there was no hope in these directions. Her rude intellect being considered, she was entitled to a great deal of credit for seizing the horses and carriages belonging to her master, as she did it for the liberation of her children.

Knowing others at the same time, who were wanting to visit Canada, she consulted with five of this class, males and females, and they mutually decided to travel together.

It is not likely that they knew much about the roads, nevertheless they reached Wilmington, Delaware, pretty direct, and ventured up into the heart of the town in carriages, looking as innocent as if they were going to a meeting to hear an old-fashioned Southern sermon – "Servants, obey your masters." Of course, the distinguished travelers were immediately reported to the noted Thomas Garrett, who was accustomed to transact the affairs of the Underground Rail Road in a cool masterly way. But, on this occasion, there was but little time for deliberation, but much need of haste to meet the emergency. He at once decided, that they must immediately be separated from the horses and carriages, and got out of Wilmington as quickly as possible. With the courage and skill, so characteristic of Garrett, the fugitives, under escort, were soon on their way to Kennett Square (a hot-bed of abolitionists and stock-holders of the Underground Rail Road), which place they reached safely. It so happened, that they reached Long Wood meeting-house in the evening, at which place a fair circle had convened. Being invited, they stayed awhile in the meeting, then, after remaining all night with one of the Kennett friends, they were brought to Downingtown early in the morning and thence, by daylight, within a short distance of Kimberton, and found succor with friend Lewis, at the old headquarters of the fugitives.

[A letter may be found from Miss G.A. Lewis, on page thirty-nine, throwing much light on this arrival.] After receiving friendly aid and advice while there, they were forwarded to the Committee in Philadelphia. Here further aid was afforded them, and as danger was quite obvious, they were completely divided and disguised, so that the Committee felt that they might safely be sent on to Canada in one of the regular trains considered most private.

Considering the condition of the slave mother and her children and friends, all concerned rejoiced, that they had had the courage to use their master's horses and vehicles as they did.

# EIGHT AND A HALF MONTHS SECRETED

WASHINGTON SOMLOR, ALIAS JAMES MOORE

But few could tell of having been eye-witnesses to outrages more revolting and disgraceful than Washington Somlor. He arrived per steamer *Pennsylvania* (secreted), directly from Norfolk, Virginia, in 1855. He was thirty-two years of age – a man of medium size and quite intelligent. A merchant by the name of Smith owned Washington.

Eight and a half months before escaping, Washington had been secreted in order to shun both master and auction-block. Smith believed in selling, flogging, cobbing, paddling, and all other kinds of torture, by which he could inflict punishment in order to make the slaves feel his power. He thus tyrannized over about twenty-five head.

Being naturally passionate, when in a brutal mood, he made his slaves suffer unmercifully. Said Washington, "On one occasion, about two months before I was secreted, he had five of the slaves (some of them women) tied across a barrel, lashed with the cow-hide and then cobbed – this was a common practice."

Such treatment was so inhuman and so incredible, that the Committee hesitated at first to give credence to the statement, and only yielded when facts and evidences were given which seemed incontestible.

The first effort to come away was made on the steamship *City of Richmond*. Within sixty miles of Philadelphia, in consequence of the ice obstruction in the river, the steamer had to go back. How sad Washington felt at thus having his hopes broken to pieces may be imagined but cannot be described. Great as was his danger, when the steamer returned to Norfolk, he was safely gotten off the boat and under the eye of officers walked away. Again he was secreted in his old doleful quarters, where he waited patiently for the Spring. It came. Again the opportunity for another trial was presented, and it was seized unhesitatingly. This time, his tried faith was rewarded with success. He came through safely to the Committee's satisfaction as well as his own. The recital of his sufferings and experience had a very inspiring effect on those who had the pleasure of seeing Wash. in Philadelphia.

Although closely secreted in Norfolk, he had, through friends, some little communication with the outside world. Among other items of information which came to his ears, was a report that his master was being pressed by his creditors, and had all his slaves advertised for sale. An item still more sad also reached his ear, to the effect that his wife had been sold away to North Carolina, and thus separated from her child, two years old. The child was given as a present to a niece of the master. While this is only a meagre portion of his interesting story, it was considered at the time sufficient to identify him should the occasion ever require it. We content ourselves, therefore, simply with giving what was recorded on the book. Wash. spent a short while in Philadelphia in order to recruit, after which, he went on North, where colored men were free.

# JAMES GRIFFIN

ALIAS THOMAS BROWN

*SLAVE-HOLDER IN MARYLAND WITH THREE COLORED WIVES.*

James was a tiller of the soil under the yoke of Joshua Hitch, who lived on a farm about seventeen miles from Baltimore. James spoke rather favorably of him; indeed, it was through a direct act of kindness on the part of his master that he procured the opportunity to make good his escape. It appeared from his story, that his master's affairs had become particularly embarrassed, and the Sheriff was making frequent visits to his house. This sign was interpreted to mean that James, if not others, would have to be sold before long. The master was much puzzled to decide which way to turn. He owned but three other adult slaves besides James, and they were females. One of them was his chief housekeeper, and with them all his social relations were of such a nature as to lead James and others to think and say that they "were all his wives." Or to use James's own language, "he had three slave women; two were sisters, and he lived with them all as his wives; two of them he was very fond of," and desired to keep them from being sold if possible. The third, he concluded he could not save, she would have to be sold. In this dilemma, he was good enough to allow James a few days' holiday, for the purpose of finding him a good master. Expressing his satisfaction and gratification, James, armed with full authority from his master to select a choice specimen, started for Baltimore.

On reaching Baltimore, however, James carefully steered clear of all slave-holders, and shrewdly turned his attention to the matter of getting an Underground Rail Road ticket for Canada. After making as much inquiry as he felt was safe, he came to the conclusion to walk of nights for a long distance. He examined his feet and legs, found that they were in good order, and his faith and hope strong enough to remove a mountain. Besides several days still remained in which he was permitted to look for a new master, and these he decided could be profitably spent in making his way towards Canada. So off he started, at no doubt a very diligent pace, for at the end of the first night's journey, he had made much headway, but at the expense of his feet.

His faith was stronger than ever. So he rested next day in the woods, concealed, of course, and the next evening started with fresh courage and renewed perseverance. Finally, he reached Columbia, Pennsylvania, and there he had the happiness to learn, that the mountain which at first had tried his faith so severely, was removed, and friendly hands were reached out and a more speedy and comfortable mode of travel advised. He was directed to the Vigilance Committee in Philadelphia, from whom he received friendly aid, and all necessary information respecting Canada and how to get there.

James was thirty-one years of age, rather a fine-looking man, of a chestnut color, and quite intelligent. He had been a married man, but for two years before his escape, he had been a widower – that is, his wife had been sold away from him to North Carolina, and in that space of time he had received only three letters from her; he had given up all hope of ever seeing her again. He had two little boys living in Baltimore, whom he was obliged to leave. Their names were Edward and William. What became of them afterwards was never known at the Philadelphia station.

James's master was a man of about fifty years of age – who had never been lawfully married, yet had a number of children on his place who were of great concern to him in the midst of other pressing embarrassments. Of course, the Committee never learned how matters were settled after James left, but, in all probability, his wives, Nancy and Mary (sisters), and Lizzie, with all the children, had to be sold.

# OWEN AND OTHO TAYLOR'S FLIGHT WITH HORSES

*THREE BROTHERS, TWO OF THEM WITH WIVES AND CHILDREN.*

About the latter part of March, 1856, Owen Taylor and his wife, Mary Ann, and their little son, Edward, together with a brother and his wife and two children, and a third brother, Benjamin, arrived from near Clear Springs, nine miles from Hagerstown, Maryland. They all left their home, or rather escaped from the prison-house, on Easter Sunday, and came *via* Harrisburg, where they were assisted and directed to the Vigilance Committee in Philadelphia. A more interesting party had not reached the Committee for a long time.

The three brothers were intelligent, and heroic, and, in the resolve to obtain freedom, not only for themselves, but for their wives and children, desperately in earnest. They had counted well the cost of this struggle for liberty, and had fully made up their minds that if interfered with by slave-catchers, somebody would have to bite the dust. That they had pledged themselves never to surrender alive, was obvious. Their travel-worn appearance, their attachment for each other, the joy that the tokens of friendship afforded them, the description they gave of incidents on the road, made an impression not soon to be effaced.

In the presence of a group like this, Sumner's great and eloquent speech on the Barbarism of Slavery, seemed almost cold and dead, – the mute appeals of these little ones in their mother's arms – the unlettered language of these young mothers, striving to save their offspring from the doom of Slavery – the resolute and manly bearing of these brothers expressed in words full of love of liberty, and of the determination to resist Slavery to the death, in defence of their wives and children – this was Sumner's speech enacted before our eyes.

Owen was about thirty-one years of age, but had experienced a deal of trouble. He had been married twice, and both wives were believed to be living. The first one, with their little child, had been sold in the Baltimore market, about three years before, the mother was sent to Louisiana, the child to South Carolina. Father, mother, and child, parted with no hope of ever seeing each other again in this world. After Owen's wife was sent South, he sent her his likeness and a dress; the latter was received, and she was greatly delighted with it, but he never heard of her having received his likeness. He likewise wrote to her, but he was not sure that she received his letters. Finally, he came to the conclusion that as she was forever dead to him, he would do well to marry again. Accordingly he took to himself another partner, the one who now accompanied him on the Underground Rail Road.

Omitting other interesting incidents, a reference to his handiwork will suffice to show the ability of Owen. Owen was a born mechanic, and his master practically tested his skill in various ways; sometimes in the blacksmith shop – at other times as a wheelwright – again at making brushes and brooms, and at leisure times he would try his hand in all these crafts. This Jack-of-all-trades was, of course, very valuable to his master. Indeed his place was hard to fill.

Henry Fiery, a farmer, "about sixty-four years of age, a stout, crusty old fellow," was the owner of Owen and his two brothers. Besides slaves, the old man was in possession of a wife, whose name was Martha, and seven children, who were pretty well grown up. One of the sons owned Owen's wife and two children. Owen declared, that they had been worked hard, while few privileges had been allowed them. Clothing of the poorest texture was only sparingly furnished. Nothing like Sunday raiment was ever given them; for these comforts they were compelled to do over-work of nights. For a long time the idea of escape had been uppermost in the minds of this party. The first of January, past, was the time "solemnly" fixed upon to "took out," but for some reason or other (not found on the record book), their strategical minds did not see the way altogether clear, and they deferred starting until Easter Sunday.

On that memorable evening, the men boldly harnessed two of Mr. Fiery's steeds and placing their wives and children in the carriage, started off *via* Hagerstown, in a direct line for Chambersburg, Pennsylvania, at a rate that allowed no grass to grow under the horses' feet. In this manner they made good time, reached Chambersburg safely, and ventured up to a hotel where they put up their horses. Here they bade their faithful beasts good-bye and "took out" for Harrisburg by another mode of travel, the cars. On their arrival they naturally fell into the hands of the Committee, who hurried them off to Philadelphia, apprising the Committee there of their approach by a dispatch sent ahead. Probably they had scarcely reached Philadelphia ere the Fierys were in hot haste after them, as far as Harrisburg, if not farther.

It hardly need be hinted, that the community in which the Fierys lived was deeply agitated for days after, as indeed it was along the entire route to Chambersburg, in consequence of this bold and successful movement. The horses were easily captured at the hotel, where they were left, but, of course, they were mute as to what had become of their drivers. The furious Fierys probably got wind of the fact, that they had made their way to Harrisburg. At any rate they made very diligent search at this point. While here prosecuting his hunting operations, Fiery managed to open communication with at least one member of the Harrisburg Committee, to whom his grievances were made known, but derived little satisfaction.

After the experience of a few weeks, the pursuers came to the conclusion, that there was no likelihood of recovering them through these agencies, or through the Fugitive Slave Law. In their despair, therefore, they resorted to another "dodge." All at once they became "sort-o'-friendly" – indeed more than half disposed to emancipate. The member of the Committee in Harrisburg had, it is probable, frequently left room for their great delusion, if he did not even go so far as to feed their hopes with plausible suggestions, that some assistance might be afforded by which an amicable settlement might be made between masters and slaves.

The following extract, from the Committee's letter, relative to this matter, is open to this inference, and may serve to throw some light on the subject:

HARRISBURG,
*April 28, '56.*

Friend Still: – Your last came to hand in due season, and I am happy to hear of the safe arrival of those gents.

I have before me the Power of Attorney of Mr. John S.

Fiery, son of Mr. Henry Fiery, of Washington county, Md., the owner of those three men, two women and three children, who arrived in your town on the 24th or 25th of March. He graciously condescends to liberate the oldest in a year, and the remainder in proportional time, if they will come back; or to sell them their time for $1,300. He is sick of the job, and is ready to make any conditions. Now, if you personally can get word to them and get them to send him a letter, in my charge, informing him of their whereabouts and prospects, I think it will be the best answer I can make him. He will return here in a week or two, to know what can be done. He offers $500 to see them.

Or if you can send me word where they are, I will endeavor to write to them for his special satisfaction; or if you cannot do either, send me your latest information, for I intend to make him spend a few more dollars, and if possible get a little sicker of this bad job. Do try and send him a few bitter pills for his weak nerves and disturbed mind.

Yours in great haste,

Jos. C. Bustill.

A subsequent letter from Mr. Bustill contains, besides other interesting Underground Rail Road matter, an item relative to the feeling of disappointment experienced by Mr. Fiery on learning that his property was in Canada.

HARRISBURG,
*May 26, '56.*

Friend Still: – I embrace the opportunity presented by the visit of our friend, John F. Williams, to drop you a few lines in relation to our future operations.

The Lightning Train was put on the Road on last Monday, and as the traveling season has commenced and this is the Southern route for Niagara Falls, I have concluded not to send by way of Auburn, except in cases of great danger; but hereafter we will use the Lightning Train, which leaves here at 1-1/2 and arrives in your city at 5 o'clock in the morning, and I will telegraph about 5-1/2 o'clock in the afternoon, so it may reach you before you close. These four are the only ones that have come since my last. The woman has been here some time waiting for her child and her beau, which she expects here about the first of June. If possible, please keep a knowledge of her whereabouts, to enable me to inform him if he comes.

*I have nothing more to send you, except that John Fiery has visited us again and much to his chagrin received the information of their being in Canada.*

Yours as ever,

Jos. C. Bustill.

Whilst the Fierys were working like beavers to re-enslave these brave fugitives, the latter were daily drinking in more and more of the spirit of freedom and were busy with schemes for the deliverance of other near kin left behind under the galling yoke.

Several very interesting letters were received from Otho Taylor, relative to a raid he designed making expressly to effect the escape of his family. The two subjoined must suffice, (others, much longer, cannot now be produced, they have probably been loaned and not returned).

*APRIL 15th, 1857.*

SIR – We arrived here safely. Mr. Syrus and his lady is well situated. They have a place for the year round 15 dollars per month. We are all well and hope that you are all the same. Now I wish to know whether you would please to send me some money to go after those people. Send it here if you please.

Yours truly,

OTHO TAYLOR.

ST. CATHARINES,
*Jan. 26, 1857.*

MR. WM. STILL: – Dear Sir – I write at this time in behalf of Otho Taylor. He is very anxious to go and get his family at Clear Spring, Washington county, Md. He would like to know if the Society there would furnish him the means to go after them from Philadelphia, that you will be running no risk in doing this. If the Society can do this, he would not be absent from P. more than three days.

He is so anxious to get his family from slavery that he is willing to do almost anything to get them to Canada. You may possibly recollect him – he was at your place last August. I think he can be trusted. If you can do something for him, he has the means to take him to your place.

Please let me know immediately if you can do this.

Respectfully yours,

M.A.H. WILSON.

Such appeals came very frequently from Canada, causing much sadness, as but little encouragement could be held out to such projects. In the first place, the danger attendant upon such expeditions was so fearful, and in the second place, our funds were so inadequate for this kind of work, that, in most cases, such appeals had to be refused. Of course, there were those whose continual coming, like the poor widow in the Gospel, could not be denied.

# CAPTAIN F. ARRIVES WITH FOURTEEN "PRIME ARTICLES" ON BOARD

Thomas Garrett announced this in the following letter:

WILMINGTON, 3d mo.,
*23d, 1856.*

DEAR FRIEND, WILLIAM STILL: – Captain Fountain has arrived all safe, with the human cargo thee was inquiring for, a few days since. I had men waiting till 12 o'clock till the Captain arrived at his berth, ready to receive them; last night they then learned, that he had landed them at the Rocks, near the old Swedes church, in the care of our efficient Pilot, who is in the employ of my friend, John Hillis, and he has them now in charge. As soon as my breakfast is over, I will see Hillis and determine what is best to be done in their case. My own opinion is, we had better send them to Hook and there put them in the cars to-night and send a pilot to take them to thy house. As Marcus Hook is in Pennsylvania, the agent of the cars runs no risk of the fine of five hundred dollars our State imposes for assisting one of God's poor out of the State by steamboat or cars.

As ever thy friend,

THOS. GARRETT.

From the tenor of Thomas Garrett's letter, the Committee was prepared for a joyful reception, knowing that Captain F. was not in the habit of doing things by the halves – that he was not in the habit of bringing numbskulls; indeed he brought none but the bravest and most intelligent. Yet notwithstanding our knowledge of his practice in this respect, when he arrived we were surprised beyond measure. The women outnumbered the men. The two young mothers – with their interesting, hearty and fine-looking children representing in blood the two races about equally – presented a very impressive spectacle.

The men had the appearance of being active, smart, and well disposed, much above the generality of slaves; but, compared with those of the opposite sex, their claims for sympathy were very faint indeed. No one could possibly avoid the conclusion, that these mothers, with their handsome daughters, were valued on the Ledger of their owners at enormously high prices; that lustful traders and sensualists had already gloated over the thought of buying them in a few short years. Probably not one of those beautiful girls would have brought less than fifteen hundred or two thousand dollars at the age of fifteen. It was therefore a great satisfaction to think, that their mothers, who knew full well to what a fate such slave girls were destined, had labored so heroically to snatch them out of this danger ere the critical hour arrived.

Rebecca Jones was about twenty-eight years of age; mulatto, good-looking, considerably above medium size, very intelligent, and a true-born heroine.

The following reward, offered by the notorious negro-trader, Hall, proved that Rebecca and her children were not to be allowed to go free, if slave-hunters could be induced by a heavy pecuniary consideration to recapture them:

> $300 REWARD is offered for the apprehension of negro woman, REBECCA JONES and her three children, and man

ISAIAH, belonging to W.W. Davidson, who have disappeared since the 20th inst. The above reward will be paid for the apprehension and delivery of the said Negroes to my Jail, by the attorney in fact of the owner, or the sum of $250 for the man alone, or $150 for the woman and three children alone.

WM. W. HALL, for the Attorney,

*feb. 1.*

Years before her escape, her mistress died in England; and as Rebecca had always understood, long before this event, that all the slaves were to be freed at the death of her mistress, she was not prepared to believe any other report. It turned out, however, as in thousands of other instances, that no will could be found, and, of course, the administrators retained the slave property, regardless of any verbal expressions respecting freeing, etc. Rebecca closely watched the course of the administrators, and in the meanwhile firmly resolved, that neither she nor her children should ever serve another master. Rather than submit, she declared that she would take the lives of her children and then her own. Notwithstanding her bold and decided stand, the report went out that she was to be sold, and that all the slaves were still to be held in bondage. Rebecca's sympathizers and friends advised her, as they thought for the best, to get a friend or gentleman to purchase her for herself. To this she replied: "Not three cents would I give, nor do I want any of my friends to buy me, not if they could get me for three cents." It would be of no use, she contended, as she was fully bent on dying, rather than remain a slave. The slave-holders evidently understood her, and were in no hurry about bringing her case to an issue – they rather gave her time to become calm. But Rebecca was inflexible.

Six years before her arrival, her husband had escaped, in company with the noted fugitive, "Shadrach." For a time after he fled, she frequently received letters from him, but for a long while he had ceased to write, and of late she had heard nothing from him.

In escaping stowed away in the boat, she suffered terribly, but faithfully endured to the end, and was only too happy when the agony was over. After resting and getting thoroughly refreshed in Philadelphia, she, with others, was forwarded to Boston, for her heart was there. Several letters were received from her, respecting her prospects, etc., from which it appears that she had gained some knowledge of her husband, although not of a satisfactory nature. At any rate she decided that she could not receive him back again. The following letter has reference to her prospects, going to California, her husband, etc.:

PARKER HOUSE, School street, Boston,
*Oct. 18th, '56.*

MY DEAR SIR: – I can hardly express the pleasure I feel at the receipt of your kind letter; but allow me to thank you for the same.

And now I will tell you my reasons for going to California. Mrs. Tarrol, a cousin of my husband, has sent for me. She says I can do much better there than in Boston. And as I have my children's welfare to look to, I have concluded to go. Of course I shall be just as likely to hear from home *there* as *here*. Please tell Mr. Bagnale I shall expect one letter from him before I leave here.

I should like to hear from my brothers and sisters once more, and let me hear every particular. You never can know how anxious I am to hear from them; do please impress this upon their minds.

I have written two letters to Dr. Lundy and never received an answer. I heard Mrs. Lundy was dead, and thought that might possibly be the reason he had not replied to me. Please tell the Doctor I should take it as a great favor if he would write me a few lines.

I suppose you think I am going to live with my husband again. Let me assure you 'tis no such thing. My mind is as firm as ever. And believe me, in going away from Boston, I am going away from him, for I have heard he is living somewhere near. He has been making inquiries about me, but that can make no difference in my feelings to him. I hope that yourself, wife and family are all quite well. Please remember me to them all. Do me the favor to give my love to all inquiring friends. I should be most happy to have any letters of introduction you may think me worthy of, and I trust I shall ever remain

Yours faithfully,

REBECCA JONES.

P.S. – I do not know if I shall go this Fall, or in the Spring. It will depend upon the letter I receive from California, but whichever it may be, I shall be happy to hear from you very soon.

Isaiah, who was a fellow-servant with Rebecca, and was included in the reward offered by Hall for Rebecca, etc., was a young man about twenty-three years of age, a mulatto, intelligent and of prepossessing manners. A purely ardent thirst for liberty prompted him to flee; although he declared that he had been treated very badly, and had even suffered severely from being shamefully "beaten." He had, however, been permitted to hire his time by the year, for which one hundred and twenty dollars were regularly demanded by his owner. Young as he was, he was a married man, with a wife and two children, to whom he was devoted. He had besides two brothers and two sisters for whom he felt a warm degree of brotherly affection; yet when the hour arrived for him to accept a chance for freedom at the apparent sacrifice of these dearest ties of kindred, he was found heroic enough for this painful ordeal, and to give up all for freedom.

Caroline Taylor, and her two little children, were also from Norfolk, and came by boat. Upon the whole, they were not less interesting than Rebecca Jones and her three little girls. Although Caroline was not in her person half so stately, nor gave such promise of heroism as Rebecca – for Caroline was rather small of stature – yet she was more refined, and quite as intelligent as Rebecca, and represented considerably more of the Anglo-Saxon blood. She was a mulatto, and her children were almost fair enough to pass for white – probably they were quadroons, hardly any one would have suspected that they had only one quarter of colored blood in their veins. For ten years Caroline had been in the habit of hiring her time at the rate of seventy-five dollars per year, with the exception of the last year, when her hire was raised to eighty-four dollars. So anxious was she to have her older girl (eleven years old) at home with her, that she also hired her time by the year, for which she was compelled to pay twenty-four dollars. As her younger child was not sufficiently grown to hire out for pay, she was permitted to have it at home with her on the conditions that she would feed, clothe and take good care of it, permitting no expense whatever to fall upon the master.

Judging from the appearance and manners of the children, their mother had, doubtless, been most faithful to them, for more handsome, well-behaved, intelligent and pleasing children could not easily be selected from either race or any station of life. The younger, Mary by name, nine years of age, attracted very great attention, by the deep interest she manifested in a poor fugitive (whom she had never seen before), at the Philadelphia station, confined to the bed and suffering excruciating pain from wounds he had received whilst escaping. Hours and hours together, during the two or three days of their sojourn, she spent of her own accord, by his bed-side, manifesting almost womanly sympathy in the most devoted and tender manner. She thus, doubtless, unconsciously imparted to the sufferer a great deal of comfort. Very many affecting incidents had come under the observation of the acting Committee, under various circumstances, but never before had they witnessed a sight more interesting, a scene more touching.

Caroline and her children were owned by Peter March, Esq., late of Norfolk, but at that time, he was living in New York, and was carrying on the iron business. He came into possession of them through his wife, who was the daughter of Caroline's former master, and almost the only heir left, in consequence of the terrible fever of the previous summer. Caroline was living under the daily fear of being sold; this, together with the task of supporting herself and two children, made her burden very grievous. Not a great while before her escape, her New York master had been on to Norfolk, expressly with a view of selling her, and asked two thousand dollars for her. This, however, he failed to get, and was still awaiting an offer.

These ill omens aroused Caroline to think more seriously over the condition of herself and children than she had ever done before, and in this state of mind she came to the conclusion, that she would strive to save herself and children by flight on the Underground Rail Road. She knew full well, that it was no faint-hearted struggle that was required of her, so she had nerved herself with the old martyr spirit to risk her all on her faith in God and Freedom, and was ready to take the consequences if she fell back into the hands of the enemy. This noble decision was the crowning act in the undertakings of thousands similarly situated. Through this faith she gained the liberty of herself and her children. Quite a number of the friends of the slave saw these interesting fugitives, and wept, and rejoiced with them.

Col. A. Cammings, in those days Publisher of the *Evening Bulletin*, for the first time, witnessed an Underground Rail Road arrival. Some time previous, in conversation with Mr. J.M. McKim, the Colonel had expressed views not altogether favorable to the Underground Rail Road; indeed he was rather inclined to apologize for slavery, if not to defend the Fugitive

Slave Law. While endeavoring somewhat tenaciously to maintain his ground, Mr. McKim opposed to him not only the now well established Anti-Slavery doctrines, but also offered as testimony Underground Rail Road facts – the results of personal knowledge from daily proofs of the heroic struggles, marvellous faith, and intense earnestness of the fugitives.

In all probability the Colonel did not feel prepared to deny wholly Mr. McKim's statement, yet, he desired to see "some" for himself. "Well," said Mr. McK., "you shall see some." So when this arrival came to hand, true to his promise, Mr. McK. called on the Colonel and invited him to accompany him to the Underground Rail Road station. He assured the Colonel that he did not want any money from him, but simply wanted to convince him of his error in the recent argument that they had held on the subject. Accordingly the Colonel accompanied him, and found that twenty-two passengers had been on hand within the past twenty-four hours, and at least sixteen or seventeen were then in his presence. It is needless to say, that such a sight admitted of no contradiction – no argument – no doubt. The facts were too self-evident. The Colonel could say but little, so complete was his amazement; but he voluntarily attested the thoroughness of his conversion by pulling out of his pocket and handing to Mr. McK. a twenty dollar gold piece to aid the passengers on to freedom.

In these hours of rest and joyful anticipation the necessities of both large and small were administered to according to their needs, before forwarding them still further. The time and attention required for so many left but little opportunity, however, for the Secretary to write their narratives. He had only evening leisure for the work. Ten or twelve of that party had to be sent off without having their stories recorded. Daniel Robertson was one of this number; his name is simply entered on the roll, and, but for letters received from him, after he passed on North, no further knowledge would have been obtained. In Petersburg, whence he escaped, he left his wife, for whose deliverance he felt bound to do everything that lay in his power, as the subjoined letters will attest:

HAVANA, Schuylkill Co., N.Y.
*August 11, 1856.*

MR. WM. STILL – Dear Sir: – I came from Virginia in March, and was at your office the last of March. My object in writing you, is to inquire what I can do, or what can be done to help my wife to escape from the same bondage that I was in. You will know by your books that I was from Petersburg, Va., and that is where my wife now is. I have received two or three letters from a lady in that place, and the last one says, that my wife's mistress is dead, and that she expects to be sold. I am very anxious to do what I can for her before it is too late, and beg of you to devise some means to get her away. Capt. the man that brought me away, knows the colored agent at Petersburg, and knows he will do all he can to forward my wife. The Capt. promised, that when I could raise one hundred dollars for him that he would deliver her in Philadelphia. Tell him that I can now raise the money, and will forward it to you at any day that he thinks that he can bring her. Please see the Captain and find when he will undertake it, and then let me know when to forward the money to you. I am at work for the Hon. Charles Cook, and can send the money any day. My wife's name is Harriet Robertson, and the agent at Petersburg knows her.

Please direct your answer, with all necessary directions, to N. Coryell, of this village, and he will see that all is right.

Very respectfully,

DANIEL ROBERTSON.

HAVANA,
*Aug. 18, 1856.*

MR. WM. STILL – Dear Sir: – Yours of the 18th, for D. Robertson, was duly received. In behalf of Daniel, I thank you kindly for the interest you manifest in him. The letters that have gone from him to his friends in Virginia, have been written by me, and sent in such a manner as we thought would best ensure safety. Yet I am well aware of the risk of writing, and have restrained him as far as possible, and the last one I wrote was to be the last, till an effort was made to reclaim his wife. Daniel is a faithful, likely man, and is well liked by all who know him. He is industrious and prudent, and is bending his whole energies toward the reclaiming his wife. He can forward to you the one hundred dollars at any day that it may be wanted, and if you can do anything to forward his interests it will be very gratefully received as an additional favor on your part. He asks for no money, but your kindly efforts, which he regards more highly than money.

Very respectfully, N. CORYELL.

The letters that have been written for him were dated "Niagara Falls, Canada West," and his friends think he is there – none of them know to the contrary – it is important that they never do know. N.C.

HAVANA,
*Sept. 29, 1856.*

MR. WM. STILL – Dear Sir: – I enclose herewith a draft on New York, payable to your order, for $100, to be paid on the delivery at Philadelphia of Daniel Robertson's wife.

You can readily see that it has been necessary for Daniel to work almost night and day to have laid up so large an amount of money, since the first of April, as this one hundred dollars. Daniel is industrious and prudent, and saves all of his earnings, above his most absolute wants. If the Captain is not successful in getting Daniel's wife, you, of course, will return the draft, without charge, as you said. I hope success will attend him, for Daniel deserves to be rewarded, if ever man did. Yours, &c.

N. CORYELL.

HAVANA,
*Jan. 2, 1857.*

DEAR SIR: – Your favor containing draft on N. York, for Daniel Robertson, came to hand on the 31st ult. Daniel begs to tender his acknowledgments for your kind interest manifested in his behalf, and says he hopes you will leave no measure untried which has any appearance of success, and that the money shall be forthcoming at a moment's notice. Daniel thinks that since Christmas, the chances for his wife's deliverance are fewer than before, for at that time he fears she was disposed of and possibly went South.

The paper sent me, with your well-written article, was received, and on reading it to Daniel, he knew some of the parties mentioned in it – he was much pleased to hear it read. Daniel spent New Year's in Elmira, about 18 miles from this place, and there he met two whom he was well acquainted with.

Yours, &c.,

N. CORYELL.

WM. STILL, Esq., Phila.

Such devotion to freedom, such untiring labor, such appeals as these letters contained awakened deep interest in the breasts of Daniel's new friends, which spoke volumes in favor of the Slave and against slave-holders. But, alas, nothing could be done to relieve the sorrowing mind of poor Daniel for the deliverance of his wife in chains. The Committee sympathized deeply with him, but could do no more. What other events followed, in Daniel's life as a fugitive, were never made known to the Committee.

Tom Page. At the time of his arrival, his name only was enrolled on the book. Yet he was not a passenger soon to be forgotten – he was but a mere boy, probably eighteen years of age; but a more apt, ready-witted, active, intelligent and self-reliant fellow is not often seen.

Judging from his smartness, under slavery, with no chances, it was easy to imagine how creditably he might with a white boy's chances have climbed the hill of art and science. Obviously he had intellect enough, if properly cultivated, to fill any station within the ordinary reach of intelligent American citizens. He could read and write remarkably well for a slave, and well did he understand his advantages in this particular; indeed if slave-holders had only been aware of the growing tendency of Tom's mind, they would have rejoiced at hearing of his departure for Canada; he was a most dangerous piece of property to be growing up amongst slaves.

After leaving the Committee and going North his uncaged mind felt the need of more education, and at the same time he was eager to make money, and do something in life. As he had no one to depend on, parents and relatives being left behind in Norfolk, he felt that he must rely upon himself, young as he was. He first took up his abode in Boston, or New Bedford, where most of the party with whom he escaped went, and where he had an aunt, and perhaps some other distant kin. There he worked and was a live young man indeed – among the foremost in ideas and notions about freedom, etc., as many letters from him bore evidence. After spending a year or more in Massachusetts, he had a desire to see how the fugitives were doing in Upper and Lower Canada, and if any better chances existed in these parts for men of his stamp.

Some of his letters, from different places, gave proof of real thought and close observation, but they were not generally saved, probably were loaned to be read by friendly eyes. Nevertheless the two subjoined will, in a measure, suffice to give some idea of his intelligence, etc.

BOSTON, Mass.,
*Feb. 25th, 1857.*

WILLIAM STILL, Esq.: – Dear Sir – I have not heard from you for some time. I take this opportunity of writing you a few lines to let you and all know that I am well at present and thank God for it. Dear Sir, I hear that the under ground railroad was in operation. I am glad to hear that. Give my best respects to your family and also to Dr. L., Mr. Warrick, Mr. Camp and familys, to Mr. Fisher, Mr. Taylor to all Friends names too numerous to mention. Please to let me know when the road arrived with another cargo. I want to come to see you all before long, if nothing happens and life lasts. Mrs. Gault requested me to learn of you if you ask Mr. Bagnal if he will see father and what he says about the children. Please to answer as soon as possible. No more at present from a friend,

THOMAS F. PAGE.

NIAGARA FALLS, N.Y.,
*Oct. 6th, '58.*

DEAR SIR: – I received your kind letter and I was very glad to hear from you and your family. This leaves me well, and I hope when this comes to hand it may find you the same. I have seen a large number of your U.G.R.R. friends in my travels through the Eastern as well as the Western States. Well there are a good many from my own city who I know – some I talk to on private matters and some I wont. Well around here there are so many – Tom, Dick, and Harry – that you do not know who your friend is. So it don't hurt any one to be careful. Well, somehow or another, I do not like Canada, or the Provinces. I have been to St. John, N.B., Lower Province, or Lower Canada, also St. Catharines, C.W., and all around the Canada side, and I do not like it at all. The people seem to be so queer – though I suppose if I had of went to Canada when I first came North to live, I might like it by this time. I was home when Aunt had her Ambrotype taken for you. She often speaks of your kindness to her. There are a number of your friends wishes you well. My little brother is going to school in Boston. The lady, Mrs. Hillard, that my Aunt lives with, thinks a good deal of him. He is very smart and I think, if he lives, he may be of some account. Do you ever see my old friend, Capt. Fountain? Please to give my love to him, and tell him to come to Boston, as there are a number of his friends that would like to see him. My best respects to all friends. I must now bring my short epistle to a close, by saying I remain your friend truly,

THOMAS F. PAGE.

While a portion of the party, on hand with him, came as passengers with Capt. P., another portion was brought by Capt.

B., both parties arriving within twelve hours of each other; and both had likewise been frozen up on the route for weeks with their respective live freight on board.

The sufferings for food, which they were called upon to endure, were beyond description. They happened to have plenty of salt fat pork, and perhaps beans, Indian meal and some potatoes for standing dishes; the more delicate necessaries did not probably last longer than the first or second week of their ice-bondage.

Without a doubt, one of these Captains left Norfolk about the twentieth of January, but did not reach Philadelphia till about the twentieth of March, having been frozen up, of course, during the greater part of that time. Men, women and children were alike sharers in the common struggle for freedom – were alike hungered, in prison, naked, and sick, but it was a fearful thing in those days for even women and children to whisper their sad lamentations in the city of Philadelphia, except to those friendly to the Underground Rail Road.

Doubtless, if these mothers, with their children and partners in tribulation, could have been seen as they arrived direct from the boats, many hearts would have melted, and many tears would have found their way down many cheeks. But at that time cotton was acknowledged to be King – the Fugitive Slave Law was supreme, and the notorious decision of Judge Taney, that "black men had no rights which white men were bound to respect," echoed the prejudices of the masses too clearly to have made it safe to reveal the fact of their arrival, or even the heart-rending condition of these Fugitives.

Nevertheless, they were not turned away empty, though at

a peril they were fed, aided, and comforted, and sent away well clothed. Indeed, so bountifully were the women and children supplied, that as they were being conveyed to the Camden and Amboy station, they looked more like a pleasuring party than like fugitives. Some of the good friends of the slave sent clothing, and likewise cheered them with their presence.

# WILLIAM AND ELLEN CRAFT

*FEMALE SLAVE IN MALE ATTIRE, FLEEING AS A PLANTER, WITH HER HUSBAND AS HER BODY SERVANT.*

A quarter of a century ago, William and Ellen Craft were slaves in the State of Georgia. With them, as with thousands of others, the desire to be free was very strong. For this jewel they were willing to make any sacrifice, or to endure any amount of suffering. In this state of mind they commenced planning. After thinking of various ways that might be tried, it occurred to William and Ellen, that one might act the part of master and the other the part of servant.

Ellen being fair enough to pass for white, of necessity would have to be transformed into a young planter for the time being. All that was needed, however, to make this important change was that she should be dressed elegantly in a fashionable suit of male attire, and have her hair cut in the style usually worn by young planters. Her profusion of dark hair offered a fine opportunity for the change. So far this plan looked very tempting. But it occurred to them that Ellen was beardless. After some mature reflection, they came to the conclusion that this difficulty could be very readily obviated by having the face muffled up as though the young planter was suffering badly with the face or toothache; thus they got rid of this trouble. Straightway, upon further reflection, several other very serious difficulties stared them in the face. For instance, in traveling, they knew that they would be under the necessity of stopping repeatedly at hotels, and that the custom of registering would have to be conformed to, unless some very good excuse could be given for not doing so.

Here they again thought much over matters, and wisely concluded that the young man had better assume the attitude of a gentleman very much indisposed. He must have his right arm placed carefully in a sling; that would be a sufficient excuse for not registering, etc. Then he must be a little lame, with a nice cane in the left hand; he must have large green spectacles over his eyes, and withal he must be very hard of hearing and dependent on his faithful servant (as was no uncommon thing with slave-holders), to look after all his wants.

William was just the man to act this part. To begin with, he was very "likely-looking;" smart, active and exceedingly attentive to his young master – indeed he was almost eyes, ears, hands and feet for him. William knew that this would please the slave-holders. The young planter would have nothing to do but hold himself subject to his ailments and put on a bold air of superiority; he was not to deign to notice anybody. If, while traveling, gentlemen, either politely or rudely, should venture to scrape acquaintance with the young planter, in his deafness he was to remain mute; the servant was to explain. In every instance when this occurred, as it actually did, the servant was fully equal to the emergency – none dreaming of the disguises in which the Underground Rail Road passengers were traveling.

They stopped at a first-class hotel in Charleston, where the young planter and his body servant were treated, as the house was wont to treat the chivalry. They stopped also at a similar hotel in Richmond, and with like results.

They knew that they must pass through Baltimore, but they did not know the obstacles that they would have to surmount in the Monumental City. They proceeded to the depot in the usual manner, and the servant asked for tickets for his master and self. Of course the master could have a ticket, but "bonds will have to be entered before you can get a ticket," said the ticket master. "It is the rule of this office to require bonds for all negroes applying for tickets to go North, and none but gentlemen of well-known responsibility will be taken," further explained the ticket master.

The servant replied, that he knew "nothing about that" – that he was "simply traveling with his young master to take care of him – he being in a very delicate state of health, so much so, that fears were entertained that he might not be able to hold out to reach Philadelphia, where he was hastening for medical treatment," and ended his reply by saying, "my master can't be detained." Without further parley, the ticket master very obligingly waived the old "rule," and furnished the requisite tickets. The mountain being thus removed, the young planter and his faithful servant were safely in the cars for the city of Brotherly Love.

Scarcely had they arrived on free soil when the rheumatism departed – the right arm was unslung – the toothache was gone – the beardless face was unmuffled – the deaf heard and spoke – the blind saw – and the lame leaped as an hart, and in the presence of a few astonished friends of the slave, the facts of this unparalleled Underground Rail Road feat were fully established by the most unquestionable evidence.

The constant strain and pressure on Ellen's nerves, however, had tried her severely, so much so, that for days afterwards, she was physically very much prostrated, although joy and gladness beamed from her eyes, which bespoke inexpressible delight within.

Never can the writer forget the impression made by their arrival. Even now, after a lapse of nearly a quarter of a century, it is easy to picture them in a private room, surrounded by a few friends – Ellen in her fine suit of black, with her cloak and high-heeled boots, looking, in every respect, like a young gentleman; in an hour after having dropped her male attire, and assumed the habiliments of her sex, the feminine only was visible in every line and feature of her structure.

Her husband, William, was thoroughly colored, but was a man of marked natural abilities, of good manners, and full of pluck, and possessed of perceptive faculties very large.

It was necessary, however, in those days, that they should seek a permanent residence, where their freedom would be more secure than in Philadelphia; therefore they were advised to go to headquarters, directly to Boston. There they would be safe, it was supposed, as it had then been about a generation since a fugitive had been taken back from the old Bay State, and through the incessant labors of William Lloyd Garrison, the great pioneer, and his faithful coadjutors, it was conceded that another fugitive slave case could never be tolerated on the free soil of Massachusetts. So to Boston they went.

On arriving, the warm hearts of abolitionists welcomed them heartily, and greeted and cheered them without let or hindrance. They did not pretend to keep their coming a secret, or hide it under a bushel; the story of their escape was heralded broadcast over the country – North and South, and indeed over the civilized world. For two years or more, not the slightest fear was entertained that they were not just as safe in Boston as if they had gone to Canada. But the day the Fugitive Bill passed, even the bravest abolitionist began to fear that a fugitive slave was no longer safe anywhere under the stars and stripes, North or South, and that William and Ellen Craft were liable to be captured at any moment by Georgia slave hunters. Many abolitionists counselled resistance to the death at all hazards. Instead of running to Canada, fugitives generally armed themselves and thus said, "Give me liberty or give me death."

William and Ellen Craft believed that it was their duty, as citizens of Massachusetts, to observe a more legal and civilized mode of conforming to the marriage rite than had been permitted them in slavery, and as Theodore Parker had shown himself a very warm friend of their's, they agreed to have their wedding over again according to the laws of a free State. After performing the ceremony, the renowned and fearless advocate of equal rights (Theodore Parker) presented William with a revolver and a dirk-knife, counselling him to use them manfully in defence of his wife and himself, if ever an attempt should be made by his owners or anybody else to re-enslave them.

But, notwithstanding all the published declarations made by abolitionists and fugitives, to the effect, that slave-holders and slave-catchers in visiting Massachusetts in pursuit of their runaway property, would be met by just such weapons as Theodore Parker presented William with, to the surprise of all Boston, the owners of William and Ellen actually had the effrontery to attempt their recapture under the Fugitive Slave Law. How it was done, and the results, taken from the *Old Liberator* (William Lloyd Garrison's organ), we copy as follows:

From the *Liberator*,
*Nov. 1, 1850.*

SLAVE-HUNTERS IN BOSTON.

Our city, for a week past, has been thrown into a state of intense excitement by the appearance of two prowling villains, named Hughes and Knight, from Macon, Georgia, for the purpose of seizing William and Ellen Craft, under the infernal Fugitive Slave Bill, and carrying them back to the hell of Slavery. Since the day of '76, there has not been such a popular demonstration on the side of human freedom in this region. The humane and patriotic contagion has infected all classes. Scarcely any other subject has been talked about in the streets, or in the social circle. On Thursday, of last week, warrants for the arrest of William and Ellen were issued by Judge Levi Woodbury, but no officer has yet been found ready or bold enough to serve them. In the meantime, the Vigilance Committee, appointed at the Faneuil Hall meeting, has not been idle. Their number has been increased to upwards of a hundred "good men and true," including some thirty or forty members of the bar; and they have been in constant session, devising every legal method to baffle the pursuing bloodhounds, and relieve the city of their hateful presence. On Saturday placards were posted up in all directions, announcing the arrival of these slave-hunters, and describing their persons. On the same day, Hughes and Knight were arrested on the charge of slander against William Craft. The Chronotype says, the damages being laid at $10,000; bail was demanded in the same sum, and was promptly furnished. By whom? is the question. An immense crowd was assembled in front of the Sheriff's office, while the bail matter was being arranged. The reporters were not admitted. It was only known that Watson Freeman, Esq., who once declared his readiness to hang any number of negroes remarkably cheap, came in, saying that the arrest was a shame, all a humbug, the trick of the damned abolitionists, and proclaimed his readiness to stand bail. John H. Pearson was also sent for, and came – the same John H. Pearson, merchant and Southern packet agent, who immortalized himself by sending back, on the 10th of September, 1846, in the bark *Niagara*, a poor fugitive slave, who came secreted in the brig *Ottoman*, from New Orleans – being himself judge, jury and executioner, to consign a fellow-being to a life of bondage – in obedience to the law of a slave State, and in violation of the law of his own. This same John H. Pearson, not contented with his previous infamy, was on hand. There is a story that the slave-hunters have been his table-guests also, and whether he bailed them or not, we don't know. What we know is, that soon after Pearson came out from the back room, where he and Knight and the Sheriff had been closeted, the Sheriff said that Knight was bailed – he would not say by whom. Knight being looked after, was not to be found. He had slipped out through a back door, and thus cheated the crowd of the pleasure of greeting him – possibly with that rough and ready affection which Barclay's brewers bestowed upon Haynau. The escape was very fortunate every way. Hughes and Knight have since been twice arrested and put under bonds of $10,000 (making $30,000 in all), charged with a conspiracy to kidnap and abduct William Craft, a peaceable citizen of Massachusetts, etc. Bail was entered by Hamilton Willis, of Willis & Co., 25 State street, and Patrick Riley, U.S. Deputy Marshal.

The following (says the Chronotype), is a *verbatim et literatim* copy of the letter sent by Knight to Craft, to entice him to the U.S. Hotel, in order to kidnap him. It shows, that the school-master owes Knight more "service and labor" than it is possible for Craft to:

BOSTON,
*Oct. 22, 1850, 11 Oclk P.M.*

Wm. Craft – Sir – I have to leave so Eirley in the moring that I cold not call according to promis, so if you want me to carry a letter home with me, you must bring it to the United States Hotel to morrow and leave it in box 44, or come your self to morro eavening after tea and bring it. let me no if you come your self by sending a note to box 44 U.S. Hotel so that I may know whether to wate after tea or not by the Bearer. If your wife wants to see me you cold bring her with you if you come your self.

JOHN KNIGHT.

P.S. I shall leave for home eirley a Thursday moring. J.K.

# Index

# TWELVE YEARS A SLAVE

SOLOMON NORTHUP

**Disclaimer**

Throughout the text, readers may find language and sentiments that appear both offensive and unacceptable. These words were duly reported by the former slave who wrote this book, and was forced to endure such dehumanizing attitudes on a daily basis. To better serve the author's original intentions and to ensure that the full impact of the writing is retained, we have decided to keep the original language in its entirety, though many segments may prove uncomfortable for the modern reader.

This edition published in 2020 by Arcturus Publishing Limited
26/27 Bickels Yard, 151–153 Bermondsey Street,
London SE1 3HA



Cover design: Peter Ridley
Cover illustration: Peter Gray

AD007616US

Printed in the UK

FSC
www.fsc.org
MIX
Paper from responsible sources
FSC® C018072

TO

HARRIET BEECHER STOWE.

WHOSE NAME,

THROUGHOUT THE WORLD, IS IDENTIFIED WITH THE GREAT REFORM:

THIS NARRATIVE, AFFORDING ANOTHER

Key to Uncle Tom's Cabin,

IS RESPECTFULLY DEDICATED

"Such dupes are men to custom, and so prone
To reverence what is ancient, and can plead
A course of long observance for its use,
That even servitude, the worst of ills,
Because delivered down from sire to son,
Is kept and guarded as a sacred thing.
But is it fit, or can it bear the shock
Of rational discussion, that a man
Compounded and made up, like other men,
Of elements tumultuous, in whom lust
And folly in as ample measure meet,
As in the bosom of the slave he rules,
Should be a despot absolute, and boast
Himself the only freeman of his land?"

COWPER.

# *Contents*

# *Introduction*

Solomon Northup was born free in Minerva, New York, in 1808. His father was a freed slave and his mother a free African-American woman. As a young man he worked as a raftsman, while developing a reputation as an accomplished fiddle player. In 1841, during a trip to Washington D.C., he was suddenly kidnapped and sold into slavery. While slavery had been outlawed in his home state of New York, it was permitted in Washington, which was at the time home to one of the most extensive slave markets in antebellum America. During the sea journey to his new master in New Orleans, he persuaded one of the sailors, John Manning, to deliver a letter to his childhood friend Henry B. Northup, describing the events. While Henry, a lawyer, was willing to help, there was little he could do without knowing Solomon's location.

Northup spent many years as a slave, during which time he was forced to endure severe beatings, much inhumane treatment, and ongoing skepticism about his claims that a black man could be free. Eventually, he made contact with a Canadian abolitionist, Samuel Bass, who visited the plantation. Bass wrote letters to Northup's family and friends, informing them of his whereabouts and the conditions he was living under. The case was soon taken up by the governor of New York, Washington Hunt. Four months after meeting Bass, Northup finally regained his freedom.

With the help of a New York lawyer, David Wilson, he published his account of his life in bondage as *Twelve Years a Slave* in 1853. It proved an immediate success and catalyzed the growing abolitionist movement. More than 30,000 copies were sold, making it one of the most widely read slave narratives of the era.

After the publication of the book, Northup brought charges of kidnapping against his tormentors. The trial was a lengthy one but ultimately the defendant was acquitted and left unpunished for his deeds. Northup spent the next few years giving lectures for the abolitionist cause. He died in 1863, but the details of his death were never recorded, leaving some to believe that he had been kidnapped again.

# *Editor's Preface*

When the editor commenced the preparation of the following narrative, he did not suppose it would reach the size of this volume. In order, however, to present all the facts which have been communicated to him, it has seemed necessary to extend it to its present length.

Many of the statements contained in the following pages are corroborated by abundant evidence—others rest entirely upon Solomon's assertion. That he has adhered strictly to the truth, the editor, at least, who has had an opportunity of detecting any contradiction or discrepancy in his statements, is well satisfied. He has invariably repeated the same story without deviating in the slightest particular, and has also carefully perused the manuscript, dictating an alteration wherever the most trivial inaccuracy has appeared.

It was Solomon's fortune, during his captivity, to be owned by several masters. The treatment he received while at the "Pine Woods" shows that among slaveholders there are men of humanity as well as of cruelty. Some of them are spoken of with emotions of gratitude—others in a spirit of bitterness. It is believed that the following account of his experience on Bayou Bœuf presents a correct picture of Slavery, in all its lights and shadows, as it now exists in that locality. Unbiased, as he conceives, by any prepossessions or prejudices, the only object of the editor has been to give a faithful history of Solomon Northup's life, as he received it from his lips.

In the accomplishment of that object, he trusts he has succeeded, notwithstanding the numerous faults of style and of expression it may be found to contain.

DAVID WILSON.

WHITEHALL, N. Y., May, 1853.

# CHAPTER I

*Introductory—Ancestry—The Northup Family—Birth And Parentage—Mintus Northup—Marriage With Anne Hampton—Good Resolutions—Champlain Canal—Rafting Excursion To Canada—Farming—The Violin—Cooking—Removal To Saratoga—Parker And Perry—Slaves And Slavery—The Children—The Beginning Of Sorrow.*

Having been born a freeman, and for more than thirty years enjoyed the blessings of liberty in a free State—and having at the end of that time been kidnapped and sold into Slavery, where I remained, until happily rescued in the month of January, 1853, after a bondage of twelve years—it has been suggested that an account of my life and fortunes would not be uninteresting to the public.

Since my return to liberty, I have not failed to perceive the increasing interest throughout the Northern States, in regard to the subject of Slavery. Works of fiction, professing to portray its features in their more pleasing as well as more repugnant aspects, have been circulated to an extent unprecedented, and, as I understand, have created a fruitful topic of comment and discussion.

I can speak of Slavery only so far as it came under my own observation—only so far as I have known and experienced it in my own person. My object is, to give a candid and truthful statement of facts: to repeat the story of my life, without exaggeration, leaving it for others to determine, whether even the pages of fiction present a picture of more cruel wrong or a severer bondage.

As far back as I have been able to ascertain, my ancestors on the paternal side were slaves in Rhode Island. They belonged to a family by the name of Northup, one of whom, removing to the State of New-York, settled at Hoosic, in Rensselaer county. He brought with him Mintus Northup, my father. On the death of this gentleman, which must have occurred some fifty years ago, my father became free, having been emancipated by a direction in his will.

Henry B. Northup, Esq., of Sandy Hill, a distinguished counselor at law, and the man to whom, under Providence, I am indebted for my present liberty, and my return to the society of my wife and children, is a relative of the family in which my forefathers were thus held to service, and from which they took the name I bear. To this fact may be attributed the persevering interest he has taken in my behalf.

Sometime after my father's liberation, he removed to the town of Minerva, Essex county, N. Y., where I was born, in the month of July, 1808. How long he remained in the latter place I have not the means of definitely ascertaining. From thence he removed to Granville, Washington county, near a place known as Slyborough, where, for some years, he labored on the farm of Clark Northup, also a relative of his old master; from thence he removed to the Alden farm, at Moss Street, a short distance north of the village of Sandy Hill; and from thence to the farm now owned by Russel Pratt, situated on the road leading from Fort Edward to Argyle, where he continued to reside until his death, which took place on the 22d day of November, 1829. He left a widow and two children—myself, and Joseph, an elder brother. The latter is still living in the county of Oswego, near the city of that name; my mother died during the period of my captivity.

Though born a slave, and laboring under the disadvantages to which my unfortunate race is subjected, my father was a man respected for his industry and integrity, as many now living, who well remember him, are ready to testify. His whole life was passed in the peaceful pursuits of agriculture, never seeking employment in those more menial positions, which seem to be especially allotted to the children of Africa. Besides giving us an education surpassing that ordinarily bestowed upon children in our condition, he acquired, by his diligence and economy, a sufficient property qualification to entitle him to the right of suffrage. He was accustomed to speak to us of his early life; and although at all times cherishing the warmest emotions of kindness, and even of affection towards the family, in whose house he had been a bondsman, he nevertheless comprehended the system of Slavery, and dwelt with sorrow on the degradation of his race. He endeavored to imbue our minds with sentiments of morality, and to teach us to place our trust and confidence in Him who regards the humblest as well as the highest of his creatures. How often since that time has the recollection of his paternal counsels occurred to me, while lying in a slave hut in the distant and sickly regions of Louisiana, smarting with the undeserved wounds which an inhuman master had inflicted, and longing only for the grave which had covered him, to shield me also from the lash of the oppressor. In the church-yard at Sandy Hill, an humble stone marks the spot where he reposes, after having worthily performed the duties appertaining to the lowly sphere wherein God had appointed him to walk.

Up to this period I had been principally engaged with my father in the labors of the farm. The leisure hours allowed me were generally either employed over my books, or playing on the violin—an amusement which was the ruling passion of my youth. It has also been the source of consolation since, affording pleasure to the simple beings with whom my lot was cast, and beguiling my own thoughts, for many hours, from the painful contemplation of my fate.

On Christmas day, 1829, I was married to Anne Hampton, a colored girl then living in the vicinity of our residence. The ceremony was performed at Fort Edward, by Timothy Eddy, Esq., a magistrate of that town, and still a prominent citizen of the place. She had resided a long time at Sandy Hill, with Mr. Baird, proprietor of the Eagle Tavern, and also in the family of Rev. Alexander Proudfit, of Salem. This gentleman for many years had presided over the Presbyterian society at the latter place, and was widely distinguished for his learning and piety. Anne still holds in grateful remembrance the exceeding kindness and the excellent counsels of that good man. She is not able to determine the exact line of her descent, but the blood of three races mingles in her veins. It is difficult to tell whether the red, white, or black predominates.

The union of them all, however, in her origin, has given her a singular but pleasing expression, such as is rarely to be seen. Though somewhat resembling, yet she cannot properly be styled a quadroon, a class to which, I have omitted to mention, my mother belonged.

I had just now passed the period of my minority, having reached the age of twenty-one years in the month of July previous. Deprived of the advice and assistance of my father, with a wife dependent upon me for support, I resolved to enter upon a life of industry; and notwithstanding the obstacle of color, and the consciousness of my lowly state, indulged in pleasant dreams of a good time coming, when the possession of some humble habitation, with a few surrounding acres, should reward my labors, and bring me the means of happiness and comfort.

From the time of my marriage to this day the love I have borne my wife has been sincere and unabated; and only those who have felt the glowing tenderness a father cherishes for his offspring, can appreciate my affection for the beloved children which have since been born to us. This much I deem appropriate and necessary to say, in order that those who read these pages, may comprehend the poignancy of those sufferings I have been doomed to bear.

Immediately upon our marriage we commenced house-keeping, in the old yellow building then standing at the southern extremity of Fort Edward village, and which has since been transformed into a modern mansion, and lately occupied by Captain Lathrop. It is known as the Fort House. In this building the courts were sometime held after the organization of the county. It was also occupied by Burgoyne in 1777, being situated near the old Fort on the left bank of the Hudson.

During the winter I was employed with others repairing the Champlain Canal, on that section over which William Van

Nortwick was superintendent. David McEachron had the immediate charge of the men in whose company I labored. By the time the canal opened in the spring, I was enabled, from the savings of my wages, to purchase a pair of horses, and other things necessarily required in the business of navigation.

Having hired several efficient hands to assist me, I entered into contracts for the transportation of large rafts of timber from Lake Champlain to Troy. Dyer Beckwith and a Mr. Bartemy, of Whitehall, accompanied me on several trips. During the season I became perfectly familiar with the art and mysteries of rafting—a knowledge which afterwards enabled me to render profitable service to a worthy master, and to astonish the simple-witted lumbermen on the banks of the Bayou Bœuf.

In one of my voyages down Lake Champlain, I was induced to make a visit to Canada. Repairing to Montreal, I visited the cathedral and other places of interest in that city, from whence I continued my excursion to Kingston and other towns, obtaining a knowledge of localities, which was also of service to me afterwards, as will appear towards the close of this narrative.

Having completed my contracts on the canal satisfactorily to myself and to my employer, and not wishing to remain idle, now that the navigation of the canal was again suspended, I entered into another contract with Medad Gunn, to cut a large quantity of wood. In this business I was engaged during the winter of 1831–32.

With the return of spring, Anne and myself conceived the project of taking a farm in the neighborhood. I had been accustomed from earliest youth to agricultural labors, and it was an occupation congenial to my tastes. I accordingly entered into arrangements for a part of the old Alden farm, on which my father formerly resided. With one cow, one swine, a yoke of fine oxen I had lately purchased of Lewis Brown, in Hartford, and other personal property and effects, we proceeded to our new home in Kingsbury. That year I planted twenty-five acres of corn, sowed large fields of oats, and commenced farming upon as large a scale as my utmost means would permit. Anne was diligent about the house affairs, while I toiled laboriously in the field.

On this place we continued to reside until 1834. In the winter season I had numerous calls to play on the violin. Wherever the young people assembled to dance, I was almost invariably there. Throughout the surrounding villages my fiddle was notorious. Anne, also, during her long residence at the Eagle Tavern, had become somewhat famous as a cook. During court weeks, and on public occasions, she was employed at high wages in the kitchen at Sherrill's Coffee House.

We always returned home from the performance of these services with money in our pockets; so that, with fiddling, cooking, and farming, we soon found ourselves in the possession of abundance, and, in fact, leading a happy and prosperous life. Well, indeed, would it have been for us had we remained on the farm at Kingsbury; but the time came when the next step was to be taken towards the cruel destiny that awaited me.

In March, 1834, we removed to Saratoga Springs. We occupied a house belonging to Daniel O'Brien, on the north side of Washington street. At that time Isaac Taylor kept a large boarding house, known as Washington Hall, at the north end of Broadway. He employed me to drive a hack, in which capacity I worked for him two years. After this time I was generally employed through the visiting season, as also was Anne, in the United States Hotel, and other public houses of the place. In winter seasons I relied upon my violin, though during the construction of the Troy and Saratoga railroad, I performed many hard days' labor upon it.

I was in the habit, at Saratoga, of purchasing articles necessary for my family at the stores of Mr. Cephas Parker and Mr. William

Perry, gentlemen towards whom, for many acts of kindness, I entertained feelings of strong regard. It was for this reason that, twelve years afterwards, I caused to be directed to them the letter, which is hereinafter inserted, and which was the means, in the hands of Mr. Northup, of my fortunate deliverance.

While living at the United States Hotel, I frequently met with slaves, who had accompanied their masters from the South. They were always well dressed and well provided for, leading apparently an easy life, with but few of its ordinary troubles to perplex them. Many times they entered into conversation with me on the subject of Slavery. Almost uniformly I found they cherished a secret desire for liberty. Some of them expressed the most ardent anxiety to escape, and consulted me on the best method of effecting it. The fear of punishment, however, which they knew was certain to attend their re-capture and return, in all cases proved sufficient to deter them from the experiment. Having all my life breathed the free air of the North, and conscious that I possessed the same feelings and affections that find a place in the white man's breast; conscious, moreover, of an intelligence equal to that of some men, at least, with a fairer skin, I was too ignorant, perhaps too independent, to conceive how any one could be content to live in the abject condition of a slave. I could not comprehend the justice of that law, or that religion, which upholds or recognizes the principle of Slavery; and never once, I am proud to say, did I fail to counsel any one who came to me, to watch his opportunity, and strike for freedom.

I continued to reside at Saratoga until the spring of 1841. The flattering anticipations which, seven years before, had seduced us from the quiet farm-house, on the east side of the Hudson, had not been realized. Though always in comfortable circumstances, we had not prospered. The society and associations at that world-renowned watering place, were not calculated to preserve the simple habits of industry and economy to which I had been accustomed, but, on the contrary, to substitute others in their stead, tending to shiftlessness and extravagance.

At this time we were the parents of three children—Elizabeth, Margaret, and Alonzo. Elizabeth, the eldest, was in her tenth year; Margaret was two years younger, and little Alonzo had just passed his fifth birth-day. They filled our house with gladness. Their young voices were music in our ears. Many an airy castle did their mother and myself build for the little innocents. When not at labor I was always walking with them, clad in their best attire, through the streets and groves of Saratoga. Their presence was my delight; and I clasped them to my bosom with as warm and tender love as if their clouded skins had been as white as snow.

Thus far the history of my life presents nothing whatever unusual—nothing but the common hopes, and loves, and labors of an obscure colored man, making his humble progress in the world. But now I had reached a turning point in my existence—reached the threshold of unutterable wrong, and sorrow, and despair. Now had I approached within the shadow of the cloud, into the thick darkness whereof I was soon to disappear, thenceforward to be hidden from the eyes of all my kindred, and shut out from the sweet light of liberty, for many a weary year.

# CHAPTER II

*The Two Strangers—The Circus Company—Departure From Saratoga—Ventriloquism And Legerdemain—Journey To New-York—Free Papers—Brown And Hamilton—The Haste To Reach The Circus—Arrival In Washington—Funeral Of Harrison—The Sudden Sickness—The Torment Of Thirst—The Receding Light—Insensibility—Chains And Darkness.*

One morning, towards the latter part of the month of March, 1841, having at that time no particular business to engage my attention, I was walking about the village of Saratoga Springs, thinking to myself where I might obtain some present employment, until the busy season should arrive. Anne, as was her usual custom, had gone over to Sandy Hill, a distance of some twenty miles, to take charge of the culinary department at Sherrill's Coffee House, during the session of the court. Elizabeth, I think, had accompanied her. Margaret and Alonzo were with their aunt at Saratoga.

On the corner of Congress street and Broadway, near the tavern, then, and for aught I know to the contrary, still kept by Mr. Moon, I was met by two gentlemen of respectable appearance, both of whom were entirely unknown to me. I have the impression that they were introduced to me by some one of my acquaintances, but who, I have in vain endeavored to recall, with the remark that I was an expert player on the violin.

At any rate, they immediately entered into conversation on that subject, making numerous inquiries touching my proficiency in that respect. My responses being to all appearances satisfactory, they proposed to engage my services for a short period, stating, at the same time, I was just such a person as their business required. Their names, as they afterwards gave them to me, were Merrill Brown and Abram Hamilton, though whether these were their true appellations, I have strong reasons to doubt. The former was a man apparently forty years of age, somewhat short and thick-set, with a countenance indicating shrewdness and intelligence. He wore a black frock coat and black hat, and said he resided either at Rochester or at Syracuse. The latter was a young man of fair complexion and light eyes, and, I should judge, had not passed the age of twenty-five. He was tall and slender, dressed in a snuff-colored coat, with glossy hat, and vest of elegant pattern. His whole apparel was in the extreme of fashion. His appearance was somewhat effeminate, but prepossessing, and there was about him an easy air, that showed he had mingled with the world. They were connected, as they informed me, with a circus company, then in the city of Washington; that they were on their way thither to rejoin it, having left it for a short time to make an excursion northward, for the purpose of seeing the country, and were paying their expenses by an occasional exhibition. They also remarked that they had found much difficulty in procuring music for their entertainments, and that if I would accompany them as far as New-York, they would give me one dollar for each day's services, and three dollars in addition for every night I played at their performances, besides sufficient to pay the expenses of my return from New-York to Saratoga.

I at once accepted the tempting offer, both for the reward it promised, and from a desire to visit the metropolis. They were anxious to leave immediately. Thinking my absence would be brief, I did not deem it necessary to write to Anne whither I had gone; in fact supposing that my return, perhaps, would be as soon as hers. So taking a change of linen and my violin, I was ready to depart. The carriage was brought round—a covered one, drawn by a pair of noble bays, altogether forming an elegant establishment. Their baggage, consisting of three large trunks, was fastened on the rack, and mounting to the driver's seat, while they took their places in the rear, I drove away from Saratoga on the road to Albany, elated with my new position, and happy as I had ever been, on any day in all my life.

We passed through Ballston, and striking the ridge road, as it is called, if my memory correctly serves me, followed it direct to Albany. We reached that city before dark, and stopped at a hotel southward from the Museum.

This night I had an opportunity of witnessing one of their performances—the only one, during the whole period I was with them. Hamilton was stationed at the door; I formed the orchestra, while Brown provided the entertainment. It consisted in throwing balls, dancing on the rope, frying pancakes in a hat, causing invisible pigs to squeal, and other like feats of ventriloquism and legerdemain. The audience was extraordinarily sparse, and not of the selectest character at that, and Hamilton's report of the proceeds presented but a "beggarly account of empty boxes."

Early next morning we renewed our journey. The burden of their conversation now was the expression of an anxiety to reach the circus without delay. They hurried forward, without again stopping to exhibit, and in due course of time, we reached New-York, taking lodgings at a house on the west side of the city, in a street running from Broadway to the river. I supposed my journey was at an end, and expected in a day or two at least, to return to my friends and family at Saratoga. Brown and Hamilton, however, began to importune me to continue with them to Washington. They alleged that immediately on their arrival, now that the summer season was approaching, the circus would set out for the north. They promised me a situation and high wages if I would accompany them. Largely did they expatiate on the advantages that would result to me, and such were the flattering representations they made, that I finally concluded to accept the offer.

The next morning they suggested that, inasmuch as we were about entering a slave State, it would be well, before leaving New-York, to procure free papers. The idea struck me as a prudent one, though I think it would scarcely have occurred to me, had they not proposed it. We proceeded at once to what I understood to be the Custom House. They made oath to certain facts showing I was a free man. A paper was drawn up and handed us, with the direction to take it to the clerk's office. We did so, and the clerk having added something to it, for which he was paid six shillings, we returned again to the Custom House. Some further formalities were gone through with before it was completed, when, paying the officer two dollars, I placed the papers in my pocket, and started with my two friends to our hotel. I thought at the time, I must confess, that the papers were scarcely worth the cost of obtaining them—the apprehension of danger to my personal safety never having suggested itself to me in the remotest manner. The clerk, to whom we were directed, I remember, made a memorandum in a large book, which, I presume, is in the office yet. A reference to the entries during the latter part of March, or first of April, 1841, I have no doubt will satisfy the incredulous, at least so far as this particular transaction is concerned.

With the evidence of freedom in my possession, the next day after our arrival in New-York, we crossed the ferry to Jersey City, and took the road to Philadelphia. Here we remained one night, continuing our journey towards Baltimore early in the morning. In due time, we arrived in the latter city, and stopped at a hotel near the railroad depot, either kept by a Mr. Rathbone, or known as the Rathbone House. All the way from New-York, their anxiety to reach the circus seemed to grow more and more intense. We left the carriage at Baltimore, and entering the cars, proceeded to Washington, at which place we arrived just at nightfall, the evening previous to the funeral of General Harrison, and stopped at Gadsby's Hotel, on Pennsylvania Avenue.

After supper they called me to their apartments, and paid me forty-three dollars, a sum greater than my wages amounted to, which act of generosity was in consequence, they said, of their not having exhibited as often as they had given me to anticipate, during our trip from Saratoga. They moreover informed me that it had been the intention of the circus company to leave Washington the next morning, but that on account of the funeral, they had concluded to remain another day. They were then, as they had been from the time of our first meeting, extremely kind. No opportunity was omitted of addressing me in the language of approbation; while, on the other hand, I was certainly much prepossessed in their favor. I gave them my confidence without reserve, and would freely have trusted them to almost any extent. Their constant conversation and manner towards me—their foresight in suggesting the idea of free papers, and a hundred other little acts, unnecessary to be repeated—all indicated that they were friends indeed, sincerely solicitous for my welfare. I know not but they were. I know not but they were innocent of the great wickedness of which I now believe them guilty. Whether they were accessory to my misfortunes—subtle and inhuman monsters in the shape of men—designedly luring me away from home and family, and liberty, for the sake of gold—those who read these pages will have the same means of determining as myself. If they were innocent, my sudden disappearance must have been unaccountable indeed; but revolving in my mind all the attending circumstances, I never yet could indulge, towards them, so charitable a supposition.

After receiving the money from them, of which they appeared to have an abundance, they advised me not to go into the streets that night, inasmuch as I was unacquainted with the customs of the city. Promising to remember their advice, I left them together, and soon after was shown by a colored servant to a sleeping room in the back part of the hotel, on the ground floor. I laid down to rest, thinking of home and wife, and children, and the long distance that stretched between us, until I fell asleep. But no good angel of pity came to my bedside, bidding me to fly—no voice of mercy forewarned me in my dreams of the trials that were just at hand.

The next day there was a great pageant in Washington. The roar of cannon and the tolling of bells filled the air, while many houses were shrouded with crape, and the streets were black with people. As the day advanced, the procession made its appearance, coming slowly through the Avenue, carriage after carriage, in long succession, while thousands upon thousands followed on foot—all moving to the sound of melancholy music. They were bearing the dead body of Harrison to the grave.

From early in the morning, I was constantly in the company of Hamilton and Brown. They were the only persons I knew in Washington. We stood together as the funeral pomp passed by. I remember distinctly how the window glass would break and rattle to the ground, after each report of the cannon they were firing in the burial ground. We went to the Capitol, and walked a long time about the grounds. In the afternoon, they strolled towards the President's House, all the time keeping me near to them, and pointing out various places of interest. As yet, I had seen nothing of the circus. In fact, I had thought of it but little, if at all, amidst the excitement of the day.

My friends, several times during the afternoon, entered drinking saloons, and called for liquor. They were by no means in the habit, however, so far as I knew them, of indulging to excess. On these occasions, after serving themselves, they would pour out a glass and hand it to me. I did not become intoxicated, as may be inferred from what subsequently occurred. Towards evening, and soon after partaking of one of these potations, I began to experience most unpleasant sensations. I felt extremely ill. My head commenced aching—a dull, heavy pain, inexpressibly disagreeable. At the supper table, I was without appetite; the sight and flavor of food was nauseous. About dark the same servant conducted me to the room I had occupied the previous night. Brown and Hamilton advised me to retire, commiserating me kindly, and expressing hopes that I would be better in the morning. Divesting myself of coat and boots merely, I threw myself upon the bed. It was impossible to sleep. The pain in my head continued to increase, until it became almost unbearable. In a short time I became thirsty. My lips were parched. I could think of nothing but water—of lakes and flowing rivers, of brooks where I had stooped to drink, and of the dripping bucket, rising with its cool and overflowing nectar, from the bottom of the well. Towards midnight, as near as I could judge, I arose, unable longer to bear such intensity of thirst. I was a stranger in the house, and knew nothing of its apartments. There was no one up, as I could observe. Groping about at random, I knew not where, I found the way at last to a kitchen in the basement. Two or three colored servants were moving through it, one of whom, a woman, gave me two glasses of water. It afforded momentary relief, but by the time I had reached my room again, the same burning desire of drink, the same tormenting thirst, had again returned. It was even more torturing than before, as was also the wild pain in my head, if such a thing could be. I was in sore distress—in most excruciating agony! I seemed to stand on the brink of madness! The memory of that night of horrible suffering will follow me to the grave.

In the course of an hour or more after my return from the kitchen, I was conscious of some one entering my room. There seemed to be several—a mingling of various voices,—but how many, or who they were, I cannot tell. Whether Brown and Hamilton were among them, is a mere matter of conjecture. I only remember, with any degree of distinctness, that I was told it was necessary to go to a physician and procure medicine, and that pulling on my boots, without coat or hat, I followed them through a long passage-way, or alley, into the open street. It ran out at right angles from Pennsylvania Avenue. On the opposite side there was a light burning in a window. My impression is there were then three persons with me, but it is altogether indefinite and vague, and like the memory of a painful dream. Going towards the light, which I imagined proceeded from a physician's office, and which seemed to recede as I advanced, is the last glimmering recollection I can now recall. From that moment I was insensible. How long I remained in that condition—whether only that night, or many days and nights—I do not know; but when consciousness returned, I found myself alone, in utter darkness, and in chains.

The pain in my head had subsided in a measure, but I was very faint and weak. I was sitting upon a low bench, made of rough boards, and without coat or hat. I was hand-cuffed. Around my ankles also were a pair of heavy fetters. One end of a chain was fastened to a large ring in the floor, the other to the fetters on my ankles. I tried in vain to stand upon my feet. Waking from such a painful trance, it was some time before I could collect my thoughts. Where was I? What was the meaning of these chains? Where were Brown and Hamilton? What had I done to deserve imprisonment in such a dungeon? I could not comprehend. There was a blank of some indefinite period, preceding my awakening in that lonely place, the events of which the utmost stretch of memory was unable to recall. I listened intently for some sign or sound of life, but nothing broke the oppressive silence, save the clinking of my chains, whenever I chanced to move. I spoke aloud, but the sound of my voice startled me. I felt of my pockets, so far as the fetters would allow—far enough, indeed, to ascertain that I had not only been robbed of liberty, but that my money and free papers were also gone! Then did the idea begin to break upon my mind, at first dim and confused, that I had been kidnapped. But that I thought was incredible. There must have been some misapprehension—some unfortunate mistake. It could not be that a free citizen of New-York, who had wronged no man, nor violated any law, should be dealt with thus inhumanly. The more I contemplated my situation, however, the more I became confirmed in my suspicions. It was a desolate thought, indeed. I felt there was no trust or mercy in unfeeling man; and commending myself to the God of the oppressed, bowed my head upon my fettered hands, and wept most bitterly.

# CHAPTER III

*Painful Meditations—James H. Burch—Williams' Slave Pen In Washington—The Lackey, Radburn—Assert My Freedom—The Anger Of The Trader—The Paddle And Cat-O'-Ninetails—The Whipping—New Acquaintances—Ray, Williams, And Randall—Arrival Of Little Emily And Her Mother In The Pen—Maternal Sorrows—The Story Of Eliza.*

Some three hours elapsed, during which time I remained seated on the low bench, absorbed in painful meditations. At length I heard the crowing of a cock, and soon a distant rumbling sound, as of carriages hurrying through the streets, came to my ears, and I knew that it was day. No ray of light, however, penetrated my prison. Finally, I heard footsteps immediately overhead, as of some one walking to and fro. It occurred to me then that I must be in an underground apartment, and the damp, mouldy odors of the place confirmed the supposition. The noise above continued for at least an hour, when, at last, I heard footsteps approaching from without. A key rattled in the lock—a strong door swung back upon its hinges, admitting a flood of light, and two men entered and stood before me. One of them was a large, powerful man, forty years of age, perhaps, with dark, chestnut-colored hair, slightly interspersed with gray. His face was full, his complexion flush, his features grossly coarse, expressive of nothing but cruelty and cunning. He was about five feet ten inches high, of full habit, and, without prejudice, I must be allowed to say, was a man whose whole appearance was sinister and repugnant. His name was James H. Burch, as I learned afterwards—a well-known slave-dealer in Washington; and then, or lately, connected in business, as a partner, with Theophilus Freeman, of New-Orleans. The person who accompanied him was a simple lackey, named Ebenezer Radburn, who acted merely in the capacity of turnkey. Both of these men still live in Washington, or did, at the time of my return through that city from slavery in January last.

The light admitted through the open door enabled me to observe the room in which I was confined. It was about twelve feet square—the walls of solid masonry. The floor was of heavy plank. There was one small window, crossed with great iron bars, with an outside shutter, securely fastened.

An iron-bound door led into an adjoining cell, or vault, wholly destitute of windows, or any means of admitting light. The furniture of the room in which I was, consisted of the wooden bench on which I sat, an old-fashioned, dirty box stove, and besides these, in either cell, there was neither bed, nor blanket, nor any other thing whatever. The door, through which Burch and Radburn entered, led through a small passage, up a flight of steps into a yard, surrounded by a brick wall ten or twelve feet high, immediately in rear of a building of the same width as itself. The yard extended rearward from the house about thirty feet. In one part of the wall there was a strongly ironed door, opening into a narrow, covered passage, leading along one side of the house into the street. The doom of the colored man, upon whom the door leading out of that narrow passage closed, was sealed. The top of the wall supported one end of a roof, which ascended inwards, forming a kind of open shed. Underneath the roof there was a crazy loft all round, where slaves, if so disposed, might sleep at night, or in inclement weather seek shelter from the storm. It was like a farmer's barnyard in most respects, save it was so constructed that the outside world could never see the human cattle that were herded there.

The building to which the yard was attached, was two stories high, fronting on one of the public streets of Washington. Its outside presented only the appearance of a quiet private residence. A stranger looking at it, would never have dreamed of its execrable uses. Strange as it may seem, within plain sight of this same house, looking down from its commanding height upon it, was the Capitol. The voices of patriotic representatives boasting of freedom and equality, and the rattling of the poor slave's chains, almost commingled. A slave pen within the very shadow of the Capitol!

* * *

Such is a correct description as it was in 1841, of Williams' slave pen in Washington, in one of the cellars of which I found myself so unaccountably confined.

"Well, my boy, how do you feel now?" said Burch, as he entered through the open door. I replied that I was sick, and inquired the cause of my imprisonment. He answered that I was his slave—that he had bought me, and that he was about to send me to New-Orleans. I asserted, aloud and boldly, that I was a free man—a resident of Saratoga, where I had a wife and children, who were also free, and that my name was Northup. I complained bitterly of the strange treatment I had received, and threatened, upon my liberation, to have satisfaction for the wrong. He denied that I was free, and with an emphatic oath, declared that I came from Georgia. Again and again I asserted I was no man's slave, and insisted upon his taking off my chains at once. He endeavored to hush me, as if he feared my voice would be overheard. But I would not be silent, and denounced the authors of my imprisonment, whoever they might be, as unmitigated villains. Finding he could not quiet me, he flew into a towering passion. With blasphemous oaths, he called me a black liar, a runaway from Georgia, and every other profane and vulgar epithet that the most indecent fancy could conceive.

During this time Radburn was standing silently by. His business was, to oversee this human, or rather inhuman stable, receiving slaves, feeding and whipping them, at the rate of two shillings a head per day. Turning to him, Burch ordered the paddle and cat-o'-ninetails to be brought in. He disappeared, and in a few moments returned with these instruments of torture. The paddle, as it is termed in slave-beating parlance, or at least the one with which I first became acquainted, and of which I now speak, was a piece of hard-wood board, eighteen or twenty inches long, moulded to the shape of an old-fashioned pudding stick, or ordinary oar. The flattened portion, which was about the size in circumference of two open hands, was bored with a small auger in numerous places. The cat was a large rope of many strands—the strands unraveled, and a knot tied at the extremity of each.

As soon as these formidable whips appeared, I was seized by both of them, and roughly divested of my clothing. My feet, as has been stated, were fastened to the floor. Drawing me over the bench, face downwards, Radburn placed his heavy foot upon the fetters, between my wrists, holding them painfully to the floor. With the paddle, Burch commenced beating me. Blow after blow was inflicted upon my naked body. When his unrelenting arm grew tired, he stopped and asked if I still insisted I was a free man. I did insist upon it, and then the blows were renewed, faster and more energetically, if possible, than before. When again tired, he would repeat the same question, and receiving the same answer, continue his cruel labor. All this time, the incarnate devil was uttering most fiendish oaths. At length the paddle broke, leaving the useless handle in his hand. Still I would not yield. All his brutal blows could not force from my lips the foul lie that I was a slave. Casting madly on the floor the handle of the broken paddle, he seized the rope. This was far more painful than the other. I struggled with all my power, but it was in vain. I prayed for mercy, but my prayer was only answered with imprecations and with stripes. I thought I must die beneath the lashes of the accursed brute. Even now the flesh crawls upon my bones, as I recall the scene. I was all on fire. My sufferings I can compare to nothing else than the burning agonies of hell!

At last I became silent to his repeated questions. I would make no reply. In fact, I was becoming almost unable to speak. Still he plied the lash without stint upon my poor body, until it seemed that the lacerated flesh was stripped from my bones at every stroke. A man with a particle of mercy in his soul would not have beaten even a dog so cruelly. At length Radburn said that it was useless to whip me any more—that I would be sore enough. Thereupon, Burch desisted, saying, with an admonitory shake of his fist in my face, and hissing the words through his firm-set teeth, that if ever I dared to utter again that I was entitled to my freedom, that I had been kidnapped, or any thing whatever of the kind, the castigation I had just received was nothing in comparison with what would follow. He swore that he would either conquer or kill me. With these consolatory words, the fetters were taken from my wrists, my feet still remaining fastened to the ring; the shutter of the little barred window, which had been opened, was again closed, and going out, locking the great door behind them, I was left in darkness as before.

In an hour, perhaps two, my heart leaped to my throat, as the key rattled in the door again. I, who had been so lonely, and who had longed so ardently to see some one, I cared not who, now shuddered at the thought of man's approach. A human face was fearful to me, especially a white one. Radburn entered, bringing with him, on a tin plate, a piece of shriveled fried pork, a slice of bread and a cup of water. He asked me how I felt, and remarked that I had received a pretty severe flogging. He remonstrated with me against the propriety of asserting my freedom. In rather a patronizing and confidential manner, he gave it to me as his advice, that the less I said on that subject the better it would be for me. The man evidently endeavored to appear kind—whether touched at the sight of my sad condition, or with the view of silencing, on my part, anyfurther expression of my rights, it is not necessary now to conjecture. He unlocked the fetters from my ankles, opened the shutters of the little window, and departed, leaving me again alone.

By this time I had become stiff and sore; my body was covered with blisters, and it was with great pain and difficulty that I could move. From the window I could observe nothing but the roof resting on the adjacent wall. At night I laid down upon the damp, hard floor, without any pillow or covering whatever. Punctually, twice a day, Radburn came in, with his pork, and bread, and water. I had but little appetite, though I was tormented with continual thirst. My wounds would not permit me to remain but a few minutes in any one position; so, sitting, or standing, or moving slowly round, I passed the days and nights. I was heart sick and discouraged. Thoughts of my family, of my wife and children, continually occupied my mind. When sleep overpowered me I dreamed of them—dreamed I was again in Saratoga—that I could see their faces, and hear their voices calling me. Awakening from the pleasant phantasms of sleep to the bitter realities around me, I could but groan and weep. Still my spirit was not broken. I indulged the anticipation of escape, and that speedily. It was impossible, I reasoned, that men could be so unjust as to detain me as a slave, when the truth of my case was known. Burch, ascertaining I was no runaway from Georgia, would certainly let me go. Though suspicions of Brown and Hamilton were not unfrequent, I could not reconcile myself to the idea that they were instrumental to my imprisonment. Surely they would seek me out—they would deliver me from thraldom. Alas! I had not then learned the measure of "man's inhumanity to man," nor to what limitless extent of wickedness he will go for the love of gain.

In the course of several days the outer door was thrown open, allowing me the liberty of the yard. There I found three slaves—one of them a lad of ten years, the others young men of about twenty and twenty-five. I was not long in forming an acquaintance, and learning their names and the particulars of their history.

The eldest was a colored man named Clemens Ray. He had lived in Washington; had driven a hack, and worked in a livery stable there for a long time. He was very intelligent, and fully comprehended his situation. The thought of going south overwhelmed him with grief. Burch had purchased him a few days before, and had placed him there until such time as he was ready to send him to the New-Orleans market. From him I learned for the first time that I was in William's Slave Pen, a place I had never heard of previously. He described to me the uses for which it was designed. I repeated to him the particulars of my unhappy story, but he could only give me the consolation of his sympathy. He also advised me to be silent henceforth on the subject of my freedom; for, knowing the character of Burch, he assured me that it would only be attended with renewed whipping. The next eldest was named John Williams. He was raised in Virginia, not far from Washington. Burch had taken him in payment of a debt, and he constantly entertained the hope that his master would redeem him—a hope that was subsequently realized. The lad was a sprightly child, that answered to the name of Randall. Most of the time he was playing about the yard, but occasionally would cry, calling for his mother, and wondering when she would come. His mother's absence seemed to be the great and only grief in his little heart. He was too young to realize his condition, and when the memory of his mother was not in his mind, he amused us with his pleasant pranks.

At night, Ray, Williams, and the boy, slept in the loft of the shed, while I was locked in the cell. Finally we were each provided with blankets, such as are used upon horses—the only bedding I was allowed to have for twelve years afterwards. Ray and Williams asked me many questions about New-York—how colored people were treated there; how they could have homes and families of their own, with none to disturb and oppress them; and Ray, especially, sighed continually for freedom. Such conversations, however, were not in the hearing of Burch, or the keeper Radburn. Aspirations such as these would have brought down the lash upon our backs.

It is necessary in this narrative, in order to present a full and truthful statement of all the principal events in the history of my life, and to portray the institution of Slavery as I have seen and known it, to speak of well-known places, and of many persons who are yet living. I am, and always was, an entire stranger in Washington and its vicinity—aside from Burch and Radburn, knowing no man there, except as I have heard of them through my enslaved companions. What I am about to say, if false, can be easily contradicted.

I remained in Williams' slave pen about two weeks. The night previous to my departure a woman was brought in, weeping bitterly, and leading by the hand a little child. They were Randall's mother and half-sister. On meeting them he was overjoyed, clinging to her dress, kissing the child, and exhibiting every demonstration of delight. The mother also clasped him in her arms, embraced him tenderly, and gazed at him fondly through her tears, calling him by many an endearing name.

Emily, the child, was seven or eight years old, of light complexion, and with a face of admirable beauty. Her hair fell in curls around her neck, while the style and richness of her dress, and the neatness of her whole appearance indicated she had been brought up in the midst of wealth. She was a sweet child indeed. The woman also was arrayed in silk, with rings upon her fingers, and golden ornaments suspended from her ears. Her air and manners, the correctness and propriety of her language—all showed, evidently, that she had sometime stood above the common level of a slave. She seemed to be amazed at finding herself in such a place as that. It was plainly a sudden and unexpected turn of fortune that had brought her there. Filling the air with her complainings, she was hustled, with the children and myself, into the cell. Language can convey but an inadequate impression of the lamentations to which she gave incessant utterance. Throwing herself upon the floor, and encircling the children in her arms, she poured forth such touching words as only maternal love and kindness can suggest. They nestled closely to her, as if *there* only was there any safety or protection. At last they slept, their heads resting upon her lap. While they slumbered, she smoothed the hair back from their little foreheads, and talked to them all night long. She called them her darlings—her sweet babes—poor innocent things, that knew not the misery they were destined to endure. Soon they would have no mother to comfort them—they would be taken from her. What would become of them? Oh! she could not live away from her little Emmy and her dear boy. They had always been good children, and had such loving ways. It would break her heart, God knew, she said, if they were taken from her; and yet she knew they meant to sell them, and, may be, they would be separated, and could never see each other any more. It was enough to melt a heart of stone to listen to the pitiful expressions of that desolate and distracted mother. Her name was Eliza; and this was the story of her life, as she afterwards related it:

She was the slave of Elisha Berry, a rich man, living in the neighborhood of Washington. She was born, I think she said, on his plantation. Years before, he had fallen into dissipated habits, and quarreled with his wife. In fact, soon after the birth of Randall, they separated. Leaving his wife and daughter in the house they had always occupied, he erected a new one near by, on the estate. Into this house he brought Eliza; and, on condition of her living with him, she and her children were to be emancipated. She resided with him there nine years, with servants to attend upon her, and provided with every comfort and luxury of life. Emily was his child! Finally, her young mistress, who had always remained with her mother at the homestead, married a Mr. Jacob Brooks. At length, for some cause, (as I gathered from her relation,) beyond Berry's control, a division of his property was made. She and her children fell to the share of Mr. Brooks. During the nine years she had lived with Berry, in consequence of the position she was compelled to occupy, she and Emily had become the object of Mrs. Berry and her daughter's hatred and dislike. Berry himself she represented as a man of naturally a kind heart, who always promised her that she should have her freedom, and who, she had no doubt, would grant it to her then, if it were only in his power. As soon as they thus came into the possession and control of the daughter, it became very manifest they would not live long together. The sight of Eliza seemed to be odious to Mrs. Brooks; neither could she bear to look upon the child, half-sister, and beautiful as she was!

The day she was led into the pen, Brooks had brought her from the estate into the city, under pretence that the time had come when her free papers were to be executed, in fulfillment of her master's promise. Elated at the prospect of immediate liberty, she decked herself and little Emmy in their best apparel, and accompanied him with a joyful heart. On their arrival in the city, instead of being baptized into the family of freemen, she was delivered to the trader Burch. The paper that was executed was a bill of sale. The hope of years was blasted in a moment. From the height of most exulting happiness to the utmost depths of wretchedness, she had that day descended. No wonder that she wept, and filled the pen with wailings and expressions of heart-rending woe.

Eliza is now dead. Far up the Red River, where it pours its waters sluggishly through the unhealthy low lands of Louisiana, she rests in the grave at last—the only resting place of the poor slave! How all her fears were realized—how she mourned day and night, and never would be comforted—how, as she predicted, her heart did indeed break, with the burden of maternal sorrow, will be seen as the narrative proceeds.

# CHAPTER IV

*Eliza's Sorrows—Preparation To Embark—Driven Through The Streets Of Washington—Hail, Columbia—The Tomb Of Washington—Clem Ray—The Breakfast On The Steamer—The Happy Birds—Aquia Creek—Fredericksburgh—Arrival In Richmond—Goodin And His Slave Pen—Robert, Of Cincinnati—David And His Wife—Mary And Lethe—Clem's Return—His Subsequent Escape To Canada—The Brig Orleans—James H. Burch.*

At intervals during the first night of Eliza's incarceration in the pen, she complained bitterly of Jacob Brooks, her young mistress' husband. She declared that had she been aware of the deception he intended to practice upon her, he never would have brought her there alive. They had chosen the opportunity of getting her away when Master Berry was absent from the plantation. He had always been kind to her. She wished that she could see him; but she knew that even he was unable now to rescue her. Then would she commence weeping again—kissing the sleeping children—talking first to one, then to the other, as they lay in their unconscious slumbers, with their heads upon her lap. So wore the long night away; and when the morning dawned, and night had come again, still she kept mourning on, and would not be consoled.

About midnight following, the cell door opened, and Burch and Radburn entered, with lanterns in their hands. Burch, with an oath, ordered us to roll up our blankets without delay, and get ready to go on board the boat. He swore we would be left unless we hurried fast. He aroused the children from their slumbers with a rough shake, and said they were d—d sleepy, it appeared. Going out into the yard, he called Clem Ray, ordering him to leave the loft and come into the cell, and bring his blanket with him. When Clem appeared, he placed us side by side, and fastened us together with hand-cuffs—my left hand to his right. John Williams had been taken out a day or two before, his master having redeemed him, greatly to his delight. Clem and I were ordered to march, Eliza and the children following. We were conducted into the yard, from thence into the covered passage, and up a flight of steps through a side door into the upper room, where I had heard the walking to and fro. Its furniture was a stove, a few old chairs, and a long table, covered with papers. It was a white-washed room, without any carpet on the floor, and seemed a sort of office. By one of the windows, I remember, hung a rusty sword, which attracted my attention. Burch's trunk was there. In obedience to his orders, I took hold of one of its handles with my unfettered hand, while he taking hold of the other, we proceeded out of the front door into the street in the same order as we had left the cell.

It was a dark night. All was quiet. I could see lights, or the reflection of them, over towards Pennsylvania Avenue, but there was no one, not even a straggler, to be seen. I was almost resolved to attempt to break away. Had I not been hand-cuffed the attempt would certainly have been made, whatever consequence might have followed. Radburn was in the rear, carrying a large stick, and hurrying up the children as fast as the little ones could walk. So we passed, hand-cuffed and in silence, through the streets of Washington—through the Capital of a nation, whose theory of government, we are told, rests on the foundation of man's inalienable right to life, *liberty*, and the pursuit of happiness! Hail! Columbia, happy land, indeed!

Reaching the steamboat, we were quickly hustled into the hold, among barrels and boxes of freight. A colored servant brought a light, the bell rung, and soon the vessel started down the Potomac, carrying us we knew not where. The bell tolled as we passed the tomb of Washington! Burch, no doubt, with uncovered head, bowed reverently before the sacred ashes of the man who devoted his illustrious life to the liberty of his country.

None of us slept that night but Randall and little Emmy. For the first time Clem Ray was wholly overcome. To him the idea of going south was terrible in the extreme. He was leaving the friends and associations of his youth—every thing that was dear and precious to his heart—in all probability never to return. He and Eliza mingled their tears together, bemoaning their cruel fate. For my own part, difficult as it was, I endeavored to keep up my spirits. I resolved in my mind a hundred plans of escape, and fully determined to make the attempt the first desperate chance that offered. I had by this time become satisfied, however, that my true policy was to say nothing further on the subject of my having been born a freeman. It would but expose me to maltreatment, and diminish the chances of liberation.

After sunrise in the morning we were called up on deck to breakfast. Burch took our hand-cuffs off, and we sat down to table. He asked Eliza if she would take a dram. She declined, thanking him politely. During the meal we were all silent—not a word passed between us. A mulatto woman who served at table seemed to take an interest in our behalf—told us to cheer up, and not to be so cast down. Breakfast over, the hand-cuffs were restored, and Burch ordered us out on the stern deck. We sat down together on some boxes, still saying nothing in Burch's presence. Occasionally a passenger would walk out to where we were, look at us for a while, then silently return.

It was a very pleasant morning. The fields along the river were covered with verdure, far in advance of what I had been accustomed to see at that season of the year. The sun shone out warmly; the birds were singing in the trees. The happy birds—I envied them. I wished for wings like them, that I might cleave the air to where my birdlings waitedvainly for their father's coming, in the cooler region of the North.

In the forenoon the steamer reached Aquia Creek. There the passengers took stages—Burch and his five slaves occupying one exclusively. He laughed with the children, and at one stopping place went so far as to purchase them a piece of gingerbread. He told me to hold up my head and look smart. That I might, perhaps, get a good master if I behaved myself. I made him no reply. His face was hateful to me, and I could not bear to look upon it. I sat in the corner, cherishing in my heart the hope, not yet extinct, of some day meeting the tyrant on the soil of my native State.

At Fredericksburgh we were transferred from the stage coach to a car, and before dark arrived in Richmond, the chief city of Virginia. At this city we were taken from the cars, and driven through the street to a slave pen, between the railroad depot and the river, kept by a Mr. Goodin. This pen is similar to Williams' in Washington, except it is somewhat larger; and besides, there were two small houses standing at opposite corners within the yard. These houses are usually found within slave yards, being used as rooms for the examination of human chattels by purchasers before concluding a bargain. Unsoundness in a slave, as well as in a horse, detracts materially from his value. If no warranty is given, a close examination is a matter of particular importance to the negro jockey.

We were met at the door of Goodin's yard by that gentleman himself—a short, fat man, with a round, plump face, black hair and whiskers, and a complexion almost as dark as some of his own negroes. He had a hard, stern look, and was perhaps about fifty years of age. Burch and he met with great cordiality. They were evidently old friends. Shaking each other warmly by the hand, Burch remarked he had brought some company, inquired at what time the brig would leave, and was answered that it would probably leave the next day at such an hour. Goodin then turned to me, took hold of my arm, turned me partly round, looked at me sharply with the air of one who considered himself a good judge of property, and as if estimating in his own mind about how much I was worth.

"Well, boy, where did you come from?"

Forgetting myself, for a moment, I answered, "From New-York."

"New-York! H—l! what have you been doing up there?" was his astonished interrogatory.

Observing Burch at this moment looking at me with an angry expression that conveyed a meaning it was not difficult to understand, I immediately said, "O, I have only been up that way a piece," in a manner intended to imply that although I might have been as far as New-York, yet I wished it distinctly understood that I did not belong to that free State, nor to any other.

Goodin then turned to Clem, and then to Eliza and the children, examining them severally, and asking various questions. He was pleased with Emily, as was every one who saw the child's sweet countenance. She was not as tidy as when I first beheld her; her hair was now somewhat disheveled; but through its unkempt and soft profusion there still beamed a little face of most surpassing loveliness. "Altogether we were a fair lot—a devilish good lot," he said, enforcing that opinion with more than one emphatic adjective not found in the Christian vocabulary. Thereupon we passed into the yard. Quite a number of slaves, as many as thirty I should say, were moving about, or sitting on benches under the shed. They were all cleanly dressed—the men with hats, the women with handkerchiefs tied about their heads.

Burch and Goodin, after separating from us, walked up the steps at the back part of the main building, and sat down upon the door sill. They entered into conversation, but the subject of it I could not hear. Presently Burch came down into the yard, unfettered me, and led me into one of the small houses.

"You told that man you came from New-York," said he.

I replied, "I told him I had been up as far as New-York, to be sure, but did not tell him I belonged there, nor that I was a freeman. I meant no harm at all, Master Burch. I would not have said it had I thought."

He looked at me a moment as if he was ready to devour me, then turning round went out. In a few minutes he returned. "If ever I hear you say a word about New-York, or about your freedom, I will be the death of you—I will kill you; you may rely on that," he ejaculated fiercely.

I doubt not he understood then better than I did, the danger and the penalty of selling a free man into slavery. He felt the necessity of closing my mouth against the crime he knew he was committing. Of course, my life would not have weighed a feather, in any emergency requiring such a sacrifice. Undoubtedly, he meant precisely what he said.

Under the shed on one side of the yard, there was constructed a rough table, while overhead were sleeping lofts—the same as in the pen at Washington. After partaking at this table of our supper of pork and bread, I was hand-cuffed to a large yellow man, quite stout and fleshy, with a countenance expressive of the utmost melancholy. He was a man of intelligence and information. Chained together, it was not long before we became acquainted with each other's history. His name was Robert. Like myself, he had been born free, and had a wife and two children in Cincinnati. He said he had come south with two men, who had hired him in the city of his residence. Without free papers, he had been seized at Fredericksburgh, placed in confinement, and beaten until he had learned, as I had, the necessity and the policy of silence. He had been in Goodin's pen about three weeks. To this man I became much attached. We could sympathize with, and understand each other. It was with tears and a heavy heart, not many days subsequently, that I saw him die, and looked for the last time upon his lifeless form!

Robert and myself, with Clem, Eliza and her children, slept that night upon our blankets, in one of the small houses in the yard. There were four others, all from the same plantation, who had been sold, and were now on their way south, who also occupied it with us. David and his wife, Caroline, both mulattoes, were exceedingly affected. They dreaded the thought of being put into the cane and cotton fields; but their greatest source of anxiety was the apprehension of being separated. Mary, a tall, lithe girl, of a most jetty black, was listless and apparently indifferent. Like many of the class, she scarcely knew there was such a word as freedom. Brought up in the ignorance of a brute, she possessed but little more than a brute's intelligence. She was one of those, and there are very many, who fear nothing but their master's lash, and know no further duty than to obey his voice. The other was Lethe. She was of an entirely different character. She had long, straight hair, and bore more the appearance of an Indian than a negro woman. She had sharp and spiteful eyes, and continually gave utterance to the language of hatred and revenge. Her husband had been sold. She knew not where she was. An exchange of masters, she was sure, could not be for the worse. She cared not whither they might carry her. Pointing to the scars upon her face, the desperate creature wished that she might see the day when she could wipe them off in some man's blood!

While we were thus learning the history of each other's wretchedness, Eliza was seated in a corner by herself, singing hymns and praying for her children. Wearied from the loss of so much sleep, I could no longer bear up against the advances of that "sweet restorer," and laying down by the side of Robert, on the floor, soon forgot my troubles, and slept until the dawn of day.

In the morning, having swept the yard, and washed ourselves, under Goodin's superintendence, we were ordered to roll up our blankets, and make ready for the continuance of our journey. Clem Ray was informed that he would go no further, Burch, for some cause, having concluded to carry him back to Washington. He was much rejoiced. Shaking hands, we parted in the slave pen at Richmond, and I have not seen him since. But, much to my surprise, since my return, I learned that he had escaped from bondage, and on his way to the free soil of Canada, lodged one night at the house of my brother-in-law in Saratoga, informing my family of the place and the condition in which he left me.

In the afternoon we were drawn up, two abreast, Robert and myself in advance, and in this order, driven by Burch and Goodin from the yard, through the streets of Richmond to the brig Orleans. She was a vessel of respectable size, full rigged, and freighted principally with tobacco. We were all on board by five o'clock. Burch brought us each a tin cup and a spoon. There were forty of us in the brig, being all, except Clem, that were in the pen.

With a small pocket knife that had not been taken from me, I began cutting the initials of my name upon the tin cup. The others immediately flocked round me, requesting me to mark theirs in a similar manner. In time, I gratified them all, of which they did not appear to be forgetful.

We were all stowed away in the hold at night, and the hatch barred down. We laid on boxes, or where-ever there was room enough to stretch our blankets on the floor.

Burch accompanied us no farther than Richmond, returning from that point to the capital with Clem. Not until the lapse of almost twelve years, to wit, in January last, in the Washington police office, did I set my eyes upon his face again.

James H. Burch was a slave-trader—buying men, women and children at low prices, and selling them at an advance. He was a speculator in human flesh—a disreputable calling—and so considered at the South. For the present he disappears from the scenes recorded in this narrative, but he will appear again before its close, not in the character of a man-whipping tyrant, but as an arrested, cringing criminal in a court of law, that failed to do him justice.

# CHAPTER V

*Arrival At Norfolk—Frederick And Maria—Arthur, The Freeman—Appointed Steward—Jim, Cuffee, And Jenny—The Storm—Bahama Banks—The Calm—The Conspiracy—The Long-Boat—The Small-Pox—Death Of Robert—Manning, The Sailor—The Meeting In The Forecastle—The Letter—Arrival At New-Orleans—Arthur's Rescue—Theophilus Freeman, The Consignee—Platt—First Night In The New-Orleans Slave Pen.*

After we were all on board, the brig Orleans proceeded down James River. Passing into Chesapeake Bay, we arrived next day opposite the city of Norfolk. While lying at anchor, a lighter approached us from the town, bringing four more slaves. Frederick, a boy of eighteen, had been born a slave, as also had Henry, who was some years older. They had both been house servants in the city. Maria was a rather genteel looking colored girl, with a faultless form, but ignorant and extremely vain. The idea of going to New-Orleans was pleasing to her. She entertained an extravagantly high opinion of her own attractions. Assuming a haughty mien, she declared to her companions, that immediately on our arrival in New-Orleans, she had no doubt, some wealthy single gentleman of good taste would purchase her at once!

But the most prominent of the four, was a man named Arthur. As the lighter approached, he struggled stoutly with his keepers. It was with main force that he was dragged aboard the brig. He protested, in a loud voice, against the treatment he was receiving, and demanded to be released. His face was swollen, and covered with wounds and bruises, and, indeed, one side of it was a complete raw sore. He was forced, with all haste, down the hatchway into the hold. I caught an outline of his story as he was borne struggling along, of which he afterwards gave me a more full relation, and it was as follows: He had long resided in the city of Norfolk, and was a free man. He had a family living there, and was a mason by trade. Having been unusually detained, he was returning late one night to his house in the suburbs of the city, when he was attacked by a gang of persons in an unfrequented street. He fought until his strength failed him. Overpowered at last, he was gagged and bound with ropes, and beaten, until he became insensible. For several days they secreted him in the slave pen at Norfolk—a very common establishment, it appears, in the cities of the South. The night before, he had been taken out and put on board the lighter, which, pushing out from shore, had awaited our arrival. For some time he continued his protestations, and was altogether irreconcilable. At length, however, he became silent. He sank into a gloomy and thoughtful mood, and appeared to be counseling with himself. There was in the man's determined face, something that suggested the thought of desperation.

After leaving Norfolk the hand-cuffs were taken off, and during the day we were allowed to remain on deck. The captain selected Robert as his waiter, and I was appointed to superintend the cooking department, and the distribution of food and water. I had three assistants, Jim, Cuffee and Jenny. Jenny's business was to prepare the coffee, which consisted of corn meal scorched in a kettle, boiled and sweetened with molasses. Jim and Cuffee baked the hoe-cake and boiled the bacon.

Standing by a table, formed of a wide board resting on the heads of the barrels, I cut and handed to each a slice of meat and a "dodger" of the bread, and from Jenny's kettle also dipped out for each a cup of the coffee. The use of plates was dispensed with, and their sable fingers took the place of knives and forks. Jim and Cuffee were very demure and attentive to business, somewhat inflated with their situation as second cooks, and without doubt feeling that there was a great responsibility resting on them. I was called steward—a name given me by the captain.

The slaves were fed twice a day, at ten and five o'clock—always receiving the same kind and quantity of fare, and in the same manner as above described. At night we were driven into the hold, and securely fastened down.

Scarcely were we out of sight of land before we were overtaken by a violent storm. The brig rolled and plunged until we feared she would go down. Some were sea-sick, others on their knees praying, while some were fast holding to each other, paralyzed with fear. The sea-sickness rendered the place of our confinement loathsome and disgusting. It would have been a happy thing for most of us—it would have saved the agony of many hundred lashes, and miserable deaths at last—had the compassionate sea snatched us that day from the clutches of remorseless men. The thought of Randall and little Emmy sinking down among the monsters of the deep, is a more pleasant contemplation than to think of them as they are now, perhaps, dragging out lives of unrequited toil.

When in sight of the Bahama Banks, at a place called Old Point Compass, or the Hole in the Wall, we were becalmed three days. There was scarcely a breath of air. The waters of the gulf presented a singularly white appearance, like lime water.

In the order of events, I come now to the relation of an occurrence, which I never call to mind but with sensations of regret. I thank God, who has since permitted me to escape from the thraldom of slavery, that through his merciful interposition I was prevented from imbruing my hands in the blood of his creatures. Let not those who have never been placed in like circumstances, judge me harshly. Until they have been chained and beaten—until they find themselves in the situation I was, borne away from home and family towards a land of bondage—let them refrain from saying what they would not do for liberty. How far I should have been justified in the sight of God and man, it is unnecessary now to speculate upon. It is enough to say that I am able to congratulate myself upon the harmless termination of an affair which threatened, for a time, to be attended with serious results.

Towards evening, on the first day of the calm, Arthur and myself were in the bow of the vessel, seated on the windlass. We were conversing together of the probable destiny that awaited us, and mourning together over our misfortunes. Arthur said, and I agreed with him, that death was far less terrible than the living prospect that was before us. For a long time we talked of our children, our past lives, and of the probabilities of escape. Obtaining possession of the brig was suggested by one of us. We discussed the possibility of our being able, in such an event, to make our way to the harbor of New-York. I knew little of the compass; but the idea of risking the experiment was eagerly entertained. The chances, for and against us, in an encounter with the crew, was canvassed. Who could be relied upon, and who could not, the proper time and manner of the attack, were all talked over and over again. From the moment the plot suggested itself I began to hope. I revolved it constantly in my mind. As difficulty after difficulty arose, some ready conceit was at hand, demonstrating how it could be overcome. While others slept, Arthur and I were maturing our plans. At length, with much caution, Robert was gradually made acquainted with our intentions. He approved of them at once, and entered into the conspiracy with a zealous spirit. There was not another slave we dared to trust. Brought up in fear and ignorance as they are, it can scarcely be conceived how servilely they will cringe before a white man's look. It was not safe to deposit so bold a secret with any of them, and finally we three resolved to take upon ourselves alone the fearful responsibility of the attempt.

At night, as has been said, we were driven into the hold, and the hatch barred down. How to reach the deck was the first difficulty that presented itself. On the bow of the brig, however, I had observed the small boat lying bottom upwards. It occurred to me that by secreting ourselves underneath it, we would not be missed from the crowd, as they were hurried down into the hold at night. I was selected to make the experiment, in order to satisfy ourselves of its feasibility. The next evening, accordingly, after supper, watching my opportunity, I hastily concealed myself beneath it. Lying close upon the deck, I could see what was going on around me, while wholly unperceived myself. In the morning, as they came up, I slipped from my hiding place without being observed. The result was entirely satisfactory.

The captain and mate slept in the cabin of the former. From Robert, who had frequent occasion, in his capacity of waiter, to make observations in that quarter, we ascertained the exact position of their respective berths. He further informed us that there were always two pistols and a cutlass lying on the table. The crew's cook slept in the cook galley on deck, a sort of vehicle on wheels, that could be moved about as convenience required, while the sailors, numbering only six, either slept in the forecastle, or in hammocks swung among the rigging.

Finally our arrangements were all completed. Arthur and I were to steal silently to the captain's cabin, seize the pistols and cutlass, and as quickly as possible despatch him and the mate. Robert, with a club, was to stand by the door leading from the deck down into the cabin, and, in case of necessity, beat back the sailors, until we could hurry to his assistance. We were to proceed then as circumstances might require. Should the attack be so sudden and successful as to prevent resistance, the hatch was to remain barred down; otherwise the slaves were to be called up, and in the crowd, and hurry, and confusion of the time, we resolved to regain our liberty or lose our lives. I was then to assume the unaccustomed place of pilot, and, steering northward, we trusted that some lucky wind might bear us to the soil of freedom.

The mate's name was Biddee, the captain's I cannot now recall, though I rarely ever forget a name once heard. The captain was a small, genteel man, erect and prompt, with a proud bearing, and looked the personification of courage. If he is still living, and these pages should chance to meet his eye, he will learn a fact connected with the voyage of the brig, from Richmond to New-Orleans, in 1841, not entered on his log-book.

We were all prepared, and impatiently waiting an opportunity of putting our designs into execution, when they were frustrated by a sad and unforeseen event. Robert was taken ill. It was soon announced that he had the small-pox. He continued to grow worse, and four days previous to our arrival in New-Orleans he died. One of the sailors sewed him in his blanket, with a large stone from the ballast at his feet, and then laying him on a hatchway, and elevating it with tackles above the railing, the inanimate body of poor Robert was consigned to the white waters of the gulf.

We were all panic-stricken by the appearance of the small-pox. The captain ordered lime to be scattered through the hold, and other prudent precautions to be taken. The death of Robert, however, and the presence of the malady, oppressed me sadly, and I gazed out over the great waste of waters with a spirit that was indeed disconsolate.

An evening or two after Robert's burial, I was leaning on the hatchway near the forecastle, full of desponding thoughts, when a sailor in a kind voice asked me why I was so down-hearted. The tone and manner of the man assured me, and I answered, because I was a freeman, and had been kidnapped. He remarked that it was enough to make any one down-hearted, and continued to interrogate me until he learned the particulars of my whole history. He was evidently much interested in my behalf, and, in the blunt speech of a sailor, swore he would aid me all he could, if it "split his timbers." I requested him to furnish me pen, ink and paper, in order that I might write to some of my friends. He promised to obtain them—but how I could use them undiscovered was a difficulty. If I could only get into the forecastle while his watch was off, and the other sailors asleep, the thing could be accomplished. The small boat instantly occurred to me. He thought we were not far from the Balize, at the mouth of the Mississippi, and it was necessary that the letter be written soon, or the opportunity would be lost. Accordingly, by arrangement, I managed the next night to secret myself again under the long-boat. His watch was off at twelve. I saw him pass into the forecastle, and in about an hour followed him. He was nodding over a table, half asleep, on which a sickly light was flickering, and on which also was a pen and sheet of paper. As I entered he aroused, beckoned me to a seat beside him, and pointed to the paper. I directed the letter to Henry B. Northup, of Sandy Hill—stating that I had been kidnapped, was then on board the brig Orleans, bound for New-Orleans; that it was then impossible for me to conjecture my ultimate destination, and requesting he would take measures to rescue me. The letter was sealed and directed, and Manning, having read it, promised to deposit it in the New-Orleans post-office. I hastened back to my place under the long-boat, and in the morning, as the slaves came up and were walking round, crept out unnoticed and mingled with them.

My good friend, whose name was John Manning, was an Englishman by birth, and a noble-hearted, generous sailor as ever walked a deck. He had lived in Boston—was a tall, well-built man, about twenty-four years old, with a face somewhat pock-marked, but full of benevolent expression.

Nothing to vary the monotony of our daily life occurred, until we reached New-Orleans. On coming to the levee, and before the vessel was made fast, I saw Manning leap on shore and hurry away into the city. As he started off he looked back over his shoulder significantly, giving me to understand the object of his errand. Presently he returned, and passing close by me, hunched me with his elbow, with a peculiar wink, as much as to say, "it is all right."

The letter, as I have since learned, reached Sandy Hill. Mr. Northup visited Albany and laid it before Governor Seward, but inasmuch as it gave no definite information as to my probable locality, it was not, at that time, deemed advisable to institute measures for my liberation. It was concluded to delay, trusting that a knowledge of where I was might eventually be obtained.

A happy and touching scene was witnessed immediately upon our reaching the levee. Just as Manning left the brig, on his way to the post-office, two men came up and called aloud for Arthur. The latter, as he recognized them, was almost crazy with delight. He could hardly be restrained from leaping over the brig's side; and when they met soon after, he grasped them by the hand, and clung to them a long, long time. They were men from Norfolk, who had come on to New-Orleans to rescue him. His kidnappers, they informed him, had been arrested, and were then confined in the Norfolk prison. They conversed a few moments with the captain, and then departed with the rejoicing Arthur.

But in all the crowd that thronged the wharf, there was no one who knew or cared for me. Not one. No familiar voice greeted my ears, nor was there a single face that I had ever seen. Soon Arthur would rejoin his family, and have the satisfaction of seeing his wrongs avenged: my family, alas, should I ever see them more? There was a feeling of utter desolation in my heart, filling it with a despairing and regretful sense, that I had not gone down with Robert to the bottom of the sea.

Very soon traders and consignees came on board. One, a tall, thin-faced man, with light complexion and a little bent, made his appearance, with a paper in his hand. Burch's gang, consisting of myself, Eliza and her children, Harry, Lethe, and some others, who had joined us at Richmond, were consigned to him. This gentleman was Mr. Theophilus Freeman. Reading from his paper, he called, "Platt." No one answered. The name was called again and again, but still there was no reply. Then Lethe was called, then Eliza, then Harry, until the list was finished, each one stepping forward as his or her name was called.

"Captain, where's Platt?" demanded Theophilus Freeman.

The captain was unable to inform him, no one being on board answering to that name.

"Who shipped *that* nigger?" he again inquired of the captain, pointing to me.

"Burch," replied the captain.

"Your name is Platt—you answer my description. Why don't you come forward?" he demanded of me, in an angry tone.

I informed him that was not my name; that I had never been called by it, but that I had no objection to it as I knew of.

"Well, I will learn you your name," said he; "and so you won't forget it either, by ——," he added.

Mr. Theophilus Freeman, by the way, was not a whit behind his partner, Burch, in the matter of blasphemy. On the vessel I had gone by the name of "Steward," and this was the first time I had ever been designated as Platt—the name forwarded by Burch to his consignee. From the vessel I observed the chain-gang at work on the levee. We passed near them as we were driven to Freeman's slave pen. This pen is very similar to Goodin's in Richmond, except the yard was enclosed by plank, standing upright, with ends sharpened, instead of brick walls.

Including us, there were now at least fifty in this pen. Depositing our blankets in one of the small buildings in the yard, and having been called up and fed, we were allowed to saunter about the enclosure until night, when we wrapped our blankets round us and laid down under the shed, or in the loft, or in the open yard, just as each one preferred.

It was but a short time I closed my eyes that night. Thought was busy in my brain. Could it be possible that I was thousands of miles from home—that I had been driven through the streets like a dumb beast—that I had been chained and beaten without mercy—that I was even then herded with a drove of slaves, a slave myself? Were the events of the last few weeks realities indeed?—or was I passing only through the dismal phases of a long, protracted dream? It was no illusion. My cup of sorrow was full to overflowing. Then I lifted up my hands to God, and in the still watches of the night, surrounded by the sleeping forms of my companions, begged for mercy on the poor, forsaken captive. To the Almighty Father of us all—the freeman and the slave—I poured forth the supplications of a broken spirit, imploring strength from on high to bear up against the burden of my troubles, until the morning light aroused the slumberers, ushering in another day of bondage.

# CHAPTER VI

*Freeman's Industry—Cleanliness And Clothes—Exercising In The Show Room—The Dance—Bob, The Fiddler—Arrival Of Customers—Slaves Examined—The Old Gentleman Of New-Orleans—Sale Of David, Caroline And Lethe—Parting Of Randall And Eliza—Small-Pox—The Hospital—Recovery And Return To Freeman's Slave Pen—The Purchaser Of Eliza, Harry And Platt—Eliza's Agony On Parting From Little Emily.*

The very amiable, pious-hearted Mr. Theophilus Freeman, partner or consignee of James H. Burch, and keeper of the slave pen in New-Orleans, was out among his animals early in the morning. With an occasional kick of the older men and women, and many a sharp crack of the whip about the ears of the younger slaves, it was not long before they were all astir, and wide awake. Mr. Theophilus Freeman bustled about in a very industrious manner, getting his property ready for the sales-room, intending, no doubt, to do that day a rousing business.

In the first place we were required to wash thoroughly, and those with beards, to shave. We were then furnished with a new suit each, cheap, but clean. The men had hat, coat, shirt, pants and shoes; the women frocks of calico, and handkerchiefs to bind about their heads. We were now conducted into a large room in the front part of the building to which the yard was attached, in order to be properly trained, before the admission of customers. The men were arranged on one side of the room, the women on the other. The tallest was placed at the head of the row, then the next tallest, and so on in the order of their respective heights. Emily was at the foot of the line of women. Freeman charged us to remember our places; exhorted us to appear smart and lively,—sometimes threatening, and again, holding out various inducements. During the day he exercised us in the art of "looking smart," and of moving to our places with exact precision.

After being fed, in the afternoon, we were again paraded and made to dance. Bob, a colored boy, who had some time belonged to Freeman, played on the violin. Standing near him, I made bold to inquire if he could play the "Virginia Reel." He answered he could not, and asked me if I could play. Replying in the affirmative, he handed me the violin. I struck up a tune, and finished it. Freeman ordered me to continue playing, and seemed well pleased, telling Bob that I far excelled him—a remark that seemed to grieve my musical companion very much.

Next day many customers called to examine Freeman's "new lot." The latter gentleman was very loquacious, dwelling at much length upon our several good points and qualities. He would make us hold up our heads, walk briskly back and forth, while customers would feel of our hands and arms and bodies, turn us about, ask us what we could do, make us open our mouths and show our teeth, precisely as a jockey examines a horse which he is about to barter for or purchase. Sometimes a man or woman was taken back to the small house in the yard, stripped, and inspected more minutely. Scars upon a slave's back were considered evidence of a rebellious or unruly spirit, and hurt his sale.

One old gentleman, who said he wanted a coachman, appeared to take a fancy to me. From his conversation with Burch, I learned he was a resident in the city. I very much desired that he would buy me, because I conceived it would not be difficult to make my escape from New-Orleans on some northern vessel. Freeman asked him fifteen hundred dollars for me. The old gentleman insisted it was too much, as times were very hard. Freeman, however, declared that I was sound and healthy, of a good constitution, and intelligent. He made it a point to enlarge upon my musical attainments. The old gentleman argued quite adroitly that there was nothing extraordinary about the nigger, and finally, to my regret, went out, saying he would call again. During the day, however, a number of sales were made. David and Caroline were purchased together by a Natchez planter. They left us, grinning broadly, and in the most happy state of mind, caused by the fact of their not being separated. Lethe was sold to a planter of Baton Rouge, her eyes flashing with anger as she was led away.

The same man also purchased Randall. The little fellow was made to jump, and run across the floor, and perform many other feats, exhibiting his activity and condition. All the time the trade was going on, Eliza was crying aloud, and wringing her hands. She besought the man not to buy him, unless he also bought herself and Emily. She promised, in that case, to be the most faithful slave that ever lived. The man answered that he could not afford it, and then Eliza burst into a paroxysm of grief, weeping plaintively. Freeman turned round to her, savagely, with his whip in his uplifted hand, ordering her to stop her noise, or he would flog her. He would not have such work—such snivelling; and unless she ceased that minute, he would take her to the yard and give her a hundred lashes. Yes, he would take the nonsense out of her pretty quick—if he didn't, might he be d—d. Eliza shrunk before him, and tried to wipe away her tears, but it was all in vain. She wanted to be with her children, she said, the little time she had to live. All the frowns and threats of Freeman, could not wholly silence the afflicted mother. She kept on begging and beseeching them, most piteously, not to separate the three. Over and over again she told them how she loved her boy. A great many times she repeated her former promises—how very faithful and obedient she would be; how hard she would labor day and night, to the last moment of her life, if he would only buy them all together. But it was of no avail; the man could not afford it. The bargain was agreed upon, and Randall must go alone. Then Eliza ran to him; embraced him passionately; kissed him again and again; told him to remember her—all the while her tears falling in the boy's face like rain.

Freeman damned her, calling her a blubbering, bawling wench, and ordered her to go to her place, and behave herself, and be somebody. He swore he wouldn't stand such stuff but a little longer. He would soon give her something to cry about, if she was not mighty careful, and *that* she might depend upon.

The planter from Baton Rouge, with his new purchases, was ready to depart.

"Don't cry, mama. I will be a good boy. Don't cry," said Randall, looking back, as they passed out of the door.

What has become of the lad, God knows. It was a mournful scene indeed. I would have cried myself if I had dared.

That night, nearly all who came in on the brig Orleans, were taken ill. They complained of violent pain in the head and back. Little Emily—a thing unusual with her—cried constantly. In the morning a physician was called in, but was unable to determine the nature of our complaint. While examining me, and asking questions touching my symptoms, I gave it as my opinion that it was an attack of small-pox—mentioning the fact of Robert's death as the reason of my belief. It might be so indeed, he thought, and he would send for the head physician of the hospital. Shortly, the head physician came—a small, light-haired man, whom they called Dr. Carr. He pronounced it small-pox, whereupon there was much alarm throughout the yard. Soon after Dr. Carr left, Eliza, Emmy, Harry and myself were put into a hack and driven to the hospital—a large white marble building, standing on the outskirts of the city. Harry and I were placed in a room in one of the upper stories. I became very sick. For three days I was entirely blind. While lying in this state one day, Bob came in, saying to Dr. Carr that Freeman had sent him over to inquire how we were getting on. Tell him, said the doctor, that Platt is very bad, but that if he survives until nine o'clock, he may recover.

I expected to die. Though there was little in the prospect before me worth living for, the near approach of death appalled me. I thought I could have been resigned to yield up my life in the bosom of my family, but to expire in the midst of strangers, under such circumstances, was a bitter reflection.

There were a great number in the hospital, of both sexes, and of all ages. In the rear of the building coffins were manufactured. When one died, the bell tolled—a signal to the undertaker to come and bear away the body to the potter's field. Many times, each day and night, the tolling bell sent forth its melancholy voice, announcing another death. But my time had not yet come. The crisis having passed, I began to revive, and at the end of two weeks and two days, returned with Harry to the pen, bearing upon my face the effects of the malady, which to this day continues to disfigure it. Eliza and Emily were also brought back next day in a hack, and again were we paraded in the sales-room, for the inspection and examination of purchasers. I still indulged the hope that the old gentleman in search of a coachman would call again, as he had promised, and purchase me. In that event I felt an abiding confidence that I would soon regain my liberty. Customer after customer entered, but the old gentleman never made his appearance.

At length, one day, while we were in the yard, Freeman came out and ordered us to our places, in the great room. A gentleman was waiting for us as we entered, and inasmuch as he will be often mentioned in the progress of this narrative, a description of his personal appearance, and my estimation of his character, at first sight, may not be out of place.

He was a man above the ordinary height, somewhat bent and stooping forward. He was a good-looking man, and appeared to have reached about the middle age of life. There was nothing repulsive in his presence; but on the other hand, there was something cheerful and attractive in his face, and in his tone of voice. The finer elements were all kindly mingled in his breast, as any one could see. He moved about among us, asking many questions, as to what we could do, and what labor we had been accustomed to; if we thought we would like to live with him, and would be good boys if he would buy us, and other interrogatories of like character.

After some further inspection, and conversation touching prices, he finally offered Freeman one thousand dollars for me, nine hundred for Harry, and seven hundred for Eliza. Whether the small-pox had depreciated our value, or from what cause Freeman had concluded to fall five hundred dollars from the price I was before held at, I cannot say. At any rate, after a little shrewd reflection, he announced his acceptance of the offer.

As soon as Eliza heard it, she was in an agony again. By this time she had become haggard and hollow-eyed with sickness and with sorrow. It would be a relief if I could consistently pass over in silence the scene that now ensued. It recalls memories more mournful and affecting than any language can portray. I have seen mothers kissing for the last time the faces of their dead offspring; I have seen them looking down into the grave, as the earth fell with a dull sound upon their coffins, hiding them from their eyes forever; but never have I seen such an exhibition of intense, unmeasured, and unbounded grief, as when Eliza was parted from her child. She broke from her place in the line of women, and rushing down where Emily was standing, caught her in her arms. The child, sensible of some impending danger, instinctively fastened her hands around her mother's neck, and nestled her little head upon her bosom. Freeman sternly ordered her to be quiet, but she did not heed him. He caught her by the arm and pulled her rudely, but she only clung the closer to the child. Then, with a volley of great oaths, he struck her such a heartless blow, that she staggered backward, and was like to fall. Oh! how piteously then did she beseech and beg and pray that they might not be separated. Why could they not be purchased together? Why not let her have one of her dear children? "Mercy, mercy, master!" she cried, falling on her knees. "Please, master, buy Emily. I can never work any if she is taken from me: I will die."

Freeman interfered again, but, disregarding him, she still plead most earnestly, telling how Randall had been taken from her—how she never would see him again, and now it was too bad—oh, God! it was too bad, too cruel, to take her away from Emily—her pride—her only darling, that could not live, it was so young, without its mother!

Finally, after much more of supplication, the purchaser of Eliza stepped forward, evidently affected, and said to Freeman he would buy Emily, and asked him what her price was.

"What is her *price*? *Buy* her?" was the responsive interrogatory of Theophilus Freeman. And instantly answering his own inquiry, he added, "I won't sell her. She's not for sale."

The man remarked he was not in need of one so young—that it would be of no profit to him, but since the mother was so fond of her, rather than see them separated, he would pay a reasonable price. But to this humane proposal Freeman was entirely deaf. He would not sell her then on any account whatever. There were heaps and piles of money to be made of her, he said, when she was a few years older. There were men enough in New-Orleans who would give five thousand dollars for such an extra, handsome, fancy piece as Emily would be, rather than not get her. No, no, he would not sell her then. She was a beauty—a picture—a doll—one of the regular bloods—none of your thick-lipped, bullet-headed, cotton-picking niggers—if she was might he be d—d.

When Eliza heard Freeman's determination not to part with Emily, she became absolutely frantic.

"I will *not* go without her. They shall *not* take her from me," she fairly shrieked, her shrieks commingling with the loud and angry voice of Freeman, commanding her to be silent.

Meantime Harry and myself had been to the yard and returned with our blankets, and were at the front door ready to leave. Our purchaser stood near us, gazing at Eliza with an expression indicative of regret at having bought her at the expense of so much sorrow. We waited some time, when, finally, Freeman, out of patience, tore Emily from her mother by main force, the two clinging to each other with all their might.

"Don't leave me, mama—don't leave me," screamed the child, as its mother was pushed harshly forward; "Don't leave me—come back, mama," she still cried, stretching forth her little arms imploringly. But she cried in vain. Out of the door and into the street we were quickly hurried. Still we could hear her calling to her mother, "Come back—don't leave me—come back, mama," until her infant voice grew faint and still more faint, and gradually died away, as distance intervened, and finally was wholly lost.

Eliza never after saw or heard of Emily or Randall. Day nor night, however, were they ever absent from her memory. In the cotton field, in the cabin, always and everywhere, she was talking of them—often *to* them, as if they were actually present. Only when absorbed in that illusion, or asleep, did she ever have a moment's comfort afterwards.

She was no common slave, as has been said. To a large share of natural intelligence which she possessed, was added a general knowledge and information on most subjects. She had enjoyed opportunities such as are afforded to very few of her oppressed class. She had been lifted up into the regions of a higher life. Freedom—freedom for herself and for her offspring, for many years had been her cloud by day, her pillar of fire by night. In her pilgrimage through the wilderness of bondage, with eyes fixed upon that hope-inspiring beacon, she had at length ascended to "the top of Pisgah," and beheld "the land of promise." In an unexpected moment she was utterly overwhelmed with disappointment and despair. The glorious vision of liberty faded from her sight as they led her away into captivity. Now "she weepeth sore in the night, and tears are on her cheeks: all her friends have dealt treacherously with her: they have become her enemies."

# CHAPTER VII

*The Steamboat Rodolph—Departure From New-Orleans—William Ford—Arrival At Alexandria, On Red River—Resolutions—The Great Pine Woods—Wild Cattle—Martin's Summer Residence—The Texas Road—Arrival At Master Ford's—Rose—Mistress Ford—Sally, And Her Children—John, The Cook—Walter, Sam, And Antony—The Mills On Indian Creek—Sabbath Days—Sam's Conversion—The Profit Of Kindness—Rafting—Adam Taydem, The Little White Man—Cascalla And His Tribe—The Indian Ball—John M. Tibeats—The Storm Approaching.*

On leaving the New-Orleans slave pen, Harry and I followed our new master through the streets, while Eliza, crying and turning back, was forced along by Freeman and his minions, until we found ourselves on board the steamboat Rodolph, then lying at the levee. In the course of half an hour we were moving briskly up the Mississippi, bound for some point on Red River. There were quite a number of slaves on board beside ourselves, just purchased in the New-Orleans market. I remember a Mr. Kelsow, who was said to be a well known and extensive planter, had in charge a gang of women.

Our master's name was William Ford. He resided then in the "Great Pine Woods," in the parish of Avoyelles, situated on the right bank of Red River, in the heart of Louisiana. He is now a Baptist preacher. Throughout the whole parish of Avoyelles, and especially along both shores of Bayou Bœuf, where he is more intimately known, he is accounted by his fellow-citizens as a worthy minister of God. In many northern minds, perhaps, the idea of a man holding his brother man in servitude, and the traffic in human flesh, may seem altogether incompatible with their conceptions of a moral or religious life. From descriptions of such men as Burch and Freeman, and others hereinafter mentioned, they are led to despise and execrate the whole class of slaveholders, indiscriminately. But I was sometime his slave, and had an opportunity of learning well his character and disposition, and it is but simple justice to him when I say, in my opinion, there never was a more kind, noble, candid, Christian man than William Ford. The influences and associations that had always surrounded him, blinded him to the inherent wrong at the bottom of the system of Slavery. He never doubted the moral right of one man holding another in subjection. Looking through the same medium with his fathers before him, he saw things in the same light. Brought up under other circumstances and other influences, his notions would undoubtedly have been different. Nevertheless, he was a model master, walking uprightly, according to the light of his understanding, and fortunate was the slave who came to his possession. Were all men such as he, Slavery would be deprived of more than half its bitterness.

We were two days and three nights on board the steamboat Rodolph, during which time nothing of particular interest occurred. I was now known as Platt, the name given me by Burch, and by which I was designated through the whole period of my servitude. Eliza was sold by the name of "Dradey." She was so distinguished in the conveyance to Ford, now on record in the recorder's office in New-Orleans.

On our passage I was constantly reflecting on my situation, and consulting with myself on the best course to pursue in order to effect my ultimate escape. Sometimes, not only then, but afterwards, I was almost on the point of disclosing fully to Ford the facts of my history. I am inclined now to the opinion it would have resulted in my benefit. This course was often considered, but through fear of its miscarriage, never put into execution, until eventually my transfer and his pecuniary embarrassments rendered it evidently unsafe. Afterwards, under other masters, unlike William Ford, I knew well enough the slightest knowledge of my real character would consign me at once to the remoter depths of Slavery. I was too costly a chattel to be lost, and was well aware that I would be taken farther on, into some by-place, over the Texan border, perhaps, and sold; that I would be disposed of as the thief disposes of his stolen horse, if my right to freedom was even whispered. So I resolved to lock the secret closely in my heart—never to utter one word or syllable as to who or what I was—trusting in Providence and my own shrewdness for deliverance.

At length we left the steamboat Rodolph at a place called Alexandria, several hundred miles from New-Orleans. It is a small town on the southern shore of Red River. Having remained there over night, we entered the morning train of cars, and were soon at Bayou Lamourie, a still smaller place, distant eighteen miles from Alexandria. At that time it was the termination of the railroad. Ford's plantation was situated on the Texas road, twelve miles from Lamourie, in the Great Pine Woods. This distance, it was announced to us, must be traveled on foot, there being public conveyances no farther. Accordingly we all set out in the company of Ford. It was an excessively hot day. Harry, Eliza, and myself were yet weak, and the bottoms of our feet were very tender from the effects of the small-pox. We proceeded slowly, Ford telling us to take our time and sit down and rest whenever we desired—a privilege that was taken advantage of quite frequently. After leaving Lamourie and crossing two plantations, one belonging to Mr. Carnell, the other to a Mr. Flint, we reached the Pine Woods, a wilderness that stretches to the Sabine River.

The whole country about Red River is low and marshy. The Pine Woods, as they are called, is comparatively upland, with frequent small intervals, however, running through them. This upland is covered with numerous trees—the white oak, the chincopin, resembling chestnut, but principally the yellow pine. They are of great size, running up sixty feet, and perfectly straight. The woods were full of cattle, very shy and wild, dashing away in herds, with a loud snuff, at our approach. Some of them were marked or branded, the rest appeared to be in their wild and untamed state. They are much smaller than northern breeds, and the peculiarity about them that most attracted my attention was their horns. They stand out from the sides of the head precisely straight, like two iron spikes.

At noon we reached a cleared piece of ground containing three or four acres. Upon it was a small, unpainted, wooden house, a corn crib, or, as we would say, a barn, and a log kitchen, standing about a rod from the house. It was the summer residence of Mr. Martin. Rich planters, having large establishments on Bayou Bœuf, are accustomed to spend the warmer season in these woods. Here they find clear water and delightful shades. In fact, these retreats are to the planters of that section of the country what Newport and Saratoga are to the wealthier inhabitants of northern cities.

We were sent around into the kitchen, and supplied with sweet potatoes, corn-bread, and bacon, while Master Ford dined with Martin in the house. There were several slaves about the premises. Martin came out and took a look at us, asking Ford the price of each, if we were green hands, and so forth, and making inquiries in relation to the slave market generally.

After a long rest we set forth again, following the Texas road, which had the appearance of being very rarely traveled. For five miles we passed through continuous woods without observing a single habitation. At length, just as the sun was sinking in the west, we entered another opening, containing some twelve or fifteen acres.

In this opening stood a house much larger than Mr. Martin's. It was two stories high, with a piazza in front. In the rear of it was also a log kitchen, poultry house, corn cribs, and several negro cabins. Near the house was a peach orchard, and gardens of orange and pomegranate trees. The space was entirely surrounded by woods, and covered with a carpet of rich, rank verdure. It was a quiet, lonely, pleasant place—literally a green spot in the wilderness. It was the residence of my master, William Ford.

As we approached, a yellow girl—her name was Rose—was standing on the piazza. Going to the door, she called her mistress, who presently came running out to meet her lord. She kissed him, and laughingly demanded if he had bought "those niggers." Ford said he had, and told us to go round to Sally's cabin and rest ourselves. Turning the corner of the house, we discovered Sally washing—her two baby children near her, rolling on the grass. They jumped up and toddled towards us, looked at us a moment like a brace of rabbits, then ran back to their mother as if afraid of us.

Sally conducted us into the cabin, told us to lay down our bundles and be seated, for she was sure that we were tired. Just then John, the cook, a boy some sixteen years of age, and blacker than any crow, came running in, looked steadily in our faces, then turning round, without saying as much as "how d'ye do," ran back to the kitchen, laughing loudly, as if our coming was a great joke indeed.

Much wearied with our walk, as soon as it was dark, Harry and I wrapped our blankets round us, and laid down upon the cabin floor. My thoughts, as usual, wandered back to my wife and children. The consciousness of my real situation; the hopelessness of any effort to escape through the wide forests of Avoyelles, pressed heavily upon me, yet my heart was at home in Saratoga.

I was awakened early in the morning by the voice of Master Ford, calling Rose. She hastened into the house to dress the children, Sally to the field to milk the cows, while John was busy in the kitchen preparing breakfast. In the meantime Harry and I were strolling about the yard, looking at our new quarters. Just after breakfast a colored man, driving three yoke of oxen, attached to a wagon load of lumber, drove into the opening. He was a slave of Ford's, named Walton, the husband of Rose. By the way, Rose was a native of Washington, and had been brought from thence five years before. She had never seen Eliza, but she had heard of Berry, and they knew the same streets, and the same people, either personally, or by reputation. They became fast friends immediately, and talked a great deal together of old times, and of friends they had left behind.

Ford was at that time a wealthy man. Besides his seat in the Pine Woods, he owned a large lumbering establishment on Indian Creek, four miles distant, and also, in his wife's right, an extensive plantation and many slaves on Bayou Bœuf.

Walton had come with his load of lumber from the mills on Indian Creek. Ford directed us to return with him, saying he would follow us as soon as possible. Before leaving, Mistress Ford called me into the store-room, and handed me, as it is there termed, a tin bucket of molasses for Harry and myself.

Eliza was still ringing her hands and deploring the loss of her children. Ford tried as much as possible to console her—told her she need not work very hard; that she might remain with Rose, and assist the madam in the house affairs.

Riding with Walton in the wagon, Harry and I became quite well acquainted with him long before reaching Indian Creek. He was a "born thrall" of Ford's, and spoke kindly and affectionately of him, as a child would speak of his own father. In answer to his inquiries from whence I came, I told him from Washington. Of that city, he had heard much from his wife, Rose, and all the way plied me with many extravagant and absurd questions.

On reaching the mills at Indian Creek, we found two more of Ford's slaves, Sam and Antony. Sam, also, was a Washingtonian, having been brought out in the same gang with Rose. He had worked on a farm near Georgetown. Antony was a blacksmith, from Kentucky, who had been in his present master's service about ten years. Sam knew Burch, and when informed that he was the trader who had sent me on from Washington, it was remarkable how well we agreed upon the subject of his superlative rascality. He had forwarded Sam, also.

On Ford's arrival at the mill, we were employed in piling lumber, and chopping logs, which occupation we continued during the remainder of the summer.

We usually spent our Sabbaths at the opening, on which days our master would gather all his slaves about him, and read and expound the Scriptures. He sought to inculcate in our minds feelings of kindness towards each other, of dependence upon God—setting forth the rewards promised unto those who lead an upright and prayerful life. Seated in the doorway of his house, surrounded by his man-servants and his maid-servants, who looked earnestly into the good man's face, he spoke of the loving kindness of the Creator, and of the life that is to come. Often did the voice of prayer ascend from his lips to heaven, the only sound that broke the solitude of the place.

In the course of the summer Sam became deeply convicted, his mind dwelling intensely on the subject of religion. His mistress gave him a Bible, which he carried with him to his work. Whatever leisure time was allowed him, he spent in perusing it, though it was only with great difficulty that he could master any part of it. I often read to him, a favor which he well repaid me by many expressions of gratitude. Sam's piety was frequently observed by white men who came to the mill, and the remark it most generally provoked was, that a man like Ford, who allowed his slaves to have Bibles, was "not fit to own a nigger."

He, however, lost nothing by his kindness. It is a fact I have more than once observed, that those who treated their slaves most leniently, were rewarded by the greatest amount of labor. I know it from my own experience. It was a source of pleasure to surprise Master Ford with a greater day's work than was required, while, under subsequent masters, there was no prompter to extra effort but the overseer's lash.

It was the desire of Ford's approving voice that suggested to me an idea that resulted to his profit. The lumber we were manufacturing was contracted to be delivered at Lamourie. It had hitherto been transported by land, and was an important item of expense. Indian Creek, upon which the mills were situated, was a narrow but deep stream emptying into Bayou Bœuf. In some places it was not more than twelve feet wide, and much obstructed with trunks of trees. Bayou Bœuf was connected with Bayou Lamourie. I ascertained the distance from the mills to the point on the latter bayou, where our lumber was to be delivered, was but a few miles less by land than by water. Provided the creek could be made navigable for rafts, it occurred to me that the expense of transportation would be materially diminished.

Adam Taydem, a little white man, who had been a soldier in Florida, and had strolled into that distant region, was foreman and superintendent of the mills. He scouted the idea; but Ford, when I laid it before him, received it favorably, and permitted me to try the experiment.

Having removed the obstructions, I made up a narrow raft, consisting of twelve cribs. At this business I think I was quite skillful, not having forgotten my experience years before on the Champlain canal. I labored hard, being extremely anxious to succeed, both from a desire to please my master, and to show Adam Taydem that my scheme was not such a visionary one as he incessantly pronounced it. One hand could manage three cribs. I took charge of the forward three, and commenced poling down the creek. In due time we entered the first bayou, and finally reached our destination in a shorter period of time than I had anticipated.

The arrival of the raft at Lamourie created a sensation, while Mr. Ford loaded me with commendations. On all sides I heard Ford's Platt pronounced the "smartest nigger in the Pine Woods"—in fact I was the Fulton of Indian Creek. I was not insensible to the praise bestowed upon me, and enjoyed, especially, my triumph over Taydem, whose half-malicious ridicule had stung my pride. From this time the entire control of bringing the lumber to Lamourie was placed in my hands until the contract was fulfilled.

# CHAPTER VII

Indian Creek, in its whole length, flows through a magnificent forest. There dwells on its shore a tribe of Indians, a remnant of the Chickasaws or Chickopees, if I remember rightly. They live in simple huts, ten or twelve feet square, constructed of pine poles and covered with bark. They subsist principally on the flesh of the deer, the coon, and opossum, all of which are plenty in these woods. Sometimes they exchange venison for a little corn and whisky with the planters on the bayous. Their usual dress is buckskin breeches and calico hunting shirts of fantastic colors, buttoned from belt to chin. They wear brass rings on their wrists, and in their ears and noses. The dress of the squaws is very similar. They are fond of dogs and horses—owning many of the latter, of a small, tough breed—and are skillful riders. Their bridles, girths and saddles were made of raw skins of animals; their stirrups of a certain kind of wood. Mounted astride their ponies, men and women, I have seen them dash out into the woods at the utmost of their speed, following narrow winding paths, and dodging trees, in a manner that eclipsed the most miraculous feats of civilized equestrianism. Circling away in various directions, the forest echoing and re-echoing with their whoops, they would presently return at the same dashing, headlong speed with which they started. Their village was on Indian Creek, known as Indian Castle, but their range extended to the Sabine River. Occasionally a tribe from Texas would come over on a visit, and then there was indeed a carnival in the "Great Pine Woods." Chief of the tribe was Cascalla; second in rank, John Baltese, his son-in-law; with both of whom, as with many others of the tribe, I became acquainted during my frequent voyages down the creek with rafts. Sam and myself would often visit them when the day's task was done. They were obedient to the chief; the word of Cascalla was their law. They were a rude but harmless people, and enjoyed their wild mode of life. They had little fancy for the open country, the cleared lands on the shores of the bayous, but preferred to hide themselves within the shadows of the forest. They worshiped the Great Spirit, loved whisky, and were happy.

On one occasion I was present at a dance, when a roving herd from Texas had encamped in their village. The entire carcass of a deer was roasting before a large fire, which threw its light a long distance among the trees under which they were assembled. When they had formed in a ring, men and squaws alternately, a sort of Indian fiddle set up an indescribable tune. It was a continuous, melancholy kind of wavy sound, with the slightest possible variation. At the first note, if indeed there was more than one note in the whole tune, they circled around, trotting after each other, and giving utterance to a guttural, sing-song noise, equally as nondescript as the music of the fiddle. At the end of the third circuit, they would stop suddenly, whoop as if their lungs would crack, then break from the ring, forming in couples, man and squaw, each jumping backwards as far as possible from the other, then forwards—which graceful feat having been twice or thrice accomplished, they would form in a ring, and go trotting round again. The best dancer appeared to be considered the one who could whoop the loudest, jump the farthest, and utter the most excruciating noise. At intervals, one or more would leave the dancing circle, and going to the fire, cut from the roasting carcass a slice of venison.

In a hole, shaped like a mortar, cut in the trunk of a fallen tree, they pounded corn with a wooden pestle, and of the meal made cake. Alternately they danced and ate. Thus were the visitors from Texas entertained by the dusky sons and daughters of the Chicopees, and such is a description, as I saw it, of an Indian ball in the Pine Woods of Avoyelles.

In the autumn, I left the mills, and was employed at the opening. One day the mistress was urging Ford to procure a loom, in order that Sally might commence weaving cloth for the winter garments of the slaves. He could not imagine where one was to be found, when I suggested that the easiest way to get one would be to make it, informing him at the same time, that I was a sort of "Jack at all trades," and would attempt it, with his permission. It was granted very readily, and I was allowed to go to a neighboring planter's to inspect one before commencing the undertaking. At length it was finishedand pronounced by Sally to be perfect. She could easily weave her task of fourteen yards, milk the cows, and have leisure time besides each day. It worked so well, I was continued in the employment of making looms, which were taken down to the plantation on the bayou.

At this time one John M. Tibeats, a carpenter, came to the opening to do some work on master's house. I was directed to quit the looms and assist him. For two weeks I was in his company, planning and matching boards for ceiling, a plastered room being a rare thing in the parish of Avoyelles.

John M. Tibeats was the opposite of Ford in all respects. He was a small, crabbed, quick-tempered, spiteful man. He had no fixed residence that I ever heard of, but passed from one plantation to another, wherever he could find employment. He was without standing in the community, not esteemed by white men, nor even respected by slaves. He was ignorant, withal, and of a revengeful disposition. He left the parish long before I did, and I know not whether he is at present alive or dead. Certain it is, it was a most unlucky day for me that brought us together. During my residence with Master Ford I had seen only the bright side of slavery. His was no heavy hand crushing us to the earth. *He* pointed upwards, and with benign and cheering words addressed us as his fellow-mortals, accountable, like himself, to the Maker of us all. I think of him with affection, and had my family been with me, could have borne his gentle servitude, without murmuring, all my days. But clouds were gathering in the horizon—forerunners of a pitiless storm that was soon to break over me. I was doomed to endure such bitter trials as the poor slave only knows, and to lead no more the comparatively happy life which I had led in the "Great Pine Woods."

# CHAPTER VIII

*Ford's Embarrassments—The Sale To Tibeats—The Chattel Mortgage—Mistress Ford's Plantation On Bayou Bœuf—Description Of The Latter—Ford's Brother-In-Law, Peter Tanner—Meeting With Eliza—She Still Mourns For Her Children—Ford's Overseer, Chapin—Tibeat's Abuse—The Keg Of Nails—The First Fight With Tibeats—His Discomfiture And Castigation—The Attempt To Hang Me—Chapin's Interference And Speech—Unhappy Reflections—Abrupt Departure Of Tibeats, Cook And Ramsay—Lawson And The Brown Mule—Message To The Pine Woods.*

William Ford unfortunately became embarrassed in his pecuniary affairs. A heavy judgment was rendered against him in consequence of his having become security for his brother, Franklin Ford, residing on Red River, above Alexandria, and who had failed to meet his liabilities. He was also indebted to John M. Tibeats to a considerable amount in consideration of his services in building the mills on Indian Creek, and also a weaving-house, corn-mill and other erections on the plantation at Bayou Bœuf, not yet completed. It was therefore necessary, in order to meet these demands, to dispose of eighteen slaves, myself among the number. Seventeen of them, including Sam and Harry, were purchased by Peter Compton, a planter also residing on Red River.

I was sold to Tibeats, in consequence, undoubtedly, of my slight skill as a carpenter. This was in the winter of 1842. The deed of myself from Freeman to Ford, as I ascertained from the public records in New-Orleans on my return, was dated June 23d, 1841. At the time of my sale to Tibeats, the price agreed to be given for me being more than the debt, Ford took a chattel mortgage of four hundred dollars. I am indebted for my life, as will hereafter be seen, to that mortgage.

I bade farewell to my good friends at the opening, and departed with my new master Tibeats. We went down to the plantation on Bayou Bœuf, distant twenty-seven miles from the Pine Woods, to complete the unfinished contract. Bayou Bœuf is a sluggish, winding stream—one of those stagnant bodies of water common in that region, setting back from Red River. It stretches from a point not far from Alexandria, in a south-easterly direction, and following its tortuous course, is more than fifty miles in length. Large cotton and sugar plantations line each shore, extending back to the borders of interminable swamps. It is alive with alligators, rendering it unsafe for swine, or unthinking slave children to stroll along its banks. Upon a bend in this bayou, a short distance from

Cheneyville, was situated the plantation of Madam Ford—her brother, Peter Tanner, a great landholder, living on the opposite side.

On my arrival at Bayou Bœuf, I had the pleasure of meeting Eliza, whom I had not seen for several months. She had not pleased Mrs. Ford, being more occupied in brooding over her sorrows than in attending to her business, and had, in consequence, been sent down to work in the field on the plantation. She had grown feeble and emaciated, and was still mourning for her children. She asked me if I had forgotten them, and a great many times inquired if I still remembered how handsome little Emily was—how much Randall loved her—and wondered if they were living still, and where the darlings could then be. She had sunk beneath the weight of an excessive grief. Her drooping form and hollow cheeks too plainly indicated that she had well nigh reached the end of her weary road.

Ford's overseer on this plantation, and who had the exclusive charge of it, was a Mr. Chapin, a kindly-disposed man, and a native of Pennsylvania. In common with others, he held Tibeats in light estimation, which fact, in connection with the four hundred dollar mortgage, was fortunate for me.

I was now compelled to labor very hard. From earliest dawn until late at night, I was not allowed to be a moment idle. Notwithstanding which, Tibeats was never satisfied. He was continually cursing and complaining. He never spoke to me a kind word. I was his faithful slave, and earned him large wages every day, and yet I went to my cabin nightly, loaded with abuse and stinging epithets.

We had completed the corn mill, the kitchen, and so forth, and were at work upon the weaving-house, when I was guilty of an act, in that State punishable with death. It was my first fight with Tibeats. The weaving-house we were erecting stood in the orchard a few rods from the residence of Chapin, or the "great house," as it was called. One night, having worked until it was too dark to see, I was ordered by Tibeats to rise very early in the morning, procure a keg of nails from Chapin, and commence putting on the clapboards. I retired to the cabin extremely tired, and having cooked a supper of bacon and corn cake, and conversed a while with Eliza, who occupied the same cabin, as also did Lawson and his wife Mary, and a slave named Bristol, laid down upon the ground floor, little dreaming of the sufferings that awaited me on the morrow. Before daylight I was on the piazza of the "great house," awaiting the appearance of overseer Chapin. To have aroused him from his slumbers and stated my errand, would have been an unpardonable boldness. At length he came out. Taking off my hat, I informed him Master Tibeats had directed me to call upon him for a keg of nails. Going into the store-room, he rolled it out, at the same time saying, if Tibeats preferred a different size, he would endeavor to furnish them, but that I might use those until further directed. Then mounting his horse, which stood saddled and bridled at the door, he rode away into the field, whither the slaves had preceded him, while I took the keg on my shoulder, and proceeding to the weaving-house, broke in the head, and commenced nailing on the clapboards.

As the day began to open, Tibeats came out of the house to where I was, hard at work. He seemed to be that morning even more morose and disagreeable than usual. He was my master, entitled by law to my flesh and blood, and to exercise over me such tyrannical control as his mean nature prompted; but there was no law that could prevent my looking upon him with intense contempt. I despised both his disposition and his intellect. I had just come round to the keg for a further supply of nails, as he reached the weaving-house.

"I thought I told you to commence putting on weather-boards this morning," he remarked.

"Yes, master, and I am about it," I replied.

"Where?" he demanded.

"On the other side," was my answer.

He walked round to the other side, examined my work for a while, muttering to himself in a fault-finding tone.

"Didn't I tell you last night to get a keg of nails of Chapin?" he broke forth again.

"Yes, master, and so I did; and overseer said he would get another size for you, if you wanted them, when he came back from the field."

Tibeats walked to the keg, looked a moment at the contents, then kicked it violently. Coming towards me in a great passion, he exclaimed,

"G—d d—n you! I thought you *knowed* something."

I made answer: "I tried to do as you told me, master. I didn't mean anything wrong. Overseer said—" But he interrupted me with such a flood of curses that I was unable to finish the sentence. At length he ran towards the house, and going to the piazza, took down one of the overseer's whips. The whip had a short wooden stock, braided over with leather, and was loaded at the butt. The lash was three feet long, or thereabouts, and made of raw-hide strands.

At first I was somewhat frightened, and my impulse was to run. There was no one about except Rachel, the cook, and Chapin's wife, and neither of them were to be seen. The rest were in the field. I knew he intended to whip me, and it was the first time any one had attempted it since my arrival at Avoyelles. I felt, moreover, that I had been faithful—that I was guilty of no wrong whatever, and deserved commendation rather than punishment. My fear changed to anger, and before he reached me I had made up my mind fully not to be whipped, let the result be life or death.

Winding the lash around his hand, and taking hold of the small end of the stock, he walked up to me, and with a malignant look, ordered me to strip.

"Master Tibeats," said I, looking him boldly in the face, "I will *not*." I was about to say something further in justification, but with concentrated vengeance, he sprang upon me, seizing me by the throat with one hand, raising the whip with the other, in the act of striking. Before the blow descended, however, I had caught him by the collar of the coat, and drawn him closely to me. Reaching down, I seized him by the ankle, and pushing him back with the other hand, he fell over on the ground. Putting one arm around his leg, and holding it to my breast, so that his head and shoulders only touched the ground, I placed my foot upon his neck. He was completely in my power. My blood was up. It seemed to course through my veins like fire. In the frenzy of my madness I snatched the whip from his hand. He struggled with all his power; swore that I should not live to see another day; and that he would tear out my heart. But his struggles and his threats were alike in vain. I cannot tell how many times I struck him. Blow after blow fell fast and heavy upon his wriggling form. At length he screamed—cried murder—and at last the blasphemous tyrant called on God for mercy. But he who had never shown mercy did not receive it. The stiff stock of the whip warped round his cringing body until my right arm ached.

Until this time I had been too busy to look about me. Desisting for a moment, I saw Mrs. Chapin looking from the window, and Rachel standing in the kitchen door. Their attitudes expressed the utmost excitement and alarm. His screams had been heard in the field. Chapin was coming as fast as he could ride. I struck him a blow or two more, then pushed him from me with such a well-directed kick that he went rolling over on the ground.

Rising to his feet, and brushing the dirt from his hair, he stood looking at me, pale with rage. We gazed at each other in silence. Not a word was uttered until Chapin galloped up to us.

"What is the matter?" he cried out.

"Master Tibeats wants to whip me for using the nails you gave me," I replied.

"What is the matter with the nails?" he inquired, turning to Tibeats.

Tibeats answered to the effect that they were too large, paying little heed, however, to Chapin's question, but still keeping his snakish eyes fastened maliciously on me.

"I am overseer here," Chapin began. "I told Platt to take them and use them, and if they were not of the proper size I would get others on returning from the field. It is not his fault. Besides, I shall furnish such nails as I please. I hope you will understand *that*, Mr. Tibeats."

Tibeats made no reply, but, grinding his teeth and shaking his fist, swore he would have satisfaction, and that it was not half over yet. Thereupon he walked away, followed by the overseer, and entered the house, the latter talking to him all the while in a suppressed tone, and with earnest gestures.

I remained where I was, doubting whether it was better to fly or abide the result, whatever it might be. Presently Tibeats came out of the house, and, saddling his horse, the only property he possessed besides myself, departed on the road to Cheneyville.

When he was gone, Chapin came out, visibly excited, telling me not to stir, not to attempt to leave the plantation on any account whatever. He then went to the kitchen, and calling Rachel out, conversed with her some time. Coming back, he again charged me with great earnestness not to run, saying my master was a rascal; that he had left on no good errand, and that there might be trouble before night. But at all events, he insisted upon it, I must not stir.

As I stood there, feelings of unutterable agony overwhelmed me. I was conscious that I had subjected myself to unimaginable punishment. The reaction that followed my extreme ebullition of anger produced the most painful sensations of regret. An unfriended, helpless slave—what could I *do*, what could I *say*, to justify, in the remotest manner, the heinous act I had committed, of resenting a *white* man's contumely and abuse. I tried to pray—I tried to beseech my Heavenly Father to sustain me in my sore extremity, but emotion choked my utterance, and I could only bow my head upon my hands and weep. For at least an hour I remained in this situation, finding relief only in tears, when, looking up, I beheld Tibeats, accompanied by two horsemen, coming down the bayou. They rode into the yard, jumped from their horses, and approached me with large whips, one of them also carrying a coil of rope.

"Cross your hands," commanded Tibeats, with the addition of such a shuddering expression of blasphemy as is not decorous to repeat.

"You need not bind me, Master Tibeats, I am ready to go with you anywhere," said I.

One of his companions then stepped forward, swearing if I made the least resistance he would break my head—he would tear me limb from limb—he would cut my black throat—and giving wide scope to other similar expressions. Perceiving any importunity altogether vain, I crossed my hands, submitting humbly to whatever disposition they might please to make of me. Thereupon Tibeats tied my wrists, drawing the rope around them with his utmost strength. Then he bound my ankles in the same manner. In the meantime the other two had slipped a cord within my elbows, running it across my back, and tying it firmly. It was utterly impossible to move hand or foot. With a remaining piece of rope Tibeats made an awkward noose, and placed it about my neck.

"Now, then," inquired one of Tibeats' companions, "where shall we hang the nigger?"

One proposed such a limb, extending from the body of a peach tree, near the spot where we were standing. His comrade objected to it, alleging it would break, and proposed another. Finally they fixed upon the latter.

During this conversation, and all the time they were binding me, I uttered not a word. Overseer Chapin, during the progress of the scene, was walking hastily back and forth on the piazza. Rachel was crying by the kitchen door, and Mrs. Chapin was stilllooking from the window. Hope died within my heart. Surely my time had come. I should never behold the light of another day—never behold the faces of my children—the sweet anticipation I had cherished with such fondness. I should that hour struggle through the fearful agonies of death! None would mourn for me—none revenge me. Soon my form would be mouldering in that distant soil, or, perhaps, be cast to the slimy reptiles that filled the stagnant waters of the bayou! Tears flowed down my cheeks, but they only afforded a subject of insulting comment for my executioners.

At length, as they were dragging me towards the tree, Chapin, who had momentarily disappeared from the piazza, came out of the house and walked towards us. He had a pistol in each hand, and as near as I can now recall to mind, spoke in a firm, determined manner, as follows:

"Gentlemen, I have a few words to say. You had better listen to them. Whoever moves that slave another foot from where he stands is a dead man. In the first place, he does not deserve this treatment. It is a shame to murder him in this manner. I never knew a more faithful boy than Platt. You, Tibeats, are in the fault yourself. You are pretty much of a scoundrel, and I know it, and you richly deserve the flogging you have received. In the next place, I have been overseer on this plantation seven years, and, in the absence of William Ford, am master here. My duty is to protect his interests, and that duty I shall perform. You are not responsible—you are a worthless fellow. Ford holds a mortgage on Platt of four hundred dollars. If you hang him he loses his debt. Until that is canceled you have no right to take his life. You have no right to take it any way. There is a law for the slave as well as for the white man. You are no better than a murderer.

"As for you," addressing Cook and Ramsay, a couple of overseers from neighboring plantations, "as for you—begone! If you have any regard for your own safety, I say, begone."

Cook and Ramsay, without a further word, mounted their horses and rode away. Tibeats, in a few minutes, evidently in fear, and overawed by the decided tone of Chapin, sneaked off like a coward, as he was, and mounting his horse, followed his companions.

I remained standing where I was, still bound, with the rope around my neck. As soon as they were gone, Chapin called Rachel, ordering her to run to the field, and tell Lawson to hurry to the house without delay, and bring the brown mule with him, an animal much prized for its unusual fleetness. Presently the boy appeared.

"Lawson," said Chapin, "you must go to the Pine Woods. Tell your master Ford to come here at once—that he must not delay a single moment. Tell him they are trying to murder Platt. Now hurry, boy. Be at the Pine Woods by noon if you kill the mule."

Chapin stepped into the house and wrote a pass. When he returned, Lawson was at the door, mounted on his mule. Receiving the pass, he plied the whip right smartly to the beast, dashed out of the yard, and turning up the bayou on a hard gallop, in less time than it has taken me to describe the scene, was out of sight.

# CHAPTER IX

*The Hot Sun—Yet Bound—The Cords Sink Into My Flesh—Chapin's Uneasiness—Speculation—Rachel, And Her Cup Of Water—Suffering Increases—The Happiness Of Slavery—Arrival Of Ford—He Cuts The Cords Which Bind Me, And Takes The Rope From My Neck—Misery—The Gathering Of The Slaves In Eliza's Cabin—Their Kindness—Rachel Repeats The Occurrences Of The Day—Lawson Entertains His Companions With An Account Of His Ride—Chapin's Apprehensions Of Tibeats—Hired To Peter Tanner—Peter Expounds The Scriptures—Description Of The Stocks.*

As the sun approached the meridian that day it became insufferably warm. Its hot rays scorched the ground. The earth almost blistered the foot that stood upon it. I was without coat or hat, standing bare-headed, exposed to its burning blaze. Great drops of perspiration rolled down my face, drenching the scanty apparel wherewith I was clothed. Over the fence, a very little way off, the peach trees cast their cool, delicious shadows on the grass. I would gladly have given a long year of service to have been enabled to exchange the heated oven, as it were, wherein I stood, for a seat beneath their branches. But I was yet bound, the rope still dangling from my neck, and standing in the same tracks where Tibeats and his comrades left me. I could not move an inch, so firmly had I been bound. To have been enabled to lean against the weaving house would have been a luxury indeed. But it was far beyond my reach, though distant less than twenty feet. I wanted to lie down, but knew I could not rise again. The ground was so parched and boiling hot I was aware it would but add to the discomfort of my situation. If I could have only moved my position, however slightly, it would have been relief unspeakable. But the hot rays of a southern sun, beating all the long summer day on my bare head, produced not half the suffering I experienced from my aching limbs. My wrists and ankles, and the cords of my legs and arms began to swell, burying the rope that bound them into the swollen flesh.

All day Chapin walked back and forth upon the stoop, but not once approached me. He appeared to be in a state of great uneasiness, looking first towards me, and then up the road, as if expecting some arrival every moment. He did not go to the field, as was his custom. It was evident from his manner that he supposed Tibeats would return with more and better armed assistance, perhaps, to renew the quarrel, and it was equally evident he had prepared his mind to defend my life at whatever hazard. Why he did not relieve me—why he suffered me to remain in agony the whole weary day, I never knew. It was not for want of sympathy, I am certain. Perhaps he wished Ford to see the rope about my neck, and the brutal manner in which I had been bound; perhaps his interference with another's property in which he had no legal interest might have been a trespass, which would have subjected him to the penalty of the law. Why Tibeats was all day absent was another mystery I never could divine. He knew well enough that Chapin would not harm him unless he persisted in his design against me. Lawson told me afterwards, that, as he passed the plantation of John David Cheney, he saw the three, and that they turned and looked after him as he flew by. I think his supposition was, that Lawson had been sent out by Overseer Chapin to arouse the neighboring planters, and to call on them to come to his assistance. He, therefore, undoubtedly, acted on the principle, that "discretion is the better part of valor," and kept away.

But whatever motive may have governed the cowardly and malignant tyrant, it is of no importance. There I still stood in the noon-tide sun, groaning with pain. From long before daylight I had not eaten a morsel. I was growing faint from pain, and thirst, and hunger. Once only, in the very hottest portion of the day, Rachel, half fearful she was acting contrary to the overseer's wishes, ventured to me, and held a cup of water to my lips. The humble creature never knew, nor could she comprehend if she had heard them, the blessings I invoked upon her, for that balmy draught. She could only say, "Oh, Platt, how I do pity you," and then hastened back to her labors in the kitchen.

Never did the sun move so slowly through the heavens—never did it shower down such fervent and fiery rays, as it did that day. At least, so it appeared to me. What my meditations were—the innumerable thoughts that thronged through my distracted brain—I will not attempt to give expression to. Suffice it to say, during the whole long day I came not to the conclusion, even once, that the southern slave, fed, clothed, whipped and protected by his master, is happier than the free colored citizen of the North. To that conclusion I have never since arrived. There are many, however, even in the Northern States, benevolent and well-disposed men, who will pronounce my opinion erroneous, and gravely proceed to substantiate the assertion with an argument. Alas! they have never drunk, as I have, from the bitter cup of slavery. Just at sunset my heart leaped with unbounded joy, as Ford came riding into the yard, his horse covered with foam. Chapin met him at the door, and after conversing a short time, he walked directly to me.

"Poor Platt, you are in a bad state," was the only expression that escaped his lips.

"Thank God!" said I, "thank God, Master Ford, that you have come at last."

Drawing a knife from his pocket, he indignantly cut the cord from my wrists, arms, and ankles, and slipped the noose from my neck. I attempted to walk, but staggered like a drunken man, and fell partially to the ground.

Ford returned immediately to the house, leaving me alone again. As he reached the piazza, Tibeats and his two friends rode up. A long dialogue followed. I could hear the sound of their voices, the mild tones of Ford mingling with the angry accents of Tibeats, but was unable to distinguish what was said. Finally the three departed again, apparently not well pleased.

I endeavored to raise the hammer, thinking to show Ford how willing I was to work, by proceeding with my labors on the weaving house, but it fell from my nerveless hand. At dark I crawled into the cabin, and laid down. I was in great misery—all sore and swollen—the slightest movement producing excruciating suffering. Soon the hands came in from the field.

Rachel, when she went after Lawson, had told them what had happened. Eliza and Mary broiled me a piece of bacon, but my appetite was gone. Then they scorched some corn meal and made coffee. It was all that I could take. Eliza consoled me and was very kind. It was not long before the cabin was full of slaves. They gathered round me, asking many questions about the difficulty with Tibeats in the morning—and the particulars of all the occurrences of the day. Then Rachel came in, and in her simple language, repeated it over again—dwelling emphatically on the kick that sent Tibeats rolling over on the ground—whereupon there was a general titter throughout the crowd. Then she described how Chapin walked out with his pistols and rescued me, and how Master Ford cut the ropes with his knife, just as if he was mad.

By this time Lawson had returned. He had to regale them with an account of his trip to the Pine Woods—how the brown mule bore him faster than a "streak o'lightnin"—how he astonished everybody as he flew along—how Master Ford started right away—how he said Platt was a good nigger, and they shouldn't kill him, concluding with pretty strong intimations that there was not another human being in the wide world, who could have created such a universal sensation on the road, or performed such a marvelous John Gilpin feat, as he had done that day on the brown mule.

The kind creatures loaded me with the expression of their sympathy—saying, Tibeats was a hard, cruel man, and hoping "Massa Ford" would get me back again. In this manner they passed the time, discussing, chatting, talking over and over again the exciting affair, until suddenly Chapin presented himself at the cabin door and called me.

"Platt," said he, "you will sleep on the floor in the great house to-night; bring your blanket with you."

I arose as quickly as I was able, took my blanket in my hand, and followed him. On the way he informed me that he should not wonder if Tibeats was back again before morning—that he intended to kill me—and that he did not mean he should do it without witnesses. Had he stabbed me to the heart in the presence of a hundred slaves, not one of them, by the laws of Louisiana, could have given evidence against him. I laid down on the floor in the "great house"—the first and the last time such a sumptuous resting place was granted me during my twelve years of bondage—and tried to sleep. Near midnight the dog began to bark. Chapin arose, looked from the window, but could discover nothing. At length the dog was quiet. As he returned to his room, he said,

"I believe, Platt, that scoundrel is skulking about the premises somewhere. If the dog barks again, and I am sleeping, wake me."

I promised to do so. After the lapse of an hour or more, the dog re-commenced his clamor, running towards the gate, then back again, all the while barking furiously.

Chapin was out of bed without waiting to be called. On this occasion, he stepped forth upon the piazza, and remained standing there a considerable length of time. Nothing, however, was to be seen, and the dog returned to his kennel. We were not disturbed again during the night. The excessive pain that I suffered, and the dread of some impending danger, prevented any rest whatever. Whether or not Tibeats did actually return to the plantation that night, seeking an opportunity to wreak his vengeance upon me, is a secret known only to himself, perhaps. I thought then, however, and have the strong impression still, that he was there. At all events, he had the disposition of an assassin—cowering before a brave man's words, but ready to strike his helpless or unsuspecting victim in the back, as I had reason afterwards to know.

At daylight in the morning, I arose, sore and weary, having rested little. Nevertheless, after partaking breakfast, which Mary and Eliza had prepared for me in the cabin, I proceeded to the weaving-house and commenced the labors of another day. It was Chapin's practice, as it is the practice of overseers generally, immediately on arising, to bestride his horse, always saddled and bridled and ready for him—the particular business of some slave—and ride into the field. This morning, on the contrary, he came to the weaving house, asking if I had seen anything of Tibeats yet. Replying in the negative, he remarked there was something not right about the fellow—there was bad blood in him—that I must keep a sharp watch of him, or he would do me wrong some day when I least expected it.

While he was yet speaking, Tibeats rode in, hitched his horse, and entered the house. I had little fear of him while Ford and Chapin were at hand, but they could not be near me always.

Oh! how heavily the weight of slavery pressed upon me then. I must toil day after day, endure abuse and taunts and scoffs, sleep on the hard ground, live on the coarsest fare, and not only this, but live the slave of a blood-seeking wretch, of whom I must stand henceforth in continued fear and dread. Why had I not died in my young years—before God had given me children to love and live for? What unhappiness and suffering and sorrow it would have prevented. I sighed for liberty; but the bondman's chain was round me, and could not be shaken off. I could only gaze wistfully towards the North, and think of the thousands of miles that stretched between me and the soil of freedom, over which a *black* freeman may not pass.

Tibeats, in the course of half an hour, walked over to the weaving-house, looked at me sharply, then returned without saying anything. Most of the forenoon he sat on the piazza, reading a newspaper and conversing with Ford. After dinner, the latter left for the Pine Woods, and it was indeed with regret that I beheld him depart from the plantation.

Once more during the day Tibeats came to me, gave me some order, and returned.

During the week the weaving-house was completed—Tibeats in the meantime making no allusion whatever to the difficulty—when I was informed he had hired me to Peter Tanner, to work under another carpenter by the name of Myers. This announcement was received with gratification, as any place was desirable that would relieve me of his hateful presence.

Peter Tanner, as the reader has already been informed, lived on the opposite shore, and was the brother of Mistress Ford. He is one of the most extensive planters on Bayou Bœuf, and owns a large number of slaves.

Over I went to Tanner's, joyfully enough. He had heard of my late difficulties—in fact, I ascertained the flogging of Tibeats was soon blazoned far and wide. This affair, together with my rafting experiment, had rendered me somewhat notorious. More than once I heard it said that Platt Ford, now Platt Tibeats—a slave's name changes with his change of master—was "a devil of a nigger." But I was destined to make a still further noise, as will presently be seen, throughout the little world of Bayou Bœuf.

Peter Tanner endeavored to impress upon me the idea that he was quite severe, though I could perceive there was a vein of good humor in the old fellow, after all.

"You're the nigger," he said to me on my arrival—"You're the nigger that flogged your master, eh? You're the nigger that kicks, and holds carpenter Tibeats by the leg, and wallops him, are ye? I'd like to see you hold me by the leg—I should. You're a 'portant character—you're a great nigger—very remarkable nigger, ain't ye? *I'd* lash you—*I'd* take the tantrums out of ye. Jest take hold of my leg, if you please. None of your pranks here, my boy, remember *that*. Now go to work, you *kickin'* rascal," concluded Peter Tanner, unable to suppress a half-comical grin at his own wit and sarcasm.

After listening to this salutation, I was taken charge of by Myers, and labored under his direction for a month, to his and my own satisfaction.

Like William Ford, his brother-in-law, Tanner was in the habit of reading the Bible to his slaves on the Sabbath, but in a somewhat different spirit. He was an impressive commentator on the New Testament. The first Sunday after my coming to the plantation, he called them together, and began to read the twelfth chapter of Luke. When he came to the 47th verse, he looked deliberately around him, and continued—"And that servant which knew his lord's *will*,"—here he paused, looking around more deliberately than before, and again proceeded—"which knew his lord's *will*, and *prepared* not himself"—here was another pause—"*prepared* not himself, neither did *according* to his will, shall be beaten with many *stripes*."

"D'ye hear that?" demanded Peter, emphatically. "*Stripes*," he repeated, slowly and distinctly, taking off his spectacles, preparatory to making a few remarks.

"That nigger that don't take care—that don't obey his lord—that's his master—d'ye see?—that *'ere* nigger shall be beaten with many stripes. Now, 'many' signifies a *great* many—forty, a hundred, a hundred and fifty lashes. *That's* Scripter!" and so Peter continued to elucidate the subject for a great length of time, much to the edification of his sable audience.

At the conclusion of the exercises, calling up three of his slaves, Warner, Will and Major, he cried out to me—

"Here, Platt, you held Tibeats by the legs; now I'll see if you can hold these rascals in the same way, till I get back from meetin'."

Thereupon he ordered them to the stocks—a common thing on plantations in the Red River country. The stocks are formed of two planks, the lower one made fast at the ends to two short posts, driven firmly into the ground. At regular distances half circles are cut in the upper edge. The other plank is fastened to one of the posts by a hinge, so that it can be opened or shut down, in the same manner as the blade of a pocket-knife is shut or opened. In the lower edge of the upper plank corresponding half circles are also cut, so that when they close, a row of holes is formed large enough to admit a negro's leg above the ankle, but not large enough to enable him to draw out his foot. The other end of the upper plank, opposite the hinge, is fastened to its post by lock and key. The slave is made to sit upon the ground, when the uppermost plank is elevated, his legs, just above the ankles, placed in the sub-half circles, and shutting it down again, and locking it, he is held secure and fast. Very often the neck instead of the ankle is enclosed. In this manner they are held during the operation of whipping.

Warner, Will and Major, according to Tanner's account of them, were melon-stealing, Sabbath-breaking niggers, and not approving of such wickedness, he felt it his duty to put them in the stocks. Handing me the key, himself, Myers, Mistress Tanner and the children entered the carriage and drove away to church at Cheneyville. When they were gone, the boys begged me to let them out. I felt sorry to see them sitting on the hot ground, and remembered my own sufferings in the sun. Upon their promise to return to the stocks at any moment they were required to do so, I consented to release them. Grateful for the lenity shown them, and in order in some measure to repay it, they could do no less, of course, than pilot me to the melon-patch. Shortly before Tanner's return, they were in the stocks again. Finally he drove up, and looking at the boys, said, with a chuckle,—

"Aha! ye havn't been strolling about much to-day, any way. *I'll* teach you what's what. *I'll* tire ye of eating water-melons on the Lord's day, ye Sabbath-breaking niggers."

Peter Tanner prided himself upon his strict religious observances: he was a deacon in the church.

But I have now reached a point in the progress of my narrative, when it becomes necessary to turn away from these light descriptions, to the more grave and weighty matter of the second battle with Master Tibeats, and the flight through the great Pacoudrie Swamp.

# CHAPTER X

*Return To Tibeats—Impossibility Of Pleasing Him—He Attacks Me With A Hatchet—The Struggle Over The Broad Axe—The Temptation To Murder Him—Escape Across The Plantation—Observations From The Fence—Tibeats Approaches, Followed By The Hounds—They Take My Track—Their Loud Yells—They Almost Overtake Me—I Reach The Water—The Hounds Confused—Moccasin Snakes—Alligators—Night In The "Great Pacoudrie Swamp"—The Sounds Of Life—North-West Course—Emerge Into The Pine Woods—The Slave And His Young Master—Arrival At Ford's—Food And Rest.*

At the end of a month, my services being no longer required at Tanner's I was sent over the bayou again to my master, whom I found engaged in building the cotton press. This was situated at some distance from the great house, in a rather retired place. I commenced working once more in company with Tibeats, being entirely alone with him most part of the time. I remembered the words of Chapin, his precautions, his advice to beware, lest in some unsuspecting moment he might injure me. They were always in my mind, so that I lived in a most uneasy state of apprehension and fear. One eye was on my work, the other on my master. I determined to give him no cause of offence, to work still more diligently, if possible, than I had done, to bear whatever abuse he might heap upon me, save bodily injury, humbly and patiently, hoping thereby to soften in some degree his manner towards me, until the blessed time might come when I should be delivered from his clutches.

The third morning after my return, Chapin left the plantation for Cheneyville, to be absent until night. Tibeats, on that morning, was attacked with one of those periodical fits of spleen and ill-humor to which he was frequently subject, rendering him still more disagreeable and venomous than usual.

It was about nine o'clock in the forenoon, when I was busily employed with the jack-plane on one of the sweeps. Tibeats was standing by the work-bench, fitting a handle into the chisel, with which he had been engaged previously in cutting the thread of the screw.

"You are not planing that down enough," said he.

"It is just even with the line," I replied.

"You're a d—d liar," he exclaimed passionately.

"Oh, well, master," I said, mildly, "I will plane it down more if you say so," at the same time proceeding to do as I supposed he desired. Before one shaving had been removed, however, he cried out, saying I had now planed it too deep—it was too small—I had spoiled the sweep entirely. Then followed curses and imprecations. I had endeavored to do exactly as he directed, but nothing would satisfy the unreasonable man. In silence and in dread I stood by the sweep, holding the jack-plane in my hand, not knowing what to do, and not daring to be idle. His anger grew more and more violent, until, finally, with an oath, such a bitter, frightful oath as only Tibeats could utter, he seized a hatchet from the work-bench and darted towards me, swearing he would cut my head open.

It was a moment of life or death. The sharp, bright blade of the hatchet glittered in the sun. In another instant it would be buried in my brain, and yet in that instant—so quick will a man's thoughts come to him in such a fearful strait—I reasoned with myself. If I stood still, my doom was certain; if I fled, ten chances to one the hatchet, flying from his hand with a too-deadly and unerring aim, would strike me in the back. There was but one course to take. Springing towards him with all my power, and meeting him full half-way, before he could bring down the blow, with one hand I caught his uplifted arm, with the other seized him by the throat. We stood looking each other in the eyes. In his I could see murder. I felt as if I had a serpent by the neck, watching the slightest relaxation of my gripe, to coil itself round my body, crushing and stinging it to death. I thought to scream aloud, trusting that some ear might catch the sound—but Chapin was away; the hands were in the field; there was no living soul in sight or hearing.

The good genius, which thus far through life has saved me from the hands of violence, at that moment suggested a lucky thought. With a vigorous and sudden kick, that brought him on one knee, with a groan, I released my hold upon his throat, snatched the hatchet, and cast it beyond reach.

Frantic with rage, maddened beyond control, he seized a white oak stick, five feet long, perhaps, and as large in circumference as his hand could grasp, which was lying on the ground. Again he rushed towards me, and again I met him, seized him about the waist, and being the stronger of the two, bore him to the earth. While in that position I obtained possession of the stick, and rising, cast it from me, also.

He likewise arose and ran for the broad-axe, on the work-bench. Fortunately, there was a heavy plank lying upon its broad blade, in such a manner that he could not extricate it, before I had sprung upon his back. Pressing him down closely and heavily on the plank, so that the axe was held more firmly to its place, I endeavored, but in vain, to break his grasp upon the handle. In that position we remained some minutes.

There have been hours in my unhappy life, many of them, when the contemplation of death as the end of earthly sorrow—of the grave as a resting place for the tired and worn out body—has been pleasant to dwell upon. But such contemplations vanish in the hour of peril. No man, in his full strength, can stand undismayed, in the presence of the "king of terrors." Life is dear to every living thing; the worm that crawls upon the ground will struggle for it. At that moment it was dear to me, enslaved and treated as I was.

Not able to unloose his hand, once more I seized him by the throat, and this time, with a vice-like gripe that soon relaxed his hold. He became pliant and unstrung. His face, that had been white with passion, was now black from suffocation. Those small serpent eyes that spat such venom, were now full of horror—two great white orbs starting from their sockets!

There was "a lurking devil" in my heart that prompted me to kill the human blood-hound on the spot—to retain the grip on his accursed throat till the breath of life was gone! I dared not murder him, and I dared not let him live. If I killed him, my life must pay the forfeit—if he lived, my life only would satisfy his vengeance. A voice within whispered me to fly. To be a wanderer among the swamps, a fugitive and a vagabond on the face of the earth, was preferable to the life that I was leading.

My resolution was soon formed, and swinging him from the work-bench to the ground, I leaped a fence near by, and hurried across the plantation, passing the slaves at work in the cotton field. At the end of a quarter of a mile I reached the wood-pasture, and it was a short time indeed that I had been running it. Climbing on to a high fence, I could see the cotton press, the great house, and the space between. It was a conspicuous position, from whence the whole plantation was in view. I saw Tibeats cross the field towards the house, and enter it—then he came out, carrying his saddle, and presently mounted his horse and galloped away.

I was desolate, but thankful. Thankful that my life was spared,—desolate and discouraged with the prospect before me. What would become of me? Who would befriend me? Whither should I fly? Oh, God! Thou who gavest me life, and implanted in my bosom the love of life—who filled it with emotions such as other men, thy creatures, have, do not forsake me. Have pity on the poor slave—let me not perish. If thou dost not protect me, I am lost—lost! Such supplications, silently and unuttered, ascended from my inmost heart to Heaven. But there was no answering voice—no sweet, low tone, coming down from on high, whispering to my soul, "It is I, be not afraid." I was the forsaken of God, it seemed—the despised and hated of men!

In about three-fourths of an hour several of the slaves shouted and made signs for me to run. Presently, looking up the bayou, I saw Tibeats and two others on horse-back, coming at a fast gait, followed by a troop of dogs. There were as many as eight or ten. Distant as I was, I knew them. They belonged on the adjoining plantation. The dogs used on Bayou Bœuf for hunting slaves are a kind of blood-hound, but a far more savage breed than is found in the Northern States. They will attack a negro, at theirmaster's bidding, and cling to him as the common bull-dog will cling to a four footed animal. Frequently their loud bay is heard in the swamps, and then there is speculation as to what point the runaway will be overhauled—the same as a New-York hunter stops to listen to the hounds coursing along the hillsides, and suggests to his companion that the fox will be taken at such a place. I never knew a slave escaping with his life from Bayou Bœuf. One reason is, they are not allowed to learn the art of swimming, and are incapable of crossing the most inconsiderable stream. In their flight they can go in no direction but a little way without coming to a bayou, when the inevitable alternative is presented, of being drowned or overtaken by the dogs. In youth I had practised in the clear streams that flow through my native district, until I had become an expert swimmer, and felt at home in the watery element.

I stood upon the fence until the dogs had reached the cotton press. In an instant more, their long, savage yells announced they were on my track. Leaping down from my position, I ran towards the swamp. Fear gave me strength, and I exerted it to the utmost. Every few moments I could hear the yelpings of the dogs. They were gaining upon me. Every howl was nearer and nearer. Each moment I expected they would spring upon my back—expected to feel their long teeth sinking into my flesh. There were so many of them, I knew they would tear me to pieces, that they would worry me, at once, to death. I gasped for breath—gasped forth a half-uttered, choking prayer to the Almighty to save me—to give me strength to reach some wide, deep bayou where I could throw them off the track, or sink into its waters. Presently I reached a thick palmetto bottom. As I fled through them they made a loud rustling noise, not loud enough, however, to drown the voices of the dogs.

Continuing my course due south, as nearly as I can judge, I came at length to water just over shoe. The hounds at that moment could not have been five rods behind me. I could hear them crashing and plunging through the palmettoes, their loud, eager yells making the whole swamp clamorous with the sound. Hope revived a little as I reached the water. If it were only deeper, they might lose the scent, and thus disconcerted, afford me the opportunity of evading them. Luckily, it grew deeper the farther I proceeded—now over my ankles—now half-way to my knees—now sinking a moment to my waist, and then emerging presently into more shallow places. The dogs had not gained upon me since I struck the water. Evidently they were confused. Now their savage intonations grew more and more distant, assuring me that I was leaving them. Finally I stopped to listen, but the long howl came booming on the air again, telling me I was not yet safe. From bog to bog, where I had stepped, they could still keep upon the track, though impeded by the water. At length, to my great joy, I came to a wide bayou, and plunging in, had soon stemmed its sluggish current to the other side. There, certainly, the dogs would be confounded—the current carrying down the stream all traces of that slight, mysterious scent, which enables the quick-smelling hound to follow in the track of the fugitive.

After crossing this bayou the water became so deep I could not run. I was now in what I afterwards learned was the "Great Pacoudrie Swamp." It was filled with immense trees—the sycamore, the gum, the cotton wood and cypress, and extends, I am informed, to the shore of the Calcasieu river. For thirty or forty miles it is without inhabitants, save wild beasts—the bear, the wild-cat, the tiger, and great slimy reptiles, that are crawling through it everywhere. Long before I reached the bayou, in fact, from the time I struck the water until I emerged from the swamp on my return, these reptiles surrounded me. I saw hundreds of moccasin snakes. Every log and bog—every trunk of a fallen tree, over which I was compelled to step or climb, was alive with them. They crawled away at my approach, but sometimes in my haste, I almost placed my hand or foot upon them. They are poisonous serpents—their bite more fatal than the rattlesnake's. Besides, I had lost one shoe, the sole having come entirely off, leaving the upper only dangling to my ankle.

I saw also many alligators, great and small, lying in the water, or on pieces of floodwood. The noise I made usually startled them, when they moved off and plunged into the deepest places. Sometimes, however, I would come directly upon a monster before observing it. In such cases, I would start back, run a short way round, and in that manner shun them. Straight forward, they will run a short distance rapidly, but do not possess the power of turning. In a crooked race, there is no difficulty in evading them.

About two o'clock in the afternoon, I heard the last of the hounds. Probably they did not cross the bayou. Wet and weary, but relieved from the sense of instant peril, I continued on, more cautious and afraid, however, of the snakes and alligators than I had been in the earlier portion of my flight. Now, before stepping into a muddy pool, I would strike the water with a stick. If the waters moved, I would go around it, if not, would venture through.

At length the sun went down, and gradually night's trailing mantle shrouded the great swamp in darkness. Still I staggered on, fearing every instant I should feel the dreadful sting of the moccasin, or be crushed within the jaws of some disturbed alligator. The dread of them now almost equaled the fear of the pursuing hounds. The moon arose after a time, its mild light creeping through the overspreading branches, loaded with long, pendent moss. I kept traveling forwards until after midnight, hoping all the while that I would soon emerge into some less desolate and dangerous region. But the water grew deeper and the walking more difficult than ever. I perceived it would be impossible to proceed much farther, and knew not, moreover, what hands I might fall into, should I succeed in reaching a human habitation. Not provided with a pass, any white man would be at liberty to arrest me, and place me in prison until such time as my master should "prove property, pay charges, and take me away." I was an estray, and if so unfortunate as to meet a law-abiding citizen of Louisiana, he would deem it his duty to his neighbor, perhaps, to put me forthwith in the pound. Really, it was difficult to determine which I had most reason to fear—dogs, alligators or men!

After midnight, however, I came to a halt. Imagination cannot picture the dreariness of the scene. The swamp was resonant with the quacking of innumerable ducks! Since the foundation of the earth, in all probability, a human footstep had never before so far penetrated the recesses of the swamp. It was not silent now—silent to a degree that rendered it oppressive,—as it was when the sun was shining in the heavens. My midnight intrusion had awakened the feathered tribes, which seemed to throng the morass in hundreds of thousands, and their garrulous throats poured forth such multitudinous sounds—there was such a fluttering of wings—such sullen plunges in the water all around me—that I was affrighted and appalled. All the fowls of the air, and all the creeping things of the earth appeared to have assembled together in that particular place, for the purpose of filling it with clamor and confusion. Not by human dwellings—not in crowded cities alone, are the sights and sounds of life. The wildest places of the earth are full of them. Even in the heart of that dismal swamp, God had provided a refuge and a dwelling place for millions of living things.

The moon had now risen above the trees, when I resolved upon a new project. Thus far I had endeavored to travel as nearly south as possible. Turning about I proceeded in a north-west direction, my object being to strike the Pine Woods in the vicinity of Master Ford's. Once within the shadow of his protection, I felt I would be comparatively safe.

My clothes were in tatters, my hands, face, and body covered with scratches, received from the sharp knots of fallen trees, and in climbing over piles of brush and floodwood. My bare foot was full of thorns. I was besmeared with muck and mud, and the green slime that had collected on the surface of the dead water, in which I had been immersed to the neck many times during the day and night. Hour after hour, and tiresome indeed had they become, I continued to plod along on my north-west course. The water began to grow less deep, and the ground more firm under my feet. At last I reached the Pacoudrie, the same wide bayou I had swam while "outward bound." I swam it again, and shortly after thought I heard a cock crow, but the sound was faint, and it might have been a mockery of the ear. The water receded from my advancing footsteps—now I had left the bogs behind me—now I was on dry land that gradually ascended to the plain, and I knew I was somewhere in the "Great Pine Woods."

Just at day-break I came to an opening—a sort of small plantation—but one I had never seen before. In the edge of the woods I came upon two men, a slave and his young master, engaged in catching wild hogs. The white man I knew would demand my pass, and not able to give him one, would take me into possession. I was too wearied to run again, and too desperate to be taken, and therefore adopted a ruse that proved entirely successful. Assuming a fierce expression, I walked directly towards him, looking him steadily in the face. As I approached, he moved backwards with an air of alarm. It was plain he was much affrighted—that he looked upon me as some infernal goblin, just arisen from the bowels of the swamp!

"Where does William Ford live?" I demanded, in no gentle tone.

"He lives seven miles from here," was the reply.

"Which is the way to his place?" I again demanded, trying to look more fiercely than ever.

"Do you see those pine trees yonder?" he asked, pointing to two, a mile distant, that rose far above their fellows, like a couple of tall sentinels, overlooking the broad expanse of forest.

"I see them," was the answer.

"At the feet of those pine trees," he continued, "runs the Texas road. Turn to the left, and it will lead you to William Ford's."

Without farther parley, I hastened forward, happy as he was, no doubt, to place the widest possible distance between us. Striking the Texas road, I turned to the left hand, as directed, and soon passed a great fire, where a pile of logs were burning. I went to it, thinking I would dry my clothes; but the gray light of the morning was fast breaking away,—some passing white man might observe me; besides, the heat overpowered me with the desire of sleep: so, lingering no longer, I continued my travels, and finally, about eight o'clock, reached the house of Master Ford.

The slaves were all absent from the quarters, at their work. Stepping on to the piazza, I knocked at the door, which was soon opened by Mistress Ford. My appearance was so changed—I was in such a wobegone and forlorn condition, she did not know me. Inquiring if Master Ford was at home, that good man made his appearance, before the question could be answered. I told him of my flight, and all the particulars connected with it. He listened attentively, and when I had concluded, spoke to me kindly and sympathetically, and taking me to the kitchen, called John, and ordered him to prepare me food. I had tasted nothing since daylight the previous morning.

When John had set the meal before me, the madam came out with a bowl of milk, and many little delicious dainties, such as rarely please the palate of a slave. I was hungry, and I was weary, but neither food nor rest afforded half the pleasure as did the blessed voices speaking kindness and consolation. It was the oil and the wine which the Good Samaritan in the "Great Pine Woods" was ready to pour into the wounded spirit of the slave, who came to him, stripped of his raiment and half-dead.

They left me in the cabin, that I might rest. Blessed be sleep! It visiteth all alike, descending as the dews of heaven on the bond and free. Soon it nestled to my bosom, driving away the troubles that oppressed it, and bearing me to that shadowy region, where I saw again the faces, and listened to the voices of my children, who, alas, for aught I knew in my waking hours, had fallen into the arms of that *other* sleep, from which they *never* would arouse.

# CHAPTER XI

*The Mistress' Garden—The Crimson And Golden Fruit—Orange And Pomegranate Trees—Return To Bayou Bœuf—Master Ford's Remarks On The Way—The Meeting With Tibeats—His Account Of The Chase—Ford Censures His Brutality—Arrival At The Plantation—Astonishment Of The Slaves On Seeing Me—The Anticipated Flogging—Kentucky John—Mr. Eldret, The Planter—Eldret's Sam—Trip To The "Big Cane Brake"—The Tradition Of "Sutton's Field"—Forest Trees—Gnats And Mosquitos—The Arrival Of Black Women In The Big Cane—Lumber Women—Sudden Appearance Of Tibeats—His Provoking Treatment—Visit To Bayou Bœuf—The Slave Pass—Southern Hospitality—The Last Of Eliza—Sale To Edwin Epps.*

After a long sleep, sometime in the afternoon I awoke, refreshed, but very sore and stiff. Sally came in and talked with me, while John cooked me some dinner. Sally was in great trouble, as well as myself, one of her children being ill, and she feared it could not survive. Dinner over, after walking about the quarters for a while, visiting Sally's cabin and looking at the sick child, I strolled into the madam's garden. Though it was a season of the year when the voices of the birds are silent, and the trees are stripped of their summer glories in more frigid climes, yet the whole variety of roses were then blooming there, and the long, luxuriant vines creeping over the frames. The crimson and golden fruit hung half hidden amidst the younger and older blossoms of the peach, the orange, the plum, and the pomegranate; for, in that region of almost perpetual warmth, the leaves are falling and the buds bursting into bloom the whole year long.

I indulged the most grateful feelings towards Master and Mistress Ford, and wishing in some manner to repay their kindness, commenced trimming the vines, and afterwards weeding out the grass from among the orange and pomegranate trees. The latter grows eight or ten feet high, and its fruit, though larger, is similar in appearance to the jelly-flower. It has the luscious flavor of the strawberry. Oranges, peaches, plums, and most other fruits are indigenous to the rich, warm soil of Avoyelles; but the apple, the most common of them all in colder latitudes, is rarely to be seen.

Mistress Ford came out presently, saying it was praise-worthy in me, but I was not in a condition to labor, and might rest myself at the quarters until master should go down to Bayou Bœuf, which would not be that day, and it might not be the next. I said to her—to be sure, I felt bad, and was stiff, and that my foot pained me, the stubs and thorns having so torn it, but thought such exercise would not hurt me, and that it was a great pleasure to work for so good a mistress. Thereupon she returned to the great house, and for three days I was diligent in the garden, cleaning the walks, weeding the flower beds, and pulling up the rank grass beneath the jessamine vines, which the gentle and generous hand of my protectress had taught to clamber along the walls.

The fourth morning, having become recruited and refreshed, Master Ford ordered me to make ready to accompany him to the bayou. There was but one saddle horse at the opening, all the others with the mules having been sent down to the plantation. I said I could walk, and bidding Sally and John goodbye, left the opening, trotting along by the horse's side.

That little paradise in the Great Pine Woods was the oasis in the desert, towards which my heart turned lovingly, during many years of bondage. I went forth from it now with regret and sorrow, not so overwhelming, however, as if it had then been given me to know that I should never return to it again.

Master Ford urged me to take his place occasionally on the horse, to rest me; but I said no, I was not tired, and it was better for me to walk than him. He said many kind and cheering things to me on the way, riding slowly, in order that I might keep pace with him. The goodness of God was manifest, he declared, in my miraculous escape from the swamp. As Daniel came forth unharmed from the den of lions, and as Jonah had been preserved in the whale's belly, even so had I been delivered from evil by the Almighty. He interrogated me in regard to the various fears and emotions I had experienced during the day and night, and if I had felt, at any time, a desire to pray. I felt forsaken of the whole world, I answered him, and was praying mentally all the while. At such times, said he, the heart of man turns instinctively towards his Maker. In prosperity, and when there is nothing to injure or make him afraid, he remembers Him not, and is ready to defy Him; but place him in the midst of dangers, cut him off from human aid, let the grave open before him—then it is, in the time of his tribulation, that the scoffer and unbelieving man turns to God for help, feeling there is no other hope, or refuge, or safety, save in his protecting arm.

So did that benignant man speak to me of this life and of the life hereafter; of the goodness and power of God, and of the vanity of earthly things, as we journeyed along the solitary road towards Bayou Bœuf.

When within some five miles of the plantation, we discovered a horseman at a distance, galloping towards us. As he came near I saw that it was Tibeats! He looked at me a moment, but did not address me, and turning about, rode along side by side with Ford. I trotted silently at their horses' heels, listening to their conversation. Ford informed him of my arrival in the Pine Woods three days before, of the sad plight I was in, and of the difficulties and dangers I had encountered.

"Well," exclaimed Tibeats, omitting his usual oaths in the presence of Ford, "I never saw such running before. I'll bet him against a hundred dollars, he'll beat any nigger in Louisiana. I offered John David Cheney twenty-five dollars to catch him, dead or alive, but he outran his dogs in a fair race. Them Cheney dogs ain't much, after all. Dunwoodie's hounds would have had him down before he touched the palmettoes. Somehow the dogs got off the track, and we had to give up the hunt. We rode the horses as far as we could, and then kept on foot till the water was three feet deep. The boys said he was drowned, sure. I allow I wanted a shot at him mightily. Ever since, I have been riding up and down the bayou, but had'nt much hope of catching him—thought he was dead, *sartin*. Oh, he's a cuss to run—that nigger is!"

In this way Tibeats ran on, describing his search in the swamp, the wonderful speed with which I had fled before the hounds, and when he had finished, Master Ford responded by saying, I had always been a willing and faithful boy with him; that he was sorry we had such trouble; that, according to Platt's story, he had been inhumanly treated, and that he, Tibeats, was himself in fault. Using hatchets and broad-axes upon slaves was shameful, and should not be allowed, he remarked. "This is no way of dealing with them, when first brought into the country. It will have a pernicious influence, and set them all running away. The swamps will be full of them. A little kindness would be far more effectual in restraining them, and rendering them obedient, than the use of such deadly weapons. Every planter on the bayou should frown upon such inhumanity. It is for the interest of all to do so. It is evident enough, Mr. Tibeats, that you and Platt cannot live together. You dislike him, and would not hesitate to kill him, and knowing it, he will run from you again through fear of his life. Now, Tibeats, you must sell him, or hire him out, at least. Unless you do so, I shall take measures to get him out of your possession."

In this spirit Ford addressed him the remainder of the distance. I opened not my mouth. On reaching the plantation they entered the great house, while I repaired to Eliza's cabin. The slaves were astonished to find me there, on returning from the field, supposing I was drowned. That night, again, they gathered about the cabin to listen to the story of my adventure. They took it for granted I would be whipped, and that it would be severe, the well-known penalty of running away being five hundred lashes.

"Poor fellow," said Eliza, taking me by the hand, "it would have been better for you if you had drowned. You have a cruel master, and he will kill you yet, I am afraid."

Lawson suggested that it might be, overseer Chapin would be appointed to inflict the punishment, in which case it would not be severe, whereupon Mary, Rachel, Bristol, and others hoped it would be Master Ford, and then it would be no whipping at all. They all pitied me and tried to console me, and were sad in view of the castigation that awaited me, except Kentucky John. There were no bounds to his laughter; he filled the cabin with cachinnations, holding his sides to prevent an explosion, and the cause of his noisy mirth was the idea of my outstripping the hounds. Somehow, he looked at the subject in a comical light. "I *know'd* dey would'nt cotch him, when he run cross de plantation. O, de lor', did'nt Platt pick his feet right up, tho', hey? When dem dogs got whar he was, he was'nt *dar*—haw, haw, haw! O, de lor' a' mity!"—and then Kentucky John relapsed into another of his boisterous fits.

Early the next morning, Tibeats left the plantation. In the course of the forenoon, while sauntering about the gin-house, a tall, good-looking man came to me, and inquired if I was Tibeats' boy, that youthful appellation being applied indiscriminately to slaves even though they may have passed the number of three score years and ten. I took off my hat, and answered that I was.

"How would you like to work for me?" he inquired.

"Oh, I would like to, very much," said I, inspired with a sudden hope of getting away from Tibeats.

"You worked under Myers at Peter Tanner's, didn't you?"

I replied I had, adding some complimentary remarks that Myers had made concerning me.

"Well, boy," said he, "I have hired you of your master to work for me in the "Big Cane Brake," thirty-eight miles from here, down on Red River."

This man was Mr. Eldret, who lived below Ford's, on the same side of the bayou. I accompanied him to his plantation, and in the morning started with his slave Sam, and a wagon-load of provisions, drawn by four mules, for the Big Cane, Eldret and Myers having preceded us on horseback. This Sam was a native of Charleston, where he had a mother, brother and sisters. He "allowed"—a common word among both black and white—that

Tibeats was a mean man, and hoped, as I most earnestly did also, that his master would buy me.

We proceeded down the south shore of the bayou, crossing it at Carey's plantation; from thence to Huff Power, passing which, we came upon the Bayou Rouge road, which runs towards Red River. After passing through Bayou Rouge Swamp, and just at sunset, turning from the highway, we struck off into the "Big Cane Brake." We followed an unbeaten track, scarcely wide enough to admit the wagon. The cane, such as are used for fishing-rods, were as thick as they could stand. A person could not be seen through them the distance of a rod. The paths of wild beasts run through them in various directions—the bear and the American tiger abounding in these brakes, and wherever there is a basin of stagnant water, it is full of alligators.

We kept on our lonely course through the "Big Cane" several miles, when we entered a clearing, known as "Sutton's Field." Many years before, a man by the name of Sutton had penetrated the wilderness of cane to this solitary place. Tradition has it, that he fled thither, a fugitive, not from service, but from justice. Here he lived alone—recluse and hermit of the swamp—with his own hands planting the seed and gathering in the harvest. One day a band of Indians stole upon his solitude, and after a bloody battle, overpowered and massacred him. For miles the country round, in the slaves' quarters, and on the piazzas of "great houses," where white children listen to superstitious tales, the story goes, that that spot, in the heart of the "Big Cane," is a haunted place. For more than a quarter of a century, human voices had rarely, if ever, disturbed the silence of the clearing. Rank and noxious weeds had overspread the once cultivated field—serpents sunned themselves on the doorway of the crumbling cabin. It was indeed a dreary picture of desolation.

Passing "Sutton's Field," we followed a new-cut road two miles farther, which brought us to its termination. We had now reached the wild lands of Mr. Eldret, where he contemplated clearing up an extensive plantation. We went to work next morning with our cane-knives, and cleared a sufficient space to allow the erection of two cabins—one for Myers and Eldret, the other for Sam, myself, and the slaves that were to join us. We were now in the midst of trees of enormous growth, whose wide-spreading branches almost shut out the light of the sun, while the space between the trunks was an impervious mass of cane, with here and there an occasional palmetto.

The bay and the sycamore, the oak and the cypress, reach a growth unparalleled, in those fertile lowlands bordering the Red River. From every tree, moreover, hang long, large masses of moss, presenting to the eye unaccustomed to them, a striking and singular appearance. This moss, in large quantities, is sent north, and there used for manufacturing purposes.

We cut down oaks, split them into rails, and with these erected temporary cabins. We covered the roofs with the broad palmetto leaf, an excellent substitute for shingles, as long as they last.

The greatest annoyance I met with here were small flies, gnats and mosquitoes. They swarmed the air. They penetrated the porches of the ear, the nose, the eyes, the mouth. They sucked themselves beneath the skin. It was impossible to brush or beat them off. It seemed, indeed, as if they would devour us—carry us away piecemeal, in their small tormenting mouths.

A lonelier spot, or one more disagreeable, than the centre of the "Big Cane Brake," it would be difficult to conceive; yet to me it was a paradise, in comparison with any other place in the company of Master Tibeats. I labored hard, and oft-times was weary and fatigued, yet I could lie down at night in peace, and arise in the morning without fear.

In the course of a fortnight, four black girls came down from Eldret's plantation—Charlotte, Fanny, Cresia and Nelly. They were all large and stout. Axes were put into their hands, and they were sent out with Sam and myself to cut trees. They were excellent choppers, the largest oak or sycamore standing but a brief season before their heavy and well-directed blows. At piling logs, they were equal to any man. There are lumberwomen as well as lumbermen in the forests of the South. In fact, in the region of the Bayou Bœuf they perform their share of all the labor required on the plantation. They plough, drag, drive team, clear wild lands, work on the highway, and so forth. Some planters, owning large cotton and sugar plantations, have none other than the labor of slave women. Such a one is Jim Burns, who lives on the north shore of the bayou, opposite the plantation of John Fogaman.

On our arrival in the brake, Eldret promised me, if I worked well, I might go up to visit my friends at Ford's in four weeks. On Saturday night of the fifth week, I reminded him of his promise, when he told me I had done so well, that I might go. I had set my heart upon it, and Eldret's announcement thrilled me with pleasure. I was to return in time to commence the labors of the day on Tuesday morning.

While indulging the pleasant anticipation of so soon meeting my old friends again, suddenly the hateful form of Tibeats appeared among us. He inquired how Myers and Platt got along together, and was told, very well, and that Platt was going up to Ford's plantation in the morning on a visit.

"Poh, poh!" sneered Tibeats; "it isn't worth while—the nigger will get unsteady. He can't go."

But Eldret insisted I had worked faithfully—that he had given me his promise, and that, under the circumstances, I ought not to be disappointed. They then, it being about dark, entered one cabin and I the other. I could not give up the idea of going; it was a sore disappointment. Before morning I resolved, if Eldret made no objection, to leave at all hazards. At daylight I was at his door, with my blanket rolled up into a bundle, and hanging on a stick over my shoulder, waiting for a pass. Tibeats came out presently in one of his disagreeable moods, washed his face, and going to a stump near by, sat down upon it, apparently busily thinking with himself. After standing there a long time, impelled by a sudden impulse of impatience, I started off.

"Are you going without a pass?" he cried out to me.

"Yes, master, I thought I would," I answered.

"How do you think you'll get there?" demanded he.

"Don't know," was all the reply I made him.

"You'd be taken and sent to jail, where you ought to be, before you got half-way there," he added, passing into the cabin as he said it. He came out soon with the pass in his hand, and calling me a "d—d nigger that deserved a hundred lashes," threw it on the ground. I picked it up, and hurried away right speedily.

A slave caught off his master's plantation without a pass, may be seized and whipped by any white man whom he meets. The one I now received was dated, and read as follows:

> "Platt has permission to go to Ford's plantation, on Bayou Bœuf, and return by Tuesday morning.
>
> JOHN M. TIBEATS."

This is the usual form. On the way, a great many demanded it, read it, and passed on. Those having the air and appearance of gentlemen, whose dress indicated the possession of wealth, frequently took no notice of me whatever; but a shabby fellow, an unmistakable loafer, never failed to hail me, and to scrutinize and examine me in the most thorough manner. Catching runaways is sometimes a money-making business. If, after advertising, no owner appears, they may be sold to the highest bidder; and certain fees are allowed the finder for his services, at all events, even if reclaimed. "A mean white," therefore,—a name applied to the species loafer—considers it a god-send to meet an unknown negro without a pass.

There are no inns along the highways in that portion of the State where I sojourned. I was wholly destitute of money, neither did I carry any provisions, on my journey from the Big Cane to Bayou Bœuf; nevertheless, with his pass in his hand, a slave need never suffer from hunger or from thirst. It is only necessary to present it to the master or overseer of a plantation, and state his wants, when he will be sent round to the kitchen and provided with food or shelter, as the case may require. The traveler stops at any house and calls for a meal with as much freedom as if it was a public tavern. It is the general custom of the country. Whatever their faults may be, it is certain the inhabitants along Red River, and around the bayous in the interior of Louisiana are not wanting in hospitality.

I arrived at Ford's plantation towards the close of the afternoon, passing the evening in Eliza's cabin, with Lawson, Rachel, and others of my acquaintance. When we left Washington Eliza's form was round and plump. She stood erect, and in her silks and jewels, presented a picture of graceful strength and elegance. Now she was but a thin shadow of her former self. Her face had become ghastly haggard, and the once straight and active form was bowed down, as if bearing the weight of a hundred years. Crouching on her cabin floor, and clad in the coarse garments of a slave, old Elisha Berry would not have recognized the mother of his child. I never saw her afterwards. Having become useless in the cotton-field, she was bartered for a trifle, to some man residing in the vicinity of Peter Compton's. Grief had gnawed remorselessly at her heart, until her strength was gone; and for that, her last master, it is said, lashed and abused her most unmercifully. But he could not whip back the departed vigor of her youth, nor straighten up that bended body to its full height, such as it was when her children were around her, and the light of freedom was shining on her path.

I learned the particulars relative to her departure from this world, from some of Compton's slaves, who had come over Red River to the bayou, to assist young Madam Tanner during the "busy season." She became at length, they said, utterly helpless, for several weeks lying on the ground floor in a dilapidated cabin, dependent upon the mercy of her fellow-thralls for an occasional drop of water, and a morsel of food. Her master did not "knock her on the head," as is sometimes done to put a suffering animal out of misery, but left her unprovided for, and unprotected, to linger through a life of pain and wretchedness to its natural close. When the hands returned from the field one night they found her dead! During the day, the Angel of the Lord, who moveth invisibly over all the earth, gathering in his harvest of departing souls, had silently entered the cabin of the dying woman, and taken her from thence. She was *free* at last!

Next day, rolling up my blanket, I started on my return to the Big Cane. After traveling five miles, at a place called Huff Power, the ever-present Tibeats met me in the road. He inquired why I was going back so soon, and when informed I was anxious to return by the time I was directed, he said I need go no farther than the next plantation, as he had that day sold me to Edwin Epps. We walked down into the yard, where we met the latter gentleman, who examined me, and asked me the usual questions propounded by purchasers. Having been duly delivered over, I was ordered to the quarters, and at the same time directed to make a hoe and axe handle for myself.

I was now no longer the property of Tibeats—his dog, his brute, dreading his wrath and cruelty day and night; and whoever or whatever my new master might prove to be, I could not, certainly, regret the change. So it was good news when the sale was announced, and with a sigh of relief I sat down for the first time in my new abode.

Tibeats soon after disappeared from that section of the country. Once afterwards, and only once, I caught a glimpse of him. It was many miles from Bayou Bœuf. He was seated in the doorway of a low groggery. I was passing, in a drove of slaves, through St. Mary's parish.

# CHAPTER XII

*Personal Appearance Of Epps—Epps, Drunk And Sober—A Glimpse Of His History—Cotton Growing—The Mode Of Ploughing And Preparing Ground—Of Planting—Of Hoeing, Of Picking, Of Treating Raw Hands—The Difference In Cotton Pickers—Patsey A Remarkable One—Tasked According To Ability—Beauty Of A Cotton Field—The Slave's Labors—Fear On Approaching The Gin-House—Weighing—"Chores"—Cabin Life—The Corn Mill—The Uses Of The Gourd—Fear Of Oversleeping—Fear Continually—Mode Of Cultivating Corn—Sweet Potatoes—Fertility Of The Soil—Fattening Hogs—Preserving Bacon—Raising Cattle—Shooting Matches—Garden Products—Flowers And Verdure.*

Edwin Epps, of whom much will be said during the remainder of this history, is a large, portly, heavy-bodied man with light hair, high cheek bones, and a Roman nose of extraordinary dimensions. He has blue eyes, a fair complexion, and is, as I should say, full six feet high. He has the sharp, inquisitive expression of a jockey. His manners are repulsive and coarse, and his language gives speedy and unequivocal evidence that he has never enjoyed the advantages of an education. He has the faculty of saying most provoking things, in that respect even excelling old Peter Tanner. At the time I came into his possession, Edwin Epps was fond of the bottle, his "sprees" sometimes extending over the space of two whole weeks. Latterly, however, he had reformed his habits, and when I left him, was as strict a specimen of temperance as could be found on Bayou Bœuf. When "in his cups," Master Epps was a roystering, blustering, noisy fellow, whose chief delight was in dancing with his "niggers," or lashing them about the yard with his long whip, just for the pleasure of hearing them screech and scream, as the great welts were planted on their backs. When sober, he was silent, reserved and cunning, not beating us indiscriminately, as in his drunken moments, but sending the end of his rawhide to some tender spot of a lagging slave, with a sly dexterity peculiar to himself.

He had been a driver and overseer in his younger years, but at this time was in possession of a plantation on Bayou Huff Power, two and a half miles from Holmesville, eighteen from Marksville, and twelve from Cheneyville. It belonged to Joseph B. Roberts, his wife's uncle, and was leased by Epps. His principal business was raising cotton, and inasmuch as some may read this book who have never seen a cotton field, a description of the manner of its culture may not be out of place.

The ground is prepared by throwing up beds or ridges, with the plough—back-furrowing, it is called. Oxen and mules, the latter almost exclusively, are used in ploughing. The women as frequently as the men perform this labor, feeding, currying, and taking care of their teams, and in all respects doing the field and stable work, precisely as do the ploughboys of the North.

The beds, or ridges, are six feet wide, that is, from water furrow to water furrow. A plough drawn by one mule is then run along the top of the ridge or center of the bed, making the drill, into which a girl usually drops the seed, which she carries in a bag hung round her neck. Behind her comes a mule and harrow, covering up the seed, so that two mules, three slaves, a plough and harrow, are employed in planting a row of cotton. This is done in the months of March and April. Corn is planted in February. When there are no cold rains, the cotton usually makes its appearance in a week. In the course of eight or ten days afterwards the first hoeing is commenced. This is performed in part, also, by the aid of the plough and mule. The plough passes as near as possible to the cotton on both sides, throwing the furrow from it. Slaves follow with their hoes, cutting up the grass and cotton, leaving hills two feet and a half apart. This is called scraping cotton. In two weeks more commences the second hoeing. This time the furrow is thrown towards the cotton. Only one stalk, the largest, is now left standing in each hill. In another fortnight it is hoed the third time, throwing the furrow towards the cotton in the same manner as before, and killing all the grass between the rows. About the first of July, when it is a foot high or thereabouts, it is hoed the fourth and last time. Now the whole space between the rows is ploughed, leaving a deep water furrow in the center. During all these hoeings the overseer or driver follows the slaves on horseback with a whip, such as has been described. The fastest hoer takes the lead row. He is usually about a rod in advance of his companions. If one of them passes him, he is whipped. If one falls behind or is a moment idle, he is whipped. In fact, the lash is flying from morning until night, the whole day long. The hoeing season thus continues from April until July, a field having no sooner been finished once, than it is commenced again.

In the latter part of August begins the cotton picking season. At this time each slave is presented with a sack. A strap is fastened to it, which goes over the neck, holding the mouth of the sack breast high, while the bottom reaches nearly to the ground. Each one is also presented with a large basket that will hold about two barrels. This is to put the cotton in when the sack is filled. The baskets are carried to the field and placed at the beginning of the rows.

When a new hand, one unaccustomed to the business, is sent for the first time into the field, he is whipped up smartly, and made for that day to pick as fast as he can possibly. At night it is weighed, so that his capability in cotton picking is known. He must bring in the same weight each night following. If it falls short, it is considered evidence that he has been laggard, and a greater or less number of lashes is the penalty.

An ordinary day's work is two hundred pounds. A slave who is accustomed to picking, is punished, if he or she brings in a less quantity than that. There is a great difference among them as regards this kind of labor. Some of them seem to have a natural knack, or quickness, which enables them to pick with great celerity, and with both hands, while others, with whatever practice or industry, are utterly unable to come up to the ordinary standard. Such hands are taken from the cotton field and employed in other business. Patsey, of whom I shall have more to say, was known as the most remarkable cotton picker on Bayou Bœuf. She picked with both hands and with such surprising rapidity, that five hundred pounds a day was not unusual for her.

Each one is tasked, therefore, according to his picking abilities, none, however, to come short of two hundred weight. I, being unskillful always in that business, would have satisfied my master by bringing in the latter quantity, while on the other hand, Patsey would surely have been beaten if she failed to produce twice as much.

The cotton grows from five to seven feet high, each stalk having a great many branches, shooting out in all directions, and lapping each other above the water furrow.

There are few sights more pleasant to the eye, than a wide cotton field when it is in the bloom. It presents an appearance of purity, like an immaculate expanse of light, new-fallen snow.

Sometimes the slave picks down one side of a row, and back upon the other, but more usually, there is one on either side, gathering all that has blossomed, leaving the unopened bolls for a succeeding picking. When the sack is filled, it is emptied into the basket and trodden down. It is necessary to be extremely careful the first time going through the field, in order not to break the branches off the stalks. The cotton will not bloom upon a broken branch. Epps never failed to inflict the severest chastisement on the unlucky servant who, either carelessly or unavoidably, was guilty in the least degree in this respect.

The hands are required to be in the cotton field as soon as it is light in the morning, and, with the exception of ten or fifteen minutes, which is given them at noon to swallow their allowance of cold bacon, they are not permitted to be a moment idle until it is too dark to see, and when the moon is full, they often times labor till the middle of the night. They do not dare to stop even at dinner time, nor return to the quarters, however late it be, until the order to halt is given by the driver.

The day's work over in the field, the baskets are "toted," or in other words, carried to the gin-house, where the cotton is weighed. No matter how fatigued and weary he may be—no matter how much he longs for sleep and rest—a slave never approaches the gin-house with his basket of cotton but with fear. If it falls short in weight—if he has not performed the full task appointed him, he knows that he must suffer. And if he has exceeded it by ten or twenty pounds, in all probability his master will measure the next day's task accordingly. So, whether he has too little or too much, his approach to the gin-house is always with fear and trembling. Most frequently they have too little, and therefore it is they are not anxious to leave the field. After weighing, follow the whippings; and then the baskets are carried to the cotton house, and their contents stored away like hay, all hands being sent in to tramp it down. If the cotton is not dry, instead of taking it to the gin-house at once, it is laid upon platforms, two feet high, and some three times as wide, covered with boards or plank, with narrow walks running between them.

This done, the labor of the day is not yet ended, by any means. Each one must then attend to his respective chores. One feeds the mules, another the swine—another cuts the wood, and so forth; besides, the packing is all done by candle light. Finally, at a late hour, they reach the quarters, sleepy and overcome with the long day's toil. Then a fire must be kindled in the cabin, the corn ground in the small hand-mill, and supper, and dinner for the next day in the field, prepared. All that is allowed them is corn and bacon, which is given out at the corncrib and smoke-house every Sunday morning. Each one receives, as his weekly, allowance, three and a half pounds of bacon, and corn enough to make a peck of meal. That is all—no tea, coffee, sugar, and with the exception of a very scanty sprinkling now and then, no salt. I can say, from a ten years' residence with Master Epps, that no slave of his is ever likely to suffer from the gout, superinduced by excessive high living. Master Epps' hogs were fed on *shelled* corn—it was thrown out to his "niggers" in the ear. The former, he thought, would fatten faster by shelling, and soaking it in the water—the latter, perhaps, if treated in the same manner, might grow too fat to labor. Master Epps was a shrewd calculator, and knew how to manage his own animals, drunk or sober.

The corn mill stands in the yard beneath a shelter. It is like a common coffee mill, the hopper holding about six quarts. There was one privilege which Master Epps granted freely to every slave he had. They might grind their corn nightly, in such small quantities as their daily wants required, or they might grind the whole week's allowance at one time, on Sundays, just as they preferred. A very generous man was Master Epps!

I kept my corn in a small wooden box, the meal in a gourd; and, by the way, the gourd is one of the most convenient and necessary utensils on a plantation. Besides supplying the place of all kinds of crockery in a slave cabin, it is used for carrying water to the fields. Another, also, contains the dinner. It dispenses with the necessity of pails, dippers, basins, and such tin and wooden superfluities altogether.

When the corn is ground, and fire is made, the bacon is taken down from the nail on which it hangs, a slice cut off and thrown upon the coals to broil. The majority of slaves have no knife, much less a fork. They cut their bacon with the axe at the woodpile. The corn meal is mixed with a little water, placed in the fire, and baked. When it is "done brown," the ashes are scraped off, and being placed upon a chip, which answers for a table, the tenant of the slave hut is ready to sit down upon the ground to supper. By this time it is usually midnight. The same fear of punishment with which they approach the gin-house, possesses them again on lying down to get a snatch of rest. It is the fear of oversleeping in the morning. Such an offence would certainly be attended with not less than twenty lashes. With a prayer that he may be on his feet and wide awake at the first sound of the horn, he sinks to his slumbers nightly.

The softest couches in the world are not to be found in the log mansion of the slave. The one whereon I reclined year after year, was a plank twelve inches wide and ten feet long. My pillow was a stick of wood. The bedding was a coarse blanket, and not a rag or shred beside. Moss might be used, were it not that it directly breeds a swarm of fleas.

The cabin is constructed of logs, without floor or window. The latter is altogether unnecessary, the crevices between the logs admitting sufficient light. In stormy weather the rain drives through them, rendering it comfortless and extremely disagreeable. The rude door hangs on great wooden hinges. In one end is constructed an awkward fire-place.

An hour before daylight the horn is blown. Then the slaves arouse, prepare their breakfast, fill a gourd with water, in another deposit their dinner of cold bacon and corn cake, and hurry to the field again. It is an offence invariably followed by a flogging, to be found at the quarters after daybreak. Then the fears and labors of another day begin; and until its close there is no such thing as rest. He fears he will be caught lagging through the day; he fears to approach the gin-house with his basket-load of cotton at night; he fears, when he lies down, that he will oversleep himself in the morning. Such is a true, faithful, unexaggerated picture and description of the slave's daily life, during the time of cotton-picking, on the shores of Bayou Bœuf.

In the month of January, generally, the fourth and last picking is completed. Then commences the harvesting of corn. This is considered a secondary crop, and receives far less attention than the cotton. It is planted, as already mentioned, in February. Corn is grown in that region for the purpose of fattening hogs and feeding slaves; very little, if any, being sent to market. It is the white variety, the ear of great size, and the stalk growing to the height of eight, and often times ten feet. In August the leaves are stripped off, dried in the sun, bound in small bundles, and stored away as provender for the mules and oxen. After this the slaves go through the field, turning down the ear, for the purpose of keeping the rains from penetrating to the grain. It is left in this condition until after cotton-picking is over, whether earlier or later. Then the ears are separated from the stalks, and deposited in the corncrib with the husks on; otherwise, stripped of the husks, the weevil would destroy it. The stalks are left standing in the field.

The Carolina, or sweet potato, is also grown in that region to some extent. They are not fed, however, to hogs or cattle, and are considered but of small importance. They are preserved by placing them upon the surface of the ground, with a slight covering of earth or cornstalks. There is not a cellar on Bayou Bœuf. The ground is so low it would fill with water. Potatoes are worth from two to three "bits," or shillings a barrel; corn, except when there is an unusual scarcity, can be purchased at the same rate.

As soon as the cotton and corn crops are secured, the stalks are pulled up, thrown into piles and burned. The ploughs are started at the same time, throwing up the beds again, preparatory to another planting. The soil, in the parishes of Rapides and Avoyelles, and throughout the whole country, so far as my observation extended, is of exceeding richness and fertility. It is a kind of marl, of a brown or reddish color. It does not require those invigorating composts necessary to more barren lands, and on the same field the same crop is grown for many successive years.

Ploughing, planting, picking cotton, gathering the corn, and pulling and burning stalks, occupies the whole of the four seasons of the year. Drawing and cutting wood, pressing cotton, fattening and killing hogs, are but incidental labors.

In the month of September or October, the hogs are run out of the swamps by dogs, and confined in pens. On a cold morning, generally about New Year's day, they are slaughtered. Each carcass is cut into six parts, and piled one above the other in salt, upon large tables in the smoke-house. In this condition it remains a fortnight, when it is hung up, and a fire built, and continued more than half the time during the remainder of the year. This thorough smoking is necessary to prevent the bacon from becoming infested with worms. In so warm a climate it is difficult to preserve it, and very many times myself and my companions have received our weekly allowance of three pounds and a half, when it was full of these disgusting vermin.

Although the swamps are overrun with cattle, they are never made the source of profit, to any considerable extent. The planter cuts his mark upon the ear, or brands his initials upon the side, and turns them into the swamps, to roam unrestricted within their almost limitless confines. They are the Spanish breed, small and spike-horned. I have known of droves being taken from Bayou Bœuf, but it is of very rare occurrence. The value of the best cows is about five dollars each. Two quarts at one milking, would be considered an unusual large quantity. They furnish little tallow, and that of a soft, inferior quality. Notwithstanding the great number of cows that throng the swamps, the planters are indebted to the North for their cheese and butter, which is purchased in the New-Orleans market. Salted beef is not an article of food either in the great house, or in the cabin.

Master Epps was accustomed to attend shooting matches for the purpose of obtaining what fresh beef he required. These sports occurred weekly at the neighboring village of Holmesville. Fat beeves are driven thither and shot at, a stipulated price being demanded for the privilege. The lucky marksman divides the flesh among his fellows, and in this manner the attending planters are supplied.

The great number of tame and untamed cattle which swarm the woods and swamps of Bayou Bœuf, most probably suggested that appellation to the French, inasmuch as the term, translated, signifies the creek or river of the wild ox.

Garden products, such as cabbages, turnips and the like, are cultivated for the use of the master and his family. They have greens and vegetables at all times and seasons of the year. "The grass withereth and the flower fadeth" before the desolating winds of autumn in the chill northern latitudes, but perpetual verdure overspreads the hot lowlands, and flowers bloom in the heart of winter, in the region of Bayou Bœuf.

There are no meadows appropriated to the cultivation of the grasses. The leaves of the corn supply a sufficiency of food for the laboring cattle, while the rest provide for themselves all the year in the ever-growing pasture.

There are many other peculiarities of climate, habit, custom, and of the manner of living and laboring at the South, but the foregoing, it is supposed, will give the reader an insight and general idea of life on a cotton plantation in Louisiana. The mode of cultivating cane, and the process of sugar manufacturing, will be mentioned in another place.

# CHAPTER XIII

*The Curious Axe-Helve—Symptoms Of Approaching Illness—Continue To Decline—The Whip Ineffectual—Confined To The Cabin—Visit By Dr. Wines—Partial Recovery—Failure At Cotton Picking—What May Be Heard On Epps' Plantation—Lashes Graduated—Epps In A Whipping Mood—Epps In A Dancing Mood—Description Of The Dance—Loss Of Rest No Excuse—Epps' Characteristics—Jim Burns—Removal From Huff Power To Bayou Bœuf—Description Of Uncle Abram; Of Wiley; Of Aunt Phebe; Of Bob, Henry, And Edward; Of Patsey; With A Genealogical Account Of Each—Something Of Their Past History, And Peculiar Characteristics—Jealousy And Lust—Patsey, The Victim.*

On my arrival at Master Epps', in obedience to his order, the first business upon which I entered was the making of an axe-helve. The handles in use there are simply a round, straight stick. I made a crooked one, shaped like those to which I had been accustomed at the North. When finished, and presented to Epps, he looked at it with astonishment, unable to determine exactly what it was. He had never before seen such a handle, and when I explained its conveniences, he was forcibly struck with the novelty of the idea. He kept it in the house a long time, and when his friends called, was wont to exhibit it as a curiosity.

It was now the season of hoeing. I was first sent into the corn-field, and afterwards set to scraping cotton. In this employment I remained until hoeing time was nearly passed, when I began to experience the symptoms of approaching illness. I was attacked with chills, which were succeeded by a burning fever. I became weak and emaciated, and frequently so dizzy that it caused me to reel and stagger like a drunken man. Nevertheless, I was compelled to keep up my row. When in health I found little difficulty in keeping pace with my fellow-laborers, but now it seemed to be an utter impossibility. Often I fell behind, when the driver's lash was sure to greet my back, infusing into my sick and drooping body a little temporary energy. I continued to decline until at length the whip became entirely ineffectual. The sharpest sting of the rawhide could not arouse me. Finally, in September, when the busy season of cotton picking was at hand, I was unable to leave my cabin. Up to this time I had received no medicine, nor any attention from my master or mistress. The old cook visited me occasionally, preparing me corn-coffee, and sometimes boiling a bit of bacon, when I had grown too feeble to accomplish it myself.

When it was said that I would die, Master Epps, unwilling to bear the loss, which the death of an animal worth a thousand dollars would bring upon him, concluded to incur the expense of sending to Holmesville for Dr. Wines. He announced to Epps that it was the effect of the climate, and there was a probability of his losing me. He directed me to eat no meat, and to partake of no more food than was absolutely necessary to sustain life. Several weeks elapsed, during which time, under the scanty diet to which I was subjected, I had partially recovered. One morning, long before I was in a proper condition to labor, Epps appeared at the cabin door, and, presenting me a sack, ordered me to the cotton field. At this time I had had no experience whatever in cotton picking. It was an awkward business indeed. While others used both hands, snatching the cotton and depositing it in the mouth of the sack, with a precision and dexterity that was incomprehensible to me, I had to seize the boll with one hand, and deliberately draw out the white, gushing blossom with the other.

Depositing the cotton in the sack, moreover, was a difficulty that demanded the exercise of both hands and eyes. I was compelled to pick it from the ground where it would fall, nearly as often as from the stalk where it had grown. I made havoc also with the branches, loaded with the yet unbroken bolls, the long, cumbersome sack swinging from side to side in a manner not allowable in the cotton field. After a most laborious day I arrived at the gin-house with my load. When the scale determined its weight to be only ninety-five pounds, not half the quantity required of the poorest picker, Epps threatened the severest flogging, but in consideration of my being a "raw hand," concluded to pardon me on that occasion. The following day, and many days succeeding, I returned at night with no better success—I was evidently not designed for that kind of labor. I had not the gift—the dexterous fingers and quick motion of Patsey, who could fly along one side of a row of cotton, stripping it of its undefiled and fleecy whiteness miraculously fast. Practice and whipping were alike unavailing, and Epps, satisfied of it at last, swore I was a disgrace—that I was not fit to associate with a cotton-picking "nigger"—that I could not pick enough in a day to pay the trouble of weighing it, and that I should go into the cotton field no more. I was now employed in cutting and hauling wood, drawing cotton from the field to the gin-house, and performed whatever other service was required. Suffice to say, I was never permitted to be idle.

It was rarely that a day passed by without one or more whippings. This occurred at the time the cotton was weighed. The delinquent, whose weight had fallen short, was taken out, stripped, made to lie upon the ground, face downwards, when he received a punishment proportioned to his offence. It is the literal, unvarnished truth, that the crack of the lash, and the shrieking of the slaves, can be heard from dark till bed time, on Epps' plantation, any day almost during the entire period of the cotton-picking season.

The number of lashes is graduated according to the nature of the case. Twenty-five are deemed a mere brush, inflicted, for instance, when a dry leaf or piece of boll is found in the cotton, or when a branch is broken in the field; fifty is the ordinary penalty following all delinquencies of the next higher grade; one hundred is called severe: it is the punishment inflicted for the serious offence of standing idle in the field; from one hundred and fifty to two hundred is bestowed upon him who quarrels with his cabin-mates, and five hundred, well laid on, besides the mangling of the dogs, perhaps, is certain to consign the poor, unpitied runaway to weeks of pain and agony.

During the two years Epps remained on the plantation at Bayou Huff Power, he was in the habit, as often as once in a fortnight at least, of coming home intoxicated from Holmesville. The shooting-matches almost invariably concluded with a debauch. At such times he was boisterous and half-crazy. Often he would break the dishes, chairs, and whatever furniture he could lay his hands on. When satisfied with his amusement in the house, he would seize the whip and walk forth into the yard. Then it behooved the slaves to be watchful and exceeding wary. The first one who came within reach felt the smart of his lash. Sometimes for hours he would keep them running in all directions, dodging around the corners of the cabins. Occasionally he would come upon one unawares, and if he succeeded in inflicting a fair, round blow, it was a feat that much delighted him. The younger children, and the aged, who had become inactive, suffered then. In the midst of the confusion he would slily take his stand behind a cabin, waiting with raised whip, to dash it into the first black face that peeped cautiously around the corner.

At other times he would come home in a less brutal humor. Then there must be a merry-making. Then all must move to the measure of a tune. Then Master Epps must needs regale his melodious ears with the music of a fiddle. Then did he become buoyant, elastic, gaily "tripping the light fantastic toe" around the piazza and all through the house.

Tibeats, at the time of my sale, had informed him I could play on the violin. He had received his information from Ford. Through the importunities of Mistress Epps, her husband had been induced to purchase me one during a visit to New-Orleans. Frequently I was called into the house to play before the family, mistress being passionately fond of music.

All of us would be assembled in the large room of the great house, whenever Epps came home in one of his dancing moods. No matter how worn out and tired we were, there must be a general dance. When properly stationed on the floor, I would strike up a tune.

"Dance, you d—d niggers, dance," Epps would shout.

Then there must be no halting or delay, no slow or languid

movements; all must be brisk, and lively, and alert. "Up and down, heel and toe, and away we go," was the order of the hour. Epps' portly form mingled with those of his dusky slaves, moving rapidly through all the mazes of the dance.

Usually his whip was in his hand, ready to fall about the ears of the presumptuous thrall, who dared to rest a moment, or even stop to catch his breath. When he was himself exhausted, there would be a brief cessation, but it would be very brief. With a slash, and crack, and flourish of the whip, he would shout again, "Dance, niggers, dance," and away they would go once more, pell-mell, while I spurred by an occasional sharp touch of the lash, sat in a corner, extracting from my violin a marvelous quick-stepping tune. The mistress often upbraided him, declaring she would return to her father's house at Cheneyville; nevertheless, there were times she could not restrain a burst of laughter, on witnessing his uproarious pranks. Frequently, we were thus detained until almost morning. Bent with excessive toil—actually suffering for a little refreshing rest, and feeling rather as if we could cast ourselves upon the earth and weep, many a night in the house of Edwin Epps have his unhappy slaves been made to dance and laugh.

Notwithstanding these deprivations in order to gratify the whim of an unreasonable master, we had to be in the field as soon as it was light, and during the day perform the ordinary and accustomed task. Such deprivations could not be urged at the scales in extenuation of any lack of weight, or in the cornfield for not hoeing with the usual rapidity. The whippings were just as severe as if we had gone forth in the morning, strengthened and invigorated by a night's repose. Indeed, after such frantic revels, he was always more sour and savage than before, punishing for slighter causes, and using the whip with increased and more vindictive energy.

Ten years I toiled for that man without reward. Ten years of my incessant labor has contributed to increase the bulk of his possessions. Ten years I was compelled to address him with down-cast eyes and uncovered head—in the attitude and language of a slave. I am indebted to him for nothing, save undeserved abuse and stripes.

Beyond the reach of his inhuman thong, and standing on the soil of the free State where I was born, thanks be to Heaven, I can raise my head once more among men. I can speak of the wrongs I have suffered, and of those who inflicted them, with upraised eyes. But I have no desire to speak of him or any other one otherwise than truthfully. Yet to speak truthfully of Edwin Epps would be to say—he is a man in whose heart the quality of kindness or of justice is not found. A rough, rude energy, united with an uncultivated mind and an avaricious spirit, are his prominent characteristics. He is known as a "nigger breaker," distinguished for his faculty of subduing the spirit of the slave, and priding himself upon his reputation in this respect, as a jockey boasts of his skill in managing a refractory horse. He looked upon a colored man, not as a human being, responsible to his Creator for the small talent entrusted to him, but as a "chattel personal," as mere live property, no better, except in value, than his mule or dog. When the evidence, clear and indisputable, was laid before him that I was a free man, and as much entitled to my liberty as he—when, on the day I left, he was informed that I had a wife and children, as dear to me as his own babes to him, he only raved and swore, denouncing the law that tore me from him, and declaring he would find out the man who had forwarded the letter that disclosed the place of my captivity, if there was any virtue or power in money, and would take his life. He thought of nothing but his loss, and cursed me for having been born free. He could have stood unmoved and seen the tongues of his poor slaves torn out by the roots—he could have seen them burned to ashes over a slow fire, or gnawed to death by dogs, if it only brought him profit. Such a hard, cruel, unjust man is Edwin Epps.

There was but one greater savage on Bayou Bœuf than he. Jim Burns' plantation was cultivated, as already mentioned, exclusively by women. That barbarian kept their backs so sore and raw, that they could not perform the customary labor demanded daily of the slave. He boasted of his cruelty, and through all the country round was accounted a more thorough-going, energetic man than even Epps. A brute himself, Jim Burns had not a particle of mercy for his subject brutes, and like a fool, whipped and scourged away the very strength upon which depended his amount of gain.

Epps remained on Huff Power two years, when, having accumulated a considerable sum of money, he expended it in the purchase of the plantation on the east bank of Bayou Bœuf, where he still continues to reside. He took possession of it in 1845, after the holidays were passed. He carried thither with him nine slaves, all of whom, except myself, and Susan, who has since died, remain there yet. He made no addition to this force, and for eight years the following were my companions in his quarters, viz: Abram, Wiley, Phebe, Bob, Henry, Edward, and Patsey. All these, except Edward, born since, were purchased out of a drove by Epps during the time he was overseer for Archy B. Williams, whose plantation is situated on the shore of Red River, not far from Alexandria.

Abram was tall, standing a full head above any common man. He is sixty years of age, and was born in Tennessee. Twenty years ago, he was purchased by a trader, carried into South Carolina, and sold to James Buford, of Williamsburgh county, in that State. In his youth he was renowned for his great strength, but age and unremitting toil have somewhat shattered his powerful frame and enfeebled his mental faculties.

Wiley is forty-eight. He was born on the estate of William Tassle, and for many years took charge of that gentleman's ferry over the Big Black River, in South Carolina.

Phebe was a slave of Buford, Tassle's neighbor, and having married Wiley, he bought the latter, at her instigation. Buford was a kind master, sheriff of the county, and in those days a man of wealth.

Bob and Henry are Phebe's children, by a former husband, their father having been abandoned to give place to Wiley. That seductive youth had insinuated himself into Phebe's affections, and therefore the faithless spouse had gently kicked her first husband out of her cabin door. Edward had been born to them on Bayou Huff Power.

Patsey is twenty-three—also from Buford's plantation. She is in no wise connected with the others, but glories in the fact that she is the offspring of a "Guinea nigger," brought over to Cuba in a slave ship, and in the course of trade transferred to Buford, who was her mother's owner.

This, as I learned from them, is a genealogical account of my master's slaves. For years they had been together. Often they recalled the memories of other days, and sighed to retrace their steps to the old home in Carolina. Troubles came upon their master Buford, which brought far greater troubles upon them. He became involved in debt, and unable to bear up against his failing fortunes, was compelled to sell these, and others of his slaves. In a chain gang they had been driven from beyond the Mississippi to the plantation of Archy B. Williams. Edwin Epps, who, for a long while had been his driver and overseer, was about establishing himself in business on his own account, at the time of their arrival, and accepted them in payment of his wages.

Old Abram was a kind-hearted being—a sort of patriarch among us, fond of entertaining his younger brethren with grave and serious discourse. He was deeply versed in such philosophy as is taught in the cabin of the slave; but the great absorbing hobby of Uncle Abram was General Jackson, whom his young master in

Tennessee had followed to the wars. He loved to wander back, in imagination, to the place where he was born, and to recount the scenes of his youth during those stirring times when the nation was in arms. He had been athletic, and more keen and powerful than the generality of his race, but now his eye had become dim, and his natural force abated. Very often, indeed, while discussing the best method of baking the hoe-cake, or expatiating at large upon the glory of Jackson, he would forget where he left his hat, or his hoe, or his basket; and then would the old man be laughed at, if Epps was absent, and whipped if he was present. So was he perplexed continually, and sighed to think that he was growing aged and going to decay. Philosophy and Jackson and forgetfulness had played the mischief with him, and it was evident that all of them combined were fast bringing down the gray hairs of Uncle Abram to the grave.

Aunt Phebe had been an excellent field hand, but latterly was put into the kitchen, where she remained, except occasionally, in a time of uncommon hurry. She was a sly old creature, and when not in the presence of her mistress or her master, was garrulous in the extreme.

Wiley, on the contrary, was silent. He performed his task without murmur or complaint, seldom indulging in the luxury of speech, except to utter a wish that he was away from Epps, and back once more in South Carolina.

Bob and Henry had reached the ages of twenty and twenty-three, and were distinguished for nothing extraordinary or unusual, while Edward, a lad of thirteen, not yet able to maintain his row in the corn or the cotton field, was kept in the great house, to wait on the little Eppses.

Patsey was slim and straight. She stood erect as the human form is capable of standing. There was an air of loftiness in her movement, that neither labor, nor weariness, nor punishment could destroy. Truly, Patsey was a splendid animal, and were it not that bondage had enshrouded her intellect in utter and everlasting darkness, would have been chief among ten thousand of her people. She could leap the highest fences, and a fleet hound it was indeed, that could outstrip her in a race. No horse could fling her from his back. She was a skillful teamster. She turned as true a furrow as the best, and at splitting rails there were none who could excel her. When the order to halt was heard at night, she would have her mules at the crib, unharnessed, fed and curried, before Uncle Abram had found his hat. Not, however, for all or any of these, was she chiefly famous. Such lightning-like motion was in her fingers as no other fingers ever possessed, and therefore it was, that in cotton picking time, Patsey was queen of the field.

She had a genial and pleasant temper, and was faithful and obedient. Naturally, she was a joyous creature, a laughing, light-hearted girl, rejoicing in the mere sense of existence. Yet Patsey wept oftener, and suffered more, than any of her companions. She had been literally excoriated. Her back bore the scars of a thousand stripes; not because she was backward in her work, nor because she was of an unmindful and rebellious spirit, but because it had fallen to her lot to be the slave of a licentious master and a jealous mistress. She shrank before the lustful eye of the one, and was in danger even of her life at the hands of the other, and between the two, she was indeed accursed. In the great house, for days together, there were high and angry words, poutings and estrangement, whereof she was the innocent cause. Nothing delighted the mistress so much as to see her suffer, and more than once, when Epps had refused to sell her, has she tempted me with bribes to put her secretly to death, and bury her body in some lonely place in the margin of the swamp. Gladly would Patsey have appeased this unforgiving spirit, if it had been in her power, but not like Joseph, dared she escape from Master Epps, leaving her garment in his hand. Patsey walked under a cloud. If she uttered a word in opposition to her master's will, the lash was resorted to at once, to bring her to subjection; if she was not watchful when about her cabin, or when walking in the yard, a billet of wood, or a broken bottle perhaps, hurled from her mistress' hand, would smite her unexpectedly in the face. The enslaved victim of lust and hate, Patsey had no comfort of her life.

These were my companions and fellow-slaves, with whom I was accustomed to be driven to the field, and with whom it has been my lot to dwell for ten years in the log cabins of Edwin Epps. They, if living, are yet toiling on the banks of Bayou Bœuf, never destined to breathe, as I now do, the blessed air of liberty, nor to shake off the heavy shackles that enthrall them, until they shall lie down forever in the dust.

# CHAPTER XIV

*Destruction Of The Cotton Crop In 1845—Demand For Laborers In St. Mary's Parish—Sent Thither In A Drove—The Order Of The March—The Grand Coteau—Hired To Judge Turner On Bayou Salle—Appointed Driver In His Sugar House—Sunday Services—Slave Furniture; How Obtained—The Party At Yarney's In Centreville—Good Fortune—The Captain Of The Steamer—His Refusal To Secrete Me—Return To Bayou Bœuf—Sight Of Tibeats—Patsey's Sorrows—Tumult And Contention—Hunting The Coon And Opossum—The Cunning Of The Latter—The Lean Condition Of The Slave—Description Of The Fish Trap—The Murder Of The Man From Natchez—Epps Challenged By Marshall—The Influence Of Slavery—The Love Of Freedom.*

The first year of Epps' residence on the bayou, 1845, the caterpillars almost totally destroyed the cotton crop throughout that region. There was little to be done, so that the slaves were necessarily idle half the time. However, there came a rumor to Bayou Bœuf that wages were high, and laborers in great demand on the sugar plantations in St. Mary's parish. This parish is situated on the coast of the Gulf of Mexico, about one hundred and forty miles from Avoyelles. The Rio Teche, a considerable stream, flows through St. Mary's to the gulf.

It was determined by the planters, on the receipt of this intelligence, to make up a drove of slaves to be sent down to Tuckapaw in St. Mary's, for the purpose of hiring them out in the cane fields. Accordingly, in the month of September, there were one hundred and forty-seven collected at Holmesville, Abram, Bob and myself among the number. Of these about one-half were women. Epps, Alonson Pierce, Henry Toler, and Addison Roberts, were the white men, selected to accompany, and take charge of the drove. They had a two-horse carriage and two saddle horses for their use. A large wagon, drawn by four horses, and driven by John, a boy belonging to Mr. Roberts, carried the blankets and provisions.

About 2 o'clock in the afternoon, having been fed, preparations were made to depart. The duty assigned me was, to take charge of the blankets and provisions, and see that none were lost by the way. The carriage proceeded in advance, the wagon following; behind this the slaves were arranged, while the two horsemen brought up the rear, and in this order the procession moved out of Holmesville.

That night we reached a Mr. McCrow's plantation, a distance of ten or fifteen miles, when we were ordered to halt. Large fires were built, and each one spreading his blanket on the ground, laid down upon it. The white men lodged in the great house. An hour before day we were aroused by the drivers coming among us, cracking their whips and ordering us to arise. Then the blankets were rolled up, and being severally delivered to me and deposited in the wagon, the procession set forth again.

The following night it rained violently. We were all drenched, our clothes saturated with mud and water. Reaching an open shed, formerly a gin-house, we found beneath it such shelter as it afforded. There was not room for all of us to lay down. There we remained, huddled together, through the night, continuing our march, as usual, in the morning. During the journey we were fed twice a day, boiling our bacon and baking our corn-cake at the fires in the same manner as in our huts. We passed through Lafayetteville, Mountsville, New-Town, to Centreville, where Bob and Uncle Abram were hired. Our number decreased as we advanced—nearly every sugar plantation requiring the services of one or more.

On our route we passed the Grand Coteau or prairie, a vast space of level, monotonous country, without a tree, except an occasional one which had been transplanted near some dilapidated dwelling. It was once thickly populated, and under cultivation, but for some cause had been abandoned. The business of the scattered inhabitants that now dwell upon it is principally raising cattle. Immense herds were feeding upon it as we passed. In the centre of the Grand Coteau one feels as if he were on the ocean, out of sight of land. As far as the eye can see, in all directions, it is but a ruined and deserted waste.

I was hired to Judge Turner, a distinguished man and extensive planter, whose large estate is situated on Bayou Salle, within a few miles of the gulf. Bayou Salle is a small stream flowing into the bay of Atchafalaya. For some days I was employed at Turner's in repairing his sugar house, when a cane knife was put into my hand, and with thirty or forty others, I was sent into the field. I found no such difficulty in learning the art of cutting cane that I had in picking cotton. It came to me naturally and intuitively, and in a short time I was able to keep up with the fastest knife. Before the cutting was over, however, Judge Turner transferred me from the field to the sugar house, to act there in the capacity of driver. From the time of the commencement of sugar making to the close, the grinding and boiling does not cease day or night. The whip was given me with directions to use it upon any one who was caught standing idle. If I failed to obey them to the letter, there was another one for my own back. In addition to this my duty was to call on and off the different gangs at the proper time. I had no regular periods of rest, and could never snatch but a few moments of sleep at a time.

It is the custom in Louisiana, as I presume it is in other slave States, to allow the slave to retain whatever compensation he may obtain for services performed on Sundays. In this way, only, are they able to provide themselves with any luxury or convenience whatever. When a slave, purchased, or kidnapped in the North, is transported to a cabin on Bayou Bœuf he is furnished with neither knife, nor fork, nor dish, nor kettle, nor any other thing in the shape of crockery, or furniture of any nature or description. He is furnished with a blanket before he reaches there, and wrapping that around him, he can either stand up, or lie down upon the ground, or on a board, if his master has no use for it. He is at liberty to find a gourd in which to keep his meal, or he can eat his corn from the cob, just as he pleases. To ask the master for a knife, or skillet, or any small convenience of the kind, would be answered with a kick, or laughed at as a joke. Whatever necessary article of this nature is found in a cabin has been purchased with Sunday money. However injurious to the morals, it is certainly a blessing to the physical condition of the slave, to be permitted to break the Sabbath. Otherwise there would be no way to provide himself with any utensils, which seem to be indispensable to him who is compelled to be his own cook.

On cane plantations in sugar time, there is no distinction as to the days of the week. It is well understood that all hands must labor on the Sabbath, and it is equally well understood that those especially who are hired, as I was to Judge Turner, and others in succeeding years, shall receive remuneration for it. It is usual, also, in the most hurrying time of cotton-picking, to require the same extra service. From this source, slaves generally are afforded an opportunity of earning sufficient to purchase a knife, a kettle, tobacco and so forth. The females, discarding the latter luxury, are apt to expend their little revenue in the purchase of gaudy ribbons, wherewithal to deck their hair in the merry season of the holidays.

I remained in St. Mary's until the first of January, during which time my Sunday money amounted to ten dollars. I met with other good fortune, for which I was indebted to my violin, my constant companion, the source of profit, and soother of my sorrows during years of servitude. There was a grand party of whites assembled at Mr. Yarney's, in Centreville, a hamlet in the vicinity of Turner's plantation. I was employed to play for them, and so well pleased were the merry-makers with my performance, that a contribution was taken for my benefit, which amounted to seventeen dollars.

With this sum in possession, I was looked upon by my fellows as a millionaire. It afforded me great pleasure to look at it—to count it over and over again, day after day. Visions of cabin furniture, of water pails, of pocket knives, new shoes and coats and hats, floated through my fancy, and up through all rose the triumphant contemplation, that I was the wealthiest "nigger" on Bayou Bœuf.

Vessels run up the Rio Teche to Centreville. While there, I was bold enough one day to present myself before the captain of a steamer, and beg permission to hide myself among the freight. I was emboldened to risk the hazard of such a step, from overhearing a conversation, in the course of which I ascertained he was a native of the North. I did not relate to him the particulars of my history, but only expressed an ardent desire to escape from slavery to a free State. He pitied me, but said it would be impossible to avoid the vigilant custom house officers in New-Orleans, and that detection would subject him to punishment, and his vessel to confiscation. My earnest entreaties evidently excited his sympathies, and doubtless he would have yielded to them, could he have done so with any kind of safety. I was compelled to smother the sudden flame that lighted up my bosom with sweet hopes of liberation, and turn my steps once more towards the increasing darkness of despair.

Immediately after this event the drove assembled at Centreville, and several of the owners having arrived and collected the monies due for our services, we were driven back to Bayou Bœuf. It was on our return, while passing through a small village, that I caught sight of Tibeats, seated in the door of a dirty grocery, looking somewhat seedy and out of repair. Passion and poor whisky, I doubt not, have ere this laid him on the shelf.

During our absence, I learned from Aunt Phebe and Patsey, that the latter had been getting deeper and deeper into trouble. The poor girl was truly an object of pity. "Old Hogjaw," the name by which Epps was called, when the slaves were by themselves, had beaten her more severely and frequently than ever. As surely as he came from Holmesville, elated with liquor—and it was often in those days—he would whip her, merely to gratify the mistress; would punish her to an extent almost beyond endurance, for an offence of which he himself was the sole and irresistible cause. In his sober moments he could not always be prevailed upon to indulge his wife's insatiable thirst for vengeance.

To be rid of Patsey—to place her beyond sight or reach, by sale, or death, or in any other manner, of late years, seemed to be the ruling thought and passion of my mistress. Patsey had been a favorite when a child, even in the great house. She had been petted and admired for her uncommon sprightliness and pleasant disposition. She had been fed many a time, so Uncle Abram said, even on biscuit and milk, when the madam, in her younger days, was wont to call her to the piazza, and fondle her as she would a playful kitten. But a sad change had come over the spirit of the woman. Now, only black and angry fiends ministered in the temple of her heart, until she could look on Patsey but with concentrated venom.

Mistress Epps was not naturally such an evil woman, after all. She was possessed of the devil, jealousy, it is true, but aside from that, there was much in her character to admire. Her father, Mr. Roberts, resided in Cheneyville, an influential and honorable man, and as much respected throughout the parish as any other citizen. She had been well educated at some institution this side the Mississippi; was beautiful, accomplished, and usually good-humored. She was kind to all of us but Patsey—frequently, in the absence of her husband, sending out to us some little dainty from her own table. In other situations—in a different society from that which exists on the shores of Bayou Bœuf, she would have been pronounced an elegant and fascinating woman. An ill wind it was that blew her into the arms of Epps.

He respected and loved his wife as much as a coarse nature like his is capable of loving, but supreme selfishness always overmastered conjugal affection.

"He loved as well as baser natures can,
But a mean heart and soul were in that man."

He was ready to gratify any whim—to grant any request she made, provided it did not cost too much. Patsey was equal to any two of his slaves in the cotton field. He could not replace her with the same money she would bring. The idea of disposing of her, therefore, could not be entertained. The mistress did not regard her at all in that light. The pride of the haughty woman was aroused; the blood of the fiery southern boiled at the sight of Patsey, and nothing less than trampling out the life of the helpless bondwoman would satisfy her.

Sometimes the current of her wrath turned upon him whom she had just cause to hate. But the storm of angry words would pass over at length, and there would be a season of calm again. At such times Patsey trembled with fear, and cried as if her heart would break, for she knew from painful experience, that if mistress should work herself to the red-hot pitch of rage, Epps would quiet her at last with a promise that Patsey should be flogged—a promise he was sure to keep. Thus did pride, and jealousy, and vengeance war with avarice and brute-passion in the mansion of my master, filling it with daily tumult and contention. Thus, upon the head of Patsey—the simpleminded slave, in whose heart God had implanted the seeds of virtue—the force of all these domestic tempests spent itself at last.

During the summer succeeding my return from St. Mary's parish, I conceived a plan of providing myself with food, which, though simple, succeeded beyond expectation. It has been followed by many others in my condition, up and down the bayou, and of such benefit has it become that I am almost persuaded to look upon myself as a benefactor. That summer the worms got into the bacon. Nothing but ravenous hunger could induce us to swallow it. The weekly allowance of meal scarcely sufficed to satisfy us. It was customary with us, as it is with all in that region, where the allowance is exhausted before Saturday night, or is in such a state as to render it nauseous and disgusting, to hunt in the swamps for coon and opossum. This, however, must be done at night, after the day's work is accomplished. There are planters whose slaves, for months at a time, have no other meat than such as is obtained in this manner. No objections are made to hunting, inasmuch as it dispenses with drafts upon the smoke-house, and because every marauding coon that is killed is so much saved from the standing corn. They are hunted with dogs and clubs, slaves not being allowed the use of fire-arms.

The flesh of the coon is palatable, but verily there is nothing in all butcherdom so delicious as a roasted 'possum. They are a round, rather long-bodied, little animal, of a whitish color, with nose like a pig, and caudal extremity like a rat. They burrow among the roots and in the hollows of the gum tree, and are clumsy and slow of motion. They are deceitful and cunning creatures. On receiving the slightest tap of a stick, they will roll over on the ground and feign death. If the hunter leaves him, in pursuit of another, without first taking particular pains to break his neck, the chances are, on his return, he is not to be found. The little animal has out witted the enemy—has "played 'possum"—and is off. But after a long and hard day's work, the weary slave feels little like going to the swamp for his supper, and half the time prefers throwing himself on the cabin floor without it. It is for the interest of the master that the servant should not suffer in health from starvation, and it is also for his interest that he should not become gross from over-feeding. In the estimation of the owner, a slave is the most serviceable when in rather a lean and lank condition, such a condition as the race-horse is in, when fitted for the course, and in that condition they are generally to be found on the sugar and cotton plantations along Red River.

# CHAPTER XIV

My cabin was within a few rods of the bayou bank, and necessity being indeed the mother of invention, I resolved upon a mode of obtaining the requisite amount of food, without the trouble of resorting nightly to the woods. This was to construct a fish trap. Having, in my mind, conceived the manner in which it could be done, the next Sunday I set about putting it into practical execution. It may be impossible for me to convey to the reader a full and correct idea of its construction, but the following will serve as a general description:

A frame between two and three feet square is made, and of a greater or less height, according to the depth of water. Boards or slats are nailed on three sides of this frame, not so closely, however, as to prevent the water circulating freely through it. A door is fitted into the fourth side, in such manner that it will slide easily up and down in the grooves cut in the two posts. A movable bottom is then so fitted that it can be raised to the top of the frame without difficulty. In the centre of the movable bottom an auger hole is bored, and into this one end of a handle or round stick is fastened on the under side so loosely that it will turn. The handle ascends from the centre of the movable bottom to the top of the frame, or as much higher as is desirable. Up and down this handle, in a great many places, are gimlet holes, through which small sticks are inserted, extending to opposite sides of the frame. So many of these small sticks are running out from the handle in all directions, that a fish of any considerable dimensions cannot pass through without hitting one of them. The frame is then placed in the water and made stationary.

The trap is "set" by sliding or drawing up the door, and kept in that position by another stick, one end of which rests in a notch on the inner side, the other end in a notch made in the handle, running up from the centre of the movable bottom. The trap is baited by rolling a handful of wet meal and cotton together until it becomes hard, and depositing it in the back part of the frame. A fish swimming through the upraised door towards the bait, necessarily strikes one of the small sticks turning the handle, which displacing the stick supporting the door, the latter falls, securing the fish within the frame. Taking hold of the top of the handle, the movable bottom is then drawn up to the surface of the water, and the fish taken out. There may have been other such traps in use before mine was constructed, but if there were I had never happened to see one. Bayou Bœuf abounds in fish of large size and excellent quality, and after this time I was very rarely in want of one for myself, or for my comrades. Thus a mine was opened—a new resource was developed, hitherto unthought of by the enslaved children of Africa, who toil and hunger along the shores of that sluggish, but prolific stream.

About the time of which I am now writing, an event occurred in our immediate neighborhood, which made a deep impression upon me, and which shows the state of society existing there, and the manner in which affronts are oftentimes avenged. Directly opposite our quarters, on the other side of the bayou, was situated the plantation of Mr. Marshall. He belonged to a family among the most wealthy and aristocratic in the country. A gentleman from the vicinity of Natchez had been negotiating with him for the purchase of the estate. One day a messenger came in great haste to our plantation, saying that a bloody and fearful battle was going on at Marshall's—that blood had been spilled—and unless the combatants were forthwith separated, the result would be disastrous.

On repairing to Marshall's house, a scene presented itself that beggars description. On the floor of one of the rooms lay the ghastly corpse of the man from Natchez, while Marshall, enraged and covered with wounds and blood, was stalking back and forth, "breathing out threatenings and slaughter." A difficulty had arisen in the course of their negotiation, high words ensued, when drawing their weapons, the deadly strife began that ended so unfortunately. Marshall was never placed in confinement. A sort of trial or investigation was had at Marksville, when he was acquitted, and returned to his plantation, rather more respected, as I thought, than ever, from the fact that the blood of a fellow being was on his soul.

Epps interested himself in his behalf, accompanying him to Marksville, and on all occasions loudly justifying him, but his services in this respect did not afterwards deter a kinsman of this same Marshall from seeking his life also. A brawl occurred between them over a gambling-table, which terminated in a deadly feud. Riding up on horseback in front of the house one day, armed with pistols and bowie knife, Marshall challenged him to come forth and make a final settlement of the quarrel, or he would brand him as a coward, and shoot him like a dog the first opportunity. Not through cowardice, nor from any conscientious scruples, in my opinion, but through the influence of his wife, he was restrained from accepting the challenge of his enemy. A reconciliation, however, was effected afterward, since which time they have been on terms of the closest intimacy.

Such occurrences, which would bring upon the parties concerned in them merited and condign punishment in the Northern States, are frequent on the bayou, and pass without notice, and almost without comment. Every man carries his bowie knife, and when two fall out, they set to work hacking and thrusting at each other, more like savages than civilized and enlightened beings.

The existence of Slavery in its most cruel form among them, has a tendency to brutalize the humane and finer feelings of their nature. Daily witnesses of human suffering—listening to the agonizing screeches of the slave—beholding him writhing beneath the merciless lash—bitten and torn by dogs—dying without attention, and buried without shroud or coffin—it cannot otherwise be expected, than that they should become brutified and reckless of human life. It is true there are many kind-hearted and good men in the parish of Avoyelles—such men as William Ford—who can look with pity upon the sufferings of a slave, just as there are, over all the world, sensitive and sympathetic spirits, who cannot look with indifference upon the sufferings of any creature which the Almighty has endowed with life. It is not the fault of the slaveholder that he is cruel, so much as it is the fault of the system under which he lives. He cannot withstand the influence of habit and associations that surround him. Taught from earliest childhood, by all that he sees and hears, that the rod is for the slave's back, he will not be apt to change his opinions in maturer years.

There may be humane masters, as there certainly are inhuman ones—there may be slaves well-clothed, well-fed, and happy, as there surely are those half-clad, half-starved and miserable; nevertheless, the institution that tolerates such wrong and inhumanity as I have witnessed, is a cruel, unjust, and barbarous one. Men may write fictions portraying lowly life as it is, or as it is not—may expatiate with owlish gravity upon the bliss of ignorance—discourse flippantly from arm chairs of the pleasures of slave life; but let them toil with him in the field—sleep with him in the cabin—feed with him on husks; let them behold him scourged, hunted, trampled on, and they will come back with another story in their mouths. Let them know the *heart* of the poor slave—learn his secret thoughts—thoughts he dare not utter in the hearing of the white man; let them sit by him in the silent watches of the night—converse with him in trustful confidence, of "life, liberty, and the pursuit of happiness," and they will find that ninety-nine out of every hundred are intelligent enough to understand their situation, and to cherish in their bosoms the love of freedom, as passionately as themselves.

# CHAPTER XV

*Labors On Sugar Plantations—The Mode Of Planting Cane—Of Hoeing Cane—Cane Ricks—Cutting Cane—Description Of The Cane Knife—Winrowing—Preparing For Succeeding Crops—Description Of Hawkins' Sugar Mill On Bayou Bœuf—The Christmas Holidays—The Carnival Season Of The Children Of Bondage—The Christmas Supper—Red, The Favorite Color—The Violin, And The Consolation It Afforded—The Christmas Dance—Lively, The Coquette—Sam Roberts, And His Rivals—Slave Songs—Southern Life As It Is—Three Days In The Year—The System Of Marriage—Uncle Abram's Contempt Of Matrimony.*

In consequence of my inability in cotton-picking, Epps was in the habit of hiring me out on sugar plantations during the season of cane-cutting and sugar-making. He received for my services a dollar a day, with the money supplying my place on his cotton plantation. Cutting cane was an employment that suited me, and for three successive years I held the lead row at Hawkins', leading a gang of from fifty to an hundred hands.

In a previous chapter the mode of cultivating cotton is described. This may be the proper place to speak of the manner of cultivating cane.

The ground is prepared in beds, the same as it is prepared for the reception of the cotton seed, except it is ploughed deeper. Drills are made in the same manner. Planting commences in January, and continues until April. It is necessary to plant a sugar field only once in three years. Three crops are taken before the seed or plant is exhausted.

Three gangs are employed in the operation. One draws the cane from the rick, or stack, cutting the top and flags from the stalk, leaving only that part which is sound and healthy. Each joint of the cane has an eye, like the eye of a potato, which sends forth a sprout when buried in the soil. Another gang lays the cane in the drill, placing two stalks side by side in such manner that joints will occur once in four or six inches. The third gang follows with hoes, drawing earth upon the stalks, and covering them to the depth, of three inches.

In four weeks, at the farthest, the sprouts appear above the ground, and from this time forward grow with great rapidity. A sugar field is hoed three times, the same as cotton, save that a greater quantity of earth is drawn to the roots. By the first of August hoeing is usually over. About the middle of September, whatever is required for seed is cut and stacked in ricks, as they are termed. In October it is ready for the mill or sugar-house, and then the general cutting begins. The blade of a cane-knife is fifteen inches long, three inches wide in the middle, and tapering towards the point and handle. The blade is thin, and in order to be at all serviceable must be kept very sharp. Every third hand takes the lead of two others, one of whom is on each side of him. The lead hand, in the first place, with a blow of his knife shears the flags from the stalk. He next cuts off the top down as far as it is green. He must be careful to sever all the green from the ripe part, inasmuch as the juice of the former sours the molasses, and renders it unsalable. Then he severs the stalk at the root, and lays it directly behind him. His right and left hand companions lay their stalks, when cut in the same manner, upon his. To every three hands there is a cart, which follows, and the stalks are thrown into it by the younger slaves, when it is drawn to the sugar-house and ground.

If the planter apprehends a frost, the cane is winrowed. Winrowing is the cutting the stalks at an early period and throwing them lengthwise in the water furrow in such a manner that the tops will cover the butts of the stalks. They will remain in this condition three weeks or a month without souring, and secure from frost. When the proper time arrives, they are taken up, trimmed and carted to the sugar-house.

In the month of January the slaves enter the field again to prepare for another crop. The ground is now strewn with the tops, and flags cut from the past year's cane. On a dry day fire is set to this combustible refuse, which sweeps over the field, leaving it bare and clean, and ready for the hoes. The earth is loosened about the roots of the old stubble, and in process of time another crop springs up from the last year's seed. It is the same the year following; but the third year the seed has exhausted its strength, and the field must be ploughed and planted again. The second year the cane is sweeter and yields more than the first, and the third year more than the second.

During the three seasons I labored on Hawkins' plantation, I was employed a considerable portion of the time in the sugar-house. He is celebrated as the producer of the finest variety of white sugar. The following is a general description of his sugar-house and the process of manufacture:

The mill is an immense brick building, standing on the shore of the bayou. Running out from the building is an open shed, at least an hundred feet in length and forty or fifty feet in width. The boiler in which the steam is generated is situated outside the main building; the machinery and engine rest on a brick pier, fifteen feet above the floor, within the body of the building. The machinery turns two great iron rollers, between two and three feet in diameter and six or eight feet in length. They are elevated above the brick pier, and roll in towards each other. An endless carrier, made of chain and wood, like leathern belts used in small mills, extends from the iron rollers out of the main building and through the entire length of the open shed. The carts in which the cane is brought from the field as fast as it is cut, are unloaded at the sides of the shed. All along the endless carrier are ranged slave children, whose business it is to place the cane upon it, when it is conveyed through the shed into the main building, where it falls between the rollers, is crushed, and drops upon another carrier that conveys it out of the main building in an opposite direction, depositing it in the top of a chimney upon a fire beneath, which consumes it. It is necessary to burn it in this manner, because otherwise it would soon fill the building, and more especially because it would soon sour and engender disease. The juice of the cane falls into a conductor underneath the iron rollers, and is carried into a reservoir. Pipes convey it from thence into five filterers, holding several hogsheads each. These filterers are filled with bone-black, a substance resembling pulverized charcoal. It is made of bones calcinated in close vessels, and is used for the purpose of decolorizing, by filtration, the cane juice before boiling. Through these five filterers it passes in succession, and then runs into a large reservoir underneath the ground floor, from whence it is carried up, by means of a steam pump, into a clarifier made of sheet iron, where it is heated by steam until it boils. From the first clarifier it is carried in pipes to a second and a third, and thence into close iron pans, through which tubes pass, filled with steam. While in a boiling state it flows through three pans in succession, and is then carried in other pipes down to the coolers on the ground floor. Coolers are wooden boxes with sieve bottoms made of the finest wire. As soon as the syrup passes into the coolers, and is met by the air, it grains, and the molasses at once escapes through the sieves into a cistern below. It is then white or loaf sugar of the finest kind—clear, clean, and as white as snow. When cool, it is taken out, packed in hogsheads, and is ready for market. The molasses is then carried from the cistern into the upper story again, and by another process converted into brown sugar.

There are larger mills, and those constructed differently from the one thus imperfectly described, but none, perhaps, more celebrated than this anywhere on Bayou Bœuf. Lambert, of New-Orleans, is a partner of Hawkins. He is a man of vast wealth, holding, as I have been told, an interest in over forty different sugar plantations in Louisiana.

The only respite from constant labor the slave has through the whole year, is during the Christmas holidays. Epps allowed us three—others allow four, five and six days, according to the measure of their generosity. It is the only time to which they look forward with any interest or pleasure. They are glad when night comes, not only because it brings them a few hours repose, but because it brings them one day nearer Christmas. It is hailed with equal delight by the old and the young; even Uncle Abram ceases to glorify Andrew Jackson, and Patsey forgets her many sorrows, amid the general hilarity of the holidays. It is the time of feasting, and frolicking, and fiddling—the carnival season with the children of bondage. They are the only days when they are allowed a little restricted liberty, and heartily indeed do they enjoy it.

It is the custom for one planter to give a "Christmas supper," inviting the slaves from neighboring plantations to join his own on the occasion; for instance, one year it is given by Epps, the next by Marshall, the next by Hawkins, and so on. Usually from three to five hundred are assembled, coming together on foot, in carts, on horseback, on mules, riding double and triple, sometimes a boy and girl, at others a girl and two boys, and at others again a boy, a girl and an old woman. Uncle Abram astride a mule, with Aunt Phebe and Patsey behind him, trotting towards a Christmas supper, would be no uncommon sight on Bayou Bœuf.

Then, too, "of all days i' the year," they array themselves in their best attire. The cotton coat has been washed clean, the stump of a tallow candle has been applied to the shoes, and if so fortunate as to possess a rimless or a crownless hat, it is placed jauntily on the head. They are welcomed with equal cordiality, however, if they come bare-headed and barefooted to the feast. As a general thing, the women wear handkerchiefs tied about their heads, but if chance has thrown in their way a fiery red ribbon, or a cast-off bonnet of their mistress' grandmother, it is sure to be worn on such occasions. Red—the deep blood red—is decidedly the favorite color among the enslaved damsels of my acquaintance. If a red ribbon does not encircle the neck, you will be certain to find all the hair of their woolly heads tied up with red strings of one sort or another.

The table is spread in the open air, and loaded with varieties of meat and piles of vegetables. Bacon and corn meal at such times are dispensed with. Sometimes the cooking is performed in the kitchen on the plantation, at others in the shade of wide branching trees. In the latter case, a ditch is dug in the ground, and wood laid in and burned until it is filled with glowing coals, over which chickens, ducks, turkeys, pigs, and not unfrequently the entire body of a wild ox, are roasted. They are furnished also with flour, of which biscuits are made, and often with peach and other preserves, with tarts, and every manner and description of pies, except the mince, that being an article of pastry as yet unknown among them. Only the slave who has lived all the years on his scanty allowance of meal and bacon, can appreciate such suppers. White people in great numbers assemble to witness the gastronomical enjoyments.

They seat themselves at the rustic table—the males on one side, the females on the other. The two between whom there may have been an exchange of tenderness, invariably manage to sit opposite; for the omnipresent Cupid disdains not to hurl his arrows into the simple hearts of slaves. Unalloyed and exulting happiness lights up the dark faces of them all. The ivory teeth, contrasting with their black complexions, exhibit two long, white streaks the whole extent of the table. All round the bountiful board a multitude of eyes roll in ecstacy. Giggling and laughter and the clattering of cutlery and crockery succeed. Cuffee's elbow hunches his neighbor's side, impelled by an involuntary impulse of delight; Nelly shakes her finger at Sambo and laughs, she knows not why, and so the fun and merriment flows on.

When the viands have disappeared, and the hungry maws of the children of toil are satisfied, then, next in the order of amusement, is the Christmas dance. My business on these gala days always was to play on the violin. The African race is a music-loving one, proverbially; and many there were among my fellow-bondsmen whose organs of tune were strikingly developed, and who could thumb the banjo with dexterity; but at the expense of appearing egotistical, I must, nevertheless, declare, that I was considered the Ole Bull of Bayou Bœuf. My master often received letters, sometimes from a distance of ten miles, requesting him to send me to play at a ball or festival of the whites. He received his compensation, and usually I also returned with many picayunes jingling in my pockets—the extra contributions of those to whose delight I had administered. In this manner I became more acquainted than I otherwise would, up and down the bayou. The young men and maidens of Holmesville always knew there was to be a jollification somewhere, whenever Platt Epps was seen passing through the town with his fiddle in his hand. "Where are you going now, Platt?" and "What is coming off to-night, Platt?" would be interrogatories issuing from every door and window, and many a time when there was no special hurry, yielding to pressing importunities, Platt would draw his bow, and sitting astride his mule, perhaps, discourse musically to a crowd of delighted children, gathered around him in the street.

Alas! had it not been for my beloved violin, I scarcely can conceive how I could have endured the long years of bondage. It introduced me to great houses—relieved me of many days' labor in the field—supplied me with conveniences for my cabin—with pipes and tobacco, and extra pairs of shoes, and oftentimes led me away from the presence of a hard master, to witness scenes of jollity and mirth. It was my companion—the friend of my bosom—triumphing loudly when I was joyful, and uttering its soft, melodious consolations when I was sad. Often, at midnight, when sleep had fled affrighted from the cabin, and my soul was disturbed and troubled with the contemplation of my fate, it would sing me a song of peace. On holy Sabbath days, when an hour or two of leisure was allowed, it would accompany me to some quiet place on the bayou bank, and, lifting up its voice, discourse kindly and pleasantly indeed. It heralded my name round the country—made me friends, who, otherwise would not have noticed me—gave me an honored seat at the yearly feasts, and secured the loudest and heartiest welcome of them all at the Christmas dance. The Christmas dance! Oh, ye pleasure-seeking sons and daughters of idleness, who move with measured step, listless and snail-like, through the slow-winding cotillon, if ye wish to look upon the celerity, if not the "poetry of motion"—upon genuine happiness, rampant and unrestrained—go down to Louisiana, and see the slaves dancing in the starlight of a Christmas night.

On that particular Christmas I have now in my mind, a description whereof will serve as a description of the day generally, Miss Lively and Mr. Sam, the first belonging to Stewart, the latter to Roberts, started the ball. It was well known that Sam cherished an ardent passion for Lively, as also did one of Marshall's and another of Carey's boys; for Lively was *lively* indeed, and a heart-breaking coquette withal. It was a victory for Sam Roberts, when, rising from the repast, she gave him her hand for the first "figure" in preference to either of his rivals. They were somewhat crest-fallen, and, shaking their heads angrily, rather intimated they would like to pitch into Mr. Sam and hurt him badly. But not an emotion of wrath ruffled the placid bosom of Samuel, as his legs flew like drum-sticks down the outside and up the middle, by the side of his bewitching partner. The whole company cheered them vociferously, and, excited with the applause, they continued "tearing down" after all the others had become exhausted and halted a moment to recover breath. But Sam's superhuman exertions overcame him finally, leaving Lively alone, yet whirling like a top. Thereupon one of Sam's rivals, Pete Marshall, dashed in, and, with might and main, leaped and shuffled and threw himself into every conceivable shape, as if determined to show Miss Lively and all the world that Sam Roberts was of no account.

Pete's affection, however, was greater than his discretion. Such violent exercise took the breath out of him directly, and he dropped like an empty bag. Then was the time for Harry Carey to try his hand; but Lively also soon out-winded him, amidst hurrahs and shouts, fully sustaining her well-earned reputation of being the "fastest gal" on the bayou.

One "set" off, another takes its place, he or she remaining longest on the floor receiving the most uproarious commendation, and so the dancing continues until broad daylight. It does not cease with the sound of the fiddle, but in that case they set up a music peculiar to themselves. This is called "patting," accompanied with one of those unmeaning songs, composed rather for its adaptation to a certain tune or measure, than for the purpose of expressing any distinct idea. The patting is performed by striking the hands on the knees, then striking the hands together, then striking the right shoulder with one hand, the left with the other—all the while keeping time with the feet, and singing, perhaps, this song:

"Harper's creek and roarin' ribber,
Thar, my dear, we'll live forebber;
Den we'll go to de Ingin nation,
All I want in dis creation,
Is pretty little wife and big plantation.

*Chorus.*
Up dat oak and down dat ribber,
Two overseers and one little nigger."

Or, if these words are not adapted to the tune called for, it may be that "Old Hog Eye" *is*—a rather solemn and startling specimen of versification, not, however, to be appreciated unless heard at the South. It runneth as follows:

"Who's been here since I've been gone?
Pretty little gal wid a josey on.
Hog Eye!
Old Hog Eye,
And Hosey too!

Never see de like since I was born,
Here come a little gal wid a josey on.
Hog Eye!
Old Hog Eye!
And Hosey too!"

Or, may be the following, perhaps, equally nonsensical, but full of melody, nevertheless, as it flows from the negro's mouth:

"Ebo Dick and Jurdan's Jo,
Them two niggers stole my yo'.
*Chorus.* Hop Jim along,
Walk Jim along,
Talk Jim along, &c.

Old black Dan, as black as tar,
He dam glad he was not dar.
Hop Jim along," &c.

During the remaining holidays succeeding Christmas, they are provided with passes, and permitted to go where they please within a limited distance, or they may remain and labor on the plantation, in which case they are paid for it. It is very rarely, however, that the latter alternative is accepted. They may be seen at these times hurrying in all directions, as happy looking mortals as can be found on the face of the earth. They are different beings from what they are in the field; the temporary relaxation, the brief deliverance from fear, and from the lash, producing an entire metamorphosis in their appearance and demeanor. In visiting, riding, renewing old friendships, or, perchance, reviving some old attachment, or pursuing whatever pleasure may suggest itself, the time is occupied. Such is "southern life as it is," *three days in the year*, as I found it—the other three hundred and sixty-two being days of weariness, and fear, and suffering, and unremitting labor.

Marriage is frequently contracted during the holidays, if such an institution may be said to exist among them. The only ceremony required before entering into that "holy estate," is to obtain the consent of the respective owners. It is usually encouraged by the masters of female slaves. Either party can have as many husbands or wives as the owner will permit, and either is at liberty to discard the other at pleasure. The law in relation to divorce, or to bigamy, and so forth, is not applicable to property, of course. If the wife does not belong on the same plantation with the husband, the latter is permitted to visit her on Saturday nights, if the distance is not too far. Uncle Abram's wife lived seven miles from Epps', on Bayou Huff Power. He had permission to visit her once a fortnight, but he was growing old, as has been said, and truth to say, had latterly well nigh forgotten her. Uncle Abram had no time to spare from his meditations on General Jackson—connubial dalliance being well enough for the young and thoughtless, but unbecoming a grave and solemn philosopher like himself.

# CHAPTER XVI

*Overseers—How They Are Armed And Accompanied—The Homicide—His Execution At Marksville—Slave-Drivers—Appointed Driver On Removing To Bayou Bœuf—Practice Makes Perfect—Epps' Attempt To Cut Platt's Throat—The Escape From Him—Protected By The Mistress—Forbids Reading And Writing—Obtain A Sheet Of Paper After Nine Years' Effort—The Letter—Armsby, The Mean White—Partially Confide In Him—His Treachery—Epps' Suspicions—How They Were Quieted—Burning The Letter—Armsby Leaves The Bayou—Disappointment And Despair.*

With the exception of my trip to St. Mary's parish, and my absence during the cane-cutting seasons, I was constantly employed on the plantation of Master Epps. He was considered but a small planter, not having a sufficient number of hands to require the services of an overseer, acting in the latter capacity himself. Not able to increase his force, it was his custom to hire during the hurry of cotton-picking.

On larger estates, employing fifty or a hundred, or perhaps two hundred hands, an overseer is deemed indispensable. These gentlemen ride into the field on horseback, without an exception, to my knowledge, armed with pistols, bowie knife, whip, and accompanied by several dogs. They follow, equipped in this fashion, in rear of the slaves, keeping a sharp lookout upon them all. The requisite qualifications in an overseer are utter heartlessness, brutality and cruelty. It is his business to produce large crops, and if that is accomplished, no matter what amount of suffering it may have cost. The presence of the dogs are necessary to overhaul a fugitive who may take to his heels, as is sometimes the case, when faint or sick, he is unable to maintain his row, and unable, also, to endure the whip. The pistols are reserved for any dangerous emergency, there having been instances when such weapons were necessary. Goaded into uncontrollable madness, even the slave will sometimes turn upon his oppressor. The gallows were standing at Marksville last January, upon which one was executed a year ago for killing his overseer. It occurred not many miles from Epps' plantation on Red River. The slave was given his task at splitting rails. In the course of the day the overseer sent him on an errand, which occupied so much time that it was not possible for him to perform the task. The next day he was called to an account, but the loss of time occasioned by the errand was no excuse, and he was ordered to kneel and bare his back for the reception of the lash. They were in the woods alone—

beyond the reach of sight or hearing. The boy submitted until maddened at such injustice, and insane with pain, he sprang to his feet, and seizing an axe, literally chopped the overseer in pieces. He made no attempt whatever at concealment, but hastening to his master, related the whole affair, and declared himself ready to expiate the wrong by the sacrifice of his life. He was led to the scaffold, and while the rope was around his neck, maintained an undismayed and fearless bearing, and with his last words justified the act.

Besides the overseer, there are drivers under him, the number being in proportion to the number of hands in the field. The drivers are black, who, in addition to the performance of their equal share of work, are compelled to do the whipping of their several gangs. Whips hang around their necks, and if they fail to use them thoroughly, are whipped themselves. They have a few privileges, however; for example, in cane-cutting the hands are not allowed to sit down long enough to eat their dinners. Carts filled with corn cake, cooked at the kitchen, are driven into the field at noon. The cake is distributed by the drivers, and must be eaten with the least possible delay.

When the slave ceases to perspire, as he often does when taxed beyond his strength, he falls to the ground and becomes entirely helpless. It is then the duty of the driver to drag him into the shade of the standing cotton or cane, or of a neighboring tree, where he dashes buckets of water upon him, and uses other means of bringing out perspiration again, when he is ordered to his place, and compelled to continue his labor.

At Huff Power, when I first came to Epps', Tom, one of Roberts' negroes, was driver. He was a burly fellow, and severe in the extreme. After Epps' removal to Bayou Bœuf, that distinguished honor was conferred upon myself. Up to the time of my departure I had to wear a whip about my neck in the field. If Epps was present, I dared not show any lenity, not having the Christian fortitude of a certain well-known Uncle Tom sufficiently to brave his wrath, by refusing to perform the office. In that way, only, I escaped the immediate martyrdom he suffered, and, withal, saved my companions much suffering, as it proved in the end. Epps, I soon found, whether actually in the field or not, had his eyes pretty generally upon us. From the piazza, from behind some adjacent tree, or other concealed point of observation, he was perpetually on the watch. If one of us had been backward or idle through the day, we were apt to be told all about it on returning to the quarters, and as it was a matter of principle with him to reprove every offence of that kind that came within his knowledge, the offender not only was certain of receiving a castigation for his tardiness, but I likewise was punished for permitting it.

If, on the other hand, he had seen me use the lash freely, the man was satisfied. "Practice makes perfect," truly; and during my eight years' experience as a driver, I learned to handle the whip with marvelous dexterity and precision, throwing the lash within a hair's breadth of the back, the ear, the nose, without, however, touching either of them. If Epps was observed at a distance, or we had reason to apprehend he was sneaking somewhere in the vicinity, I would commence plying the lash vigorously, when, according to arrangement, they would squirm and screech as if in agony, although not one of them had in fact been even grazed. Patsey would take occasion, if he made his appearance presently, to mumble in his hearing some complaints that Platt was lashing them the whole time, and Uncle Abram, with an appearance of honesty peculiar to himself, would declare roundly I had just whipped them worse than General Jackson whipped the enemy at New-Orleans. If Epps was not drunk, and in one of his beastly humors, this was, in general, satisfactory. If he was, some one or more of us must suffer, as a matter of course. Sometimes his violence assumed a dangerous form, placing the lives of his human stock in jeopardy. On one occasion the drunken madman thought to amuse himself by cutting my throat.

He had been absent at Holmesville, in attendance at a shooting-match, and none of us were aware of his return. While hoeing by the side of Patsey, she exclaimed, in a low voice, suddenly, "Platt, d'ye see old Hog-Jaw beckoning me to come to him?"

Glancing sideways, I discovered him in the edge of the field, motioning and grimacing, as was his habit when half-intoxicated. Aware of his lewd intentions, Patsey began to cry. I whispered her not to look up, and to continue at her work, as if she had not observed him. Suspecting the truth of the matter, however, he soon staggered up to me in a great rage.

"What did you say to Pats?" he demanded, with an oath. I made him some evasive answer, which only had the effect of increasing his violence.

"How long have you owned this plantation, *say*, you d——d nigger?" he inquired, with a malicious sneer, at the same time taking hold of my shirt collar with one hand, and thrusting the other into his pocket. "Now I'll cut your black throat; that's what I'll do," drawing his knife from his pocket as he said it. But with one hand he was unable to open it, until finally seizing the blade in his teeth, I saw he was about to succeed, and felt the necessity of escaping from him, for in his present reckless state, it was evident he was not joking, by any means. My shirt was open in front, and as I turned round quickly and sprang from him, while he still retained his gripe, it was stripped entirely from my back. There was no difficulty now in eluding him. He would chase me until out of breath, then stop until it was recovered, swear, and renew the chase again. Now he would command me to come to him, now endeavor to coax me, but I was careful to keep at a respectful distance. In this manner we made the circuit of the field several times, he making desperate plunges, and I always dodging them, more amused than frightened, well knowing that when his sober senses returned, he would laugh at his own drunken folly. At length I observed the mistress standing by the yard fence, watching our half-serious, half-comical manœuvres. Shooting past him, I ran directly to her. Epps, on discovering her, did not follow. He remained about the field an hour or more, during which time I stood by the mistress, having related the particulars of what had taken place. Now, *she* was aroused again, denouncing her husband and Patsey about equally. Finally, Epps came towards the house, by this time nearly sober, walking demurely, with his hands behind his back, and attempting to look as innocent as a child.

As he approached, nevertheless, Mistress Epps began to berate him roundly, heaping upon him many rather disrespectful epithets, and demanding for what reason he had attempted to cut my throat. Epps made wondrous strange of it all, and to my surprise, swore by all the saints in the calendar he had not spoken to me that day.

"Platt, you lying nigger, *have* I?" was his brazen appeal to me.

It is not safe to contradict a master, even by the assertion of a truth. So I was silent, and when he entered the house I returned to the field, and the affair was never after alluded to.

Shortly after this time a circumstance occurred that came nigh divulging the secret of my real name and history, which I had so long and carefully concealed, and upon which I was convinced depended my final escape. Soon after he purchased me, Epps asked me if I could write and read, and on being informed that I had received some instruction in those branches of education, he assured me, with emphasis, if he evercaught me with a book, or with pen and ink, he would give me a hundred lashes. He said he wanted me to understand that he bought "niggers" to work and not to educate. He never inquired a word of my past life, or from whence I came. The mistress, however, cross-examined me frequently about Washington, which she supposed was my native city, and more than once remarked that I did not talk nor act like the other "niggers," and she was sure I had seen more of the world than I admitted.

My great object always was to invent means of getting a letter secretly into the post-office, directed to some of my friends or family at the North. The difficulty of such an achievement cannot be comprehended by one unacquainted with the severe restrictions imposed upon me. In the first place, I was deprived of pen, ink, and paper. In the second place, a slave cannot leave his plantation without a pass, nor will a post-master mail a letter for one without written instructions from his owner. I was in slavery nine years, and always watchful and on the alert, before I met with the good fortune of obtaining a sheet of paper. While Epps was in New-Orleans, one winter, disposing of his cotton, the mistress sent me to Holmesville, with an order for several articles, and among the rest a quantity of foolscap. I appropriated a sheet, concealing it in the cabin, under the board on which I slept.

After various experiments I succeeded in making ink, by boiling white maple bark, and with a feather plucked from the wing of a duck, manufactured a pen. When all were asleep in the cabin, by the light of the coals, lying upon my plank couch, I managed to complete a somewhat lengthy epistle. It was directed to an old acquaintance at Sandy Hill, stating my condition, and urging him to take measures to restore me to liberty. This letter I kept a long time, contriving measures by which it could be safely deposited in the post-office. At length, a low fellow, by the name of Armsby, hitherto a stranger, came into the neighborhood, seeking a situation as overseer. He applied to Epps, and was about the plantation for several days. He next went over to Shaw's, near by, and remained with him several weeks. Shaw was generally surrounded by such worthless characters, being himself noted as a gambler and unprincipled man. He had made a wife of his slave Charlotte, and a brood of young mulattoes were growing up in his house. Armsby became so much reduced at last, that he was compelled to labor with the slaves. A white man working in the field is a rare and unusual spectacle on Bayou Bœuf. I improved every opportunity of cultivating his acquaintance privately, desiring to obtain his confidence so far as to be willing to intrust the letter to his keeping. He visited Marksville repeatedly, he informed me, a town some twenty miles distant, and there, I proposed to myself, the letter should be mailed.

Carefully deliberating on the most proper manner of approaching him on the subject, I concluded finally to ask him simply if he would deposit a letter for me in the Marksville post-office the next time he visited that place, without disclosing to him that the letter was written, or any of the particulars it contained; for I had fears that he might betray me, and knew that some inducement must be held out to him of a pecuniary nature, before it would be safe to confide in him. As late as one o'clock one night I stole noiselessly from my cabin, and, crossing the field to Shaw's, found him sleeping on the piazza. I had but a few picayunes—the proceeds of my fiddling performances, but all I had in the world I promised him if he would do me the favor required. I begged him not to expose me if he could not grant the request. He assured me, upon his honor, he would deposit it in the Marksville post-office, and that he would keep it an inviolable secret forever. Though the letter was in my pocket at the time, I dared not then deliver it to him, but stating I would have it written in a day or two, bade him good night, and returned to my cabin. It was impossible for me to expel the suspicions I entertained, and all night I lay awake, revolving in my mind the safest course to pursue. I was willing to risk a great deal to accomplish my purpose, but should the letter by any means fall into the hands of Epps, it would be a death-blow to my aspirations. I was "perplexed in the extreme."

My suspicions were well-founded, as the sequel demonstrated. The next day but one, while scraping cotton in the field, Epps seated himself on the line fence between Shaw's plantation and his own, in such a position as to overlook the scene of our labors. Presently Armsby made his appearance, and, mounting the fence, took a seat beside him. They remained two or three hours, all of which time I was in an agony of apprehension.

That night, while broiling my bacon, Epps entered the cabin with his rawhide in his hand.

"Well, boy," said he, "I understand I've got a larned nigger, that writes letters, and tries to get white fellows to mail 'em. Wonder if you know who he is?"

My worst fears were realized, and although it may not be considered entirely creditable, even under the circumstances, yet a resort to duplicity and downright falsehood was the only refuge that presented itself.

"Don't know nothing about it, Master Epps," I answered him, assuming an air of ignorance and surprise; "Don't know nothing at all about it, sir."

"Wan't you over to Shaw's night before last?" he inquired.

"No, master," was the reply.

"Hav'nt you asked that fellow, Armsby, to mail a letter for you at Marksville?"

"Why, Lord, master, I never spoke three words to him in all my life. I don't know what you mean."

"Well," he continued, "Armsby told me to-day the devil was among my niggers; that I had one that needed close watching or he would run away; and when I axed him why, he said you come over to Shaw's, and waked him up in the night, and wanted him to carry a letter to Marksville. What have you got to say to that, ha?"

"All I've got to say, master," I replied, "is, there is no truth in it. How could I write a letter without any ink or paper? There is nobody I want to write to, 'cause I haint got no friends living as I know of. That Armsby is a lying, drunken fellow, they say, and nobody believes him anyway. You know I always tell the truth, and that I never go off the plantation without a pass. Now, master, I can see what that Armsby is after, plain enough. Did'nt he want you to hire him for an overseer?"

"Yes, he wanted me to hire him," answered Epps.

"That's it," said I, "he wants to make you believe we're all going to run away, and then he thinks you'll hire an overseer to watch us. He just made that story out of whole cloth, 'cause he wants to get a situation. It's all a lie, master, you may depend on't."

Epps mused awhile, evidently impressed with the plausibility of my theory, and exclaimed,

"I'm d—d, Platt, if I don't believe you tell the truth. He must take me for a soft, to think he can come it over me with them kind of yarns, musn't he? Maybe he thinks he can fool me; maybe he thinks I don't know nothing—can't take care of my own niggers, eh! Soft soap old Epps, eh! Ha, ha, ha! D—n Armsby! Set the dogs on him, Platt," and with many other comments descriptive of Armsby's general character, and his capability of taking care of his own business, and attending to his own "niggers," Master Epps left the cabin. As soon as he was gone I threw the letter in the fire, and, with a desponding and despairing heart, beheld the epistle which had cost me so much anxiety and thought, and which I fondly hoped would have been my forerunner to the land of freedom, writhe and shrivel on its bed of coals, and dissolve into smoke and ashes. Armsby, the treacherous wretch, was driven from Shaw's plantation not long subsequently, much to my relief, for I feared he might renew his conversation, and perhaps induce Epps to credit him.

I knew not now whither to look for deliverance. Hopes sprang up in my heart only to be crushed and blighted. The summer of my life was passing away; I felt I was growing prematurely old; that a few years more, and toil, and grief, and the poisonous miasmas of the swamps would accomplish their work upon me—would consign me to the grave's embrace, to moulder and be forgotten. Repelled, betrayed, cut off from the hope of succor, I could only prostrate myself upon the earth and groan in unutterable anguish. The hope of rescue was the only light that cast a ray of comfort on my heart. That was now flickering, faint and low; another breath of disappointment would extinguish it altogether, leaving me to grope in midnight darkness to the end of life.

# CHAPTER XVII

*Wiley Disregards The Counsels Of Aunt Phebe And Uncle Abram, And Is Caught By The Patrollers—The Organization And Duties Of The Latter—Wiley Runs Away—Speculations In Regard To Him—His Unexpected Return—His Capture On Red River, And Confinement In Alexandria Jail—Discovered By Joseph B. Roberts—Subduing Dogs In Anticipation Of Escape—The Fugitives In The Great Pine Woods—Captured By Adam Taydem And The Indians—Augustus Killed By Dogs—Nelly, Eldret's Slave Woman—The Story Of Celeste—The Concerted Movement—Lew Cheney, The Traitor—The Idea Of Insurrection.*

The year 1850, down to which time I have now arrived, omitting many occurrences uninteresting to the reader, was an unlucky year for my companion Wiley, the husband of Phebe, whose taciturn and retiring nature has thus far kept him in the background. Notwithstanding Wiley seldom opened his mouth, and revolved in his obscure and unpretending orbit without a grumble, nevertheless the warm elements of sociality were strong in the bosom of that silent "nigger." In the exuberance of his self-reliance, disregarding the philosophy of Uncle Abram, and setting the counsels of Aunt Phebe utterly at naught, he had the fool-hardiness to essay a nocturnal visit to a neighboring cabin without a pass.

So attractive was the society in which he found himself, that Wiley took little note of the passing hours, and the light began to break in the east before he was aware. Speeding homeward as fast as he could run, he hoped to reach the quarters before the horn would sound; but, unhappily, he was spied on the way by a company of patrollers.

How it is in other dark places of slavery, I do not know, but on Bayou Bœuf there is an organization of patrollers, as they are styled, whose business it is to seize and whip any slave they may find wandering from the plantation. They ride on horseback, headed by a captain, armed, and accompanied by dogs. They have the right, either by law, or by general consent, to inflict discretionary chastisement upon a black man caught beyond the boundaries of his master's estate without a pass, and even to shoot him, if he attempts to escape. Each company has a certain distance to ride up and down the bayou. They are compensated by the planters, who contribute in proportion to the number of slaves they own. The clatter of their horses' hoofs dashing by can be heard at all hours of the night, and frequently they may be seen driving a slave before them, or leading him by a rope fastened around his neck, to his owner's plantation.

Wiley fled before one of these companies, thinking he could reach his cabin before they could overtake him; but one of their dogs, a great ravenous hound, griped him by the leg, and held him fast. The patrollers whipped him severely, and brought him, aprisoner, to Epps. From him he received another flagellation still more severe, so that the cuts of the lash and the bites of the dog rendered him sore, stiff and miserable, insomuch he was scarcely able to move. It was impossible in such a state to keep up his row, and consequently there was not an hour in the day but Wiley felt the sting of his master's rawhide on his raw and bleeding back. His sufferings became intolerable, and finally he resolved to run away. Without disclosing his intentions to run away even to his wife Phebe, he proceeded to make arrangements for carrying his plan into execution. Having cooked his whole week's allowance, he cautiously left the cabin on a Sunday night, after the inmates of the quarters were asleep. When the horn sounded in the morning, Wiley did not make his appearance. Search was made for him in the cabins, in the corn-crib, in the cotton-house, and in every nook and corner of the premises. Each of us was examined, touching any knowledge we might have that could throw light upon his sudden disappearance or present whereabouts. Epps raved and stormed, and mounting his horse, galloped to neighboring plantations, making inquiries in all directions. The search was fruitless. Nothing whatever was elicited, going to show what had become of the missing man. The dogs were led to the swamp, but were unable to strike his trail. They would circle away through the forest, their noses to the ground, but invariably returned in a short time to the spot from whence they started.

Wiley had escaped, and so secretly and cautiously as to elude and baffle all pursuit. Days and even weeks passed away, and nothing could be heard of him. Epps did nothing but curse and swear. It was the only topic of conversation among us when alone. We indulged in a great deal of speculation in regard to him, one suggesting he might have been drowned in some bayou, inasmuch as he was a poor swimmer; another, that perhaps he might have been devoured by alligators, or stung by the venomous moccasin, whose bite is certain and sudden death. The warm and hearty sympathies of us all, however, were with poor Wiley, wherever he might be. Many an earnest prayer ascended from the lips of Uncle Abram, beseeching safety for the wanderer.

In about three weeks, when all hope of ever seeing him again was dismissed, to our surprise, he one day appeared among us. On leaving the plantation, he informed us, it was his intention to make his way back to South Carolina—to the old quarters of Master Buford. During the day he remained secreted, sometimes in the branches of a tree, and at night pressed forward through the swamps. Finally, one morning, just at dawn, he reached the shore of Red River. While standing on the bank, considering how he could cross it, a white man accosted him, and demanded a pass. Without one, and evidently a runaway, he was taken to Alexandria, the shire town of the parish of Rapides, and confined in prison. It happened several days after that Joseph B. Roberts, uncle of Mistress Epps, was in Alexandria, and going into the jail, recognized him. Wiley had worked on his plantation, when Epps resided at Huff Power. Paying the jail fee, and writing him a pass, underneath which was a note to Epps, requesting him not to whip him on his return, Wiley was sent back to Bayou Bœuf. It was the hope that hung upon this request, and which Roberts assured him would be respected by his master, that sustained him as he approached the house. The request, however, as may be readily supposed, was entirely disregarded. After being kept in suspense three days, Wiley was stripped, and compelled to endure one of those inhuman floggings to which the poor slave is so often subjected. It was the first and last attempt of Wiley to run away. The long scars upon his back, which he will carry with him to the grave, perpetually remind him of the dangers of such a step.

There was not a day throughout the ten years I belonged to Epps that I did not consult with myself upon the prospect of escape. I laid many plans, which at the time I considered excellent ones, but one after the other they were all abandoned. No man who has never been placed in such a situation, can comprehend the thousand obstacles thrown in the way of the flying slave. Every white man's hand is raised against him—the patrollers are watching for him—the hounds are ready to follow on his track, and the nature of the country is such as renders it impossible to pass through it with any safety. I thought, however, that the time might come, perhaps, when I should be running through the swamps again. I concluded, in that case, to be prepared for Epps' dogs, should they pursue me. He possessed several, one of which was a notorious slave-hunter, and the most fierce and savage of his breed. While out hunting the coon or the opossum, I never allowed an opportunity to escape, when alone, of whipping them severely. In this manner I succeeded at length in subduing them completely. They feared me, obeying my voice at once when others had no control over them whatever. Had they followed and overtaken me, I doubt not they would have shrank from attacking me.

Notwithstanding the certainty of being captured, the woods and swamps are, nevertheless, continually filled with runaways. Many of them, when sick, or so worn out as to be unable to perform their tasks, escape into the swamps, willing to suffer the punishment inflicted for such offences, in order to obtain a day or two of rest.

While I belonged to Ford, I was unwittingly the means of disclosing the hiding-place of six or eight, who had taken up their residence in the "Great Pine Woods." Adam Taydem frequently sent me from the mills over to the opening after provisions. The whole distance was then a thick pine forest. About ten o'clock of a beautiful moonlight night, while walking along the Texas road, returning to the mills, carrying a dressed pig in a bag swung over my shoulder, I heard footsteps behind me, and turning round, beheld two black men in the dress of slaves approaching at a rapid pace. When within a short distance, one of them raised a club, as if intending to strike me; the other snatched at the bag. I managed to dodge them both, and seizing a pine knot, hurled it with such force against the head of one of them that he was prostrated apparently senseless to the ground. Just then two more made their appearance from one side of the road. Before they could grapple me, however, I succeeded in passing them, and taking to my heels, fled, much affrighted, towards the mills. When Adam was informed of the adventure, he hastened straightway to the Indian village, and arousing Cascalla and several of his tribe, started in pursuit of the highwaymen. I accompanied them to the scene of attack, when we discovered a puddle of blood in the road, where the man whom I had smitten with the pine knot had fallen. After searching carefully through the woods a long time, one of Cascalla's men discovered a smoke curling up through the branches of several prostrate pines, whose tops had fallen together. The rendezvous was cautiously surrounded, and all of them taken prisoners. They had escaped from a plantation in the vicinity of Lamourie, and had been secreted there three weeks. They had no evil design upon me, except to frighten me out of my pig. Having observed me passing towards Ford's just at night-fall, and suspecting the nature of my errand, they had followed me, seen me butcher and dress the porker, and start on my return. They had been pinched for food, and were driven to this extremity by necessity. Adam conveyed them to the parish jail, and was liberally rewarded.

Not unfrequently the runaway loses his life in the attempt to escape. Epps' premises were bounded on one side by Carey's, a very extensive sugar plantation. He cultivates annually at least fifteen hundred acres of cane, manufacturing twenty-two or twenty-three hundred hogsheads of sugar; an hogshead and a half being the usual yield of an acre. Besides this he also cultivates five or six hundred acres of corn and cotton. He owned last year one hundred and fifty-three field hands, besides nearly as many children, and yearly hires a drove during the busy season from this side the Mississippi.

One of his negro drivers, a pleasant, intelligent boy, was named Augustus. During the holidays, and occasionally while at work in adjoining fields, I had an opportunity of making his acquaintance, which eventually ripened into a warm and mutual attachment. Summer before last he was so unfortunate as to incur the displeasure of the overseer, a coarse, heartless brute, who whipped him most cruelly. Augustus ran away. Reaching a cane rick on Hawkins' plantation, he secreted himself in the top of it. All Carey's dogs were put upon his track—some fifteen of them—and soon scented his footsteps to the hiding place. They surrounded the rick, baying and scratching, but could not reach him. Presently, guided by the clamor of the hounds, the pursuers rode up, when the overseer, mounting on to the rick, drew him forth. As he rolled down to the ground the whole pack plunged upon him, and before they could be beaten off, had gnawed and mutilated his body in the most shocking manner, their teeth having penetrated to the bone in an hundred places. He was taken up, tied upon a mule, and carried home. But this was Augustus' last trouble. He lingered until the next day, when death sought the unhappy boy, and kindly relieved him from his agony.

It was not unusual for slave women as well as slave men to endeavor to escape. Nelly, Eldret's girl, with whom I lumbered for a time in the "Big Cane Brake," lay concealed in Epps' corn crib three days. At night, when his family were asleep, she would steal into the quarters for food, and return to the crib again. We concluded it would no longer be safe for us to allow her to remain, and accordingly she retraced her steps to her own cabin.

But the most remarkable instance of a successful evasion of dogs and hunters was the following: Among Carey's girls was one by the name of Celeste. She was nineteen or twenty, and far whiter than her owner, or any of his offspring. It required a close inspection to distinguish in her features the slightest trace of African blood. A stranger would never have dreamed that she was the descendant of slaves. I was sitting in my cabin late at night, playing a low air on my violin, when the door opened carefully, and Celeste stood before me. She was pale and haggard. Had an apparition arisen from the earth, I could not have been more startled.

"Who are you?" I demanded, after gazing at her a moment.

"I'm hungry; give me some bacon," was her reply.

My first impression was that she was some deranged young mistress, who, escaping from home, was wandering, she knew not whither, and had been attracted to my cabin by the sound of the violin. The coarse cotton slave dress she wore, however, soon dispelled such a supposition.

"What is your name?" I again interrogated.

"My name is Celeste," she answered. "I belong to Carey, and have been two days among the palmettoes. I am sick and can't work, and would rather die in the swamp than be whipped to death by the overseer. Carey's dogs won't follow me. They have tried to set them on. There's a secret between them and Celeste, and they wont mind the devilish orders of the overseer. Give me some meat—I'm starving."

I divided my scanty allowance with her, and while partaking of it, she related how she had managed to escape, and described the place of her concealment. In the edge of the swamp, not half a mile from Epps' house, was a large space, thousands of acres in extent, thickly covered with palmetto. Tall trees, whose long arms interlocked each other, formed a canopy above them, so dense as to exclude the beams of the sun. It was like twilight always, even in the middle of the brightest day. In the centre of this great space, which nothing but serpents very often explore—a sombre and solitary spot—Celeste had erected a rude hut of dead branches that had fallen to the ground, and covered it with the leaves of the palmetto. This was the abode she had selected. She had no fear of Carey's dogs, any more than I had of Epps'. It is a fact, which I have never been able to explain, that there are those whose tracks the hounds will absolutely refuse to follow. Celeste was one of them.

For several nights she came to my cabin for food. On one occasion our dogs barked as she approached, which aroused Epps, and induced him to reconnoitre the premises. He did not discover her, but after that it was not deemed prudent for her to come to the yard. When all was silent I carried provisions to a certain spot agreed upon, where she would find them.

In this manner Celeste passed the greater part of the summer. She regained her health, and became strong and hearty. At all seasons of the year the howlings of wild animals can be heard at night along the borders of the swamps. Several times they had made her a midnight call, awakening her from slumber with a growl. Terrified by such unpleasant salutations, she finally concluded to abandon her lonely dwelling; and, accordingly, returning to her master, was scourged, her neck meanwhile being fastened in the stocks, and sent into the field again.

The year before my arrival in the country there was a concerted movement among a number of slaves on Bayou Bœuf, that terminated tragically indeed. It was, I presume, a matter of newspaper notoriety at the time, but all the knowledge I have of it, has been derived from the relation of those living at that period in the immediate vicinity of the excitement. It has become a subject of general and unfailing interest in every slave-hut on the bayou, and will doubtless go down to succeeding generations as their chief tradition. Lew Cheney, with whom I became acquainted—a shrewd, cunning negro, more intelligent than the generality of his race, but unscrupulous and full of treachery—conceived the project of organizing a company sufficiently strong to fight their way against all opposition, to the neighboring territory of Mexico.

A remote spot, far within the depths of the swamp, back of Hawkins' plantation, was selected as the rallying point. Lew flitted from one plantation to another, in the dead of night, preaching a crusade to Mexico, and, like Peter the Hermit, creating a furor of excitement wherever he appeared. At length a large number of runaways were assembled; stolen mules, and corn gathered from the fields, and bacon filched from smoke-houses, had been conveyed into the woods. The expedition was about ready to proceed, when their hiding place was discovered. Lew Cheney, becoming convinced of the ultimate failure of his project, in order to curry favor with his master, and avoid the consequences which he foresaw would follow, deliberately determined to sacrifice all his companions. Departing secretly from the encampment, he proclaimed among the planters the number collected in the swamp, and, instead of stating truly the object they had in view, asserted their intention was to emerge from their seclusion the first favorable opportunity, and murder every white person along the bayou.

Such an announcement, exaggerated as it passed from mouth to mouth, filled the whole country with terror. The fugitives were surrounded and taken prisoners, carried in chains to Alexandria, and hung by the populace. Not only those, but many who were suspected, though entirely innocent, were taken from the field and from the cabin, and without the shadow of process or form of trial, hurried to the scaffold. The planters on Bayou Bœuf finally rebelled against such reckless destruction of property, but it was not until a regiment of soldiers had arrived from some fort on the Texan frontier, demolished the gallows, and opened the doors of the Alexandria prison, that the indiscriminate slaughter was stayed. Lew Cheney escaped, and was even rewarded for his treachery. He is still living, but his name is despised and execrated by all his race throughout the parishes of Rapides and Avoyelles.

Such an idea as insurrection, however, is not new among the enslaved population of Bayou Bœuf. More than once I have joined in serious consultation, when the subject has been discussed, and there have been times when a word from me would have placed hundreds of my fellow-bondsmen in an attitude of defiance. Without arms or ammunition, or even with them, I saw such a step would result in certain defeat, disaster and death, and always raised my voice against it.

During the Mexican war I well remember the extravagant hopes that were excited. The news of victory filled the great house with rejoicing, but produced only sorrow and disappointment in the cabin. In my opinion—and I have had opportunity to know something of the feeling of which I speak—there are not fifty slaves on the shores of Bayou Bœuf, but would hail with unmeasured delight the approach of an invading army.

They are deceived who flatter themselves that the ignorant and debased slave has no conception of the magnitude of his wrongs. They are deceived who imagine that he arises from his knees, with back lacerated and bleeding, cherishing only a spirit of meekness and forgiveness. A day may come—it *will* come, if his prayer is heard—a terrible day of vengeance, when the master in his turn will cry in vain for mercy.

# CHAPTER XVIII

*O'Niel, The Tanner—Conversation With Aunt Phebe Overheard—Epps In The Tanning Business—Stabbing Of Uncle Abram—The Ugly Wound—Epps Is Jealous—Patsey Is Missing—Her Return From Shaw's—Harriet, Shaw's Black Wife—Epps Enraged—Patsey Denies His Charges—She Is Tied Down Naked To Four Stakes—The Inhuman Flogging—Flaying Of Patsey—The Beauty Of The Day—The Bucket Of Salt Water—The Dress Stiff With Blood—Patsey Grows Melancholy—Her Idea Of God And Eternity—Of Heaven And Freedom—The Effect Of Slave-Whipping—Epps' Oldest Son—"The Child Is Father To The Man."*

Wiley suffered severely at the hands of Master Epps, as has been related in the preceding chapter, but in this respect he fared no worse than his unfortunate companions. "Spare the rod," was an idea scouted by our master. He was constitutionally subject to periods of ill-humor, and at such times, however little provocation there might be, a certain amount of punishment was inflicted. The circumstances attending the last flogging but one that I received, will show how trivial a cause was sufficient with him for resorting to the whip.

A Mr. O'Niel, residing in the vicinity of the Big Pine Woods, called upon Epps for the purpose of purchasing me. He was a tanner and currier by occupation, transacting an extensive business, and intended to place me at service in some department of his establishment, provided he bought me. Aunt Phebe, while preparing the dinner-table in the great house, overheard their conversation. On returning to the yard at night, the old woman ran to meet me, designing, of course, to overwhelm me with the news. She entered into a minute repetition of all she had heard, and Aunt Phebe was one whose ears never failed to drink in every word of conversation uttered in her hearing. She enlarged upon the fact that "Massa Epps was g'wine to sell me to a tanner ober in de Pine Woods," so long and loudly as to attract the attention of the mistress, who, standing unobserved on the piazza at the time, was listening to our conversation.

"Well, Aunt Phebe," said I, "I'm glad of it. I'm tired of scraping cotton, and would rather be a tanner. I hope he'll buy me."

O'Niel did not effect a purchase, however, the parties differing as to price, and the morning following his arrival, departed homewards. He had been gone but a short time, when Epps made his appearance in the field. Now nothing will more violently enrage a master, especially Epps, than the intimation of one of his servants that he would like to leave him. Mistress Epps had repeated to him my expressions to Aunt Phebe the evening previous, as I learned from the latter afterwards, the mistress having mentioned to her that she had overheard us. On entering the field, Epps walked directly to me.

"So, Platt, you're tired of scraping cotton, are you? You would like to change your master, eh? You're fond of moving round—traveler—ain't ye? Ah, yes—like to travel for your health, may be? Feel above cotton-scraping, I s'pose. So you're going into the tanning business? Good business—devilish fine business. Enterprising nigger! B'lieve I'll go into that business myself. Down on your knees, and strip that rag off your back! I'll try my hand at tanning."

I begged earnestly, and endeavored to soften him with excuses, but in vain. There was no other alternative; so kneeling down, I presented my bare back for the application of the lash.

"How do you like *tanning*?" he exclaimed, as the rawhide descended upon my flesh. "How do you like *tanning*?" he repeated at every blow. In this manner he gave me twenty or thirty lashes, incessantly giving utterance to the word "tanning," in one form of expression or another. When sufficiently "tanned," he allowed me to arise, and with a half-malicious laugh assured me, if I still fancied the business, he would give me further instruction in it whenever I desired. This time, he remarked, he had only given me a short lesson in "*tanning*"—the next time he would "curry me down."

Uncle Abram, also, was frequently treated with great brutality, although he was one of the kindest and most faithful creatures in the world. He was my cabin-mate for years. There was a benevolent expression in the old man's face, pleasant to behold. He regarded us with a kind of parental feeling, always counseling us with remarkable gravity and deliberation.

Returning from Marshall's plantation one afternoon, whither I had been sent on some errand of the mistress, I found him lying on the cabin floor, his clothes saturated with blood. He informed me that he had been stabbed! While spreading cotton on the scaffold, Epps came home intoxicated from Holmesville. He found fault with every thing, giving many orders so directly contrary that it was impossible to execute any of them. Uncle Abram, whose faculties were growing dull, became confused, and committed some blunder of no particular consequence. Epps was so enraged thereat, that, with drunken recklessness, he flew upon the old man, and stabbed him in the back. It was a long, ugly wound, but did not happen to penetrate far enough to result fatally. It was sewed up by the mistress, who censured her husband with extreme severity, not only denouncing his inhumanity, but declaring that she expected nothing else than that he would bring the family to poverty—that he would kill all the slaves on the plantation in some of his drunken fits.

It was no uncommon thing with him to prostrate Aunt Phebe with a chair or stick of wood; but the most cruel whipping that ever I was doomed to witness—one I can never recall with any other emotion than that of horror—was inflicted on the unfortunate Patsey.

It has been seen that the jealousy and hatred of Mistress Epps made the daily life of her young and agile slave completely miserable. I am happy in the belief that on numerous occasions I was the means of averting punishment from the inoffensive girl. In Epps' absence the mistress often ordered me to whip her without the remotest provocation. I would refuse, saying that I feared my master's displeasure, and several times ventured to remonstrate with her against the treatment Patsey received. I endeavored to impress her with the truth that the latter was not responsible for the acts of which she complained, but that she being a slave, and subject entirely to her master's will, he alone was answerable.

At length "the green-eyed monster" crept into the soul of Epps also, and then it was that he joined with his wrathful wife in an infernal jubilee over the girl's miseries.

On a Sabbath day in hoeing time, not long ago, we were on the bayou bank, washing our clothes, as was our usual custom. Presently Patsey was missing. Epps called aloud, but there was no answer. No one had observed her leaving the yard, and it was a wonder with us whither she had gone. In the course of a couple of hours she was seen approaching from the direction of Shaw's. This man, as has been intimated, was a notorious profligate, and withal not on the most friendly terms with Epps. Harriet, his black wife, knowing Patsey's troubles, was kind to her, in consequence of which the latter was in the habit of going over to see her every opportunity. Her visits were prompted by friendship merely, but the suspicion gradually entered the brain of Epps, that another and a baser passion led her thither—that it was not Harriet she desired to meet, but rather the unblushing libertine, his neighbor. Patsey found her master in a fearful rage on her return. His violence so alarmed her that at first she attempted to evade direct answers to his questions, which only served to increase his suspicions. She finally, however, drew herself up proudly, and in a spirit of indignation boldly denied his charges.

"Missus don't give me soap to wash with, as she does the rest," said Patsey, "and you know why. I went over to Harriet's to get a piece," and saying this, she drew it forth from a pocket in her dress and exhibited it to him. "That's what I went to Shaw's for, Massa Epps," continued she; "the Lord knows that was all."

"You lie, you black wench!" shouted Epps.

"I *don't* lie, massa. If you kill me, I'll stick to that."

"Oh! I'll fetch you down. I'll learn you to go to Shaw's. I'll take the starch out of ye," he muttered fiercely through his shut teeth.

Then turning to me, he ordered four stakes to be driven into the ground, pointing with the toe of his boot to the places where he wanted them. When the stakes were driven down, he ordered her to be stripped of every article of dress. Ropes were then brought, and the naked girl was laid upon her face, her wrists and feet each tied firmly to a stake. Stepping to the piazza, he took down a heavy whip, and placing it in my hands, commanded me to lash her. Unpleasant as it was, I was compelled to obey him. Nowhere that day, on the face of the whole earth, I venture to say, was there such a demoniac exhibition witnessed as then ensued.

Mistress Epps stood on the piazza among her children, gazing on the scene with an air of heartless satisfaction. The slaves were huddled together at a little distance, their countenances indicating the sorrow of their hearts. Poor Patsey prayed piteously for mercy, but her prayers were vain. Epps ground his teeth, and stamped upon the ground, screaming at me, like a mad fiend, to strike *harder*.

"Strike harder, or *your* turn will come next, you scoundrel," he yelled.

"Oh, mercy, massa!—oh! have mercy, *do*. Oh, God! pity me," Patsey exclaimed continually, struggling fruitlessly, and the flesh quivering at every stroke.

When I had struck her as many as thirty times, I stopped, and turned round toward Epps, hoping he was satisfied; but with bitter oaths and threats, he ordered me to continue. I inflicted ten or fifteen blows more. By this time her back was covered with long welts, intersecting each other like net work. Epps was yet furious and savage as ever, demanding if she would like to go to Shaw's again, and swearing he would flog her until she wished she was in h—l. Throwing down the whip, I declared I could punish her no more. He ordered me to go on, threatening me with a severer flogging than she had received, in case of refusal. My heart revolted at the inhuman scene, and risking the consequences, I absolutely refused to raise the whip. He then seized it himself, and applied it with ten-fold greater force than I had. The painful cries and shrieks of the tortured Patsey, mingling with the loud and angry curses of Epps, loaded the air. She was terribly lacerated—I may say, without exaggeration, literally flayed. The lash was wet with blood, which flowed down her sides and dropped upon the ground. At length she ceased struggling. Her head sank listlessly on the ground. Her screams and supplications gradually decreased and died away into a low moan. She no longer writhed and shrank beneath the lash when it bit out small pieces of her flesh. I thought that she was dying!

It was the Sabbath of the Lord. The fields smiled in the warm sunlight—the birds chirped merrily amidst the foliage of the trees—peace and happiness seemed to reign everywhere, save in the bosoms of Epps and his panting victim and the silent witnesses around him. The tempestuous emotions that were raging there were little in harmony with the calm and quiet beauty of the day. I could look on Epps only with unutterable loathing and abhorrence, and thought within myself—"Thou devil, sooner or later, somewhere in the course of eternal justice, thou shalt answer for this sin!"

Finally, he ceased whipping from mere exhaustion, and ordered Phebe to bring a bucket of salt and water. After washing her thoroughly with this, I was told to take her to her cabin. Untying the ropes, I raised her in my arms. She was unable to stand, and as her head rested on my shoulder, she repeated many times, in a faint voice scarcely perceptible, "Oh, Platt—oh, Platt!" but nothing further. Her dress was replaced, but it clung to her back, and was soon stiff with blood. We laid her on some boards in the hut, where she remained a long time, with eyes closed and groaning in agony. At night Phebe applied melted tallow to her wounds, and so far as we were able, all endeavored to assist and console her. Day after day she lay in her cabin upon her face, the sores preventing her resting in any other position.

A blessed thing it would have been for her—days and weeks and months of misery it would have saved her—had she never lifted up her head in life again. Indeed, from that time forward she was not what she had been. The burden of a deep melancholy weighed heavily on her spirits. She no longer moved with that buoyant and elastic step—there was not that mirthful sparkle in her eyes that formerly distinguished her. The bounding vigor—the sprightly, laughter-loving spirit of her youth, were gone. She fell into a mournful and desponding mood, and oftentimes would start up in her sleep, and with raised hands, plead for mercy. She became more silent than she was, toiling all day in our midst, not uttering a word. A care-worn, pitiful expression settled on her face, and it was her humor now to weep, rather than rejoice. If ever there was a broken heart—one crushed and blighted by the rude grasp of suffering and misfortune—it was Patsey's.

She had been reared no better than her master's beast—looked upon merely as a valuable and handsome animal—and consequently possessed but a limited amount of knowledge. And yet a faint light cast its rays over her intellect, so that it was not wholly dark. She had a dim perception of God and of eternity, and a still more dim perception of a Saviour who had died even for such as her. She entertained but confused notions of a future life—not comprehending the distinction between the corporeal and spiritual existence. Happiness, in her mind, was exemption from stripes—from labor—from the cruelty of masters and overseers. Her idea of the joy of heaven was simply *rest*, and is fully expressed in these lines of a melancholy bard:

"I ask no paradise on high,
With cares on earth oppressed,
The only heaven for which I sigh,
Is rest, eternal rest."

It is a mistaken opinion that prevails in some quarters, that the slave does not understand the term—does not comprehend the idea of freedom. Even on Bayou Bœuf, where I conceive slavery exists in its most abject and cruel form—where it exhibits features altogether unknown in more northern States—the most ignorant of them generally know full well its meaning. They understand the privileges and exemptions that belong to it—that it would bestow upon them the fruits of their own labors, and that it would secure to them the enjoyment of domestic happiness. They do not fail to observe the difference between their own condition and the meanest white man's, and to realize the injustice of the laws which place it in his power not only to appropriate the profits of their industry, but to subject them to unmerited and unprovoked punishment, without remedy, or the right to resist, or to remonstrate.

Patsey's life, especially after her whipping, was one long dream of liberty. Far away, to her fancy an immeasurable distance, she knew there was a land of freedom. A thousand times she had heard that somewhere in the distant North there were no slaves—no masters. In her imagination it was an enchanted region, the Paradise of the earth. To dwell where the black man may work for himself—live in his own cabin—till his own soil, was a blissful dream of Patsey's—a dream, alas! the fulfillment of which she can never realize.

The effect of these exhibitions of brutality on the household of the slave-holder, is apparent. Epps' oldest son is an intelligent lad of ten or twelve years of age. It is pitiable, sometimes, to see him chastising, for instance, the venerable Uncle Abram. He will call the old man to account, and if in his childish judgment it is necessary, sentence him to a certain number of lashes, which he proceeds to inflict with much gravity and deliberation. Mounted on his pony, he often rides into the field with his whip, playing the overseer, greatly to his father's delight. Without discrimination, at such times, he applies the rawhide, urging the slaves forward with shouts, and occasional expressions of profanity, while the old man laughs, and commends him as a thorough-going boy.

"The child is father to the man," and with such training, whatever may be his natural disposition, it cannot well be otherwise than that, on arriving at maturity, the sufferings and miseries of the slave will be looked upon with entire indifference. The influence of the iniquitous system necessarily fosters an unfeeling and cruel spirit, even in the bosoms of those who, among their equals, are regarded as humane and generous.

Young Master Epps possessed some noble qualities, yet no process of reasoning could lead him to comprehend, that in the eye of the Almighty there is no distinction of color. He looked upon the black man simply as an animal, differing in no respect from any other animal, save in the gift of speech and the possession of somewhat higher instincts, and, therefore, the more valuable. To work like his father's mules—to be whipped and kicked and scourged through life—to address the white man with hat in hand, and eyes bent servilely on the earth, in his mind, was the natural and proper destiny of the slave. Brought up with such ideas—in the notion that we stand without the pale of humanity—no wonder the oppressors of my people are a pitiless and unrelenting race.

# CHAPTER XIX

*Avery, Of Bayou Rouge—Peculiarity Of Dwellings—Epps Builds A New House—Bass, The Carpenter—His Noble Qualities—His Personal Appearance And Eccentricities—Bass And Epps Discuss The Question Of Slavery—Epps' Opinion Of Bass—I Make Myself Known To Him—Our Conversation—His Surprise—The Midnight Meeting On The Bayou Bank—Bass' Assurances—Declares War Against Slavery—Why I Did Not Disclose My History—Bass Writes Letters—Copy Of His Letter To Messrs. Parker And Perry—The Fever Of Suspense—Disappointments—Bass Endeavors To Cheer Me—My Faith In Him.*

In the month of June, 1852, in pursuance of a previous contract, Mr. Avery, a carpenter of Bayou Rouge, commenced the erection of a house for Master Epps. It has previously been stated that there are no cellars on Bayou Bœuf; on the other hand, such is the low and swampy nature of the ground, the great houses are usually built upon spiles. Another peculiarity is, the rooms are not plastered, but the ceiling and sides are covered with matched cypress boards, painted such color as most pleases the owner's taste. Generally the plank and boards are sawed by slaves with whip-saws, there being no water-power upon which mills might be built within many miles. When the planter erects for himself a dwelling, therefore, there is plenty of extra work for his slaves. Having had some experience under Tibeats as a carpenter, I was taken from the field altogether, on the arrival of Avery and his hands.

Among them was one to whom I owe an immeasurable debt of gratitude. Only for him, in all probability, I should have ended my days in slavery. He was my deliverer—a man whose true heart overflowed with noble and generous emotions. To the last moment of my existence I shall remember him with feelings of thankfulness. His name was Bass, and at that time he resided in Marksville. It will be difficult to convey a correct impression of his appearance or character. He was a large man, between forty and fifty years old, of light complexion and light hair. He was very cool and self-possessed, fond of argument, but always speaking with extreme deliberation. He was that kind of person whose peculiarity of manner was such that nothing he uttered ever gave offence. What would be intolerable, coming from the lips of another, could be said by him with impunity. There was not a man on Red River, perhaps, that agreed with him on the subject of politics or religion, and not a man, I venture to say, who discussed either of those subjects half as much. It seemed to be taken for granted that he would espouse the unpopular side of every local question, and it always created amusement rather than displeasure among his auditors, to listen to the ingenious and original manner in which he maintained the controversy. He was a bachelor—an "old bachelor," according to the true acceptation of the term—having no kindred living, as he knew of, in the world. Neither had he any permanent abiding place—wandering from one State to another, as his fancy dictated. He had lived in Marksville three or four years, and in the prosecution of his business as a carpenter; and in consequence, likewise, of his peculiarities, was quite extensively known throughout the parish of Avoyelles. He was liberal to a fault; and his many acts of kindness and transparent goodness of heart rendered him popular in the community, the sentiment of which he unceasingly combated.

He was a native of Canada, from whence he had wandered in early life, and after visiting all the principal localities in the northern and western States, in the course of his peregrinations, arrived in the unhealthy region of the Red River. His last removal was from Illinois. Whither he has now gone, I regret to be obliged to say, is unknown to me. He gathered up his effects and departed quietly from Marksville the day before I did, the suspicions of his instrumentality in procuring my liberation rendering such a step necessary. For the commission of a just and righteous act he would undoubtedly have suffered death, had he remained within reach of the slave-whipping tribe on Bayou Bœuf.

One day, while working on the new house, Bass and Epps became engaged in a controversy, to which, as will be readily supposed, I listened with absorbing interest. They were discussing the subject of Slavery.

"I tell you what it is Epps," said Bass, "it's all wrong—all wrong, sir—there's no justice nor righteousness in it. I wouldn't own a slave if I was rich as Crœsus, which I am not, as is perfectly well understood, more particularly among my creditors. *There's* another humbug—the credit system—humbug, sir; no credit—no debt. Credit leads a man into temptation. Cash down is the only thing that will deliver him from evil. But this question of *Slavery*; what *right* have you to your niggers when you come down to the point?"

"What right!" said Epps, laughing; "why, I bought 'em, and paid for 'em."

"Of *course* you did; the law says you have the right to hold a nigger, but begging the law's pardon, it *lies*. Yes, Epps, when the law says that it's a *liar*, and the truth is not in it. Is every thing right because the law allows it? Suppose they'd pass a law taking away your liberty and making you a slave?"

"Oh, that ain't a supposable case," said Epps, still laughing; "hope you don't compare me to a nigger, Bass."

"Well," Bass answered gravely, "no, not exactly. But I have seen niggers before now as good as I am, and I have no acquaintance with any white man in these parts that I consider a whit better than myself. Now, in the sight of God, what is the difference, Epps, between a white man and a black one?"

"All the difference in the world," replied Epps. "You might as well ask what the difference is between a white man and a baboon. Now, I've seen one of them critters in Orleans that knowed just as much as any nigger I've got. You'd call them feller citizens, I s'pose?"—and Epps indulged in a loud laugh at his own wit.

"Look here, Epps," continued his companion; "you can't laugh me down in that way. Some men are witty, and some ain't so witty as they think they are. Now let me ask you a question. Are all men created free and equal as the Declaration of Independence holds they are?"

"Yes," responded Epps, "but all men, niggers, and monkeys *ain't*;" and hereupon he broke forth into a more boisterous laugh than before.

"There are monkeys among white people as well as black, when you come to that," coolly remarked Bass. "I know some white men that use arguments no sensible monkey would. But let that pass. These niggers are human beings. If they don't know as much as their masters, whose fault is it? They are not *allowed* to know anything. You have books and papers, and can go where you please, and gather intelligence in a thousand ways. But your slaves have no privileges. You'd whip one of them if caught reading a book. They are held in bondage, generation after generation, deprived of mental improvement, and who can expect them to possess much knowledge? If they are not brought down to a level with the brute creation, you slaveholders will never be blamed for it. If they are baboons, or stand no higher in the scale of intelligence than such animals, you and men like you will have to answer for it. There's a sin, a fearful sin, resting on this nation, that will not go unpunished forever. There will be a reckoning yet—yes, Epps, there's a day coming that will burn as an oven. It may be sooner or it may be later, but it's a coming as sure as the Lord is just."

"If you lived up among the Yankees in New-England," said Epps, "I expect you'd be one of them cursed fanatics that know more than the constitution, and go about peddling clocks and coaxing niggers to run away."

"If I was in New-England," returned Bass, "I would be just what I am here. I would say that Slavery was an iniquity, and ought to be abolished. I would say there was no reason nor justice in the law, or the constitution that allows one man to hold another man in bondage. It would be hard for you to lose your property, to be sure, but it wouldn't be half as hard as it would be to lose your liberty. You have no more right to your freedom, in exact justice, than Uncle Abram yonder. Talk about black skin, and black blood; why, how many slaves are there on this bayou as white as either of us? And what difference is there in the color of the soul? Pshaw! the whole system is as absurd as it is cruel. You may own niggers and behanged, but I wouldn't own one for the best plantation in Louisiana."

"You like to hear yourself talk, Bass, better than any man I know of. You would argue that black was white, or white black, if any body would contradict you. Nothing suits you in this world, and I don't believe you will be satisfied with the next, if you should have your choice in them."

Conversations substantially like the foregoing were not unusual between the two after this; Epps drawing him out more for the purpose of creating a laugh at his expense, than with a view of fairly discussing the merits of the question. He looked upon Bass, as a man ready to say anything merely for the pleasure of hearing his own voice; as somewhat self-conceited, perhaps, contending against his faith and judgment, in order, simply, to exhibit his dexterity in argumentation.

He remained at Epps' through the summer, visiting Marksville generally once a fortnight. The more I saw of him, the more I became convinced he was a man in whom I could confide. Nevertheless, my previous ill-fortune had taught me to be extremely cautious. It was not my place to speak to a white man except when spoken to, but I omitted no opportunity of throwing myself in his way, and endeavored constantly in every possible manner to attract his attention. In the early part of August he and myself were at work alone in the house, the other carpenters having left, and Epps being absent in the field. Now was the time, if ever, to broach the subject, and I resolved to do it, and submit to whatever consequences might ensue. We were busily at work in the afternoon, when I stopped suddenly and said—

"Master Bass, I want to ask you what part of the country you came from?"

"Why, Platt, what put that into your head?" he answered. "You wouldn't know if I should tell you." After a moment or two he added—"I was born in Canada; now guess where that is."

"Oh, I know where Canada is," said I, "I have been there myself."

"Yes, I expect you are well acquainted all through that country," he remarked, laughing incredulously.

"As sure as I live, Master Bass," I replied, "I have been there. I have been in Montreal and Kingston, and Queenston, and a great many places in Canada, and I have been in York State, too—in Buffalo, and Rochester, and Albany, and can tell you the names of the villages on the Erie canal and the Champlain canal."

Bass turned round and gazed at me a long time without uttering a syllable.

"How came you here?" he inquired, at length. "Master Bass," I answered, "if justice had been done, I never would have been here."

"Well, how's this?" said he. "Who are you? You have been in Canada sure enough; I know all the places you mention. How did you happen to get here? Come, tell me all about it."

"I have no friends here," was my reply, "that I can put confidence in. I am afraid to tell you, though I don't believe you would tell Master Epps if I should."

He assured me earnestly he would keep every word I might speak to him a profound secret, and his curiosity was evidently strongly excited. It was a long story, I informed him, and would take some time to relate it. Master Epps would be back soon, but if he would see me that night after all were asleep, I would repeat it to him. He consented readily to the arrangement, and directed me to come into the building where we were then at work, and I would find him there. About midnight, when all was still and quiet, I crept cautiously from my cabin, and silently entering the unfinished building, found him awaiting me.

After further assurances on his part that I should not be betrayed, I began a relation of the history of my life and misfortunes. He was deeply interested, asking numerous questions in reference to localities and events. Having ended my story I besought him to write to some of my friends at the North, acquainting them with my situation, and begging them to forward free papers, or take such steps as they might consider proper to secure my release. He promised to do so, but dwelt upon the danger of such an act in case of detection, and now impressed upon me the great necessity of strict silence and secresy. Before we parted our plan of operation was arranged.

We agreed to meet the next night at a specified place among the high weeds on the bank of the bayou, some distance from master's dwelling. There he was to write down on paper the names and address of several persons, old friends in the North, to whom he would direct letters during his next visit to Marksville. It was not deemed prudent to meet in the new house, inasmuch as the light it would be necessary to use might possibly be discovered. In the course of the day I managed to obtain a few matches and a piece of candle, unperceived, from the kitchen, during a temporary absence of Aunt Phebe. Bass had pencil and paper in his tool chest.

At the appointed hour we met on the bayou bank, and creeping among the high weeds, I lighted the candle, while he drew forth pencil and paper and prepared for business. I gave him the names of William Perry, Cephas Parker and Judge Marvin, all of Saratoga Springs, Saratoga county, New-York. I had been employed by the latter in the United States Hotel, and had transacted business with the former to a considerable extent, and trusted that at least one of them would be still living at that place. He carefully wrote the names, and then remarked, thoughtfully—

"It is so many years since you left Saratoga, all these men may be dead, or may have removed. You say you obtained papers at the custom house in New-York. Probably there is a record of them there, and I think it would be well to write and ascertain."

I agreed with him, and again repeated the circumstances related heretofore, connected with my visit to the custom house with Brown and Hamilton. We lingered on the bank of the bayou an hour or more, conversing upon the subject which now engrossed our thoughts. I could no longer doubt his fidelity, and freely spoke to him of the many sorrows I had borne in silence, and so long. I spoke of my wife and children, mentioning their names and ages, and dwelling upon the unspeakable happiness it would be to clasp them to my heart once more before I died. I caught him by the hand, and with tears and passionate entreaties implored him to befriend me—to restore me to my kindred and to liberty—promising I would weary Heaven the remainder of my life with prayers that it would bless and prosper him. In the enjoyment of freedom—surrounded by the associations of youth, and restored to the bosom of my family—that promise is not yet forgotten, nor shall it ever be so long as I have strength to raise my imploring eyes on high.

"Oh, blessings on his kindly voice and on his silver hair,
And blessings on his whole life long, until he meet me there."

He overwhelmed me with assurances of friendship and faithfulness, saying he had never before taken so deep an interest in the fate of any one. He spoke of himself in a somewhat mournful tone, as a lonely man, a wanderer about the world—that he was growing old, and must soon reach the end of his earthly journey, and lie down to his final rest without kith or kin to mourn for him, or to remember him—that his life was of little value to himself, and henceforth should be devoted to the accomplishment of my liberty, and to an unceasing warfare against the accursed shame of Slavery.

After this time we seldom spoke to, or recognized each other. He was, moreover, less free in his conversation with Epps on the subject of Slavery. The remotest suspicion that there was any unusual intimacy—any secret understanding between us—never once entered the mind of Epps, or any other person, white or black, on the plantation.

I am often asked, with an air of incredulity, how I succeeded so many years in keeping from my daily and constant companions the knowledge of my true name and history. The terrible lesson Burch taught me, impressed indelibly upon my mind the danger and uselessness of asserting I was a freeman. There was no possibility of any slave being able to assist me, while, on the other hand, there *was* a possibility of his exposing me. When it is recollected the whole current of my thoughts, for twelve years, turned to the contemplation of escape, it will not be wondered at, that I was always cautious and on my guard. It would have been an act of folly to have proclaimed my *right* to freedom; it would only have subjected me to severer scrutiny—probably have consigned me to some more distant and inaccessible region than even Bayou Bœuf. Edwin Epps was a person utterly regardless of a black man's rights or wrongs—utterly destitute of any natural sense of justice, as I well knew. It was important, therefore, not only as regarded my hope of deliverance, but also as regarded the few personal privileges I was permitted to enjoy, to keep from him the history of my life.

The Saturday night subsequent to our interview at the water's edge, Bass went home to Marksville. The next day, being Sunday, he employed himself in his own room writing letters. One he directed to the Collector of Customs at New-York, another to Judge Marvin, and another to Messrs. Parker and Perry jointly. The latter was the one which led to my recovery. He subscribed my true name, but in the postscript intimated I was not the writer. The letter itself shows that he considered himself engaged in a dangerous undertaking—no less than running "the risk of his life, if detected." I did not see the letter before it was mailed, but have since obtained a copy, which is here inserted:

"Bayou Bœuf, August 15, 1852.

"Mr. William Perry or Mr. Cephas Parker:

"Gentlemen—It having been a long time since I have seen or heard from you, and not knowing that you are living, it is with uncertainty that I write to you, but the necessity of the case must be my excuse.

"Having been born free, just across the river from you, I am certain you must know me, and I am here now a slave. I wish you to obtain free papers for me, and forward them to me at Marksville, Louisiana, Parish of Avoyelles, and oblige

"Yours,

SOLOMON NORTHUP.

"The way I came to be a slave, I was taken sick in Washington City, and was insensible for some time. When I recovered my reason, I was robbed of my free-papers, and in irons on my way to this State, and have never been able to get any one to write for me until now; and he that is writing for me runs the risk of his life if detected."

The allusion to myself in the work recently issued, entitled "A Key to Uncle Tom's Cabin," contains the first part of this letter, omitting the postscript. Neither are the full names of the gentlemen to whom it is directed correctly stated, there being a slight discrepancy, probably a typographical error. To the postscript more than to the body of the communication am I indebted for my liberation, as will presently be seen.

When Bass returned from Marksville he informed me of what he had done. We continued our midnight consultations, never speaking to each other through the day, excepting as it was necessary about the work. As nearly as he was able to ascertain, it would require two weeks for the letter to reach Saratoga in due course of mail, and the same length of time for an answer to return. Within six weeks, at the farthest, we concluded, an answer would arrive, if it arrived at all. A great many suggestions were now made, and a great deal of conversation took place between us, as to the most safe and proper course to pursue on receipt of the free papers. They would stand between him and harm, in case we were overtaken and arrested leaving the country altogether. It would be no infringement of law, however much it might provoke individual hostility, to assist a freeman to regain his freedom.

At the end of four weeks he was again at Marksville, but no answer had arrived. I was sorely disappointed, but still reconciled myself with the reflection that sufficient length of time had not yet elapsed—that there might have been delays—and that I could not reasonably expect one so soon. Six, seven, eight, and ten weeks passed by, however, and nothing came. I was in a fever of suspense whenever Bass visited Marksville, and could scarcely close my eyes until his return. Finally my master's house was finished, and the time came when Bass must leave me. The night before his departure I was wholly given up to despair. I had clung to him as a drowning man clings to the floating spar, knowing if it slips from his grasp he must forever sink beneath the waves. The all-glorious hope, upon which I had laid such eager hold, was crumbling to ashes in my hands. I felt as if sinking down, down, amidst the bitter waters of Slavery, from the unfathomable depths of which I should never rise again.

The generous heart of my friend and benefactor was touched with pity at the sight of my distress. He endeavored to cheer me up, promising to return the day before Christmas, and if no intelligence was received in the meantime, some further step would be undertaken to effect our design. He exhorted me to keep up my spirits—to rely upon his continued efforts in my behalf, assuring me, in most earnest and impressive language, that my liberation should, from thenceforth, be the chief object of his thoughts.

In his absence the time passed slowly indeed. I looked forward to Christmas with intense anxiety and impatience. I had about given up the expectation of receiving any answer to the letters. They might have miscarried, or might have been misdirected. Perhaps those at Saratoga, to whom they had been addressed, were all dead; perhaps, engaged in their pursuits, they did not consider the fate of an obscure, unhappy black man of sufficient importance to be noticed. My whole reliance was in Bass. The faith I had in him was continually re-assuring me, and enabled me to stand up against the tide of disappointment that had overwhelmed me.

So wholly was I absorbed in reflecting upon my situation and prospects, that the hands with whom I labored in the field often observed it. Patsey would ask me if I was sick, and Uncle Abram, and Bob, and Wiley frequently expressed a curiosity to know what I could be thinking about so steadily. But I evaded their inquiries with some light remark, and kept my thoughts locked closely in my breast.

# CHAPTER XX

*Bass Faithful To His Word—His Arrival On Christmas Eve—The Difficulty Of Obtaining An Interview—The Meeting In The Cabin—Non-Arrival Of The Letter—Bass Announces His Intention To Proceed North—Christmas—Conversation Between Epps And Bass—Young Mistress M'Coy, The Beauty Of Bayou Bœuf—The "Ne Plus Ultra" Of Dinners—Music And Dancing—Presence Of The Mistress—Her Exceeding Beauty—The Last Slave Dance—William Pierce—Oversleep Myself—The Last Whipping—Despondency—The Cold Morning—Epps' Threats—The Passing Carriage—Strangers Approaching Through The Cotton-Field—Last Hour On Bayou Bœuf.*

Faithful to his word, the day before Christmas, just at nightfall, Bass came riding into the yard.

"How are you," said Epps, shaking him by the hand, "glad to see you."

He would not have been *very* glad had he known the object of his errand.

"Quite well, quite well," answered Bass. "Had some business out on the bayou, and concluded to call and see you, and stay over night."

Epps ordered one of the slaves to take charge of his horse, and with much talk and laughter they passed into the house together; not, however, until Bass had looked at me significantly, as much as to say, "Keep dark, we understand each other." It was ten o'clock at night before the labors of the day were performed, when I entered the cabin. At that time Uncle Abram and Bob occupied it with me. I laid down upon my board and feigned I was asleep. When my companions had fallen into a profound slumber, I moved stealthily out of the door, and watched, and listened attentively for some sign or sound from Bass. There I stood until long after midnight, but nothing could be seen or heard. As I suspected, he dared not leave the house, through fear of exciting the suspicion of some of the family. I judged, correctly, he would rise earlier than was his custom, and take the opportunity of seeing me before Epps was up. Accordingly I aroused Uncle Abram an hour sooner than usual, and sent him into the house to build a fire, which, at that season of the year, is a part of Uncle Abram's duties.

I also gave Bob a violent shake, and asked him if he intended to sleep till noon, saying master would be up before the mules were fed. He knew right well the consequence that would follow such an event, and, jumping to his feet, was at the horse-pasture in a twinkling.

Presently, when both were gone, Bass slipped into the cabin.

"No letter yet, Platt," said he. The announcement fell upon my heart like lead.

"Oh, *do* write again, Master Bass," I cried; "I will give you the names of a great many I know. Surely they are not all dead. Surely some one will pity me."

"No use," Bass replied, "no use. I have made up my mind to that. I fear the Marksville post-master will mistrust something, I have inquired so often at his office. Too uncertain—too dangerous."

"Then it is all over," I exclaimed. "Oh, my God, how can I end my days here!"

"You're not going to end them here," he said, "unless you die very soon. I've thought this matter all over, and have come to a determination. There are more ways than one to manage this business, and a better and surer way than writing letters. I have a job or two on hand which can be completed by March or April. By that time I shall have a considerable sum of money, and then, Platt, I am going to Saratoga myself."

I could scarcely credit my own senses as the words fell from his lips. But he assured me, in a manner that left no doubt of the sincerity of his intention, that if his life was spared until spring, he should certainly undertake the journey.

"I have lived in this region long enough," he continued; "I may as well be in one place as another. For a long time I have been thinking of going back once more to the place where I was born. I'm tired of Slavery as well as you. If I can succeed in getting you away from here, it will be a good act that I shall like to think of all my life. And I *shall* succeed, Platt; I'm *bound* to do it. Now let me tell you what I want. Epps will be up soon, and it won't do to be caught here. Think of a great many men at Saratoga and Sandy Hill, and in that neighborhood, who once knew you. I shall make excuse to come here again in the course of the winter, when

I will write down their names. I will then know who to call on when I go north. Think of all you can. Cheer up! Don't be discouraged. I'm with you, life or death. Good-bye. God bless you," and saying this he left the cabin quickly, and entered the great house.

It was Christmas morning—the happiest day in the whole year for the slave. That morning he need not hurry to the field, with his gourd and cotton-bag. Happiness sparkled in the eyes and overspread the countenances of all. The time of feasting and dancing had come. The cane and cotton fields were deserted. That day the clean dress was to be donned—the red ribbon displayed; there were to be re-unions, and joy and laughter, and hurrying to and fro. It was to be a day of *liberty* among the children of Slavery. Wherefore they were happy, and rejoiced.

After breakfast Epps and Bass sauntered about the yard, conversing upon the price of cotton, and various other topics.

"Where do your niggers hold Christmas?" Bass inquired.

"Platt is going to Tanners to-day. His fiddle is in great demand. They want him at Marshall's Monday, and Miss Mary McCoy, on the old Norwood plantation, writes me a note that she wants him to play for her niggers Tuesday."

"He is rather a smart boy, ain't he?" said Bass. "Come here, Platt," he added, looking at me as I walked up to them, as if he had never thought before to take any special notice of me.

"Yes," replied Epps, taking hold of my arm and feeling it, "there isn't a bad joint in him. There ain't a boy on the bayou worth more than he is—perfectly sound, and no bad tricks. D—n him, he isn't like other niggers; doesn't look like 'em—don't act like 'em. I was offered seventeen hundred dollars for him last week."

"And didn't take it?" Bass inquired, with an air of surprise.

"Take it—no; devilish clear of it. Why, he's a reg'lar genius;

can make a plough beam, wagon tongue—anything, as well as you can. Marshall wanted to put up one of his niggers agin him and raffle for them, but I told him I would see the devil have him first."

"I don't see anything remarkable about him," Bass observed.

"Why, just feel of him, now," Epps rejoined. "You don't see a boy very often put together any closer than he is. He's a thin-skin'd cuss, and won't bear as much whipping as some; but he's got the muscle in him, and no mistake."

Bass felt of me, turned me round, and made a thorough examination, Epps all the while dwelling on my good points. But his visitor seemed to take but little interest finally in the subject, and consequently it was dropped. Bass soon departed, giving me another sly look of recognition and significance, as he trotted out of the yard.

When he was gone I obtained a pass, and started for Tanner's—not Peter Tanner's, of whom mention has previously been made, but a relative of his. I played during the day and most of the night, spending the next day, Sunday, in my cabin. Monday I crossed the bayou to Douglas Marshall's, all Epps' slaves accompanying me, and on Tuesday went to the old Norwood place, which is the third plantation above Marshall's, on the same side of the water.

This estate is now owned by Miss Mary McCoy, a lovely girl, some twenty years of age. She is the beauty and the glory of Bayou Bœuf. She owns about a hundred working hands, besides a great many house servants, yard boys, and young children. Her brother-in-law, who resides on the adjoining estate, is her general agent. She is beloved by all her slaves, and good reason indeed have they to be thankful that they have fallen into such gentle hands. Nowhere on the bayou are there such feasts, such merry-making, as at young Madam McCoy's. Thither, more than to any other place, do the old and the young for miles around love to repair in the time of the Christmas holidays; for nowhere else can they find such delicious repasts; nowhere else can they hear a voice speaking to them so pleasantly. No one is so well beloved—no one fills so large a space in the hearts of a thousand slaves, as young Madam McCoy, the orphan mistress of the old Norwood estate.

On my arrival at her place, I found two or three hundred had assembled. The table was prepared in a long building, which she had erected expressly for her slaves to dance in. It was covered with every variety of food the country afforded, and was pronounced by general acclamation to be the rarest of dinners. Roast turkey, pig, chicken, duck, and all kinds of meat, baked, boiled, and broiled, formed a line the whole length of the extended table, while the vacant spaces were filled with tarts, jellies, and frosted cake, and pastry of many kinds. The young mistress walked around the table, smiling and saying a kind word to each one, and seemed to enjoy the scene exceedingly.

When the dinner was over the tables were removed to make room for the dancers. I tuned my violin and struck up a lively air; while some joined in a nimble reel, others patted and sang their simple but melodious songs, filling the great room with music mingled with the sound of human voices and the clatter of many feet.

In the evening the mistress returned, and stood in the door a long time, looking at us. She was magnificently arrayed. Her dark hair and eyes contrasted strongly with her clear and delicate complexion. Her form was slender but commanding, and her movement was a combination of unaffected dignity and grace. As she stood there, clad in her rich apparel, her face animated with pleasure, I thought I had never looked upon a human being half so beautiful. I dwell with delight upon the description of this fair and gentle lady, not only because she inspired me with emotions of gratitude and admiration, but because I would have the reader understand that all slave-owners on Bayou Bœuf are not like Epps, or Tibeats, or Jim Burns. Occasionally can be found, rarely it may be, indeed, a good man like William Ford, or an angel of kindness like young Mistress McCoy.

Tuesday concluded the three holidays Epps yearly allowed us. On my way home, Wednesday morning, while passing the plantation of William Pierce, that gentleman hailed me, saying he had received a line from Epps, brought down by William Varnell, permitting him to detain me for the purpose of playing for his slaves that night. It was the last time I was destined to witness a slave dance on the shores of Bayou Bœuf. The party at Pierce's continued their jollification until broad daylight, when I returned to my master's house, somewhat wearied with the loss of rest, but rejoicing in the possession of numerous bits and picayunes, which the whites, who were pleased with my musical performances, had contributed.

On Saturday morning, for the first time in years, I overslept myself. I was frightened on coming out of the cabin to find the slaves were already in the field. They had preceded me some fifteen minutes. Leaving my dinner and water-gourd, I hurried after them as fast as I could move. It was not yet sunrise, but Epps was on the piazza as I left the hut, and cried out to me that it was a pretty time of day to be getting up. By extra exertion my row was up when he came out after breakfast. This, however, was no excuse for the offence of oversleeping. Bidding me strip and lie down, he gave me ten or fifteen lashes, at the conclusion of which he inquired if I thought, after that, I could get up sometime in the *morning*. I expressed myself quite positively that I *could*, and, with back stinging with pain, went about my work.

The following day, Sunday, my thoughts were upon Bass, and

the probabilities and hopes which hung upon his action and determination. I considered the uncertainty of life; that if it should be the will of God that he should die, my prospect of deliverance, and all expectation of happiness in this world, would be wholly ended and destroyed. My sore back, perhaps, did not have a tendency to render me unusually cheerful. I felt down-hearted and unhappy all day long, and when I laid down upon the hard board at night, my heart was oppressed with such a load of grief, it seemed that it must break.

Monday morning, the third of January, 1853, we were in the field betimes. It was a raw, cold morning, such as is unusual in that region. I was in advance, Uncle Abram next to me, behind him Bob, Patsey and Wiley, with our cotton-bags about our necks. Epps happened (a rare thing, indeed,) to come out that morning without his whip. He swore, in a manner that would shame a pirate, that we were doing nothing. Bob ventured to say that his fingers were so numb with cold he couldn't pick fast. Epps cursed himself for not having brought his rawhide, and declared that when he came out again he would warm us well; yes, he would make us all hotter than that fiery realm in which I am sometimes compelled to believe he will himself eventually reside.

With these fervent expressions, he left us. When out of hearing, we commenced talking to each other, saying how hard it was to be compelled to keep up our tasks with numb fingers; how unreasonable master was, and speaking of him generally in no flattering terms. Our conversation was interrupted by a carriage passing rapidly towards the house. Looking up, we saw two men approaching us through the cotton-field.

Having now brought down this narrative to the last hour I was to spend on Bayou Bœuf—having gotten through my last cotton picking, and about to bid Master Epps farewell—I must beg the reader to go back with me to the month of August; to follow Bass' letter on its long journey to Saratoga; to learn the effect it produced—and that, while I was repining and despairing in the slave hut of Edwin Epps, through the friendship of Bass and the goodness of Providence, all things were working together for my deliverance.

# CHAPTER XXI

*The Letter Reaches Saratoga—Is Forwarded To Anne—Is Laid Before Henry B. Northup—The Statute Of May 14, 1840—Its Provisions—Anne's Memorial To The Governor—The Affidavits Accompanying It—Senator Soule's Letter—Departure Of The Agent Appointed By The Governor—Arrival At Marksville—The Hon. John P. Waddill—The Conversation On New-York Politics—It Suggests A Fortunate Idea—The Meeting With Bass—The Secret Out—Legal Proceedings Instituted—Departure Of Northup And The Sheriff From Marksville For Bayou Bœuf—Arrangements On The Way—Reach Epps' Plantation—Discover His Slaves In The Cotton Field—The Meeting—The Farewell.*

I am indebted to Mr. Henry B. Northup and others for many of the particulars contained in this chapter.

The letter written by Bass, directed to Parker and Perry, and which was deposited in the post-office in Marksville on the 15th day of August, 1852, arrived at Saratoga in the early part of September. Some time previous to this, Anne had removed to Glens Falls, Warren county, where she had charge of the kitchen in Carpenter's Hotel. She kept house, however, lodging with our children, and was only absent from them during such time as the discharge of her duties in the hotel required.

Messrs. Parker and Perry, on receipt of the letter, forwarded it immediately to Anne. On reading it the children were all excitement, and without delay hastened to the neighboring village of Sandy Hill, to consult Henry B. Northup, and obtain his advice and assistance in the matter.

Upon examination, that gentleman found among the statutes of the State an act providing for the recovery of free citizens from slavery. It was passed May 14, 1840, and is entitled "An act more effectually to protect the free citizens of this State from being kidnapped or reduced to slavery." It provides that it shall be the duty of the Governor, upon the receipt of satisfactory information that any free citizen or inhabitant of this State, is wrongfully held in another State or Territory of the United States, upon the allegation or pretence that such person is a slave, or by color of any usage or rule of law is deemed or taken to be a slave, to take such measures to procure the restoration of such person to liberty, as he shall deem necessary. And to that end, he is authorized to appoint and employ an agent, and directed to furnish him with such credentials and instructions as will be likely to accomplish the object of his appointment. It requires the agent so appointed to proceed to collect the proper proof to establish the right of such person to his freedom; to perform such journeys, take such measures, institute such legal proceedings, &c., as may be necessary to return such person to this State, and charges all expenses incurred in carrying the act into effect, upon moneys not otherwise appropriated in the treasury.

It was necessary to establish two facts to the satisfaction of the Governor: First, that I was a free citizen of New-York; and secondly, that I was wrongfully held in bondage. As to the first point, there was no difficulty, all the older inhabitants in the vicinity being ready to testify to it. The second point rested entirely upon the letter to Parker and Perry, written in an unknown hand, and upon the letter penned on board the brig Orleans, which, unfortunately, had been mislaid or lost.

A memorial was prepared, directed to his excellency, Governor Hunt, setting forth her marriage, my departure to Washington city; the receipt of the letters; that I was a free citizen, and such other facts as were deemed important, and was signed and verified by Anne. Accompanying this memorial were several affidavits of prominent citizens of Sandy Hill and Fort Edward, corroborating fully the statements it contained, and also a request of several well known gentlemen to the Governor, that Henry B. Northup be appointed agent under the legislative act.

On reading the memorial and affidavits, his excellency took a lively interest in the matter, and on the 23d day of November, 1852, under the seal of the State, "constituted, appointed and employed Henry B. Northup, Esq., an agent, with full power to effect" my restoration, and to take such measures as would be most likely to accomplish it, and instructing him to proceed to Louisiana with all convenient dispatch.

The pressing nature of Mr. Northup's professional and political engagements delayed his departure until December. On the fourteenth day of that month he left Sandy Hill, and proceeded to Washington. The Hon. Pierre Soule, Senator in Congress from

Louisiana, Hon. Mr. Conrad, Secretary of War, and Judge Nelson, of the Supreme Court of the United States, upon hearing a statement of the facts, and examining his commission, and certified copies of the memorial and affidavits, furnished him with open letters to gentlemen in Louisiana, strongly urging their assistance in accomplishing the object of his appointment.

Senator Soule especially interested himself in the matter, insisting, in forcible language, that it was the duty and interest of every planter in his State to aid in restoring me to freedom, and trusted the sentiments of honor and justice in the bosom of every citizen of the commonwealth would enlist him at once in my behalf. Having obtained these valuable letters, Mr. Northup returned to Baltimore, and proceeded from thence to Pittsburgh. It was his original intention, under advice of friends at Washington, to go directly to New-Orleans, and consult the authorities of that city. Providentially, however, on arriving at the mouth of Red River, he changed his mind. Had he continued on, he would not have met with Bass, in which case the search for me would probably have been fruitless.

Taking passage on the first steamer that arrived, he pursued his journey up Red River, a sluggish, winding stream, flowing through a vast region of primitive forests and impenetrable swamps, almost wholly destitute of inhabitants. About nine o'clock in the forenoon, January 1st, 1853, he left the steamboat at Marksville, and proceeded directly to Marksville Court House, a small village four miles in the interior.

From the fact that the letter to Messrs. Parker and Perry was post-marked at Marksville, it was supposed by him that I was in that place or its immediate vicinity. On reaching this town, he at once laid his business before the Hon. John P. Waddill, a legal gentleman of distinction, and a man of fine genius and most noble impulses. After reading the letters and documents presented him, and listening to a representation of the circumstances under which I had been carried away into captivity, Mr. Waddill at once proffered his services, and entered into the affair with great zeal and earnestness. He, in common with others of like elevated character, looked upon the kidnapper with abhorrence. The title of his fellow parishioners and clients to the property which constituted the larger proportion of their wealth, not only depended upon the good faith in which slave sales were transacted, but he was a man in whose honorable heart emotions of indignation were aroused by such an instance of injustice.

Marksville, although occupying a prominent position, and standing out in impressive italics on the map of Louisiana, is, in fact, but a small and insignificant hamlet. Aside from the tavern, kept by a jolly and generous boniface, the court house, inhabited by lawless cows and swine in the seasons of vacation, and a high gallows, with its dissevered rope dangling in the air, there is little to attract the attention of the stranger.

Solomon Northup was a name Mr. Waddill had never heard, but he was confident that if there was a slave bearing that appellation in Marksville or vicinity, his black boy Tom would know him. Tom was accordingly called, but in all his extensive circle of acquaintances there was no such personage.

The letter to Parker and Perry was dated at Bayou Bœuf. At this place, therefore, the conclusion was, I must be sought. But here a difficulty suggested itself, of a very grave character indeed. Bayou Bœuf, at its nearest point, was twenty-three miles distant, and was the name applied to the section of country extending between fifty and a hundred miles, on both sides of that stream. Thousands and thousands of slaves resided upon its shores, the remarkable richness and fertility of the soil having attracted thither a great number of planters. The information in the letter was so vague and indefinite as to render it difficult to conclude upon any specific course of proceeding. It was finally determined, however, as the only plan that presented any prospect of success, that Northup and the brother of Waddill, a student in the office of the latter, should repair to the Bayou, and traveling up one side and down the other its whole length, inquire at each plantation for me. Mr. Waddill tendered the use of his carriage, and it was definitely arranged that they should start upon the excursion early Monday morning.

It will be seen at once that this course, in all probability, would have resulted unsuccessfully. It would have been impossible for them to have gone into the fields and examine all the gangs at work. They were not aware that I was known only as Platt; and had they inquired of Epps himself, he would have stated truly that he knew nothing of Solomon Northup.

The arrangement being adopted, however, there was nothing further to be done until Sunday had elapsed. The conversation between Messrs. Northup and Waddill, in the course of the afternoon, turned upon New-York politics.

"I can scarcely comprehend the nice distinctions and shades of political parties in your State," observed Mr. Waddill. "I read of soft-shells and hard-shells, hunkers and barnburners, woolly-heads and silver-grays, and am unable to understand the precise difference between them. Pray, what is it?"

Mr. Northup, re-filling his pipe, entered into quite an elaborate narrative of the origin of the various sections of parties, and concluded by saying there was another party in New-York, known as free-soilers or abolitionists. "You have seen none of those in this part of the country, I presume?" Mr. Northup remarked.

"Never, but one," answered Waddill, laughingly. "We have one here in Marksville, an eccentric creature, who preaches abolitionism as vehemently as any fanatic at the North. He is a generous, inoffensive man, but always maintaining the wrong side of an argument. It affords us a deal of amusement. He is an excellent mechanic, and almost indispensable in this community. He is a carpenter. His name is Bass."

Some further good-natured conversation was had at the expense of Bass' peculiarities, when Waddill all at once fell into a reflective mood, and asked for the mysterious letter again.

"Let me see—l-e-t m-e s-e-e!" he repeated, thoughtfully to himself, running his eyes over the letter once more. "'Bayou Bœuf, August 15.' August 15—post-marked here. 'He that is writing for me—' Where did Bass work last summer?" he inquired, turning suddenly to his brother. His brother was unable to inform him, but rising, left the office, and soon returned with the intelligence that "Bass worked last summer somewhere on Bayou Bœuf."

"He is the man," bringing down his hand emphatically on the table, "who can tell us all about Solomon Northup," exclaimed Waddill.

Bass was immediately searched for, but could not be found. After some inquiry, it was ascertained he was at the landing on Red River. Procuring a conveyance, young Waddill and Northup were not long in traversing the few miles to the latter place. On their arrival, Bass was found, just on the point of leaving, to be absent a fortnight or more. After an introduction, Northup begged the privilege of speaking to him privately a moment. They walked together towards the river, when the following conversation ensued:

"Mr. Bass," said Northup, "allow me to ask you if you were on Bayou Bœuf last August?"

"Yes, sir, I was there in August," was the reply.

"Did you write a letter for a colored man at that place to some gentleman in Saratoga Springs?"

"Excuse me, sir, if I say that is none of your business," answered Bass, stopping and looking his interrogator searchingly in the face.

"Perhaps I am rather hasty, Mr. Bass; I beg your pardon; but I have come from the State of New-York to accomplish the purpose the writer of a letter dated the 15th of August, post-marked at Marksville, had in view. Circumstances have led me to think that you are perhaps the man who wrote it. I am in search of Solomon Northup. If you know him, I beg you to inform me frankly where he is, and I assure you the source of any information you may give me shall not be divulged, if you desire it not to be."

A long time Bass looked his new acquaintance steadily in the eyes, without opening his lips. He seemed to be doubting in his own mind if there was not an attempt to practice some deception upon him. Finally he said, deliberately—

"I have done nothing to be ashamed of. I am the man who wrote the letter. If you have come to rescue Solomon Northup, I am glad to see you."

"When did you last see him, and where is he?" Northup inquired.

"I last saw him Christmas, a week ago to-day. He is the slave of Edwin Epps, a planter on Bayou Bœuf, near Holmesville. He is not known as Solomon Northup; he is called Platt."

The secret was out—the mystery was unraveled. Through the thick, black cloud, amid whose dark and dismal shadows I had walked twelve years, broke the star that was to light me back to liberty. All mistrust and hesitation were soon thrown aside, and the two men conversed long and freely upon the subject uppermost in their thoughts. Bass expressed the interest he had taken in my behalf—his intention of going north in the Spring, and declaring that he had resolved to accomplish my emancipation, if it were in his power. He described the commencement and progress of his acquaintance with me, and listened with eager curiosity to the account given him of my family, and the history of my early life. Before separating, he drew a map of the bayou on a strip of paper with a piece of red chalk, showing the locality of Epps' plantation, and the road leading most directly to it.

Northup and his young companion returned to Marksville, where it was determined to commence legal proceedings to test the question of my right to freedom. I was made plaintiff, Mr. Northup acting as my guardian, and Edwin Epps defendant. The process to be issued was in the nature of replevin, directed to the sheriff of the parish, commanding him to take me into custody, and detain me until the decision of the court. By the time the papers were duly drawn up, it was twelve o'clock at night—too late to obtain the necessary signature of the Judge, who resided some distance out of town. Further business was therefore suspended until Monday morning.

Everything, apparently, was moving along swimmingly, until Sunday afternoon, when Waddill called at Northup's room to express his apprehension of difficulties they had not expected to encounter. Bass had become alarmed, and had placed his affairs in the hands of a person at the landing, communicating to him his intention of leaving the State. This person had betrayed the confidence reposed in him to a certain extent, and a rumor began to float about the town, that the stranger at the hotel, who had been observed in the company of lawyer Waddill, was after one of old Epps' slaves, over on the bayou. Epps was known at Marksville, having frequent occasion to visit that place during the session of the courts, and the fear entertained by Mr. Northup's adviser was, that intelligence would be conveyed to him in the night, giving him an opportunity of secreting me before the arrival of the sheriff.

This apprehension had the effect of expediting matters considerably. The sheriff, who lived in one direction from the village, was requested to hold himself in readiness immediately after midnight, while the Judge was informed he would be called upon at the same time. It is but justice to say, that the authorities at Marksville cheerfully rendered all the assistance in their power.

As soon after midnight as bail could be perfected, and the Judge's signature obtained, a carriage, containing Mr. Northup and the sheriff, driven by the landlord's son, rolled rapidly out of the village of Marksville, on the road towards Bayou Bœuf.

It was supposed that Epps would contest the issue involving my right to liberty, and it therefore suggested itself to Mr. Northup, that the testimony of the sheriff, describing my first meeting with the former, might perhaps become material on the trial. It was accordingly arranged during the ride, that, before I had an opportunity of speaking to Mr. Northup, the sheriff should propound to me certain questions agreed upon, such as the number and names of my children, the name of my wife before marriage, of places I knew at the North, and so forth. If my answers corresponded with the statements given him, the evidence must necessarily be considered conclusive.

At length, shortly after Epps had left the field, with the consoling assurance that he would soon return and *warm* us, as was stated in the conclusion of the preceding chapter, they came in sight of the plantation, and discovered us at work. Alighting from the carriage, and directing the driver to proceed to the great house, with instructions not to mention to any one the object of their errand until they met again, Northup and the sheriff turned from the highway, and came towards us across the cotton field. We observed them, on looking up at the carriage—one several rods in advance of the other. It was a singular and unusual thing to see white men approaching us in that manner, and especially at that early hour in the morning, and Uncle Abram and Patsey made some remarks, expressive of their astonishment. Walking up to Bob, the sheriff inquired:

"Where's the boy they call Platt?"

"Thar he is, massa," answered Bob, pointing to me, and twitching off his hat.

I wondered to myself what business he could possibly have with me, and turning round, gazed at him until he had approached within a step. During my long residence on the bayou, I had become familiar with the face of every planter within many miles; but this man was an utter stranger—certainly I had never seen him before.

"Your name is Platt, is it?" he asked.

"Yes, master," I responded.

Pointing towards Northup, standing a few rods distant, he demanded—"Do you know that man?"

I looked in the direction indicated, and as my eyes rested on his countenance, a world of images thronged my brain; a multitude of well-known faces—Anne's, and the dear children's, and my old dead father's; all the scenes and associations of childhood and youth; all the friends of other and happier days, appeared and disappeared, flitting and floating like dissolving shadows before the vision of my imagination, until at last the perfect memory of the man recurred to me, and throwing up my hands towards Heaven, I exclaimed, in a voice louder than I could utter in a less exciting moment—

"*Henry B. Northup!* Thank God—thank God!"

In an instant I comprehended the nature of his business, and felt that the hour of my deliverance was at hand. I started towards him, but the sheriff stepped before me.

"Stop a moment," said he; "have you any other name than Platt?"

"Solomon Northup is my name, master," I replied.

"Have you a family?" he inquired.

"I *had* a wife and three children."

"What were your children's names?"

"Elizabeth, Margaret and Alonzo."

"And your wife's name before her marriage?"

"Anne Hampton."

"Who married you?"

"Timothy Eddy, of Fort Edward."

"Where does that gentleman live?" again pointing to Northup, who remained standing in the same place where I had first recognized him.

"He lives in Sandy Hill, Washington county, New-York," was the reply.

He was proceeding to ask further questions, but I pushed past him, unable longer to restrain myself. I seized my old acquaintance by both hands. I could not speak. I could not refrain from tears.

"Sol," he said at length, "I'm glad to see you."

I essayed to make some answer, but emotion choked all utterance, and I was silent. The slaves, utterly confounded, stood gazing upon the scene, their open mouths and rolling eyes indicating the utmost wonder and astonishment. For ten years I had dwelt among them, in the field and in the cabin, borne the same hardships, partaken the same fare, mingled my griefs with theirs, participated in the same scanty joys; nevertheless, not until this hour, the last I was to remain among them, had the remotest suspicion of my true name, or the slightest knowledge of my real history, been entertained by any one of them.

Not a word was spoken for several minutes, during which time I clung fast to Northup, looking up into his face, fearful I should awake and find it all a dream.

"Throw down that sack," Northup added, finally; "your cotton-picking days are over. Come with us to the man you live with."

I obeyed him, and walking between him and the sheriff, we moved towards the great house. It was not until we had proceeded some distance that I had recovered my voice sufficiently to ask if my family were all living. He informed me he had seen Anne, Margaret and Elizabeth but a short time previously; that Alonzo was still living, and all were well. My mother, however, I could never see again. As I began to recover in some measure from the sudden and great excitement which so overwhelmed me, I grew faint and weak, insomuch it was with difficulty I could walk. The sheriff took hold of my arm and assisted me, or I think I should have fallen. As we entered the yard, Epps stood by the gate, conversing with the driver. That young man, faithful to his instructions, was entirely unable to give him the least information in answer to his repeated inquiries of what was going on. By the time we reached him he was almost as much amazed and puzzled as Bob or Uncle Abram.

Shaking hands with the sheriff, and receiving an introduction to Mr. Northup, he invited them into the house, ordering me, at the same time, to bring in some wood. It was some time before I succeeded in cutting an armful, having, somehow, unaccountably lost the power of wielding the axe with any manner of precision. When I entered with it at last, the table was strewn with papers, from one of which Northup was reading. I was probably longer than necessity required, in placing the sticks upon the fire, being particular as to the exact position of each individual one of them. I heard the words, "the said Solomon Northup," and "the deponent further says," and "free citizen of New-York," repeated frequently, and from these expressions understood that the secret I had so long retained from Master and Mistress Epps, was finally developing. I lingered as long as prudence permitted, and was about leaving the room, when Epps inquired,

"Platt, do you know this gentleman?"

"Yes, master," I replied, "I have known him as long as I can remember."

"Where does he live?"

"He lives in New-York."

"Did you ever live there?"

"Yes, master—born and bred there."

"You was free, then. Now you d——d nigger," he exclaimed, "why did you not tell me that when I bought you?"

"Master Epps," I answered, in a somewhat different tone than the one in which I had been accustomed to address him—"Master Epps, you did not take the trouble to ask me; besides, I told one of my owners—the man that kidnapped me—that I was free, and was whipped almost to death for it."

"It seems there has been a letter written for you by somebody. Now, who is it?" he demanded, authoritatively. I made no reply.

"I say, who wrote that letter?" he demanded again.

"Perhaps I wrote it myself," I said.

"You haven't been to Marksville post-office and back before light, I know."

He insisted upon my informing him, and I insisted I would not. He made many vehement threats against the man, whoever he might be, and intimated the bloody and savage vengeance he would wreak upon him, when he found him out. His whole manner and language exhibited a feeling of anger towards the unknown person who had written for me, and of fretfulness at the idea of losing so much property. Addressing Mr. Northup, he swore if he had only had an hour's notice of his coming, he would have saved him the trouble of taking me back to New-York; that he would have run me into the swamp, or some other place out of the way, where all the sheriffs on earth couldn't have found me.

I walked out into the yard, and was entering the kitchen door, when something struck me in the back. Aunt Phebe, emerging from the back door of the great house with a pan of potatoes, had thrown one of them with unnecessary violence, thereby giving me to understand that she wished to speak to me a moment confidentially. Running up to me, she whispered in my ear with great earnestness,

"Lor a' mity, Platt! what d'ye think? Dem two men come after ye. Heard 'em tell massa you free—got wife and tree children back thar whar you come from. Goin' wid 'em? Fool if ye don't—wish I could go," and Aunt Phebe ran on in this manner at a rapid rate.

Presently Mistress Epps made her appearance in the kitchen. She said many things to me, and wondered why I had not told her who I was. She expressed her regret, complimenting me by saying she had rather lose any other servant on the plantation. Had Patsey that day stood in my place, the measure of my mistress' joy would have overflowed. Now there was no one left who could mend a chair or a piece of furniture—no one who was of any use about the house—no one who could play for her on the violin—and Mistress Epps was actually affected to tears.

Epps had called to Bob to bring up his saddle horse. The other slaves, also, overcoming their fear of the penalty, had left their work and come to the yard. They were standing behind the cabins, out of sight of Epps. They beckoned me to come to them, and with all the eagerness of curiosity, excited to the highest pitch, conversed with and questioned me. If I could repeat the exact words they uttered, with the same emphasis—if I could paint their several attitudes, and the expression of their countenances—it would be indeed an interesting picture. In their estimation, I had suddenly arisen to an immeasurable height—had become a being of immense importance.

The legal papers having been served, and arrangements made with Epps to meet them the next day at Marksville, Northup and the sheriff entered the carriage to return to the latter place. As I was about mounting to the driver's seat, the sheriff said I ought to bid Mr. and Mrs. Epps good-bye. I ran back to the piazza where they were standing, and taking off my hat, said,

"Good-bye, missis."

"Good-bye, Platt," said Mrs. Epps, kindly.

"Good-bye, master."

"Ah! you d—d nigger," muttered Epps, in a surly, malicious tone of voice, "you needn't feel so cussed tickled—you ain't gone yet—I'll see about this business at Marksville to-morrow."

I was only a "*nigger*" and knew my place, but felt as strongly as if I had been a white man, that it would have been an inward comfort, had I dared to have given him a parting kick. On my way back to the carriage, Patsey ran from behind a cabin and threw her arms about my neck.

"Oh! Platt," she cried, tears streaming down her face, "you're goin' to be free—you're goin' way off yonder where we'll neber see ye any more. You've saved me a good many whippins, Platt; I'm glad you're goin' to be free—but oh! de Lord, de Lord! what'll become of me?"

I disengaged myself from her, and entered the carriage. The driver cracked his whip and away we rolled. I looked back and saw Patsey, with drooping head, half reclining on the ground; Mrs. Epps was on the piazza; Uncle Abram, and Bob, and Wiley, and Aunt Phebe stood by the gate, gazing after me. I waved my hand, but the carriage turned a bend of the bayou, hiding them from my eyes forever.

We stopped a moment at Carey's sugar house, where a great number of slaves were at work, such an establishment being a curiosity to a Northern man. Epps dashed by us on horseback at full speed—on the way, as we learned next day, to the "Pine Woods," to see William Ford, who had brought me into the country.

Tuesday, the fourth of January, Epps and his counsel, the Hon. H. Taylor, Northup, Waddill, the Judge and sheriff of Avoyelles, and myself, met in a room in the village of Marksville. Mr. Northup stated the facts in regard to me, and presented his commission, and the affidavits accompanying it. The sheriff described the scene in the cotton field. I was also interrogated at great length. Finally, Mr. Taylor assured his client that he was satisfied, and that litigation would not only be expensive, but utterly useless. In accordance with his advice, a paper was drawn up and signed by the proper parties, wherein Epps acknowledged he was satisfied of my right to freedom, and formally surrendered me to the authorities of New-York. It was also stipulated that it be entered of record in the recorder's office of Avoyelles.

Mr. Northup and myself immediately hastened to the landing, and taking passage on the first steamer that arrived, were soon floating down Red River, up which, with such desponding thoughts, I had been borne twelve years before.

**Footnotes:**

See Appendix A.

See Appendix B.

See Appendix C.

# CHAPTER XXII

*Arrival In New-Orleans—Glimpse Of Freeman—Genois, The Recorder—His Description Of Solomon—Reach Charleston—Interrupted By Custom House Officers—Pass Through Richmond—Arrival In Washington—Burch Arrested—Shekels And Thorn—Their Testimony—Burch Acquitted—Arrest Of Solomon—Burch Withdraws The Complaint—The Higher Tribunal—Departure From Washington—Arrival At Sandy Hill—Old Friends And Familiar Scenes—Proceed To Glens Falls—Meeting With Anne, Margaret And Elizabeth—Solomon Northup Staunton—Incidents—Conclusion.*

As the steamer glided on its way towards New-Orleans, *perhaps* I was not happy—*perhaps* there was no difficulty in restraining myself from dancing round the deck—perhaps I did not feel grateful to the man who had come so many hundred miles for me—perhaps I did not light his pipe, and wait and watch his word, and run at his slightest bidding. If I didn't—well, no matter.

We tarried at New-Orleans two days. During that time I pointed out the locality of Freeman's slave pen, and the room in which Ford purchased me. We happened to meet Theophilus in the street, but I did not think it worth while to renew acquaintance with him. From respectable citizens we ascertained he had become a low, miserable rowdy—a broken-down, disreputable man.

We also visited the recorder, Mr. Genois, to whom Senator Soule's letter was directed, and found him a man well deserving the wide and honorable reputation that he bears. He very generously furnished us with a sort of legal pass, over his signature and seal of office, and as it contains the recorder's description of my personal appearance, it may not be amiss to insert it here. The following is a copy:

"*State of Louisiana—City of New-Orleans*:
Recorder's Office, Second District.

"To all to whom these presents shall come:—

"This is to certify that Henry B. Northup, Esquire, of the county of Washington, New-York, has produced before me due evidence of the freedom of Solomon, a mulatto man, aged about forty-two years, five feet, seven inches and six lines, woolly hair, and chestnut eyes, who is a native born of the State of New-York. That the said Northup, being about bringing the said Solomon to his native place, through the southern routes, the civil authorities are requested to let the aforesaid colored man Solomon pass unmolested, he demeaning well and properly.

"Given under my hand and the seal of the city of New-Orleans this 7th January, 1853.

[L. S.]

"TH. GENOIS, Recorder."

On the 8th we came to Lake Pontchartrain, by railroad, and, in due time, following the usual route, reached Charleston. After going on board the steamboat, and paying our passage at this city, Mr. Northup was called upon by a custom-house officer to explain why he had not registered his servant. He replied that he had no servant—that, as the agent of New-York, he was accompanying a free citizen of that State from slavery to freedom, and did not desire nor intend to make any registry whatever. I conceived from his conversation and manner, though I may perhaps be entirely mistaken, that no great pains would be taken to avoid whatever difficulty the Charleston officials might deem proper to create. At length, however, we were permitted to proceed, and, passing through Richmond, where I caught a glimpse of Goodin's pen, arrived in Washington January 17th, 1853.

We ascertained that both Burch and Radburn were still residing in that city. Immediately a complaint was entered with a police magistrate of Washington, against James H. Burch, for kidnapping and selling me into slavery. He was arrested upon a warrant issued by Justice Goddard, and returned before Justice Mansel, and held to bail in the sum of three thousand dollars. When first arrested, Burch was much excited, exhibiting the utmost fear and alarm, and before reaching the justice's office on Louisiana Avenue, and before knowing the precise nature of the complaint, begged the police to permit him to consult Benjamin O. Shekels, a slave trader of seventeen years' standing, and his former partner. The latter became his bail.

At ten o'clock, the 18th of January, both parties appeared before the magistrate. Senator Chase, of Ohio, Hon. Orville Clark, of Sandy Hill, and Mr. Northup acted as counsel for the prosecution, and Joseph H. Bradley for the defence.

Gen. Orville Clark was called and sworn as a witness, and testified that he had known me from childhood, and that I was a free man, as was my father before me. Mr. Northup then testified to the same, and proved the facts connected with his mission to Avoyelles.

Ebenezer Radburn was then sworn for the prosecution, and testified he was forty-eight years old; that he was a resident of Washington, and had known Burch fourteen years; that in 1841 he was keeper of Williams' slave pen; that he remembered the fact of my confinement in the pen that year. At this point it was admitted by the defendant's counsel, that I had been placed in the pen by Burch in the spring of 1841, and hereupon the prosecution rested.

Benjamin O. Shekels was then offered as a witness by the prisoner. Benjamin is a large, coarse-featured man, and the reader may perhaps get a somewhat correct conception of him by reading the exact language he used in answer to the first question of defendant's lawyer. He was asked the place of his nativity, and his reply, uttered in a sort of rowdyish way, was in these very words—

"I was born in Ontario county, New-York, and *weighed fourteen pounds*!"

Benjamin was a prodigious baby! He further testified that he kept the Steamboat Hotel in Washington in 1841, and saw me there in the spring of that year. He was proceeding to state what he had heard two men say, when Senator Chase raised a legal objection, to wit, that the sayings of third persons, being hearsay, was improper evidence. The objection was overruled by the Justice, and Shekels continued, stating that two men came to his hotel and represented they had a colored man for sale; that they had an interview with Burch; that they stated they came from Georgia, but he did not remember the county; that they gave a full history of the boy, saying he was a bricklayer, and played on the violin; that Burch remarked he would purchase if they could agree; that they went out and brought the boy in, and that I was the same person. He further testified, with as much unconcern as if it was the truth, that I represented I was born and bred in Georgia; that one of the young men with me was my master; that I exhibited a great deal of regret at parting with him, and he believed "got into tears!"—nevertheless, that I insisted my master had a right to sell me; that he *ought* to sell me; and the remarkable reason I gave was, according to Shekels, because he, my master, "had been gambling and on a spree!"

He continued, in these words, copied from the minutes taken on the examination: "Burch interrogated the boy in the usual manner, told him if he purchased him he should send him south. The boy said he had no objection, that in fact he would like to go south. Burch paid $650 for him, to my knowledge. I don't know what name was given him, but think it was not Solomon. Did not know the name of either of the two men. They were in my tavern two or three hours, during which time the boy played on the violin. The bill of sale was signed in my bar-room. It was a *printed blank, filled up by Burch*. Before 1838 Burch was my partner. Our business was buying and selling slaves. After that time he was a partner of Theophilus Freeman, of New-Orleans. Burch bought here—Freeman sold there!"

Shekels, before testifying, had heard my relation of the circumstances connected with the visit to Washington with Brown and Hamilton, and therefore, it was, undoubtedly, he spoke of "two men," and of my playing on the violin. Such was his fabrication, utterly untrue, and yet there was found in Washington a man who endeavored to corroborate him.

Benjamin A. Thorn testified he was at Shekels' in 1841, and saw a colored boy playing on a fiddle. "Shekels said he was for sale. Heard his master tell him he should sell him. The boy acknowledged to me he was a slave. I was not present when the money was paid. Will not swear positively this is the boy. The master *came near shedding tears: I think the boy did*! I have been engaged in the business of taking slaves south, off and on, for twenty years. When I can't do that I do something else."

I was then offered as a witness, but, objection being made, the court decided my evidence inadmissible. It was rejected solely on the ground that I was a colored man—the fact of my being a free citizen of New-York not being disputed.

Shekels having testified there was a bill of sale executed, Burch was called upon by the prosecution to produce it, inasmuch as such a paper would corroborate the testimony of Thorn and Shekels. The prisoner's counsel saw the necessity of exhibiting it, or giving some reasonable explanation for its non-production. To effect the latter, Burch himself was offered as a witness in his own behalf. It was contended by counsel for the people, that such testimony should not be allowed—that it was in contravention of every rule of evidence, and if permitted would defeat the ends of justice. His testimony, however, was received by the court! He made oath that such a bill of sale had been drawn up and signed, *but he had lost it, and did not know what had become of it*! Thereupon the magistrate was requested to dispatch a police officer to Burch's residence, with directions to bring his books, containing his bills of sales for the year 1841. The request was granted, and before any measure could be taken to prevent it, the officer had obtained possession of the books, and brought them into court. The sales for the year 1841 were found, and carefully examined, but no sale of myself, by any name, was discovered!

Upon this testimony the court held the fact to be established, that Burch came innocently and honestly by me, and accordingly he was discharged.

An attempt was then made by Burch and his satellites, to fasten upon me the charge that I had conspired with the two white men to defraud him—with what success, appears in an extract taken from an article in the New-York Times, published a day or two subsequent to the trial: "The counsel for the defendant had drawn up, before the defendant was discharged, an affidavit, signed by Burch, and had a warrant out against the colored man for a conspiracy with the two white men before referred to, to defraud Burch out of six hundred and twenty-five dollars. The warrant was served, and the colored man arrested and brought before officer Goddard. Burch and his witnesses appeared in court, and H. B. Northup appeared as counsel for the colored man, stating he was ready to proceed as counsel on the part of the defendant, and asking no delay whatever. Burch, after consulting privately a short time with Shekels, stated to the magistrate that he wished him to dismiss the complaint, as he would not proceed farther with it. Defendant's counsel stated to the magistrate that if the complaint was withdrawn, it must be without the request or consent of the defendant. Burch then asked the magistrate to let him have the complaint and the warrant, and he took them. The counsel for the defendant objected to his receiving them, and insisted they should remain as part of the records of the court, and that the court should endorse the proceedings which had been had under the process. Burch delivered them up, and the court rendered a judgment of discontinuance by the request of the prosecutor, and filed it in his office."

There may be those who will affect to believe the statement of the slave-trader—those, in whose minds his allegations will weigh heavier than mine. I am a poor colored man—one of a down-trodden and degraded race, whose humble voice may not be heeded by the oppressor—but *knowing* the truth, and with a full sense of my accountability, I do solemnly declare before men, and before God, that any charge or assertion, that I conspired directly or indirectly with any person or persons to sell myself; that any other account of my visit to Washington, my capture and imprisonment in Williams' slave pen, than is contained in these pages, is utterly and absolutely false. I never played on the violin in Washington. I never was in the Steamboat Hotel, and never saw Thorn or Shekels, to my knowledge, in my life, until last January. The story of the trio of slave-traders is a fabrication as absurd as it is base and unfounded. Were it true, I should not have turned aside on my way back to liberty for the purpose of prosecuting Burch. I should have *avoided* rather than sought him. I should have known that such a step would have resulted in rendering me infamous. Under the circumstances—longing as I did to behold my family, and elated with the prospect of returning home—it is an outrage upon probability to suppose I would have run the hazard, not only of exposure, but of a criminal prosecution and conviction, by voluntarily placing myself in the position I did, if the statements of Burch and his confederates contain a particle of truth. I took pains to seek him out, to confront him in a court of law, charging him with the crime of kidnapping; and the only motive that impelled me to this step, was a burning sense of the wrong he had inflicted upon me, and a desire to bring him to justice. He was acquitted, in the manner, and by such means as have been described. A human tribunal has permitted him to escape; but there is another and a higher tribunal, where false testimony will not prevail, and where I am willing, so far at least as these statements are concerned, to be judged at last.

We left Washington on the 20th of January, and proceeding by the way of Philadelphia, New-York, and Albany, reached Sandy Hill in the night of the 21st. My heart overflowed with happiness as I looked around upon old familiar scenes, and found myself in the midst of friends of other days. The following morning I started, in company with several acquaintances, for Glens Falls, the residence of Anne and our children.

As I entered their comfortable cottage, Margaret was the first that met me. She did not recognize me. When I left her, she was but seven years old, a little prattling girl, playing with her toys. Now she was grown to womanhood—was married, with a bright-eyed boy standing by her side. Not forgetful of his enslaved, unfortunate grand-father, she had named the child Solomon Northup Staunton. When told who I was, she was overcome with emotion, and unable to speak. Presently Elizabeth entered the room, and Anne came running from the hotel, having been informed of my arrival. They embraced me, and with tears flowing down their cheeks, hung upon my neck. But I draw a veil over a scene which can better be imagined than described.

When the violence of our emotions had subsided to a sacred joy—when the household gathered round the fire, that sent out its warm and crackling comfort through the room, we conversed of the thousand events that had occurred—the hopes and fears, the joys and sorrows, the trials and troubles we had each experienced during the long separation. Alonzo was absent in the western part of the State. The boy had written to his mother a short time previous, of the prospect of his obtaining sufficient money to purchase my freedom. From his earliest years, that had been the chief object of his thoughts and his ambition. They knew I was in bondage. The letter written on board the brig, and Clem Ray himself, had given them that information. But where I was, until the arrival of Bass' letter, was a matter of conjecture. Elizabeth and Margaret once returned from school—so Anne informed me—weeping bitterly. On inquiring the cause of the children's sorrow, it was found that, while studying geography, their attention had been attracted to the picture of slaves working in the cotton-field, and an overseer following them with his whip. It reminded them of the sufferings their father might be, and, as it happened, actually *was*, enduring in the South. Numerous incidents, such as these, were related—incidents showing they still held me in constant remembrance, but not, perhaps, of sufficient interest to the reader, to be recounted.

My narrative is at an end. I have no comments to make upon the subject of Slavery. Those who read this book may form their own opinions of the "peculiar institution." What it may be in other States, I do not profess to know; what it is in the region of Red River, is truly and faithfully delineated in these pages. This is no fiction, no exaggeration. If I have failed in anything, it has been in presenting to the reader too prominently the bright side of the picture. I doubt not hundreds have been as unfortunate as myself; that hundreds of free citizens have been kidnapped and sold into slavery, and are at this moment wearing out their lives on plantations in Texas and Louisiana. But I forbear. Chastened and subdued in spirit by the sufferings I have borne, and thankful to that good Being through whose mercy I have been restored to happiness and liberty, I hope henceforward to lead an upright though lowly life, and rest at last in the church yard where my father sleeps.

# *Roaring River.*

## *A Refrain Of The Red River Plantation.*

"Harper's creek and roarin' ribber,
Thar, my dear, we'll live forebber;
Den we'll go to de Ingin nation,
All I want in dis creation,
Is pretty little wife and big plantation.
CHORUS.
Up dat oak and down dat ribber,
Two overseers and one little nigger."

# *Appendices*

## *Appendix A.*

CHAP. 375.

*An act more effectually to protect the free citizens of this State from being kidnapped, or reduced to Slavery.*

The People of the State of New-York, represented in Senate and Assembly, do enact as follows:

[Passed May 14, 1840.]

§ 1. Whenever the Governor of this State shall receive information satisfactory to him that any free citizen or any inhabitant of this State has been kidnapped or transported away out of this State, into any other State or Territory of the United States, for the purpose of being there held in slavery; or that such free citizen or inhabitant is wrongfully seized, imprisoned or held in slavery in any of the States or Territories of the United States, on the allegation or pretence that such a person is a slave, or by color of any usage or rule of law prevailing in such State or Territory, is deemed or taken to be a slave, or not entitled of right to the personal liberty belonging to a citizen; it shall be the duty of the said Governor to take such measures as he shall deem necessary to procure such person to be restored to his liberty and returned to this State. The Governor is hereby authorized to appoint and employ such agent or agents as he shall deem necessary to effect the restoration and return of such person; and shall furnish the said agent with such credentials and instructions as will be likely to accomplish the object of his appointment. The Governor may determine the compensation to be allowed to such agent for his services besides his necessary expenses.

§ 2. Such agent shall proceed to collect the proper proof to establish the right of such person to his freedom, and shall perform such journeys, take such measures, institute and procure to be prosecuted such legal proceedings, under the direction of the Governor, as shall be necessary to procure such person to be restored to his liberty and returned to this State.

§ 3. The accounts for all services and expenses incurred in carrying this act into effect shall be audited by the Comptroller, and paid by the Treasurer on his warrant, out of any moneys in the treasury of this State not otherwise appropriated. The Treasurer may advance, on the warrant of the Comptroller, to such agent, such sum or sums as the Governor shall certify to be reasonable advances to enable him to accomplish the purposes of his appointment, for which advance such agent shall account, on the final audit of his warrant.

§ 4. This act shall take effect immediately.

## *Appendix B.*

### MEMORIAL OF ANNE.

*To His Excellency, the Governor of*
*the State of New-York:*

The memorial of Anne Northup, of the village of Glens Falls, in the county of Warren, State aforesaid, respectfully sets forth—

That your memorialist, whose maiden name was Anne Hampton, was forty-four years old on the 14th day of March last, and was married to Solomon Northup, then of Fort Edward, in the county of Washington and State aforesaid, on the 25th day of December, A. D. 1828, by Timothy Eddy, then a Justice of the Peace. That the said Solomon, after such marriage, lived and kept house with your memorialist in said town until 1830, when he removed with his said family to the town of Kingsbury in said county, and remained there about three years, and then removed to Saratoga Springs in the State aforesaid, and continued to reside in said Saratoga Springs and the adjoining town until about the year 1841, as near as the time can be recollected, when the said Solomon started to go to the city of Washington, in the District of Columbia, since which time your memorialist has never seen her said husband.

And your memorialist further states, that in the year 1841 she received information by a letter directed to Henry B. Northup, Esq., of Sandy Hill, Washington county, New-York, and post-marked at New-Orleans, that said Solomon had been kidnapped in Washington, put on board of a vessel, and was then in such vessel in New-Orleans, but could not tell how he came in that situation, nor what his destination was.

That your memorialist ever since the last mentioned period has been wholly unable to obtain any information of where the said Solomon was, until the month of September last, when another letter was received from the said Solomon, post-marked at Marksville, in the parish of Avoyelles, in the State of Louisiana, stating that he was held there as a slave, which statement your memorialist believes to be true.

That the said Solomon is about forty-five years of age, and never resided out of the State of New-York, in which State he was born, until the time he went to Washington city, as before stated. That the said Solomon Northup is a free citizen of the State of New-York, and is now wrongfully held in slavery, in or near Marksville, in the parish of Avoyelles, in the State of Louisiana, one of the United States of America, on the allegation or pretence that the said Solomon is a slave.

And your memorialist further states that Mintus Northup was the reputed father of said Solomon, and was a negro, and died at Fort Edward, on the 22d day of November, 1829; that the mother of said Solomon was a mulatto, or three quarters white, and died in the county of Oswego, New-York, some five or six years ago, as your memorialist was informed and believes, and never was a slave.

That your memorialist and her family are poor and wholly unable to pay or sustain any portion of the expenses of restoring the said Solomon to his freedom.

Your excellency is entreated to employ such agent or agents as shall be deemed necessary to effect the restoration and return of said Solomon Northup, in pursuance of an act of the Legislature of the State of New-York, passed May 14th, 1840, entitled "An act more effectually to protect the free citizens of this State from being kidnappd or reduced to slavery." And your memorialist will ever pray.

(Signed,)
ANNE NORTHUP.
Dated November 19, 1852.

State of New-York:
Washington county, ss.

Anne Northup, of the village of Glens Falls, in the county of Warren, in said State, being duly sworn, doth depose and say that she signed the above memorial, and that the statements therein contained are true.

(Signed,)
ANNE NORTHUP.

Subscribed and sworn before me this
19th November, 1852.
Charles Hughes, Justice Peace.

We recommend that the Governor appoint Henry B. Northup, of the village of Sandy Hill, Washington county, New-York, as one of the agents to procure the restoration and return of Solomon Northup, named in the foregoing memorial of Anne Northup.

Dated at Sandy Hill, Washington Co., N. Y.,
November 20, 1852.
(Signed.)
PETER HOLBROOK, DANIEL SWEET, B. F. HOAG,
ALMON CLARK, CHARLES HUGHES,
BENJAMIN FERRIS, E. D. BAKER,
JOSIAH H. BROWN, ORVILLE CLARK.

STATE OF NEW-YORK:
Washington County, ss:

Josiah Hand, of the village of Sandy Hill, in said county, being duly sworn, says, he is fifty-seven years old, and was born in said village, and has always resided there; that he has known Mintus Northup and his son Solomon, named in the annexed memorial of Anne Northup, since previous to the year 1816; that Mintus Northup then, and until the time of his death, cultivated a farm in the towns of Kingsbury and Fort Edward, from the time deponent first knew him until he died; that said Mintus and his wife, the mother of said Solomon Northup, were reported to be free citizens of New-York, and deponent believes they were so free; that said Solomon Northup was born in said county of Washington, as deponent believes, and was married Dec. 25th, 1828, in Fort Edward aforesaid, and his said wife and three children—two daughters and one son—are now living in Glens Falls, Warren county, New-York, and that the said Solomon Northup always resided in said county of Washington, and its immediate vicinity, until about 1841, since which time deponent has not seen him, but deponent has been credibly informed, and as he verily believes truly, the said Solomon is now wrongfully held as a slave in the State of Louisiana. And deponent further says that Anne Northup, named in the said memorial, is entitled to credit, and deponent believes the statements contained in her said memorial are true.

(Signed,)
JOSIAH HAND.

Subscribed and sworn before me this
19th day of November, 1852,
CHARLES HUGHES, Justice Peace.

STATE OF NEW-YORK:
Washington county, ss:

Timothy Eddy, of Fort Edward, in said county, being duly sworn, says he is now over—years old, and has been a resident of said town more than—years last past, and that he was well acquainted with Solomon Northup, named in the annexed memorial of Anne Northup, and with his father, Mintus Northup, who was a negro,—the wife of said Mintus was a mulatto woman; that said Mintus Northup and his said wife and family, two sons, Joseph and Solomon, resided in said town of Fort Edward for several years before the year 1828, and said Mintus died in said town A. D. 1829, as deponent believes. And deponent further says that he was a Justice of the Peace in said town in the year 1828, and as such Justice of the Peace, he, on the 25th day of Dec'r, 1828, joined the said Solomon Northup in marriage with Anne Hampton, who is the same person who has subscribed the annexed memorial. And deponent expressly says, that said Solomon was a free citizen of the State of New-York, and always lived in said State, until about the year A. D. 1840, since which time deponent has not seen him, but has recently been informed, and as deponent believes truly, that said Solomon Northup is wrongfully held in slavery in or near Marksville, in the parish of Avoyelles, in the State of Louisiana. And deponent further says, that said Mintus Northup was nearly sixty years old at the time of his death, and was, for more than thirty years next prior to his death, a free citizen of the State of New-York.

And this deponent further says, that Anne Northup, the wife of said Solomon Northup, is of good character and reputation, and her statements, as contained in the memorial hereto annexed, are entitled to full credit.

(Signed,)

TIMOTHY EDDY.

Subscribed and sworn before me this
19th day of November, 1852,
TIM'Y STOUGHTON, Justice.

STATE OF NEW-YORK:
Washington County, ss:

Henry B. Northup, of the village of Sandy Hill, in said county, being duly sworn, says, that he is forty-seven years old, and has always lived in said county; that he knew Mintus Northup, named in the annexed memorial, from deponent's earliest recollection until the time of his death, which occurred at Fort Edward, in said county, in 1829; that deponent knew the children of said Mintus, viz, Solomon and Joseph; that they were both born in the county of Washington aforesaid, as deponent believes; that deponent was well acquainted with said Solomon, who is the same person named in the annexed memorial of Anne Northup, from his childhood; and that said Solomon always resided in said county of Washington and the adjoining counties until about the year 1841; that said Solomon could read and write; that said Solomon and his mother and father were free citizens of the State of New-York; that sometime about the year 1841 this deponent received a letter from said Solomon, post-marked New-Orleans, stating that while on business at Washington city, he had been kidnapped, and his free papers taken from him, and he was then on board a vessel, in irons, and was claimed as a slave, and that he did not know his destination, which the deponent believes to be true, and he urged this deponent to assist in procuring his restoration to freedom; that deponent has lost or mislaid said letter, and cannot find it; that deponent has since endeavored to find where said Solomon was, but could get no farther trace of him until Sept. last, when this deponent ascertained by a letter purporting to have been written by the direction of said Solomon, that said Solomon was held and claimed as a slave in or near Marksville, in the parish of Avoyelles, Louisiana, and that this deponent verily believes that such information is true, and that said Solomon is now wrongfully held in slavery at Marksville aforesaid.

(Signed,)
HENRY B. NORTHUP.

Subscribed and sworn to before me
this 20th day of November, 1852,
CHARLES HUGHES, J. P.

STATE OF NEW-YORK:
Washington County, ss

Nicholas C. Northup, of the village of Sandy Hill, in said county, being duly sworn, doth depose and say, that he is now fifty-eight years of age, and has known Solomon Northup, mentioned in the annexed memorial of Ann Northup, ever since he was born. And this deponent saith that said Solomon is now about forty-five years old, and was born in the county of Washington aforesaid, or in the county of Essex, in said State, and always resided in the State of New-York until about the year 1841, since which time deponent has not seen him or known where he was, until a few weeks since, deponent was informed, and believes truly, that said Solomon was held in slavery in the State of Louisiana. Deponent further says, that said Solomon was married in the town of Fort Edward, in said county, about twenty-four years ago, and that his wife and two daughters and one son now reside in the village of Glens Falls, county of Warren, in said State of New-York. And this deponent swears positively that said Solomon Northup is a citizen of said State of New-York, and was born free, and from his earliest infancy lived and resided in the counties of Washington, Essex, Warren and Saratoga, in the State of New-York, and that his said wife and children have never resided out of said counties since the time said Solomon was married; that deponent knew the father of said Solomon Northup; that said father was a negro, named Mintus Northup, and died in the town of Fort Edward, in the county of Washington, State of New-York, on the 22d day of November, A. D. 1829, and was buried in the grave-yard in Sandy Hill aforesaid; that for more than thirty years before his death he lived in the counties of Essex, Washington and Rensselaer and State of New-York, and left a wife and two sons, Joseph and the said Solomon, him surviving; that the mother of said Solomon was a mulatto woman, and is now dead, and died, as deponent believes, in Oswego county, New-York, within five or six years past. And this deponent further states, that the mother of the said Solomon Northup was not a slave at the time of the birth of said Solomon Northup, and has not been a slave at any time within the last fifty years.

(Signed,)
N. C. NORTHUP.

Subscribed and sworn before me this 19th day
of November, 1852. CHARLES HUGHES, Justice Peace.

STATE OF NEW-YORK:
Washington County, ss.

Orville Clark, of the village of Sandy Hill, in the county of Washington, State of New-York, being duly sworn, doth depose and say—that he, this deponent, is over fifty years of age; that in the years 1810 and 1811, or most of the time of those years, this deponent resided at Sandy Hill, aforesaid, and at Glens Falls; that this deponent then knew Mintus Northup, a black or colored man; he was then a free man, as this deponent believes and always understood; that the wife of said Mintus Northup, and mother of Solomon, was a free woman; that from the year 1818 until the time of the death of said Mintus Northup, about the year 1829, this deponent was very well acquainted with the said Mintus Northup; that he was a respectable man in the community in which he resided, and was a free man, so taken and esteemed by all his acquaintances; that this deponent has also been and was acquainted with his son Solomon Northup, from the said year 1818 until he left this part of the country, about the year 1840 or 1841; that he married Anne Hampton, daughter of William Hampton, a near neighbor of this deponent; that the said Anne, wife of said Solomon, is now living and resides in this vicinity; that the said Mintus Northup and William Hampton were both reputed and esteemed in this community as respectable men. And this deponent saith that the said Mintus Northup and his family, and the said William Hampton and his family, from the earliest recollection and acquaintance of this deponent with him (as far back as 1810,) were always reputed, esteemed, and taken to be, and this deponent believes, truly so, free citizens of the State of New-York. This deponent knows the said William Hampton, under the laws of this State, was entitled to vote at our elections, and he believes the said Mintus Northup also was entitled as a free citizen with the property qualification. And this deponent further saith, that the said Solomon Northup, son of said Mintus, and husband of said Anne Hampton, when he left this State, was at the time thereof a free citizen of the State of New-York. And this deponent further saith, that said Anne Hampton, wife of Solomon

Northup, is a respectable woman, of good character, and I would believe her statements, and do believe the facts set forth in her memorial to his excellency, the Governor, in relation to her said husband, are true.

(Signed,)

ORVILLE CLARK.

Sworn before me, November 19th, 1852.

U. G. PARIS, Justice of the Peace.

STATE OF NEW-YORK:

Washington County, ss.

Benjamin Ferris, of the village of Sandy Hill, in said county, being duly sworn, doth depose and say—that he is now fifty-seven years old, and has resided in said village forty-five years; that he was well acquainted with Mintus Northup, named in the annexed memorial of Anne Northup, from the year 1816 to the time of his death, which occurred at Fort Edward, in the fall of 1829; that he knew the children of the said Mintus, namely, Joseph Northup and Solomon Northup, and that the said Solomon is the same person named in said memorial; that said Mintus resided in the said county of Washington to the time of his death, and was, during all that time, a free citizen of the said State of New-York, as deponent verily believes; that said memorialist, Anne Northup, is a woman of good character, and the statement contained in her memorial is entitled to credit.

(Signed)

BENJAMIN FERRIS.

Sworn before me, November
19th, 1852.

U. G. Paris, Justice of the Peace.

State of New-York:
Executive Chamber, Albany, Nov. 30, 1852.

I hereby certify that the foregoing is a correct copy of certain proofs filed in the Executive Department, upon which I have appointed Henry B. Northup an Agent of this State, to take proper proceedings in behalf of Solomon Northup, there in mentioned.
(Signed,)
WASHINGTON HUNT.

By the Governor.
J. F. R., Private Secretary.

State of New-York:
Executive Department.
Washington Hunt, *Governor of the State of New-York, to whom it may concern, greeting*:

Whereas, I have received information on oath, which is satisfactory to me, that Solomon Northup, who is a free citizen of this State, is wrongfully held in slavery, in the State of Louisiana:

And whereas, it is made my duty, by the laws of this State, to take such measures as I shall deem necessary to procure any citizen so wrongfully held in slavery, to be restored to his liberty and returned to this State:

Be it known, that in pursuance of chapter 375 of the laws of this State, passed in 1840, I have constituted, appointed and employed Henry B. Northup, Esquire, of the county of Washington, in this State, an Agent, with full power to effect the restoration of said Solomon Northup, and the said Agent is hereby authorized and empowered to institute such proper and legal proceedings, to procure such evidence, retain such counsel, and finally to take such measures as will be most likely to accomplish the object of his said appointment.

He is also instructed to proceed to the State of Louisiana with all convenient dispatch, to execute the agency hereby created.

[L. S.] In witness whereof, I have hereunto subscribed my name, and affixed the privy seal of the State, at Albany, this 23d day of November, in the year of our Lord 1852.

(Signed,)

WASHINGTON HUNT.

James F. Ruggles, Private Secretary.

## *Appendix C.*

STATE OF LOUISIANA:
Parish of Avoyelles.

Before me, Aristide Barbin, Recorder of the parish of Avoyelles, personally came and appeared Henry B. Northup, of the county of Washington, State of New-York, who hath declared that by virtue of a commission to him as agent of the State of New-York, given and granted by his excellency, Washington Hunt, Governor of the said State of New-York, bearing date the 23d day of November, 1852, authorizing and empowering him, the said Northup, to pursue and recover from slavery a free man of color, called Solomon Northup, who is a free citizen of the State of New-York, and who was kidnapped and sold into slavery, in the State of Louisiana, and now in the possession of Edwin Epps, of the State of Louisiana, of the Parish of Avoyelles; he, the said agent, hereto signing, acknowledges that the said Edwin has this day given and surrendered to him as such agent, the said Solomon Northup, free man of color, as aforesaid, in order that he be restored to his freedom, and carried back to the said State of New-York, pursuant to said commission, the said Edwin Epps being satisfied from the proofs produced by said agent, that the said Solomon Northup is entitled to his freedom. The parties consenting that a certified copy of said power of attorney be annexed to this act.

Done and signed at Marksville, parish of Avoyelles, this fourth day of January, one thousand eight hundred and fifty-three, in the presence of the undersigned, legal and competent witnesses, who have also hereto signed.

(Signed,)
HENRY B. NORTHUP.

EDWIN EPPS.
ADE. BARBIN, Recorder.

Witnesses:
H. TAYLOR,
JOHN P. WADDILL.

STATE OF LOUISIANA:
Parish of Avoyelles.

I do hereby certify the foregoing to be a true and correct copy of the original on file and of record in my office.

[L. S.] Given under my hand and seal of office as Recorder in and for the parish of Avoyelles, this 4th day of January, A. D. 1853.

(Signed,)
ADE. BARBIN, Recorder.

# INCIDENTS IN THE LIFE OF A SLAVE GIRL

HARRIET JACOBS

**Disclaimer**
Throughout the text, readers may find language and sentiments that appear both offensive and unacceptable. These words were duly reported by the former slave who wrote this book, and was forced to endure such dehumanizing attitudes on a daily basis. To better serve the author's original intentions and to ensure that the full impact of the writing is retained, we have decided to keep the original language in its entirety, though many segments may prove uncomfortable for the modern reader.

This edition published in 2020 by Arcturus Publishing Limited
26/27 Bickels Yard, 151–153 Bermondsey Street,
London SE1 3HA



Cover design: Peter Ridley
Cover illustration: Peter Gray

AD008697US

Printed in the UK

FSC
www.fsc.org
MIX
Paper from
responsible sources
FSC® C018072

# CONTENTS

*"Northerners know nothing at all about Slavery. They think it is perpetual bondage only. They have no conception of the depth of* degradation *involved in that word, SLAVERY; if they had, they would never cease their efforts until so horrible a system was overthrown."*

A Woman Of North Carolina

*"Rise up, ye women that are at ease! Hear my voice, ye careless daughters!*

*Give ear unto my speech."*

Isaiah XXXII. 9

# INTRODUCTION BY THE EDITOR

The author of the following autobiography is personally known to me, and her conversation and manners inspire me with confidence. During the last seventeen years, she has lived the greater part of the time with a distinguished family in New York, and has so deported herself as to be highly esteemed by them. This fact is sufficient, without further credentials of her character. I believe those who know her will not be disposed to doubt her veracity, though some incidents in her story are more romantic than fiction.

At her request, I have revised her manuscript; but such changes as I have made have been mainly for purposes of condensation and orderly arrangement. I have not added any thing to the incidents, or changed the import of her very pertinent remarks. With trifling exceptions, both the ideas and the language are her own. I pruned excrescences a little, but otherwise I had no reason for changing her lively and dramatic way of telling her own story. The names of both persons and places are known to me; but for good reasons I suppress them.

It will naturally excite surprise that a woman reared in Slavery should be able to write so well. But circumstances will explain this. In the first place, nature endowed her with quick perceptions. Secondly, the mistress, with whom she lived till she was twelve years old, was a kind, considerate friend, who taught her to read and spell. Thirdly, she was placed in favorable circumstances after she came to the North; having frequent intercourse with intelligent persons, who felt a friendly interest in her welfare, and were disposed to give her opportunities for self-improvement.

I am well aware that many will accuse me of indecorum for presenting these pages to the public; for the experiences of this intelligent and much-injured woman belong to a class which some call delicate subjects, and others indelicate. This peculiar phase of Slavery has generally been kept veiled; but the public ought to be made acquainted with its monstrous features, and I willingly take the responsibility of presenting them with the veil withdrawn. I do this for the sake of my sisters in bondage, who are suffering wrongs so foul, that our ears are too delicate to listen to them. I do it with the hope of arousing conscientious and reflecting women at the North to a sense of their duty in the exertion of moral influence on the question of Slavery, on all possible occasions. I do it with the hope that every man who reads this narrative will swear solemnly before God that, so far as he has power to prevent it, no fugitive from Slavery shall ever be sent back to suffer in that loathsome den of corruption and cruelty.

*L. Maria Child*

# PREFACE BY THE AUTHOR

Reader be assured this narrative is no fiction. I am aware that some of my adventures may seem incredible; but they are, nevertheless, strictly true. I have not exaggerated the wrongs inflicted by Slavery; on the contrary, my descriptions fall far short of the facts. I have concealed the names of places, and given persons fictitious names. I had no motive for secrecy on my own account, but I deemed it kind and considerate towards others to pursue this course.

I wish I were more competent to the task I have undertaken. But I trust my readers will excuse deficiencies in consideration of circumstances. I was born and reared in Slavery; and I remained in a Slave State twenty-seven years. Since I have been at the North, it has been necessary for me to work diligently for my own support, and the education of my children. This has not left me much leisure to make up for the loss of early opportunities to improve myself; and it has compelled me to write these pages at irregular intervals, whenever I could snatch an hour from household duties.

When I first arrived in Philadelphia, Bishop Paine advised me to publish a sketch of my life, but I told him I was altogether incompetent to such an undertaking. Though I have improved my mind somewhat since that time, I still remain of the same opinion; but I trust my motives will excuse what might otherwise seem presumptuous. I have not written my experiences in order to attract attention to myself; on the contrary, it would have been more pleasant to me to have been silent about my own history. Neither do I care to excite sympathy for my own sufferings. But I do earnestly desire to arouse the women of the North to a realizing sense of the condition of two millions of women at the South, still in bondage, suffering what I suffered, and most of them far worse. I want to add my testimony to that of abler pens to convince the people of the Free States what Slavery really is. Only by experience can any one realize how deep, and dark, and foul is that pit of abominations. May the blessing of God rest on this imperfect effort in behalf of my persecuted people!

*Linda Brent [Pseudonym of Harriet Jacobs]*

# I. CHILDHOOD

I was born a slave; but I never knew it till six years of happy childhood had passed away. My father was a carpenter, and considered so intelligent and skilful in his trade, that, when buildings out of the common line were to be erected, he was sent for from long distances, to be head workman. On condition of paying his mistress two hundred dollars a year, and supporting himself, he was allowed to work at his trade, and manage his own affairs. His strongest wish was to purchase his children; but, though he several times offered his hard earnings for that purpose, he never succeeded. In complexion my parents were a light shade of brownish yellow, and were termed mulattoes. They lived together in a comfortable home; and, though we were all slaves, I was so fondly shielded that I never dreamed I was a piece of merchandise, trusted to them for safe keeping, and liable to be demanded of them at any moment. I had one brother, William, who was two years younger than myself—a bright, affectionate child. I had also a great treasure in my maternal grandmother, who was a remarkable woman in many respects. She was the daughter of a planter in South Carolina, who, at his death, left her mother and his three children free, with money to go to St. Augustine, where they had relatives. It was during the Revolutionary War; and they were captured on their passage, carried back, and sold to different purchasers. Such was the story my grandmother used to tell me; but I do not remember all the particulars. She was a little girl when she was captured and sold to the keeper of a large hotel. I have often heard her tell how hard she fared during childhood. But as she grew older she evinced so much intelligence, and was so faithful, that her master and mistress could not help seeing it was for their interest to take care of such a valuable piece of property. She became an indispensable personage in the household, officiating in all capacities, from cook and wet nurse to seamstress. She was much praised for her cooking; and her nice crackers became so famous in the neighborhood that many people were desirous of obtaining them. In consequence of numerous requests of this kind, she asked permission of her mistress to bake crackers at night, after all the household work was done; and she obtained leave to do it, provided she would clothe herself and her children from the profits. Upon these terms, after working hard all day for her mistress, she began her midnight bakings, assisted by her two oldest children. The business proved profitable; and each year she laid by a little, which was saved for a fund to purchase her children. Her master died, and the property was divided among his heirs. The widow had her dower in the hotel which she continued to keep open. My grandmother remained in her service as a slave; but her children were divided among her master's children. As she had five, Benjamin, the youngest one, was sold, in order that each heir might have an equal portion of dollars and cents. There was so little difference in our ages that he seemed more like my brother than my uncle. He was a bright, handsome lad, nearly white; for he inherited the complexion my grandmother had derived from Anglo-Saxon ancestors. Though only ten years old, seven hundred and twenty dollars were paid for him. His sale was a terrible blow to my grandmother, but she was naturally hopeful, and she went to work with renewed energy, trusting in time to be able to purchase some of her children. She had laid up three hundred dollars, which her mistress one day begged as a loan, promising to pay her soon. The reader probably knows that no promise or writing given to a slave is legally binding; for, according to Southern laws, a slave, *being* property, can *hold* no property. When my grandmother lent her hard earnings to her mistress, she trusted solely to her honor. The honor of a slaveholder to a slave!

To this good grandmother I was indebted for many comforts. My brother Willie and I often received portions of the crackers, cakes, and preserves, she made to sell; and after we ceased to be children we were indebted to her for many more important services.

Such were the unusually fortunate circumstances of my early childhood. When I was six years old, my mother died; and then, for the first time, I learned, by the talk around me, that I was a slave. My mother's mistress was the daughter of my grandmother's mistress. She was the foster sister of my mother; they were both nourished at my grandmother's breast. In fact, my mother had been weaned at three months old, that the babe of the mistress might obtain sufficient food. They played together as children; and, when they became women, my mother was a most faithful servant to her whiter foster sister. On her death-bed her mistress promised that her children should never suffer for any thing; and during her lifetime she kept her word. They all spoke kindly of my dead mother, who had been a slave merely in name, but in nature was noble and womanly. I grieved for her, and my young mind was troubled with the thought who would now take care of me and my little brother. I was told that my home was now to be with her mistress; and I found it a happy one. No toilsome or disagreeable duties were imposed on me. My mistress was so kind to me that I was always glad to do her bidding, and proud to labor for her as much as my young years would permit. I would sit by her side for hours, sewing diligently, with a heart as free from care as that of any free-born white child. When she thought I was tired, she would send me out to run and jump; and away I bounded, to gather berries or flowers to decorate her room. Those were happy days—too happy to last. The slave child had no thought for the morrow; but there came that blight, which too surely waits on every human being born to be a chattel.

When I was nearly twelve years old, my kind mistress sickened and died. As I saw the cheek grow paler, and the eye more glassy, how earnestly I prayed in my heart that she might live! I loved her; for she had been almost like a mother to me. My prayers were not answered. She died, and they buried her in the little churchyard, where, day after day, my tears fell upon her grave.

I was sent to spend a week with my grandmother. I was now old enough to begin to think of the future; and again and again I asked myself what they would do with me. I felt sure I should never find another mistress so kind as the one who was gone. She had promised my dying mother that her children should never suffer for any thing; and when I remembered that, and recalled her many proofs of attachment to me, I could not help having some hopes that she had left me free. My friends were almost certain it would be so. They thought she would be sure to do it, on account of my mother's love and faithful service. But, alas! we all know that the memory of a faithful slave does not avail much to save her children from the auction block.

After a brief period of suspense, the will of my mistress was read, and we learned that she had bequeathed me to her sister's daughter, a child of five years old. So vanished our hopes. My mistress had taught me the precepts of God's Word: "Thou shalt love thy neighbor as thyself." "Whatsoever ye would that men should do unto you, do ye even so unto them." But I was her slave, and I suppose she did not recognize me as her neighbor. I would give much to blot out from my memory that one great wrong. As a child, I loved my mistress; and, looking back on the happy days I spent with her, I try to think with less bitterness of this act of injustice. While I was with her, she taught me to read and spell; and for this privilege, which so rarely falls to the lot of a slave, I bless her memory.

She possessed but few slaves; and at her death those were all distributed among her relatives. Five of them were my grandmother's children, and had shared the same milk that nourished her mother's children. Notwithstanding my grandmother's long and faithful service to her owners, not one of her children escaped the auction block. These God-breathing machines are no more, in the sight of their masters, than the cotton they plant, or the horses they tend.

# II. THE NEW MASTER AND MISTRESS

Dr. Flint, a physician in the neighborhood, had married the sister of my mistress, and I was now the property of their little daughter. It was not without murmuring that I prepared for my new home; and what added to my unhappiness, was the fact that my brother William was purchased by the same family. My father, by his nature, as well as by the habit of transacting business as a skillful mechanic, had more of the feelings of a freeman than is common among slaves. My brother was a spirited boy; and being brought up under such influences, he daily detested the name of master and mistress. One day, when his father and his mistress both happened to call him at the same time, he hesitated between the two; being perplexed to know which had the strongest claim upon his obedience. He finally concluded to go to his mistress. When my father reproved him for it, he said, "You both called me, and I didn't know which I ought to go to first."

"You are *my* child," replied our father, "and when I call you, you should come immediately, if you have to pass through fire and water."

Poor Willie! He was now to learn his first lesson of obedience to a master. Grandmother tried to cheer us with hopeful words, and they found an echo in the credulous hearts of youth.

When we entered our new home we encountered cold looks, cold words, and cold treatment. We were glad when the night came. On my narrow bed I moaned and wept, I felt so desolate and alone.

I had been there nearly a year, when a dear little friend of mine was buried. I heard her mother sob, as the clods fell on the coffin of her only child, and I turned away from the grave, feeling thankful that I still had something left to love. I met my grandmother, who said, "Come with me, Linda;" and from her tone I knew that something sad had happened. She led me apart from the people, and then said, "My child, your father is dead." Dead! How could I believe it? He had died so suddenly I had not even heard that he was sick. I went home with my grandmother. My heart rebelled against God, who had taken from me mother, father, mistress, and friend. The good grandmother tried to comfort me. "Who knows the ways of God?" said she. "Perhaps they have been kindly taken from the evil days to come." Years afterwards I often thought of this. She promised to be a mother to her grandchildren, so far as she might be permitted to do so; and strengthened by her love, I returned to my master's. I thought I should be allowed to go to my father's house the next morning; but I was ordered to go for flowers, that my mistress's house might be decorated for an evening party. I spent the day gathering flowers and weaving them into festoons, while the dead body of my father was lying within a mile of me. What cared my owners for that? he was merely a piece of property. Moreover, they thought he had spoiled his children, by teaching them to feel that they were human beings. This was blasphemous doctrine for a slave to teach; presumptuous in him, and dangerous to the masters.

The next day I followed his remains to a humble grave beside that of my dear mother. There were those who knew my father's worth, and respected his memory.

My home now seemed more dreary than ever. The laugh of the little slave-children sounded harsh and cruel. It was selfish to feel so about the joy of others. My brother moved about with a very grave face. I tried to comfort him, by saying, "Take courage, Willie; brighter days will come by and by."

"You don't know any thing about it, Linda," he replied. "We shall have to stay here all our days; we shall never be free."

I argued that we were growing older and stronger, and that perhaps we might, before long, be allowed to hire our own time, and then we could earn money to buy our freedom. William declared this was much easier to say than to do; moreover, he did not intend to *buy* his freedom. We held daily controversies upon this subject.

Little attention was paid to the slaves' meals in Dr. Flint's house. If they could catch a bit of food while it was going, well and good. I gave myself no trouble on that score, for on my various errands I passed my grandmother's house, where there was always something to spare for me. I was frequently threatened with punishment if I stopped there; and my grandmother, to avoid detaining me, often stood at the gate with something for my breakfast or dinner. I was indebted to *her* for all my comforts, spiritual or temporal. It was *her* labor that supplied my scanty wardrobe. I have a vivid recollection of the linsey-woolsey dress given me every winter by Mrs. Flint. How I hated it! It was one of the badges of slavery.

While my grandmother was thus helping to support me from her hard earnings, the three hundred dollars she had lent her mistress were never repaid. When her mistress died, her son-in-law, Dr. Flint, was appointed executor. When grandmother applied to him for payment, he said the estate was insolvent, and the law prohibited payment. It did not, however, prohibit him from retaining the silver candelabra, which had been purchased with that money. I presume they will be handed down in the family, from generation to generation.

My grandmother's mistress had always promised her that, at her death, she should be free; and it was said that in her will she made good the promise. But when the estate was settled, Dr. Flint told the faithful old servant that, under existing circumstances, it was necessary she should be sold.

On the appointed day, the customary advertisement was posted up, proclaiming that there would be a "public sale of negroes, horses, &c." Dr. Flint called to tell my grandmother that he was unwilling to wound her feelings by putting her up at auction, and that he would prefer to dispose of her at private sale. My grandmother saw through his hypocrisy; she understood very well that he was ashamed of the job. She was a very spirited woman, and if he was base enough to sell her, when her mistress intended she should be free, she was determined the public should know it. She had for a long time supplied many families with crackers and preserves; consequently, "Aunt Marthy," as she was called, was generally known, and every body who knew her respected her intelligence and good character. Her long and faithful service in the family was also well known, and the intention of her mistress to leave her free. When the day of sale came, she took her place among the chattels, and at the first call she sprang upon the auction-block. Many voices called out, "Shame! Shame! Who is going to sell *you*, Aunt Marthy? Don't stand there! That is no place for *you*." Without saying a word, she quietly awaited her fate. No one bid for her. At last, a feeble voice said, "Fifty dollars." It came from a maiden lady, seventy years old, the sister of my grandmother's deceased mistress. She had lived forty years under the same roof with my grandmother; she knew how faithfully she had served her owners, and how cruelly she had been defrauded of her rights; and she resolved to protect her. The auctioneer waited for a higher bid; but her wishes were respected; no one bid above her. She could neither read nor write; and when the bill of sale was made out, she signed it with a cross. But what consequence was that, when she had a big heart overflowing with human kindness? She gave the old servant her freedom.

At that time, my grandmother was just fifty years old. Laborious years had passed since then; and now my brother and I were slaves to the man who had defrauded her of her money, and tried to defraud her of her freedom. One of my mother's sisters, called Aunt Nancy, was also a slave in his family. She was a kind, good aunt to me; and supplied the place of both housekeeper and waiting maid to her mistress. She was, in fact, at the beginning and end of every thing.

Mrs. Flint, like many southern women, was totally deficient in energy. She had not strength to superintend her household affairs; but her nerves were so strong, that she could sit in her easy chair and see a woman whipped, till the blood trickled from every stroke of the lash. She was a member of the church; but partaking of the Lord's supper did not seem to put her in a Christian frame of mind. If dinner was not served at the exact time on that particular Sunday, she would station herself in the kitchen, and wait till it was dished, and then spit in all the kettles and pans that had been used for cooking. She did this to prevent the cook and her children from eking out their meagre fare with the remains of the gravy and other scrapings. The slaves could get nothing to eat except what she chose to give them. Provisions were weighed out by the pound and ounce, three times a day. I can assure you she gave them no chance to eat wheat bread from her flour barrel. She knew how many biscuits a quart of flour would make, and exactly what size they ought to be.

Dr. Flint was an epicure. The cook never sent a dinner to his table without fear and trembling; for if there happened to be a dish not to his liking, he would either order her to be whipped, or compel her to eat every mouthful of it in his presence. The poor, hungry creature might not have objected to eating it; but she did object to having her master cram it down her throat till she choked.

They had a pet dog, that was a nuisance in the house. The cook was ordered to make some Indian mush for him. He refused to eat, and when his head was held over it, the froth flowed from his mouth into the basin. He died a few minutes after. When Dr. Flint came in, he said the mush had not been well cooked, and that was the reason the animal would not eat it. He sent for the cook, and compelled her to eat it. He thought that the woman's stomach was stronger than the dog's; but her sufferings afterwards proved that he was mistaken. This poor woman endured many cruelties from her master and mistress; sometimes she was locked up, away from her nursing baby, for a whole day and night.

When I had been in the family a few weeks, one of the plantation slaves was brought to town, by order of his master. It was near night when he arrived, and Dr. Flint ordered him to be taken to the work house, and tied up to the joist, so that his feet would just escape the ground. In that situation he was to wait till the doctor had taken his tea. I shall never forget that night. Never before, in my life, had I heard hundreds of blows fall, in succession, on a human being. His piteous groans, and his "O, pray don't, massa," rang in my ear for months afterwards. There were many conjectures as to the cause of this terrible punishment. Some said master accused him of stealing corn; others said the slave had quarrelled with his wife, in presence of the overseer, and had accused his master of being the father of her child. They were both black, and the child was very fair.

I went into the work house next morning, and saw the cowhide still wet with blood, and the boards all covered with gore. The poor man lived, and continued to quarrel with his wife. A few months afterwards Dr. Flint handed them both over to a slave-trader. The guilty man put their value into his pocket, and had the satisfaction of knowing that they were out of sight and hearing. When the mother was delivered into the trader's hands, she said. "You *promised* to treat me well." To which he replied, "You have let your tongue run too far; damn you!" She had forgotten that it was a crime for a slave to tell who was the father of her child.

From others than the master persecution also comes in such cases. I once saw a young slave girl dying soon after the birth of a child nearly white. In her agony she cried out, "O Lord, come and take me!" Her mistress stood by, and mocked at her like an incarnate fiend. "You suffer, do you?" she exclaimed. "I am glad of it. You deserve it all, and more too."

The girl's mother said, "The baby is dead, thank God; and I hope my poor child will soon be in heaven, too."

"Heaven!" retorted the mistress. "There is no such place for the like of her and her bastard."

The poor mother turned away, sobbing. Her dying daughter called her, feebly, and as she bent over her, I heard her say, "Don't grieve so, mother; God knows all about it; and HE will have mercy upon me."

Her sufferings, afterwards, became so intense, that her mistress felt unable to stay; but when she left the room, the scornful smile was still on her lips. Seven children called her mother. The poor black woman had but the one child, whose eyes she saw closing in death, while she thanked God for taking her away from the greater bitterness of life.

# III. THE SLAVES' NEW YEAR'S DAY

Dr. Flint owned a fine residence in town, several farms, and about fifty slaves, besides hiring a number by the year.

Hiring-day at the south takes place on the 1st of January. On the 2d, the slaves are expected to go to their new masters. On a farm, they work until the corn and cotton are laid. They then have two holidays. Some masters give them a good dinner under the trees. This over, they work until Christmas eve. If no heavy charges are meantime brought against them, they are given four or five holidays, whichever the master or overseer may think proper. Then comes New Year's eve; and they gather together their little alls, or more properly speaking, their little nothings, and wait anxiously for the dawning of day. At the appointed hour the grounds are thronged with men, women, and children, waiting, like criminals, to hear their doom pronounced. The slave is sure to know who is the most humane, or cruel master, within forty miles of him.

It is easy to find out, on that day, who clothes and feeds his slaves well; for he is surrounded by a crowd, begging, "Please, massa, hire me this year. I will work *very* hard, massa."

If a slave is unwilling to go with his new master, he is whipped, or locked up in jail, until he consents to go, and promises not to run away during the year. Should he chance to change his mind, thinking it justifiable to violate an extorted promise, woe unto him if he is caught! The whip is used till the blood flows at his feet; and his stiffened limbs are put in chains, to be dragged in the field for days and days!

If he lives until the next year, perhaps the same man will hire him again, without even giving him an opportunity of going to the hiring-ground. After those for hire are disposed of, those for sale are called up.

O, you happy free women, contrast *your* New Year's day with that of the poor bond-woman! With you it is a pleasant season, and the light of the day is blessed. Friendly wishes meet you every where, and gifts are showered upon you. Even hearts that have been estranged from you soften at this season, and lips that have been silent echo back, "I wish you a happy New Year." Children bring their little offerings, and raise their rosy lips for a caress. They are your own, and no hand but that of death can take them from you.

But to the slave mother New Year's day comes laden with peculiar sorrows. She sits on her cold cabin floor, watching the children who may all be torn from her the next morning; and often does she wish that she and they might die before the day dawns. She may be an ignorant creature, degraded by the system that has brutalized her from childhood; but she has a mother's instincts, and is capable of feeling a mother's agonies.

On one of these sale days, I saw a mother lead seven children to the auction-block. She knew that *some* of them would be taken from her; but they took *all*. The children were sold to a slave-trader, and their mother was bought by a man in her own town. Before night her children were all far away. She begged the trader to tell her where he intended to take them; this he refused to do. How *could* he, when he knew he would sell them, one by one, wherever he could command the highest price? I met that mother in the street, and her wild, haggard face lives to-day in my mind. She wrung her hands in anguish, and exclaimed, "Gone! All gone! Why *don't* God kill me?" I had no words wherewith to comfort her. Instances of this kind are of daily, yea, of hourly occurrence.

Slaveholders have a method, peculiar to their institution, of getting rid of *old* slaves, whose lives have been worn out in their service. I knew an old woman, who for seventy years faithfully served her master. She had become almost helpless, from hard labor and disease. Her owners moved to Alabama, and the old black woman was left to be sold to any body who would give twenty dollars for her.

# IV. THE SLAVE WHO DARED TO FEEL LIKE A MAN

Two years had passed since I entered Dr. Flint's family, and those years had brought much of the knowledge that comes from experience, though they had afforded little opportunity for any other kinds of knowledge.

My grandmother had, as much as possible, been a mother to her orphan grandchildren. By perseverance and unwearied industry, she was now mistress of a snug little home, surrounded with the necessaries of life. She would have been happy could her children have shared them with her. There remained but three children and two grandchildren, all slaves. Most earnestly did she strive to make us feel that it was the will of God: that He had seen fit to place us under such circumstances; and though it seemed hard, we ought to pray for contentment.

It was a beautiful faith, coming from a mother who could not call her children her own. But I, and Benjamin, her youngest boy, condemned it. We reasoned that it was much more the will of God that we should be situated as she was. We longed for a home like hers. There we always found sweet balsam for our troubles. She was so loving, so sympathizing! She always met us with a smile, and listened with patience to all our sorrows. She spoke so hopefully, that unconsciously the clouds gave place to sunshine. There was a grand big oven there, too, that baked bread and nice things for the town, and we knew there was always a choice bit in store for us.

But, alas! Even the charms of the old oven failed to reconcile us to our hard lot. Benjamin was now a tall, handsome lad, strongly and gracefully made, and with a spirit too bold and daring for a slave. My brother William, now twelve years old, had the same aversion to the word master that he had when he was an urchin of seven years. I was his confidant. He came to me with all his troubles. I remember one instance in particular. It was on a lovely spring morning, and when I marked the sunlight dancing here and there, its beauty seemed to mock my sadness. For my master, whose restless, craving, vicious nature roved about day and night, seeking whom to devour, had just left me, with stinging, scorching words; words that scathed ear and brain like fire. O, how I despised him! I thought how glad I should be, if some day when he walked the earth, it would open and swallow him up, and disencumber the world of a plague.

When he told me that I was made for his use, made to obey his command in *every* thing; that I was nothing but a slave, whose will must and should surrender to his, never before had my puny arm felt half so strong.

So deeply was I absorbed in painful reflections afterwards, that I neither saw nor heard the entrance of any one, till the voice of William sounded close beside me. "Linda," said he, "what makes you look so sad? I love you. O, Linda, isn't this a bad world? Every body seems so cross and unhappy. I wish I had died when poor father did."

I told him that every body was *not* cross, or unhappy; that those who had pleasant homes, and kind friends, and who were not afraid to love them, were happy. But we, who were slave-children, without father or mother, could not expect to be happy. We must be good; perhaps that would bring us contentment.

"Yes," he said, "I try to be good; but what's the use? They are all the time troubling me." Then he proceeded to relate his afternoon's difficulty with young master Nicholas. It seemed that the brother of master Nicholas had pleased himself with making up stories about William. Master Nicholas said he should be flogged, and he would do it. Whereupon he went to work; but William fought bravely, and the young master, finding he was getting the better of him, undertook to tie his hands behind him. He failed in that likewise. By dint of kicking and fisting, William came out of the skirmish none the worse for a few scratches.

He continued to discourse, on his young master's *meanness*; how he whipped the *little* boys, but was a perfect coward when a tussle ensued between him and white boys of his own size. On such occasions he always took to his legs. William had other charges to make against him. One was his rubbing up pennies with quicksilver, and passing them off for quarters of a dollar on an old man who kept a fruit stall. William was often sent to buy fruit, and he earnestly inquired of me what he ought to do under such circumstances. I told him it was certainly wrong to deceive the old man, and that it was his duty to tell him of the impositions practised by his young master. I assured him the old man would not be slow to comprehend the whole, and there the matter would end. William thought it might with the old man, but not with *him*. He said he did not mind the smart of the whip, but he did not like the *idea* of being whipped.

While I advised him to be good and forgiving I was not unconscious of the beam in my own eye. It was the very knowledge of my own shortcomings that urged me to retain, if possible, some sparks of my brother's God-given nature. I had not lived fourteen years in slavery for nothing. I had felt, seen, and heard enough, to read the characters, and question the motives, of those around me. The war of my life had begun; and though one of God's most powerless creatures, I resolved never to be conquered. Alas, for me!

If there was one pure, sunny spot for me, I believed it to be in Benjamin's heart, and in another's, whom I loved with all the ardor of a girl's first love. My owner knew of it, and sought in every way to render me miserable. He did not resort to corporal punishment, but to all the petty, tyrannical ways that human ingenuity could devise.

I remember the first time I was punished. It was in the month of February. My grandmother had taken my old shoes, and replaced them with a new pair. I needed them; for several inches of snow had fallen, and it still continued to fall. When I walked through Mrs. Flint's room, their creaking grated harshly on her refined nerves. She called me to her, and asked what I had about me that made such a horrid noise. I told her it was my new shoes. "Take them off," said she; "and if you put them on again, I'll throw them into the fire."

I took them off, and my stockings also. She then sent me a long distance, on an errand. As I went through the snow, my bare feet tingled. That night I was very hoarse; and I went to bed thinking the next day would find me sick, perhaps dead. What was my grief on waking to find myself quite well!

I had imagined if I died, or was laid up for some time, that my mistress would feel a twinge of remorse that she had so hated "the little imp," as she styled me. It was my ignorance of that mistress that gave rise to such extravagant imaginings.

Dr. Flint occasionally had high prices offered for me; but he always said, "She don't belong to me. She is my daughter's property, and I have no right to sell her." Good, honest man! My young mistress was still a child, and I could look for no protection from her. I loved her, and she returned my affection. I once heard her father allude to her attachment to me, and his wife promptly replied that it proceeded from fear. This put unpleasant doubts into my mind. Did the child feign what she did not feel? or was her mother jealous of the mite of love she bestowed on me? I concluded it must be the latter. I said to myself, "Surely, little children are true."

One afternoon I sat at my sewing, feeling unusual depression of spirits. My mistress had been accusing me of an offence, of which I assured her I was perfectly innocent; but I saw, by the contemptuous curl of her lip, that she believed I was telling a lie.

I wondered for what wise purpose God was leading me through such thorny paths, and whether still darker days were in store for me. As I sat musing thus, the door opened softly, and William came in. "Well, brother," said I, "what is the matter this time?"

"O Linda, Ben and his master have had a dreadful time!" said he.

My first thought was that Benjamin was killed. "Don't be frightened, Linda," said William; "I will tell you all about it."

It appeared that Benjamin's master had sent for him, and he did not immediately obey the summons. When he did, his master was angry, and began to whip him. He resisted. Master and slave fought, and finally the master was thrown. Benjamin had cause to tremble; for he had thrown to the ground his master—one of the richest men in town. I anxiously awaited the result.

That night I stole to my grandmother's house; and Benjamin also stole thither from his master's. My grandmother had gone to spend a day or two with an old friend living in the country.

"I have come," said Benjamin, "to tell you good by. I am going away."

I inquired where.

"To the north," he replied.

I looked at him to see whether he was in earnest. I saw it all in his firm, set mouth. I implored him not to go, but he paid no heed to my words. He said he was no longer a boy, and every day made his yoke more galling. He had raised his hand against his master, and was to be publicly whipped for the offence. I reminded him of the poverty and hardships he must encounter among strangers. I told him he might be caught and brought back; and that was terrible to think of.

He grew vexed, and asked if poverty and hardships with freedom, were not preferable to our treatment in slavery. "Linda," he continued, "we are dogs here; foot-balls, cattle, every thing that's mean. No, I will not stay. Let them bring me back. We don't die but once."

He was right; but it was hard to give him up. "Go," said I, "and break your mother's heart."

I repented of my words ere they were out.

"Linda," said he, speaking as I had not heard him speak that evening, "how *could* you say that? Poor mother! be kind to her, Linda; and you, too, cousin Fanny."

Cousin Fanny was a friend who had lived some years with us.

Farewells were exchanged, and the bright, kind boy, endeared to us by so many acts of love, vanished from our sight.

It is not necessary to state how he made his escape. Suffice it to say, he was on his way to New York when a violent storm overtook the vessel. The captain said he must put into the nearest port. This alarmed Benjamin, who was aware that he would be advertised in every port near his own town. His embarrassment was noticed by the captain. To port they went. There the advertisement met the captain's eye. Benjamin so exactly answered its description, that the captain laid hold on him, and bound him in chains. The storm passed, and they proceeded to New York. Before reaching that port Benjamin managed to get off his chains and throw them overboard. He escaped from the vessel, but was pursued, captured, and carried back to his master.

When my grandmother returned home and found her youngest child had fled, great was her sorrow; but, with characteristic piety, she said, "God's will be done." Each morning, she inquired if any news had been heard from her boy. Yes, news *was* heard. The master was rejoicing over a letter, announcing the capture of his human chattel.

That day seems but as yesterday, so well do I remember it. I saw him led through the streets in chains, to jail. His face was ghastly pale, yet full of determination. He had begged one of the sailors to go to his mother's house and ask her not to meet him. He said the sight of her distress would take from him all self-control. She yearned to see him, and she went; but she screened herself in the crowd, that it might be as her child had said.

We were not allowed to visit him; but we had known the jailer for years, and he was a kind-hearted man. At midnight he opened the jail door for my grandmother and myself to enter, in disguise. When we entered the cell not a sound broke the stillness. "Benjamin, Benjamin!" whispered my grandmother. No answer. "Benjamin!" she again faltered. There was a jingle of chains. The moon had just risen, and cast an uncertain light through the bars of the window. We knelt down and took Benjamin's cold hands in ours. We did not speak. Sobs were heard, and Benjamin's lips were unsealed; for his mother was weeping on his neck. How vividly does memory bring back that sad night! Mother and son talked together. He asked her pardon for the suffering he had caused her. She said she had nothing to forgive; she could not blame his desire for freedom. He told her that when he was captured, he broke away, and was about casting himself into the river, when thoughts of *her* came over him, and he desisted. She asked if he did not also think of God. I fancied I saw his face grow fierce in the moonlight. He answered, "No, I did not think of him. When a man is hunted like a wild beast he forgets there is a God, a heaven. He forgets every thing in his struggle to get beyond the reach of the bloodhounds."

"Don't talk so, Benjamin," said she. "Put your trust in God. Be humble, my child, and your master will forgive you."

"Forgive me for *what*, mother? For not letting him treat me like a dog? No! I will never humble myself to him. I have worked for him for nothing all my life, and I am repaid with stripes and imprisonment. Here I will stay till I die, or till he sells me."

The poor mother shuddered at his words. I think he felt it; for when he next spoke, his voice was calmer. "Don't fret about me, mother. I ain't worth it," said he. "I wish I had some of your goodness. You bear every thing patiently, just as though you thought it was all right. I wish I could."

She told him she had not always been so; once, she was like him;

but when sore troubles came upon her, and she had no arm to lean upon, she learned to call on God, and he lightened her burdens. She besought him to do likewise.

We overstaid our time, and were obliged to hurry from the jail.

Benjamin had been imprisoned three weeks, when my grandmother went to intercede for him with his master. He was immovable. He said Benjamin should serve as an example to the rest of his slaves; he should be kept in jail till he was subdued, or be sold if he got but one dollar for him. However, he afterwards relented in some degree. The chains were taken off, and we were allowed to visit him.

As his food was of the coarsest kind, we carried him as often as possible a warm supper, accompanied with some little luxury for the jailer.

Three months elapsed, and there was no prospect of release or of a purchaser. One day he was heard to sing and laugh. This piece of indecorum was told to his master, and the overseer was ordered to re-chain him. He was now confined in an apartment with other prisoners, who were covered with filthy rags. Benjamin was chained near them, and was soon covered with vermin. He worked at his chains till he succeeded in getting out of them. He passed them through the bars of the window, with a request that they should be taken to his master, and he should be informed that he was covered with vermin.

This audacity was punished with heavier chains, and prohibition of our visits.

My grandmother continued to send him fresh changes of clothes. The old ones were burned up. The last night we saw him in jail his mother still begged him to send for his master, and beg his pardon. Neither persuasion nor argument could turn him from his purpose. He calmly answered, "I am waiting his time."

Those chains were mournful to hear.

Another three months passed, and Benjamin left his prison walls. We that loved him waited to bid him a long and last farewell. A slave trader had bought him. You remember, I told you what price he brought when ten years of age. Now he was more than twenty years old, and sold for three hundred dollars. The master had been blind to his own interest. Long confinement had made his face too pale, his form too thin; moreover, the trader had heard something of his character, and it did not strike him as suitable for a slave. He said he would give any price if the handsome lad was a girl. We thanked God that he was not.

Could you have seen that mother clinging to her child, when they fastened the irons upon his wrists; could you have heard her heart-rending groans, and seen her bloodshot eyes wander wildly from face to face, vainly pleading for mercy; could you have witnessed that scene as I saw it, you would exclaim, *Slavery is damnable*!

Benjamin, her youngest, her pet, was forever gone! She could not realize it. She had had an interview with the trader for the purpose of ascertaining if Benjamin could be purchased. She was told it was impossible, as he had given bonds not to sell him till he was out of the state. He promised that he would not sell him till he reached New Orleans.

With a strong arm and unvaried trust, my grandmother began her work of love. Benjamin must be free. If she succeeded, she knew they would still be separated; but the sacrifice was not too great. Day and night she labored. The trader's price would treble that he gave; but she was not discouraged.

She employed a lawyer to write to a gentleman, whom she knew, in New Orleans. She begged him to interest himself for Benjamin, and he willingly favored her request. When he saw Benjamin, and stated his business, he thanked him; but said he preferred to wait a while before making the trader an offer. He knew he had tried to obtain a high price for him, and had invariably failed. This encouraged him to make another effort for freedom. So one morning, long before day, Benjamin was missing. He was riding over the blue billows, bound for Baltimore.

For once his white face did him a kindly service. They had no suspicion that it belonged to a slave; otherwise, the law would have been followed out to the letter, and the *thing* rendered back to slavery. The brightest skies are often overshadowed by the darkest clouds. Benjamin was taken sick, and compelled to remain in Baltimore three weeks. His strength was slow in returning; and his desire to continue his journey seemed to retard his recovery. How could he get strength without air and exercise? He resolved to venture on a short walk. A by-street was selected, where he thought himself secure of not being met by any one that knew him; but a voice called out, "Halloo, Ben, my boy! what are you doing *here*!"

His first impulse was to run; but his legs trembled so that he could not stir. He turned to confront his antagonist, and behold, there stood his old master's next door neighbor! He thought it was all over with him now; but it proved otherwise. That man was a miracle. He possessed a goodly number of slaves, and yet was not quite deaf to that mystic clock, whose ticking is rarely heard in the slaveholder's breast.

"Ben, you are sick," said he. "Why, you look like a ghost. I guess I gave you something of a start. Never mind, Ben, I am not going to touch you. You had a pretty tough time of it, and you may go on your way rejoicing for all me. But I would advise you to get out of this place plaguy quick, for there are several gentlemen here from our town." He described the nearest and safest route to New York, and added, "I shall be glad to tell your mother I have seen you. Good by, Ben."

Benjamin turned away, filled with gratitude, and surprised that the town he hated contained such a gem—a gem worthy of a purer setting.

This gentleman was a Northerner by birth, and had married a southern lady. On his return, he told my grandmother that he had seen her son, and of the service he had rendered him.

Benjamin reached New York safely, and concluded to stop there until he had gained strength enough to proceed further. It happened that my grandmother's only remaining son had sailed for the same city on business for his mistress. Through God's providence, the brothers met. You may be sure it was a happy meeting. "O Phil," exclaimed Benjamin, "I am here at last." Then he told him how near he came to dying, almost in sight of free land, and how he prayed that he might live to get one breath of free air. He said life was worth something now, and it would be hard to die. In the old jail he had not valued it; once, he was tempted to destroy it; but something, he did not know what, had prevented him; perhaps it was fear. He had heard those who profess to be religious declare there was no heaven for self-murderers; and as his life had been pretty hot here, he did not desire a continuation of the same in another world. "If I die now," he exclaimed, "thank God, I shall die a freeman!"

He begged my uncle Phillip not to return south; but stay and work with him, till they earned enough to buy those at home. His brother told him it would kill their mother if he deserted her in her trouble. She had pledged her house, and with difficulty had raised money to buy him. Would he be bought?

"No, never!" he replied. "Do you suppose, Phil, when I have got so far out of their clutches, I will give them one red cent? No! And do you suppose I would turn mother out of her home in her old age? That I would let her pay all those hard-earned dollars for me, and never to see me? For you know she will stay south as long as her other children are slaves. What a good mother! Tell her to buy *you*, Phil. You have been a comfort to her, and I have been a trouble. And Linda, poor Linda; what'll become of her? Phil, you don't know what a life they lead her. She has told me something about it, and I wish old Flint was dead, or a better man. When I was in jail, he asked her if she didn't want *him* to ask my master to forgive me, and take me home again. She told him, No; that I didn't want to go back. He got mad, and said we were all alike. I never despised my own master half as much as I do that man. There is many a worse slaveholder than my master; but for all that I would not be his slave."

While Benjamin was sick, he had parted with nearly all his clothes to pay necessary expenses. But he did not part with a little pin I fastened in his bosom when we parted. It was the most valuable thing I owned, and I thought none more worthy to wear it. He had it still.

His brother furnished him with clothes, and gave him what money he had.

They parted with moistened eyes; and as Benjamin turned away, he said, "Phil, I part with all my kindred." And so it proved. We never heard from him again.

Uncle Phillip came home; and the first words he uttered when he entered the house were, "Mother, Ben is free! I have seen him in New York." She stood looking at him with a bewildered air. "Mother, don't you believe it?" he said, laying his hand softly upon her shoulder. She raised her hands, and exclaimed, "God be praised! Let us thank him." She dropped on her knees, and poured forth her heart in prayer. Then Phillip must sit down and repeat to her every word Benjamin had said. He told her all; only he forbore to mention how sick and pale her darling looked. Why should he distress her when she could do him no good?

The brave old woman still toiled on, hoping to rescue some of her other children. After a while she succeeded in buying Phillip. She paid eight hundred dollars, and came home with the precious document that secured his freedom. The happy mother and son sat together by the old hearthstone that night, telling how proud they were of each other, and how they would prove to the world that they could take care of themselves, as they had long taken care of others. We all concluded by saying, "He that is *willing* to be a slave, let him be a slave."

# V. THE TRIALS OF GIRLHOOD

During the first years of my service in Dr. Flint's family, I was accustomed to share some indulgences with the children of my mistress. Though this seemed to me no more than right, I was grateful for it, and tried to merit the kindness by the faithful discharge of my duties. But I now entered on my fifteenth year—a sad epoch in the life of a slave girl. My master began to whisper foul words in my ear. Young as I was, I could not remain ignorant of their import. I tried to treat them with indifference or contempt. The master's age, my extreme youth, and the fear that his conduct would be reported to my grandmother, made him bear this treatment for many months. He was a crafty man, and resorted to many means to accomplish his purposes. Sometimes he had stormy, terrific ways, that made his victims tremble; sometimes he assumed a gentleness that he thought must surely subdue. Of the two, I preferred his stormy moods, although they left me trembling. He tried his utmost to corrupt the pure principles my grandmother had instilled. He peopled my young mind with unclean images, such as only a vile monster could think of. I turned from him with disgust and hatred. But he was my master. I was compelled to live under the same roof with him—where I saw a man forty years my senior daily violating the most sacred commandments of nature. He told me I was his property; that I must be subject to his will in all things. My soul revolted against the mean tyranny. But where could I turn for protection? No matter whether the slave girl be as black as ebony or as fair as her mistress. In either case, there is no shadow of law to protect her from insult, from violence, or even from death; all these are inflicted by fiends who bear the shape of men. The mistress, who ought to protect the helpless victim, has no other feelings towards her but those of jealousy and rage. The degradation, the wrongs, the vices, that grow out of slavery, are more than I can describe. They are greater than you would willingly believe. Surely, if you credited one half the truths that are told you concerning the helpless millions suffering in this cruel bondage, you at the north would not help to tighten the yoke. You surely would refuse to do for the master, on your own soil, the mean and cruel work which trained bloodhounds and the lowest class of whites do for him at the south.

Every where the years bring to all enough of sin and sorrow; but in slavery the very dawn of life is darkened by these shadows. Even the little child, who is accustomed to wait on her mistress and her children, will learn, before she is twelve years old, why it is that her mistress hates such and such a one among the slaves. Perhaps the child's own mother is among those hated ones. She listens to violent outbreaks of jealous passion, and cannot help understanding what is the cause. She will become prematurely knowing in evil things. Soon she will learn to tremble when she hears her master's footfall. She will be compelled to realize that she is no longer a child. If God has bestowed beauty upon her, it will prove her greatest curse. That which commands admiration in the white woman only hastens the degradation of the female slave. I know that some are too much brutalized by slavery to feel the humiliation of their position; but many slaves feel it most acutely, and shrink from the memory of it. I cannot tell how much I suffered in the presence of these wrongs, nor how I am still pained by the retrospect. My master met me at every turn, reminding me that I belonged to him, and swearing by heaven and earth that he would compel me to submit to him. If I went out for a breath of fresh air, after a day of unwearied toil, his footsteps dogged me. If I knelt by my mother's grave, his dark shadow fell on me even there. The light heart which nature had given me became heavy with sad forebodings. The other slaves in my master's house noticed the change. Many of them pitied me; but none dared to ask the cause. They had no need to inquire. They knew too well the guilty practices under that roof; and they were aware that to speak of them was an offence that never went unpunished.

I longed for some one to confide in. I would have given the world to have laid my head on my grandmother's faithful bosom, and told her all my troubles. But Dr. Flint swore he would kill me, if I was not as silent as the grave. Then, although my grandmother was all in all to me, I feared her as well as loved her. I had been accustomed to look up to her with a respect bordering upon awe. I was very young, and felt shamefaced about telling her such impure things, especially as I knew her to be very strict on such subjects. Moreover, she was a woman of a high spirit. She was usually very quiet in her demeanor; but if her indignation was once roused, it was not very easily quelled. I had been told that she once chased a white gentleman with a loaded pistol, because he insulted one of her daughters. I dreaded the consequences of a violent outbreak; and both pride and fear kept me silent. But though I did not confide in my grandmother, and even evaded her vigilant watchfulness and inquiry, her presence in the neighborhood was some protection to me. Though she had been a slave, Dr. Flint was afraid of her. He dreaded her scorching rebukes. Moreover, she was known and patronized by many people; and he did not wish to have his villany made public. It was lucky for me that I did not live on a distant plantation, but in a town not so large that the inhabitants were ignorant of each other's affairs. Bad as are the laws and customs in a slaveholding community, the doctor, as a professional man, deemed it prudent to keep up some outward show of decency.

O, what days and nights of fear and sorrow that man caused me! Reader, it is not to awaken sympathy for myself that I am telling you truthfully what I suffered in slavery. I do it to kindle a flame of compassion in your hearts for my sisters who are still in bondage, suffering as I once suffered.

I once saw two beautiful children playing together. One was a fair white child; the other was her slave, and also her sister. When I saw them embracing each other, and heard their joyous laughter, I turned sadly away from the lovely sight. I foresaw the inevitable blight that would fall on the little slave's heart. I knew how soon her laughter would be changed to sighs. The fair child grew up to be a still fairer woman. From childhood to womanhood her pathway was blooming with flowers, and overarched by a sunny sky. Scarcely one day of her life had been clouded when the sun rose on her happy bridal morning.

How had those years dealt with her slave sister, the little playmate of her childhood? She, also, was very beautiful; but the flowers and sunshine of love were not for her. She drank the cup of sin, and shame, and misery, whereof her persecuted race are compelled to drink.

In view of these things, why are ye silent, ye free men and women of the north? Why do your tongues falter in maintenance of the right? Would that I had more ability! But my heart is so full, and my pen is so weak! There are noble men and women who plead for us, striving to help those who cannot help themselves. God bless them! God give them strength and courage to go on! God bless those, every where, who are laboring to advance the cause of humanity!

# VI. THE JEALOUS MISTRESS

I would ten thousand times rather that my children should be the half-starved paupers of Ireland than to be the most pampered among the slaves of America. I would rather drudge out my life on a cotton plantation, till the grave opened to give me rest, than to live with an unprincipled master and a jealous mistress. The felon's home in a penitentiary is preferable. He may repent, and turn from the error of his ways, and so find peace; but it is not so with a favorite slave. She is not allowed to have any pride of character. It is deemed a crime in her to wish to be virtuous.

Mrs. Flint possessed the key to her husband's character before I was born. She might have used this knowledge to counsel and to screen the young and the innocent among her slaves; but for them she had no sympathy. They were the objects of her constant suspicion and malevolence. She watched her husband with unceasing vigilance; but he was well practised in means to evade it. What he could not find opportunity to say in words he manifested in signs. He invented more than were ever thought of in a deaf and dumb asylum. I let them pass, as if I did not understand what he meant; and many were the curses and threats bestowed on me for my stupidity. One day he caught me teaching myself to write. He frowned, as if he was not well pleased; but I suppose he came to the conclusion that such an accomplishment might help to advance his favorite scheme. Before long, notes were often slipped into my hand. I would return them, saying, "I can't read them, sir." "Can't you?" he replied; "then I must read them to you." He always finished the reading by asking, "Do you understand?" Sometimes he would complain of the heat of the tea room, and order his supper to be placed on a small table in the piazza. He would seat himself there with a well-satisfied smile, and tell me to stand by and brush away the flies. He would eat very slowly, pausing between the mouthfuls. These intervals were employed in describing the happiness I was so foolishly throwing away, and in threatening me with the penalty that finally awaited my stubborn disobedience. He boasted much of the forbearance he had exercised towards me, and reminded me that there was a limit to his patience. When I succeeded in avoiding opportunities for him to talk to me at home, I was ordered to come to his office, to do some errand. When there, I was obliged to stand and listen to such language as he saw fit to address to me. Sometimes I so openly expressed my contempt for him that he would become violently enraged, and I wondered why he did not strike me. Circumstanced as he was, he probably thought it was better policy to be forebearing. But the state of things grew worse and worse daily. In desperation I told him that I must and would apply to my grandmother for protection. He threatened me with death, and worse than death, if I made any complaint to her. Strange to say, I did not despair. I was naturally of a buoyant disposition, and always I had a hope of somehow getting out of his clutches. Like many a poor, simple slave before me, I trusted that some threads of joy would yet be woven into my dark destiny.

I had entered my sixteenth year, and every day it became more apparent that my presence was intolerable to Mrs. Flint. Angry words frequently passed between her and her husband. He had never punished me himself, and he would not allow any body else to punish me. In that respect, she was never satisfied; but, in her angry moods, no terms were too vile for her to bestow upon me. Yet I, whom she detested so bitterly, had far more pity for her than he had, whose duty it was to make her life happy. I never wronged her, or wished to wrong her, and one word of kindness from her would have brought me to her feet.

After repeated quarrels between the doctor and his wife, he announced his intention to take his youngest daughter, then four years old, to sleep in his apartment. It was necessary that a servant should sleep in the same room, to be on hand if the child stirred. I was selected for that office, and informed for what purpose that arrangement had been made. By managing to keep within sight of people, as much as possible, during the day time, I had hitherto succeeded in eluding my master, though a razor was often held to my throat to force me to change this line of policy. At night I slept by the side of my great aunt, where I felt safe. He was too prudent to come into her room. She was an old woman, and had been in the family many years. Moreover, as a married man, and a professional man, he deemed it necessary to save appearances in some degree. But he resolved to remove the obstacle in the way of his scheme; and he thought he had planned it so that he should evade suspicion. He was well aware how much I prized my refuge by the side of my old aunt, and he determined to dispossess me of it. The first night the doctor had the little child in his room alone. The next morning, I was ordered to take my station as nurse the following night. A kind Providence interposed in my favor. During the day Mrs. Flint heard of this new arrangement, and a storm followed. I rejoiced to hear it rage.

After a while my mistress sent for me to come to her room. Her first question was, "Did you know you were to sleep in the doctor's room?"

"Yes, ma'am."

"Who told you?"

"My master."

"Will you answer truly all the questions I ask?"

"Yes, ma'am."

"Tell me, then, as you hope to be forgiven, are you innocent of what I have accused you?"

"I am."

She handed me a Bible, and said, "Lay your hand on your heart, kiss this holy book, and swear before God that you tell me the truth."

I took the oath she required, and I did it with a clear conscience.

"You have taken God's holy word to testify your innocence," said she. "If you have deceived me, beware! Now take this stool, sit down, look me directly in the face, and tell me all that has passed between your master and you."

I did as she ordered. As I went on with my account her color changed frequently, she wept, and sometimes groaned. She spoke in tones so sad, that I was touched by her grief. The tears came to my eyes; but I was soon convinced that her emotions arose from anger and wounded pride. She felt that her marriage vows were desecrated, her dignity insulted; but she had no compassion for the poor victim of her husband's perfidy. She pitied herself as a martyr; but she was incapable of feeling for the condition of shame and misery in which her unfortunate, helpless slave was placed.

Yet perhaps she had some touch of feeling for me; for when the conference was ended, she spoke kindly, and promised to protect me.

I should have been much comforted by this assurance if I could have had confidence in it; but my experiences in slavery had filled me with distrust. She was not a very refined woman, and had not much control over her passions. I was an object of her jealousy, and, consequently, of her hatred; and I knew I could not expect kindness or confidence from her under the circumstances in which I was placed. I could not blame her. Slaveholders' wives feel as other women would under similar circumstances. The fire of her temper kindled from small sparks, and now the flame became so intense that the doctor was obliged to give up his intended arrangement.

I knew I had ignited the torch, and I expected to suffer for it afterwards; but I felt too thankful to my mistress for the timely aid she rendered me to care much about that. She now took me to sleep in a room adjoining her own. There I was an object of her especial care, though not to her especial comfort, for she spent many a sleepless night to watch over me. Sometimes I woke up, and found her bending over me. At other times she whispered in my ear, as though it was her husband who was speaking to me, and listened to hear what I would answer. If she startled me, on such occasions, she would glide stealthily away; and the next morning she would tell me I had been talking in my sleep, and ask who I was talking to. At last, I began to be fearful for my life. It had been often threatened; and you can imagine, better than I can describe, what an unpleasant sensation it must produce to wake up in the dead of night and find a jealous woman bending over you. Terrible as this experience was, I had fears that it would give place to one more terrible.

My mistress grew weary of her vigils; they did not prove satisfactory. She changed her tactics. She now tried the trick of accusing my master of crime, in my presence, and gave my name as the author of the accusation. To my utter astonishment, he replied, "I don't believe it; but if she did acknowledge it, you tortured her into exposing me." Tortured into exposing him! Truly, Satan had no difficulty in distinguishing the color of his soul! I understood his object in making this false representation. It was to show me that I gained nothing by seeking the protection of my mistress; that the power was still all in his own hands. I pitied Mrs. Flint. She was a second wife, many years the junior of her husband; and the hoary-headed miscreant was enough to try the patience of a wiser and better woman. She was completely foiled, and knew not how to proceed. She would gladly have had me flogged for my supposed false oath; but, as I have already stated, the doctor never allowed any one to whip me. The old sinner was politic. The application of the lash might have led to remarks that would have exposed him in the eyes of his children and grandchildren. How often did I rejoice that I lived in a town where all the inhabitants knew each other! If I had been on a remote plantation, or lost among the multitude of a crowded city, I should not be a living woman at this day.

The secrets of slavery are concealed like those of the Inquisition. My master was, to my knowledge, the father of eleven slaves. But did the mothers dare to tell who was the father of their children? Did the other slaves dare to allude to it, except in whispers among themselves? No, indeed! They knew too well the terrible consequences.

My grandmother could not avoid seeing things which excited her suspicions. She was uneasy about me, and tried various ways to buy me; but the never-changing answer was always repeated: "Linda does not belong to *me*. She is my daughter's property, and I have no legal right to sell her." The conscientious man! He was too scrupulous to *sell* me; but he had no scruples whatever about committing a much greater wrong against the helpless young girl placed under his guardianship, as his daughter's property. Sometimes my persecutor would ask me whether I would like to be sold. I told him I would rather be sold to any body than to lead such a life as I did. On such occasions he would assume the air of a very injured individual, and reproach me for my ingratitude. "Did I not take you into the house, and make you the companion of my own children?" he would say. "Have *I* ever treated you like a negro? I have never allowed you to be punished, not even to please your mistress. And this is the recompense I get, you ungrateful girl!" I answered that he had reasons of his own for screening me from punishment, and that the course he pursued made my mistress hate me and persecute me. If I wept, he would say, "Poor child! Don't cry! don't cry! I will make peace for you with your mistress. Only let me arrange matters in my own way. Poor, foolish girl! you don't know what is for your own good. I would cherish you. I would make a lady of you. Now go, and think of all I have promised you."

I did think of it.

Reader, I draw no imaginary pictures of southern homes. I am telling you the plain truth. Yet when victims make their escape from the wild beast of Slavery, northerners consent to act the part of bloodhounds, and hunt the poor fugitive back into his den, "full of dead men's bones, and all uncleanness." Nay, more, they are not only willing, but proud, to give their daughters in marriage to slaveholders. The poor girls have romantic notions of a sunny clime, and of the flowering vines that all the year round shade a happy home. To what disappointments are they destined! The young wife soon learns that the husband in whose hands she has placed her happiness pays no regard to his marriage vows. Children of every shade of complexion play with her own fair babies, and too well she knows that they are born unto him of his own household. Jealousy and hatred enter the flowery home, and it is ravaged of its loveliness.

Southern women often marry a man knowing that he is the father of many little slaves. They do not trouble themselves about it. They regard such children as property, as marketable as the pigs on the plantation; and it is seldom that they do not make them aware of this by passing them into the slave-trader's hands as soon as possible, and thus getting them out of their sight. I am glad to say there are some honorable exceptions.

I have myself known two southern wives who exhorted their husbands to free those slaves towards whom they stood in a "parental relation;" and their request was granted. These husbands blushed before the superior nobleness of their wives' natures. Though they had only counselled them to do that which it was their duty to do, it commanded their respect, and rendered their conduct more exemplary. Concealment was at an end, and confidence took the place of distrust.

Though this bad institution deadens the moral sense, even in white women, to a fearful extent, it is not altogether extinct. I have heard southern ladies say of Mr. Such a one, "He not only thinks it no disgrace to be the father of those little niggers, but he is not ashamed to call himself their master. I declare, such things ought not to be tolerated in any decent society!"

# VII. THE LOVER

Why does the slave ever love? Why allow the tendrils of the heart to twine around objects which may at any moment be wrenched away by the hand of violence? When separations come by the hand of death, the pious soul can bow in resignation, and say, "Not my will, but thine be done, O Lord!" But when the ruthless hand of man strikes the blow, regardless of the misery he causes, it is hard to be submissive. I did not reason thus when I was a young girl. Youth will be youth. I loved and I indulged the hope that the dark clouds around me would turn out a bright lining. I forgot that in the land of my birth the shadows are too dense for light to penetrate. A land

> Where laughter is not mirth; nor thought the mind;
> Nor words a language; nor e'en men mankind.
> Where cries reply to curses, shrieks to blows,
> And each is tortured in his separate hell.

There was in the neighborhood a young colored carpenter; a free born man. We had been well acquainted in childhood, and frequently met together afterwards. We became mutually attached, and he proposed to marry me. I loved him with all the ardor of a young girl's first love. But when I reflected that I was a slave, and that the laws gave no sanction to the marriage of such, my heart sank within me. My lover wanted to buy me; but I knew that Dr. Flint was too willful and arbitrary a man to consent to that arrangement. From him, I was sure of experiencing all sort of opposition, and I had nothing to hope from my mistress. She would have been delighted to have got rid of me, but not in that way. It would have relieved her mind of a burden if she could have seen me sold to some distant state, but if I was married near home I should be just as much in her husband's power as I had previously been,—for the husband of a slave has no power to protect her. Moreover, my mistress, like many others, seemed to think that slaves had no right to any family ties of their own; that they were created merely to wait upon the family of the mistress. I once heard her abuse a young slave girl, who told her that a colored man wanted to make her his wife. "I will have you peeled and pickled, my lady," said she, "if I ever hear you mention that subject again. Do you suppose that I will have you tending *my* children with the children of that nigger?" The girl to whom she said this had a mulatto child, of course not acknowledged by its father. The poor black man who loved her would have been proud to acknowledge his helpless offspring.

Many and anxious were the thoughts I revolved in my mind. I was at a loss what to do. Above all things, I was desirous to spare my lover the insults that had cut so deeply into my own soul. I talked with my grandmother about it, and partly told her my fears. I did not dare to tell her the worst. She had long suspected all was not right, and if I confirmed her suspicions I knew a storm would rise that would prove the overthrow of all my hopes.

This love-dream had been my support through many trials; and I could not bear to run the risk of having it suddenly dissipated. There was a lady in the neighborhood, a particular friend of Dr. Flint's, who often visited the house. I had a great respect for her, and she had always manifested a friendly interest in me. Grandmother thought she would have great influence with the doctor. I went to this lady, and told her my story. I told her I was aware that my lover's being a free-born man would prove a great objection; but he wanted to buy me; and if Dr. Flint would consent to that arrangement, I felt sure he would be willing to pay any reasonable price. She knew that Mrs. Flint disliked me; therefore, I ventured to suggest that perhaps my mistress would approve of my being sold, as that would rid her of me. The lady listened with kindly sympathy, and promised to do her utmost to promote my wishes. She had an interview with the doctor, and I believe she pleaded my cause earnestly; but it was all to no purpose.

How I dreaded my master now! Every minute I expected to be summoned to his presence; but the day passed, and I heard nothing from him. The next morning, a message was brought to me: "Master wants you in his study." I found the door ajar, and I stood a moment gazing at the hateful man who claimed a right to rule me, body and soul. I entered, and tried to appear calm. I did not want him to know how my heart was bleeding. He looked fixedly at me, with an expression which seemed to say, "I have half a mind to kill you on the spot." At last he broke the silence, and that was a relief to both of us.

"So you want to be married, do you?" said he, "and to a free nigger."

"Yes, sir."

"Well, I'll soon convince you whether I am your master, or the nigger fellow you honor so highly. If you *must* have a husband, you may take up with one of my slaves."

What a situation I should be in, as the wife of one of *his* slaves, even if my heart had been interested!

I replied, "Don't you suppose, sir, that a slave can have some preference about marrying? Do you suppose that all men are alike to her?"

"Do you love this nigger?" said he, abruptly.

"Yes, sir."

"How dare you tell me so!" he exclaimed, in great wrath. After a slight pause, he added, "I supposed you thought more of yourself; that you felt above the insults of such puppies."

I replied, "If he is a puppy, I am a puppy, for we are both of the negro race. It is right and honorable for us to love each other. The man you call a puppy never insulted me, sir; and he would not love me if he did not believe me to be a virtuous woman."

He sprang upon me like a tiger, and gave me a stunning blow. It was the first time he had ever struck me; and fear did not enable me to control my anger. When I had recovered a little from the effects, I exclaimed, "You have struck me for answering you honestly. How I despise you!"

There was silence for some minutes. Perhaps he was deciding what should be my punishment; or, perhaps, he wanted to give me time to reflect on what I had said, and to whom I had said it. Finally, he asked, "Do you know what you have said?"

"Yes, sir; but your treatment drove me to it."

"Do you know that I have a right to do as I like with you,—that I can kill you, if I please?"

"You have tried to kill me, and I wish you had; but you have no right to do as you like with me."

"Silence!" he exclaimed, in a thundering voice. "By heavens, girl, you forget yourself too far! Are you mad? If you are, I will soon bring you to your senses. Do you think any other master would bear what I have borne from you this morning? Many masters would have killed you on the spot. How would you like to be sent to jail for your insolence?"

"I know I have been disrespectful, sir," I replied; "but you drove me to it; I couldn't help it. As for the jail, there would be more peace for me there than there is here."

"You deserve to go there," said he, "and to be under such treatment, that you would forget the meaning of the word *peace*. It would do you good. It would take some of your high notions out of you. But I am not ready to send you there yet, notwithstanding your ingratitude for all my kindness and forbearance. You have been the plague of my life. I have wanted to make you happy, and I have been repaid with the basest ingratitude; but though you have proved yourself incapable of appreciating my kindness, I will be lenient towards you, Linda. I will give you one more chance to redeem your character. If you behave yourself and do as I require, I will forgive you and treat you as I always have done; but if you disobey me, I will punish you as I would the meanest slave on my plantation. Never let me hear that fellow's name mentioned again. If I ever know of your speaking to him, I will cowhide you both; and if I catch him lurking about my premises, I will shoot him as soon as I would a dog. Do you hear what I say? I'll teach you a lesson about marriage and free niggers! Now go, and let this be the last time I have occasion to speak to you on this subject."

Reader, did you ever hate? I hope not. I never did but once; and I trust I never shall again. Somebody has called it "the atmosphere of hell;" and I believe it is so.

For a fortnight the doctor did not speak to me. He thought to mortify me; to make me feel that I had disgraced myself by receiving the honorable addresses of a respectable colored man, in preference to the base proposals of a white man. But though his lips disdained to address me, his eyes were very loquacious. No animal ever watched its prey more narrowly than he watched me. He knew that I could write, though he had failed to make me read his letters; and he was now troubled lest I should exchange letters with another man. After a while he became weary of silence; and I was sorry for it. One morning, as he passed through the hall, to leave the house, he contrived to thrust a note into my hand. I thought I had better read it, and spare myself the vexation of having him read it to me. It expressed regret for the blow he had given me, and reminded me that I myself was wholly to blame for it. He hoped I had become convinced of the injury I was doing myself by incurring his displeasure. He wrote that he had made up his mind to go to Louisiana; that he should take several slaves with him, and intended I should be one of the number. My mistress would remain where she was; therefore I should have nothing to fear from that quarter. If I merited kindness from him, he assured me that it would be lavishly bestowed. He begged me to think over the matter, and answer the following day.

The next morning I was called to carry a pair of scissors to his room. I laid them on the table, with the letter beside them. He thought it was my answer, and did not call me back. I went as usual to attend my young mistress to and from school. He met me in the street, and ordered me to stop at his office on my way back. When I entered, he showed me his letter, and asked me why I had not answered it. I replied, "I am your daughter's property, and it is in your power to send me, or take me, wherever you please." He said he was very glad to find me so willing to go, and that we should start early in the autumn. He had a large practice in the town, and I rather thought he had made up the story merely to frighten me. However that might be, I was determined that I would never go to Louisiana with him.

Summer passed away, and early in the autumn Dr. Flint's eldest son was sent to Louisiana to examine the country, with a view to emigrating. That news did not disturb me. I knew very well that I should not be sent with *him*. That I had not been taken to the plantation before this time, was owing to the fact that his son was there. He was jealous of his son; and jealousy of the overseer had kept him from punishing me by sending me into the fields to work. Is it strange, that I was not proud of these protectors? As for the overseer, he was a man for whom I had less respect than I had for a bloodhound.

Young Mr. Flint did not bring back a favorable report of Louisiana, and I heard no more of that scheme. Soon after this, my lover met me at the corner of the street, and I stopped to speak to him. Looking up, I saw my master watching us from his window. I hurried home, trembling with fear. I was sent for, immediately, to go to his room. He met me with a blow. "When is mistress to be married?" said he, in a sneering tone. A shower of oaths and imprecations followed. How thankful I was that my lover was a free man! that my tyrant had no power to flog him for speaking to me in the street!

Again and again I revolved in my mind how all this would end. There was no hope that the doctor would consent to sell me on any terms. He had an iron will, and was determined to keep me, and to conquer me. My lover was an intelligent and religious man. Even if he could have obtained permission to marry me while I was a slave, the marriage would give him no power to protect me from my master. It would have made him miserable to witness the insults I should have been subjected to. And then, if we had children, I knew they must "follow the condition of the mother." What a terrible blight that would be on the heart of a free, intelligent father! For *his* sake, I felt that I ought not to link his fate with my own unhappy destiny. He was going to Savannah to see about a little property left him by an uncle; and hard as it was to bring my feelings to it, I earnestly entreated him not to come back. I advised him to go to the Free States, where his tongue would not be tied, and where his intelligence would be of more avail to him. He left me, still hoping the day would come when I could be bought. With me the lamp of hope had gone out. The dream of my girlhood was over. I felt lonely and desolate.

Still I was not stripped of all. I still had my good grandmother, and my affectionate brother. When he put his arms round my neck, and looked into my eyes, as if to read there the troubles I dared not tell, I felt that I still had something to love. But even that pleasant emotion was chilled by the reflection that he might be torn from me at any moment, by some sudden freak of my master. If he had known how we loved each other, I think he would have exulted in separating us. We often planned together how we could get to the north. But, as William remarked, such things are easier said than done. My movements were very closely watched, and we had no means of getting any money to defray our expenses. As for grandmother, she was strongly opposed to her children's undertaking any such project. She had not forgotten poor Benjamin's sufferings, and she was afraid that if another child tried to escape, he would have a similar or a worse fate. To me, nothing seemed more dreadful than my present life. I said to myself, "William *must* be free. He shall go to the north, and I will follow him." Many a slave sister has formed the same plans.

# VIII. WHAT SLAVES ARE TAUGHT TO THINK OF THE NORTH

Slaveholders pride themselves upon being honorable men; but if you were to hear the enormous lies they tell their slaves, you would have small respect for their veracity. I have spoken plain English. Pardon me. I cannot use a milder term. When they visit the north, and return home, they tell their slaves of the runaways they have seen, and describe them to be in the most deplorable condition. A slaveholder once told me that he had seen a runaway friend of mine in New York, and that she besought him to take her back to her master, for she was literally dying of starvation; that many days she had only one cold potato to eat, and at other times could get nothing at all. He said he refused to take her, because he knew her master would not thank him for bringing such a miserable wretch to his house. He ended by saying to me, "This is the punishment she brought on herself for running away from a kind master."

This whole story was false. I afterwards staid with that friend in New York, and found her in comfortable circumstances. She had never thought of such a thing as wishing to go back to slavery. Many of the slaves believe such stories, and think it is not worth while to exchange slavery for such a hard kind of freedom. It is difficult to persuade such that freedom could make them useful men, and enable them to protect their wives and children. If those heathen in our Christian land had as much teaching as some Hindoos, they would think otherwise. They would know that liberty is more valuable than life. They would begin to understand their own capabilities, and exert themselves to become men and women.

But while the Free States sustain a law which hurls fugitives back into slavery, how can the slaves resolve to become men? There are some who strive to protect wives and daughters from the insults of their masters; but those who have such sentiments have had advantages above the general mass of slaves. They have been partially civilized and Christianized by favorable circumstances. Some are bold enough to *utter* such sentiments to their masters. O, that there were more of them!

Some poor creatures have been so brutalized by the lash that they will sneak out of the way to give their masters free access to their wives and daughters. Do you think this proves the black man to belong to an inferior order of beings? What would *you* be, if you had been born and brought up a slave, with generations of slaves for ancestors? I admit that the black man *is* inferior. But what is it that makes him so? It is the ignorance in which white men compel him to live; it is the torturing whip that lashes manhood out of him; it is the fierce bloodhounds of the South, and the scarcely less cruel human bloodhounds of the north, who enforce the Fugitive Slave Law. *They* do the work.

Southern gentlemen indulge in the most contemptuous expressions about the Yankees, while they, on their part, consent to do the vilest work for them, such as the ferocious bloodhounds and the despised negro-hunters are employed to do at home. When southerners go to the north, they are proud to do them honor; but the northern man is not welcome south of Mason and Dixon's line, unless he suppresses every thought and feeling at variance with their "peculiar institution." Nor is it enough to be silent. The masters are not pleased, unless they obtain a greater degree of subservience than that; and they are generally accommodated. Do they respect the northerner for this? I trow not. Even the slaves despise "a northern man with southern principles;" and that is the class they generally see. When northerners go to the south to reside, they prove very apt scholars. They soon imbibe the sentiments and disposition of their neighbors, and generally go beyond their teachers. Of the two, they are proverbially the hardest masters.

They seem to satisfy their consciences with the doctrine that God created the Africans to be slaves. What a libel upon the heavenly Father, who "made of one blood all nations of men!" And then who *are* Africans? Who can measure the amount of Anglo-Saxon blood coursing in the veins of American slaves?

I have spoken of the pains slaveholders take to give their slaves a bad opinion of the north; but, notwithstanding this, intelligent slaves are aware that they have many friends in the Free States. Even the most ignorant have some confused notions about it. They knew that I could read; and I was often asked if I had seen any thing in the newspapers about white folks over in the big north, who were trying to get their freedom for them. Some believe that the abolitionists have already made them free, and that it is established by law, but that their masters prevent the law from going into effect. One woman begged me to get a newspaper and read it over. She said her husband told her that the black people had sent word to the queen of 'Merica that they were all slaves; that she didn't believe it, and went to Washington city to see the president about it. They quarrelled; she drew her sword upon him, and swore that he should help her to make them all free.

That poor, ignorant woman thought that America was governed by a Queen, to whom the President was subordinate. I wish the President was subordinate to Queen Justice.

# IX. SKETCHES OF NEIGHBORING SLAVEHOLDERS

There was a planter in the country, not far from us, whom I will call Mr. Litch. He was an ill-bred, uneducated man, but very wealthy. He had six hundred slaves, many of whom he did not know by sight. His extensive plantation was managed by well-paid overseers. There was a jail and a whipping post on his grounds; and whatever cruelties were perpetrated there, they passed without comment. He was so effectually screened by his great wealth that he was called to no account for his crimes, not even for murder.

Various were the punishments resorted to. A favorite one was to tie a rope round a man's body, and suspend him from the ground. A fire was kindled over him, from which was suspended a piece of fat pork. As this cooked, the scalding drops of fat continually fell on the bare flesh. On his own plantation, he required very strict obedience to the eighth commandment. But depredations on the neighbors were allowable, provided the culprit managed to evade detection or suspicion. If a neighbor brought a charge of theft against any of his slaves, he was browbeaten by the master, who assured him that his slaves had enough of every thing at home, and had no inducement to steal. No sooner was the neighbor's back turned, than the accused was sought out, and whipped for his lack of discretion. If a slave stole from him even a pound of meat or a peck of corn, if detection followed, he was put in chains and imprisoned, and so kept till his form was attentuated by hunger and suffering.

A freshet once bore his wine cellar and meat house miles away from the plantation. Some slaves followed, and secured bits of meat and bottles of wine. Two were detected; a ham and some liquor being found in their huts. They were summoned by their master. No words were used, but a club felled them to the ground. A rough box was their coffin, and their interment was a dog's burial. Nothing was said.

Murder was so common on his plantation that he feared to be alone after nightfall. He might have believed in ghosts.

His brother, if not equal in wealth, was at least equal in cruelty. His bloodhounds were well trained. Their pen was spacious, and a terror to the slaves. They were let loose on a runway, and, if they tracked him, they literally tore the flesh from his bones. When this slaveholder died, his shrieks and groans were so frightful that they appalled his own friends. His last words were, "I am going to hell; bury my money with me."

After death his eyes remained open. To press the lids down, silver dollars were laid on them. These were buried with him. From this circumstance, a rumor went abroad that his coffin was filled with money. Three times his grave was opened, and his coffin taken out. The last time, his body was found on the ground, and a flock of buzzards were pecking at it. He was again interred, and a sentinel set over his grave. The perpetrators were never discovered.

Cruelty is contagious in uncivilized communities. Mr. Conant, a neighbor of Mr. Litch, returned from town one evening in a partial state of intoxication. His body servant gave him some offence. He was divested of his clothes, except his shirt, whipped, and tied to a large tree in front of the house. It was a stormy night in winter. The wind blew bitterly cold, and the boughs of the old tree crackled under falling sleet. A member of the family, fearing he would freeze to death, begged that he might be taken down; but the master would not relent. He remained there three hours; and, when he was cut down, he was more dead than alive. Another slave, who stole a pig from this master, to appease his hunger, was terribly flogged. In desperation, he tried to run away. But at the end of two miles, he was so faint with loss of blood, he thought he was dying. He had a wife, and he longed to see her once more. Too sick to walk, he crept back that long distance on his hands and knees. When he reached his master's, it was night. He had not strength to rise and open the gate. He moaned, and tried to call for help. I had a friend living in the same family. At last his cry reached her. She went out and found the prostrate man at the gate. She ran back to the house for assistance, and two men returned with her. They carried him in, and laid him on the floor. The back of his shirt was one clot of blood. By means of lard, my friend loosened it from the raw flesh. She bandaged him, gave him cool drink, and left him to rest. The master said he deserved a hundred more lashes.

When his own labor was stolen from him, he had stolen food to appease his hunger. This was his crime.

Another neighbor was a Mrs. Wade. At no hour of the day was there cessation of the lash on her premises. Her labors began with the dawn, and did not cease till long after nightfall. The barn was her particular place of torture. There she lashed the slaves with the might of a man. An old slave of hers once said to me, "It is hell in missis's house. 'Pears I can never get out. Day and night I prays to die."

The mistress died before the old woman, and, when dying, entreated her husband not to permit any one of her slaves to look on her after death. A slave who had nursed her children, and had still a child in her care, watched her chance, and stole with it in her arms to the room where lay her dead mistress. She gazed a while on her, then raised her hand and dealt two blows on her face, saying, as she did so, "The devil is got you *now*!" She forgot that the child was looking on. She had just begun to talk; and she said to her father, "I did see ma, and mammy did strike ma, so," striking her own face with her little hand. The master was startled. He could not imagine how the nurse could obtain access to the room where the corpse lay; for he kept the door locked. He questioned her. She confessed that what the child had said was true, and told how she had procured the key. She was sold to Georgia.

In my childhood I knew a valuable slave, named Charity, and loved her, as all children did. Her young mistress married, and took her to Louisiana. Her little boy, James, was sold to a good sort of master. He became involved in debt, and James was sold again to a wealthy slaveholder, noted for his cruelty. With this man he grew up to manhood, receiving the treatment of a dog. After a severe whipping, to save himself from further infliction of the lash, with which he was threatened, he took to the woods. He was in a most miserable condition—cut by the cowskin, half naked, half starved, and without the means of procuring a crust of bread.

Some weeks after his escape, he was captured, tied, and carried back to his master's plantation. This man considered punishment in his jail, on bread and water, after receiving hundreds of lashes, too mild for the poor slave's offence. Therefore he decided, after the overseer should have whipped him to his satisfaction, to have him placed between the screws of the cotton gin, to stay as long as he had been in the woods. This wretched creature was cut with the whip from his head to his feet, then washed with strong brine, to prevent the flesh from mortifying, and make it heal sooner than it otherwise would. He was then put into the cotton gin, which was screwed down, only allowing him room to turn on his side when he could not lie on his back. Every morning a slave was sent with a piece of bread and bowl of water, which was placed within reach of the poor fellow. The slave was charged, under penalty of severe punishment, not to speak to him.

Four days passed, and the slave continued to carry the bread and water. On the second morning, he found the bread gone, but the water untouched. When he had been in the press four days and five night, the slave informed his master that the water had not been used for four mornings, and that horrible stench came from the gin house. The overseer was sent to examine into it. When the press was unscrewed, the dead body was found partly eaten by rats and vermin. Perhaps the rats that devoured his bread had gnawed him before life was extinct. Poor Charity! Grandmother and I often asked each other how her affectionate heart would bear the news, if she should ever hear of the murder of her son. We had known her husband, and knew that James was like him in manliness and intelligence. These were the qualities that made it so hard for him to be a plantation slave. They put him into a rough box, and buried him with less feeling than would have been manifested for an old house dog. Nobody asked any questions. He was a slave; and the feeling was that the master had a right to do what he pleased with his own property. And what did *he* care for the value of a slave? He had hundreds of them. When they had finished their daily toil, they must hurry to eat their little morsels, and be ready to extinguish their pine knots before nine o'clock, when the overseer went his patrol rounds. He entered every cabin, to see that men and their wives had gone to bed together, lest the men, from over-fatigue, should fall asleep in the chimney corner, and remain there till the morning horn called them to their daily task. Women are considered of no value, unless they continually increase their owner's stock. They are put on a par with animals. This same master shot a woman through the head, who had run away and been brought back to him. No one called him to account for it. If a slave resisted being whipped, the bloodhounds were unpacked, and set upon him, to tear his flesh from his bones. The master who did these things was highly educated, and styled a perfect gentleman. He also boasted the name and standing of a Christian, though Satan never had a truer follower.

I could tell of more slaveholders as cruel as those I have described. They are not exceptions to the general rule. I do not say there are no humane slaveholders. Such characters do exist, notwithstanding the hardening influences around them. But they are "like angels' visits—few and far between."

I knew a young lady who was one of these rare specimens. She was an orphan, and inherited as slaves a woman and her six children. Their father was a free man. They had a comfortable home of their own, parents and children living together. The mother and eldest daughter served their mistress during the day, and at night returned to their dwelling, which was on the premises. The young lady was very pious, and there was some reality in her religion. She taught her slaves to lead pure lives, and wished them to enjoy the fruit of their own industry. *Her* religion was not a garb put on for Sunday, and laid aside till Sunday returned again. The eldest daughter of the slave mother was promised in marriage to a free man; and the day before the wedding this good mistress emancipated her, in order that her marriage might have the sanction of *law*.

Report said that this young lady cherished an unrequited affection for a man who had resolved to marry for wealth. In the course of time a rich uncle of hers died. He left six thousand dollars to his two sons by a colored woman, and the remainder of his property to this orphan niece. The metal soon attracted the magnet. The lady and her weighty purse became his. She offered to manumit her slaves—telling them that her marriage might make unexpected changes in their destiny, and she wished to insure their happiness. They refused to take their freedom, saying that she had always been their best friend, and they could not be so happy any where as with her. I was not surprised. I had often seen them in their comfortable home, and thought that the whole town did not contain a happier family. They had never felt slavery; and, when it was too late, they were convinced of its reality.

When the new master claimed this family as his property, the father became furious, and went to his mistress for protection. "I can do nothing for you now, Harry," said she. "I no longer have the power I had a week ago. I have succeeded in obtaining the freedom of your wife; but I cannot obtain it for your children." The unhappy father swore that nobody should take his children from him. He concealed them in the woods for some days; but they were discovered and taken. The father was put in jail, and the two oldest boys sold to Georgia. One little girl, too young to be of service to her master, was left with the wretched mother. The other three were carried to their master's plantation. The eldest soon became a mother; and when the slaveholder's wife looked at the babe, she wept bitterly. She knew that her own husband had violated the purity she had so carefully inculcated. She had a second child by her master, and then he sold her and his offspring to his brother. She bore two children to the brother and was sold again. The next sister went crazy. The life she was compelled to lead drove her mad. The third one became the mother of five daughters. Before the birth of the fourth the pious mistress died. To the last, she rendered every kindness to the slaves that her unfortunate circumstances permitted. She passed away peacefully, glad to close her eyes on a life which had been made so wretched by the man she loved.

This man squandered the fortune he had received, and sought to retrieve his affairs by a second marriage; but, having retired after a night of drunken debauch, he was found dead in the morning. He was called a good master; for he fed and clothed his slaves better than most masters, and the lash was not heard on his plantation so frequently as on many others. Had it not been for slavery, he would have been a better man, and his wife a happier woman.

No pen can give an adequate description of the all-pervading corruption produced by slavery. The slave girl is reared in an atmosphere of licentiousness and fear. The lash and the foul talk of her master and his sons are her teachers. When she is fourteen or fifteen, her owner, or his sons, or the overseer, or perhaps all of them, begin to bribe her with presents. If these fail to accomplish their purpose, she is whipped or starved into submission to their will. She may have had religious principles inculcated by some pious mother or grandmother, or some good mistress; she may have a lover, whose good opinion and peace of mind are dear to her heart; or the profligate men who have power over her may be exceedingly odious to her. But resistance is hopeless.

> The poor worm
> Shall prove her contest vain. Life's little day
> Shall pass, and she is gone!

The slaveholder's sons are, of course, vitiated, even while boys, by the unclean influences every where around them. Nor do the master's daughters always escape. Severe retributions sometimes come upon him for the wrongs he does to the daughters of the slaves. The white daughters early hear their parents quarrelling about some female slave. Their curiosity is excited, and they soon learn the cause. They are attended by the young slave girls whom their father has corrupted; and they hear such talk as should never meet youthful ears, or any other ears. They know that the woman slaves are subject to their father's authority in all things; and in some cases they exercise the same authority over the men slaves. I have myself seen the master of such a household whose head was bowed down in shame; for it was known in the neighborhood that his daughter had selected one of the meanest slaves on his plantation to be the father of his first grandchild. She did not make her advances to her equals, nor even to her father's more intelligent servants. She selected the most brutalized, over whom her authority could be exercised with less fear of exposure. Her father, half frantic with rage, sought to revenge himself on the offending black man; but his daughter, foreseeing the storm that would arise, had given him free papers, and sent him out of the state.

In such cases the infant is smothered, or sent where it is never seen by any who know its history. But if the white parent is the *father*, instead of the mother, the offspring are unblushingly reared for the market. If they are girls, I have indicated plainly enough what will be their inevitable destiny.

You may believe what I say; for I write only that whereof I know.

I was twenty-one years in that cage of obscene birds. I can testify, from my own experience and observation, that slavery is a curse to the whites as well as to the blacks. It makes white fathers cruel and sensual; the sons violent and licentious; it contaminates the daughters, and makes the wives wretched. And as for the colored race, it needs an abler pen than mine to describe the extremity of their sufferings, the depth of their degradation.

Yet few slaveholders seem to be aware of the widespread moral ruin occasioned by this wicked system. Their talk is of blighted cotton crops—not of the blight on their children's souls.

If you want to be fully convinced of the abominations of slavery, go on a southern plantation, and call yourself a negro trader. Then there will be no concealment; and you will see and hear things that will seem to you impossible among human beings with immortal souls.

# X. A PERILOUS PASSAGE IN THE SLAVE GIRL'S LIFE

After my lover went away, Dr. Flint contrived a new plan. He seemed to have an idea that my fear of my mistress was his greatest obstacle. In the blandest tones, he told me that he was going to build a small house for me, in a secluded place, four miles away from the town. I shuddered; but I was constrained to listen, while he talked of his intention to give me a home of my own, and to make a lady of me. Hitherto, I had escaped my dreaded fate, by being in the midst of people. My grandmother had already had high words with my master about me. She had told him pretty plainly what she thought of his character, and there was considerable gossip in the neighborhood about our affairs, to which the open-mouthed jealousy of Mrs. Flint contributed not a little. When my master said he was going to build a house for me, and that he could do it with little trouble and expense, I was in hopes something would happen to frustrate his scheme; but I soon heard that the house was actually begun. I vowed before my Maker that I would never enter it: I had rather toil on the plantation from dawn till dark; I had rather live and die in jail, than drag on, from day to day, through such a living death. I was determined that the master, whom I so hated and loathed, who had blighted the prospects of my youth, and made my life a desert, should not, after my long struggle with him, succeed at last in trampling his victim under his feet. I would do any thing, every thing, for the sake of defeating him. What *could* I do? I thought and thought, till I became desperate, and made a plunge into the abyss.

And now, reader, I come to a period in my unhappy life, which I would gladly forget if I could. The remembrance fills me with sorrow and shame. It pains me to tell you of it; but I have promised to tell you the truth, and I will do it honestly, let it cost me what it may. I will not try to screen myself behind the plea of compulsion from a master; for it was not so. Neither can I plead ignorance or thoughtlessness. For years, my master had done his utmost to pollute my mind with foul images, and to destroy the pure principles inculcated by my grandmother, and the good mistress of my childhood.

The influences of slavery had had the same effect on me that they had on other young girls; they had made me prematurely knowing, concerning the evil ways of the world. I knew what I did, and I did it with deliberate calculation.

But, O, ye happy women, whose purity has been sheltered from childhood, who have been free to choose the objects of your affection, whose homes are protected by law, do not judge the poor desolate slave girl too severely! If slavery had been abolished, I, also, could have married the man of my choice; I could have had a home shielded by the laws; and I should have been spared the painful task of confessing what I am now about to relate; but all my prospects had been blighted by slavery. I wanted to keep myself pure; and, under the most adverse circumstances, I tried hard to preserve my self-respect; but I was struggling alone in the powerful grasp of the demon Slavery; and the monster proved too strong for me. I felt as if I was forsaken by God and man; as if all my efforts must be frustrated; and I became reckless in my despair.

I have told you that Dr. Flint's persecutions and his wife's jealousy had given rise to some gossip in the neighborhood. Among others, it chanced that a white unmarried gentleman had obtained some knowledge of the circumstances in which I was placed. He knew my grandmother, and often spoke to me in the street. He became interested for me, and asked questions about my master, which I answered in part. He expressed a great deal of sympathy, and a wish to aid me. He constantly sought opportunities to see me, and wrote to me frequently. I was a poor slave girl, only fifteen years old.

So much attention from a superior person was, of course, flattering; for human nature is the same in all. I also felt grateful for his sympathy, and encouraged by his kind words. It seemed to me a great thing to have such a friend. By degrees, a more tender feeling crept into my heart. He was an educated and eloquent gentleman; too eloquent, alas, for the poor slave girl who trusted in him. Of course I saw whither all this was tending. I knew the impassable gulf between us; but to be an object of interest to a man who is not married, and who is not her master, is agreeable to the pride and feelings of a slave, if her miserable situation has left her any pride or sentiment. It seems less degrading to give one's self, than to submit to compulsion. There is something akin to freedom in having a lover who has no control over you, except that which he gains by kindness and attachment. A master may treat you as rudely as he pleases, and you dare not speak; moreover, the wrong does not seem so great with an unmarried man, as with one who has a wife to be made unhappy. There may be sophistry in all this; but the condition of a slave confuses all principles of morality, and, in fact, renders the practice of them impossible.

When I found that my master had actually begun to build the lonely cottage, other feelings mixed with those I have described. Revenge, and calculations of interest, were added to flattered vanity and sincere gratitude for kindness. I knew nothing would enrage Dr. Flint so much as to know that I favored another, and it was something to triumph over my tyrant even in that small way. I thought he would revenge himself by selling me, and I was sure my friend, Mr. Sands, would buy me. He was a man of more generosity and feeling than my master, and I thought my freedom could be easily obtained from him. The crisis of my fate now came so near that I was desperate. I shuddered to think of being the mother of children that should be owned by my old tyrant. I knew that as soon as a new fancy took him, his victims were sold far off to get rid of them; especially if they had children. I had seen several women sold, with babies at the breast. He never allowed his offspring by slaves to remain long in sight of himself and his wife. Of a man who was not my master I could ask to have my children well supported; and in this case, I felt confident I should obtain the boon. I also felt quite sure that they would be made free. With all these thoughts revolving in my mind, and seeing no other way of escaping the doom I so much dreaded, I made a headlong plunge. Pity me, and pardon me, O virtuous reader! You never knew what it is to be a slave; to be entirely unprotected by law or custom; to have the laws reduce you to the condition of a chattel, entirely subject to the will of another. You never exhausted your ingenuity in avoiding the snares, and eluding the power of a hated tyrant; you never shuddered at the sound of his footsteps, and trembled within hearing of his voice. I know I did wrong. No one can feel it more sensibly than I do. The painful and humiliating memory will haunt me to my dying day. Still, in looking back, calmly, on the events of my life, I feel that the slave woman ought not to be judged by the same standard as others.

The months passed on. I had many unhappy hours. I secretly mourned over the sorrow I was bringing on my grandmother, who had so tried to shield me from harm. I knew that I was the greatest comfort of her old age, and that it was a source of pride to her that I had not degraded myself, like most of the slaves. I wanted to confess to her that I was no longer worthy of her love; but I could not utter the dreaded words.

As for Dr. Flint, I had a feeling of satisfaction and triumph in the thought of telling *him*. From time to time he told me of his intended arrangements, and I was silent. At last, he came and told me the cottage was completed, and ordered me to go to it. I told him I would never enter it. He said, "I have heard enough of such talk as that. You shall go, if you are carried by force; and you shall remain there."

I replied, "I will never go there. In a few months I shall be a mother."

He stood and looked at me in dumb amazement, and left the house without a word. I thought I should be happy in my triumph over him. But now that the truth was out, and my relatives would hear of it, I felt wretched. Humble as were their circumstances, they had pride in my good character. Now, how could I look at them in the face? My self-respect was gone! I had resolved that I would be virtuous, though I was a slave. I had said, "Let the storm beat! I will brave it till I die." And now, how humiliated I felt!

I went to my grandmother. My lips moved to make confession, but the words stuck in my throat. I sat down in the shade of a tree at her door and began to sew. I think she saw something unusual was the matter with me. The mother of slaves is very watchful. She knows there is no security for her children. After they have entered their teens she lives in daily expectation of trouble. This leads to many questions. If the girl is of a sensitive nature, timidity keeps her from answering truthfully, and this well-meant course has a tendency to drive her from maternal counsels. Presently, in came my mistress, like a mad woman, and accused me concerning her husband. My grandmother, whose suspicions had been previously awakened, believed what she said. She exclaimed, "O Linda! Has it come to this?

I had rather see you dead than to see you as you now are. You are a disgrace to your dead mother." She tore from my fingers my mother's wedding ring and her silver thimble. "Go away!" she exclaimed, "and never come to my house, again." Her reproaches fell so hot and heavy, that they left me no chance to answer. Bitter tears, such as the eyes never shed but once, were my only answer. I rose from my seat, but fell back again, sobbing. She did not speak to me; but the tears were running down her furrowed cheeks, and they scorched me like fire. She had always been so kind to me! *So* kind! How I longed to throw myself at her feet, and tell her all the truth! But she had ordered me to go, and never to come there again. After a few minutes, I mustered strength, and started to obey her. With what feelings did I now close that little gate, which I used to open with such an eager hand in my childhood! It closed upon me with a sound I never heard before.

Where could I go? I was afraid to return to my master's. I walked on recklessly, not caring where I went, or what would become of me. When I had gone four or five miles, fatigue compelled me to stop. I sat down on the stump of an old tree. The stars were shining through the boughs above me. How they mocked me, with their bright, calm light! The hours passed by, and as I sat there alone a chilliness and deadly sickness came over me. I sank on the ground. My mind was full of horrid thoughts. I prayed to die; but the prayer was not answered. At last, with great effort I roused myself, and walked some distance further, to the house of a woman who had been a friend of my mother. When I told her why I was there, she spoke soothingly to me; but I could not be comforted. I thought I could bear my shame if I could only be reconciled to my grandmother. I longed to open my heart to her. I thought if she could know the real state of the case, and all I had been bearing for years, she would perhaps judge me less harshly. My friend advised me to send for her. I did so; but days of agonizing suspense passed before she came. Had she utterly forsaken me? No. She came at last. I knelt before her, and told her the things that had poisoned my life; how long I had been persecuted; that I saw no way of escape; and in an hour of extremity I had become desperate. She listened in silence. I told her I would bear any thing and do any thing, if in time I had hopes of obtaining her forgiveness. I begged of her to pity me, for my dead mother's sake. And she did pity me. She did not say, "I forgive you;" but she looked at me lovingly, with her eyes full of tears. She laid her old hand gently on my head, and murmured, "Poor child! Poor child!"

# XI. THE NEW TIE TO LIFE

I returned to my good grandmother's house. She had an interview with Mr. Sands. When she asked him why he could not have left her one ewe lamb,—whether there were not plenty of slaves who did not care about character,—he made no answer, but he spoke kind and encouraging words. He promised to care for my child, and to buy me, be the conditions what they might.

I had not seen Dr. Flint for five days. I had never seen him since I made the avowal to him. He talked of the disgrace I had brought on myself; how I had sinned against my master, and mortified my old grandmother. He intimated that if I had accepted his proposals, he, as a physician, could have saved me from exposure. He even condescended to pity me. Could he have offered wormwood more bitter? He, whose persecutions had been the cause of my sin!

"Linda," said he, "though you have been criminal towards me, I feel for you, and I can pardon you if you obey my wishes. Tell me whether the fellow you wanted to marry is the father of your child. If you deceive me, you shall feel the fires of hell."

I did not feel as proud as I had done. My strongest weapon with him was gone. I was lowered in my own estimation, and had resolved to bear his abuse in silence. But when he spoke contemptuously of the lover who had always treated me honorably; when I remembered that but for *him* I might have been a virtuous, free, and happy wife, I lost my patience. "I have sinned against God and myself," I replied; "but not against you."

He clinched his teeth, and muttered, "Curse you!" He came towards me, with ill-suppressed rage, and exclaimed, "You obstinate girl! I could grind your bones to powder! You have thrown yourself away on some worthless rascal. You are weak-minded, and have been easily persuaded by those who don't care a straw for you. The future will settle accounts between us. You are blinded now; but hereafter you will be convinced that your master was your best friend. My lenity towards you is a proof of it. I might have punished you in many ways. I might have whipped till you fell dead under the lash. But I wanted you to live; I would have bettered your condition. Others cannot do it. You are my slave. Your mistress, disgusted by your conduct, forbids you to return to the house; therefore I leave you here for the present; but I shall see you often. I will call to-morrow."

He came with frowning brows, that showed a dissatisfied state of mind. After asking about my health, he inquired whether my board was paid, and who visited me. He then went on to say that he had neglected his duty; that as a physician there were certain things that he ought to have explained to me. Then followed talk such as would have made the most shameless blush. He ordered me to stand up before him. I obeyed. "I command you," said he, "to tell me whether the father of your child is white or black." I hesitated. "Answer me this instant!" he exclaimed. I did answer. He sprang upon me like a wolf, and grabbed my arm as if he would have broken it. "Do you love him?" said he, in a hissing tone.

"I am thankful that I do not despise him," I replied.

He raised his hand to strike me; but it fell again. I don't know what arrested the blow. He sat down, with lips tightly compressed. At last he spoke. "I came here," said he, "to make you a friendly proposition; but your ingratitude chafes me beyond endurance. You turn aside all my good intentions towards you. I don't know what it is that keeps me from killing you." Again he rose, as if he had a mind to strike me.

But he resumed. "On one condition I will forgive your insolence and crime. You must henceforth have no communication of any kind with the father of your child. You must not ask any thing from him, or receive any thing from him. I will take care of you and your child. You had better promise this at once, and not wait till you are deserted by him. This is the last act of mercy I shall show towards you."

I said something about being unwilling to have my child supported by a man who had cursed it and me also. He rejoined, that a woman who had sunk to my level had no right to expect any thing else. He asked, for the last time, would I accept his kindness? I answered that I would not.

"Very well," said he; "then take the consequences of your wayward course. Never look to me for help. You are my slave, and shall always be my slave. I will never sell you, that you may depend upon."

Hope died away in my heart as he closed the door after him. I had calculated that in his rage he would sell me to a slave-trader; and I knew the father of my child was on the watch to buy me.

About this time my uncle Phillip was expected to return from a voyage. The day before his departure I had officiated as bridesmaid to a young friend. My heart was then ill at ease, but my smiling countenance did not betray it. Only a year had passed; but what fearful changes it had wrought! My heart had grown gray in misery. Lives that flash in sunshine, and lives that are born in tears, receive their hue from circumstances. None of us know what a year may bring forth.

I felt no joy when they told me my uncle had come. He wanted to see me, though he knew what had happened. I shrank from him at first; but at last consented that he should come to my room. He received me as he always had done. O, how my heart smote me when I felt his tears on my burning cheeks! The words of my grandmother came to my mind,—"Perhaps your mother and father are taken from the evil days to come." My disappointed heart could now praise God that it was so. But why, thought I, did my relatives ever cherish hopes for me? What was there to save me from the usual fate of slave girls? Many more beautiful and more intelligent than I had experienced a similar fate, or a far worse one. How could they hope that I should escape?

My uncle's stay was short, and I was not sorry for it. I was too ill in mind and body to enjoy my friends as I had done. For some weeks I was unable to leave my bed. I could not have any doctor but my master, and I would not have him sent for. At last, alarmed by my increasing illness, they sent for him. I was very weak and nervous; and as soon as he entered the room, I began to scream. They told him my state was very critical. He had no wish to hasten me out of the world, and he withdrew.

When my babe was born, they said it was premature. It weighed only four pounds; but God let it live. I heard the doctor say I could not survive till morning. I had often prayed for death; but now I did not want to die, unless my child could die too. Many weeks passed before I was able to leave my bed. I was a mere wreck of my former self. For a year there was scarcely a day when I was free from chills and fever. My babe also was sickly. His little limbs were often racked with pain. Dr. Flint continued his visits, to look after my health; and he did not fail to remind me that my child was an addition to his stock of slaves.

I felt too feeble to dispute with him, and listened to his remarks in silence. His visits were less frequent; but his busy spirit could not remain quiet. He employed my brother in his office; and he was made the medium of frequent notes and messages to me. William was a bright lad, and of much use to the doctor. He had learned to put up medicines, to leech, cup, and bleed. He had taught himself to read and spell. I was proud of my brother, and the old doctor suspected as much. One day, when I had not seen him for several weeks, I heard his steps approaching the door. I dreaded the encounter, and hid myself. He inquired for me, of course; but I was nowhere to be found. He went to his office, and despatched William with a note. The color mounted to my brother's face when he gave it to me; and he said, "Don't you hate me, Linda, for bringing you these things?" I told him I could not blame him; he was a slave, and obliged to obey his master's will. The note ordered me to come to his office. I went. He demanded to know where I was when he called. I told him I was at home. He flew into a passion, and said he knew better. Then he launched out upon his usual themes,—my crimes against him, and my ingratitude for his forbearance. The laws were laid down to me anew, and I was dismissed. I felt humiliated that my brother should stand by, and listen to such language as would be addressed only to a slave. Poor boy! He was powerless to defend me; but I saw the tears, which he vainly strove to keep back. The manifestation of feeling irritated the doctor. William could do nothing to please him. One morning he did not arrive at the office so early as usual; and that circumstance afforded his master an opportunity to vent his spleen. He was put in jail. The next day my brother sent a trader to the doctor, with a request to be sold. His master was greatly incensed at what he called his insolence. He said he had put him there, to reflect upon his bad conduct, and he certainly was not giving any evidence of repentance. For two days he harassed himself to find somebody to do his office work; but every thing went wrong without William. He was released, and ordered to take his old stand, with many threats, if he was not careful about his future behavior.

As the months passed on, my boy improved in health. When he was a year old, they called him beautiful. The little vine was taking deep root in my existence, though its clinging fondness excited a mixture of love and pain. When I was most sorely oppressed I found a solace in his smiles. I loved to watch his infant slumbers; but always there was a dark cloud over my enjoyment. I could never forget that he was a slave. Sometimes I wished that he might die in infancy. God tried me. My darling became very ill. The bright eyes grew dull, and the little feet and hands were so icy cold that I thought death had already touched them. I had prayed for his death, but never so earnestly as I now prayed for his life; and my prayer was heard. Alas, what mockery it is for a slave mother to try to pray back her dying child to life! Death is better than slavery. It was a sad thought that I had no name to give my child. His father caressed him and treated him kindly, whenever he had a chance to see him. He was not unwilling that he should bear his name; but he had no legal claim to it; and if I had bestowed it upon him, my master would have regarded it as a new crime, a new piece of insolence, and would, perhaps, revenge it on the boy. O, the serpent of Slavery has many and poisonous fangs!

# XII. FEAR OF INSURRECTION

Not far from this time Nat Turner's insurrection broke out; and the news threw our town into great commotion. Strange that they should be alarmed, when their slaves were so "contented and happy"! But so it was.

It was always the custom to have a muster every year. On that occasion every white man shouldered his musket. The citizens and the so-called country gentlemen wore military uniforms. The poor whites took their places in the ranks in every-day dress, some without shoes, some without hats. This grand occasion had already passed; and when the slaves were told there was to be another muster, they were surprised and rejoiced. Poor creatures! They thought it was going to be a holiday. I was informed of the true state of affairs, and imparted it to the few I could trust. Most gladly would I have proclaimed it to every slave; but I dared not. All could not be relied on. Mighty is the power of the torturing lash.

By sunrise, people were pouring in from every quarter within twenty miles of the town. I knew the houses were to be searched; and I expected it would be done by country bullies and the poor whites. I knew nothing annoyed them so much as to see colored people living in comfort and respectability; so I made arrangements for them with especial care. I arranged every thing in my grandmother's house as neatly as possible. I put white quilts on the beds, and decorated some of the rooms with flowers. When all was arranged, I sat down at the window to watch. Far as my eye could reach, it rested on a motley crowd of soldiers. Drums and fifes were discoursing martial music. The men were divided into companies of sixteen, each headed by a captain. Orders were given, and the wild scouts rushed in every direction, wherever a colored face was to be found.

It was a grand opportunity for the low whites, who had no negroes of their own to scourge. They exulted in such a chance to exercise a little brief authority, and show their subserviency to the slaveholders; not reflecting that the power which trampled on the colored people also kept themselves in poverty, ignorance, and moral degradation. Those who never witnessed such scenes can hardly believe what I know was inflicted at this time on innocent men, women, and children, against whom there was not the slightest ground for suspicion. Colored people and slaves who lived in remote parts of the town suffered in an especial manner. In some cases the searchers scattered powder and shot among their clothes, and then sent other parties to find them, and bring them forward as proof that they were plotting insurrection. Every where men, women, and children were whipped till the blood stood in puddles at their feet. Some received five hundred lashes; others were tied hands and feet, and tortured with a bucking paddle, which blisters the skin terribly. The dwellings of the colored people, unless they happened to be protected by some influential white person, who was nigh at hand, were robbed of clothing and every thing else the marauders thought worth carrying away. All day long these unfeeling wretches went round, like a troop of demons, terrifying and tormenting the helpless. At night, they formed themselves into patrol bands, and went wherever they chose among the colored people, acting out their brutal will. Many women hid themselves in woods and swamps, to keep out of their way. If any of the husbands or fathers told of these outrages, they were tied up to the public whipping post, and cruelly scourged for telling lies about white men. The consternation was universal. No two people that had the slightest tinge of color in their faces dared to be seen talking together.

I entertained no positive fears about our household, because we were in the midst of white families who would protect us. We were ready to receive the soldiers whenever they came. It was not long before we heard the tramp of feet and the sound of voices. The door was rudely pushed open; and in they tumbled, like a pack of hungry wolves. They snatched at every thing within their reach. Every box, trunk, closet, and corner underwent a thorough examination. A box in one of the drawers containing some silver change was eagerly pounced upon. When I stepped forward to take it from them, one of the soldiers turned and said angrily, "What d'ye foller us fur? D'ye s'pose white folks is come to steal?"

I replied, "You have come to search; but you have searched that box, and I will take it, if you please."

At that moment I saw a white gentleman who was friendly to us; and I called to him, and asked him to have the goodness to come in and stay till the search was over. He readily complied. His entrance into the house brought in the captain of the company, whose business it was to guard the outside of the house, and see that none of the inmates left it. This officer was Mr. Litch, the wealthy slaveholder whom I mentioned, in the account of neighboring planters, as being notorious for his cruelty. He felt above soiling his hands with the search. He merely gave orders; and, if a bit of writing was discovered, it was carried to him by his ignorant followers, who were unable to read.

My grandmother had a large trunk of bedding and table cloths. When that was opened, there was a great shout of surprise; and one exclaimed, "Where'd the damned niggers git all dis sheet an' table clarf?"

My grandmother, emboldened by the presence of our white protector said, "You may be sure we didn't pilfer 'em from *your* houses."

"Look here, mammy," said a grim-looking fellow without any coat, "you seem to feel mighty gran' 'cause you got all them 'ere fixens. White folks oughter have 'em all."

His remarks were interrupted by a chorus of voices shouting, "We's got 'em! We's got 'em! Dis 'ere yaller gal's got letters!"

There was a general rush for the supposed letter, which, upon examination, proved to be some verses written to me by a friend. In packing away my things, I had overlooked them. When their captain informed them of their contents, they seemed much disappointed. He inquired of me who wrote them. I told him it was one of my friends. "Can you read them?" he asked. When I told him I could, he swore, and raved, and tore the paper into bits. "Bring me all your letters!" said he, in commanding tone. I told him I had none. "Don't be afraid," he continued, in an insinuating way. "Bring them all to me. Nobody shall do you any harm." Seeing I did not move to obey him, his pleasant tone changed to oaths and threats. "Who writes to you? half free niggers?" inquired he. I replied, "O, no; most of my letters are from white people. Some request me to burn them after they are read, and some I destroy without reading."

An exclamation of surprise from some of the company put a stop to our conversation. Some silver spoons which ornamented an old-fashioned buffet had just been discovered. My grandmother was in the habit of preserving fruit for many ladies in the town, and of preparing suppers for parties; consequently she had many jars of preserves. The closet that contained these was next invaded, and the contents tasted. One of them, who was helping himself freely, tapped his neighbor on the shoulder, and said, "Wal done! Don't wonder de niggers want to kill all de white folks, when dey live on 'sarves" [meaning preserves]. I stretched out my hand to take the jar, saying, "You were not sent here to search for sweetmeats."

"And what *were* we sent for?" said the captain, bristling up to me. I evaded the question.

The search of the house was completed, and nothing found to condemn us. They next proceeded to the garden, and knocked about every bush and vine, with no better success. The captain called his men together, and, after a short consultation, the order to march was given. As they passed out of the gate, the captain turned back, and pronounced a malediction on the house. He said it ought to be burned to the ground, and each of its inmates receive thirty-nine lashes. We came out of this affair very fortunately; not losing any thing except some wearing apparel.

Towards evening the turbulence increased. The soldiers, stimulated by drink, committed still greater cruelties. Shrieks and shouts continually rent the air. Not daring to go to the door, I peeped under the window curtain. I saw a mob dragging along a number of colored people, each white man, with his musket upraised, threatening instant death if they did not stop their shrieks. Among the prisoners was a respectable old colored minister. They had found a few parcels of shot in his house, which his wife had for years used to balance her scales. For this they were going to shoot him on Court House Green. What a spectacle was that for a civilized country! A rabble, staggering under intoxication, assuming to be the administrators of justice!

The better class of the community exerted their influence to save the innocent, persecuted people; and in several instances they succeeded, by keeping them shut up in jail till the excitement abated. At last the white citizens found that their own property was not safe from the lawless rabble they had summoned to protect them. They rallied the drunken swarm, drove them back into the country, and set a guard over the town.

The next day, the town patrols were commissioned to search colored people that lived out of the city; and the most shocking outrages were committed with perfect impunity. Every day for a fortnight, if I looked out, I saw horsemen with some poor panting negro tied to their saddles, and compelled by the lash to keep up with their speed, till they arrived at the jail yard. Those who had been whipped too unmercifully to walk were washed with brine, tossed into a cart, and carried to jail. One black man, who had not fortitude to endure scourging, promised to give information about the conspiracy. But it turned out that he knew nothing at all. He had not even heard the name of Nat Turner. The poor fellow had, however, made up a story, which augmented his own sufferings and those of the colored people.

The day patrol continued for some weeks, and at sundown a night guard was substituted. Nothing at all was proved against the colored people, bond or free. The wrath of the slaveholders was somewhat appeased by the capture of Nat Turner. The imprisoned were released. The slaves were sent to their masters, and the free were permitted to return to their ravaged homes. Visiting was strictly forbidden on the plantations. The slaves begged the privilege of again meeting at their little church in the woods, with their burying ground around it. It was built by the colored people, and they had no higher happiness than to meet there and sing hymns together, and pour out their hearts in spontaneous prayer. Their request was denied, and the church was demolished. They were permitted to attend the white churches, a certain portion of the galleries being appropriated to their use. There, when every body else had partaken of the communion, and the benediction had been pronounced, the minister said, "Come down, now, my colored friends." They obeyed the summons, and partook of the bread and wine, in commemoration of the meek and lowly Jesus, who said, "God is your Father, and all ye are brethren."

# XIII. THE CHURCH AND SLAVERY

After the alarm caused by Nat Turner's insurrection had subsided, the slaveholders came to the conclusion that it would be well to give the slaves enough of religious instruction to keep them from murdering their masters. The Episcopal clergyman offered to hold a separate service on Sundays for their benefit. His colored members were very few, and also very respectable—a fact which I presume had some weight with him. The difficulty was to decide on a suitable place for them to worship. The Methodist and Baptist churches admitted them in the afternoon; but their carpets and cushions were not so costly as those at the Episcopal church. It was at last decided that they should meet at the house of a free colored man, who was a member.

I was invited to attend, because I could read. Sunday evening came, and, trusting to the cover of night, I ventured out. I rarely ventured out by daylight, for I always went with fear, expecting at every turn to encounter Dr. Flint, who was sure to turn me back, or order me to his office to inquire where I got my bonnet, or some other article of dress. When the Rev. Mr. Pike came, there were some twenty persons present. The reverend gentleman knelt in prayer, then seated himself, and requested all present, who could read, to open their books, while he gave out the portions he wished them to repeat or respond to.

His text was, "Servants, be obedient to them that are your masters according to the flesh, with fear and trembling, in singleness of your heart, as unto Christ."

Pious Mr. Pike brushed up his hair till it stood upright, and, in deep, solemn tones, began: "Hearken, ye servants! Give strict heed unto my words. You are rebellious sinners. Your hearts are filled with all manner of evil. 'Tis the devil who tempts you. God is angry with you, and will surely punish you, if you don't forsake your wicked ways. You that live in town are eyeservants behind your master's back. Instead of serving your masters faithfully, which is pleasing in the sight of your heavenly Master, you are idle, and shirk your work. God sees you. You tell lies. God hears you. Instead of being engaged in worshipping him, you are hidden away somewhere, feasting on your master's substance; tossing coffee-grounds with some wicked fortuneteller, or cutting cards with another old hag. Your masters may not find you out, but God sees you, and will punish you. O, the depravity of your hearts! When your master's work is done, are you quietly together, thinking of the goodness of God to such sinful creatures? No; you are quarrelling, and tying up little bags of roots to bury under the doorsteps to poison each other with. God sees you. You men steal away to every grog shop to sell your master's corn, that you may buy rum to drink. God sees you. You sneak into the back streets, or among the bushes, to pitch coppers. Although your masters may not find you out, God sees you; and he will punish you. You must forsake your sinful ways, and be faithful servants. Obey your old master and your young master—your old mistress and your young mistress. If you disobey your earthly master, you offend your heavenly Master. You must obey God's commandments. When you go from here, don't stop at the corners of the streets to talk, but go directly home, and let your master and mistress see that you have come."

The benediction was pronounced. We went home, highly amused at brother Pike's gospel teaching, and we determined to hear him again. I went the next Sabbath evening, and heard pretty much a repetition of the last discourse. At the close of the meeting, Mr. Pike informed us that he found it very inconvenient to meet at the friend's house, and he should be glad to see us, every Sunday evening, at his own kitchen.

I went home with the feeling that I had heard the Reverend Mr. Pike for the last time. Some of his members repaired to his house, and found that the kitchen sported two tallow candles; the first time, I am sure, since its present occupant owned it, for the servants never had any thing but pine knots. It was so long before the reverend gentleman descended from his comfortable parlor that the slaves left, and went to enjoy a Methodist shout. They never seem so happy as when shouting and singing at religious meetings. Many of them are sincere, and nearer to the gate of heaven than sanctimonious Mr. Pike, and other long-faced Christians, who see wounded Samaritans, and pass by on the other side.

The slaves generally compose their own songs and hymns; and they do not trouble their heads much about the measure. They often sing the following verses:

Old Satan is one busy ole man;
He rolls dem blocks all in my way;
But Jesus is my bosom friend;
He rolls dem blocks away.

If I had died when I was young,
Den how my stam'ring tongue would have sung;
But I am ole, and now I stand
A narrow chance for to tread dat heavenly land.

I well remember one occasion when I attended a Methodist class meeting. I went with a burdened spirit, and happened to sit next a poor, bereaved mother, whose heart was still heavier than mine. The class leader was the town constable—a man who bought and sold slaves, who whipped his brethren and sisters of the church at the public whipping post, in jail or out of jail. He was ready to perform that Christian office any where for fifty cents. This white-faced, black-hearted brother came near us, and said to the stricken woman, "Sister, can't you tell us how the Lord deals with your soul? Do you love him as you did formerly?"

She rose to her feet, and said, in piteous tones, "My Lord and Master, help me! My load is more than I can bear. God has hid himself from me, and I am left in darkness and misery." Then, striking her breast, she continued, "I can't tell you what is in here! They've got all my children. Last week they took the last one. God only knows where they've sold her. They let me have her sixteen years, and then—O! O! Pray for her brothers and sisters! I've got nothing to live for now. God make my time short!"

She sat down, quivering in every limb. I saw that constable class leader become crimson in the face with suppressed laughter, while he held up his handkerchief, that those who were weeping for the poor woman's calamity might not see his merriment. Then, with assumed gravity, he said to the bereaved mother, "Sister, pray to the

Lord that every dispensation of his divine will may be sanctified to the good of your poor needy soul!"

The congregation struck up a hymn, and sung as though they were as free as the birds that warbled round us,—

> Ole Satan thought he had a mighty aim;
> He missed my soul, and caught my sins.
> Cry Amen, cry Amen, cry Amen to God!
>
> He took my sins upon his back;
> Went muttering and grumbling down to hell.
> Cry Amen, cry Amen, cry Amen to God!
>
> Ole Satan's church is here below.
> Up to God's free church I hope to go.
> Cry Amen, cry Amen, cry Amen to God!

Precious are such moments to the poor slaves. If you were to hear them at such times, you might think they were happy. But can that hour of singing and shouting sustain them through the dreary week, toiling without wages, under constant dread of the lash?

The Episcopal clergyman, who, ever since my earliest recollection, had been a sort of god among the slaveholders, concluded, as his family was large, that he must go where money was more abundant. A very different clergyman took his place. The change was very agreeable to the colored people, who said, "God has sent us a good man this time." They loved him, and their children followed him for a smile or a kind word. Even the slaveholders felt his influence. He brought to the rectory five slaves. His wife taught them to read and write, and to be useful to her and themselves. As soon as he was settled, he turned his attention to the needy slaves around him. He urged upon his parishioners the duty of having a meeting expressly for them every Sunday, with a sermon adapted to their comprehension. After much argument and importunity, it was finally agreed that they might occupy the gallery of the church on Sunday evenings. Many colored people, hitherto unaccustomed to attend church, now gladly went to hear the gospel preached. The sermons were simple, and they understood them. Moreover, it was the first time they had ever been addressed as human beings. It was not long before his white parishioners began to be dissatisfied. He was accused of preaching better sermons to the negroes than he did to them. He honestly confessed that he bestowed more pains upon those sermons than upon any others; for the slaves were reared in such ignorance that it was a difficult task to adapt himself to their comprehension. Dissensions arose in the parish. Some wanted he should preach to them in the evening, and to the slaves in the afternoon. In the midst of these disputings his wife died, after a very short illness. Her slaves gathered round her dying bed in great sorrow. She said, "I have tried to do you good and promote your happiness; and if I have failed, it has not been for want of interest in your welfare. Do not weep for me; but prepare for the new duties that lie before you. I leave you all free. May we meet in a better world." Her liberated slaves were sent away, with funds to establish them comfortably. The colored people will long bless the memory of that truly Christian woman. Soon after her death her husband preached his farewell sermon, and many tears were shed at his departure.

Several years after, he passed through our town and preached to his former congregation. In his afternoon sermon he addressed the colored people. "My friends," said he, "it affords me great happiness to have an opportunity of speaking to you again. For two years I have been striving to do something for the colored people of my own parish; but nothing is yet accomplished. I have not even preached a sermon to them. Try to live according to the word of God, my friends. Your skin is darker than mine; but God judges men by their hearts, not by the color of their skins." This was strange doctrine from a southern pulpit. It was very offensive to slaveholders. They said he and his wife had made fools of their slaves, and that he preached like a fool to the negroes.

I knew an old black man, whose piety and childlike trust in God were beautiful to witness. At fifty-three years old he joined the Baptist church. He had a most earnest desire to learn to read. He thought he should know how to serve God better if he could only read the Bible. He came to me, and begged me to teach him. He said he could not pay me, for he had no money; but he would bring me nice fruit when the season for it came. I asked him if he didn't know it was contrary to law; and that slaves were whipped and imprisoned for teaching each other to read. This brought the tears into his eyes. "Don't be troubled, uncle Fred," said I. "I have no thoughts of refusing to teach you. I only told you of the law, that you might know the danger, and be on your guard." He thought he could plan to come three times a week without its being suspected. I selected a quiet nook, where no intruder was likely to penetrate, and there I taught him his A, B, C. Considering his age, his progress was astonishing. As soon as he could spell in two syllables he wanted to spell out words in the Bible. The happy smile that illuminated his face put joy into my heart. After spelling out a few words, he paused, and said, "Honey, it 'pears when I can read dis good book I shall be nearer to God. White man is got all de sense. He can larn easy. It ain't easy for ole black man like me. I only wants to read dis book, dat I may know how to live; den I hab no fear 'bout dying."

I tried to encourage him by speaking of the rapid progress he had made.

"Hab patience, child," he replied. "I larns slow."

I had no need of patience. His gratitude, and the happiness imparted, were more than a recompense for all my trouble.

At the end of six months he had read through the New Testament, and could find any text in it. One day, when he had recited unusually well, I said, "Uncle Fred, how do you manage to get your lessons so well?"

"Lord bress you, chile," he replied. "You nebber gibs me a lesson dat I don't pray to God to help me to understan' what I spells and what I reads. And he *does* help me, chile. Bress his holy name!"

There are thousands, who, like good uncle Fred, are thirsting for the water of life; but the law forbids it, and the churches withhold it. They send the Bible to heathen abroad, and neglect the heathen at home. I am glad that missionaries go out to the dark corners of the earth; but I ask them not to overlook the dark corners at home. Talk to American slaveholders as you talk to savages in Africa. Tell *them* it was wrong to traffic in men. Tell them it is sinful to sell their own children, and atrocious to violate their own daughters. Tell them that all men are brethren, and that man has no right to shut out the light of knowledge from his brother. Tell them they are answerable to God for sealing up the Fountain of Life from souls that are thirsting for it.

There are men who would gladly undertake such missionary work as this; but, alas! their number is small. They are hated by the south, and would be driven from its soil, or dragged to prison to die, as others have been before them. The field is ripe for the harvest, and awaits the reapers. Perhaps the great grandchildren of uncle Fred may have freely imparted to them the divine treasures, which he sought by stealth, at the risk of the prison and the scourge.

Are doctors of divinity blind, or are they hypocrites? I suppose some are the one, and some the other; but I think if they felt the interest in the poor and the lowly, that they ought to feel, they would not be so *easily* blinded. A clergyman who goes to the south, for the first time, has usually some feeling, however vague, that slavery is wrong. The slaveholder suspects this, and plays his game accordingly. He makes himself as agreeable as possible; talks on theology, and other kindred topics. The reverend gentleman is asked to invoke a blessing on a table loaded with luxuries. After dinner he walks round the premises, and sees the beautiful groves and flowering vines, and the comfortable huts of favored household slaves. The southerner invites him to talk with those slaves. He asks them if they want to be free, and they say, "O, no, massa." This is sufficient to satisfy him. He comes home to publish a "South Side View of Slavery," and to complain of the exaggerations of abolitionists. He assures people that he has been to the south, and seen slavery for himself; that it is a beautiful "patriarchal institution;" that the slaves don't want their freedom; that they have hallelujah meetings and other religious privileges.

What does *he* know of the half-starved wretches toiling from dawn till dark on the plantations? of mothers shrieking for their children, torn from their arms by slave traders? of young girls dragged down into moral filth? of pools of blood around the whipping post? of hounds trained to tear human flesh? of men screwed into cotton gins to die? The slaveholder showed him none of these things, and the slaves dared not tell of them if he had asked them.

There is a great difference between Christianity and religion at the south. If a man goes to the communion table, and pays money into the treasury of the church, no matter if it be the price of blood, he is called religious. If a pastor has offspring by a woman not his wife, the church dismiss him, if she is a white woman; but if she is colored, it does not hinder his continuing to be their good shepherd.

When I was told that Dr. Flint had joined the Episcopal church, I was much surprised. I supposed that religion had a purifying effect on the character of men; but the worst persecutions I endured from him were after he was a communicant. The conversation of the doctor, the day after he had been confirmed, certainly gave *me* no indication that he had "renounced the devil and all his works." In answer to some of his usual talk, I reminded him that he had just joined the church. "Yes, Linda," said he. "It was proper for me to do so. I am getting in years, and my position in society requires it, and it puts an end to all the damned slang. You would do well to join the church, too, Linda."

"There are sinners enough in it already," rejoined I. "If I could be allowed to live like a Christian, I should be glad."

"You can do what I require; and if you are faithful to me, you will be as virtuous as my wife," he replied.

I answered that the Bible didn't say so.

His voice became hoarse with rage. "How dare you preach to me about your infernal Bible!" he exclaimed. "What right have you, who are my negro, to talk to me about what you would like and what you wouldn't like? I am your master, and you shall obey me."

No wonder the slaves sing,—

> Ole Satan's church is here below;
> Up to God's free church I hope to go.

# XIV. ANOTHER LINK TO LIFE

I had not returned to my master's house since the birth of my child. The old man raved to have me thus removed from his immediate power; but his wife vowed, by all that was good and great, she would kill me if I came back; and he did not doubt her word. Sometimes he would stay away for a season. Then he would come and renew the old threadbare discourse about his forbearance and my ingratitude. He labored, most unnecessarily, to convince me that I had lowered myself. The venomous old reprobate had no need of descanting on that theme. I felt humiliated enough. My unconscious babe was the ever-present witness of my shame. I listened with silent contempt when he talked about my having forfeited *his* good opinion; but I shed bitter tears that I was no longer worthy of being respected by the good and pure. Alas! slavery still held me in its poisonous grasp. There was no chance for me to be respectable. There was no prospect of being able to lead a better life.

Sometimes, when my master found that I still refused to accept what he called his kind offers, he would threaten to sell my child. "Perhaps that will humble you," said he.

Humble *me*! Was I not already in the dust? But his threat lacerated my heart. I knew the law gave him power to fulfil it; for slaveholders have been cunning enough to enact that "the child shall follow the condition of the *mother*," not of the *father*, thus taking care that licentiousness shall not interfere with avarice. This reflection made me clasp my innocent babe all the more firmly to my heart. Horrid visions passed through my mind when I thought of his liability to fall into the slave trader's hands. I wept over him, and said, "O my child! perhaps they will leave you in some cold cabin to die, and then throw you into a hole, as if you were a dog."

When Dr. Flint learned that I was again to be a mother, he was exasperated beyond measure. He rushed from the house, and returned with a pair of shears. I had a fine head of hair; and he often railed about my pride of arranging it nicely. He cut every hair close to my head, storming and swearing all the time. I replied to some of his abuse, and he struck me. Some months before, he had pitched me down stairs in a fit of passion; and the injury I received was so serious that I was unable to turn myself in bed for many days. He then said, "Linda, I swear by God I will never raise my hand against you again;" but I knew that he would forget his promise.

After he discovered my situation, he was like a restless spirit from the pit. He came every day; and I was subjected to such insults as no pen can describe. I would not describe them if I could; they were too low, too revolting. I tried to keep them from my grandmother's knowledge as much as I could. I knew she had enough to sadden her life, without having my troubles to bear. When she saw the doctor treat me with violence, and heard him utter oaths terrible enough to palsy a man's tongue, she could not always hold her peace. It was natural and motherlike that she should try to defend me; but it only made matters worse.

When they told me my new-born babe was a girl, my heart was heavier than it had ever been before. Slavery is terrible for men; but it is far more terrible for women. Superadded to the burden common to all, *they* have wrongs, and sufferings, and mortifications peculiarly their own.

Dr. Flint had sworn that he would make me suffer, to my last day, for this new crime against *him*, as he called it; and as long as he had me in his power he kept his word. On the fourth day after the birth of my babe, he entered my room suddenly, and commanded me to rise and bring my baby to him. The nurse who took care of me had gone out of the room to prepare some nourishment, and I was alone. There was no alternative. I rose, took up my babe, and crossed the room to where he sat. "Now stand there," said he, "till I tell you to go back!" My child bore a strong resemblance to her father, and to the deceased Mrs. Sands, her grandmother. He noticed this; and while I stood before him, trembling with weakness, he heaped upon me and my little one every vile epithet he could think of. Even the grandmother in her grave did not escape his curses. In the midst of his vituperations I fainted at his feet. This recalled him to his senses. He took the baby from my arms, laid it on the bed, dashed cold water in my face, took me up, and shook me violently, to restore my consciousness before any one entered the room. Just then my grandmother came in, and he hurried out of the house. I suffered in consequence of this treatment; but I begged my friends to let me die, rather than send for the doctor. There was nothing I dreaded so much as his presence. My life was spared; and I was glad for the sake of my little ones. Had it not been for these ties to life, I should have been glad to be released by death, though I had lived only nineteen years.

Always it gave me a pang that my children had no lawful claim to a name. Their father offered his; but, if I had wished to accept the offer, I dared not while my master lived. Moreover, I knew it would not be accepted at their baptism. A Christian name they were at least entitled to; and we resolved to call my boy for our dear good Benjamin, who had gone far away from us.

My grandmother belonged to the church; and she was very desirous of having the children christened. I knew Dr. Flint would forbid it, and I did not venture to attempt it. But chance favored me. He was called to visit a patient out of town, and was obliged to be absent during Sunday. "Now is the time," said my grandmother; "we will take the children to church, and have them christened."

When I entered the church, recollections of my mother came over me, and I felt subdued in spirit. There she had presented me for baptism, without any reason to feel ashamed. She had been married, and had such legal rights as slavery allows to a slave. The vows had at least been sacred to *her*, and she had never violated them. I was glad she was not alive, to know under what different circumstances her grandchildren were presented for baptism. Why had my lot been so different from my mother's? *Her* master had died when she was a child; and she remained with her mistress till she married. She was never in the power of any master; and thus she escaped one class of the evils that generally fall upon slaves.

When my baby was about to be christened, the former mistress of my father stepped up to me, and proposed to give it her Christian name. To this I added the surname of my father, who had himself no legal right to it; for my grandfather on the paternal side was a white gentleman. What tangled skeins are the genealogies of slavery! I loved my father; but it mortified me to be obliged to bestow his name on my children.

When we left the church, my father's old mistress invited me to go home with her. She clasped a gold chain round my baby's neck. I thanked her for this kindness; but I did not like the emblem. I wanted no chain to be fastened on my daughter, not even if its links were of gold. How earnestly I prayed that she might never feel the weight of slavery's chain, whose iron entereth into the soul!

# XV. CONTINUED PERSECUTIONS

My children grew finely; and Dr. Flint would often say to me, with an exulting smile. "These brats will bring me a handsome sum of money one of these days."

I thought to myself that, God being my helper, they should never pass into his hands. It seemed to me I would rather see them killed than have them given up to his power. The money for the freedom of myself and my children could be obtained; but I derived no advantage from that circumstance. Dr. Flint loved money, but he loved power more. After much discussion, my friends resolved on making another trial. There was a slaveholder about to leave for Texas, and he was commissioned to buy me. He was to begin with nine hundred dollars, and go up to twelve. My master refused his offers. "Sir," said he, "she don't belong to me. She is my daughter's property, and I have no right to sell her. I mistrust that you come from her paramour. If so, you may tell him that he cannot buy her for any money; neither can he buy her children."

The doctor came to see me the next day, and my heart beat quicker as he entered. I never had seen the old man tread with so majestic a step. He seated himself and looked at me with withering scorn. My children had learned to be afraid of him. The little one would shut her eyes and hide her face on my shoulder whenever she saw him; and Benny, who was now nearly five years old, often inquired, "What makes that bad man come here so many times? Does he want to hurt us?" I would clasp the dear boy in my arms, trusting that he would be free before he was old enough to solve the problem. And now, as the doctor sat there so grim and silent, the child left his play and came and nestled up by me. At last my tormentor spoke. "So you are left in disgust, are you?" said he. "It is no more than I expected. You remember I told you years ago that you would be treated so. So he is tired of you? Ha! ha! ha! The virtuous madam don't like to hear about it, does she? Ha! ha! ha!" There was a sting in his calling me virtuous madam. I no longer had the power of answering him as I had formerly done. He continued: "So it seems you are trying to get up another intrigue. Your new paramour came to me, and offered to buy you; but you may be assured you will not succeed. You are mine; and you shall be mine for life. There lives no human being that can take you out of slavery. I would have done it; but you rejected my kind offer."

I told him I did not wish to get up any intrigue; that I had never seen the man who offered to buy me.

"Do you tell me I lie?" exclaimed he, dragging me from my chair. "Will you say again that you never saw that man?"

I answered, "I do say so."

He clinched my arm with a volley of oaths. Ben began to scream, and I told him to go to his grandmother.

"Don't you stir a step, you little wretch!" said he. The child drew nearer to me, and put his arms round me, as if he wanted to protect me. This was too much for my enraged master. He caught him up and hurled him across the room. I thought he was dead, and rushed towards him to take him up.

"Not yet!" exclaimed the doctor. "Let him lie there till he comes to."

"Let me go! Let me go!" I screamed, "or I will raise the whole house." I struggled and got away; but he clinched me again. Somebody opened the door, and he released me. I picked up my insensible child, and when I turned my tormentor was gone. Anxiously, I bent over the little form, so pale and still; and when the brown eyes at last opened, I don't know whether I was very happy. All the doctor's former persecutions were renewed. He came morning, noon, and night. No jealous lover ever watched a rival more closely than he watched me and the unknown slaveholder, with whom he accused me of wishing to get up an intrigue. When my grandmother was out of the way he searched every room to find him.

In one of his visits, he happened to find a young girl, whom he had sold to a trader a few days previous. His statement was, that he sold her because she had been too familiar with the overseer. She had had a bitter life with him, and was glad to be sold. She had no mother, and no near ties. She had been torn from all her family years before. A few friends had entered into bonds for her safety, if the trader would allow her to spend with them the time that intervened between her sale and the gathering up of his human stock. Such a favor was rarely granted. It saved the trader the expense of board and jail fees, and though the amount was small, it was a weighty consideration in a slavetrader's mind.

Dr. Flint always had an aversion to meeting slaves after he had sold them. He ordered Rose out of the house; but he was no longer her master, and she took no notice of him. For once the crushed Rose was the conqueror. His gray eyes flashed angrily upon her; but that was the extent of his power. "How came this girl here?" he exclaimed. "What right had you to allow it, when you knew I had sold her?"

I answered, "This is my grandmother's house, and Rose came to see her. I have no right to turn any body out of doors, that comes here for honest purposes."

He gave me the blow that would have fallen upon Rose if she had still been his slave. My grandmother's attention had been attracted by loud voices, and she entered in time to see a second blow dealt. She was not a woman to let such an outrage, in her own house, go unrebuked. The doctor undertook to explain that I had been insolent. Her indignant feelings rose higher and higher, and finally boiled over in words. "Get out of my house!" she exclaimed. "Go home, and take care of your wife and children, and you will have enough to do, without watching my family."

He threw the birth of my children in her face, and accused her of sanctioning the life I was leading. She told him I was living with her by compulsion of his wife; that he needn't accuse her, for he was the one to blame; he was the one who had caused all the trouble. She grew more and more excited as she went on. "I tell you what, Dr. Flint," said she, "you ain't got many more years to live, and you'd better be saying your prayers. It will take 'em all, and more too, to wash the dirt off your soul."

"Do you know whom you are talking to?" he exclaimed.

She replied, "Yes, I know very well who I am talking to."

He left the house in a great rage. I looked at my grandmother. Our eyes met. Their angry expression had passed away, but she looked sorrowful and weary—weary of incessant strife. I wondered that it did not lessen her love for me; but if it did she never showed it. She was always kind, always ready to sympathize with my troubles. There might have been peace and contentment in that humble home if it had not been for the demon Slavery.

The winter passed undisturbed by the doctor. The beautiful spring came; and when Nature resumes her loveliness, the human soul is apt to revive also. My drooping hopes came to life again with the flowers. I was dreaming of freedom again; more for my children's sake than my own. I planned and I planned. Obstacles hit against plans. There seemed no way of overcoming them; and yet I hoped.

Back came the wily doctor. I was not at home when he called. A friend had invited me to a small party, and to gratify her I went. To my great consternation, a messenger came in haste to say that Dr. Flint was at my grandmother's, and insisted on seeing me. They did not tell him where I was, or he would have come and raised a disturbance in my friend's house. They sent me a dark wrapper, I threw it on and hurried home. My speed did not save me; the doctor had gone away in anger. I dreaded the morning, but I could not delay it; it came, warm and bright. At an early hour the doctor came and asked me where I had been last night. I told him. He did not believe me, and sent to my friend's house to ascertain the facts. He came in the afternoon to assure me he was satisfied that I had spoken the truth. He seemed to be in a facetious mood, and I expected some jeers were coming. "I suppose you need some recreation," said he, "but I am surprised at your being there, among those negroes. It was not the place for *you*. Are you *allowed* to visit such people?"

I understood this covert fling at the white gentleman who was my friend; but I merely replied, "I went to visit my friends, and any company they keep is good enough for me."

He went on to say, "I have seen very little of you of late, but my interest in you is unchanged. When I said I would have no more mercy on you I was rash. I recall my words. Linda, you desire freedom for yourself and your children, and you can obtain it only through me. If you agree to what I am about to propose, you and they shall be free. There must be no communication of any kind between you and their father. I will procure a cottage, where you and the children can live together. Your labor shall be light, such as sewing for my family. Think what is offered you, Linda—a home and freedom! Let the past be forgotten. If I have been harsh with you at times, your wilfulness drove me to it. You know I exact obedience from my own children, and I consider you as yet a child."

He paused for an answer, but I remained silent.

"Why don't you speak?" said he. "What more do you wait for?"

"Nothing, sir."

"Then you accept my offer?"

"No, sir."

His anger was ready to break loose; but he succeeded in curbing it, and replied, "You have answered without thought. But I must let you know there are two sides to my proposition; if you reject the bright side, you will be obliged to take the dark one. You must either accept my offer, or you and your children shall be sent to your young master's plantation, there to remain till your young mistress is married; and your children shall fare like the rest of the negro children. I give you a week to consider it."

He was shrewd; but I knew he was not to be trusted. I told him I was ready to give my answer now.

"I will not receive it now," he replied. "You act too much from impulse. Remember that you and your children can be free a week from to-day if you choose."

On what a monstrous chance hung the destiny of my children! I knew that my master's offer was a snare, and that if I entered it escape would be impossible. As for his promise, I knew him so well that I was sure if he gave me free papers, they would be so managed as to have no legal value. The alternative was inevitable. I resolved to go to the plantation. But then I thought how completely I should be in his power, and the prospect was appalling. Even if I should kneel before him, and implore him to spare me, for the sake of my children, I knew he would spurn me with his foot, and my weakness would be his triumph.

Before the week expired, I heard that young Mr. Flint was about to be married to a lady of his own stamp. I foresaw the position I should occupy in his establishment. I had once been sent to the plantation for punishment, and fear of the son had induced the father to recall me very soon. My mind was made up; I was resolved that I would foil my master and save my children, or I would perish in the attempt. I kept my plans to myself; I knew that friends would try to dissuade me from them, and I would not wound their feelings by rejecting their advice.

On the decisive day the doctor came, and said he hoped I had made a wise choice.

"I am ready to go to the plantation, sir," I replied.

"Have you thought how important your decision is to your children?" said he.

I told him I had.

"Very well. Go to the plantation, and my curse go with you," he replied. "Your boy shall be put to work, and he shall soon be sold; and your girl shall be raised for the purpose of selling well. Go your own ways!" He left the room with curses, not to be repeated.

As I stood rooted to the spot, my grandmother came and said, "Linda, child, what did you tell him?"

I answered that I was going to the plantation.

"*Must* you go?" said she. "Can't something be done to stop it?"

I told her it was useless to try; but she begged me not to give up. She said she would go to the doctor, and remind him how long and how faithfully she had served in the family, and how she had taken her own baby from her breast to nourish his wife. She would tell him I had been out of the family so long they would not miss me; that she would pay them for my time, and the money would procure a woman who had more strength for the situation than I had. I begged her not to go; but she persisted in saying, "He will listen to *me*, Linda." She went, and was treated as I expected. He coolly listened to what she said, but denied her request. He told her that what he did was for my good, that my feelings were entirely above my situation, and that on the plantation I would receive treatment that was suitable to my behavior.

My grandmother was much cast down. I had my secret hopes; but I must fight my battle alone. I had a woman's pride, and a mother's love for my children; and I resolved that out of the darkness of this hour a brighter dawn should rise for them. My master had power and law on his side; I had a determined will. There is might in each.

# XVI. SCENES AT THE PLANTATION

Early the next morning I left my grandmother's with my youngest child. My boy was ill, and I left him behind. I had many sad thoughts as the old wagon jolted on. Hitherto, I had suffered alone; now, my little one was to be treated as a slave. As we drew near the great house, I thought of the time when I was formerly sent there out of revenge. I wondered for what purpose I was now sent. I could not tell. I resolved to obey orders so far as duty required; but within myself, I determined to make my stay as short as possible. Mr. Flint was waiting to receive us, and told me to follow him up stairs to receive orders for the day. My little Ellen was left below in the kitchen. It was a change for her, who had always been so carefully tended. My young master said she might amuse herself in the yard. This was kind of him, since the child was hateful to his sight. My task was to fit up the house for the reception of the bride. In the midst of sheets, tablecloths, towels, drapery, and carpeting, my head was as busy planning, as were my fingers with the needle. At noon I was allowed to go to Ellen. She had sobbed herself to sleep. I heard Mr. Flint say to a neighbor, "I've got her down here, and I'll soon take the town notions out of her head. My father is partly to blame for her nonsense. He ought to have broke her in long ago." The remark was made within my hearing, and it would have been quite as manly to have made it to my face. He *had* said things to my face which might, or might not, have surprised his neighbor if he had known of them. He was "a chip of the old block."

I resolved to give him no cause to accuse me of being too much of a lady, so far as work was concerned. I worked day and night, with wretchedness before me. When I lay down beside my child, I felt how much easier it would be to see her die than to see her master beat her about, as I daily saw him beat other little ones. The spirit of the mothers was so crushed by the lash, that they stood by, without courage to remonstrate. How much more must I suffer, before I should be "broke in" to that degree?

I wished to appear as contented as possible. Sometimes I had an opportunity to send a few lines home; and this brought up recollections that made it difficult, for a time, to seem calm and indifferent to my lot. Notwithstanding my efforts, I saw that Mr. Flint regarded me with a suspicious eye. Ellen broke down under the trials of her new life. Separated from me, with no one to look after her, she wandered about, and in a few days cried herself sick. One day, she sat under the window where I was at work, crying that weary cry which makes a mother's heart bleed. I was obliged to steel myself to bear it. After a while it ceased. I looked out, and she was gone. As it was near noon, I ventured to go down in search of her. The great house was raised two feet above the ground. I looked under it, and saw her about midway, fast asleep. I crept under and drew her out. As I held her in my arms, I thought how well it would be for her if she never waked up; and I uttered my thought aloud. I was startled to hear some one say, "Did you speak to me?" I looked up, and saw Mr. Flint standing beside me. He said nothing further, but turned, frowning, away. That night he sent Ellen a biscuit and a cup of sweetened milk. This generosity surprised me. I learned afterwards, that in the afternoon he had killed a large snake, which crept from under the house; and I supposed that incident had prompted his unusual kindness.

The next morning the old cart was loaded with shingles for town. I put Ellen into it, and sent her to her grandmother. Mr. Flint said I ought to have asked his permission. I told him the child was sick, and required attention which I had no time to give. He let it pass; for he was aware that I had accomplished much work in a little time.

I had been three weeks on the plantation, when I planned a visit home. It must be at night, after every body was in bed. I was six miles from town, and the road was very dreary. I was to go with a young man, who, I knew, often stole to town to see his mother. One night, when all was quiet, we started. Fear gave speed to our steps, and we were not long in performing the journey. I arrived at my grandmother's. Her bed room was on the first floor, and the window was open, the weather being warm. I spoke to her and she awoke. She let me in and closed the window, lest some late passer-by should see me. A light was brought, and the whole household gathered round me, some smiling and some crying. I went to look at my children, and thanked God for their happy sleep. The tears fell as I leaned over them. As

I moved to leave, Benny stirred. I turned back, and whispered, "Mother is here." After digging at his eyes with his little fist, they opened, and he sat up in bed, looking at me curiously. Having satisfied himself that it was I, he exclaimed, "O mother! you ain't dead, are you? They didn't cut off your head at the plantation, did they?"

My time was up too soon, and my guide was waiting for me. I laid Benny back in his bed, and dried his tears by a promise to come again soon. Rapidly we retraced our steps back to the plantation. About half way we were met by a company of four patrols. Luckily we heard their horse's hoofs before they came in sight, and we had time to hide behind a large tree. They passed, hallooing and shouting in a manner that indicated a recent carousal. How thankful we were that they had not their dogs with them! We hastened our footsteps, and when we arrived on the plantation we heard the sound of the hand-mill. The slaves were grinding their corn. We were safely in the house before the horn summoned them to their labor. I divided my little parcel of food with my guide, knowing that he had lost the chance of grinding his corn, and must toil all day in the field.

Mr. Flint often took an inspection of the house, to see that no one was idle. The entire management of the work was trusted to me, because he knew nothing about it; and rather than hire a superintendent he contented himself with my arrangements. He had often urged upon his father the necessity of having me at the plantation to take charge of his affairs, and make clothes for the slaves; but the old man knew him too well to consent to that arrangement.

When I had been working a month at the plantation, the great aunt of Mr. Flint came to make him a visit. This was the good old lady who paid fifty dollars for my grandmother, for the purpose of making her free, when she stood on the auction block. My grandmother loved this old lady, whom we all called Miss Fanny. She often came to take tea with us. On such occasions the table was spread with a snow-white cloth, and the china cups and silver spoons were taken from the old-fashioned buffet. There were hot muffins, tea rusks, and delicious sweetmeats. My grandmother kept two cows, and the fresh cream was Miss Fanny's delight. She invariably declared that it was the best in town. The old ladies had cosey times together. They would work and chat, and sometimes, while talking over old times, their spectacles would get dim with tears, and would have to be taken off and wiped. When Miss Fanny bade us good by, her bag was filled with grandmother's best cakes, and she was urged to come again soon.

There had been a time when Dr. Flint's wife came to take tea with us, and when her children were also sent to have a feast of "Aunt Marthy's" nice cooking. But after I became an object of her jealousy and spite, she was angry with grandmother for giving a shelter to me and my children. She would not even speak to her in the street. This wounded my grandmother's feelings, for she could not retain ill will against the woman whom she had nourished with her milk when a babe. The doctor's wife would gladly have prevented our intercourse with Miss Fanny if she could have done it, but fortunately she was not dependent on the bounty of the Flints. She had enough to be independent; and that is more than can ever be gained from charity, however lavish it may be.

Miss Fanny was endeared to me by many recollections, and I was rejoiced to see her at the plantation. The warmth of her large, loyal heart made the house seem pleasanter while she was in it. She staid a week, and I had many talks with her. She said her principal object in coming was to see how I was treated, and whether any thing could be done for me. She inquired whether she could help me in any way. I told her I believed not. She condoled with me in her own peculiar way; saying she wished that I and all my grandmother's family were at rest in our graves, for not until then should she feel any peace about us. The good old soul did not dream that I was planning to bestow peace upon her, with regard to myself and my children; not by death, but by securing our freedom.

Again and again I had traversed those dreary twelve miles, to and from the town; and all the way, I was meditating upon some means of escape for myself and my children. My friends had made every effort that ingenuity could devise to effect our purchase, but all their plans had proved abortive. Dr. Flint was suspicious, and determined not to loosen his grasp upon us. I could have made my escape alone; but it was more for my helpless children than for myself that I longed for freedom. Though the boon would have been precious to me, above all price, I would not have taken it at the expense of leaving them in slavery. Every trial I endured, every sacrifice I made for their sakes, drew them closer to my heart, and gave me fresh courage to beat back the dark waves that rolled and rolled over me in a seemingly endless night of storms.

The six weeks were nearly completed, when Mr. Flint's bride was expected to take possession of her new home. The arrangements were all completed, and Mr. Flint said I had done well. He expected to leave home on Saturday, and return with his bride the following Wednesday. After receiving various orders from him, I ventured to ask permission to spend Sunday in town. It was granted; for which favor I was thankful. It was the first I had ever asked of him, and I intended it should be the last. I needed more than one night to accomplish the project I had in view; but the whole of Sunday would give me an opportunity. I spent the Sabbath with my grandmother. A calmer, more beautiful day never came down out of heaven. To me it was a day of conflicting emotions. Perhaps it was the last day I should ever spend under that dear, old sheltering roof! Perhaps these were the last talks I should ever have with the faithful old friend of my whole life! Perhaps it was the last time I and my children should be together! Well, better so, I thought, than that they should be slaves. I knew the doom that awaited my fair baby in slavery, and I determined to save her from it, or perish in the attempt. I went to make this vow at the graves of my poor parents, in the burying-ground of the slaves. "There the wicked cease from troubling, and there the weary be at rest. There the prisoners rest together; they hear not the voice of the oppressor; the servant is free from his master." I knelt by the graves of my parents, and thanked God, as I had often done before, that they had not lived to witness my trials, or to mourn over my sins. I had received my mother's blessing when she died; and in many an hour of tribulation I had seemed to hear her voice, sometimes chiding me, sometimes whispering loving words into my wounded heart. I have shed many and bitter tears, to think that when I am gone from my children they cannot remember me with such entire satisfaction as I remembered my mother.

The graveyard was in the woods, and twilight was coming on. Nothing broke the death-like stillness except the occasional twitter of a bird. My spirit was overawed by the solemnity of the scene. For more than ten years I had frequented this spot, but never had it seemed to me so sacred as now. A black stump, at the head of my mother's grave, was all that remained of a tree my father had planted. His grave was marked by a small wooden board, bearing his name, the letters of which were nearly obliterated. I knelt down and kissed them, and poured forth a prayer to God for guidance and support in the perilous step I was about to take. As I passed the wreck of the old meeting house, where, before Nat Turner's time, the slaves had been allowed to meet for worship, I seemed to hear my father's voice come from it, bidding me not to tarry till I reached freedom or the grave. I rushed on with renovated hopes. My trust in God had been strengthened by that prayer among the graves.

My plan was to conceal myself at the house of a friend, and remain there a few weeks till the search was over. My hope was that the doctor would get discouraged, and, for fear of losing my value, and also of subsequently finding my children among the missing, he would consent to sell us; and I knew somebody would buy us. I had done all in my power to make my children comfortable during the time I expected to be separated from them. I was packing my things, when grandmother came into the room, and asked what I was doing. "I am putting my things in order," I replied. I tried to look and speak cheerfully; but her watchful eye detected something beneath the surface. She drew me towards her, and asked me to sit down. She looked earnestly at me, and said, "Linda, do you want to kill your old grandmother? Do you mean to leave your little, helpless children? I am old now, and cannot do for your babies as I once did for you."

I replied, that if I went away, perhaps their father would be able to secure their freedom.

"Ah, my child," said she, "don't trust too much to him. Stand by your own children, and suffer with them till death. Nobody respects a mother who forsakes her children; and if you leave them, you will never have a happy moment. If you go, you will make me miserable the short time I have to live. You would be taken and brought back, and your sufferings would be dreadful. Remember poor Benjamin. Do give it up, Linda. Try to bear a little longer. Things may turn out better than we expect."

My courage failed me, in view of the sorrow I should bring on that faithful, loving old heart. I promised that I would try longer, and that I would take nothing out of her house without her knowledge.

Whenever the children climbed on my knee, or laid their heads on my lap, she would say, "Poor little souls! what would you do without a mother? She don't love you as I do." And she would hug them to her own bosom, as if to reproach me for my want of affection; but she knew all the while that I loved them better than my life. I slept with her that night, and it was the last time. The memory of it haunted me for many a year.

On Monday I returned to the plantation, and busied myself with preparations for the important day. Wednesday came. It was a beautiful day, and the faces of the slaves were as bright as the sunshine. The poor creatures were merry. They were expecting little presents from the bride, and hoping for better times under her administration. I had no such hopes for them. I knew that the young wives of slaveholders often thought their authority and importance would be best established and maintained by cruelty; and what I had heard of young Mrs. Flint gave me no reason to expect that her rule over them would be less severe than that of the master and overseer. Truly, the colored race are the most cheerful and forgiving people on the face of the earth. That their masters sleep in safety is owing to their superabundance of heart; and yet they look upon their sufferings with less pity than they would bestow on those of a horse or a dog.

I stood at the door with others to receive the bridegroom and bride. She was a handsome, delicate-looking girl, and her face flushed with emotion at sight of her new home. I thought it likely that visions of a happy future were rising before her. It made me sad; for I knew how soon clouds would come over her sunshine. She examined every part of the house, and told me she was delighted with the arrangements I had made. I was afraid old Mrs. Flint had tried to prejudice her against me, and I did my best to please her.

All passed off smoothly for me until dinner time arrived. I did not mind the embarrassment of waiting on a dinner party, for the first time in my life, half so much as I did the meeting with Dr. Flint and his wife, who would be among the guests. It was a mystery to me why Mrs. Flint had not made her appearance at the plantation during all the time I was putting the house in order. I had not met her, face to face, for five years, and I had no wish to see her now. She was a praying woman, and, doubtless, considered my present position a special answer to her prayers. Nothing could please her better than to see me humbled and trampled upon. I was just where she would have me—in the power of a hard, unprincipled master. She did not speak to me when she took her seat at table; but her satisfied, triumphant smile, when I handed her plate, was more eloquent than words. The old doctor was not so quiet in his demonstrations. He ordered me here and there, and spoke with peculiar emphasis when he said "your *mistress*." I was drilled like a disgraced soldier. When all was over, and the last key turned, I sought my pillow, thankful that God had appointed a season of rest for the weary.

The next day my new mistress began her housekeeping. I was not exactly appointed maid of all work; but I was to do whatever I was told. Monday evening came. It was always a busy time. On that night the slaves received their weekly allowance of food. Three pounds of meat, a peck of corn, and perhaps a dozen herring were allowed to each man. Women received a pound and a half of meat, a peck of corn, and the same number of herring. Children over twelve years old had half the allowance of the women. The meat was cut and weighed by the foreman of the field hands, and piled on planks before the meat house. Then the second foreman went behind the building, and when the first foreman called out, "Who takes this piece of meat?" he answered by calling somebody's name. This method was resorted to as a means of preventing partiality in distributing the meat. The young mistress came out to see how things were done on her plantation, and she soon gave a specimen of her character. Among those in waiting for their allowance was a very old slave, who had faithfully served the Flint family through three generations. When he hobbled up to get his bit of meat, the mistress said he was too old to have any allowance; that when niggers were too old to work, they ought to be fed on grass. Poor old man! He suffered much before he found rest in the grave.

My mistress and I got along very well together. At the end of a week, old Mrs. Flint made us another visit, and was closeted a long time with her daughter-in-law. I had my suspicions what was the subject of the conference. The old doctor's wife had been informed that I could leave the plantation on one condition, and she was very desirous to keep me there. If she had trusted me, as I deserved to be trusted by her, she would have had no fears of my accepting that condition. When she entered her carriage to return home, she said to young Mrs. Flint, "Don't neglect to send for them as quick as possible." My heart was on the watch all the time, and I at once concluded that she spoke of my children. The doctor came the next day, and as I entered the room to spread the tea table, I heard him say, "Don't wait any longer. Send for them to-morrow." I saw through the plan. They thought my children's being there would fetter me to the spot, and that it was a good place to break us all in to abject submission to our lot as slaves. After the doctor left, a gentleman called, who had always manifested friendly feelings towards my grandmother and her family. Mr. Flint carried him over the plantation to show him the results of labor performed by men and women who were unpaid, miserably clothed, and half famished. The cotton crop was all they thought of. It was duly admired, and the gentleman returned with specimens to show his friends. I was ordered to carry water to wash his hands. As I did so, he said, "Linda, how do you like your new home?" I told him I liked it as well as I expected. He replied, "They don't think you are contented, and to-morrow they are going to bring your children to be with you. I am sorry for you, Linda. I hope they will treat you kindly." I hurried from the room, unable to thank him. My suspicions were correct. My children were to be brought to the plantation to be "broke in."

To this day I feel grateful to the gentleman who gave me this timely information. It nerved me to immediate action.

# XVII. THE FLIGHT

Mr. Flint was hard pushed for house servants, and rather than lose me he had restrained his malice. I did my work faithfully, though not, of course, with a willing mind. They were evidently afraid I should leave them. Mr. Flint wished that I should sleep in the great house instead of the servants' quarters. His wife agreed to the proposition, but said I mustn't bring my bed into the house, because it would scatter feathers on her carpet. I knew when I went there that they would never think of such a thing as furnishing a bed of any kind for me and my little ones. I therefore carried my own bed, and now I was forbidden to use it. I did as I was ordered. But now that I was certain my children were to be put in their power, in order to give them a stronger hold on me, I resolved to leave them that night. I remembered the grief this step would bring upon my dear old grandmother, and nothing less than the freedom of my children would have induced me to disregard her advice. I went about my evening work with trembling steps. Mr. Flint twice called from his chamber door to inquire why the house was not locked up. I replied that I had not done my work. "You have had time enough to do it," said he. "Take care how you answer me!"

I shut all the windows, locked all the doors, and went up to the third story, to wait till midnight. How long those hours seemed, and how fervently I prayed that God would not forsake me in this hour of utmost need! I was about to risk every thing on the throw of a die; and if I failed, O what would become of me and my poor children? They would be made to suffer for my fault.

At half past twelve I stole softly down stairs. I stopped on the second floor, thinking I heard a noise. I felt my way down into the parlor, and looked out of the window. The night was so intensely dark that I could see nothing. I raised the window very softly and jumped out. Large drops of rain were falling, and the darkness bewildered me. I dropped on my knees, and breathed a short prayer to God for guidance and protection. I groped my way to the road, and rushed towards the town with almost lightning speed. I arrived at my grandmother's house, but dared not see her. She would say, "Linda, you are killing me;" and I knew that would unnerve me. I tapped softly at the window of a room, occupied by a woman, who had lived in the house several years. I knew she was a faithful friend, and could be trusted with my secret. I tapped several times before she heard me. At last she raised the window, and I whispered, "Sally, I have run away. Let me in, quick." She opened the door softly, and said in low tones, "For God's sake, don't. Your grandmother is trying to buy you and de chillern. Mr. Sands was here last week. He tole her he was going away on business, but he wanted her to go ahead about buying you and de chillern, and he would help her all he could. Don't run away, Linda. Your grandmother is all bowed down wid trouble now."

I replied, "Sally, they are going to carry my children to the plantation to-morrow; and they will never sell them to any body so long as they have me in their power. Now, would you advise me to go back?"

"No, chile, no," answered she. "When dey finds you is gone, dey won't want de plague ob de chillern; but where is you going to hide? Dey knows ebery inch ob dis house."

I told her I had a hiding-place, and that was all it was best for her to know. I asked her to go into my room as soon as it was light, and take all my clothes out of my trunk, and pack them in hers; for I knew Mr. Flint and the constable would be there early to search my room. I feared the sight of my children would be too much for my full heart; but I could not go into the uncertain future without one last look. I bent over the bed where lay my little Benny and baby Ellen. Poor little ones! fatherless and motherless! Memories of their father came over me. He wanted to be kind to them; but they were not all to him, as they were to my womanly heart. I knelt and prayed for the innocent little sleepers. I kissed them lightly, and turned away.

As I was about to open the street door, Sally laid her hand on my shoulder, and said, "Linda, is you gwine all alone? Let me call your uncle."

"No, Sally," I replied, "I want no one to be brought into trouble on my account."

I went forth into the darkness and rain. I ran on till I came to the house of the friend who was to conceal me.

Early the next morning Mr. Flint was at my grandmother's inquiring for me. She told him she had not seen me, and supposed I was at the plantation. He watched her face narrowly, and said, "Don't you know any thing about her running off?" She assured him that she did not. He went on to say, "Last night she ran off without the least provocation. We had treated her very kindly. My wife liked her. She will soon be found and brought back. Are her children with you?" When told that they were, he said, "I am very glad to hear that. If they are here, she cannot be far off. If I find out that any of my niggers have had any thing to do with this damned business, I'll give 'em five hundred lashes." As he started to go to his father's, he turned round and added, persuasively, "Let her be brought back, and she shall have her children to live with her."

The tidings made the old doctor rave and storm at a furious rate. It was a busy day for them. My grandmother's house was searched from top to bottom. As my trunk was empty, they concluded I had taken my clothes with me. Before ten o'clock every vessel northward bound was thoroughly examined, and the law against harboring fugitives was read to all on board. At night a watch was set over the town. Knowing how distressed my grandmother would be, I wanted to send her a message; but it could not be done. Every one who went in or out of her house was closely watched. The doctor said he would take my children, unless she became responsible for them; which of course she willingly did. The next day was spent in searching. Before night, the following advertisement was posted at every corner, and in every public place for miles round:—

> $300 REWARD! Ran away from the subscriber, an intelligent, bright, mulatto girl, named Linda, 21 years of age. Five feet four inches high. Dark eyes, and black hair inclined to curl; but it can be made straight. Has a decayed spot on a front tooth. She can read and write, and in all probability will try to get to the Free States. All persons

are forbidden, under penalty of law, to harbor or employ said slave. $150 will be given to whoever takes her in the state, and $300 if taken out of the state and delivered to me, or lodged in jail.

DR. FLINT.

# XVIII. MONTHS OF PERIL

The search for me was kept up with more perseverence than I had anticipated. I began to think that escape was impossible. I was in great anxiety lest I should implicate the friend who harbored me. I knew the consequences would be frightful; and much as I dreaded being caught, even that seemed better than causing an innocent person to suffer for kindness to me. A week had passed in terrible suspense, when my pursuers came into such close vicinity that I concluded they had tracked me to my hiding-place. I flew out of the house, and concealed myself in a thicket of bushes. There I remained in an agony of fear for two hours. Suddenly, a reptile of some kind seized my leg. In my fright, I struck a blow which loosened its hold, but I could not tell whether I had killed it; it was so dark, I could not see what it was; I only knew it was something cold and slimy. The pain I felt soon indicated that the bite was poisonous. I was compelled to leave my place of concealment, and I groped my way back into the house. The pain had become intense, and my friend was startled by my look of anguish. I asked her to prepare a poultice of warm ashes and vinegar, and I applied it to my leg, which was already much swollen. The application gave me some relief, but the swelling did not abate. The dread of being disabled was greater than the physical pain I endured. My friend asked an old woman, who doctored among the slaves, what was good for the bite of a snake or a lizard. She told her to steep a dozen coppers in vinegar, over night, and apply the cankered vinegar to the inflamed part.[1]

I had succeeded in cautiously conveying some messages to my relatives. They were harshly threatened, and despairing of my having a chance to escape, they advised me to return to my master, ask his forgiveness, and let him make an example of me. But such counsel had no influence with me. When I started upon this hazardous undertaking, I had resolved that, come what would, there should be

---

[Footnote 1: The poison of a snake is a powerful acid, and is counteracted by powerful alkalies, such as potash, ammonia, &c. The Indians are accustomed to apply wet ashes, or plunge the limb into strong lie. White men, employed to lay out railroads in snaky places, often carry ammonia with them as an antidote.—EDITOR.]

no turning back. "Give me liberty, or give me death," was my motto. When my friend contrived to make known to my relatives the painful situation I had been in for twenty-four hours, they said no more about my going back to my master. Something must be done, and that speedily; but where to return for help, they knew not. God in his mercy raised up "a friend in need."

Among the ladies who were acquainted with my grandmother, was one who had known her from childhood, and always been very friendly to her. She had also known my mother and her children, and felt interested for them. At this crisis of affairs she called to see my grandmother, as she not unfrequently did. She observed the sad and troubled expression of her face, and asked if she knew where Linda was, and whether she was safe. My grandmother shook her head, without answering. "Come, Aunt Martha," said the kind lady, "tell me all about it. Perhaps I can do something to help you." The husband of this lady held many slaves, and bought and sold slaves. She also held a number in her own name; but she treated them kindly, and would never allow any of them to be sold. She was unlike the majority of slaveholders' wives. My grandmother looked earnestly at her. Something in the expression of her face said "Trust me!" and she did trust her. She listened attentively to the details of my story, and sat thinking for a while. At last she said, "Aunt Martha, I pity you both. If you think there is any chance of Linda's getting to the Free States, I will conceal her for a time. But first you must solemnly promise that my name shall never be mentioned. If such a thing should become known, it would ruin me and my family. No one in my house must know of it, except the cook. She is so faithful that I would trust my own life with her; and I know she likes Linda. It is a great risk; but I trust no harm will come of it. Get word to Linda to be ready as soon as it is dark, before the patrols are out. I will send the housemaids on errands, and Betty shall go to meet Linda." The place where we were to meet was designated and agreed upon. My grandmother was unable to thank the lady for this noble deed; overcome by her emotions, she sank on her knees and sobbed like a child.

I received a message to leave my friend's house at such an hour, and go to a certain place where a friend would be waiting for me. As a matter of prudence no names were mentioned. I had no means of conjecturing who I was to meet, or where I was going. I did not like to move thus blindfolded, but I had no choice. It would not do for me to remain where I was. I disguised myself, summoned up courage to meet the worst, and went to the appointed place. My friend Betty was there; she was the last person I expected to see. We hurried along in silence. The pain in my leg was so intense that it seemed as if I should drop but fear gave me strength. We reached the house and entered unobserved. Her first words were: "Honey, now you is safe. Dem devils ain't coming to search *dis* house. When I get you into missis' safe place, I will bring some nice hot supper. I specs you need it after all dis skeering." Betty's vocation led her to think eating the most important thing in life. She did not realize that my heart was too full for me to care much about supper.

The mistress came to meet us, and led me up stairs to a small room over her own sleeping apartment. "You will be safe here, Linda," said she; "I keep this room to store away things that are out of use. The girls are not accustomed to be sent to it, and they will not suspect any thing unless they hear some noise. I always keep it locked, and Betty shall take care of the key. But you must be very careful, for my sake as well as your own; and you must never tell my secret; for it would ruin me and my family. I will keep the girls busy in the morning, that Betty may have a chance to bring your breakfast; but it will not do for her to come to you again till night. I will come to see you sometimes. Keep up your courage. I hope this state of things will not last long." Betty came with the "nice hot supper," and the mistress hastened down stairs to keep things straight till she returned. How my heart overflowed with gratitude! Words choked in my throat; but I could have kissed the feet of my benefactress. For that deed of Christian womanhood, may God forever bless her!

I went to sleep that night with the feeling that I was for the present the most fortunate slave in town. Morning came and filled my little cell with light. I thanked the heavenly Father for this safe retreat. Opposite my window was a pile of feather beds. On the top of these I could lie perfectly concealed, and command a view of the street through which Dr. Flint passed to his office. Anxious as I was, I felt a gleam of satisfaction when I saw him. Thus far I had outwitted him, and I triumphed over it. Who can blame slaves for being cunning?

They are constantly compelled to resort to it. It is the only weapon of the weak and oppressed against the strength of their tyrants.

I was daily hoping to hear that my master had sold my children; for I knew who was on the watch to buy them. But Dr. Flint cared even more for revenge than he did for money. My brother William and the good aunt who had served in his family twenty years, and my little Benny, and Ellen, who was a little over two years old, were thrust into jail, as a means of compelling my relatives to give some information about me. He swore my grandmother should never see one of them again till I was brought back. They kept these facts from me for several days. When I heard that my little ones were in a loathsome jail, my first impulse was to go to them. I was encountering dangers for the sake of freeing them, and must I be the cause of their death? The thought was agonizing. My benefactress tried to soothe me by telling me that my aunt would take good care of the children while they remained in jail. But it added to my pain to think that the good old aunt, who had always been so kind to her sister's orphan children, should be shut up in prison for no other crime than loving them. I suppose my friends feared a reckless movement on my part, knowing, as they did, that my life was bound up in my children. I received a note from my brother William. It was scarcely legible, and ran thus: "Wherever you are, dear sister, I beg of you not to come here. We are all much better off than you are. If you come, you will ruin us all. They would force you to tell where you had been, or they would kill you. Take the advice of your friends; if not for the sake of me and your children, at least for the sake of those you would ruin."

Poor William! He also must suffer for being my brother. I took his advice and kept quiet. My aunt was taken out of jail at the end of a month, because Mrs. Flint could not spare her any longer. She was tired of being her own housekeeper. It was quite too fatiguing to order her dinner and eat it too. My children remained in jail, where brother William did all he could for their comfort. Betty went to see them sometimes, and brought me tidings. She was not permitted to enter the jail; but William would hold them up to the grated window while she chatted with them. When she repeated their prattle, and told me how they wanted to see their ma, my tears would flow. Old Betty would exclaim, "Lors, chile! what's you crying 'bout? Dem young uns vil kill you dead. Don't be so chick'n hearted! If you does, you vil nebber git thro' dis world."

Good old soul! She had gone through the world childless. She had never had little ones to clasp their arms round her neck; she had never seen their soft eyes looking into hers; no sweet little voices had called her mother; she had never pressed her own infants to her heart, with the feeling that even in fetters there was something to live for. How could she realize my feelings? Betty's husband loved children dearly, and wondered why God had denied them to him. He expressed great sorrow when he came to Betty with the tidings that Ellen had been taken out of jail and carried to Dr. Flint's. She had the measles a short time before they carried her to jail, and the disease had left her eyes affected. The doctor had taken her home to attend to them. My children had always been afraid of the doctor and his wife. They had never been inside of their house. Poor little Ellen cried all day to be carried back to prison. The instincts of childhood are true. She knew she was loved in the jail. Her screams and sobs annoyed Mrs. Flint. Before night she called one of the slaves, and said, "Here, Bill, carry this brat back to the jail. I can't stand her noise. If she would be quiet I should like to keep the little minx. She would make a handy waiting-maid for my daughter by and by. But if she staid here, with her white face, I suppose I should either kill her or spoil her. I hope the doctor will sell them as far as wind and water can carry them. As for their mother, her ladyship will find out yet what she gets by running away. She hasn't so much feeling for her children as a cow has for its calf. If she had, she would have come back long ago, to get them out of jail, and save all this expense and trouble. The good-for-nothing hussy! When she is caught, she shall stay in jail, in irons, for one six months, and then be sold to a sugar plantation. I shall see her broke in yet. What do you stand there for, Bill? Why don't you go off with the brat? Mind, now, that you don't let any of the niggers speak to her in the street!"

When these remarks were reported to me, I smiled at Mrs. Flint's saying that she should either kill my child or spoil her. I thought to myself there was very little danger of the latter. I have always considered it as one of God's special providences that Ellen screamed till she was carried back to jail.

That same night Dr. Flint was called to a patient, and did not return till near morning. Passing my grandmother's, he saw a light in the house, and thought to himself, "Perhaps this has something to do with Linda." He knocked, and the door was opened. "What calls you up so early?" said he. "I saw your light, and I thought I would just stop and tell you that I have found out where Linda is. I know where to put my hands on her, and I shall have her before twelve o'clock." When he had turned away, my grandmother and my uncle looked anxiously at each other. They did not know whether or not it was merely one of the doctor's tricks to frighten them. In their uncertainty, they thought it was best to have a message conveyed to my friend Betty. Unwilling to alarm her mistress, Betty resolved to dispose of me herself. She came to me, and told me to rise and dress quickly. We hurried down stairs, and across the yard, into the kitchen. She locked the door, and lifted up a plank in the floor. A buffalo skin and a bit of carpet were spread for me to lie on, and a quilt thrown over me. "Stay dar," said she, "till I sees if dey know 'bout you. Dey say dey vil put thar hans on you afore twelve o'clock. If dey *did* know whar you are, dey won't know *now*. Dey'll be disapinted dis time. Dat's all I got to say. If dey comes rummagin 'mong *my* tings, de'll get one bressed sarssin from dis 'ere nigger." In my shallow bed I had but just room enough to bring my hands to my face to keep the dust out of my eyes; for Betty walked over me twenty times in an hour, passing from the dresser to the fireplace. When she was alone, I could hear her pronouncing anathemas over Dr. Flint and all his tribe, every now and then saying, with a chuckling laugh, "Dis nigger's too cute for 'em dis time." When the housemaids were about, she had sly ways of drawing them out, that I might hear what they would say. She would repeat stories she had heard about my being in this, or that, or the other place. To which they would answer, that I was not fool enough to be staying round there; that I was in Philadelphia or New York before this time. When all were abed and asleep, Betty raised the plank, and said, "Come out, chile; come out. Dey don't know nottin 'bout you. Twas only white folks' lies, to skeer de niggers."

Some days after this adventure I had a much worse fright. As I sat very still in my retreat above stairs, cheerful visions floated through my mind. I thought Dr. Flint would soon get discouraged, and would be willing to sell my children, when he lost all hopes of making them the means of my discovery. I knew who was ready to buy them. Suddenly I heard a voice that chilled my blood. The sound was too familiar to me, it had been too dreadful, for me not to recognize at once my old master. He was in the house, and I at once concluded he had come to seize me. I looked round in terror. There was no way of escape. The voice receded. I supposed the constable was with him, and they were searching the house. In my alarm I did not forget the trouble I was bringing on my generous benefactress. It seemed as if I were born to bring sorrow on all who befriended me, and that was the bitterest drop in the bitter cup of my life. After a while I heard approaching footsteps; the key was turned in my door. I braced myself against the wall to keep from falling. I ventured to look up, and there stood my kind benefactress alone. I was too much overcome to speak, and sunk down upon the floor.

"I thought you would hear your master's voice," she said; "and knowing you would be terrified, I came to tell you there is nothing to fear. You may even indulge in a laugh at the old gentleman's expense. He is so sure you are in New York, that he came to borrow five hundred dollars to go in pursuit of you. My sister had some money to loan on interest. He has obtained it, and proposes to start for New York to-night. So, for the present, you see you are safe. The doctor will merely lighten his pocket hunting after the bird he has left behind."

# XIX. THE CHILDREN SOLD

The Doctor came back from New York, of course without accomplishing his purpose. He had expended considerable money, and was rather disheartened. My brother and the children had now been in jail two months, and that also was some expense. My friends thought it was a favorable time to work on his discouraged feelings. Mr. Sands sent a speculator to offer him nine hundred dollars for my brother William, and eight hundred for the two children. These were high prices, as slaves were then selling; but the offer was rejected. If it had been merely a question of money, the doctor would have sold any boy of Benny's age for two hundred dollars; but he could not bear to give up the power of revenge. But he was hard pressed for money, and he revolved the matter in his mind. He knew that if he could keep Ellen till she was fifteen, he could sell her for a high price; but I presume he reflected that she might die, or might be stolen away. At all events, he came to the conclusion that he had better accept the slave-trader's offer. Meeting him in the street, he inquired when he would leave town. "To-day, at ten o'clock," he replied. "Ah, do you go so soon?" said the doctor. "I have been reflecting upon your proposition, and I have concluded to let you have the three negroes if you will say nineteen hundred dollars." After some parley, the trader agreed to his terms. He wanted the bill of sale drawn up and signed immediately, as he had a great deal to attend to during the short time he remained in town. The doctor went to the jail and told William he would take him back into his service if he would promise to behave himself but he replied that he would rather be sold. "And you *shall* be sold, you ungrateful rascal!" exclaimed the doctor. In less than an hour the money was paid, the papers were signed, sealed, and delivered, and my brother and children were in the hands of the trader.

It was a hurried transaction; and after it was over, the doctor's characteristic caution returned. He went back to the speculator, and said, "Sir, I have come to lay you under obligations of a thousand dollars not to sell any of those negroes in this state." "You come too late," replied the trader; "our bargain is closed." He had, in fact, already sold them to Mr. Sands, but he did not mention it. The doctor required him to put irons on "that rascal, Bill," and to pass through the back streets when he took his gang out of town. The trader was privately instructed to concede to his wishes. My good old aunt went to the jail to bid the children good by, supposing them to be the speculator's property, and that she should never see them again. As she held Benny in her lap, he said, "Aunt Nancy, I want to show you something." He led her to the door and showed her a long row of marks, saying, "Uncle Will taught me to count. I have made a mark for every day I have been here, and it is sixty days. It is a long time; and the speculator is going to take me and Ellen away. He's a bad man. It's wrong for him to take grandmother's children. I want to go to my mother."

My grandmother was told that the children would be restored to her, but she was requested to act as if they were really to be sent away. Accordingly, she made up a bundle of clothes and went to the jail. When she arrived, she found William handcuffed among the gang, and the children in the trader's cart. The scene seemed too much like reality. She was afraid there might have been some deception or mistake. She fainted, and was carried home.

When the wagon stopped at the hotel, several gentlemen came out and proposed to purchase William, but the trader refused their offers, without stating that he was already sold. And now came the trying hour for that drove of human beings, driven away like cattle, to be sold they knew not where. Husbands were torn from wives, parents from children, never to look upon each other again this side the grave. There was wringing of hands and cries of despair.

Dr. Flint had the supreme satisfaction of seeing the wagon leave town, and Mrs. Flint had the gratification of supposing that my children were going "as far as wind and water would carry them." According to agreement, my uncle followed the wagon some miles, until they came to an old farm house. There the trader took the irons from William, and as he did so, he said, "You are a damned clever fellow. I should like to own you myself. Them gentlemen that wanted to buy you said you was a bright, honest chap, and I must git you a good home. I guess your old master will swear to-morrow, and call himself an old fool for selling the children. I reckon he'll never git their mammy back again. I expect she's made tracks for the north. Good by, old boy. Remember, I have done you a good turn. You must thank me by coaxing all the pretty gals to go with me next fall. That's going to be my last trip. This trading in niggers is a bad business for a fellow that's got any heart. Move on, you fellows!" And the gang went on, God alone knows where.

Much as I despise and detest the class of slave-traders, whom I regard as the vilest wretches on earth, I must do this man the justice to say that he seemed to have some feeling. He took a fancy to William in the jail, and wanted to buy him. When he heard the story of my children, he was willing to aid them in getting out of Dr. Flint's power, even without charging the customary fee.

My uncle procured a wagon and carried William and the children back to town. Great was the joy in my grandmother's house! The curtains were closed, and the candles lighted. The happy grandmother cuddled the little ones to her bosom. They hugged her, and kissed her, and clapped their hands, and shouted. She knelt down and poured forth one of her heartfelt prayers of thanksgiving to God. The father was present for a while; and though such a "parental relation" as existed between him and my children takes slight hold on the hearts or consciences of slaveholders, it must be that he experienced some moments of pure joy in witnessing the happiness he had imparted.

I had no share in the rejoicings of that evening. The events of the day had not come to my knowledge. And now I will tell you something that happened to me; though you will, perhaps, think it illustrates the superstition of slaves. I sat in my usual place on the floor near the window, where I could hear much that was said in the street without being seen. The family had retired for the night, and all was still. I sat there thinking of my children, when I heard a low strain of music. A band of serenaders were under the window, playing "Home, sweet home." I listened till the sounds did not seem like music, but like the moaning of children. It seemed as if my heart would burst. I rose from my sitting posture, and knelt. A streak of moonlight was on the floor before me, and in the midst of it appeared the forms of my two children. They vanished; but I had seen them distinctly. Some will call it a dream, others a vision. I know not how to account for it, but it made a strong impression on my mind, and I felt certain something had happened to my little ones.

I had not seen Betty since morning. Now I heard her softly turning the key. As soon as she entered, I clung to her, and begged her to let me know whether my children were dead, or whether they were sold; for I had seen their spirits in my room, and I was sure something had happened to them. "Lor, chile," said she, putting her arms round me, "you's got de high-sterics. I'll sleep wid you to-night, 'cause you'll make a noise, and ruin missis. Something has stirred you up mightily. When you is done cryin, I'll talk wid you. De chillern is well, and mighty happy. I seed 'em myself. Does dat satisfy you? Dar, chile, be still! Somebody vill hear you." I tried to obey her. She lay down, and was soon sound asleep; but no sleep would come to my eyelids.

At dawn, Betty was up and off to the kitchen. The hours passed on, and the vision of the night kept constantly recurring to my thoughts. After a while I heard the voices of two women in the entry. In one of them I recognized the housemaid. The other said to her, "Did you know Linda Brent's children was sold to the speculator yesterday. They say ole massa Flint was mighty glad to see 'em drove out of town; but they say they've come back agin. I 'spect it's all their daddy's doings. They say he's bought William too. Lor! how it will take hold of ole massa Flint! I'm going roun' to aunt Marthy's to see 'bout it."

I bit my lips till the blood came to keep from crying out. Were my children with their grandmother, or had the speculator carried them off? The suspense was dreadful. Would Betty *never* come, and tell me the truth about it? At last she came, and I eagerly repeated what I had overheard. Her face was one broad, bright smile. "Lor, you foolish ting!" said she. "I'se gwine to tell you all 'bout it. De gals is eating thar breakfast, and missus tole me to let her tell you; but, poor creeter! t'aint right to keep you waitin', and I'se gwine to tell you. Brudder, chillern, all is bought by de daddy! I'se laugh more dan nuff, tinking 'bout ole massa Flint. Lor, how he *vill* swar! He's got ketched dis time, any how; but I must be getting out o' dis, or dem gals vill come and ketch *me*."

Betty went off laughing; and I said to myself, "Can it be true that my children are free? I have not suffered for them in vain. Thank God!"

Great surprise was expressed when it was known that my children had returned to their grandmother's. The news spread through the town, and many a kind word was bestowed on the little ones.

Dr. Flint went to my grandmother's to ascertain who was the owner of my children, and she informed him. "I expected as much," said he. "I am glad to hear it. I have had news from Linda lately, and I shall soon have her. You need never expect to see *her* free. She shall be my slave as long as I live, and when I am dead she shall be the slave of my children. If I ever find out that you or Phillip had anything to do with her running off I'll kill him. And if I meet William in the street, and he presumes to look at me, I'll flog him within an inch of his life. Keep those brats out of my sight!"

As he turned to leave, my grandmother said something to remind him of his own doings. He looked back upon her, as if he would have been glad to strike her to the ground.

I had my season of joy and thanksgiving. It was the first time since my childhood that I had experienced any real happiness. I heard of the old doctor's threats, but they no longer had the same power to trouble me. The darkest cloud that hung over my life had rolled away. Whatever slavery might do to me, it could not shackle my children. If I fell a sacrifice, my little ones were saved. It was well for me that my simple heart believed all that had been promised for their welfare. It is always better to trust than to doubt.

# XX. NEW PERILS

The doctor, more exasperated than ever, again tried to revenge himself on my relatives. He arrested uncle Phillip on the charge of having aided my flight. He was carried before a court, and swore truly that he knew nothing of my intention to escape, and that he had not seen me since I left my master's plantation. The doctor then demanded that he should give bail for five hundred dollars that he would have nothing to do with me. Several gentlemen offered to be security for him; but Mr. Sands told him he had better go back to jail, and he would see that he came out without giving bail.

The news of his arrest was carried to my grandmother, who conveyed it to Betty. In the kindness of her heart, she again stowed me away under the floor; and as she walked back and forth, in the performance of her culinary duties, she talked apparently to herself, but with the intention that I should hear what was going on. I hoped that my uncle's imprisonment would last but few days; still I was anxious. I thought it likely Dr. Flint would do his utmost to taunt and insult him, and I was afraid my uncle might lose control of himself, and retort in some way that would be construed into a punishable offence; and I was well aware that in court his word would not be taken against any white man's. The search for me was renewed. Something had excited suspicions that I was in the vicinity. They searched the house I was in. I heard their steps and their voices. At night, when all were asleep, Betty came to release me from my place of confinement. The fright I had undergone, the constrained posture, and the dampness of the ground, made me ill for several days. My uncle was soon after taken out of prison; but the movements of all my relatives, and of all our friends, were very closely watched.

We all saw that I could not remain where I was much longer. I had already staid longer than was intended, and I knew my presence must be a source of perpetual anxiety to my kind benefactress. During this time, my friends had laid many plans for my escape, but the extreme vigilance of my persecutors made it impossible to carry them into effect.

One morning I was much startled by hearing somebody trying to get into my room. Several keys were tried, but none fitted. I instantly conjectured it was one of the housemaids; and I concluded she must either have heard some noise in the room, or have noticed the entrance of Betty. When my friend came, at her usual time, I told her what had happened. "I knows who it was," said she. "'Pend upon it, 'twas dat Jenny. Dat nigger allers got de debble in her." I suggested that she might have seen or heard something that excited her curiosity.

"Tut! tut! chile!" exclaimed Betty, "she ain't seen notin', nor hearn notin'. She only 'spects something. Dat's all. She wants to fine out who hab cut and make my gownd. But she won't nebber know. Dat's sartin. I'll git missis to fix her."

I reflected a moment, and said, "Betty, I must leave here to-night."

"Do as you tink best, poor chile," she replied. "I'se mighty 'fraid dat 'ere nigger vill pop on you some time."

She reported the incident to her mistress, and received orders to keep Jenny busy in the kitchen till she could see my uncle Phillip. He told her he would send a friend for me that very evening. She told him she hoped I was going to the north, for it was very dangerous for me to remain any where in the vicinity. Alas, it was not an easy thing, for one in my situation, to go to the north. In order to leave the coast quite clear for me, she went into the country to spend the day with her brother, and took Jenny with her. She was afraid to come and bid me good by, but she left a kind message with Betty. I heard her carriage roll from the door, and I never again saw her who had so generously befriended the poor, trembling fugitive! Though she was a slaveholder, to this day my heart blesses her!

I had not the slightest idea where I was going. Betty brought me a suit of sailor's clothes,—jacket, trowsers, and tarpaulin hat. She gave me a small bundle, saying I might need it where I was going. In cheery tones, she exclaimed, "I'se *so* glad you is gwine to free parts! Don't forget ole Betty. P'raps I'll come 'long by and by."

I tried to tell her how grateful I felt for all her kindness. But she interrupted me. "I don't want no tanks, honey. I'se glad I could help you, and I hope de good Lord vill open de path for you. I'se gwine wid you to de lower gate. Put your hands in your pockets, and walk ricketty, like de sailors."

I performed to her satisfaction. At the gate I found Peter, a young colored man, waiting for me. I had known him for years. He had been an apprentice to my father, and had always borne a good character. I was not afraid to trust to him. Betty bade me a hurried good by, and we walked off. "Take courage, Linda," said my friend Peter. "I've got a dagger, and no man shall take you from me, unless he passes over my dead body."

It was a long time since I had taken a walk out of doors, and the fresh air revived me. It was also pleasant to hear a human voice speaking to me above a whisper. I passed several people whom I knew, but they did not recognize me in my disguise. I prayed internally that, for Peter's sake, as well as my own, nothing might occur to bring out his dagger. We walked on till we came to the wharf. My aunt Nancy's husband was a seafaring man, and it had been deemed necessary to let him into our secret. He took me into his boat, rowed out to a vessel not far distant, and hoisted me on board. We three were the only occupants of the vessel. I now ventured to ask what they proposed to do with me. They said I was to remain on board till near dawn, and then they would hide me in Snaky Swamp, till my uncle Phillip had prepared a place of concealment for me. If the vessel had been bound north, it would have been of no avail to me, for it would certainly have been searched. About four o'clock, we were again seated in the boat, and rowed three miles to the swamp. My fear of snakes had been increased by the venomous bite I had received, and I dreaded to enter this hiding place. But I was in no situation to choose, and I gratefully accepted the best that my poor, persecuted friends could do for me.

Peter landed first, and with a large knife cut a path through bamboos and briers of all descriptions. He came back, took me in his arms, and carried me to a seat made among the bamboos. Before we reached it, we were covered with hundreds of mosquitos. In an hour's time they had so poisoned my flesh that I was a pitiful sight to behold. As the light increased, I saw snake after snake crawling round us. I had been accustomed to the sight of snakes all my life, but these were larger than any I had ever seen. To this day I shudder when I remember that morning. As evening approached, the number of snakes increased so much that we were continually obliged to thrash them with sticks to keep them from crawling over us. The bamboos were so high and so thick that it was impossible to see beyond a very short distance.

Just before it became dark we procured a seat nearer to the entrance of the swamp, being fearful of losing our way back to the boat. It was not long before we heard the paddle of oars, and the low whistle, which had been agreed upon as a signal. We made haste to enter the boat, and were rowed back to the vessel. I passed a wretched night; for the heat of the swamp, the mosquitos, and the constant terror of snakes, had brought on a burning fever. I had just dropped asleep, when they came and told me it was time to go back to that horrid swamp. I could scarcely summon courage to rise. But even those large, venomous snakes were less dreadful to my imagination than the white men in that community called civilized. This time Peter took a quantity of tobacco to burn, to keep off the mosquitos. It produced the desired effect on them, but gave me nausea and severe headache. At dark we returned to the vessel. I had been so sick during the day, that Peter declared I should go home that night, if the devil himself was on patrol. They told me a place of concealment had been provided for me at my grandmother's. I could not imagine how it was possible to hide me in her house, every nook and corner of which was known to the Flint family. They told me to wait and see. We were rowed ashore, and went boldly through the streets, to my grandmother's. I wore my sailor's clothes, and had blackened my face with charcoal. I passed several people whom I knew. The father of my children came so near that I brushed against his arm; but he had no idea who it was.

"You must make the most of this walk," said my friend Peter, "for you may not have another very soon."

I thought his voice sounded sad. It was kind of him to conceal from me what a dismal hole was to be my home for a long, long time.

# XXI. THE LOOPHOLE OF RETREAT

A small shed had been added to my grandmother's house years ago. Some boards were laid across the joists at the top, and between these boards and the roof was a very small garret, never occupied by any thing but rats and mice. It was a pent roof, covered with nothing but shingles, according to the southern custom for such buildings. The garret was only nine feet long and seven wide. The highest part was three feet high, and sloped down abruptly to the loose board floor. There was no admission for either light or air. My uncle Phillip, who was a carpenter, had very skilfully made a concealed trap-door, which communicated with the storeroom. He had been doing this while I was waiting in the swamp. The storeroom opened upon a piazza. To this hole I was conveyed as soon as I entered the house. The air was stifling; the darkness total. A bed had been spread on the floor. I could sleep quite comfortably on one side; but the slope was so sudden that I could not turn on my other without hitting the roof. The rats and mice ran over my bed; but I was weary, and I slept such sleep as the wretched may, when a tempest has passed over them. Morning came. I knew it only by the noises I heard; for in my small den day and night were all the same. I suffered for air even more than for light. But I was not comfortless. I heard the voices of my children. There was joy and there was sadness in the sound. It made my tears flow. How I longed to speak to them! I was eager to look on their faces; but there was no hole, no crack, through which I could peep. This continued darkness was oppressive. It seemed horrible to sit or lie in a cramped position day after day, without one gleam of light. Yet I would have chosen this, rather than my lot as a slave, though white people considered it an easy one; and it was so compared with the fate of others. I was never cruelly overworked; I was never lacerated with the whip from head to foot; I was never so beaten and bruised that I could not turn from one side to the other; I never had my heel-strings cut to prevent my running away; I was never chained to a log and forced to drag it about, while I toiled in the fields from morning till night; I was never branded with hot iron, or torn by bloodhounds. On the contrary, I had always been kindly treated, and tenderly cared for, until I came into the hands of Dr. Flint. I had never wished for freedom till then. But though my life in slavery was comparatively devoid of hardships, God pity the woman who is compelled to lead such a life!

My food was passed up to me through the trap-door my uncle had contrived; and my grandmother, my uncle Phillip, and aunt Nancy would seize such opportunities as they could, to mount up there and chat with me at the opening. But of course this was not safe in the daytime. It must all be done in darkness. It was impossible for me to move in an erect position, but I crawled about my den for exercise. One day I hit my head against something, and found it was a gimlet. My uncle had left it sticking there when he made the trap-door. I was as rejoiced as Robinson Crusoe could have been at finding such a treasure. It put a lucky thought into my head. I said to myself, "Now I will have some light. Now I will see my children." I did not dare to begin my work during the daytime, for fear of attracting attention. But I groped round; and having found the side next the street, where I could frequently see my children, I stuck the gimlet in and waited for evening. I bored three rows of holes, one above another; then I bored out the interstices between. I thus succeeded in making one hole about an inch long and an inch broad. I sat by it till late into the night, to enjoy the little whiff of air that floated in. In the morning I watched for my children. The first person I saw in the street was Dr. Flint. I had a shuddering, superstitious feeling that it was a bad omen. Several familiar faces passed by. At last I heard the merry laugh of children, and presently two sweet little faces were looking up at me, as though they knew I was there, and were conscious of the joy they imparted. How I longed to *tell* them I was there!

My condition was now a little improved. But for weeks I was tormented by hundreds of little red insects, fine as a needle's point, that pierced through my skin, and produced an intolerable burning. The good grandmother gave me herb teas and cooling medicines, and finally I got rid of them. The heat of my den was intense, for nothing but thin shingles protected me from the scorching summer's sun. But I had my consolations. Through my peeping-hole I could watch the children, and when they were near enough, I could hear their talk. Aunt Nancy brought me all the news she could hear at Dr. Flint's. From her I learned that the doctor had written to New York to a colored woman, who had been born and raised in our neighborhood, and had breathed his contaminating atmosphere. He offered her a reward if she could find out any thing about me. I know not what was the nature of her reply; but he soon after started for New York in haste, saying to his family that he had business of importance to transact. I peeped at him as he passed on his way to the steamboat. It was a satisfaction to have miles of land and water between us, even for a little while; and it was a still greater satisfaction to know that he believed me to be in the Free States. My little den seemed less dreary than it had done. He returned, as he did from his former journey to New York, without obtaining any satisfactory information. When he passed our house next morning, Benny was standing at the gate. He had heard them say that he had gone to find me, and he called out, "Dr. Flint, did you bring my mother home? I want to see her." The doctor stamped his foot at him in a rage, and exclaimed, "Get out of the way, you little damned rascal! If you don't, I'll cut off your head."

Benny ran terrified into the house, saying, "You can't put me in jail again. I don't belong to you now." It was well that the wind carried the words away from the doctor's ear. I told my grandmother of it, when we had our next conference at the trap-door, and begged of her not to allow the children to be impertinent to the irascible old man.

Autumn came, with a pleasant abatement of heat. My eyes had become accustomed to the dim light, and by holding my book or work in a certain position near the aperture I contrived to read and sew. That was a great relief to the tedious monotony of my life. But when winter came, the cold penetrated through the thin shingle roof, and I was dreadfully chilled. The winters there are not so long, or so severe, as in northern latitudes; but the houses are not built to shelter from cold, and my little den was peculiarly comfortless. The kind grandmother brought me bedclothes and warm drinks. Often I was obliged to lie in bed all day to keep comfortable; but with all my precautions, my shoulders and feet were frostbitten. O, those long, gloomy days, with no object for my eye to rest upon, and no thoughts to occupy my mind, except the dreary past and the uncertain future! I was thankful when there came a day sufficiently mild for me to wrap myself up and sit at the loophole to watch the passers by. Southerners have the habit of stopping and talking in the streets, and I heard many conversations not intended to meet my ears. I heard slave-hunters planning how to catch some poor fugitive. Several times I heard allusions to Dr. Flint, myself, and the history of my children, who, perhaps, were playing near the gate. One would say, "I wouldn't move my little finger to catch her, as old Flint's property." Another would say, "I'll catch *any* nigger for the reward. A man ought to have what belongs to him, if he *is* a damned brute." The opinion was often expressed that I was in the Free States. Very rarely did any one suggest that I might be in the vicinity. Had the least suspicion rested on my grandmother's house, it would have been burned to the ground. But it was the last place they thought of. Yet there was no place, where slavery existed, that could have afforded me so good a place of concealment.

Dr. Flint and his family repeatedly tried to coax and bribe my children to tell something they had heard said about me. One day the doctor took them into a shop, and offered them some bright little silver pieces and gay handkerchiefs if they would tell where their mother was. Ellen shrank away from him, and would not speak; but Benny spoke up, and said, "Dr. Flint, I don't know where my mother is. I guess she's in New York; and when you go there again, I wish you'd ask her to come home, for I want to see her; but if you put her in jail, or tell her you'll cut her head off, I'll tell her to go right back."

# XXII. CHRISTMAS FESTIVITIES

Christmas was approaching. Grandmother brought me materials, and I busied myself making some new garments and little playthings for my children. Were it not that hiring day is near at hand, and many families are fearfully looking forward to the probability of separation in a few days, Christmas might be a happy season for the poor slaves. Even slave mothers try to gladden the hearts of their little ones on that occasion. Benny and Ellen had their Christmas stockings filled. Their imprisoned mother could not have the privilege of witnessing their surprise and joy. But I had the pleasure of peeping at them as they went into the street with their new suits on. I heard Benny ask a little playmate whether Santa Claus brought him any thing. "Yes," replied the boy; "but Santa Claus ain't a real man. It's the children's mothers that put things into the stockings." "No, that can't be," replied Benny, "for Santa Claus brought Ellen and me these new clothes, and my mother has been gone this long time."

How I longed to tell him that his mother made those garments, and that many a tear fell on them while she worked!

Every child rises early on Christmas morning to see the Johnkannaus. Without them, Christmas would be shorn of its greatest attraction. They consist of companies of slaves from the plantations, generally of the lower class. Two athletic men, in calico wrappers, have a net thrown over them, covered with all manner of bright-colored stripes. Cows' tails are fastened to their backs, and their heads are decorated with horns. A box, covered with sheepskin, is called the gumbo box. A dozen beat on this, while other strike triangles and jawbones, to which bands of dancers keep time. For a month previous they are composing songs, which are sung on this occasion. These companies, of a hundred each, turn out early in the morning, and are allowed to go round till twelve o'clock, begging for contributions. Not a door is left unvisited where there is the least chance of obtaining a penny or a glass of rum. They do not drink while they are out, but carry the rum home in jugs, to have a carousal. These Christmas donations frequently amount to twenty or thirty dollars. It is seldom that any white man or child refuses to give them a trifle. If he does, they regale his ears with the following song:—

Poor massa, so dey say;
Down in de heel, so dey say;
Got no money, so dey say;
Not one shillin, so dey say;
God A'mighty bress you, so dey say.

Christmas is a day of feasting, both with white and colored people. Slaves, who are lucky enough to have a few shillings, are sure to spend them for good eating; and many a turkey and pig is captured, without saying, "By your leave, sir." Those who cannot obtain these, cook a 'possum, or a raccoon, from which savory dishes can be made. My grandmother raised poultry and pigs for sale and it was her established custom to have both a turkey and a pig roasted for Christmas dinner.

On this occasion, I was warned to keep extremely quiet, because two guests had been invited. One was the town constable, and the other was a free colored man, who tried to pass himself off for white, and who was always ready to do any mean work for the sake of currying favor with white people. My grandmother had a motive for inviting them. She managed to take them all over the house. All the rooms on the lower floor were thrown open for them to pass in and out; and after dinner, they were invited up stairs to look at a fine mocking bird my uncle had just brought home. There, too, the rooms were all thrown open that they might look in. When I heard them talking on the piazza, my heart almost stood still. I knew this colored man had spent many nights hunting for me. Every body knew he had the blood of a slave father in his veins; but for the sake of passing himself off for white, he was ready to kiss the slaveholders' feet. How I despised him! As for the constable, he wore no false colors. The duties of his office were despicable, but he was superior to his companion, inasmuch as he did not pretend to be what he was not. Any white man, who could raise money enough to buy a slave, would have considered himself degraded by being a constable; but the office enabled its possessor to exercise authority. If he found any slave out after nine o'clock, he could whip him as much as he liked; and that was a privilege to be coveted. When the guests were ready to depart, my grandmother gave each of them some of her nice pudding, as a present for their wives. Through my peep-hole I saw them go out of the gate, and I was glad when it closed after them. So passed the first Christmas in my den.

# XXIII. STILL IN PRISON

When spring returned, and I took in the little patch of green the aperture commanded, I asked myself how many more summers and winters I must be condemned to spend thus. I longed to draw in a plentiful draught of fresh air, to stretch my cramped limbs, to have room to stand erect, to feel the earth under my feet again. My relatives were constantly on the lookout for a chance of escape; but none offered that seemed practicable, and even tolerably safe. The hot summer came again, and made the turpentine drop from the thin roof over my head.

During the long nights I was restless for want of air, and I had no room to toss and turn. There was but one compensation; the atmosphere was so stifled that even mosquitos would not condescend to buzz in it. With all my detestation of Dr. Flint, I could hardly wish him a worse punishment, either in this world or that which is to come, than to suffer what I suffered in one single summer. Yet the laws allowed *him* to be out in the free air, while I, guiltless of crime, was pent up here, as the only means of avoiding the cruelties the laws allowed him to inflict upon me! I don't know what kept life within me. Again and again, I thought I should die before long; but I saw the leaves of another autumn whirl through the air, and felt the touch of another winter. In summer the most terrible thunder storms were acceptable, for the rain came through the roof, and I rolled up my bed that it might cool the hot boards under it. Later in the season, storms sometimes wet my clothes through and through, and that was not comfortable when the air grew chilly. Moderate storms I could keep out by filling the chinks with oakum.

But uncomfortable as my situation was, I had glimpses of things out of doors, which made me thankful for my wretched hiding-place. One day I saw a slave pass our gate, muttering, "It's his own, and he can kill it if he will." My grandmother told me that woman's history. Her mistress had that day seen her baby for the first time, and in the lineaments of its fair face she saw a likeness to her husband. She turned the bondwoman and her child out of doors, and forbade her ever to return. The slave went to her master, and told him what had happened. He promised to talk with her mistress, and make it all right. The next day she and her baby were sold to a Georgia trader.

Another time I saw a woman rush wildly by, pursued by two men. She was a slave, the wet nurse of her mistress's children. For some trifling offence her mistress ordered her to be stripped and whipped. To escape the degradation and the torture, she rushed to the river, jumped in, and ended her wrongs in death.

Senator Brown, of Mississippi, could not be ignorant of many such facts as these, for they are of frequent occurrence in every Southern State. Yet he stood up in the Congress of the United States, and declared that slavery was "a great moral, social, and political blessing; a blessing to the master, and a blessing to the slave!"

I suffered much more during the second winter than I did during the first. My limbs were benumbed by inaction, and the cold filled them with cramp. I had a very painful sensation of coldness in my head; even my face and tongue stiffened, and I lost the power of speech. Of course it was impossible, under the circumstances, to summon any physician. My brother William came and did all he could for me. Uncle Phillip also watched tenderly over me; and poor grandmother crept up and down to inquire whether there were any signs of returning life. I was restored to consciousness by the dashing of cold water in my face, and found myself leaning against my brother's arm, while he bent over me with streaming eyes. He afterwards told me he thought I was dying, for I had been in an unconscious state sixteen hours. I next became delirious, and was in great danger of betraying myself and my friends. To prevent this, they stupefied me with drugs. I remained in bed six weeks, weary in body and sick at heart. How to get medical advice was the question. William finally went to a Thompsonian doctor, and described himself as having all my pains and aches. He returned with herbs, roots, and ointment. He was especially charged to rub on the ointment by a fire; but how could a fire be made in my little den? Charcoal in a furnace was tried, but there was no outlet for the gas, and it nearly cost me my life. Afterwards coals, already kindled, were brought up in an iron pan, and placed on bricks. I was so weak, and it was so long since I had enjoyed the warmth of a fire, that those few coals actually made me weep. I think the medicines did me some good; but my recovery was very slow. Dark thoughts passed through my mind as I lay there day after day. I tried to be thankful for my little cell, dismal as it was, and even to love it, as part of the price I had paid for the redemption of my children. Sometimes I thought God was a compassionate Father, who would forgive my sins for the sake of my sufferings. At other times, it seemed to me there was no justice or mercy in the divine government. I asked why the curse of slavery was permitted to exist, and why I had been so persecuted and wronged from youth upward. These things took the shape of mystery, which is to this day not so clear to my soul as I trust it will be hereafter.

In the midst of my illness, grandmother broke down under the weight and anxiety and toil. The idea of losing her, who had always been my best friend and a mother to my children, was the sorest trial I had yet had. O, how earnestly I prayed that she might recover! How hard it seemed, that I could not tend upon her, who had so long and so tenderly watched over me!

One day the screams of a child nerved me with strength to crawl to my peeping-hole, and I saw my son covered with blood. A fierce dog, usually kept chained, had seized and bitten him. A doctor was sent for, and I heard the groans and screams of my child while the wounds were being sewed up. O, what torture to a mother's heart, to listen to this and be unable to go to him!

But childhood is like a day in spring, alternately shower and sunshine. Before night Benny was bright and lively, threatening the destruction of the dog; and great was his delight when the doctor told him the next day that the dog had bitten another boy and been shot. Benny recovered from his wounds; but it was long before he could walk.

When my grandmother's illness became known, many ladies, who were her customers, called to bring her some little comforts, and to inquire whether she had every thing she wanted. Aunt Nancy one night asked permission to watch with her sick mother, and Mrs. Flint replied, "I don't see any need of your going. I can't spare you." But when she found other ladies in the neighborhood were so attentive, not wishing to be outdone in Christian charity, she also sallied forth, in magnificent condescension, and stood by the bedside of her who had loved her in her infancy, and who had been repaid by such grievous wrongs. She seemed surprised to find her so ill, and scolded uncle Phillip for not sending for Dr. Flint. She herself sent for him immediately, and he came. Secure as I was in my retreat, I should have been terrified if I had known he was so near me. He pronounced my grandmother in a very critical situation, and said if her attending physician wished it, he would visit her. Nobody wished to have him coming to the house at all hours, and we were not disposed to give him a chance to make out a long bill.

As Mrs. Flint went out, Sally told her the reason Benny was lame was, that a dog had bitten him. "I'm glad of it," replied she. "I wish he had killed him. It would be good news to send to his mother. *Her* day will come. The dogs will grab *her* yet." With these Christian words she and her husband departed, and, to my great satisfaction, returned no more.

I learned from uncle Phillip, with feelings of unspeakable joy and gratitude, that the crisis was passed and grandmother would live. I could now say from my heart, "God is merciful. He has spared me the anguish of feeling that I caused her death."

# XXIV. THE CANDIDATE FOR CONGRESS

The summer had nearly ended, when Dr. Flint made a third visit to New York, in search of me. Two candidates were running for Congress, and he returned in season to vote. The father of my children was the Whig candidate. The doctor had hitherto been a stanch Whig; but now he exerted all his energies for the defeat of Mr. Sands. He invited large parties of men to dine in the shade of his trees, and supplied them with plenty of rum and brandy. If any poor fellow drowned his wits in the bowl, and, in the openness of his convivial heart, proclaimed that he did not mean to vote the Democratic ticket, he was shoved into the street without ceremony.

The doctor expended his liquor in vain. Mr. Sands was elected; an event which occasioned me some anxious thoughts. He had not emancipated my children, and if he should die they would be at the mercy of his heirs. Two little voices, that frequently met my ear, seemed to plead with me not to let their father depart without striving to make their freedom secure. Years had passed since I had spoken to him. I had not even seen him since the night I passed him, unrecognized, in my disguise of a sailor. I supposed he would call before he left, to say something to my grandmother concerning the children, and I resolved what course to take.

The day before his departure for Washington I made arrangements, toward evening, to get from my hiding-place into the storeroom below. I found myself so stiff and clumsy that it was with great difficulty I could hitch from one resting place to another. When I reached the storeroom my ankles gave way under me, and I sank exhausted on the floor. It seemed as if I could never use my limbs again. But the purpose I had in view roused all the strength I had. I crawled on my hands and knees to the window, and, screened behind a barrel, I waited for his coming. The clock struck nine, and I knew the steamboat would leave between ten and eleven. My hopes were failing. But presently I heard his voice, saying to some one, "Wait for me a moment. I wish to see aunt Martha." When he came out, as he passed the window, I said, "Stop one moment, and let me speak for my children." He started, hesitated, and then passed on, and went out of the gate. I closed the shutter I had partially opened, and sank down behind the barrel. I had suffered much; but seldom had I experienced a keener pang than I then felt. Had my children, then, become of so little consequence to him? And had he so little feeling for their wretched mother that he would not listen a moment while she pleaded for them? Painful memories were so busy within me, that I forgot I had not hooked the shutter, till I heard some one opening it. I looked up. He had come back. "Who called me?" said he, in a low tone. "I did," I replied. "Oh, Linda," said he, "I knew your voice; but I was afraid to answer, lest my friend should hear me. Why do you come here? Is it possible you risk yourself in this house? They are mad to allow it. I shall expect to hear that you are all ruined," I did not wish to implicate him, by letting him know my place of concealment; so I merely said, "I thought you would come to bid grandmother good by, and so I came here to speak a few words to you about emancipating my children. Many changes may take place during the six months you are gone to Washington, and it does not seem right for you to expose them to the risk of such changes. I want nothing for myself; all I ask is, that you will free my children, or authorize some friend to do it, before you go."

He promised he would do it, and also expressed a readiness; to make any arrangements whereby I could be purchased.

I heard footsteps approaching, and closed the shutter hastily. I wanted to crawl back to my den, without letting the family know what I had done; for I knew they would deem it very imprudent. But he stepped back into the house, to tell my grandmother that he had spoken with me at the storeroom window, and to beg of her not to allow me to remain in the house over night. He said it was the height of madness for me to be there; that we should certainly all be ruined. Luckily, he was in too much of a hurry to wait for a reply, or the dear old woman would surely have told him all.

I tried to go back to my den, but found it more difficult to go up than I had to come down. Now that my mission was fulfilled, the little strength that had supported me through it was gone, and I sank helpless on the floor. My grandmother, alarmed at the risk I had run, came into the storeroom in the dark, and locked the door behind her. "Linda," she whispered, "where are you?"

"I am here by the window," I replied. "I *couldn't* have him go away without emancipating the children. Who knows what may happen?"

"Come, come, child," said she, "it won't do for you to stay here another minute. You've done wrong; but I can't blame you, poor thing!"

I told her I could not return without assistance, and she must call my uncle. Uncle Phillip came, and pity prevented him from scolding me. He carried me back to my dungeon, laid me tenderly on the bed, gave me some medicine, and asked me if there was any thing more he could do. Then he went away, and I was left with my own thoughts—starless as the midnight darkness around me.

My friends feared I should become a cripple for life; and I was so weary of my long imprisonment that, had it not been for the hope of serving my children, I should have been thankful to die; but, for their sakes, I was willing to bear on.

# XXV. COMPETITION IN CUNNING

Dr. Flint had not given me up. Every now and then he would say to my grandmother that I would yet come back, and voluntarily surrender myself; and that when I did, I could be purchased by my relatives, or any one who wished to buy me. I knew his cunning nature too well not to perceive that this was a trap laid for me; and so all my friends understood it. I resolved to match my cunning against his cunning. In order to make him believe that I was in New York, I resolved to write him a letter dated from that place. I sent for my friend Peter, and asked him if he knew any trustworthy seafaring person, who would carry such a letter to New York, and put it in the post office there. He said he knew one that he would trust with his own life to the ends of the world. I reminded him that it was a hazardous thing for him to undertake. He said he knew it, but he was willing to do any thing to help me. I expressed a wish for a New York paper, to ascertain the names of some of the streets. He run his hand into his pocket, and said, "Here is half a one, that was round a cap I bought of a pedler yesterday." I told him the letter would be ready the next evening. He bade me good by, adding, "Keep up your spirits, Linda; brighter days will come by and by."

My uncle Phillip kept watch over the gate until our brief interview was over. Early the next morning, I seated myself near the little aperture to examine the newspaper. It was a piece of the New York Herald; and, for once, the paper that systematically abuses the colored people, was made to render them a service. Having obtained what information I wanted concerning streets and numbers, I wrote two letters, one to my grandmother, the other to Dr. Flint. I reminded him how he, a gray-headed man, had treated a helpless child, who had been placed in his power, and what years of misery he had brought upon her. To my grandmother, I expressed a wish to have my children sent to me at the north, where I could teach them to respect themselves, and set them a virtuous example; which a slave mother was not allowed to do at the south. I asked her to direct her answer to a certain street in Boston, as I did not live in New York, though

I went there sometimes. I dated these letters ahead, to allow for the time it would take to carry them, and sent a memorandum of the date to the messenger. When my friend came for the letters, I said, "God bless and reward you, Peter, for this disinterested kindness. Pray be careful. If you are detected, both you and I will have to suffer dreadfully. I have not a relative who would dare to do it for me." He replied, "You may trust to me, Linda. I don't forget that your father was my best friend, and I will be a friend to his children so long as God lets me live."

It was necessary to tell my grandmother what I had done, in order that she might be ready for the letter, and prepared to hear what Dr. Flint might say about my being at the north. She was sadly troubled. She felt sure mischief would come of it. I also told my plan to aunt Nancy, in order that she might report to us what was said at Dr. Flint's house. I whispered it to her through a crack, and she whispered back, "I hope it will succeed. I shan't mind being a slave all *my* life, if I can only see you and the children free."

I had directed that my letters should be put into the New York post office on the 20th of the month. On the evening of the 24th my aunt came to say that Dr. Flint and his wife had been talking in a low voice about a letter he had received, and that when he went to his office he promised to bring it when he came to tea. So I concluded I should hear my letter read the next morning. I told my grandmother Dr. Flint would be sure to come, and asked her to have him sit near a certain door, and leave it open, that I might hear what he said. The next morning I took my station within sound of that door, and remained motionless as a statue. It was not long before I heard the gate slam, and the well-known footsteps enter the house. He seated himself in the chair that was placed for him, and said, "Well, Martha, I've brought you a letter from Linda. She has sent me a letter, also. I know exactly where to find her; but I don't choose to go to Boston for her. I had rather she would come back of her own accord, in a respectable manner. Her uncle Phillip is the best person to go for her. With *him*, she would feel perfectly free to act. I am willing to pay his expenses going and returning. She shall be sold to her friends. Her children are free; at least I suppose they are; and when you obtain her freedom, you'll make a happy family. I suppose, Martha, you have no objection to my reading to you the letter Linda has written to you."

He broke the seal, and I heard him read it. The old villain! He had suppressed the letter I wrote to grandmother, and prepared a substitute of his own, the purport of which was as follows:—

> Dear Grandmother: I have long wanted to write to you; but the disgraceful manner in which I left you and my children made me ashamed to do it. If you knew how much I have suffered since I ran away, you would pity and forgive me. I have purchased freedom at a dear rate. If any arrangement could be made for me to return to the south without being a slave, I would gladly come. If not, I beg of you to send my children to the north. I cannot live any longer without them. Let me know in time, and I will meet them in New York or Philadelphia, whichever place best suits my uncle's convenience. Write as soon as possible to your unhappy daughter,
>
> LINDA.

"It is very much as I expected it would be," said the old hypocrite, rising to go. "You see the foolish girl has repented of her rashness, and wants to return. We must help her to do it, Martha. Talk with Phillip about it. If he will go for her, she will trust to him, and come back. I should like an answer to-morrow. Good morning, Martha."

As he stepped out on the piazza, he stumbled over my little girl. "Ah, Ellen, is that you?" he said, in his most gracious manner. "I didn't see you. How do you do?"

"Pretty well, sir," she replied. "I heard you tell grandmother that my mother is coming home. I want to see her."

"Yes, Ellen, I am going to bring her home very soon," rejoined he; "and you shall see her as much as you like, you little curly-headed nigger."

This was as good as a comedy to me, who had heard it all; but grandmother was frightened and distressed, because the doctor wanted my uncle to go for me.

The next evening Dr. Flint called to talk the matter over. My uncle told him that from what he had heard of Massachusetts, he judged he should be mobbed if he went there after a runaway slave. "All stuff and nonsense, Phillip!" replied the doctor. "Do you suppose I want you to kick up a row in Boston? The business can all be done quietly. Linda writes that she wants to come back. You are her relative, and she would trust *you*. The case would be different if I went. She might object to coming with *me*; and the damned abolitionists, if they knew I was her master, would not believe me, if I told them she had begged to go back. They would get up a row; and I should not like to see Linda dragged through the streets like a common negro. She has been very ungrateful to me for all my kindness; but I forgive her, and want to act the part of a friend towards her. I have no wish to hold her as my slave. Her friends can buy her as soon as she arrives here."

Finding that his arguments failed to convince my uncle, the doctor "let the cat out of the bag," by saying that he had written to the mayor of Boston, to ascertain whether there was a person of my description at the street and number from which my letter was dated. He had omitted this date in the letter he had made up to read to my grandmother. If I had dated from New York, the old man would probably have made another journey to that city. But even in that dark region, where knowledge is so carefully excluded from the slave, I had heard enough about Massachusetts to come to the conclusion that slaveholders did not consider it a comfortable place to go in search of a runaway. That was before the Fugitive Slave Law was passed; before Massachusetts had consented to become a "nigger hunter" for the south.

My grandmother, who had become skittish by seeing her family always in danger, came to me with a very distressed countenance, and said, "What will you do if the mayor of Boston sends him word that you haven't been there? Then he will suspect the letter was a trick; and maybe he'll find out something about it, and we shall all get into trouble. O Linda, I wish you had never sent the letters."

"Don't worry yourself, Grandmother," said I. "The mayor of Boston won't trouble himself to hunt niggers for Dr. Flint. The letters will do good in the end. I shall get out of this dark hole some time or other."

"I hope you will, child," replied the good, patient old friend. "You have been here a long time; almost five years; but whenever you do go, it will break your old grandmother's heart. I should be expecting every day to hear that you were brought back in irons and put in jail. God help you, poor child! Let us be thankful that some time or other we shall go 'where the wicked cease from troubling, and the weary are at rest.'" My heart responded, Amen.

The fact that Dr. Flint had written to the mayor of Boston convinced me that he believed my letter to be genuine, and of course that he had no suspicion of my being any where in the vicinity. It was a great object to keep up this delusion, for it made me and my friends feel less anxious, and it would be very convenient whenever there was a chance to escape. I resolved, therefore, to continue to write letters from the north from time to time.

Two or three weeks passed, and as no news came from the mayor of Boston, grandmother began to listen to my entreaty to be allowed to leave my cell, sometimes, and exercise my limbs to prevent my becoming a cripple. I was allowed to slip down into the small storeroom, early in the morning, and remain there a little while. The room was all filled up with barrels, except a small open space under my trap-door. This faced the door, the upper part of which was of glass, and purposely left uncurtained, that the curious might look in. The air of this place was close; but it was so much better than the atmosphere of my cell, that I dreaded to return. I came down as soon as it was light, and remained till eight o'clock, when people began to be about, and there was danger that some one might come on the piazza. I had tried various applications to bring warmth and feeling into my limbs, but without avail. They were so numb and stiff that it was a painful effort to move; and had my enemies come upon me during the first mornings I tried to exercise them a little in the small unoccupied space of the storeroom, it would have been impossible for me to have escaped.

# XXVI. IMPORTANT ERA IN MY BROTHER'S LIFE

I missed the company and kind attentions of my brother William, who had gone to Washington with his master, Mr. Sands. We received several letters from him, written without any allusion to me, but expressed in such a manner that I knew he did not forget me. I disguised my hand, and wrote to him in the same manner. It was a long session; and when it closed, William wrote to inform us that Mr. Sands was going to the north, to be gone some time, and that he was to accompany him. I knew that his master had promised to give him his freedom, but no time had been specified. Would William trust to a slave's chances? I remembered how we used to talk together, in our young days, about obtaining our freedom, and I thought it very doubtful whether he would come back to us.

Grandmother received a letter from Mr. Sands, saying that William had proved a most faithful servant, and he would also say a valued friend; that no mother had ever trained a better boy. He said he had travelled through the Northern States and Canada; and though the abolitionists had tried to decoy him away, they had never succeeded. He ended by saying they should be at home shortly.

We expected letters from William, describing the novelties of his journey, but none came. In time, it was reported that Mr. Sands would return late in the autumn, accompanied by a bride. Still no letters from William. I felt almost sure I should never see him again on southern soil; but had he no word of comfort to send to his friends at home? to the poor captive in her dungeon? My thoughts wandered through the dark past, and over the uncertain future. Alone in my cell, where no eye but God's could see me, I wept bitter tears. How earnestly I prayed to him to restore me to my children, and enable me to be a useful woman and a good mother!

At last the day arrived for the return of the travellers. Grandmother had made loving preparations to welcome her absent boy back to the old hearthstone. When the dinner table was laid, William's place occupied its old place. The stage coach went by empty. My grandmother waited dinner. She thought perhaps he was necessarily detained by his master. In my prison I listened anxiously, expecting every moment to hear my dear brother's voice and step. In the course of the afternoon a lad was sent by Mr. Sands to tell grandmother that William did not return with him; that the abolitionists had decoyed him away. But he begged her not to feel troubled about it, for he felt confident she would see William in a few days. As soon as he had time to reflect he would come back, for he could never expect to be so well off at the north as he had been with him.

If you had seen the tears, and heard the sobs, you would have thought the messenger had brought tidings of death instead of freedom. Poor old grandmother felt that she should never see her darling boy again. And I was selfish. I thought more of what I had lost, than of what my brother had gained. A new anxiety began to trouble me. Mr. Sands had expended a good deal of money, and would naturally feel irritated by the loss he had incurred. I greatly feared this might injure the prospects of my children, who were now becoming valuable property. I longed to have their emancipation made certain. The more so, because their master and father was now married. I was too familiar with slavery not to know that promises made to slaves, though with kind intentions, and sincere at the time, depend upon many contingencies for their fulfillment.

Much as I wished William to be free, the step he had taken made me sad and anxious. The following Sabbath was calm and clear; so beautiful that it seemed like a Sabbath in the eternal world. My grandmother brought the children out on the piazza, that I might hear their voices. She thought it would comfort me in my despondency; and it did. They chatted merrily, as only children can. Benny said, "Grandmother, do you think uncle Will has gone for good? Won't he ever come back again? May be he'll find mother. If he does, *won't* she be glad to see him! Why don't you and uncle Phillip, and all of us, go and live where mother is? I should like it; wouldn't you, Ellen?"

"Yes, I should like it," replied Ellen; "but how could we find her? Do you know the place, grandmother? I don't remember how mother looked—do you, Benny?"

Benny was just beginning to describe me when they were interrupted by an old slave woman, a near neighbor, named Aggie. This poor creature had witnessed the sale of her children, and seen them carried off to parts unknown, without any hopes of ever hearing from them again. She saw that my grandmother had been weeping, and she said, in a sympathizing tone, "What's the matter, aunt Marthy?"

"O Aggie," she replied, "it seems as if I shouldn't have any of my children or grandchildren left to hand me a drink when I'm dying, and lay my old body in the ground. My boy didn't come back with Mr. Sands. He staid at the north."

Poor old Aggie clapped her hands for joy. "Is *dat* what you's crying fur?" she exclaimed. "Git down on your knees and bress de Lord! I don't know whar my poor chillern is, and I nebber 'spect to know. You don't know whar poor Linda's gone to; but you *do* know whar her brudder is. He's in free parts; and dat's de right place. Don't murmur at de Lord's doings but git down on your knees and tank him for his goodness."

My selfishness was rebuked by what poor Aggie said. She rejoiced over the escape of one who was merely her fellow-bondman, while his own sister was only thinking what his good fortune might cost her children. I knelt and prayed God to forgive me; and I thanked him from my heart, that one of my family was saved from the grasp of slavery.

It was not long before we received a letter from William. He wrote that Mr. Sands had always treated him kindly, and that he had tried to do his duty to him faithfully. But ever since he was a boy, he had longed to be free; and he had already gone through enough to convince him he had better not lose the chance that offered. He concluded by saying, "Don't worry about me, dear grandmother. I shall think of you always; and it will spur me on to work hard and try to do right. When I have earned money enough to give you a home, perhaps you will come to the north, and we can all live happy together."

Mr. Sands told my uncle Phillip the particulars about William's leaving him. He said, "I trusted him as if he were my own brother, and treated him as kindly. The abolitionists talked to him in several places; but I had no idea they could tempt him. However, I don't blame William. He's young and inconsiderate, and those Northern rascals decoyed him. I must confess the scamp was very bold about it. I met him coming down the steps of the Astor House with his trunk on his shoulder, and I asked him where he was going. He said he was going to change his old trunk. I told him it was rather shabby, and asked if he didn't need some money. He said, No, thanked me, and went off. He did not return so soon as I expected; but I waited patiently. At last I went to see if our trunks were packed, ready for our journey. I found them locked, and a sealed note on the table informed me where I could find the keys. The fellow even tried to be religious. He wrote that he hoped God would always bless me, and reward me for my kindness; that he was not unwilling to serve me; but he wanted to be a free man; and that if I thought he did wrong, he hoped I would forgive him. I intended to give him his freedom in five years. He might have trusted me. He has shown himself ungrateful; but I shall not go for him, or send for him. I feel confident that he will soon return to me."

I afterwards heard an account of the affair from William himself. He had not been urged away by abolitionists. He needed no information they could give him about slavery to stimulate his desire for freedom. He looked at his hands, and remembered that they were once in irons. What security had he that they would not be so again? Mr. Sands was kind to him; but he might indefinitely postpone the promise he had made to give him his freedom. He might come under pecuniary embarrassments, and his property be seized by creditors; or he might die, without making any arrangements in his favor. He had too often known such accidents to happen to slaves who had kind masters, and he wisely resolved to make sure of the present opportunity to own himself. He was scrupulous about taking any money from his master on false pretences; so he sold his best clothes to pay for his passage to Boston. The slaveholders pronounced him a base, ungrateful wretch, for thus requiting his master's indulgence. What would *they* have done under similar circumstances?

When Dr. Flint's family heard that William had deserted Mr. Sands, they chuckled greatly over the news. Mrs. Flint made her usual manifestations of Christian feeling, by saying, "I'm glad of it. I hope he'll never get him again. I like to see people paid back in their own coin. I reckon Linda's children will have to pay for it. I should be glad to see them in the speculator's hands again, for I'm tired of seeing those little niggers march about the streets."

# XXVII. NEW DESTINATION FOR THE CHILDREN

Mrs. Flint proclaimed her intention of informing Mrs. Sands who was the father of my children. She likewise proposed to tell her what an artful devil I was; that I had made a great deal of trouble in her family; that when Mr. Sands was at the north, she didn't doubt I had followed him in disguise, and persuaded William to run away. She had some reason to entertain such an idea; for I had written from the north, from time to time, and I dated my letters from various places. Many of them fell into Dr. Flint's hands, as I expected they would; and he must have come to the conclusion that I travelled about a good deal. He kept a close watch over my children, thinking they would eventually lead to my detection.

A new and unexpected trial was in store for me. One day, when Mr. Sands and his wife were walking in the street, they met Benny. The lady took a fancy to him, and exclaimed, "What a pretty little negro! Whom does he belong to?"

Benny did not hear the answer; but he came home very indignant with the stranger lady, because she had called him a negro. A few days afterwards, Mr. Sands called on my grandmother, and told her he wanted her to take the children to his house. He said he had informed his wife of his relation to them, and told her they were motherless; and she wanted to see them.

When he had gone, my grandmother came and asked what I would do. The question seemed a mockery. What *could* I do? They were Mr. Sands's slaves, and their mother was a slave, whom he had represented to be dead. Perhaps he thought I was. I was too much pained and puzzled to come to any decision; and the children were carried without my knowledge.

Mrs. Sands had a sister from Illinois staying with her. This lady, who had no children of her own, was so much pleased with Ellen, that she offered to adopt her, and bring her up as she would a daughter. Mrs. Sands wanted to take Benjamin. When grandmother reported this to me, I was tried almost beyond endurance. Was this all I was to gain by what I had suffered for the sake of having my children free? True, the prospect *seemed* fair; but I knew too well how lightly slaveholders held such "parental relations." If pecuniary troubles should come, or if the new wife required more money than could conveniently be spared, my children might be thought of as a convenient means of raising funds. I had no trust in thee, O Slavery! Never should I know peace till my children were emancipated with all due formalities of law.

I was too proud to ask Mr. Sands to do any thing for my own benefit; but I could bring myself to become a supplicant for my children. I resolved to remind him of the promise he had made me, and to throw myself upon his honor for the performance of it. I persuaded my grandmother to go to him, and tell him I was not dead, and that I earnestly entreated him to keep the promise he had made me; that I had heard of the recent proposals concerning my children, and did not feel easy to accept them; that he had promised to emancipate them, and it was time for him to redeem his pledge. I knew there was some risk in thus betraying that I was in the vicinity; but what will not a mother do for her children? He received the message with surprise, and said, "The children are free. I have never intended to claim them as slaves. Linda may decide their fate. In my opinion, they had better be sent to the north. I don't think they are quite safe here. Dr. Flint boasts that they are still in his power. He says they were his daughter's property, and as she was not of age when they were sold, the contract is not legally binding."

So, then, after all I had endured for their sakes, my poor children were between two fires; between my old master and their new master! And I was powerless. There was no protecting arm of the law for me to invoke. Mr. Sands proposed that Ellen should go, for the present, to some of his relatives, who had removed to Brooklyn, Long Island. It was promised that she should be well taken care of, and sent to school. I consented to it, as the best arrangement I could make for her. My grandmother, of course, negotiated it all; and Mrs. Sands knew of no other person in the transaction. She proposed that they should take Ellen with them to Washington, and keep her till they had a good chance of sending her, with friends, to Brooklyn. She had an infant daughter. I had had a glimpse of it, as the nurse passed with it in her arms. It was not a pleasant thought to me, that the bondwoman's child should tend her free-born sister; but there was no alternative. Ellen was made ready for the journey. O, how it tried my heart to send her away, so young, alone, among strangers! Without a mother's love to shelter her from the storms of life; almost without memory of a mother! I doubted whether she and Benny would have for me the natural affection that children feel for a parent. I thought to myself that I might perhaps never see my daughter again, and I had a great desire that she should look upon me, before she went, that she might take my image with her in her memory. It seemed to me cruel to have her brought to my dungeon. It was sorrow enough for her young heart to know that her mother was a victim of slavery, without seeing the wretched hiding-place to which it had driven her. I begged permission to pass the last night in one of the open chambers, with my little girl. They thought I was crazy to think of trusting such a young child with my perilous secret. I told them I had watched her character, and I felt sure she would not betray me; that I was determined to have an interview, and if they would not facilitate it, I would take my own way to obtain it. They remonstrated against the rashness of such a proceeding; but finding they could not change my purpose, they yielded. I slipped through the trap-door into the storeroom, and my uncle kept watch at the gate, while I passed into the piazza and went up stairs, to the room I used to occupy. It was more than five years since I had seen it; and how the memories crowded on me! There I had taken shelter when my mistress drove me from her house; there came my old tyrant, to mock, insult, and curse me; there my children were first laid in my arms; there I had watched over them, each day with a deeper and sadder love; there I had knelt to God, in anguish of heart, to forgive the wrong I had done. How vividly it all came back! And after this long, gloomy interval, I stood there such a wreck!

In the midst of these meditations, I heard footsteps on the stairs. The door opened, and my uncle Phillip came in, leading Ellen by the hand. I put my arms round her, and said, "Ellen, my dear child, I am your mother." She drew back a little, and looked at me; then, with sweet confidence, she laid her cheek against mine, and I folded her to the heart that had been so long desolated. She was the first to speak. Raising her head, she said, inquiringly, "You really *are* my mother?" I told her I really was; that during all the long time she had not seen me, I had loved her most tenderly; and that now she was going away, I wanted to see her and talk with her, that she might remember me. With a sob in her voice, she said, "I'm glad you've come to see me; but why didn't you ever come before? Benny and I have wanted so much to see you! He remembers you, and sometimes he tells me about you. Why didn't you come home when Dr. Flint went to bring you?"

I answered, "I couldn't come before, dear. But now that I am with you, tell me whether you like to go away." "I don't know," said she, crying. "Grandmother says I ought not to cry; that I am going to a good place, where I can learn to read and write, and that by and by I can write her a letter. But I shan't have Benny, or grandmother, or uncle Phillip, or any body to love me. Can't you go with me? O, *do* go, dear mother!"

I told her I couldn't go now; but sometime I would come to her, and then she and Benny and I would live together, and have happy times. She wanted to run and bring Benny to see me now. I told her he was going to the north, before long, with uncle Phillip, and then I would come to see him before he went away. I asked if she would like to have me stay all night and sleep with her. "O, yes," she replied. Then, turning to her uncle, she said, pleadingly, "*May* I stay? Please, uncle! She is my own mother." He laid his hand on her head, and said, solemnly, "Ellen, this is the secret you have promised grandmother never to tell. If you ever speak of it to any body, they will never let you see your grandmother again, and your mother can never come to Brooklyn." "Uncle," she replied, "I will never tell." He told her she might stay with me; and when he had gone, I took her in my arms and told her I was a slave, and that was the reason she must never say she had seen me. I exhorted her to be a good child, to try to please the people where she was going, and that God would raise her up friends. I told her to say her prayers, and remember always to pray for her poor mother, and that God would permit us to meet again. She wept, and I did not check her tears. Perhaps she would never again have a chance to pour her tears into a mother's bosom. All night she nestled in my arms, and I had no inclination to slumber. The moments were too precious to lose any of them. Once, when I thought she was asleep, I kissed her forehead softly, and she said, "I am not asleep, dear mother."

Before dawn they came to take me back to my den. I drew aside the window curtain, to take a last look of my child. The moonlight shone on her face, and I bent over her, as I had done years before, that wretched night when I ran away. I hugged her close to my throbbing heart; and tears, too sad for such young eyes to shed, flowed down her cheeks, as she gave her last kiss, and whispered in my ear, "Mother, I will never tell." And she never did.

When I got back to my den, I threw myself on the bed and wept there alone in the darkness. It seemed as if my heart would burst. When the time for Ellen's departure drew nigh, I could hear neighbors and friends saying to her, "Good by, Ellen. I hope your poor mother will find you out. *Won't* you be glad to see her!" She replied, "Yes, ma'am;" and they little dreamed of the weighty secret that weighed down her young heart. She was an affectionate child, but naturally very reserved, except with those she loved, and I felt secure that my secret would be safe with her. I heard the gate close after her, with such feelings as only a slave mother can experience. During the day my meditations were very sad. Sometimes I feared I had been very selfish not to give up all claim to her, and let her go to Illinois, to be adopted by Mrs. Sands's sister. It was my experience of slavery that decided me against it. I feared that circumstances might arise that would cause her to be sent back. I felt confident that I should go to New York myself; and then I should be able to watch over her, and in some degree protect her.

Dr. Flint's family knew nothing of the proposed arrangement till after Ellen was gone, and the news displeased them greatly. Mrs. Flint called on Mrs. Sands's sister to inquire into the matter. She expressed her opinion very freely as to the respect Mr. Sands showed for his wife, and for his own character, in acknowledging those "young niggers." And as for sending Ellen away, she pronounced it to be just as much stealing as it would be for him to come and take a piece of furniture out of her parlor. She said her daughter was not of age to sign the bill of sale, and the children were her property; and when she became of age, or was married, she could take them, wherever she could lay hands on them.

Miss Emily Flint, the little girl to whom I had been bequeathed, was now in her sixteenth year. Her mother considered it all right and honorable for her, or her future husband, to steal my children; but she did not understand how any body could hold up their heads in respectable society, after they had purchased their own children, as Mr. Sands had done. Dr. Flint said very little. Perhaps he thought that Benny would be less likely to be sent away if he kept quiet. One of my letters, that fell into his hands, was dated from Canada; and he seldom spoke of me now. This state of things enabled me to slip down into the storeroom more frequently, where I could stand upright, and move my limbs more freely.

Days, weeks, and months passed, and there came no news of Ellen. I sent a letter to Brooklyn, written in my grandmother's name, to inquire whether she had arrived there. Answer was returned that she had not. I wrote to her in Washington; but no notice was taken of it. There was one person there, who ought to have had some sympathy with the anxiety of the child's friends at home; but the links of such relations as he had formed with me, are easily broken and cast away as rubbish. Yet how protectingly and persuasively he once talked to the poor, helpless slave girl! And how entirely I trusted him! But now suspicions darkened my mind. Was my child dead, or had they deceived me, and sold her?

If the secret memoirs of many members of Congress should be published, curious details would be unfolded. I once saw a letter from a member of Congress to a slave, who was the mother of six of his children. He wrote to request that she would send her children away from the great house before his return, as he expected to be accompanied by friends. The woman could not read, and was obliged to employ another to read the letter. The existence of the colored children did not trouble this gentleman, it was only the fear that friends might recognize in their features a resemblance to him.

At the end of six months, a letter came to my grandmother, from Brooklyn. It was written by a young lady in the family, and announced that Ellen had just arrived. It contained the following message from her: "I do try to do just as you told me to, and I pray for you every night and morning." I understood that these words were meant for me; and they were a balsam to my heart. The writer closed her letter by saying, “Ellen is a nice little girl, and we shall like to have her with us. My cousin, Mr. Sands, has given her to me, to be my little waiting maid. I shall send her to school, and I hope some day she will write to you herself.” This letter perplexed and troubled me. Had my child’s father merely placed her there till she was old enough to support herself? Or had he given her to his cousin, as a piece of property? If the last idea was correct, his cousin might return to the south at any time, and hold Ellen as a slave. I tried to put away from me the painful thought that such a foul wrong could have been done to us. I said to myself, “Surely there must be *some* justice in man;” then I remembered, with a sigh, how slavery perverted all the natural feelings of the human heart. It gave me a pang to look on my light-hearted boy. He believed himself free; and to have him brought under the yoke of slavery, would be more than I could bear. How I longed to have him safely out of the reach of its power!

# XXVIII. AUNT NANCY

I have mentioned my great-aunt, who was a slave in Dr. Flint's family, and who had been my refuge during the shameful persecutions I suffered from him. This aunt had been married at twenty years of age; that is, as far as slaves *can* marry. She had the consent of her master and mistress, and a clergyman performed the ceremony. But it was a mere form, without any legal value. Her master or mistress could annul it any day they pleased. She had always slept on the floor in the entry, near Mrs. Flint's chamber door, that she might be within call. When she was married, she was told she might have the use of a small room in an outhouse. Her mother and her husband furnished it. He was a seafaring man, and was allowed to sleep there when he was at home. But on the wedding evening, the bride was ordered to her old post on the entry floor.

Mrs. Flint, at that time, had no children; but she was expecting to be a mother, and if she should want a drink of water in the night, what could she do without her slave to bring it? So my aunt was compelled to lie at her door, until one midnight she was forced to leave, to give premature birth to a child. In a fortnight she was required to resume her place on the entry floor, because Mrs. Flint's babe needed her attentions. She kept her station there through summer and winter, until she had given premature birth to six children; and all the while she was employed as night-nurse to Mrs. Flint's children. Finally, toiling all day, and being deprived of rest at night, completely broke down her constitution, and Dr. Flint declared it was impossible she could ever become the mother of a living child. The fear of losing so valuable a servant by death, now induced them to allow her to sleep in her little room in the out-house, except when there was sickness in the family. She afterwards had two feeble babes, one of whom died in a few days, and the other in four weeks. I well remember her patient sorrow as she held the last dead baby in her arms. "I wish it could have lived," she said; "it is not the will of God that any of my children should live. But I will try to be fit to meet their little spirits in heaven."

Aunt Nancy was housekeeper and waiting-maid in Dr. Flint's family. Indeed, she was the *factotum* of the household. Nothing went on well without her. She was my mother's twin sister, and, as far as was in her power, she supplied a mother's place to us orphans. I slept with her all the time I lived in my old master's house, and the bond between us was very strong. When my friends tried to discourage me from running away, she always encouraged me. When they thought I had better return and ask my master's pardon, because there was no possibility of escape, she sent me word never to yield. She said if I persevered I might, perhaps, gain the freedom of my children; and even if I perished in doing it, that was better than to leave them to groan under the same persecutions that had blighted my own life. After I was shut up in my dark cell, she stole away, whenever she could, to bring me the news and say something cheering. How often did I kneel down to listen to her words of consolation, whispered through a crack! "I am old, and have not long to live," she used to say; "and I could die happy if I could only see you and the children free. You must pray to God, Linda, as I do for you, that he will lead you out of this darkness." I would beg her not to worry herself on my account; that there was an end of all suffering sooner or later, and that whether I lived in chains or in freedom, I should always remember her as the good friend who had been the comfort of my life. A word from her always strengthened me; and not me only. The whole family relied upon her judgement, and were guided by her advice.

I had been in my cell six years when my grandmother was summoned to the bedside of this, her last remaining daughter. She was very ill, and they said she would die. Grandmother had not entered Dr. Flint's house for several years. They had treated her cruelly, but she thought nothing of that now. She was grateful for permission to watch by the death-bed of her child. They had always been devoted to each other; and now they sat looking into each other's eyes, longing to speak of the secret that had weighed so much on the hearts of both. My aunt had been stricken with paralysis. She lived but two days, and the last day she was speechless. Before she lost the power of utterance, she told her mother not to grieve if she could not speak to her; that she would try to hold up her hand; to let her know that all was well with her. Even the hard-hearted doctor was a little softened when he saw the dying woman try to smile on the aged mother, who was kneeling by her side. His eyes moistened for a moment, as he said she had always been a faithful servant, and they should never be able to supply her place. Mrs. Flint took to her bed, quite overcome by the shock. While my grandmother sat alone with the dead, the doctor came in, leading his youngest son, who had always been a great pet with aunt Nancy, and was much attached to her. "Martha," said he, "aunt Nancy loved this child, and when he comes where you are, I hope you will be kind to him, for her sake." She replied, "Your wife was my foster-child, Dr. Flint, the foster-sister of my poor Nancy, and you little know me if you think I can feel any thing but good will for her children."

"I wish the past could be forgotten, and that we might never think of it," said he; "and that Linda would come to supply her aunt's place. She would be worth more to us than all the money that could be paid for her. I wish it for your sake also, Martha. Now that Nancy is taken away from you, she would be a great comfort to your old age."

He knew he was touching a tender chord. Almost choking with grief, my grandmother replied, "It was not I that drove Linda away. My grandchildren are gone; and of my nine children only one is left. God help me!"

To me, the death of this kind relative was an inexpressible sorrow. I knew that she had been slowly murdered; and I felt that my troubles had helped to finish the work. After I heard of her illness, I listened constantly to hear what news was brought from the great house; and the thought that I could not go to her made me utterly miserable. At last, as uncle Phillip came into the house, I heard some one inquire, "How is she?" and he answered, "She is dead." My little cell seemed whirling round, and I knew nothing more till I opened my eyes and found uncle Phillip bending over me. I had no need to ask any questions. He whispered, "Linda, she died happy." I could not weep. My fixed gaze troubled him. "Don't look *so*," he said. "Don't add to my poor mother's trouble. Remember how much she has to bear, and that we ought to do all we can to comfort her." Ah, yes, that blessed old grandmother, who for seventy-three years had borne the pelting storms of a slave-mother's life. She did indeed need consolation!

Mrs. Flint had rendered her poor foster-sister childless, apparently without any compunction; and with cruel selfishness had ruined her health by years of incessant, unrequited toil, and broken rest. But now she became very sentimental. I suppose she thought it would be a beautiful illustration of the attachment existing between slaveholder and slave, if the body of her old worn-out servant was buried at her feet. She sent for the clergyman and asked if he had any objection to burying aunt Nancy in the doctor's family burial-place. No colored person had ever been allowed interment in the white people's burying-ground, and the minister knew that all the deceased of your family reposed together in the old graveyard of the slaves. He therefore replied, "I have no objection to complying with your wish; but perhaps aunt Nancy's *mother* may have some choice as to where her remains shall be deposited."

It had never occurred to Mrs. Flint that slaves could have any feelings. When my grandmother was consulted, she at once said she wanted Nancy to lie with all the rest of her family, and where her own old body would be buried. Mrs. Flint graciously complied with her wish, though she said it was painful to her to have Nancy buried away from *her*. She might have added with touching pathos, "I was so long *used* to sleep with her lying near me, on the entry floor."

My uncle Phillip asked permission to bury his sister at his own expense; and slaveholders are always ready to grant *such* favors to slaves and their relatives. The arrangements were very plain, but perfectly respectable. She was buried on the Sabbath, and Mrs. Flint's minister read the funeral service. There was a large concourse of colored people, bond and free, and a few white persons who had always been friendly to our family. Dr. Flint's carriage was in the procession; and when the body was deposited in its humble resting place, the mistress dropped a tear, and returned to her carriage, probably thinking she had performed her duty nobly.

It was talked of by the slaves as a mighty grand funeral. Northern travellers, passing through the place, might have described this tribute of respect to the humble dead as a beautiful feature in the "patriarchal institution;" a touching proof of the attachment between slaveholders and their servants; and tender-hearted Mrs. Flint would have confirmed this impression, with handkerchief at her eyes. *We* could have told them a different story. We could have given them a chapter of wrongs and sufferings, that would have touched their hearts, if they *had* any hearts to feel for the colored people. We could have told them how the poor old slave-mother had toiled, year after year, to earn eight hundred dollars to buy her son Phillip's right to his own earnings; and how that same Phillip paid the expenses of the funeral, which they regarded as doing so much credit to the master. We could also have told them of a poor, blighted young creature, shut up in a living grave for years, to avoid the tortures that would be inflicted on her, if she ventured to come out and look on the face of her departed friend.

All this, and much more, I thought of, as I sat at my loophole, waiting for the family to return from the grave; sometimes weeping, sometimes falling asleep, dreaming strange dreams of the dead and the living.

It was sad to witness the grief of my bereaved grandmother. She had always been strong to bear, and now, as ever, religious faith supported her. But her dark life had become still darker, and age and trouble were leaving deep traces on her withered face. She had four places to knock for me to come to the trapdoor, and each place had a different meaning. She now came oftener than she had done, and talked to me of her dead daughter, while tears trickled slowly down her furrowed cheeks. I said all I could to comfort her; but it was a sad reflection, that instead of being able to help her, I was a constant source of anxiety and trouble. The poor old back was fitted to its burden. It bent under it, but did not break.

# XXIX. PREPARATIONS FOR ESCAPE

I hardly expect that the reader will credit me, when I affirm that I lived in that little dismal hole, almost deprived of light and air, and with no space to move my limbs, for nearly seven years. But it is a fact; and to me a sad one, even now; for my body still suffers from the effects of that long imprisonment, to say nothing of my soul. Members of my family, now living in New York and Boston, can testify to the truth of what I say.

Countless were the nights that I sat late at the little loophole scarcely large enough to give me a glimpse of one twinkling star. There, I heard the patrols and slave-hunters conferring together about the capture of runaways, well knowing how rejoiced they would be to catch me.

Season after season, year after year, I peeped at my children's faces, and heard their sweet voices, with a heart yearning all the while to say, "Your mother is here." Sometimes it appeared to me as if ages had rolled away since I entered upon that gloomy, monotonous existence. At times, I was stupefied and listless; at other times I became very impatient to know when these dark years would end, and I should again be allowed to feel the sunshine, and breathe the pure air.

After Ellen left us, this feeling increased. Mr. Sands had agreed that Benny might go to the north whenever his uncle Phillip could go with him; and I was anxious to be there also, to watch over my children, and protect them so far as I was able. Moreover, I was likely to be drowned out of my den, if I remained much longer; for the slight roof was getting badly out of repair, and uncle Phillip was afraid to remove the shingles, lest some one should get a glimpse of me. When storms occurred in the night, they spread mats and bits of carpet, which in the morning appeared to have been laid out to dry; but to cover the roof in the daytime might have attracted attention. Consequently, my clothes and bedding were often drenched; a process by which the pains and aches in my cramped and stiffened limbs were greatly increased. I revolved various plans of escape in my mind, which I sometimes imparted to my grandmother, when she came to whisper with me at the trap-door. The kind-hearted old woman had an intense sympathy for runaways. She had known too much of the cruelties inflicted on those who were captured. Her memory always flew back at once to the sufferings of her bright and handsome son, Benjamin, the youngest and dearest of her flock. So, whenever I alluded to the subject, she would groan out, "O, don't think of it, child. You'll break my heart." I had no good old aunt Nancy now to encourage me; but my brother William and my children were continually beckoning me to the north.

And now I must go back a few months in my story. I have stated that the first of January was the time for selling slaves, or leasing them out to new masters. If time were counted by heart-throbs, the poor slaves might reckon years of suffering during that festival so joyous to the free. On the New Year's day preceding my aunt's death, one of my friends, named Fanny, was to be sold at auction, to pay her master's debts. My thoughts were with her during all the day, and at night I anxiously inquired what had been her fate. I was told that she had been sold to one master, and her four little girls to another master, far distant; that she had escaped from her purchaser, and was not to be found. Her mother was the old Aggie I have spoken of. She lived in a small tenement belonging to my grandmother, and built on the same lot with her own house. Her dwelling was searched and watched, and that brought the patrols so near me that I was obliged to keep very close in my den. The hunters were somehow eluded; and not long afterwards Benny accidentally caught sight of Fanny in her mother's hut. He told his grandmother, who charged him never to speak of it, explaining to him the frightful consequences; and he never betrayed the trust. Aggie little dreamed that my grandmother knew where her daughter was concealed, and that the stooping form of her old neighbor was bending under a similar burden of anxiety and fear; but these dangerous secrets deepened the sympathy between the two old persecuted mothers.

My friend Fanny and I remained many weeks hidden within call of each other; but she was unconscious of the fact. I longed to have her share my den, which seemed a more secure retreat than her own; but I had brought so much trouble on my grandmother, that it seemed wrong to ask her to incur greater risks. My restlessness increased. I had lived too long in bodily pain and anguish of spirit. Always I was in dread that by some accident, or some contrivance, slavery would succeed in snatching my children from me. This thought drove me nearly frantic, and I determined to steer for the North Star at all hazards. At this crisis, Providence opened an unexpected way for me to escape. My friend Peter came one evening, and asked to speak with me. "Your day has come, Linda," said he. "I have found a chance for you to go to the Free States. You have a fortnight to decide." The news seemed too good to be true; but Peter explained his arrangements, and told me all that was necessary was for me to say I would go. I was going to answer him with a joyful yes, when the thought of Benny came to my mind. I told him the temptation was exceedingly strong, but I was terribly afraid of Dr. Flint's alleged power over my child, and that I could not go and leave him behind. Peter remonstrated earnestly. He said such a good chance might never occur again; that Benny was free, and could be sent to me; and that for the sake of my children's welfare I ought not to hesitate a moment. I told him I would consult with uncle Phillip. My uncle rejoiced in the plan, and bade me go by all means. He promised, if his life was spared, that he would either bring or send my son to me as soon as I reached a place of safety. I resolved to go, but thought nothing had better be said to my grandmother till very near the time of departure. But my uncle thought she would feel it more keenly if I left here so suddenly. "I will reason with her," said he, "and convince her how necessary it is, not only for your sake, but for hers also. You cannot be blind to the fact that she is sinking under her burdens." I was not blind to it. I knew that my concealment was an ever-present source of anxiety, and that the older she grew the more nervously fearful she was of discovery. My uncle talked with her, and finally succeeded in persuading her that it was absolutely necessary for me to seize the chance so unexpectedly offered.

The anticipation of being a free woman proved almost too much for my weak frame. The excitement stimulated me, and at the same time bewildered me. I made busy preparations for my journey, and for my son to follow me. I resolved to have an interview with him before I went, that I might give him cautions and advice, and tell him how anxiously I should be waiting for him at the north. Grandmother stole up to me as often as possible to whisper words of counsel. She insisted upon writing to Dr. Flint, as soon as I arrived in the Free States, and asking him to sell me to her. She said she would sacrifice her house, and all she had in the world, for the sake of having me safe with my children in any part of the world. If she could only live to know *that* she could die in peace. I promised the dear old faithful friend that I would write to her as soon as I arrived, and put the letter in a safe way to reach her; but in my own mind I resolved that not another cent of her hard earnings should be spent to pay rapacious slaveholders for what they called their property. And even if I had not been unwilling to buy what I had already a right to possess, common humanity would have prevented me from accepting the generous offer, at the expense of turning my aged relative out of house and home, when she was trembling on the brink of the grave.

I was to escape in a vessel; but I forbear to mention any further particulars. I was in readiness, but the vessel was unexpectedly detained several days. Meantime, news came to town of a most horrible murder committed on a fugitive slave, named James. Charity, the mother of this unfortunate young man, had been an old acquaintance of ours. I have told the shocking particulars of his death, in my description of some of the neighboring slaveholders. My grandmother, always nervously sensitive about runaways, was terribly frightened. She felt sure that a similar fate awaited me, if I did not desist from my enterprise. She sobbed, and groaned, and entreated me not to go. Her excessive fear was somewhat contagious, and my heart was not proof against her extreme agony. I was grievously disappointed, but I promised to relinquish my project.

When my friend Peter was apprised of this, he was both disappointed and vexed. He said, that judging from our past experience, it would be a long time before I had such another chance to throw away. I told him it need not be thrown away; that I had a friend concealed near by, who would be glad enough to take the place that had been provided for me. I told him about poor Fanny, and the kind-hearted, noble fellow, who never turned his back upon any body in distress, white or black, expressed his readiness to help her. Aggie was much surprised when she found that we knew her secret. She was rejoiced to hear of such a chance for Fanny, and arrangements were made for her to go on board the vessel the next night. They both supposed that I had long been at the north, therefore my name was not mentioned in the transaction. Fanny was carried on board at the appointed time, and stowed away in a very small cabin. This accommodation had been purchased at a price that would pay for a voyage to England. But when one proposes to go to fine old England, they stop to calculate whether they can afford the cost of the pleasure; while in making a bargain to escape from slavery, the trembling victim is ready to say, "Take all I have, only don't betray me!"

The next morning I peeped through my loophole, and saw that it was dark and cloudy. At night I received news that the wind was ahead, and the vessel had not sailed. I was exceedingly anxious about Fanny, and Peter too, who was running a tremendous risk at my instigation. Next day the wind and weather remained the same. Poor Fanny had been half dead with fright when they carried her on board, and I could readily imagine how she must be suffering now. Grandmother came often to my den, to say how thankful she was I did not go. On the third morning she rapped for me to come down to the storeroom. The poor old sufferer was breaking down under her weight of trouble. She was easily flurried now. I found her in a nervous, excited state, but I was not aware that she had forgotten to lock the door behind her, as usual. She was exceedingly worried about the detention of the vessel. She was afraid all would be discovered, and then Fanny, and Peter, and I, would all be tortured to death, and Phillip would be utterly ruined, and her house would be torn down. Poor Peter! If he should die such a horrible death as the poor slave James had lately done, and all for his kindness in trying to help me, how dreadful it would be for us all! Alas, the thought was familiar to me, and had sent many a sharp pang through my heart. I tried to suppress my own anxiety, and speak soothingly to her. She brought in some allusion to aunt Nancy, the dear daughter she had recently buried, and then she lost all control of herself. As she stood there, trembling and sobbing, a voice from the piazza called out, "Whar is you, aunt Marthy?" Grandmother was startled, and in her agitation opened the door, without thinking of me. In stepped Jenny, the mischievous housemaid, who had tried to enter my room, when I was concealed in the house of my white benefactress. "I's bin huntin ebery whar for you, aunt Marthy," said she. "My missis wants you to send her some crackers." I had slunk down behind a barrel, which entirely screened me, but I imagined that Jenny was looking directly at the spot, and my heart beat violently. My grandmother immediately thought what she had done, and went out quickly with Jenny to count the crackers locking the door after her. She returned to me, in a few minutes, the perfect picture of despair. "Poor child!" she exclaimed, "my carelessness has ruined you. The boat ain't gone yet. Get ready immediately, and go with Fanny. I ain't got another word to say against it now; for there's no telling what may happen this day."

Uncle Phillip was sent for, and he agreed with his mother in thinking that Jenny would inform Dr. Flint in less than twenty-four hours. He advised getting me on board the boat, if possible; if not, I had better keep very still in my den, where they could not find me without tearing the house down. He said it would not do for him to move in the matter, because suspicion would be immediately excited; but he promised to communicate with Peter. I felt reluctant to apply to him again, having implicated him too much already; but there seemed to be no alternative. Vexed as Peter had been by my indecision, he was true to his generous nature, and said at once that he would do his best to help me, trusting I should show myself a stronger woman this time.

He immediately proceeded to the wharf, and found that the wind had shifted, and the vessel was slowly beating down stream. On some pretext of urgent necessity, he offered two boatmen a dollar apiece to catch up with her. He was of lighter complexion than the boatmen he hired, and when the captain saw them coming so rapidly, he thought officers were pursuing his vessel in search of the runaway slave he had on board. They hoisted sails, but the boat gained upon them, and the indefatigable Peter sprang on board.

The captain at once recognized him. Peter asked him to go below, to speak about a bad bill he had given him. When he told his errand, the captain replied, "Why, the woman's here already; and I've put her where you or the devil would have a tough job to find her."

"But it is another woman I want to bring," said Peter. "*She* is in great distress, too, and you shall be paid any thing within reason, if you'll stop and take her."

"What's her name?" inquired the captain. "Linda," he replied.

"That's the name of the woman already here," rejoined the captain. "By George! I believe you mean to betray me."

"O!" exclaimed Peter, "God knows I wouldn't harm a hair of your head. I am too grateful to you. But there really *is* another woman in great danger. Do have the humanity to stop and take her!"

After a while they came to an understanding. Fanny, not dreaming I was any where about in that region, had assumed my name, though she called herself Johnson. "Linda is a common name," said Peter, "and the woman I want to bring is Linda Brent."

The captain agreed to wait at a certain place till evening, being handsomely paid for his detention.

Of course, the day was an anxious one for us all. But we concluded that if Jenny had seen me, she would be too wise to let her mistress know of it; and that she probably would not get a chance to see Dr. Flint's family till evening, for I knew very well what were the rules in that household. I afterwards believed that she did not see me; for nothing ever came of it, and she was one of those base characters that would have jumped to betray a suffering fellow being for the sake of thirty pieces of silver.

I made all my arrangements to go on board as soon as it was dusk. The intervening time I resolved to spend with my son. I had not spoken to him for seven years, though I had been under the same roof, and seen him every day, when I was well enough to sit at the loophole. I did not dare to venture beyond the storeroom; so they brought him there, and locked us up together, in a place concealed from the piazza door. It was an agitating interview for both of us. After we had talked and wept together for a little while, he said, "Mother, I'm glad you're going away. I wish I could go with you. I knew you was here; and I have been *so* afraid they would come and catch you!" I was greatly surprised, and asked him how he had found it out.

He replied, "I was standing under the eaves, one day, before Ellen went away, and I heard somebody cough up over the wood shed. I don't know what made me think it was you, but I did think so. I missed Ellen, the night before she went away; and grandmother brought her back into the room in the night; and I thought maybe she'd been to see *you*, before she went, for I heard grandmother whisper to her, 'Now go to sleep; and remember never to tell.'"

I asked him if he ever mentioned his suspicions to his sister. He said he never did; but after he heard the cough, if he saw her playing with other children on that side of the house, he always tried to coax her round to the other side, for fear they would hear me cough, too. He said he had kept a close lookout for Dr. Flint, and if he saw him speak to a constable, or a patrol, he always told grandmother. I now recollected that I had seen him manifest uneasiness, when people were on that side of the house, and I had at the time been puzzled to conjecture a motive for his actions. Such prudence may seem extraordinary in a boy of twelve years, but slaves, being surrounded by mysteries, deceptions, and dangers, early learn to be suspicious and watchful, and prematurely cautious and cunning. He had never asked a question of grandmother, or uncle Phillip, and I had often heard him chime in with other children, when they spoke of my being at the north.

I told him I was now really going to the Free States, and if he was a good, honest boy, and a loving child to his dear old grandmother, the Lord would bless him, and bring him to me, and we and Ellen would live together. He began to tell me that grandmother had not eaten any thing all day. While he was speaking, the door was unlocked, and she came in with a small bag of money, which she wanted me to take. I begged her to keep a part of it, at least, to pay for Benny's being sent to the north; but she insisted, while her tears were falling fast, that I should take the whole. "You may be sick among strangers," she said, "and they would send you to the poorhouse to die." Ah, that good grandmother!

For the last time I went up to my nook. Its desolate appearance no longer chilled me, for the light of hope had risen in my soul. Yet, even with the blessed prospect of freedom before me, I felt very sad at leaving forever that old homestead, where I had been sheltered so long by the dear old grandmother; where I had dreamed my first young dream of love; and where, after that had faded away, my children came to twine themselves so closely round my desolate heart. As the hour approached for me to leave, I again descended to the storeroom. My grandmother and Benny were there. She took me by the hand,

and said, "Linda, let us pray." We knelt down together, with my child pressed to my heart, and my other arm round the faithful, loving old friend I was about to leave forever. On no other occasion has it ever been my lot to listen to so fervent a supplication for mercy and protection. It thrilled through my heart, and inspired me with trust in God.

Peter was waiting for me in the street. I was soon by his side, faint in body, but strong of purpose. I did not look back upon the old place, though I felt that I should never see it again.

# XXX. NORTHWARD BOUND

I never could tell how we reached the wharf. My brain was all of a whirl, and my limbs tottered under me. At an appointed place we met my uncle Phillip, who had started before us on a different route, that he might reach the wharf first, and give us timely warning if there was any danger. A row-boat was in readiness. As I was about to step in, I felt something pull me gently, and turning round I saw Benny, looking pale and anxious. He whispered in my ear, "I've been peeping into the doctor's window, and he's at home. Good by, mother. Don't cry; I'll come." He hastened away. I clasped the hand of my good uncle, to whom I owed so much, and of Peter, the brave, generous friend who had volunteered to run such terrible risks to secure my safety. To this day I remember how his bright face beamed with joy, when he told me he had discovered a safe method for me to escape. Yet that intelligent, enterprising, noble-hearted man was a chattel! liable, by the laws of a country that calls itself civilized, to be sold with horses and pigs! We parted in silence. Our hearts were all too full for words!

Swiftly the boat glided over the water. After a while, one of the sailors said, "Don't be down-hearted, madam. We will take you safely to your husband, in ——." At first I could not imagine what he meant; but I had presence of mind to think that it probably referred to something the captain had told him; so I thanked him, and said I hoped we should have pleasant weather.

When I entered the vessel the captain came forward to meet me. He was an elderly man, with a pleasant countenance. He showed me to a little box of a cabin, where sat my friend Fanny. She started as if she had seen a spectre. She gazed on me in utter astonishment, and exclaimed, "Linda, can this be *you*? or is it your ghost?" When we were locked in each other's arms, my overwrought feelings could no longer be restrained. My sobs reached the ears of the captain, who came and very kindly reminded us, that for his safety, as well as our own, it would be prudent for us not to attract any attention. He said that when there was a sail in sight he wished us to keep below; but at other times, he had no objection to our being on deck. He assured us that he would keep a good lookout, and if we acted prudently, he thought we should be in no danger. He had represented us as women going to meet our husbands in ——. We thanked him, and promised to observe carefully all the directions he gave us.

Fanny and I now talked by ourselves, low and quietly, in our little cabin. She told me of the suffering she had gone through in making her escape, and of her terrors while she was concealed in her mother's house. Above all, she dwelt on the agony of separation from all her children on that dreadful auction day. She could scarcely credit me, when I told her of the place where I had passed nearly seven years. "We have the same sorrows," said I. "No," replied she, "you are going to see your children soon, and there is no hope that I shall ever even hear from mine."

The vessel was soon under way, but we made slow progress. The wind was against us. I should not have cared for this, if we had been out of sight of the town; but until there were miles of water between us and our enemies, we were filled with constant apprehensions that the constables would come on board. Neither could I feel quite at ease with the captain and his men. I was an entire stranger to that class of people, and I had heard that sailors were rough, and sometimes cruel. We were so completely in their power, that if they were bad men, our situation would be dreadful. Now that the captain was paid for our passage, might he not be tempted to make more money by giving us up to those who claimed us as property? I was naturally of a confiding disposition, but slavery had made me suspicious of every body. Fanny did not share my distrust of the captain or his men. She said she was afraid at first, but she had been on board three days while the vessel lay in the dock, and nobody had betrayed her, or treated her otherwise than kindly.

The captain soon came to advise us to go on deck for fresh air. His friendly and respectful manner, combined with Fanny's testimony, reassured me, and we went with him. He placed us in a comfortable seat, and occasionally entered into conversation. He told us he was a Southerner by birth, and had spent the greater part of his life in the Slave States, and that he had recently lost a brother who traded in slaves. "But," said he, "it is a pitiable and degrading business, and I always felt ashamed to acknowledge my brother in connection with it." As we passed Snaky Swamp, he pointed to it, and said, "There is a slave territory that defies all the laws." I thought of the terrible days I had spent there, and though it was not called Dismal Swamp, it made me feel very dismal as I looked at it.

I shall never forget that night. The balmy air of spring was so refreshing! And how shall I describe my sensations when we were fairly sailing on Chesapeake Bay? O, the beautiful sunshine! the exhilarating breeze! And I could enjoy them without fear or restraint. I had never realized what grand things air and sunlight are till I had been deprived of them.

Ten days after we left land we were approaching Philadelphia. The captain said we should arrive there in the night, but he thought we had better wait till morning, and go on shore in broad daylight, as the best way to avoid suspicion.

I replied, "You know best. But will you stay on board and protect us?"

He saw that I was suspicious, and he said he was sorry, now that he had brought us to the end of our voyage, to find I had so little confidence in him. Ah, if he had ever been a slave he would have known how difficult it was to trust a white man. He assured us that we might sleep through the night without fear; that he would take care we were not left unprotected. Be it said to the honor of this captain, Southerner as he was, that if Fanny and I had been white ladies, and our passage lawfully engaged, he could not have treated us more respectfully. My intelligent friend, Peter, had rightly estimated the character of the man to whose honor he had intrusted us.

The next morning I was on deck as soon as the day dawned. I called Fanny to see the sun rise, for the first time in our lives, on free soil; for such I *then* believed it to be. We watched the reddening sky, and saw the great orb come up slowly out of the water, as it seemed. Soon the waves began to sparkle, and every thing caught the beautiful glow. Before us lay the city of strangers. We looked at each other, and the eyes of both were moistened with tears. We had escaped from slavery, and we supposed ourselves to be safe from the hunters. But we were alone in the world, and we had left dear ties behind us; ties cruelly sundered by the demon Slavery.

# XXXI. INCIDENTS IN PHILADELPHIA

I had heard that the poor slave had many friends at the north. I trusted we should find some of them. Meantime, we would take it for granted that all were friends, till they proved to the contrary. I sought out the kind captain, thanked him for his attentions, and told him I should never cease to be grateful for the service he had rendered us. I gave him a message to the friends I had left at home, and he promised to deliver it. We were placed in a row-boat, and in about fifteen minutes were landed on a wood wharf in Philadelphia. As I stood looking round, the friendly captain touched me on the shoulder, and said, "There is a respectable-looking colored man behind you. I will speak to him about the New York trains, and tell him you wish to go directly on." I thanked him, and asked him to direct me to some shops where I could buy gloves and veils. He did so, and said he would talk with the colored man till I returned. I made what haste I could. Constant exercise on board the vessel, and frequent rubbing with salt water, had nearly restored the use of my limbs. The noise of the great city confused me, but I found the shops, and bought some double veils and gloves for Fanny and myself. The shopman told me they were so many levies. I had never heard the word before, but I did not tell him so. I thought if he knew I was a stranger he might ask me where I came from. I gave him a gold piece, and when he returned the change, I counted it, and found out how much a levy was. I made my way back to the wharf, where the captain introduced me to the colored man, as the Rev. Jeremiah Durham, minister of Bethel church. He took me by the hand, as if I had been an old friend. He told us we were too late for the morning cars to New York, and must wait until the evening, or the next morning. He invited me to go home with him, assuring me that his wife would give me a cordial welcome; and for my friend he would provide a home with one of his neighbors. I thanked him for so much kindness to strangers, and told him if I must be detained, I should like to hunt up some people who formerly went from our part of the country. Mr. Durham insisted that I should dine with him, and then he would assist me in finding my friends. The sailors came to bid us good by. I shook their hardy hands, with tears in my eyes. They had all been kind to us, and they had rendered us a greater service than they could possibly conceive of.

I had never seen so large a city, or been in contact with so many people in the streets. It seemed as if those who passed looked at us with an expression of curiosity. My face was so blistered and peeled, by sitting on deck, in wind and sunshine, that I thought they could not easily decide to what nation I belonged.

Mrs. Durham met me with a kindly welcome, without asking any questions. I was tired, and her friendly manner was a sweet refreshment. God bless her! I was sure that she had comforted other weary hearts, before I received her sympathy. She was surrounded by her husband and children, in a home made sacred by protecting laws. I thought of my own children, and sighed.

After dinner Mr. Durham went with me in quest of the friends I had spoken of. They went from my native town, and I anticipated much pleasure in looking on familiar faces. They were not at home, and we retracted our steps through streets delightfully clean. On the way, Mr. Durham observed that I had spoken to him of a daughter I expected to meet; that he was surprised, for I looked so young he had taken me for a single woman. He was approaching a subject on which I was extremely sensitive. He would ask about my husband next, I thought, and if I answered him truly, what would he think of me? I told him I had two children, one in New York the other at the south. He asked some further questions, and I frankly told him some of the most important events of my life. It was painful for me to do it; but I would not deceive him. If he was desirous of being my friend, I thought he ought to know how far I was worthy of it. "Excuse me, if I have tried your feelings," said he. "I did not question you from idle curiosity. I wanted to understand your situation, in order to know whether I could be of any service to you, or your little girl. Your straight-forward answers do you credit; but don't answer every body so openly. It might give some heartless people a pretext for treating you with contempt."

That word *contempt* burned me like coals of fire. I replied, "God alone knows how I have suffered; and He, I trust, will forgive me. If I am permitted to have my children, I intend to be a good mother, and to live in such a manner that people cannot treat me with contempt."

"I respect your sentiments," said he. "Place your trust in God, and be governed by good principles, and you will not fail to find friends."

When we reached home, I went to my room, glad to shut out the world for a while. The words he had spoken made an indelible impression upon me. They brought up great shadows from the mournful past. In the midst of my meditations I was startled by a knock at the door. Mrs. Durham entered, her face all beaming with kindness, to say that there was an anti-slavery friend down stairs, who would like to see me. I overcame my dread of encountering strangers, and went with her. Many questions were asked concerning my experiences, and my escape from slavery; but I observed how careful they all were not to say any thing that might wound my feelings. How gratifying this was, can be fully understood only by those who have been accustomed to be treated as if they were not included within the pale of human beings. The anti-slavery friend had come to inquire into my plans, and to offer assistance, if needed. Fanny was comfortably established, for the present, with a friend of Mr. Durham. The Anti-Slavery Society agreed to pay her expenses to New York. The same was offered to me, but I declined to accept it, telling them that my grandmother had given me sufficient to pay my expenses to the end of my journey. We were urged to remain in Philadelphia a few days, until some suitable escort could be found for us. I gladly accepted the proposition, for I had a dread of meeting slaveholders, and some dread also of railroads. I had never entered a railroad car in my life, and it seemed to me quite an important event.

That night I sought my pillow with feelings I had never carried to it before. I verily believed myself to be a free woman. I was wakeful for a long time, and I had no sooner fallen asleep, than I was roused by fire-bells. I jumped up, and hurried on my clothes. Where I came from, every body hastened to dress themselves on such occasions. The white people thought a great fire might be used as a good opportunity for insurrection, and that it was best to be in readiness; and the colored people were ordered out to labor in extinguishing the flames. There was but one engine in our town, and colored women and children were often required to drag it to the river's edge and fill it. Mrs. Durham's daughter slept in the same room with me, and seeing that she slept through all the din, I thought it was my duty to wake her. "What's the matter?" said she, rubbing her eyes.

"They're screaming fire in the streets, and the bells are ringing," I replied.

"What of that?" said she, drowsily. "We are used to it. We never get up, without the fire is very near. What good would it do?"

I was quite surprised that it was not necessary for us to go and help fill the engine. I was an ignorant child, just beginning to learn how things went on in great cities.

At daylight, I heard women crying fresh fish, berries, radishes, and various other things. All this was new to me. I dressed myself at an early hour, and sat at the window to watch that unknown tide of life. Philadelphia seemed to me a wonderfully great place. At the breakfast table, my idea of going out to drag the engine was laughed over, and I joined in the mirth.

I went to see Fanny, and found her so well contented among her new friends that she was in no haste to leave. I was also very happy with my kind hostess. She had had advantages for education, and was vastly my superior. Every day, almost every hour, I was adding to my little stock of knowledge. She took me out to see the city as much as she deemed prudent. One day she took me to an artist's room, and showed me the portraits of some of her children. I had never seen any paintings of colored people before, and they seemed to be beautiful.

At the end of five days, one of Mrs. Durham's friends offered to accompany us to New York the following morning. As I held the hand of my good hostess in a parting clasp, I longed to know whether her husband had repeated to her what I had told him. I supposed he had, but she never made any allusion to it. I presume it was the delicate silence of womanly sympathy.

When Mr. Durham handed us our tickets, he said, "I am afraid you will have a disagreeable ride; but I could not procure tickets for the first-class cars."

Supposing I had not given him money enough, I offered more. "O, no," said he, "they could not be had for any money. They don't allow colored people to go in the first-class cars."

This was the first chill to my enthusiasm about the Free States. Colored people were allowed to ride in a filthy box, behind white people, at the south, but there they were not required to pay for the privilege. It made me sad to find how the north aped the customs of slavery.

We were stowed away in a large, rough car, with windows on each side, too high for us to look out without standing up. It was crowded with people, apparently of all nations. There were plenty of beds and cradles, containing screaming and kicking babies. Every other man had a cigar or pipe in his mouth, and jugs of whiskey were handed round freely. The fumes of the whiskey and the dense tobacco smoke were sickening to my senses, and my mind was equally nauseated by the coarse jokes and ribald songs around me. It was a very disagreeable ride. Since that time there has been some improvement in these matters.

# XXXII. THE MEETING OF MOTHER AND DAUGHTER

When we arrived in New York, I was half crazed by the crowd of coachmen calling out, "Carriage, ma'am?" We bargained with one to take us to Sullivan Street for twelve shillings. A burly Irishman stepped up and said, "I'll tak' ye for sax shillings." The reduction of half the price was an object to us, and we asked if he could take us right away. "Troth an I will, ladies," he replied. I noticed that the hackmen smiled at each other, and I inquired whether his conveyance was decent. "Yes, it's dacent it is, marm. Devil a bit would I be after takin' ladies in a cab that was not dacent." We gave him our checks. He went for the baggage, and soon reappeared, saying, "This way, if you plase, ladies." We followed, and found our trunks on a truck, and we were invited to take our seats on them. We told him that was not what we bargained for, and he must take the trunks off. He swore they should not be touched till we had paid him six shillings. In our situation it was not prudent to attract attention, and I was about to pay him what he required, when a man near by shook his head for me not to do it. After a great ado we got rid of the Irishman, and had our trunks fastened on a hack. We had been recommended to a boarding-house in Sullivan Street, and thither we drove. There Fanny and I separated. The Anti-Slavery Society provided a home for her, and I afterwards heard of her in prosperous circumstances. I sent for an old friend from my part of the country, who had for some time been doing business in New York. He came immediately. I told him I wanted to go to my daughter, and asked him to aid me in procuring an interview.

I cautioned him not to let it be known to the family that I had just arrived from the south, because they supposed I had been at the north seven years. He told me there was a colored woman in Brooklyn who came from the same town I did, and I had better go to her house, and have my daughter meet me there. I accepted the proposition thankfully, and he agreed to escort me to Brooklyn. We crossed Fulton ferry, went up Myrtle Avenue, and stopped at the house he designated. I was just about to enter, when two girls passed. My friend called my attention to them. I turned, and recognized in the eldest, Sarah, the daughter of a woman who used to live with my grandmother, but who had left the south years ago. Surprised and rejoiced at this unexpected meeting, I threw my arms round her, and inquired concerning her mother.

"You take no notice of the other girl," said my friend. I turned, and there stood my Ellen! I pressed her to my heart, then held her away from me to take a look at her. She had changed a good deal in the two years since I parted from her. Signs of neglect could be discerned by eyes less observing than a mother's. My friend invited us all to go into the house; but Ellen said she had been sent of an errand, which she would do as quickly as possible, and go home and ask Mrs. Hobbs to let her come and see me. It was agreed that I should send for her the next day. Her companion, Sarah, hastened to tell her mother of my arrival. When I entered the house, I found the mistress of it absent, and I waited for her return. Before I saw her, I heard her saying, "Where is Linda Brent? I used to know her father and mother." Soon Sarah came with her mother. So there was quite a company of us, all from my grandmother's neighborhood. These friends gathered round me and questioned me eagerly. They laughed, they cried, and they shouted. They thanked God that I had got away from my persecutors and was safe on Long Island. It was a day of great excitement. How different from the silent days I had passed in my dreary den!

The next morning was Sunday. My first waking thoughts were occupied with the note I was to send to Mrs. Hobbs, the lady with whom Ellen lived. That I had recently come into that vicinity was evident; otherwise I should have sooner inquired for my daughter. It would not do to let them know I had just arrived from the south, for that would involve the suspicion of my having been harbored there, and might bring trouble, if not ruin, on several people.

I like a straightforward course, and am always reluctant to resort to subterfuges. So far as my ways have been crooked, I charge them all upon slavery. It was that system of violence and wrong which now left me no alternative but to enact a falsehood. I began my note by stating that I had recently arrived from Canada, and was very desirous to have my daughter come to see me. She came and brought a message from Mrs. Hobbs, inviting me to her house, and assuring me that I need not have any fears. The conversation I had with my child did not leave my mind at ease. When I asked if she was well treated, she answered yes; but there was no heartiness in the tone, and it seemed to me that she said it from an unwillingness to have me troubled on her account. Before she left me, she asked very earnestly, "Mother, will you take me to live with you?" It made me sad to think that I could not give her a home till I went to work and earned the means; and that might take me a long time. When she was placed with Mrs. Hobbs, the agreement was that she should be sent to school She had been there two years, and was now nine years old, and she scarcely knew her letters. There was no excuse for this, for there were good public schools in Brooklyn, to which she could have been sent without expense.

She staid with me till dark, and I went home with her. I was received in a friendly manner by the family, and all agreed in saying that Ellen was a useful, good girl. Mrs. Hobbs looked me coolly in the face, and said, "I suppose you know that my cousin, Mr. Sands, has *given* her to my eldest daughter. She will make a nice waiting-maid for her when she grows up." I did not answer a word. How *could* she, who knew by experience the strength of a mother's love, and who was perfectly aware of the relation Mr. Sands bore to my children,—how *could* she look me in the face, while she thrust such a dagger into my heart?

I was no longer surprised that they had kept her in such a state of ignorance. Mr. Hobbs had formerly been wealthy, but he had failed, and afterwards obtained a subordinate situation in the Custom House. Perhaps they expected to return to the south some day; and Ellen's knowledge was quite sufficient for a slave's condition. I was impatient to go to work and earn money, that I might change the uncertain position of my children. Mr. Sands had not kept his promise to emancipate them. I had also been deceived about Ellen. What security had I with regard to Benjamin? I felt that I had none.

I returned to my friend's house in an uneasy state of mind. In order to protect my children, it was necessary that I should own myself. I called myself free, and sometimes felt so; but I knew I was insecure. I sat down that night and wrote a civil letter to Dr. Flint, asking him to state the lowest terms on which he would sell me; and as I belonged by law to his daughter, I wrote to her also, making a similar request.

Since my arrival at the north I had not been unmindful of my dear brother William. I had made diligent inquiries for him, and having heard of him in Boston, I went thither. When I arrived there, I found he had gone to New Bedford. I wrote to that place, and was informed he had gone on a whaling voyage, and would not return for some months. I went back to New York to get employment near Ellen. I received an answer from Dr. Flint, which gave me no encouragement. He advised me to return and submit myself to my rightful owners, and then any request I might make would be granted. I lent this letter to a friend, who lost it; otherwise I would present a copy to my readers.

# XXXIII. A HOME FOUND

My greatest anxiety now was to obtain employment. My health was greatly improved, though my limbs continued to trouble me with swelling whenever I walked much. The greatest difficulty in my way was, that those who employed strangers required a recommendation; and in my peculiar position, I could, of course, obtain no certificates from the families I had so faithfully served.

One day an acquaintance told me of a lady who wanted a nurse for her babe, and I immediately applied for the situation. The lady told me she preferred to have one who had been a mother, and accustomed to the care of infants. I told her I had nursed two babes of my own. She asked me many questions, but, to my great relief, did not require a recommendation from my former employers. She told me she was an English woman, and that was a pleasant circumstance to me, because I had heard they had less prejudice against color than Americans entertained. It was agreed that we should try each other for a week. The trial proved satisfactory to both parties, and I was engaged for a month.

The heavenly Father had been most merciful to me in leading me to this place. Mrs. Bruce was a kind and gentle lady, and proved a true and sympathizing friend. Before the stipulated month expired, the necessity of passing up and down stairs frequently, caused my limbs to swell so painfully, that I became unable to perform my duties. Many ladies would have thoughtlessly discharged me; but Mrs. Bruce made arrangements to save me steps, and employed a physician to attend upon me. I had not yet told her that I was a fugitive slave. She noticed that I was often sad, and kindly inquired the cause. I spoke of being separated from my children, and from relatives who were dear to me; but I did not mention the constant feeling of insecurity which oppressed my spirits. I longed for some one to confide in; but I had been so deceived by white people, that I had lost all confidence in them. If they spoke kind words to me, I thought it was for some selfish purpose. I had entered this family with the distrustful feelings I had brought with me out of slavery; but ere six months had passed, I found that the gentle deportment of Mrs. Bruce and the smiles of her lovely babe were thawing my chilled heart. My narrow mind also began to expand under the influences of her intelligent conversation, and the opportunities for reading, which were gladly allowed me whenever I had leisure from my duties. I gradually became more energetic and more cheerful.

The old feeling of insecurity, especially with regard to my children, often threw its dark shadow across my sunshine. Mrs. Bruce offered me a home for Ellen; but pleasant as it would have been, I did not dare to accept it, for fear of offending the Hobbs family. Their knowledge of my precarious situation placed me in their power; and I felt that it was important for me to keep on the right side of them, till, by dint of labor and economy, I could make a home for my children. I was far from feeling satisfied with Ellen's situation. She was not well cared for. She sometimes came to New York to visit me; but she generally brought a request from Mrs. Hobbs that I would buy her a pair of shoes, or some article of clothing. This was accompanied by a promise of payment when Mr. Hobbs's salary at the Custom House became due; but some how or other the pay-day never came. Thus many dollars of my earnings were expended to keep my child comfortably clothed. That, however, was a slight trouble, compared with the fear that their pecuniary embarrassments might induce them to sell my precious young daughter. I knew they were in constant communication with Southerners, and had frequent opportunities to do it. I have stated that when Dr. Flint put Ellen in jail, at two years old, she had an inflammation of the eyes, occasioned by measles. This disease still troubled her; and kind Mrs. Bruce proposed that she should come to New York for a while, to be under the care of Dr. Elliott, a well known oculist. It did not occur to me that there was any thing improper in a mother's making such a request; but Mrs. Hobbs was very angry, and refused to let her go. Situated as I was, it was not politic to insist upon it. I made no complaint, but I longed to be entirely free to act a mother's part towards my children. The next time I went over to Brooklyn, Mrs. Hobbs, as if to apologize for her anger, told me she had employed her own physician to attend to Ellen's eyes, and that she had refused my request because she did not consider it safe to trust her in New York. I accepted the explanation in silence; but she had told me that my child *belonged* to her daughter, and I suspected that her real motive was a fear of my conveying her property away from her. Perhaps I did her injustice; but my knowledge of Southerners made it difficult for me to feel otherwise.

Sweet and bitter were mixed in the cup of my life, and I was thankful that it had ceased to be entirely bitter. I loved Mrs. Bruce's babe. When it laughed and crowed in my face, and twined its little tender arms confidingly about my neck, it made me think of the time when Benny and Ellen were babies, and my wounded heart was soothed. One bright morning, as I stood at the window, tossing baby in my arms, my attention was attracted by a young man in sailor's dress, who was closely observing every house as he passed. I looked at him earnestly. Could it be my brother William? It *must* be he—and yet, how changed! I placed the baby safely, flew down stairs, opened the front door, beckoned to the sailor, and in less than a minute I was clasped in my brother's arms. How much we had to tell each other! How we laughed, and how we cried, over each other's adventures! I took him to Brooklyn, and again saw him with Ellen, the dear child whom he had loved and tended so carefully, while I was shut up in my miserable den. He staid in New York a week. His old feelings of affection for me and Ellen were as lively as ever. There are no bonds so strong as those which are formed by suffering together.

# XXXIV. THE OLD ENEMY AGAIN

My young mistress, Miss Emily Flint, did not return any answer to my letter requesting her to consent to my being sold. But after a while, I received a reply, which purported to be written by her younger brother. In order rightly to enjoy the contents of this letter, the reader must bear in mind that the Flint family supposed I had been at the north many years. They had no idea that I knew of the doctor's three excursions to New York in search of me; that I had heard his voice, when he came to borrow five hundred dollars for that purpose; and that I had seen him pass on his way to the steamboat. Neither were they aware that all the particulars of aunt Nancy's death and burial were conveyed to me at the time they occurred. I have kept the letter, of which I herewith subjoin a copy:—

"Your letter to sister was received a few days ago. I gather from it that you are desirous of returning to your native place, among your friends and relatives. We were all gratified with the contents of your letter; and let me assure you that if any members of the family have had any feeling of resentment towards you, they feel it no longer. We all sympathize with you in your unfortunate condition, and are ready to do all in our power to make you contented and happy. It is difficult for you to return home as a free person. If you were purchased by your grandmother, it is doubtful whether you would be permitted to remain, although it would be lawful for you to do so. If a servant should be allowed to purchase herself, after absenting herself so long from her owners, and return free, it would have an injurious effect. From your letter, I think your situation must be hard and uncomfortable. Come home. You have it in your power to be reinstated in our affections. We would receive you with open arms and tears of joy. You need not apprehend any unkind treatment, as we have not put ourselves to any trouble or expense to get you. Had we done so, perhaps we should feel otherwise. You know my sister was always attached to you, and that you were never treated as a slave. You were never put to hard work, nor exposed to field labor. On the contrary, you were taken into the house, and treated as one of us, and almost as free; and we, at least, felt that you were above disgracing yourself by running away. Believing you may be induced to come home voluntarily has induced me to write for my sister. The family will be rejoiced to see you; and your poor old grandmother expressed a great desire to have you come, when she heard your letter read. In her old age she needs the consolation of having her children round her. Doubtless you have heard of the death of your aunt. She was a faithful servant, and a faithful member of the Episcopal church. In her Christian life she taught us how to live—and, O, too high the price of knowledge, she taught us how to die! Could you have seen us round her death bed, with her mother, all mingling our tears in one common stream, you would have thought the same heartfelt tie existed between a master and his servant, as between a mother and her child. But this subject is too painful to dwell upon. I must bring my letter to a close. If you are contented to stay away from your old grandmother, your child, and the friends who love you, stay where you are. We shall never trouble ourselves to apprehend you. But should you prefer to come home, we will do all that we can to make you happy. If you do not wish to remain in the family, I know that father, by our persuasion, will be induced to let you be purchased by any person you may choose in our community. You will please answer this as soon as possible, and let us know your decision. Sister sends much love to you. In the mean time believe me your sincere friend and well wisher."

This letter was signed by Emily's brother, who was as yet a mere lad. I knew, by the style, that it was not written by a person of his age, and though the writing was disguised, I had been made too unhappy by it, in former years, not to recognize at once the hand of Dr. Flint. O, the hypocrisy of slaveholders! Did the old fox suppose I was goose enough to go into such a trap? Verily, he relied too much on "the stupidity of the African race." I did not return the family of Flints any thanks for their cordial invitation—a remissness for which I was, no doubt, charged with base ingratitude.

Not long afterwards I received a letter from one of my friends at the south, informing me that Dr. Flint was about to visit the north. The letter had been delayed, and I supposed he might be already on the way. Mrs. Bruce did not know I was a fugitive. I told her that important business called me to Boston, where my brother then was, and asked permission to bring a friend to supply my place as nurse, for a fortnight. I started on my journey immediately; and as soon as I arrived, I wrote to my grandmother that if Benny came, he must be sent to Boston. I knew she was only waiting for a good chance to send him north, and, fortunately, she had the legal power to do so, without asking leave of any body. She was a free woman; and when my children were purchased, Mr. Sands preferred to have the bill of sale drawn up in her name. It was conjectured that he advanced the money, but it was not known. At the south, a gentleman may have a shoal of colored children without any disgrace; but if he is known to purchase them, with the view of setting them free, the example is thought to be dangerous to their "peculiar institution," and he becomes unpopular.

There was a good opportunity to send Benny in a vessel coming directly to New York. He was put on board with a letter to a friend, who was requested to see him off to Boston. Early one morning, there was a loud rap at my door, and in rushed Benjamin, all out of breath. "O mother!" he exclaimed, "here I am! I run all the way; and I come all alone. How d'you do?"

O reader, can you imagine my joy? No, you cannot, unless you have been a slave mother. Benjamin rattled away as fast as his tongue could go. "Mother, why don't you bring Ellen here? I went over to Brooklyn to see her, and she felt very bad when I bid her good by. She said, 'O Ben, I wish I was going too.' I thought she'd know ever so much; but she don't know so much as I do; for I can read, and she can't. And, mother, I lost all my clothes coming. What can I do to get some more? I 'spose free boys can get along here at the north as well as white boys."

I did not like to tell the sanguine, happy little fellow how much he was mistaken. I took him to a tailor, and procured a change of clothes. The rest of the day was spent in mutual asking and answering of questions, with the wish constantly repeated that the good old grandmother was with us, and frequent injunctions from Benny to write to her immediately, and be sure to tell her every thing about his voyage, and his journey to Boston.

Dr. Flint made his visit to New York, and made every exertion to call upon me, and invite me to return with him, but not being able to ascertain where I was, his hospitable intentions were frustrated, and the affectionate family, who were waiting for me with "open arms," were doomed to disappointment.

As soon as I knew he was safely at home, I placed Benjamin in the care of my brother William, and returned to Mrs. Bruce. There I remained through the winter and spring, endeavoring to perform my duties faithfully, and finding a good degree of happiness in the attractions of baby Mary, the considerate kindness of her excellent mother, and occasional interviews with my darling daughter.

But when summer came, the old feeling of insecurity haunted me. It was necessary for me to take little Mary out daily, for exercise and fresh air, and the city was swarming with Southerners, some of whom might recognize me. Hot weather brings out snakes and slaveholders, and I like one class of the venomous creatures as little as I do the other. What a comfort it is, to be free to *say* so!

# XXXV. PREJUDICE AGAINST COLOR

It was a relief to my mind to see preparations for leaving the city. We went to Albany in the steamboat Knickerbocker. When the gong sounded for tea, Mrs. Bruce said, "Linda, it is late, and you and baby had better come to the table with me." I replied, "I know it is time baby had her supper, but I had rather not go with you, if you please. I am afraid of being insulted." "O no, not if you are with *me*," she said. I saw several white nurses go with their ladies, and I ventured to do the same. We were at the extreme end of the table. I was no sooner seated, than a gruff voice said, "Get up! You know you are not allowed to sit here." I looked up, and, to my astonishment and indignation, saw that the speaker was a colored man. If his office required him to enforce the by-laws of the boat, he might, at least, have done it politely. I replied, "I shall not get up, unless the captain comes and takes me up." No cup of tea was offered me, but Mrs. Bruce handed me hers and called for another. I looked to see whether the other nurses were treated in a similar manner. They were all properly waited on.

Next morning, when we stopped at Troy for breakfast, every body was making a rush for the table. Mrs. Bruce said, "Take my arm, Linda, and we'll go in together." The landlord heard her, and said, "Madam, will you allow your nurse and baby to take breakfast with my family?" I knew this was to be attributed to my complexion; but he spoke courteously, and therefore I did not mind it.

At Saratoga we found the United States Hotel crowded, and Mr. Bruce took one of the cottages belonging to the hotel. I had thought, with gladness, of going to the quiet of the country, where I should meet few people, but here I found myself in the midst of a swarm of Southerners. I looked round me with fear and trembling, dreading to see some one who would recognize me. I was rejoiced to find that we were to stay but a short time.

We soon returned to New York, to make arrangements for spending the remainder of the summer at Rockaway. While the laundress was putting the clothes in order, I took an opportunity to go over to

Brooklyn to see Ellen. I met her going to a grocery store, and the first words she said, were, "O, mother, don't go to Mrs. Hobbs's. Her brother, Mr. Thorne, has come from the south, and may be he'll tell where you are." I accepted the warning. I told her I was going away with Mrs. Bruce the next day, and would try to see her when I came back.

Being in servitude to the Anglo-Saxon race, I was not put into a "Jim Crow car," on our way to Rockaway, neither was I invited to ride through the streets on the top of trunks in a truck; but every where I found the same manifestations of that cruel prejudice, which so discourages the feelings, and represses the energies of the colored people. We reached Rockaway before dark, and put up at the Pavilion—a large hotel, beautifully situated by the sea-side—a great resort of the fashionable world. Thirty or forty nurses were there, of a great variety of nations. Some of the ladies had colored waiting-maids and coachmen, but I was the only nurse tinged with the blood of Africa. When the tea bell rang, I took little Mary and followed the other nurses. Supper was served in a long hall. A young man, who had the ordering of things, took the circuit of the table two or three times, and finally pointed me to a seat at the lower end of it. As there was but one chair, I sat down and took the child in my lap. Whereupon the young man came to me and said, in the blandest manner possible, "Will you please to seat the little girl in the chair, and stand behind it and feed her? After they have done, you will be shown to the kitchen, where you will have a good supper."

This was the climax! I found it hard to preserve my self-control, when I looked round, and saw women who were nurses, as I was, and only one shade lighter in complexion, eyeing me with a defiant look, as if my presence were a contamination. However, I said nothing. I quietly took the child in my arms, went to our room, and refused to go to the table again. Mr. Bruce ordered meals to be sent to the room for little Mary and I. This answered for a few days; but the waiters of the establishment were white, and they soon began to complain, saying they were not hired to wait on negroes. The landlord requested Mr. Bruce to send me down to my meals, because his servants rebelled against bringing them up, and the colored servants of other boarders were dissatisfied because all were not treated alike.

My answer was that the colored servants ought to be dissatisfied with *themselves*, for not having too much self-respect to submit to such treatment; that there was no difference in the price of board for colored and white servants, and there was no justification for difference of treatment. I staid a month after this, and finding I was resolved to stand up for my rights, they concluded to treat me well. Let every colored man and woman do this, and eventually we shall cease to be trampled under foot by our oppressors.

# XXXVI. THE HAIRBREADTH ESCAPE

After we returned to New York, I took the earliest opportunity to go and see Ellen. I asked to have her called down stairs; for I supposed Mrs. Hobbs's southern brother might still be there, and I was desirous to avoid seeing him, if possible. But Mrs. Hobbs came to the kitchen, and insisted on my going up stairs. "My brother wants to see you," said she, "and he is sorry you seem to shun him. He knows you are living in New York. He told me to say to you that he owes thanks to good old aunt Martha for too many little acts of kindness for him to be base enough to betray her grandchild."

This Mr. Thorne had become poor and reckless long before he left the south, and such persons had much rather go to one of the faithful old slaves to borrow a dollar, or get a good dinner, than to go to one whom they consider an equal. It was such acts of kindness as these for which he professed to feel grateful to my grandmother. I wished he had kept at a distance, but as he was here, and knew where I was, I concluded there was nothing to be gained by trying to avoid him; on the contrary, it might be the means of exciting his ill will. I followed his sister up stairs. He met me in a very friendly manner, congratulated me on my escape from slavery, and hoped I had a good place, where I felt happy.

I continued to visit Ellen as often as I could. She, good thoughtful child, never forgot my hazardous situation, but always kept a vigilant lookout for my safety. She never made any complaint about her own inconveniences and troubles; but a mother's observing eye easily perceived that she was not happy. On the occasion of one of my visits I found her unusually serious. When I asked her what was the matter, she said nothing was the matter. But I insisted upon knowing what made her look so very grave. Finally, I ascertained that she felt troubled about the dissipation that was continually going on in the house. She was sent to the store very often for rum and brandy, and she felt ashamed to ask for it so often; and Mr. Hobbs and Mr. Thorne drank a great deal, and their hands trembled so that they had to call her to pour out the liquor for them. "But for all that," said she, "Mr. Hobbs is good to me, and I can't help liking him. I feel sorry for him." I tried to comfort her, by telling her that I had laid up a hundred dollars, and that before long I hoped to be able to give her and Benjamin a home, and send them to school. She was always desirous not to add to my troubles more than she could help, and I did not discover till years afterwards that Mr. Thorne's intemperance was not the only annoyance she suffered from him. Though he professed too much gratitude to my grandmother to injure any of her descendants, he had poured vile language into the ears of her innocent great-grandchild.

I usually went to Brooklyn to spend Sunday afternoon. One Sunday, I found Ellen anxiously waiting for me near the house. "O, mother," said she, "I've been waiting for you this long time. I'm afraid Mr. Thorne has written to tell Dr. Flint where you are. Make haste and come in. Mrs. Hobbs will tell you all about it!"

The story was soon told. While the children were playing in the grape-vine arbor, the day before, Mr. Thorne came out with a letter in his hand, which he tore up and scattered about. Ellen was sweeping the yard at the time, and having her mind full of suspicions of him, she picked up the pieces and carried them to the children, saying, "I wonder who Mr. Thorne has been writing to."

"I'm sure I don't know, and don't care," replied the oldest of the children; "and I don't see how it concerns you."

"But it does concern me," replied Ellen; "for I'm afraid he's been writing to the south about my mother."

They laughed at her, and called her a silly thing, but good-naturedly put the fragments of writing together, in order to read them to her. They were no sooner arranged, than the little girl exclaimed, "I declare, Ellen, I believe you are right."

The contents of Mr. Thorne's letter, as nearly as I can remember, were as follows: "I have seen your slave, Linda, and conversed with her. She can be taken very easily, if you manage prudently. There are enough of us here to swear to her identity as your property. I am a patriot, a lover of my country, and I do this as an act of justice to the laws." He concluded by informing the doctor of the street and number where I lived. The children carried the pieces to Mrs. Hobbs, who immediately went to her brother's room for an explanation. He was not to be found. The servants said they saw him go out with a letter in his hand, and they supposed he had gone to the post office. The natural inference was, that he had sent to Dr. Flint a copy of those fragments. When he returned, his sister accused him of it, and he did not deny the charge. He went immediately to his room, and the next morning he was missing. He had gone over to New York, before any of the family were astir.

It was evident that I had no time to lose; and I hastened back to the city with a heavy heart. Again I was to be torn from a comfortable home, and all my plans for the welfare of my children were to be frustrated by that demon Slavery! I now regretted that I never told Mrs. Bruce my story. I had not concealed it merely on account of being a fugitive; that would have made her anxious, but it would have excited sympathy in her kind heart. I valued her good opinion, and I was afraid of losing it, if I told her all the particulars of my sad story. But now I felt that it was necessary for her to know how I was situated. I had once left her abruptly, without explaining the reason, and it would not be proper to do it again. I went home resolved to tell her in the morning. But the sadness of my face attracted her attention, and, in answer to her kind inquiries, I poured out my full heart to her, before bed time. She listened with true womanly sympathy, and told me she would do all she could to protect me. How my heart blessed her!

Early the next morning, Judge Vanderpool and Lawyer Hopper were consulted. They said I had better leave the city at once, as the risk would be great if the case came to trial. Mrs. Bruce took me in a carriage to the house of one of her friends, where she assured me I should be safe until my brother could arrive, which would be in a few days. In the interval my thoughts were much occupied with Ellen. She was mine by birth, and she was also mine by Southern law, since my grandmother held the bill of sale that made her so. I did not feel that she was safe unless I had her with me. Mrs. Hobbs, who felt badly about her brother's treachery, yielded to my entreaties, on condition that she should return in ten days. I avoided making any promise. She came to me clad in very thin garments, all outgrown, and with a school satchel on her arm, containing a few articles. It was late in October, and I knew the child must suffer; and not daring to go out in the streets to purchase any thing, I took off my own flannel skirt and converted it into one for her. Kind Mrs. Bruce came to bid me good by, and when she saw that I had taken off my clothing for my child, the tears came to her eyes. She said, "Wait for me, Linda," and went out. She soon returned with a nice warm shawl and hood for Ellen. Truly, of such souls as hers are the kingdom of heaven.

My brother reached New York on Wednesday. Lawyer Hopper advised us to go to Boston by the Stonington route, as there was less Southern travel in that direction. Mrs. Bruce directed her servants to tell all inquirers that I formerly lived there, but had gone from the city.

We reached the steamboat Rhode Island in safety. That boat employed colored hands, but I knew that colored passengers were not admitted to the cabin. I was very desirous for the seclusion of the cabin, not only on account of exposure to the night air, but also to avoid observation. Lawyer Hopper was waiting on board for us. He spoke to the stewardess, and asked, as a particular favor, that she would treat us well. He said to me, "Go and speak to the captain yourself by and by. Take your little girl with you, and I am sure that he will not let her sleep on deck." With these kind words and a shake of the hand he departed.

The boat was soon on her way, bearing me rapidly from the friendly home where I had hoped to find security and rest. My brother had left me to purchase the tickets, thinking that I might have better success than he would. When the stewardess came to me, I paid what she asked, and she gave me three tickets with clipped corners. In the most unsophisticated manner I said, "You have made a mistake; I asked you for cabin tickets. I cannot possibly consent to sleep on deck with my little daughter." She assured me there was no mistake. She said on some of the routes colored people were allowed to sleep in the cabin, but not on this route, which was much travelled by the wealthy. I asked her to show me to the captain's office, and she said she would after tea. When the time came, I took Ellen by the hand and went to the captain, politely requesting him to change our tickets, as we should be very uncomfortable on deck. He said it was contrary to their custom, but he would see that we had berths below; he would also try to obtain comfortable seats for us in the cars; of that he was not certain, but he would speak to the conductor about it, when the boat arrived. I thanked him, and returned to the ladies' cabin. He came afterwards and told me that the conductor of the cars was on board, that he had spoken to him, and he had promised to take care of us. I was very much surprised at receiving so much kindness. I don't know whether the pleasing face of my little girl had won his heart, or whether the stewardess inferred from Lawyer Hopper's manner that I was a fugitive, and had pleaded with him in my behalf.

When the boat arrived at Stonington, the conductor kept his promise, and showed us to seats in the first car, nearest the engine. He asked us to take seats next the door, but as he passed through, we ventured to move on toward the other end of the car. No incivility was offered us, and we reached Boston in safety.

The day after my arrival was one of the happiest of my life. I felt as if I was beyond the reach of the bloodhounds; and, for the first time during many years, I had both my children together with me. They greatly enjoyed their reunion, and laughed and chatted merrily. I watched them with a swelling heart. Their every motion delighted me.

I could not feel safe in New York, and I accepted the offer of a friend, that we should share expenses and keep house together. I represented to Mrs. Hobbs that Ellen must have some schooling, and must remain with me for that purpose. She felt ashamed of being unable to read or spell at her age, so instead of sending her to school with Benny, I instructed her myself till she was fitted to enter an intermediate school. The winter passed pleasantly, while I was busy with my needle, and my children with their books.

# XXXVII. A VISIT TO ENGLAND

In the spring, sad news came to me. Mrs. Bruce was dead. Never again, in this world, should I see her gentle face, or hear her sympathizing voice. I had lost an excellent friend, and little Mary had lost a tender mother. Mr. Bruce wished the child to visit some of her mother's relatives in England, and he was desirous that I should take charge of her. The little motherless one was accustomed to me, and attached to me, and I thought she would be happier in my care than in that of a stranger. I could also earn more in this way than I could by my needle. So I put Benny to a trade, and left Ellen to remain in the house with my friend and go to school.

We sailed from New York, and arrived in Liverpool after a pleasant voyage of twelve days. We proceeded directly to London, and took lodgings at the Adelaide Hotel. The supper seemed to me less luxurious than those I had seen in American hotels; but my situation was indescribably more pleasant. For the first time in my life I was in a place where I was treated according to my deportment, without reference to my complexion. I felt as if a great millstone had been lifted from my breast. Ensconced in a pleasant room, with my dear little charge, I laid my head on my pillow, for the first time, with the delightful consciousness of pure, unadulterated freedom.

As I had constant care of the child, I had little opportunity to see the wonders of that great city; but I watched the tide of life that flowed through the streets, and found it a strange contrast to the stagnation in our Southern towns. Mr. Bruce took his little daughter to spend some days with friends in Oxford Crescent, and of course it was necessary for me to accompany her. I had heard much of the systematic method of English education, and I was very desirous that my dear Mary should steer straight in the midst of so much propriety. I closely observed her little playmates and their nurses, being ready to take any lessons in the science of good management. The children were more rosy than American children, but I did not see that they differed materially in other respects. They were like all children—sometimes docile and sometimes wayward.

We next went to Steventon, in Berkshire. It was a small town, said to be the poorest in the county. I saw men working in the fields for six shillings, and seven shillings, a week, and women for sixpence, and sevenpence, a day, out of which they boarded themselves. Of course they lived in the most primitive manner; it could not be otherwise, where a woman's wages for an entire day were not sufficient to buy a pound of meat. They paid very low rents, and their clothes were made of the cheapest fabrics, though much better than could have been procured in the United States for the same money. I had heard much about the oppression of the poor in Europe. The people I saw around me were, many of them, among the poorest poor. But when I visited them in their little thatched cottages, I felt that the condition of even the meanest and most ignorant among them was vastly superior to the condition of the most favored slaves in America. They labored hard; but they were not ordered out to toil while the stars were in the sky, and driven and slashed by an overseer, through heat and cold, till the stars shone out again. Their homes were very humble; but they were protected by law. No insolent patrols could come, in the dead of night, and flog them at their pleasure. The father, when he closed his cottage door, felt safe with his family around him. No master or overseer could come and take from him his wife, or his daughter. They must separate to earn their living; but the parents knew where their children were going, and could communicate with them by letters. The relations of husband and wife, parent and child, were too sacred for the richest noble in the land to violate with impunity. Much was being done to enlighten these poor people. Schools were established among them, and benevolent societies were active in efforts to ameliorate their condition. There was no law forbidding them to learn to read and write; and if they helped each other in spelling out the Bible, they were in no danger of thirty-nine lashes, as was the case with myself and poor, pious, old uncle Fred. I repeat that the most ignorant and the most destitute of these peasants was a thousand fold better off than the most pampered American slave.

I do not deny that the poor are oppressed in Europe. I am not disposed to paint their condition so rose-colored as the Hon. Miss Murray paints the condition of the slaves in the United States. A small portion of *my* experience would enable her to read her own pages with anointed eyes. If she were to lay aside her title, and, instead of visiting among the fashionable, become domesticated, as a poor governess, on some plantation in Louisiana or Alabama, she would see and hear things that would make her tell quite a different story.

My visit to England is a memorable event in my life, from the fact of my having there received strong religious impressions. The contemptuous manner in which the communion had been administered to colored people, in my native place; the church membership of Dr. Flint, and others like him; and the buying and selling of slaves, by professed ministers of the gospel, had given me a prejudice against the Episcopal church. The whole service seemed to me a mockery and a sham. But my home in Steventon was in the family of a clergyman, who was a true disciple of Jesus. The beauty of his daily life inspired me with faith in the genuineness of Christian professions. Grace entered my heart, and I knelt at the communion table, I trust, in true humility of soul.

I remained abroad ten months, which was much longer than I had anticipated. During all that time, I never saw the slightest symptom of prejudice against color. Indeed, I entirely forgot it, till the time came for us to return to America.

# XXXVIII. RENEWED INVITATIONS TO GO SOUTH

We had a tedious winter passage, and from the distance spectres seemed to rise up on the shores of the United States. It is a sad feeling to be afraid of one's native country. We arrived in New York safely, and I hastened to Boston to look after my children. I found Ellen well, and improving at her school; but Benny was not there to welcome me. He had been left at a good place to learn a trade, and for several months every thing worked well. He was liked by the master, and was a favorite with his fellow-apprentices; but one day they accidentally discovered a fact they had never before suspected—that he was colored! This at once transformed him into a different being. Some of the apprentices were Americans, others American-born Irish; and it was offensive to their dignity to have a "nigger" among them, after they had been told that he *was* a "nigger." They began by treating him with silent scorn, and finding that he returned the same, they resorted to insults and abuse. He was too spirited a boy to stand that, and he went off. Being desirous to do something to support himself, and having no one to advise him, he shipped for a whaling voyage. When I received these tidings I shed many tears, and bitterly reproached myself for having left him so long. But I had done it for the best, and now all I could do was to pray to the heavenly Father to guide and protect him.

Not long after my return, I received the following letter from Miss Emily Flint, now Mrs. Dodge:—

"In this you will recognize the hand of your friend and mistress. Having heard that you had gone with a family to Europe, I have waited to hear of your return to write to you. I should have answered the letter you wrote to me long since, but as I could not then act independently of my father, I knew there could be nothing done satisfactory to you. There were persons here who were willing to buy you and run the risk of getting you. To this I would not consent. I have always been attached to you, and would not like to see you the slave of another, or have unkind treatment. I am married now, and can protect you. My husband expects to move to Virginia this spring, where we think of settling. I am very anxious that you should come and live with me. If you are not willing to come, you may purchase yourself; but I should prefer having you live with me. If you come, you may, if you like, spend a month with your grandmother and friends, then come to me in Norfolk, Virginia. Think this over, and write as soon as possible, and let me know the conclusion. Hoping that your children are well, I remain your friend and mistress."

Of course I did not write to return thanks for this cordial invitation. I felt insulted to be thought stupid enough to be caught by such professions.

"Come up into my parlor," said the spider to the fly;
"'Tis the prettiest little parlor that ever you did spy."

It was plain that Dr. Flint's family were apprised of my movements, since they knew of my voyage to Europe. I expected to have further trouble from them; but having eluded them thus far, I hoped to be as successful in future. The money I had earned, I was desirous to devote to the education of my children, and to secure a home for them. It seemed not only hard, but unjust, to pay for myself. I could not possibly regard myself as a piece of property. Moreover, I had worked many years without wages, and during that time had been obliged to depend on my grandmother for many comforts in food and clothing. My children certainly belonged to me; but though Dr. Flint had incurred no expense for their support, he had received a large sum of money for them. I knew the law would decide that I was his property, and would probably still give his daughter a claim to my children; but I regarded such laws as the regulations of robbers, who had no rights that I was bound to respect.

The Fugitive Slave Law had not then passed. The judges of Massachusetts had not then stooped under chains to enter her courts of justice, so called. I knew my old master was rather skittish of Massachusetts. I relied on her love of freedom, and felt safe on her soil. I am now aware that I honored the old Commonwealth beyond her deserts.

# XXXIX. THE CONFESSION

For two years my daughter and I supported ourselves comfortably in Boston. At the end of that time, my brother William offered to send Ellen to a boarding school. It required a great effort for me to consent to part with her, for I had few near ties, and it was her presence that made my two little rooms seem home-like. But my judgment prevailed over my selfish feelings. I made preparations for her departure. During the two years we had lived together I had often resolved to tell her something about her father; but I had never been able to muster sufficient courage. I had a shrinking dread of diminishing my child's love. I knew she must have curiosity on the subject, but she had never asked a question. She was always very careful not to say any thing to remind me of my troubles. Now that she was going from me, I thought if I should die before she returned, she might hear my story from some one who did not understand the palliating circumstances; and that if she were entirely ignorant on the subject, her sensitive nature might receive a rude shock.

When we retired for the night, she said, "Mother, it is very hard to leave you alone. I am almost sorry I am going, though I do want to improve myself. But you will write to me often; won't you, mother?"

I did not throw my arms round her. I did not answer her. But in a calm, solemn way, for it cost me great effort, I said, "Listen to me, Ellen; I have something to tell you!" I recounted my early sufferings in slavery, and told her how nearly they had crushed me. I began to tell her how they had driven me into a great sin, when she clasped me in her arms, and exclaimed, "O, don't, mother! Please don't tell me any more."

I said, "But, my child, I want you to know about your father."

"I know all about it, mother," she replied; "I am nothing to my father, and he is nothing to me. All my love is for you. I was with him five months in Washington, and he never cared for me. He never spoke to me as he did to his little Fanny. I knew all the time he was my father, for Fanny's nurse told me so, but she said I must never tell any body, and I never did. I used to wish he would take me in his arms and kiss me, as he did Fanny; or that he would sometimes smile at me, as he did at her. I thought if he was my own father, he ought to love me. I was a little girl then, and didn't know any better. But now I never think any thing about my father. All my love is for you." She hugged me closer as she spoke, and I thanked God that the knowledge I had so much dreaded to impart had not diminished the affection of my child. I had not the slightest idea she knew that portion of my history. If I had, I should have spoken to her long before; for my pent-up feelings had often longed to pour themselves out to some one I could trust. But I loved the dear girl better for the delicacy she had manifested towards her unfortunate mother.

The next morning, she and her uncle started on their journey to the village in New York, where she was to be placed at school. It seemed as if all the sunshine had gone away. My little room was dreadfully lonely. I was thankful when a message came from a lady, accustomed to employ me, requesting me to come and sew in her family for several weeks. On my return, I found a letter from brother William. He thought of opening an anti-slavery reading room in Rochester, and combining with it the sale of some books and stationery; and he wanted me to unite with him. We tried it, but it was not successful. We found warm anti-slavery friends there, but the feeling was not general enough to support such an establishment. I passed nearly a year in the family of Isaac and Amy Post, practical believers in the Christian doctrine of human brotherhood. They measure a man's worth by his character, not by his complexion. The memory of those beloved and honored friends will remain with me to my latest hour.

# XL. THE FUGITIVE SLAVE LAW

My brother, being disappointed in his project, concluded to go to California; and it was agreed that Benjamin should go with him. Ellen liked her school, and was a great favorite there. They did not know her history, and she did not tell it, because she had no desire to make capital out of their sympathy. But when it was accidentally discovered that her mother was a fugitive slave, every method was used to increase her advantages and diminish her expenses.

I was alone again. It was necessary for me to be earning money, and I preferred that it should be among those who knew me. On my return from Rochester, I called at the house of Mr. Bruce, to see Mary, the darling little babe that had thawed my heart, when it was freezing into a cheerless distrust of all my fellow-beings. She was growing a tall girl now, but I loved her always. Mr. Bruce had married again, and it was proposed that I should become nurse to a new infant. I had but one hesitation, and that was my feeling of insecurity in New York, now greatly increased by the passage of the Fugitive Slave Law. However, I resolved to try the experiment. I was again fortunate in my employer. The new Mrs. Bruce was an American, brought up under aristocratic influences, and still living in the midst of them; but if she had any prejudice against color, I was never made aware of it; and as for the system of slavery, she had a most hearty dislike of it. No sophistry of Southerners could blind her to its enormity. She was a person of excellent principles and a noble heart. To me, from that hour to the present, she has been a true and sympathizing friend. Blessings be with her and hers!

About the time that I reentered the Bruce family, an event occurred of disastrous import to the colored people. The slave Hamlin, the first fugitive that came under the new law, was given up by the bloodhounds of the north to the bloodhounds of the south. It was the beginning of a reign of terror to the colored population. The great city rushed on in its whirl of excitement, taking no note of the "short and simple annals of the poor." But while fashionables were listening to the thrilling voice of Jenny Lind in Metropolitan Hall, the thrilling voices of poor hunted colored people went up, in an agony of supplication, to the Lord, from Zion's church. Many families, who had lived in the city for twenty years, fled from it now. Many a poor washerwoman, who, by hard labor, had made herself a comfortable home, was obliged to sacrifice her furniture, bid a hurried farewell to friends, and seek her fortune among strangers in Canada. Many a wife discovered a secret she had never known before—that her husband was a fugitive, and must leave her to insure his own safety. Worse still, many a husband discovered that his wife had fled from slavery years ago, and as "the child follows the condition of its mother," the children of his love were liable to be seized and carried into slavery. Every where, in those humble homes, there was consternation and anguish. But what cared the legislators of the "dominant race" for the blood they were crushing out of trampled hearts?

When my brother William spent his last evening with me, before he went to California, we talked nearly all the time of the distress brought on our oppressed people by the passage of this iniquitous law; and never had I seen him manifest such bitterness of spirit, such stern hostility to our oppressors. He was himself free from the operation of the law; for he did not run from any Slaveholding State, being brought into the Free States by his master. But I was subject to it; and so were hundreds of intelligent and industrious people all around us. I seldom ventured into the streets; and when it was necessary to do an errand for Mrs. Bruce, or any of the family, I went as much as possible through back streets and by-ways. What a disgrace to a city calling itself free, that inhabitants, guiltless of offence, and seeking to perform their duties conscientiously, should be condemned to live in such incessant fear, and have nowhere to turn for protection! This state of things, of course, gave rise to many impromptu vigilance committees. Every colored person, and every friend of their persecuted race, kept their eyes wide open. Every evening I examined the newspapers carefully, to see what Southerners had put up at the hotels. I did this for my own sake, thinking my young mistress and her husband might be among the list; I wished also to give information to others, if necessary; for if many were "running to and fro," I resolved that "knowledge should be increased."

This brings up one of my Southern reminiscences, which I will here briefly relate. I was somewhat acquainted with a slave named Luke, who belonged to a wealthy man in our vicinity. His master died, leaving a son and daughter heirs to his large fortune. In the division of the slaves, Luke was included in the son's portion. This young man became a prey to the vices growing out of the "patriarchal institution"; and when he went to the north, to complete his education, he carried his vices with him. He was brought home, deprived of the use of his limbs, by excessive dissipation. Luke was appointed to wait upon his bed-ridden master, whose despotic habits were greatly increased by exasperation at his own helplessness. He kept a cowhide beside him, and, for the most trivial occurrence, he would order his attendant to bare his back, and kneel beside the couch, while he whipped him till his strength was exhausted. Some days he was not allowed to wear any thing but his shirt, in order to be in readiness to be flogged. A day seldom passed without his receiving more or less blows. If the slightest resistance was offered, the town constable was sent for to execute the punishment, and Luke learned from experience how much more the constable's strong arm was to be dreaded than the comparatively feeble one of his master. The arm of his tyrant grew weaker, and was finally palsied; and then the constable's services were in constant requisition. The fact that he was entirely dependent on Luke's care, and was obliged to be tended like an infant, instead of inspiring any gratitude or compassion towards his poor slave, seemed only to increase his irritability and cruelty. As he lay there on his bed, a mere degraded wreck of manhood, he took into his head the strangest freaks of despotism; and if Luke hesitated to submit to his orders, the constable was immediately sent for. Some of these freaks were of a nature too filthy to be repeated. When I fled from the house of bondage, I left poor Luke still chained to the bedside of this cruel and disgusting wretch.

One day, when I had been requested to do an errand for Mrs. Bruce, I was hurrying through back streets, as usual, when I saw a young man approaching, whose face was familiar to me. As he came nearer, I recognized Luke. I always rejoiced to see or hear of any one who had escaped from the black pit; I was peculiarly glad to see him on Northern soil, though I no longer called it *free* soil. I well remembered what a desolate feeling it was to be alone among strangers, and I went up to him and greeted him cordially. At first, he did not know me; but when I mentioned my name, he remembered all about me. I told him of the Fugitive Slave Law, and asked him if he did not know that New York was a city of kidnappers.

He replied, "De risk ain't so bad for me, as 'tis fur you. 'Cause I runned away from de speculator, and you runned away from de massa. Dem speculators vont spen dar money to come here fur a runaway, if dey ain't sartin sure to put dar hans right on him. An I tell you I's tuk good car 'bout dat. I had too hard times down dar, to let 'em ketch dis nigger."

He then told me of the advice he had received, and the plans he had laid. I asked if he had money enough to take him to Canada. "'Pend upon it, I hab," he replied. "I tuk car fur dat. I'd bin workin all my days fur dem cussed whites, an got no pay but kicks and cuffs. So I tought dis nigger had a right to money nuff to bring him to de Free States. Massa Henry he lib till ebery body vish him dead; an ven he did die, I knowed de debbil would hab him, an vouldn't vant him to bring his money 'long too. So I tuk some of his bills, and put 'em in de pocket of his ole trousers. An ven he was buried, dis nigger ask fur dem ole trousers, an dey gub 'em to me." With a low, chuckling laugh, he added, "You see I didn't *steal* it; dey *gub* it to me. I tell you, I had mighty hard time to keep de speculator from findin it; but he didn't git it."

This is a fair specimen of how the moral sense is educated by slavery. When a man has his wages stolen from him, year after year, and the laws sanction and enforce the theft, how can he be expected to have more regard to honesty than has the man who robs him? I have become somewhat enlightened, but I confess that I agree with poor, ignorant, much-abused Luke, in thinking he had a *right* to that money, as a portion of his unpaid wages. He went to Canada forthwith, and I have not since heard from him.

All that winter I lived in a state of anxiety. When I took the children out to breathe the air, I closely observed the countenances of all I met. I dreaded the approach of summer, when snakes and slaveholders make their appearance. I was, in fact, a slave in New York, as subject to slave laws as I had been in a Slave State. Strange incongruity in a State called free!

Spring returned, and I received warning from the south that Dr. Flint knew of my return to my old place, and was making preparations to have me caught. I learned afterwards that my dress, and that of Mrs. Bruce's children, had been described to him by some of the Northern tools, which slaveholders employ for their base purposes, and then indulge in sneers at their cupidity and mean servility.

I immediately informed Mrs. Bruce of my danger, and she took prompt measures for my safety. My place as nurse could not be supplied immediately, and this generous, sympathizing lady proposed that I should carry her baby away. It was a comfort to me to have the child with me; for the heart is reluctant to be torn away from every object it loves. But how few mothers would have consented to have one of their own babes become a fugitive, for the sake of a poor, hunted nurse, on whom the legislators of the country had let loose the bloodhounds! When I spoke of the sacrifice she was making, in depriving herself of her dear baby, she replied, "It is better for you to have baby with you, Linda; for if they get on your track, they will be obliged to bring the child to me; and then, if there is a possibility of saving you, you shall be saved."

This lady had a very wealthy relative, a benevolent gentleman in many respects, but aristocratic and pro-slavery. He remonstrated with her for harboring a fugitive slave; told her she was violating the laws of her country; and asked her if she was aware of the penalty. She replied, "I am very well aware of it. It is imprisonment and one thousand dollars fine. Shame on my country that it *is* so! I am ready to incur the penalty. I will go to the state's prison, rather than have any poor victim torn from *my* house, to be carried back to slavery."

The noble heart! The brave heart! The tears are in my eyes while I write of her. May the God of the helpless reward her for her sympathy with my persecuted people!

I was sent into New England, where I was sheltered by the wife of a senator, whom I shall always hold in grateful remembrance. This honorable gentleman would not have voted for the Fugitive Slave Law, as did the senator in "Uncle Tom's Cabin;" on the contrary, he was strongly opposed to it; but he was enough under its influence to be afraid of having me remain in his house many hours. So I was sent into the country, where I remained a month with the baby. When it was supposed that Dr. Flint's emissaries had lost track of me, and given up the pursuit for the present, I returned to New York.

# XLI. FREE AT LAST

Mrs. Bruce, and every member of her family, were exceedingly kind to me. I was thankful for the blessings of my lot, yet I could not always wear a cheerful countenance. I was doing harm to no one; on the contrary, I was doing all the good I could in my small way; yet I could never go out to breathe God's free air without trepidation at my heart. This seemed hard; and I could not think it was a right state of things in any civilized country.

From time to time I received news from my good old grandmother. She could not write; but she employed others to write for her. The following is an extract from one of her last letters:—

"Dear Daughter: I cannot hope to see you again on earth; but I pray to God to unite us above, where pain will no more rack this feeble body of mine; where sorrow and parting from my children will be no more. God has promised these things if we are faithful unto the end. My age and feeble health deprive me of going to church now; but God is with me here at home. Thank your brother for his kindness. Give much love to him, and tell him to remember the Creator in the days of his youth, and strive to meet me in the Father's kingdom. Love to Ellen and Benjamin. Don't neglect him. Tell him for me, to be a good boy. Strive, my child, to train them for God's children. May he protect and provide for you, is the prayer of your loving old mother."

These letters both cheered and saddened me. I was always glad to have tidings from the kind, faithful old friend of my unhappy youth; but her messages of love made my heart yearn to see her before she died, and I mourned over the fact that it was impossible. Some months after I returned from my flight to New England, I received a letter from her, in which she wrote, "Dr. Flint is dead. He has left a distressed family. Poor old man! I hope he made his peace with God."

I remembered how he had defrauded my grandmother of the hard earnings she had loaned; how he had tried to cheat her out of the freedom her mistress had promised her, and how he had persecuted her children; and I thought to myself that she was a better Christian than I was, if she could entirely forgive him. I cannot say, with truth, that the news of my old master's death softened my feelings towards him. There are wrongs which even the grave does not bury. The man was odious to me while he lived, and his memory is odious now.

His departure from this world did not diminish my danger. He had threatened my grandmother that his heirs should hold me in slavery after he was gone; that I never should be free so long as a child of his survived. As for Mrs. Flint, I had seen her in deeper afflictions than I supposed the loss of her husband would be, for she had buried several children; yet I never saw any signs of softening in her heart. The doctor had died in embarrassed circumstances, and had little to will to his heirs, except such property as he was unable to grasp. I was well aware what I had to expect from the family of Flints; and my fears were confirmed by a letter from the south, warning me to be on my guard, because Mrs. Flint openly declared that her daughter could not afford to lose so valuable a slave as I was.

I kept close watch of the newspapers for arrivals; but one Saturday night, being much occupied, I forgot to examine the Evening Express as usual. I went down into the parlor for it, early in the morning, and found the boy about to kindle a fire with it. I took it from him and examined the list of arrivals. Reader, if you have never been a slave, you cannot imagine the acute sensation of suffering at my heart, when I read the names of Mr. and Mrs. Dodge, at a hotel in Courtland Street. It was a third-rate hotel, and that circumstance convinced me of the truth of what I had heard, that they were short of funds and had need of my value, as *they* valued me; and that was by dollars and cents. I hastened with the paper to Mrs. Bruce. Her heart and hand were always open to every one in distress, and she always warmly sympathized with mine. It was impossible to tell how near the enemy was. He might have passed and repassed the house while we were sleeping. He might at that moment be waiting to pounce upon me if I ventured out of doors. I had never seen the husband of my young mistress, and therefore I could not distinguish him from any other stranger. A carriage was hastily ordered; and, closely veiled, I followed Mrs. Bruce, taking the baby again with me into exile. After various turnings and crossings, and returnings, the carriage stopped at the house of one of Mrs. Bruce's friends, where I was kindly received. Mrs. Bruce returned immediately, to instruct the domestics what to say if any one came to inquire for me.

It was lucky for me that the evening paper was not burned up before I had a chance to examine the list of arrivals. It was not long after Mrs. Bruce's return to her house, before several people came to inquire for me. One inquired for me, another asked for my daughter Ellen, and another said he had a letter from my grandmother, which he was requested to deliver in person.

They were told, "She *has* lived here, but she has left."

"How long ago?"

"I don't know, sir."

"Do you know where she went?"

"I do not, sir." And the door was closed.

This Mr. Dodge, who claimed me as his property, was originally a Yankee pedler in the south; then he became a merchant, and finally a slaveholder. He managed to get introduced into what was called the first society, and married Miss Emily Flint. A quarrel arose between him and her brother, and the brother cowhided him. This led to a family feud, and he proposed to remove to Virginia. Dr. Flint left him no property, and his own means had become circumscribed, while a wife and children depended upon him for support. Under these circumstances, it was very natural that he should make an effort to put me into his pocket.

I had a colored friend, a man from my native place, in whom I had the most implicit confidence. I sent for him, and told him that Mr. and Mrs. Dodge had arrived in New York. I proposed that he should call upon them to make inquiries about his friends at the south, with whom Dr. Flint's family were well acquainted. He thought there was no impropriety in his doing so, and he consented. He went to the hotel, and knocked at the door of Mr. Dodge's room, which was opened by the gentleman himself, who gruffly inquired, "What brought you here? How came you to know I was in the city?"

"Your arrival was published in the evening papers, sir; and I called to ask Mrs. Dodge about my friends at home. I didn't suppose it would give any offence."

"Where's that negro girl, that belongs to my wife?"

"What girl, sir?"

"You know well enough. I mean Linda, that ran away from

Dr. Flint's plantation, some years ago. I dare say you've seen her, and know where she is."

"Yes, sir, I've seen her, and know where she is. She is out of your reach, sir."

"Tell me where she is, or bring her to me, and I will give her a chance to buy her freedom."

"I don't think it would be of any use, sir. I have heard her say she would go to the ends of the earth, rather than pay any man or woman for her freedom, because she thinks she has a right to it. Besides, she couldn't do it, if she would, for she has spent her earnings to educate her children."

This made Mr. Dodge very angry, and some high words passed between them. My friend was afraid to come where I was; but in the course of the day I received a note from him. I supposed they had not come from the south, in the winter, for a pleasure excursion; and now the nature of their business was very plain.

Mrs. Bruce came to me and entreated me to leave the city the next morning. She said her house was watched, and it was possible that some clew to me might be obtained. I refused to take her advice. She pleaded with an earnest tenderness, that ought to have moved me; but I was in a bitter, disheartened mood. I was weary of flying from pillar to post. I had been chased during half my life, and it seemed as if the chase was never to end. There I sat, in that great city, guiltless of crime, yet not daring to worship God in any of the churches. I heard the bells ringing for afternoon service, and, with contemptuous sarcasm, I said, "Will the preachers take for their text, 'Proclaim liberty to the captive, and the opening of prison doors to them that are bound'? or will they preach from the text, 'Do unto others as ye would they should do unto you'?" Oppressed Poles and Hungarians could find a safe refuge in that city; John Mitchell was free to proclaim in the City Hall his desire for "a plantation well stocked with slaves;" but there I sat, an oppressed American, not daring to show my face. God forgive the black and bitter thoughts I indulged on that Sabbath day! The Scripture says, "Oppression makes even a wise man mad;" and I was not wise.

I had been told that Mr. Dodge said his wife had never signed away her right to my children, and if he could not get me, he would take them. This it was, more than any thing else, that roused such a tempest in my soul. Benjamin was with his uncle William in California, but my innocent young daughter had come to spend a vacation with me. I thought of what I had suffered in slavery at her age, and my heart was like a tiger's when a hunter tries to seize her young.

Dear Mrs. Bruce! I seem to see the expression of her face, as she turned away discouraged by my obstinate mood. Finding her expostulations unavailing, she sent Ellen to entreat me. When ten o'clock in the evening arrived and Ellen had not returned, this watchful and unwearied friend became anxious. She came to us in a carriage, bringing a well-filled trunk for my journey—trusting that by this time I would listen to reason. I yielded to her, as I ought to have done before.

The next day, baby and I set out in a heavy snow storm, bound for New England again. I received letters from the City of Iniquity, addressed to me under an assumed name. In a few days one came from Mrs. Bruce, informing me that my new master was still searching for me, and that she intended to put an end to this persecution by buying my freedom. I felt grateful for the kindness that prompted this offer, but the idea was not so pleasant to me as might have been expected. The more my mind had become enlightened, the more difficult it was for me to consider myself an article of property; and to pay money to those who had so grievously oppressed me seemed like taking from my sufferings the glory of triumph. I wrote to Mrs. Bruce, thanking her, but saying that being sold from one owner to another seemed too much like slavery; that such a great obligation could not be easily cancelled; and that I preferred to go to my brother in California.

Without my knowledge, Mrs. Bruce employed a gentleman in New York to enter into negotiations with Mr. Dodge. He proposed to pay three hundred dollars down, if Mr. Dodge would sell me, and enter into obligations to relinquish all claim to me or my children forever after. He who called himself my master said he scorned so small an offer for such a valuable servant. The gentleman replied, "You can do as you choose, sir. If you reject this offer you will never get any thing; for the woman has friends who will convey her and her children out of the country."

Mr. Dodge concluded that "half a loaf was better than no bread," and he agreed to the proffered terms. By the next mail I received this brief letter from Mrs. Bruce: "I am rejoiced to tell you that the money for your freedom has been paid to Mr. Dodge. Come home to-morrow. I long to see you and my sweet babe."

My brain reeled as I read these lines. A gentleman near me said, "It's true; I have seen the bill of sale." "The bill of sale!" Those words struck me like a blow. So I was *sold* at last! A human being *sold* in the free city of New York! The bill of sale is on record, and future generations will learn from it that women were articles of traffic in New York, late in the nineteenth century of the Christian religion. It may hereafter prove a useful document to antiquaries, who are seeking to measure the progress of civilization in the United States. I well know the value of that bit of paper; but much as I love freedom, I do not like to look upon it. I am deeply grateful to the generous friend who procured it, but I despise the miscreant who demanded payment for what never rightfully belonged to him or his.

I had objected to having my freedom bought, yet I must confess that when it was done I felt as if a heavy load had been lifted from my weary shoulders. When I rode home in the cars I was no longer afraid to unveil my face and look at people as they passed. I should have been glad to have met Daniel Dodge himself; to have had him seen me and known me, that he might have mourned over the untoward circumstances which compelled him to sell me for three hundred dollars.

When I reached home, the arms of my benefactress were thrown round me, and our tears mingled. As soon as she could speak, she said, "O Linda, I'm *so* glad it's all over! You wrote to me as if you thought you were going to be transferred from one owner to another. But I did not buy you for your services. I should have done just the same, if you had been going to sail for California to-morrow. I should, at least, have the satisfaction of knowing that you left me a free woman."

My heart was exceedingly full. I remembered how my poor father had tried to buy me, when I was a small child, and how he had been disappointed. I hoped his spirit was rejoicing over me now. I remembered how my good old grandmother had laid up her earnings to purchase me in later years, and how often her plans had been frustrated. How that faithful, loving old heart would leap for joy, if she could look on me and my children now that we were free! My relatives had been foiled in all their efforts, but God had raised me up a friend among strangers, who had bestowed on me the precious, long-desired boon. Friend! It is a common word, often lightly used. Like other good and beautiful things, it may be tarnished by careless handling; but when I speak of Mrs. Bruce as my friend, the word is sacred.

My grandmother lived to rejoice in my freedom; but not long after, a letter came with a black seal. She had gone "where the wicked cease from troubling, and the weary are at rest."

Time passed on, and a paper came to me from the south, containing an obituary notice of my uncle Phillip. It was the only case I ever knew of such an honor conferred upon a colored person. It was written by one of his friends, and contained these words: "Now that death has laid him low, they call him a good man and a useful citizen; but what are eulogies to the black man, when the world has faded from his vision? It does not require man's praise to obtain rest in God's kingdom." So they called a colored man a *citizen*! Strange words to be uttered in that region!

Reader, my story ends with freedom; not in the usual way, with marriage. I and my children are now free! We are as free from the power of slaveholders as are the white people of the north; and though that, according to my ideas, is not saying a great deal, it is a vast improvement in *my* condition. The dream of my life is not yet realized. I do not sit with my children in a home of my own, I still long for a hearthstone of my own, however humble. I wish it for my children's sake far more than for my own. But God so orders circumstances as to keep me with my friend Mrs. Bruce. Love, duty, gratitude, also bind me to her side. It is a privilege to serve her who pities my oppressed people, and who has bestowed the inestimable boon of freedom on me and my children.

It has been painful to me, in many ways, to recall the dreary years I passed in bondage. I would gladly forget them if I could. Yet the retrospection is not altogether without solace; for with those gloomy recollections come tender memories of my good old grandmother, like light, fleecy clouds floating over a dark and troubled sea.

# APPENDIX

The following statement is from Amy Post, a member of the Society of Friends in the State of New York, well known and highly respected by friends of the poor and the oppressed. As has been already stated, in the preceding pages, the author of this volume spent some time under her hospitable roof.

L.M.C.

"The author of this book is my highly-esteemed friend. If its readers knew her as I know her, they could not fail to be deeply interested in her story. She was a beloved inmate of our family nearly the whole of the year 1849. She was introduced to us by her affectionate and conscientious brother, who had previously related to us some of the almost incredible events in his sister's life. I immediately became much interested in Linda; for her appearance was prepossessing, and her deportment indicated remarkable delicacy of feeling and purity of thought.

"As we became acquainted, she related to me, from time to time some of the incidents in her bitter experiences as a slave-woman. Though impelled by a natural craving for human sympathy, she passed through a baptism of suffering, even in recounting her trials to me, in private confidential conversations. The burden of these memories lay heavily upon her spirit—naturally virtuous and refined. I repeatedly urged her to consent to the publication of her narrative; for I felt that it would arouse people to a more earnest work for the disinthralment of millions still remaining in that soul-crushing condition, which was so unendurable to her. But her sensitive spirit shrank from publicity. She said, "You know a woman can whisper her cruel wrongs in the ear of a dear friend much easier than she can record them for the world to read." Even in talking with me, she wept so much, and seemed to suffer such mental agony, that I felt her story was too sacred to be drawn from her by inquisitive questions, and I left her free to tell as much, or as little, as she chose. Still, I urged upon her the duty of publishing her experience, for the sake of the good it might do; and, at last, she undertook the task.

“Having been a slave so large a portion of her life, she is unlearned; she is obliged to earn her living by her own labor, and she has worked untiringly to procure education for her children; several times she has been obliged to leave her employments, in order to fly from the man-hunters and woman-hunters of our land; but she pressed through all these obstacles and overcame them. After the labors of the day were over, she traced secretly and wearily, by the midnight lamp, a truthful record of her eventful life.

“This Empire State is a shabby place of refuge for the oppressed; but here, through anxiety, turmoil, and despair, the freedom of Linda and her children was finally secured, by the exertions of a generous friend. She was grateful for the boon; but the idea of having been *bought* was always galling to a spirit that could never acknowledge itself to be a chattel. She wrote to us thus, soon after the event: “I thank you for your kind expressions in regard to my freedom; but the freedom I had before the money was paid was dearer to me. God gave me *that* freedom; but man put God’s image in the scales with the paltry sum of three hundred dollars. I served for my liberty as faithfully as Jacob served for Rachel. At the end, he had large possessions; but I was robbed of my victory; I was obliged to resign my crown, to rid myself of a tyrant.”

“Her story, as written by herself, cannot fail to interest the reader. It is a sad illustration of the condition of this country, which boasts of its civilization, while it sanctions laws and customs which make the experiences of the present more strange than any fictions of the past.

AMY POST,

“Rochester, N.Y., Oct. 30th, 1859.”

The following testimonial is from a man who is now a highly respectable colored citizen of Boston.

L.M.C.

“This narrative contains some incidents so extraordinary, that, doubtless, many persons, under whose eyes it may chance to fall, will be ready to believe that it is colored highly, to serve a special purpose. But, however it may be regarded by the incredulous, I know that it is full of living truths. I have been well acquainted with the author from my boyhood. The circumstances recounted in her history are perfectly familiar to me. I knew of her treatment from her master; of the imprisonment of her children; of their sale and redemption; of her seven years' concealment; and of her subsequent escape to the North. I am now a resident of Boston, and am a living witness to the truth of this interesting narrative.

George W. Lowther."

# UP FROM SLAVERY

BOOKER T.
WASHINGTON

**Disclaimer**

Throughout the text, readers may find language and sentiments that appear both offensive and unacceptable. These words were duly reported by the former slave who wrote this book, and was forced to endure such dehumanizing attitudes on a daily basis. To better serve the author's original intentions and to ensure that the full impact of the writing is retained, we have decided to keep the original language in its entirety, though many segments may prove uncomfortable for the modern reader.

This edition published in 2020 by Arcturus Publishing Limited
26/27 Bickels Yard, 151–153 Bermondsey Street,
London SE1 3HA



Cover design: Peter Ridley
Cover illustration: Peter Gray

AD006012US

Printed in the UK

FSC www.fsc.org MIX Paper from responsible sources FSC® C018072

*This volume is dedicated to my Wife*
Margaret James Washington

*And to my Brother*
John H. Washington

*Whose patience, fidelity, and hard work*
*have gone far to make the work at Tuskegee successful*

# CONTENTS

# INTRODUCTION

At the end of the 19th century, slavery had been abolished in the United States, but the battle for African-American civil rights was only just beginning. Booker T. Washington was one of the most visible leaders of the emerging civil rights movement, focusing on the importance of education and hard work to achieve racial equality.

Washington was born into slavery in Virginia in 1856. His mother, a slave, and his father, a white man from another plantation, were separated until emancipation in 1865. After the civil war, the family was reunited in West Virginia. The Reconstruction Era that followed was a traumatic period for much of the South. Over this time, the Republican party sought to restructure the society in the former confederate states, providing new opportunities for black men and women in politics and economic life. A backlash from disenchanted southern legislatures meant that conditions improved little for the majority of newly freed slaves. Most were trapped into plantation economies dependent on sharecropping and confronted with racism and discrimination at every turn. For several years, Washington toiled in the coal mines of West Virginia. There was little chance for black men and women in the south to educate themselves and escape the grinding poverty of life. Booker T. Washington proposed to change that.

By 1872, he had finally saved up enough money to attend the newly created Hampton Normal and Agricultural Institute. It had been set up by General Samuel Armstrong, but it was a 500-mile journey away and Washington could only support himself through the year by working as a janitor in his free time. Fortunately, the founder of the institute soon recognized his qualities and made it his mission to sponsor Booker. Washington graduated in 1875 and began teaching. In 1881, Washington was given his chance to make a real difference. Armstrong recommended him as the next head of the Tuskegee Institute in Alabama.

Washington was often in conflict with his fellow civil rights activists. His focus on self-improvement and his unwillingness to challenge the status quo, in particular his acceptance of segregation, rubbed people like W. E. B. DuBois the wrong way. Nonetheless, his conciliatory approach was very effective. Two presidents, Theodore Roosevelt and William Taft, turned to Washington for advice on racial affairs.

He intended his autobiography, *Up from Slavery*, to act as an example for African-Americans across the country, who could be inspired by his tale of hard work and determination to receive a good education. First published in 1901, it tells the tale of a slave born into obscurity who rises to become the most famous black man in America. Through numerous obstacles and constant challenges, he fought tirelessly for the rights of his race and did everything he could to show that black men were every bit the equal of white men.

# INTRODUCTION BY WALTER H. PAGE

The details of Mr. Washington's early life, as frankly set down in *Up from Slavery*, do not give quite a whole view of his education. He had the training that a coloured youth receives at Hampton, which, indeed, the autobiography does explain. But the reader does not get his intellectual pedigree, for Mr. Washington himself, perhaps, does not as clearly understand it as another man might. The truth is he had a training during the most impressionable period of his life that was very extraordinary, such a training as few men of his generation have had. To see its full meaning one must start in the Hawaiian Islands half a century or more ago.[1] There Samuel Armstrong, a youth of missionary parents, earned enough money to pay his expenses at an American college. Equipped with this small sum and the earnestness that the undertaking implied, he came to Williams College when Dr. Mark Hopkins was president. Williams College had many good things for youth in that day, as it has in this, but the greatest was the strong personality of its famous president. Every student does not profit by a great teacher; but perhaps no young man ever came under the influence of Dr. Hopkins, whose whole nature was so ripe for profit by such an experience as young Armstrong. He lived in the family of President Hopkins, and thus had a training that was wholly out of the common; and this training had much to do with the development of his own strong character, whose originality and force we are only beginning to appreciate.

In turn, Samuel Armstrong, the founder of Hampton Institute, took up his work as a trainer of youth. He had very raw material, and doubtless most of his pupils failed to get the greatest lessons from him; but, as he had been a peculiarly receptive pupil of Dr. Hopkins, so Booker Washington became a peculiarly receptive pupil

1 For this interesting view of Mr. Washington's education, I am indebted to Robert C. Ogden, Esq., Chairman of the Board of Trustees of Hampton Institute and the intimate friend of General Armstrong during the whole period of his educational work.

of his. To the formation of Mr. Washington's character, then, went the missionary zeal of New England, influenced by one of the strongest personalities in modern education, and the wide-reaching moral earnestness of General Armstrong himself. These influences are easily recognizable in Mr. Washington to-day by men who knew Dr. Hopkins and General Armstrong.

I got the cue to Mr. Washington's character from a very simple incident many years ago. I had never seen him, and I knew little about him, except that he was the head of a school at Tuskegee, Alabama. I had occasion to write to him, and I addressed him as "The Rev. Booker T. Washington." In his reply there was no mention of my addressing him as a clergyman. But when I had occasion to write to him again, and persisted in making him a preacher, his second letter brought a postscript: "I have no claim to 'Rev.'" I knew most of the coloured men who at that time had become prominent as leaders of their race, but I had not then known one who was neither a politician nor a preacher; and I had not heard of the head of an important coloured school who was not a preacher. "A new kind of man in the coloured world," I said to myself— "a new kind of man surely if he looks upon his task as an economic one instead of a theological one." I wrote him an apology for mistaking him for a preacher.

The first time that I went to Tuskegee I was asked to make an address to the school on Sunday evening. I sat upon the platform of the large chapel and looked forth on a thousand coloured faces, and the choir of a hundred or more behind me sang a familiar religious melody, and the whole company joined in the chorus with unction. I was the only white man under the roof, and the scene and the songs made an impression on me that I shall never forget. Mr. Washington arose and asked them to sing one after another of the old melodies that I had heard all my life; but I had never before heard them sung by a thousand voices nor by the voices of educated Negroes. I had associated them with the Negro of the past, not with the Negro who was struggling upward. They brought to my mind the plantation, the cabin, the slave, not the freedman in quest of education. But on the plantation and in the cabin they had never been sung as these thousand students sang them. I saw again all the old plantations that I had ever seen; the whole history of the Negro ran through my mind; and the inexpressible pathos of his life found expression in these songs as I had never before felt it.

And the future? These were the ambitious youths of the race, at work with an earnestness that put to shame the conventional student life of most educational institutions. Another song rolled up along the rafters. And as soon as silence came, I found myself in front of this extraordinary mass of faces, thinking not of them, but of that long and unhappy chapter in our country's history which followed the one great structural mistake of the Fathers of the Republic; thinking of the one continuous great problem that generations of statesmen had wrangled over, and a million men fought about, and that had so dwarfed the mass of English men in the Southern States as to hold them back a hundred years behind their fellows in every other part of the world—in England, in Australia, and in the Northern and Western States; I was thinking of this dark shadow that had oppressed every large-minded statesman from Jefferson to Lincoln. These thousand young men and women about me were victims of it. I, too, was an innocent victim of it. The whole Republic was a victim of that fundamental error of importing Africa into America. I held firmly to the first article of my faith that the Republic must stand fast by the principle of a fair ballot; but I recalled the wretched mess that Reconstruction had made of it; I recalled the low level of public life in all the "black" States. Every effort of philanthropy seemed to have miscarried, every effort at correcting abuses seemed of doubtful value, and the race friction seemed to become severer. Here was the century-old problem in all its pathos seated singing before me. Who were the more to be pitied—these innocent victims of an ancient wrong, or I and men like me, who had inherited the problem? I had long ago thrown aside illusions and theories, and was willing to meet the facts face to face, and to do whatever in God's name a man might do towards saving the next generation from such a burden. But I felt the weight of twenty well-nigh hopeless years of thought and reading and observation; for the old difficulties remained and new ones had sprung up. Then

I saw clearly that the way out of a century of blunders had been made by this man who stood beside me and was introducing me to this audience. Before me was the material he had used. All about me was the indisputable evidence that he had found the natural line of development. He had shown the way. Time and patience and encouragement and work would do the rest.

It was then more clearly than ever before that I understood the patriotic significance of Mr. Washington's work. It is this conception of it and of him that I have ever since carried with me. It is on this that his claim to our gratitude rests.

To teach the Negro to read, whether English, or Greek, or Hebrew, butters no parsnips. To make the Negro work, that is what his master did in one way and hunger has done in another; yet both these left Southern life where they found it. But to teach the Negro to do skilful work, as men of all the races that have risen have worked,—responsible work, which *is* education and character; and most of all when Negroes so teach Negroes to do this that they will teach others with a missionary zeal that puts all ordinary philanthropic efforts to shame,—this is to change the whole economic basis of life and the whole character of a people.

The plan itself is not a new one. It was worked out at Hampton Institute, but it was done at Hampton by white men. The plan had, in fact, been many times theoretically laid down by thoughtful students of Southern life. Handicrafts were taught in the days of slavery on most well-managed plantations. But Tuskegee is, nevertheless, a brand-new chapter in the history of the Negro, and in the history of the knottiest problem we have ever faced. It not only makes "a carpenter of a man; it makes a man of a carpenter." In one sense, therefore, it is of greater value than any other institution for the training of men and women that we have, from Cambridge to Palo Alto. It is almost the only one of which it may be said that it points the way to a new epoch in a large area of our national life.

To work out the plan on paper, or at a distance—that is one thing. For a white man to work it out—that too, is an easy thing. For a coloured man to work it out in the South, where, in its constructive period, he was necessarily misunderstood by his own people as well as by the whites, and where he had to adjust it at every step to the strained race relations—that is so very different and more difficult a thing that the man who did it put the country under lasting obligations to him.

It was not and is not a mere educational task. Anybody could teach boys trades and give them an elementary education. Such tasks have been done since the beginning of civilization. But this task had to be done with the rawest of raw material, done within the civilization of the dominant race, and so done as not to run across race lines and social lines that are the strongest forces in the community. It had to be done for the benefit of the whole community. It had to be done, moreover, without local help, in the face of the direst poverty, done by begging, and done in spite of the ignorance of one race and the prejudice of the other.

No man living had a harder task, and a task that called for more wisdom to do it right. The true measure of Mr. Washington's success is, then, not his teaching the pupils of Tuskegee, nor even gaining the support of philanthropic persons at a distance, but this—that every Southern white man of character and of wisdom has been won to a cordial recognition of the value of the work, even men who held and still hold to the conviction that a mere book education for the Southern blacks under present conditions is a positive evil. This is a demonstration of the efficiency of the Hampton-Tuskegee idea that stands like the demonstration of the value of democratic institutions themselves—a demonstration made so clear in spite of the greatest odds that it is no longer open to argument.

Consider the change that has come in twenty years in the discussion of the Negro problem. Two or three decades ago social philosophers and statisticians and well-meaning philanthropists were still talking and writing about the deportation of the Negroes, or about their settlement within some restricted area, or about their settling in all parts of the Union, or about their decline through their neglect of their children, or about their rapid multiplication till they should expel the whites from the South—of every sort of nonsense under heaven. All this has given place to the simple plan of an indefinite extension among the neglected classes of both races of the

Hampton-Tuskegee system of training. The "problem" in one sense has disappeared. The future will have for the South swift or slow development of its masses and of its soil in proportion to the swift or slow development of this kind of training. This change of view is a true measure of Mr. Washington's work.

The literature of the Negro in America is colossal, from political oratory through abolitionism to *Uncle Tom's Cabin* and *Cotton is King*—a vast mass of books which many men have read to the waste of good years (and I among them); but the only books that I have read a second time or ever care again to read in the whole list (most of them by tiresome and unbalanced "reformers") are *Uncle Remus* and *Up from Slavery*; for these are the great literature of the subject. One has all the best of the past, the other foreshadows a better future; and the men who wrote them are the only men who have written of the subject with that perfect frankness and perfect knowledge and perfect poise whose other name is genius.

Mr. Washington has won a world-wide fame at an early age. His story of his own life already has the distinction of translation into more languages, I think, than any other American book; and I suppose that he has as large a personal acquaintance among men of influence as any private citizen now living.

His own teaching at Tuskegee is unique. He lectures to his advanced students on the art of right living, not out of text-books, but straight out of life. Then he sends them into the country to visit Negro families. Such a student will come back with a minute report of the way in which the family that he has seen lives, what their earnings are, what they do well and what they do ill; and he will explain how they might live better. He constructs a definite plan for the betterment of that particular family out of the resources that they have. Such a student, if he be bright, will profit more by an experience like this than he could profit by all the books on sociology and economics that ever were written. I talked with a boy at Tuskegee who had made such a study as this, and I could not keep from contrasting his knowledge and enthusiasm with what I heard in a class room at a Negro university in one of the Southern cities, which is conducted on the idea that a college course will save the soul. Here the class was reciting a lesson from an abstruse text-book on economics, reciting it by rote, with so obvious a failure to assimilate it that the waste of labour was pitiful.

I asked Mr. Washington years ago what he regarded as the most important result of his work, and he replied:

"I do not know which to put first, the effect of Tuskegee's work on the Negro, or the effect on the attitude of the white man to the Negro."

The race divergence under the system of miseducation was fast getting wider. Under the influence of the Hampton-Tuskegee idea the races are coming into a closer sympathy and into an honourable and helpful relation. As the Negro becomes economically independent, he becomes a responsible part of the Southern life; and the whites so recognize him. And this must be so from the nature of things. There is nothing artificial about it. It is development in a perfectly natural way. And the Southern whites not only so recognize it, but they are imitating it in the teaching of the neglected masses of their own race. It has thus come about that the school is taking a more direct and helpful hold on life in the South than anywhere else in the country. Education is not a thing apart from life—not a "system," nor a philosophy; it is direct teaching how to live and how to work.

To say that Mr. Washington has won the gratitude of all thoughtful Southern white men, is to say that he has worked with the highest practical wisdom at a large constructive task; for no plan for the up-building of the freedman could succeed that ran counter to Southern opinion. To win the support of Southern opinion and to shape it was a necessary part of the task; and in this he has so well succeeded that the South has a sincere and high regard for him. He once said to me that he recalled the day, and remembered it thankfully, when he grew large enough to regard a Southern white man as he regarded a Northern one. It is well for our common country that the day is come when he and his work are regarded as highly in the South as in any other part of the Union. I think that no man of our generation has a more noteworthy achievement to his credit than this; and it is an achievement of moral earnestness of the strong character of a man who has done a great national service.

Walter H. Page

# PREFACE

This volume is the outgrowth of a series of articles, dealing with incidents in my life, which were published consecutively in the *Outlook*. While they were appearing in that magazine I was constantly surprised at the number of requests which came to me from all parts of the country, asking that the articles be permanently preserved in book form. I am most grateful to the *Outlook* for permission to gratify these requests.

I have tried to tell a simple, straightforward story, with no attempt at embellishment. My regret is that what I have attempted to do has been done so imperfectly. The greater part of my time and strength is required for the executive work connected with the Tuskegee Normal and Industrial Institute, and in securing the money necessary for the support of the institution. Much of what I have said has been written on board trains, or at hotels or railroad stations while I have been waiting for trains, or during the moments that I could spare from my work while at Tuskegee. Without the painstaking and generous assistance of Mr. Max Bennett Thrasher I could not have succeeded in any satisfactory degree.

# CHAPTER I

## *A Slave Among Slaves*

I was born a slave on a plantation in Franklin County, Virginia. I am not quite sure of the exact place or exact date of my birth, but at any rate I suspect I must have been born somewhere and at some time. As nearly as I have been able to learn, I was born near a cross-roads post-office called Hale's Ford, and the year was 1858 or 1859. I do not know the month or the day. The earliest impressions I can now recall are of the plantation and the slave quarters—the latter being the part of the plantation where the slaves had their cabins.

My life had its beginning in the midst of the most miserable, desolate, and discouraging surroundings. This was so, however, not because my owners were especially cruel, for they were not, as compared with many others. I was born in a typical log cabin, about fourteen by sixteen feet square. In this cabin I lived with my mother and a brother and sister till after the Civil War, when we were all declared free.

Of my ancestry I know almost nothing. In the slave quarters, and even later, I heard whispered conversations among the coloured people of the tortures which the slaves, including, no doubt, my ancestors on my mother's side, suffered in the middle passage of the slave ship while being conveyed from Africa to America. I have been unsuccessful in securing any information that would throw any accurate light upon the history of my family beyond my mother. She, I remember, had a half-brother and a half-sister. In the days of slavery not very much attention was given to family history and family records—that is, black family records. My mother, I suppose, attracted the attention of a purchaser who was afterward my owner and hers. Her addition to the slave family attracted about as much attention as the purchase of a new horse or cow. Of my father I know even less than of my mother. I do not even know his name. I have heard reports to the effect that he was a white man who lived on one of the near-by plantations. Whoever he was, I never heard of his taking the least interest in me or providing in any way for my rearing. But I do not find especial fault with him. He was simply another unfortunate victim of the institution which the Nation unhappily had engrafted upon it at that time.

The cabin was not only our living-place, but was also used as the kitchen for the plantation. My mother was the plantation cook. The cabin was without glass windows; it had only openings in the side which let in the light, and also the cold, chilly air of winter. There was a door to the cabin—that is, something that was called a door—but the uncertain hinges by which it was hung, and the large cracks in it, to say nothing of the fact that it was too small, made the room a very uncomfortable one. In addition to these openings there was, in the lower right-hand corner of the room, the "cat-hole," —a contrivance which almost every mansion or cabin in Virginia possessed during the ante-bellum period. The "cat-hole" was a square opening, about seven by eight inches, provided for the purpose of letting the cat pass in and out of the house at will during the night. In the case of our particular cabin I could never understand the necessity for this convenience, since there were at least a half-dozen other places in the cabin that would have accommodated the cats. There was no wooden floor in our cabin, the naked earth being used as a floor. In the centre of the earthen floor there was a large, deep opening covered with boards, which was used as a place in which to store sweet potatoes during the winter. An impression of this potato-hole is very distinctly engraved upon my memory, because I recall that during the process of putting the potatoes in or taking them out I would often come into possession of one or two, which I roasted and thoroughly enjoyed. There was no cooking-stove on our plantation, and all the cooking for the whites and slaves my mother had to do over an open fireplace, mostly in pots and "skillets." While the poorly built cabin caused us to suffer with cold in the winter, the heat from the open fireplace in summer was equally trying.

The early years of my life, which were spent in the little cabin, were not very different from those of thousands of other slaves. My mother, of course, had little time in which to give attention to the training of her children during the day. She snatched a few moments for our care in the early morning before her work began, and at night after the day's work was done. One of my earliest recollections is that of my mother cooking a chicken late at night, and awakening her children for the purpose of feeding them. How or where she got it I do not know. I presume, however, it was procured from our owner's farm. Some people may call this theft. If such a thing were to happen now, I should condemn it as theft myself. But taking place at the time it did, and for the reason that it did, no one could ever make me believe that my mother was guilty of thieving. She was simply a victim of the system of slavery. I cannot remember having slept in a bed until after our family was declared free by the Emancipation Proclamation. Three children—John, my older brother, Amanda, my sister, and myself—had a pallet on the dirt floor, or, to be more correct, we slept in and on a bundle of filthy rags laid upon the dirt floor.

I was asked not long ago to tell something about the sports and pastimes that I engaged in during my youth. Until that question was asked it had never occurred to me that there was no period of my life that was devoted to play. From the time that I can remember anything, almost every day of my life had been occupied in some kind of labour; though I think I would now be a more useful man if I had had time for sports. During the period that I spent in slavery I was not large enough to be of much service, still I was occupied most of the time in cleaning the yards, carrying water to the men in the fields, or going to the mill to which I used to take the corn, once a week, to be ground. The mill was about three miles from the plantation. This work I always dreaded. The heavy bag of corn would be thrown across the back of the horse, and the corn divided about evenly on each side; but in some way, almost without exception, on these trips, the corn would so shift as to become unbalanced and would fall off the horse, and often I would fall with it. As I was not strong enough to reload the corn upon the horse, I would have to wait, sometimes for many hours, till a chance passer-by came along who would help me out of my trouble. The hours while waiting for some one were usually spent in crying. The time consumed in this way made me late in reaching the mill, and by the time I got my corn ground and reached home it would be far into the night. The road was a lonely one, and often led through dense forests. I was always frightened. The woods were said to be full of soldiers who had deserted from the army, and I had been told that the first thing a deserter did to a Negro boy when he found him alone was to cut off his ears. Besides, when I was late in getting home I knew I would always get a severe scolding or a flogging.

I had no schooling whatever while I was a slave, though I remember on several occasions I went as far as the schoolhouse door with one of my young mistresses to carry her books. The picture of several dozen boys and girls in a schoolroom engaged in study made a deep impression upon me, and I had the feeling that to get into a schoolhouse and study in this way would be about the same as getting into paradise.

So far as I can now recall, the first knowledge that I got of the fact that we were slaves, and that freedom of the slaves was being discussed, was early one morning before day, when I was awakened by my mother kneeling over her children and fervently praying that Lincoln and his armies might be successful, and that one day she and her children might be free. In this connection I have never been able to understand how the slaves throughout the South, completely ignorant as were the masses so far as books or newspapers were concerned, were able to keep themselves so accurately and completely informed about the great National questions that were agitating the country. From the time that Garrison, Lovejoy, and others began to agitate for freedom, the slaves throughout the South kept in close touch with the progress of the movement. Though I was a mere child during the preparation for the Civil War and during the war itself, I now recall the many late-at-night whispered discussions that I heard my mother and the other slaves on the plantation indulge in. These discussions showed that they understood the situation, and that they kept themselves informed of events by what was termed the "grapevine" telegraph.

During the campaign when Lincoln was first a candidate for the Presidency, the slaves on our far-off plantation, miles from any railroad or large city or daily newspaper, knew what the issues involved were.

When war was begun between the North and the South, every slave on our plantation felt and knew that, though other issues were discussed, the primal one was that of slavery. Even the most ignorant members of my race on the remote plantations felt in their hearts, with a certainty that admitted of no doubt, that the freedom of the slaves would be the one great result of the war, if the Northern armies conquered. Every success of the Federal armies and every defeat of the Confederate forces was watched with the keenest and most intense interest. Often the slaves got knowledge of the results of great battles before the white people received it. This news was usually gotten from the coloured man who was sent to the post-office for the mail. In our case the post-office was about three miles from the plantation, and the mail came once or twice a week. The man who was sent to the office would linger about the place long enough to get the drift of the conversation from the group of white people who naturally congregated there, after receiving their mail, to discuss the latest news. The mail-carrier on his way back to our master's house would as naturally retail the news that he had secured among the slaves, and in this way they often heard of important events before the white people at the "big house," as the master's house was called.

I cannot remember a single instance during my childhood or early boyhood when our entire family sat down to the table together, and God's blessing was asked, and the family ate a meal in a civilized manner. On the plantation in Virginia, and even later, meals were gotten by the children very much as dumb animals get theirs. It was a piece of bread here and a scrap of meat there. It was a cup of milk at one time and some potatoes at another. Sometimes a portion of our family would eat out of the skillet or pot, while some one else would eat from a tin plate held on the knees, and often using nothing but the hands with which to hold the food. When I had grown to sufficient size, I was required to go to the "big house" at meal-times to fan the flies from the table by means of a large set of paper fans operated by a pulley. Naturally much of the conversation of the white people turned upon the subject of freedom and the war, and I absorbed a good deal of it. I remember that at one time I saw two of my young mistresses and some lady visitors eating ginger-cakes, in the yard. At that time those cakes seemed to me to be absolutely the most tempting and desirable things that I had ever seen; and I then and there resolved that, if I ever got free, the height of my ambition would be reached if I could get to the point where I could secure and eat ginger-cakes in the way that I saw those ladies doing.

Of course as the war was prolonged the white people, in many cases, often found it difficult to secure food for themselves. I think the slaves felt the deprivation less than the whites, because the usual diet for slaves was corn bread and pork, and these could be raised on the plantation; but coffee, tea, sugar, and other articles which the whites had been accustomed to use could not be raised on the plantation, and the conditions brought about by the war frequently made it impossible to secure these things. The whites were often in great straits. Parched corn was used for coffee, and a kind of black molasses was used instead of sugar. Many times nothing was used to sweeten the so-called tea and coffee.

The first pair of shoes that I recall wearing were wooden ones. They had rough leather on the top, but the bottoms, which were about an inch thick, were of wood. When I walked they made a fearful noise, and besides this they were very inconvenient, since there was no yielding to the natural pressure of the foot. In wearing them one presented an exceedingly awkward appearance. The most trying ordeal that I was forced to endure as a slave boy, however, was the wearing of a flax shirt. In the portion of Virginia where I lived it was common to use flax as part of the clothing for the slaves. That part of the flax from which our clothing was made was largely the refuse, which of course was the cheapest and roughest part. I can scarcely imagine any torture, except, perhaps, the pulling of a tooth, that is equal to that caused by putting on a new flax shirt for the first time. It is almost equal to the feeling that one would experience if he had a dozen or more chestnut burrs, or a hundred small pin-points, in contact with his flesh. Even to this day I can recall accurately the tortures that I underwent when putting on one of these garments. The fact that my flesh was soft and tender added to the pain. But I had no choice. I had to wear the flax shirt or none; and had it been left to me to choose, I should have chosen to wear no covering. In connection with the flax shirt, my brother John, who is several years older than I am, performed one of the most generous acts that I ever heard of one slave relative doing for another. On several occasions when I was being forced to wear a new flax shirt, he generously agreed to put it on in my stead and wear it for several days, till it was "broken in." Until I had grown to be quite a youth this single garment was all that I wore.

One may get the idea, from what I have said, that there was bitter feeling toward the white people on the part of my race, because of the fact that most of the white population was away fighting in a war which would result in keeping the Negro in slavery if the South was successful. In the case of the slaves on our place this was not true, and it was not true of any large portion of the slave population in the South where the Negro was treated with anything like decency. During the Civil War one of my young masters was killed, and two were severely wounded. I recall the feeling of sorrow which existed among the slaves when they heard of the death of "Mars' Billy." It was no sham sorrow, but real. Some of the slaves had nursed "Mars' Billy"; others had played with him when he was a child. "Mars' Billy" had begged for mercy in the case of others when the overseer or master was thrashing them. The sorrow in the slave quarter was only second to that in the "big house." When the two young masters were brought home wounded, the sympathy of the slaves was shown in many ways. They were just as anxious to assist in the nursing as the family relatives of the wounded. Some of the slaves would even beg for the privilege of sitting up at night to nurse their wounded masters. This tenderness and sympathy on the part of those held in bondage was a result of their kindly and generous nature. In order to defend and protect the women and children who were left on the plantations when the white males went to war, the slaves would have laid down their lives. The slave who was selected to sleep in the "big house" during the absence of the males was considered to have the place of honour. Any one attempting to harm "young Mistress" or "old Mistress" during the night would have had to cross the dead body of the slave to do so. I do not know how many have noticed it, but I think that it will be found to be true that there are few instances, either in slavery or freedom, in which a member of my race has been known to betray a specific trust.

As a rule, not only did the members of my race entertain no feelings of bitterness against the whites before and during the war, but there are many instances of Negroes tenderly carrying for their former masters and mistresses who for some reason have become poor and dependent since the war. I know of instances where the former masters of slaves have for years been supplied with money by their former slaves to keep them from suffering. I have known of still other cases in which the former slaves have assisted in the education of the descendants of their former owners. I know of a case on a large plantation in the South in which a young white man, the son of the former owner of the estate, has become so reduced in purse and self-control by reason of drink that he is a pitiable creature; and yet, notwithstanding the poverty of the coloured people themselves on this plantation, they have for years supplied this young white man with the necessities of life. One sends him a little coffee or sugar, another a little meat, and so on. Nothing that the coloured people possess is too good for the son of "old Mars' Tom," who will perhaps never be permitted to suffer while any remain on the place who knew directly or indirectly of "old Mars' Tom."

I have said that there are few instances of a member of my race betraying a specific trust. One of the best illustrations of this which I know of is in the case of an ex-slave from Virginia whom I met not long ago in a little town in the state of Ohio. I found that this man had made a contract with his master, two or three years previous to the Emancipation Proclamation, to the effect that the slave was to be permitted to buy himself, by paying so much per year for his body; and while he was paying for himself, he was to be permitted to labour where and for whom he pleased. Finding that he could secure better wages in Ohio, he went there. When freedom came, he was still in debt to his master some three hundred dollars. Notwithstanding that the Emancipation Proclamation freed him from any obligation to his master, this black man walked the greater portion of the distance back to where his old master lived in Virginia, and placed the last dollar, with interest, in his hands. In talking to me about this, the man told me that he knew that he did not have to pay the debt, but that he had given his word to the master, and his word he had never broken.

He felt that he could not enjoy his freedom till he had fulfilled his promise.

From some things that I have said one may get the idea that some of the slaves did not want freedom. This is not true. I have never seen one who did not want to be free, or one who would return to slavery.

I pity from the bottom of my heart any nation or body of people that is so unfortunate as to get entangled in the net of slavery. I have long since ceased to cherish any spirit of bitterness against the Southern white people on account of the enslavement of my race. No one section of our country was wholly responsible for its introduction, and, besides, it was recognized and protected for years by the General Government. Having once got its tentacles fastened on to the economic and social life of the Republic, it was no easy matter for the country to relieve itself of the institution. Then, when we rid ourselves of prejudice, or racial feeling, and look facts in the face, we must acknowledge that, notwithstanding the cruelty and moral wrong of slavery, the ten million Negroes inhabiting this country, who themselves or whose ancestors went through the school of American slavery, are in a stronger and more hopeful condition, materially, intellectually, morally, and religiously, than is true of an equal number of black people in any other portion of the globe. This is so to such an extent that Negroes in this country, who themselves or whose forefathers went through the school of slavery, are constantly returning to Africa as missionaries to enlighten those who remained in the fatherland. This I say, not to justify slavery—on the other hand, I condemn it as an institution, as we all know that in America it was established for selfish and financial reasons, and not from a missionary motive—but to call attention to a fact, and to show how Providence so often uses men and institutions to accomplish a purpose. When persons ask me in these days how, in the midst of what sometimes seem hopelessly discouraging conditions, I can have such faith in the future of my race in this country, I remind them of the wilderness through which and out of which, a good Providence has already led us.

Ever since I have been old enough to think for myself, I have entertained the idea that, notwithstanding the cruel wrongs inflicted upon us, the black man got nearly as much out of slavery as the white man did. The hurtful influences of the institution were not by any means confined to the Negro. This was fully illustrated by the life upon our own plantation. The whole machinery of slavery was so constructed as to cause labour, as a rule, to be looked upon as a badge of degradation, of inferiority. Hence labour was something that both races on the slave plantation sought to escape. The slave system on our place, in a large measure, took the spirit of self-reliance and self-help out of the white people. My old master had many boys and girls, but not one, so far as I know, ever mastered a single trade or special line of productive industry. The girls were not taught to cook, sew, or to take care of the house. All of this was left to the slaves. The slaves, of course, had little personal interest in the life of the plantation, and their ignorance prevented them from learning how to do things in the most improved and thorough manner. As a result of the system, fences were out of repair, gates were hanging half off the hinges, doors creaked, window-panes were out, plastering had fallen but was not replaced, weeds grew in the yard. As a rule, there was food for whites and blacks, but inside the house, and on the dining-room table, there was wanting that delicacy and refinement of touch and finish which can make a home the most convenient, comfortable, and attractive place in the world. Withal there was a waste of food and other materials which was sad. When freedom came, the slaves were almost as well fitted to begin life anew as the master, except in the matter of book-learning and ownership of property. The slave owner and his sons had mastered no special industry. They unconsciously had imbibed the feeling that manual labour was not the proper thing for them. On the other hand, the slaves, in many cases, had mastered some handicraft, and none were ashamed, and few unwilling, to labour.

Finally the war closed, and the day of freedom came. It was a momentous and eventful day to all upon our plantation. We had been expecting it. Freedom was in the air, and had been for months. Deserting soldiers returning to their homes were to be seen every day. Others who had been discharged, or whose regiments had been paroled, were constantly passing near our place. The "grape-vine telegraph" was kept busy night and day. The news and mutterings of great events were swiftly carried from one plantation to another. In the fear of "Yankee" invasions, the silverware and other valuables were taken from the "big house," buried in the woods, and guarded by trusted slaves. Woe be to any one who would have attempted to disturb the buried treasure. The slaves would give the Yankee soldiers food, drink, clothing—anything but that which had been specifically intrusted to their care and honour. As the great day drew nearer, there was more singing in the slave quarters than usual. It was bolder, had more ring, and lasted later into the night. Most of the verses of the plantation songs had some reference to freedom. True, they had sung those same verses before, but they had been careful to explain that the "freedom" in these songs referred to the next world, and had no connection with life in this world. Now they gradually threw off the mask, and were not afraid to let it be known that the "freedom" in their songs meant freedom of the body in this world. The night before the eventful day, word was sent to the slave quarters to the effect that something unusual was going to take place at the "big house" the next morning. There was little, if any, sleep that night. All was excitement and expectancy. Early the next morning word was sent to all the slaves, old and young, to gather at the house. In company with my mother, brother, and sister, and a large number of other slaves, I went to the master's house. All of our master's family were either standing or seated on the veranda of the house, where they could see what was to take place and hear what was said. There was a feeling of deep interest, or perhaps sadness, on their faces, but not bitterness. As I now recall the impression they made upon me, they did not at the moment seem to be sad because of the loss of property, but rather because of parting with those whom they had reared and who were in many ways very close to them. The most distinct thing that I now recall in connection with the scene was that some man who seemed to be a stranger (a United States officer, I presume) made a little speech and then read a rather long paper—the Emancipation Proclamation, I think. After the reading we were told that we were all free, and could go when and where we pleased. My mother, who was standing by my side, leaned over and kissed her children, while tears of joy ran down her cheeks. She explained to us what it all meant, that this was the day for which she had been so long praying, but fearing that she would never live to see.

For some minutes there was great rejoicing, and thanksgiving, and wild scenes of ecstasy. But there was no feeling of bitterness. In fact, there was pity among the slaves for our former owners. The wild rejoicing on the part of the emancipated coloured people lasted but for a brief period, for I noticed that by the time they returned to their cabins there was a change in their feelings. The great responsibility of being free, of having charge of themselves, of having to think and plan for themselves and their children, seemed to take possession of them. It was very much like suddenly turning a youth of ten or twelve years out into the world to provide for himself. In a few hours the great questions with which the Anglo-Saxon race had been grappling for centuries had been thrown upon these people to be solved. These were the questions of a home, a living, the rearing of children, education, citizenship, and the establishment and support of churches. Was it any wonder that within a few hours the wild rejoicing ceased and a feeling of deep gloom seemed to pervade the slave quarters? To some it seemed that, now that they were in actual possession of it, freedom was a more serious thing than they had expected to find it. Some of the slaves were seventy or eighty years old; their best days were gone. They had no strength with which to earn a living in a strange place and among strange people, even if they had been sure where to find a new place of abode. To this class the problem seemed especially hard. Besides, deep down in their hearts there was a strange and peculiar attachment to "old Marster" and "old Missus," and to their children, which they found it hard to think of breaking off. With these they had spent in some cases nearly a half-century, and it was no light thing to think of parting. Gradually, one by one, stealthily at first, the older slaves began to wander from the slave quarters back to the "big house" to have a whispered conversation with their former owners as to the future.

# CHAPTER II

## *Boyhood Days*

After the coming of freedom there were two points upon which practically all the people on our place were agreed, and I found that this was generally true throughout the South: that they must change their names, and that they must leave the old plantation for at least a few days or weeks in order that they might really feel sure that they were free.

In some way a feeling got among the coloured people that it was far from proper for them to bear the surname of their former owners, and a great many of them took other surnames. This was one of the first signs of freedom. When they were slaves, a coloured person was simply called "John" or "Susan." There was seldom occasion for more than the use of the one name. If "John" or "Susan" belonged to a white man by the name of "Hatcher," sometimes he was called "John Hatcher," or as often "Hatcher's John." But there was a feeling that "John Hatcher" or "Hatcher's John" was not the proper title by which to denote a freeman; and so in many cases "John Hatcher" was changed to "John S. Lincoln" or "John S. Sherman," the initial "S" standing for no name, it being simply a part of what the coloured man proudly called his "entitles."

As I have stated, most of the coloured people left the old plantation for a short while at least, so as to be sure, it seemed, that they could leave and try their freedom on to see how it felt. After they had remained away for a while, many of the older slaves, especially, returned to their old homes and made some kind of contract with their former owners by which they remained on the estate.

My mother's husband, who was the stepfather of my brother John and myself, did not belong to the same owners as did my mother. In fact, he seldom came to our plantation. I remember seeing him there perhaps once a year, that being about Christmas time. In some way, during the war, by running away and following the Federal soldiers, it seems, he found his way into the new state of West Virginia. As soon as freedom was declared, he sent for my mother to come to the Kanawha Valley, in West Virginia. At that time a journey from Virginia over the mountains to West Virginia was rather a tedious and in some cases a painful undertaking. What little clothing and few household goods we had were placed in a cart, but the children walked the greater portion of the distance, which was several hundred miles.

I do not think any of us ever had been very far from the plantation, and the taking of a long journey into another state was quite an event. The parting from our former owners and the members of our own race on the plantation was a serious occasion. From the time of our parting till their death we kept up a correspondence with the older members of the family, and in later years we have kept in touch with those who were the younger members. We were several weeks making the trip, and most of the time we slept in the open air and did our cooking over a log fire out-of-doors. One night I recall that we camped near an abandoned log cabin, and my mother decided to build a fire in that for cooking, and afterward to make a "pallet" on the floor for our sleeping. Just as the fire had gotten well started a large black snake fully a yard and a half long dropped down the chimney and ran out on the floor. Of course we at once abandoned that cabin. Finally we reached our destination—a little town called Malden, which is about five miles from Charleston, the present capital of the state.

At that time salt-mining was the great industry in that part of West Virginia, and the little town of Malden was right in the midst of the salt-furnaces. My stepfather had already secured a job at a salt-furnace, and he had also secured a little cabin for us to live in. Our new house was no better than the one we had left on the old plantation in Virginia. In fact, in one respect it was worse. Notwithstanding the poor condition of our plantation cabin, we were at all times sure of pure air. Our new home was in the midst of a cluster of cabins crowded closely together, and as there were no sanitary regulations, the filth about the cabins was often intolerable. Some of our neighbours were coloured people, and some were the poorest and most ignorant and degraded white people. It was a motley mixture. Drinking, gambling, quarrels, fights, and shockingly immoral practices were frequent. All who lived in the little town were in one way or another connected with the salt business. Though I was a mere child, my stepfather put me and my brother at work in one of the furnaces. Often I began work as early as four o'clock in the morning.

The first thing I ever learned in the way of book knowledge was while working in this salt-furnace. Each salt-packer had his barrels marked with a certain number. The number allotted to my stepfather was "18." At the close of the day's work the boss of the packers would come around and put "18" on each of our barrels, and I soon learned to recognize that figure wherever I saw it, and after a while got to the point where I could make that figure, though I knew nothing about any other figures or letters.

From the time that I can remember having any thoughts about anything, I recall that I had an intense longing to learn to read. I determined, when quite a small child, that, if I accomplished nothing else in life, I would in some way get enough education to enable me to read common books and newspapers. Soon after we got settled in some manner in our new cabin in West Virginia, I induced my mother to get hold of a book for me. How or where she got it I do not know, but in some way she procured an old copy of Webster's "blue-back" spelling-book, which contained the alphabet, followed by such meaningless words as "ab," "ba," "ca," "da." I began at once to devour this book, and I think that it was the first one I ever had in my hands. I had learned from somebody that the way to begin to read was to learn the alphabet, so I tried in all the ways I could think of to learn it,—all of course without a teacher, for I could find no one to teach me. At that time there was not a single member of my race anywhere near us who could read, and I was too timid to approach any of the white people. In some way, within a few weeks, I mastered the greater portion of the alphabet. In all my efforts to learn to read my mother shared fully my ambition, and sympathized with me and aided me in every way that she could. Though she was totally ignorant, she had high ambitions for her children, and a large fund of good, hard, common sense, which seemed to enable her to meet and master every situation. If I have done anything in life worth attention, I feel sure that I inherited the disposition from my mother.

In the midst of my struggles and longing for an education, a young coloured boy who had learned to read in the state of Ohio came to Malden. As soon as the coloured people found out that he could read, a newspaper was secured, and at the close of nearly every day's work this young man would be surrounded by a group of men and women who were anxious to hear him read the news contained in the papers. How I used to envy this man! He seemed to me to be the one young man in all the world who ought to be satisfied with his attainments.

About this time the question of having some kind of a school opened for the coloured children in the village began to be discussed by members of the race. As it would be the first school for Negro children that had ever been opened in that part of Virginia, it was, of course, to be a great event, and the discussion excited the wildest interest. The most perplexing question was where to find a teacher. The young man from Ohio who had learned to read the papers was considered, but his age was against him. In the midst of the discussion about a teacher, another young coloured man from Ohio, who had been a soldier, in some way found his way into town. It was soon learned that he possessed considerable education, and he was engaged by the coloured people to teach their first school. As yet no free schools had been started for coloured people in that section, hence each family agreed to pay a certain amount per month, with the understanding that the teacher was to "board 'round"—that is, spend a day with each family. This was not bad for the teacher, for each family tried to provide the very best on the day the teacher was to be its guest. I recall that I looked forward with an anxious appetite to the "teacher's day" at our little cabin.

This experience of a whole race beginning to go to school for the first time, presents one of the most interesting studies that has ever occurred in connection with the development of any race. Few people who were not right in the midst of the scenes can form any exact idea of the intense desire which the people of my race showed for an education. As I have stated, it was a whole race trying to go to school. Few were too young, and none too old, to make the attempt to learn. As fast as any kind of teachers could be secured, not only were day-schools filled, but night-schools as well. The great ambition of the older people was to try to learn to read the Bible before they died. With this end in view men and women who were fifty or seventy-five years old would often be found in the night-school. Some day-schools were formed soon after freedom, but the principal book studied in the Sunday-school was the spelling-book. Day-school, night-school, Sunday-school, were always crowded, and often many had to be turned away for want of room.

The opening of the school in the Kanawha Valley, however, brought to me one of the keenest disappointments that I ever experienced. I had been working in a salt-furnace for several months, and my step-father had discovered that I had a financial value, and so, when the school opened, he decided that he could not spare me from my work. This decision seemed to cloud my every ambition. The disappointment was made all the more severe by reason of the fact that my place of work was where I could see the happy children passing to and from school mornings and afternoons. Despite this disappointment, however, I determined that I would learn something, anyway. I applied myself with greater earnestness than ever to the mastering of what was in the "blue-back" speller.

My mother sympathized with me in my disappointment, and sought to comfort me in all the ways she could, and to help me find a way to learn. After a while I succeeded in making arrangements with the teacher to give me some lessons at night, after the day's work was done. These night lessons were so welcome that I think I learned more at night than the other children did during the day. My own experiences in the night-school gave me faith in the night-school idea, with which, in after years, I had to do both at Hampton and Tuskegee. But my boyish heart was still set upon going to the day-school, and I let no opportunity slip to push my case. Finally I won, and was permitted to go to the school in the day for a few months, with the understanding that I was to rise early in the morning and work in the furnace till nine o'clock, and return immediately after school closed in the afternoon for at least two more hours of work.

The schoolhouse was some distance from the furnace, and as I had to work till nine o'clock, and the school opened at nine, I found myself in a difficulty. School would always be begun before I reached it, and sometimes my class had recited. To get around this difficulty I yielded to a temptation for which most people, I suppose, will condemn me; but since it is a fact, I might as well state it. I have great faith in the power and influence of facts. It is seldom that anything is permanently gained by holding back a fact. There was a large clock in a little office in the furnace. This clock, of course, all the hundred or more workmen depended upon to regulate their hours of beginning and ending the day's work. I got the idea that the way for me to reach school on time was to move the clock hands from half-past eight up to the nine o'clock mark. This I found myself doing morning after morning, till the furnace "boss" discovered that something was wrong, and locked the clock in a case. I did not mean to inconvenience anybody. I simply meant to reach that schoolhouse in time.

When, however, I found myself at the school for the first time, I also found myself confronted with two other difficulties. In the first place, I found that all the other children wore hats or caps on their heads, and I had neither hat nor cap. In fact, I do not remember that up to the time of going to school I had ever worn any kind of covering upon my head, nor do I recall that either I or anybody else had even thought anything about the need of covering for my head. But, of course, when I saw how all the other boys were dressed, I began to feel quite uncomfortable. As usual, I put the case before my mother, and she explained to me that she had no money with which to buy a "store hat," which was a rather new institution at that time among the members of my race and was considered quite the thing for young and old to own, but that she would find a way to help me out of the difficulty. She accordingly got two pieces of "homespun" (jeans) and sewed them together, and I was soon the proud possessor of my first cap.

The lesson that my mother taught me in this has always remained with me, and I have tried as best as I could to teach it to others. I have always felt proud, whenever I think of the incident, that my mother had strength of character enough not to be led into the temptation of seeming to be that which she was not—of trying to impress my schoolmates and others with the fact that she was able to buy me a "store hat" when she was not. I have always felt proud that she refused to go into debt for that which she did not have the money to pay for. Since that time I have owned many kinds of caps and hats, but never one of which I have felt so proud as of the cap made of the two pieces of cloth sewed together by my mother. I have noted the fact, but without satisfaction, I need not add, that several of the boys who began their careers with "store hats" and who were my schoolmates and used to join in the sport that was made of me because I had only a "homespun" cap, have ended their careers in the penitentiary, while others are not able now to buy any kind of hat.

My second difficulty was with regard to my name, or rather *a* name. From the time when I could remember anything, I had been called simply "Booker." Before going to school it had never occurred to me that it was needful or appropriate to have an additional name. When I heard the schoolroll called, I noticed that all of the children had at least two names, and some of them indulged in what seemed to me the extravagance of having three. I was in deep perplexity, because I knew that the teacher would demand of me at least two names, and I had only one. By the time the occasion came for the enrolling of my name, an idea occurred to me which I thought would make me equal to the situation; and so, when the teacher asked me what my full name was, I calmly told him "Booker Washington," as if I had been called by that name all my life; and by that name I have since been known. Later in my life I found that my mother had given me the name of "Booker Taliaferro" soon after I was born, but in some way that part of my name seemed to disappear and for a long while was forgotten, but as soon as I found out about it I revived it, and made my full name "Booker Taliaferro Washington." I think there are not many men in our country who have had the privilege of naming themselves in the way that I have.

More than once I have tried to picture myself in the position of a boy or man with an honoured and distinguished ancestry which I could trace back through a period of hundreds of years, and who had not only inherited a name, but fortune and a proud family homestead;

and yet I have sometimes had the feeling that if I had inherited these, and had been a member of a more popular race, I should have been inclined to yield to the temptation of depending upon my ancestry and my colour to do that for me which I should do for myself. Years ago I resolved that because I had no ancestry myself I would leave a record of which my children would be proud, and which might encourage them to still higher effort.

The world should not pass judgment upon the Negro, and especially the Negro youth, too quickly or too harshly. The Negro boy has obstacles, discouragements, and temptations to battle with that are little known to those not situated as he is. When a white boy undertakes a task, it is taken for granted that he will succeed. On the other hand, people are usually surprised if the Negro boy does not fail. In a word, the Negro youth starts out with the presumption against him.

The influence of ancestry, however, is important in helping forward any individual or race, if too much reliance is not placed upon it. Those who constantly direct attention to the Negro youth's moral weaknesses, and compare his advancement with that of white youths, do not consider the influence of the memories which cling about the old family homesteads. I have no idea, as I have stated elsewhere, who my grandmother was. I have, or have had, uncles and aunts and cousins, but I have no knowledge as to where most of them are. My case will illustrate that of hundreds of thousands of black people in every part of our country. The very fact that the white boy is conscious that, if he fails in life, he will disgrace the whole family record, extending back through many generations, is of tremendous value in helping him to resist temptations. The fact that the individual has behind and surrounding him proud family history and connection serves as a stimulus to help him to overcome obstacles when striving for success.

The time that I was permitted to attend school during the day was short, and my attendance was irregular. It was not long before I had to stop attending day-school altogether, and devote all of my time again to work. I resorted to the night-school again. In fact, the greater part of the education I secured in my boyhood was gathered through the night-school after my day's work was done. I had difficulty often in securing a satisfactory teacher. Sometimes, after I had secured some one to teach me at night, I would find, much to my disappointment, that the teacher knew but little more than I did. Often I would have to walk several miles at night in order to recite my night-school lessons. There was never a time in my youth, no matter how dark and discouraging the days might be, when one resolve did not continually remain with me, and that was a determination to secure an education at any cost.

Soon after we moved to West Virginia, my mother adopted into our family, notwithstanding our poverty, an orphan boy, to whom afterward we gave the name of James B. Washington. He has ever since remained a member of the family.

After I had worked in the salt-furnace for some time, work was secured for me in a coal-mine which was operated mainly for the purpose of securing fuel for the salt-furnace. Work in the coal-mine I always dreaded. One reason for this was that any one who worked in a coal-mine was always unclean, at least while at work, and it was a very hard job to get one's skin clean after the day's work was over. Then it was fully a mile from the opening of the coal-mine to the face of the coal, and all, of course, was in the blackest darkness. I do not believe that one ever experiences anywhere else such darkness as he does in a coal-mine. The mine was divided into a large number of different "rooms" or departments, and, as I never was able to learn the location of all these "rooms," I many times found myself lost in the mine. To add to the horror of being lost, sometimes my light would go out, and then, if I did not happen to have a match, I would wander about in the darkness until by chance I found some one to give me a light. The work was not only hard, but it was dangerous. There was always the danger of being blown to pieces by a premature explosion of powder, or of being crushed by falling slate. Accidents from one or the other of these causes were frequently occurring, and this kept me in constant fear. Many children of the tenderest years were compelled then, as is now true I fear, in most coal-mining districts, to spend a large part of their lives in these coal-mines, with little opportunity to get an education; and, what is worse, I have often noted that, as a rule, young boys who begin life in a coal-mine are often physically and mentally dwarfed. They soon lose ambition to do anything else than to continue as a coal-miner.

In those days, and later as a young man, I used to try to picture in my imagination the feelings and ambitions of a white boy with absolutely no limit placed upon his aspirations and activities. I used to envy the white boy who had no obstacles placed in the way of his becoming a Congressman, Governor, Bishop, or President by reason of the accident of his birth or race. I used to picture the way that I would act under such circumstances; how I would begin at the bottom and keep rising until I reached the highest round of success.

In later years, I confess that I do not envy the white boy as I once did. I have learned that success is to be measured not so much by the position that one has reached in life as by the obstacles which he has overcome while trying to succeed. Looked at from this standpoint, I almost reached the conclusion that often the Negro boy's birth and connection with an unpopular race is an advantage, so far as real life is concerned. With few exceptions, the Negro youth must work harder and must perform his tasks even better than a white youth in order to secure recognition. But out of the hard and unusual struggle through which he is compelled to pass, he gets a strength, a confidence, that one misses whose pathway is comparatively smooth by reason of birth and race.

From any point of view, I had rather be what I am, a member of the Negro race, than be able to claim membership with the most favoured of any other race. I have always been made sad when I have heard members of any race claiming rights or privileges, or certain badges of distinction, on the ground simply that they were members of this or that race, regardless of their own individual worth or attainments. I have been made to feel sad for such persons because I am conscious of the fact that mere connection with what is known as a superior race will not permanently carry an individual forward unless he has individual worth, and mere connection with what is regarded as an inferior race will not finally hold an individual back if he possesses intrinsic, individual merit. Every persecuted individual and race should get much consolation out of the great human law, which is universal and eternal, that merit, no matter under what skin found, is, in the long run, recognized and rewarded. This I have said here, not to call attention to myself as an individual, but to the race to which I am proud to belong.

# CHAPTER III

## *The Struggle for an Education*

One day, while at work in the coal-mine, I happened to overhear two miners talking about a great school for coloured people somewhere in Virginia. This was the first time that I had ever heard anything about any kind of school or college that was more pretentious than the little coloured school in our town.

In the darkness of the mine I noiselessly crept as close as I could to the two men who were talking. I heard one tell the other that not only was the school established for the members of any race, but that opportunities were provided by which poor but worthy students could work out all or a part of the cost of a board, and at the same time be taught some trade or industry.

As they went on describing the school, it seemed to me that it must be the greatest place on earth, and not even Heaven presented more attractions for me at that time than did the Hampton Normal and Agricultural Institute in Virginia, about which these men were talking. I resolved at once to go to that school, although I had no idea where it was, or how many miles away, or how I was going to reach it; I remembered only that I was on fire constantly with one ambition, and that was to go to Hampton. This thought was with me day and night.

After hearing of the Hampton Institute, I continued to work for a few months longer in the coal-mine. While at work there, I heard of a vacant position in the household of General Lewis Ruffner, the owner of the salt-furnace and coal-mine. Mrs. Viola Ruffner, the wife of General Ruffner, was a "Yankee" woman from Vermont. Mrs. Ruffner had a reputation all through the vicinity for being very strict with her servants, and especially with the boys who tried to serve her. Few of them remained with her more than two or three weeks. They all left with the same excuse: she was too strict. I decided, however, that I would rather try Mrs. Ruffner's house than remain in the coal-mine, and so my mother applied to her for the vacant position. I was hired at a salary of $5 per month.

I had heard so much about Mrs. Ruffner's severity that I was almost afraid to see her, and trembled when I went into her presence. I had not lived with her many weeks, however, before I began to understand her. I soon began to learn that, first of all, she wanted everything kept clean about her, that she wanted things done promptly and systematically, and that at the bottom of everything she wanted absolute honesty and frankness. Nothing must be sloven or slipshod; every door, every fence, must be kept in repair.

I cannot now recall how long I lived with Mrs. Ruffner before going to Hampton, but I think it must have been a year and a half. At any rate, I here repeat what I have said more than once before, that the lessons that I learned in the home of Mrs. Ruffner were as valuable to me as any education I have ever gotten anywhere else. Even to this day I never see bits of paper scattered around a house or in the street that I do not want to pick them up at once. I never see a filthy yard that I do not want to clean it, a paling off of a fence that I do not want to put it on, an unpainted or unwhitewashed house that I do not want to paint or whitewash it, or a button off one's clothes, or a grease-spot on them or on a floor, that I do not want to call attention to it.

From fearing Mrs. Ruffner I soon learned to look upon her as one of my best friends. When she found that she could trust me she did so implicitly. During the one or two winters that I was with her she gave me an opportunity to go to school for an hour in the day during a portion of the winter months, but most of my studying was done at night, sometimes alone, sometimes under some one whom I could hire to teach me. Mrs. Ruffner always encouraged and sympathized with me in all my efforts to get an education. It was while living with her that I began to get together my first library. I secured a dry-goods box, knocked out one side of it, put some shelves in it, and began putting into it every kind of book that I could get my hands upon, and called it my "library."

Notwithstanding my success at Mrs. Ruffner's I did not give up the idea of going to the Hampton Institute. In the fall of 1872 I determined to make an effort to get there, although, as I have stated, I had no definite idea of the direction in which Hampton was, or of what it would cost to go there. I do not think that any one thoroughly sympathized with me in my ambition to go to Hampton unless it was my mother, and she was troubled with a grave fear that I was starting out on a "wild-goose chase." At any rate, I got only a half-hearted consent from her that I might start. The small amount of money that I had earned had been consumed by my stepfather and the remainder of the family, with the exception of a very few dollars, and so I had very little with which to buy clothes and pay my travelling expenses. My brother John helped me all that he could, but of course that was not a great deal, for his work was in the coal-mine, where he did not earn much, and most of what he did earn went in the direction of paying the household expenses.

Perhaps the thing that touched and pleased me most in connection with my starting for Hampton was the interest that many of the older coloured people took in the matter. They had spent the best days of their lives in slavery, and hardly expected to live to see the time when they would see a member of their race leave home to attend a boarding-school. Some of these older people would give me a nickel, others a quarter, or a handkerchief.

Finally the great day came, and I started for Hampton. I had only a small, cheap satchel that contained a few articles of clothing I could get. My mother at the time was rather weak and broken in health. I hardly expected to see her again, and thus our parting was all the more sad. She, however, was very brave through it all. At that time there were no through trains connecting that part of West Virginia with eastern Virginia. Trains ran only a portion of the way, and the remainder of the distance was travelled by stage-coaches.

The distance from Malden to Hampton is about five hundred miles. I had not been away from home many hours before it began to grow painfully evident that I did not have enough money to pay my fair to Hampton. One experience I shall long remember. I had been travelling over the mountains most of the afternoon in an old-fashioned stage-coach, when, late in the evening, the coach stopped for the night at a common, unpainted house called a hotel. All the other passengers except myself were whites. In my ignorance I supposed that the little hotel existed for the purpose of accommodating the passengers who travelled on the stage-coach. The difference that the colour of one's skin would make I had not thought anything about. After all the other passengers had been shown rooms and were getting ready for supper, I shyly presented myself before the man at the desk. It is true I had practically no money in my pocket with which to pay for bed or food, but I had hoped in some way to beg my way into the good graces of the landlord, for at that season in the mountains of Virginia the weather was cold, and I wanted to get indoors for the night. Without asking as to whether I had any money, the man at the desk firmly refused to even consider the matter of providing me with food or lodging. This was my first experience in finding out what the colour of my skin meant. In some way I managed to keep warm by walking about, and so got through the night. My whole soul was so bent upon reaching Hampton that I did not have time to cherish any bitterness toward the hotel-keeper.

By walking, begging rides both in wagons and in the cars, in some way, after a number of days, I reached the city of Richmond, Virginia, about eighty-two miles from Hampton. When I reached there, tired, hungry, and dirty, it was late in the night. I had never been in a large city, and this rather added to my misery. When I reached Richmond, I was completely out of money. I had not a single acquaintance in the place, and, being unused to city ways, I did not know where to go. I applied at several places for lodging, but they all wanted money, and that was what I did not have. Knowing nothing else better to do, I walked the streets. In doing this I passed by many a food-stands where fried chicken and half-moon apple pies were piled high and made to present a most tempting appearance. At that time it seemed to me that I would have promised all that I expected to possess in the future to have gotten hold of one of those chicken legs or one of those pies. But I could not get either of these, nor anything else to eat.

I must have walked the streets till after midnight. At last I became so exhausted that I could walk no longer. I was tired, I was hungry, I was everything but discouraged. Just about the time when I reached extreme physical exhaustion, I came upon a portion of a street where the board sidewalk was considerably elevated. I waited for a few minutes, till I was sure that no passers-by could see me, and then crept under the sidewalk and lay for the night upon the ground, with my satchel of clothing for a pillow. Nearly all night I could hear the tramp of feet over my head. The next morning I found myself somewhat refreshed, but I was extremely hungry, because it had been a long time since I had had sufficient food. As soon as it became light enough for me to see my surroundings I noticed that I was near a large ship, and that this ship seemed to be unloading a cargo of pig iron. I went at once to the vessel and asked the captain to permit me to help unload the vessel in order to get money for food. The captain, a white man, who seemed to be kind-hearted, consented. I worked long enough to earn money for my breakfast, and it seems to me, as I remember it now, to have been about the best breakfast that I have ever eaten.

My work pleased the captain so well that he told me if I desired I could continue working for a small amount per day. This I was very glad to do. I continued working on this vessel for a number of days. After buying food with the small wages I received there was not much left to add on the amount I must get to pay my way to Hampton. In order to economize in every way possible, so as to be sure to reach Hampton in a reasonable time, I continued to sleep under the same sidewalk that gave me shelter the first night I was in Richmond. Many years after that the coloured citizens of Richmond very kindly tendered me a reception at which there must have been two thousand people present. This reception was held not far from the spot where I slept the first night I spent in the city, and I must confess that my mind was more upon the sidewalk that first gave me shelter than upon the recognition, agreeable and cordial as it was.

When I had saved what I considered enough money with which to reach Hampton, I thanked the captain of the vessel for his kindness, and started again. Without any unusual occurrence I reached Hampton, with a surplus of exactly fifty cents with which to begin my education. To me it had been a long, eventful journey; but the first sight of the large, three-story, brick school building seemed to have rewarded me for all that I had undergone in order to reach the place. If the people who gave the money to provide that building could appreciate the influence the sight of it had upon me, as well as upon thousands of other youths, they would feel all the more encouraged to make such gifts. It seemed to me to be the largest and most beautiful building I had ever seen. The sight of it seemed to give me new life. I felt that a new kind of existence had now begun—that life would now have a new meaning. I felt that I had reached the promised land, and I resolved to let no obstacle prevent me from putting forth the highest effort to fit myself to accomplish the most good in the world.

As soon as possible after reaching the grounds of the Hampton Institute, I presented myself before the head teacher for an assignment to a class. Having been so long without proper food, a bath, and a change of clothing, I did not, of course, make a very favourable impression upon her, and I could see at once that there were doubts in her mind about the wisdom of admitting me as a student. I felt that I could hardly blame her if she got the idea that I was a worthless loafer or tramp. For some time she did not refuse to admit me, neither did she decide in my favour, and I continued to linger about her, and to impress her in all the ways I could with my worthiness. In the meantime I saw her admitting other students, and that added greatly to my discomfort, for I felt, deep down in my heart, that I could do as well as they, if I could only get a chance to show what was in me.

After some hours had passed, the head teacher said to me: "The adjoining recitation-room needs sweeping. Take the broom and sweep it."

It occurred to me at once that here was my chance. Never did I receive an order with more delight. I knew that I could sweep, for Mrs. Ruffner had thoroughly taught me how to do that when I lived with her.

I swept the recitation-room three times. Then I got a dusting-cloth and dusted it four times. All the woodwork around the walls, every bench, table, and desk, I went over four times with my dusting-cloth. Besides, every piece of furniture had been moved and every closet and corner in the room had been thoroughly cleaned. I had the feeling that in a large measure my future depended upon the impression I made upon the teacher in the cleaning of that room. When I was through, I reported to the head teacher. She was a "Yankee" woman who knew just where to look for dirt. She went into the room and inspected the floor and closets; then she took her handkerchief and rubbed it on the woodwork about the walls, and over the table and benches. When she was unable to find one bit of dirt on the floor, or a particle of dust on any of the furniture, she quietly remarked, "I guess you will do to enter this institution."

I was one of the happiest souls on Earth. The sweeping of that room was my college examination, and never did any youth pass an examination for entrance into Harvard or Yale that gave him more genuine satisfaction. I have passed several examinations since then, but I have always felt that this was the best one I ever passed.

I have spoken of my own experience in entering the Hampton Institute. Perhaps few, if any, had anything like the same experience that I had, but about the same period there were hundreds who found their way to Hampton and other institutions after experiencing something of the same difficulties that I went through. The young men and women were determined to secure an education at any cost.

The sweeping of the recitation-room in the manner that I did it seems to have paved the way for me to get through Hampton. Miss Mary F. Mackie, the head teacher, offered me a position as janitor. This, of course, I gladly accepted, because it was a place where I could work out nearly all the cost of my board. The work was hard and taxing but I stuck to it. I had a large number of rooms to care for, and had to work late into the night, while at the same time I had to rise by four o'clock in the morning, in order to build the fires and have a little time in which to prepare my lessons. In all my career at Hampton, and ever since I have been out in the world, Miss Mary F. Mackie, the head teacher to whom I have referred, proved one of my strongest and most helpful friends. Her advice and encouragement were always helpful in strengthening to me in the darkest hour.

I have spoken of the impression that was made upon me by the buildings and general appearance of the Hampton Institute, but I have not spoken of that which made the greatest and most lasting impression on me, and that was a great man—the noblest, rarest human being that it has ever been my privilege to meet. I refer to the late General Samuel C. Armstrong.

It has been my fortune to meet personally many of what are called great characters, both in Europe and America, but I do not hesitate to say that I never met any man who, in my estimation, was the equal of General Armstrong. Fresh from the degrading influences of the slave plantation and the coal-mines, it was a rare privilege for me to be permitted to come into direct contact with such a character as General Armstrong. I shall always remember that the first time I went into his presence he made the impression upon me of being a perfect man: I was made to feel that there was something about him that was superhuman. It was my privilege to know the General personally from the time I entered Hampton till he died, and the more I saw of him the greater he grew in my estimation. One might have removed from Hampton all the buildings, class-rooms, teachers, and industries, and given the men and women there the opportunity of coming into daily contact with General Armstrong, and that alone would have been a liberal education. The older I grow, the more I am convinced that there is no education which one can get from books and costly apparatus that is equal to that which can be gotten from contact with great men and women. Instead of studying books so constantly, how I wish that our schools and colleges might learn to study men and things!

General Armstrong spent two of the last six months of his life in my home at Tuskegee. At that time he was paralyzed to the extent that he had lost control of his body and voice in a very large degree. Notwithstanding his affliction, he worked almost constantly night and day for the cause to which he had given his life. I never saw a man who so completely lost sight of himself. I do not believe he ever had a selfish thought. He was just as happy in trying to assist some other institution in the South as he was when working for Hampton. Although he fought the Southern white man in the Civil War, I never heard him utter a bitter word against him afterward. On the other hand, he was constantly seeking to find ways by which he could be of service to the Southern whites.

It would be difficult to describe the hold that he had upon the students at Hampton, or the faith they had in him. In fact, he was worshipped by his students. It never occurred to me that General Armstrong could fail in anything that he undertook. There is almost no request that he could have made that would not have been complied with. When he was a guest at my home in Alabama, and was so badly paralyzed that he had to be wheeled about in an invalid's chair, I recall that one of the General's former students had occasion to push his chair up a long, steep hill that taxed his strength to the utmost. When the top of the hill was reached, the former pupil, with a glow of happiness on his face, exclaimed, "I am so glad that I have been permitted to do something that was real hard for the General before he dies!" While I was a student at Hampton, the dormitories became so crowded that it was impossible to find room for all who wanted to be admitted. In order to help remedy the difficulty, the General conceived the plan of putting up tents to be used as rooms. As soon as it became known that General Armstrong would be pleased if some of the older students would live in the tents during the winter, nearly every student in school volunteered to go.

I was one of the volunteers. The winter that we spent in those tents was an intensely cold one, and we suffered severely—how much I am sure General Armstrong never knew, because we made no complaints. It was enough for us to know that we were pleasing General Armstrong, and that we were making it possible for an additional number of students to secure an education. More than once, during a cold night, when a stiff gale would be blowing, our tent was lifted bodily, and we would find ourselves in the open air. The General would usually pay a visit to the tents early in the morning, and his earnest, cheerful, encouraging voice would dispel any feeling of despondency.

I have spoken of my admiration for General Armstrong, and yet he was but a type of that Christlike body of men and women who went into the Negro schools at the close of the war by the hundreds to assist in lifting up my race. The history of the world fails to show a higher, purer, and more unselfish class of men and women than those who found their way into those Negro schools.

Life at Hampton was a constant revelation to me; was constantly taking me into a new world. The matter of having meals at regular hours, of eating on a tablecloth, using a napkin, the use of the bathtub and of the tooth-brush, as well as the use of sheets upon the bed, were all new to me.

I sometimes feel that almost the most valuable lesson I got at the Hampton Institute was in the use and value of the bath. I learned there for the first time some of its value, not only in keeping the body healthy, but in inspiring self-respect and promoting virtue. In all my travels in the South and elsewhere since leaving Hampton I have always in some way sought my daily bath. To get it sometimes when I have been the guest of my own people in a single-roomed cabin has not always been easy to do, except by slipping away to some stream in the woods. I have always tried to teach my people that some provision for bathing should be a part of every house.

For some time, while a student at Hampton, I possessed but a single pair of socks, but when I had worn these till they became soiled, I would wash them at night and hang them by the fire to dry, so that I might wear them again the next morning.

The charge for my board at Hampton was ten dollars per month. I was expected to pay a part of this in cash and to work out the remainder. To meet this cash payment, as I have stated, I had just fifty cents when I reached the institution. Aside from a very few dollars that my brother John was able to send me once in a while, I had no money with which to pay my board. I was determined from the first to make my work as janitor so valuable that my services would be indispensable. This I succeeded in doing to such an extent that I was soon informed that I would be allowed the full cost of my board in return for my work. The cost of tuition was seventy dollars a year. This, of course, was wholly beyond my ability to provide. If I had been compelled to pay the seventy dollars for tuition, in addition to providing for my board, I would have been compelled to leave the Hampton school. General Armstrong, however, very kindly got Mr. S. Griffitts Morgan, of New Bedford, Mass., to defray the cost of my tuition during the whole time that I was at Hampton. After I finished the course at Hampton and had entered upon my lifework at Tuskegee, I had the pleasure of visiting Mr. Morgan several times.

After having been for a while at Hampton, I found myself in difficulty because I did not have books and clothing. Usually, however, I got around the trouble about books by borrowing from those who were more fortunate than myself. As to clothes, when I reached Hampton I had practically nothing. Everything that I possessed was in a small hand satchel. My anxiety about clothing was increased because of the fact that General Armstrong made a personal inspection of the young men in ranks, to see that their clothes were clean. Shoes had to be polished, there must be no buttons off the clothing, and no grease-spots. To wear one suit of clothes continually, while at work and in the schoolroom, and at the same time keep it clean, was rather a hard problem for me to solve. In some way I managed to get on till the teachers learned that I was in earnest and meant to succeed, and then some of them were kind enough to see that I was partly supplied with second-hand clothing that had been sent in barrels from the North. These barrels proved a blessing to hundreds of poor but deserving students. Without them I question whether I should ever have gotten through Hampton.

When I first went to Hampton I do not recall that I had ever slept in a bed that had two sheets on it. In those days there were not many buildings there, and room was very precious. There were seven other boys in the same room with me; most of them, however, students who had been there for some time. The sheets were quite a puzzle to me. The first night I slept under both of them, and the second night I slept on top of them; but by watching the other boys I learned my lesson in this, and have been trying to follow it ever since and to teach it to others.

I was among the youngest of the students who were in Hampton at the time. Most of the students were men and women—some as old as forty years of ago. As I now recall the scene of my first year, I do not believe that one often has the opportunity of coming into contact with three or four hundred men and women who were so tremendously in earnest as these men and women were. Every hour was occupied in study or work. Nearly all had had enough actual contact with the world to teach them the need of education. Many of the older ones were, of course, too old to master the text-books very thoroughly, and it was often sad to watch their struggles; but they made up in earnest much of what they lacked in books. Many of them were as poor as I was, and, besides having to wrestle with their books, they had to struggle with a poverty which prevented their having the necessities of life. Many of them had aged parents who were dependent upon them, and some of them were men who had wives whose support in some way they had to provide for.

The great and prevailing idea that seemed to take possession of every one was to prepare himself to lift up the people at his home. No one seemed to think of himself. And the officers and teachers, what a rare set of human beings they were! They worked for the students night and day, in seasons and out of season. They seemed happy only when they were helping the students in some manner. Whenever it is written—and I hope it will be—the part that the Yankee teachers played in the education of the Negroes immediately after the war will make one of the most thrilling parts of the history of this country. The time is not far distant when the whole South will appreciate this service in a way that it has not yet been able to do.

# CHAPTER IV

## *Helping Others*

At the end of my first year at Hampton I was confronted with another difficulty. Most of the students went home to spend their vacation. I had no money with which to go home, but I had to go somewhere. In those days very few students were permitted to remain at the school during vacation. It made me feel very sad and homesick to see the other students preparing to leave and starting for home. I not only had no money with which to go home, but I had none with which to go anywhere.

In some way, however, I had gotten hold of an extra, second-hand coat which I thought was a pretty valuable coat. This I decided to sell, in order to get a little money for travelling expenses. I had a good deal of boyish pride, and I tried to hide, as far as I could, from the other students the fact that I had no money and nowhere to go. I made it known to a few people in the town of Hampton that I had this coat to sell, and, after a good deal of persuading, one coloured man promised to come to my room to look the coat over and consider the matter of buying it. This cheered my drooping spirits considerably. Early the next morning my prospective customer appeared. After looking the garment over carefully, he asked me how much I wanted for it. I told him I thought it was worth three dollars. He seemed to agree with me as to price, but remarked in the most matter-of-fact way: "I tell you what I will do; I will take the coat, and will pay you five cents, cash down, and pay you the rest of the money just as soon as I can get it." It is not hard to imagine what my feelings were at the time.

With this disappointment I gave up all hope of getting out of the town of Hampton for my vacation work. I wanted very much to go where I might secure work that would at least pay me enough to purchase some much-needed clothing and other necessities. In a few days practically all the students and teachers had left for their homes, and this served to depress my spirits even more.

After trying for several days in and near the town of Hampton, I finally secured work in a restaurant at Fortress Monroe. The wages, however, were very little more than my board. At night, and between meals, I found considerable time for study and reading; and in this direction I improved myself very much during the summer.

When I left school at the end of my first year, I owed the institution sixteen dollars that I had not been able to work out. It was my greatest ambition during the summer to save money enough with which to pay this debt. I felt that this was a debt of honour, and that I could hardly bring myself to the point of even trying to enter school again till it was paid. I economized in every way that I could think of—did my own washing, and went without necessary garments—but still I found my summer vacation ending and I did not have the sixteen dollars.

One day, during the last week of my stay in the restaurant, I found under one of the tables a crisp, new ten-dollar bill. I could hardly contain myself, I was so happy. As it was not my place of business I felt it to be the proper thing to show the money to the proprietor. This I did. He seemed as glad as I was, but he coolly explained to me that, as it was his place of business, he had a right to keep the money, and he proceeded to do so. This, I confess, was another pretty hard blow to me. I will not say that I became discouraged, for as I now look back over my life I do not recall that I ever became discouraged over anything that I set out to accomplish. I have begun everything with the idea that I could succeed, and I never had much patience with the multitudes of people who are always ready to explain why one cannot succeed. I determined to face the situation just as it was. At the end of the week I went to the treasurer of the Hampton Institute, General J.F.B. Marshall, and told him frankly my condition. To my gratification he told me that I could re-enter the institution, and that he would trust me to pay the debt when I could. During the second year I continued to work as a janitor.

The education that I received at Hampton out of the text-books was but a small part of what I learned there. One of the things that impressed itself upon me deeply, the second year, was the unselfishness of the teachers. It was hard for me to understand how any individuals could bring themselves to the point where they could be so happy in working for others. Before the end of the year, I think I began learning that those who are happiest are those who do the most for others. This lesson I have tried to carry with me ever since.

I also learned a valuable lesson at Hampton by coming into contact with the best breeds of live stock and fowls. No student, I think, who has had the opportunity of doing this could go out into the world and content himself with the poorest grades.

Perhaps the most valuable thing that I got out of my second year was an understanding of the use and value of the Bible. Miss Nathalie Lord, one of the teachers, from Portland, Me., taught me how to use and love the Bible. Before this I had never cared a great deal about it, but now I learned to love to read the Bible, not only for the spiritual help which it gives, but on account of it as literature. The lessons taught me in this respect took such a hold upon me that at the present time, when I am at home, no matter how busy I am, I always make it a rule to read a chapter or a portion of a chapter in the morning, before beginning the work of the day.

Whatever ability I may have as a public speaker I owe in a measure to Miss Lord. When she found out that I had some inclination in this direction, she gave me private lessons in the matter of breathing, emphasis, and articulation. Simply to be able to talk in public for the sake of talking has never had the least attraction to me. In fact, I consider that there is nothing so empty and unsatisfactory as mere abstract public speaking; but from my early childhood I have had a desire to do something to make the world better, and then to be able to speak to the world about that thing.

The debating societies at Hampton were a constant source of delight to me. These were held on Saturday evening; and during my whole life at Hampton I do not recall that I missed a single meeting. I not only attended the weekly debating society, but was instrumental in organizing an additional society. I noticed that between the time when supper was over and the time to begin evening study there were about twenty minutes which the young men usually spent in idle gossip. About twenty of us formed a society for the purpose of utilizing this time in debate or in practice in public speaking. Few persons ever derived more happiness or benefit from the use of twenty minutes of time than we did in this way.

At the end of my second year at Hampton, by the help of some money sent me by my mother and brother John, supplemented by a small gift from one of the teachers at Hampton, I was enabled to return to my home in Malden, West Virginia, to spend my vacation. When I reached home I found that the salt-furnaces were not running, and that the coal-mine was not being operated on account of the miners being out on "strike." This was something which, it seemed, usually occurred whenever the men got two or three months ahead in their savings. During the strike, of course, they spent all that they had saved, and would often return to work in debt at the same wages, or would move to another mine at considerable expense. In either case, my observations convinced me that the miners were worse off at the end of the strike. Before the days of strikes in that section of the country, I knew miners who had considerable money in the bank, but as soon as the professional labour agitators got control, the savings of even the more thrifty ones began disappearing.

My mother and the other members of my family were, of course, much rejoiced to see me and to note the improvement that I had made during my two years' absence. The rejoicing on the part of all classes of the coloured people, and especially the older ones, over my return, was almost pathetic. I had to pay a visit to each family and take a meal with each, and at each place tell the story of my experiences at Hampton. In addition to this I had to speak before the church and Sunday-school, and at various other places. The thing that I was most in search of, though, work, I could not find. There was no work on account of the strike. I spent nearly the whole of the first month of my vacation in an effort to find something to do by which I could earn money to pay my way back to Hampton and save a little money to use after reaching there.

Toward the end of the first month, I went to a place a considerable distance from my home, to try to find employment. I did not succeed, and it was night before I got started on my return. When I had gotten within a mile or so of my home I was so completely tired out that I could not walk any farther, and I went into an old, abandoned house to spend the remainder of the night. About three o'clock in the morning my brother John found me asleep in this house, and broke to me, as gently as he could, the sad news that our dear mother had died during the night.

This seemed to me the saddest and blankest moment in my life. For several years my mother had not been in good health, but I had no idea, when I parted from her the previous day, that I should never see her alive again. Besides that, I had always had an intense desire to be with her when she did pass away. One of the chief ambitions which spurred me on at Hampton was that I might be able to get to be in a position in which I could better make my mother comfortable and happy. She had so often expressed the wish that she might be permitted to live to see her children educated and started out in the world.

In a very short time after the death of my mother our little home was in confusion. My sister Amanda, although she tried to do the best she could, was too young to know anything about keeping house, and my stepfather was not able to hire a housekeeper. Sometimes we had food cooked for us, and sometimes we did not. I remember that more than once a can of tomatoes and some crackers constituted a meal. Our clothing went uncared for, and everything about our home was soon in a tumble-down condition. It seems to me that this was the most dismal period of my life.

My good friend, Mrs. Ruffner, to whom I have already referred, always made me welcome at her home, and assisted me in many ways during this trying period. Before the end of the vacation she gave me some work, and this, together with work in a coal-mine at some distance from my home, enabled me to earn a little money.

At one time it looked as if I would have to give up the idea of returning to Hampton, but my heart was so set on returning that I determined not to give up going back without a struggle. I was very anxious to secure some clothes for the winter, but in this I was disappointed, except for a few garments which my brother John secured for me. Notwithstanding my need of money and clothing, I was very happy in the fact that I had secured enough money to pay my travelling expenses back to Hampton. Once there, I knew that I could make myself so useful as a janitor that I could in some way get through the school year.

Three weeks before the time for the opening of the term at Hampton, I was pleasantly surprised to receive a letter from my good friend Miss Mary F. Mackie, the lady principal, asking me to return to Hampton two weeks before the opening of the school, in order that I might assist her in cleaning the buildings and getting things in order for the new school year. This was just the opportunity I wanted. It gave me a chance to secure a credit in the treasurer's office. I started for Hampton at once.

During these two weeks I was taught a lesson which I shall never forget. Miss Mackie was a member of one of the oldest and most cultured families of the North, and yet for two weeks she worked by my side cleaning windows, dusting rooms, putting beds in order, and what not. She felt that things would not be in condition for the opening of school unless every window-pane was perfectly clean, and she took the greatest satisfaction in helping to clean them herself. The work which I have described she did every year that I was at Hampton.

It was hard for me at this time to understand how a woman of her education and social standing could take such delight in performing such service, in order to assist in the elevation of an unfortunate race. Ever since then I have had no patience with any school for my race in the South which did not teach its students the dignity of labour.

During my last year at Hampton every minute of my time that was not occupied with my duties as janitor was devoted to hard study. I was determined, if possible, to make such a record in my class as would cause me to be placed on the "honour roll" of Commencement speakers. This I was successful in doing. It was June of 1875 when I finished the regular course of study at Hampton. The greatest benefits that I got out of my at the Hampton Institute, perhaps, may be classified under two heads:—

First was contact with a great man, General S.C. Armstrong, who, I repeat, was, in my opinion, the rarest, strongest, and most beautiful character that it has ever been my privilege to meet.

Second, at Hampton, for the first time, I learned what education was expected to do for an individual. Before going there I had a good deal of the then rather prevalent idea among our people that to secure an education meant to have a good, easy time, free from all necessity for manual labour. At Hampton I not only learned that it was not a disgrace to labour, but learned to love labour, not alone for its financial value, but for labour's own sake and for the independence and self-reliance which the ability to do something which the world wants done brings. At that institution I got my first taste of what it meant to live a life of unselfishness, my first knowledge of the fact that the happiest individuals are those who do the most to make others useful and happy.

I was completely out of money when I graduated. In company with our other Hampton students, I secured a place as a table waiter in a summer hotel in Connecticut, and managed to borrow enough money with which to get there. I had not been in this hotel long before I found out that I knew practically nothing about waiting on a hotel table. The head waiter, however, supposed that I was an accomplished waiter. He soon gave me charge of the table at which their sat four or five wealthy and rather aristocratic people. My ignorance of how to wait upon them was so apparent that they scolded me in such a severe manner that I became frightened and left their table, leaving them sitting there without food. As a result of this I was reduced from the position of waiter to that of a dish-carrier.

But I determined to learn the business of waiting, and did so within a few weeks and was restored to my former position. I have had the satisfaction of being a guest in this hotel several times since I was a waiter there.

At the close of the hotel season I returned to my former home in Malden, and was elected to teach the coloured school at that place. This was the beginning of one of the happiest periods of my life. I now felt that I had the opportunity to help the people of my home town to a higher life. I felt from the first that mere book education was not all that the young people of that town needed. I began my work at eight o'clock in the morning, and, as a rule, it did not end until ten o'clock at night. In addition to the usual routine of teaching,

I taught the pupils to comb their hair, and to keep their hands and faces clean, as well as their clothing. I gave special attention to teaching them the proper use of the tooth-brush and the bath. In all my teaching I have watched carefully the influence of the tooth-brush, and I am convinced that there are few single agencies of civilization that are more far-reaching.

There were so many of the older boys and girls in the town, as well as men and women, who had to work in the daytime and still were craving an opportunity for an education, that I soon opened a night-school. From the first, this was crowded every night, being about as large as the school that I taught in the day. The efforts of some of the men and women, who in many cases were over fifty years of age, to learn, were in some cases very pathetic.

My day and night school work was not all that I undertook. I established a small reading-room and a debating society. On Sundays I taught two Sunday-schools, one in the town of Malden in the afternoon, and the other in the morning at a place three miles distant from Malden. In addition to this, I gave private lessons to several young men whom I was fitting to send to the Hampton Institute. Without regard to pay and with little thought of it, I taught any one who wanted to learn anything that I could teach him. I was supremely happy in the opportunity of being able to assist somebody else. I did receive, however, a small salary from the public fund, for my work as a public-school teacher.

During the time that I was a student at Hampton my older brother, John, not only assisted me all that he could, but worked all of the time in the coal-mines in order to support the family. He willingly neglected his own education that he might help me. It was my earnest wish to help him to prepare to enter Hampton, and to save money to assist him in his expenses there. Both of these objects I was successful in accomplishing. In three years my brother finished the course at Hampton, and he is now holding the important position of Superintendent of Industries at Tuskegee. When he returned from Hampton, we both combined our efforts and savings to send our adopted brother, James, through the Hampton Institute. This we succeeded in doing, and he is now the postmaster at the Tuskegee

Institute. The year 1877, which was my second year of teaching in Malden, I spent very much as I did the first.

It was while my home was at Malden that what was known as the "Ku Klux Klan" was in the height of its activity. The "Ku Klux" were bands of men who had joined themselves together for the purpose of regulating the conduct of the coloured people, especially with the object of preventing the members of the race from exercising any influence in politics. They corresponded somewhat to the "patrollers" of whom I used to hear a great deal during the days of slavery, when I was a small boy. The "patrollers" were bands of white men—usually young men—who were organized largely for the purpose of regulating the conduct of the slaves at night in such matters as preventing the slaves from going from one plantation to another without passes, and for preventing them from holding any kind of meetings without permission and without the presence at these meetings of at least one white man.

Like the "patrollers" the "Ku Klux" operated almost wholly at night. They were, however, more cruel than the "patrollers." Their objects, in the main, were to crush out the political aspirations of the Negroes, but they did not confine themselves to this, because school-houses as well as churches were burned by them, and many innocent persons were made to suffer. During this period not a few coloured people lost their lives.

As a young man, the acts of these lawless bands made a great impression upon me. I saw one open battle take place at Malden between some of the coloured and white people. There must have been not far from a hundred persons engaged on each side; many on both sides were seriously injured, among them General Lewis Ruffner, the husband of my friend Mrs. Viola Ruffner. General Ruffner tried to defend the coloured people, and for this he was knocked down and so seriously wounded that he never completely recovered. It seemed to me as I watched this struggle between members of the two races, that there was no hope for our people in this country. The "Ku Klux" period was, I think, the darkest part of the Reconstruction days.

I have referred to this unpleasant part of the history of the South simply for the purpose of calling attention to the great change that has taken place since the days of the "Ku Klux." To-day there are no such organizations in the South, and the fact that such ever existed is almost forgotten by both races. There are few places in the South now where public sentiment would permit such organizations to exist.

# CHAPTER V

## *The Reconstruction Period*

The years from 1867 to 1878 I think may be called the period of Reconstruction. This included the time that I spent as a student at Hampton and as a teacher in West Virginia. During the whole of the Reconstruction period two ideas were constantly agitating in the minds of the coloured people, or, at least, in the minds of a large part of the race. One of these was the craze for Greek and Latin learning, and the other was a desire to hold office.

It could not have been expected that a people who had spent generations in slavery, and before that generations in the darkest heathenism, could at first form any proper conception of what an education meant. In every part of the South, during the Reconstruction period, schools, both day and night, were filled to overflowing with people of all ages and conditions, some being as far along in age as sixty and seventy years. The ambition to secure an education was most praiseworthy and encouraging. The idea, however, was too prevalent that, as soon as one secured a little education, in some unexplainable way he would be free from most of the hardships of the world, and, at any rate, could live without manual labour. There was a further feeling that a knowledge, however little, of the Greek and Latin languages would make one a very superior human being, something bordering almost on the supernatural. I remember that the first coloured man whom I saw who knew something about foreign languages impressed me at the time as being a man of all others to be envied.

Naturally, most of our people who received some little education became teachers or preachers. While among those two classes there were many capable, earnest, godly men and women, still a large proportion took up teaching or preaching as an easy way to make a living. Many became teachers who could do little more than write their names. I remember there came into our neighbourhood one of this class, who was in search of a school to teach, and the question arose while he was there as to the shape of the earth and how he could teach the children concerning the subject. He explained his position in the matter by saying that he was prepared to teach that the earth was either flat or round, according to the preference of a majority of his patrons.

The ministry was the profession that suffered most—and still suffers, though there has been great improvement—on account of not only ignorant but in many cases immoral men who claimed that they were "called to preach." In the earlier days of freedom almost every coloured man who learned to read would receive "a call to preach" within a few days after he began reading. At my home in West Virginia the process of being called to the ministry was a very interesting one. Usually the "call" came when the individual was sitting in church. Without warning the one called would fall upon the floor as if struck by a bullet, and would lie there for hours, speechless and motionless. Then the news would spread all through the neighbourhood that this individual had received a "call." If he were inclined to resist the summons, he would fall or be made to fall a second or third time. In the end he always yielded to the call. While I wanted an education badly, I confess that in my youth I had a fear that when I had learned to read and write very well I would receive one of these "calls"; but, for some reason, my call never came.

When we add the number of wholly ignorant men who preached or "exhorted" to that of those who possessed something of an education, it can be seen at a glance that the supply of ministers was large. In fact, some time ago I knew a certain church that had a total membership of about two hundred, and eighteen of that number were ministers. But, I repeat, in many communities in the South the character of the ministry is being improved, and I believe that within the next two or three decades a very large proportion of the unworthy ones will have disappeared. The "calls" to preach, I am glad to say, are not nearly so numerous now as they were formerly, and the calls to some industrial occupation are growing more numerous. The improvement that has taken place in the character of the teachers is even more marked than in the case of the ministers.

During the whole of the Reconstruction period our people

throughout the South looked to the Federal Government for everything, very much as a child looks to its mother. This was not unnatural. The central government gave them freedom, and the whole Nation had been enriched for more than two centuries by the labour of the Negro. Even as a youth, and later in manhood, I had the feeling that it was cruelly wrong in the central government, at the beginning of our freedom, to fail to make some provision for the general education of our people in addition to what the states might do, so that the people would be the better prepared for the duties of citizenship.

It is easy to find fault, to remark what might have been done, and perhaps, after all, and under all the circumstances, those in charge of the conduct of affairs did the only thing that could be done at the time. Still, as I look back now over the entire period of our freedom, I cannot help feeling that it would have been wiser if some plan could have been put in operation which would have made the possession of a certain amount of education or property, or both, a test for the exercise of the franchise, and a way provided by which this test should be made to apply honestly and squarely to both the white and black races.

Though I was but little more than a youth during the period of Reconstruction, I had the feeling that mistakes were being made, and that things could not remain in the condition that they were in then very long. I felt that the Reconstruction policy, so far as it related to my race, was in a large measure on a false foundation, was artificial and forced. In many cases it seemed to me that the ignorance of my race was being used as a tool with which to help white men into office, and that there was an element in the North which wanted to punish the Southern white men by forcing the Negro into positions over the heads of the Southern whites. I felt that the Negro would be the one to suffer for this in the end. Besides, the general political agitation drew the attention of our people away from the more fundamental matters of perfecting themselves in the industries at their doors and in securing property.

The temptations to enter political life were so alluring that I came very near yielding to them at one time, but I was kept from doing so by the feeling that I would be helping in a more substantial way by assisting in the laying of the foundation of the race through a generous education of the hand, head, and heart. I saw coloured men who were members of the state legislatures, and county officers, who, in some cases, could not read or write, and whose morals were as weak as their education. Not long ago, when passing through the streets of a certain city in the South, I heard some brick-masons calling out, from the top of a two-story brick building on which they were working, for the "Governor" to "hurry up and bring up some more bricks." Several times I heard the command, "Hurry up, Governor!" "Hurry up, Governor!" My curiosity was aroused to such an extent that I made inquiry as to who the "Governor" was, and soon found that he was a coloured man who at one time had held the position of Lieutenant-Governor of his state.

But not all the coloured people who were in office during Reconstruction were unworthy of their positions, by any means. Some of them, like the late Senator B.K. Bruce, Governor Pinchback, and many others, were strong, upright, useful men. Neither were all the class designated as carpetbaggers dishonourable men. Some of them, like ex-Governor Bullock, of Georgia, were men of high character and usefulness.

Of course the coloured people, so largely without education, and wholly without experience in government, made tremendous mistakes, just as many people similarly situated would have done. Many of the Southern whites have a feeling that, if the Negro is permitted to exercise his political rights now to any degree, the mistakes of the Reconstruction period will repeat themselves. I do not think this would be true, because the Negro is a much stronger and wiser man than he was thirty-five years ago, and he is fast learning the lesson that he cannot afford to act in a manner that will alienate his Southern white neighbours from him. More and more I am convinced that the final solution of the political end of our race problem will be for each state that finds it necessary to change the law bearing upon the franchise to make the law apply with absolute honesty, and without opportunity for double dealing or evasion, to both races alike. Any other course my daily observation in the South convinces me, will be unjust to the Negro, unjust to the white man, and unfair to the rest of the state in the Union, and will be, like slavery, a sin that at some time we shall have to pay for.

In the fall of 1878, after having taught school in Malden for two years, and after I had succeeded in preparing several of the young men and women, besides my two brothers, to enter the Hampton Institute, I decided to spend some months in study at Washington, D.C. I remained there for eight months. I derived a great deal of benefit from the studies which I pursued, and I came into contact with some strong men and women. At the institution I attended there was no industrial training given to the students, and I had an opportunity of comparing the influence of an institution with no industrial training with that of one like the Hampton Institute, that emphasizes the industries. At this school I found the students, in most cases, had more money, were better dressed, wore the latest style of all manner of clothing, and in some cases were more brilliant mentally. At Hampton it was a standing rule that, while the institution would be responsible for securing some one to pay the tuition for the students, the men and women themselves must provide for their own board, books, clothing, and room wholly by work, or partly by work and partly in cash. At the institution at which I now was, I found that a large portion of the students by some means had their personal expenses paid for them. At Hampton the student was constantly making the effort through the industries to help himself, and that very effort was of immense value in character-building. The students at the other school seemed to be less self-dependent. They seemed to give more attention to mere outward appearances. In a word, they did not appear to me to be beginning at the bottom, on a real, solid foundation, to the extent that they were at Hampton. They knew more about Latin and Greek when they left school, but they seemed to know less about life and its conditions as they would meet it at their homes. Having lived for a number of years in the midst of comfortable surroundings, they were not as much inclined as the Hampton students to go into the country districts of the South, where there was little of comfort, to take up work for our people, and they were more inclined to yield to the temptation to become hotel waiters and Pullman-car porters as their life-work.

During the time I was a student at Washington the city was crowded with coloured people, many of whom had recently come from the South. A large proportion of these people had been drawn to Washington because they felt that they could lead a life of ease there. Others had secured minor government positions, and still another large class was there in the hope of securing Federal positions. A number of coloured men—some of them very strong and brilliant—were in the House of Representatives at that time, and one, the Hon. B.K. Bruce, was in the Senate. All this tended to make Washington an attractive place for members of the coloured race. Then, too, they knew that at all times they could have the protection of the law in the District of Columbia. The public schools in Washington for coloured people were better then than they were elsewhere. I took great interest in studying the life of our people there closely at that time. I found that while among them there was a large element of substantial, worthy citizens, there was also a superficiality about the life of a large class that greatly alarmed me. I saw young coloured men who were not earning more than four dollars a week spend two dollars or more for a buggy on Sunday to ride up and down Pennsylvania Avenue in, in order that they might try to convince the world that they were worth thousands. I saw other young men who received seventy-five or one hundred dollars per month from the Government, who were in debt at the end of every month. I saw men who but a few months previous were members of Congress, then without employment and in poverty. Among a large class there seemed to be a dependence upon the Government for every conceivable thing. The members of this class had little ambition to create a position for themselves, but wanted the Federal officials to create one for them. How many times I wished then, and have often wished since, that by some power of magic I might remove the great bulk of these people into the county districts and plant them upon the soil, upon the solid and never deceptive foundation of Mother Nature, where all nations and races that have ever succeeded have gotten their start,—a start that at first may be slow and toilsome, but one that nevertheless is real.

In Washington I saw girls whose mothers were earning their living by laundrying. These girls were taught by their mothers, in rather a crude way it is true, the industry of laundrying. Later, these girls entered the public schools and remained there perhaps six or eight years. When the public school course was finally finished, they wanted more costly dresses, more costly hats and shoes. In a word, while their wants have been increased, their ability to supply their wants had not been increased in the same degree. On the other hand, their six or eight years of book education had weaned them away from the occupation of their mothers. The result of this was in too many cases that the girls went to the bad. I often thought how much wiser it would have been to give these girls the same amount of maternal training—and I favour any kind of training, whether in the languages or mathematics, that gives strength and culture to the mind —but at the same time to give them the most thorough training in the latest and best methods of laundrying and other kindred occupations.

# CHAPTER VI

## *Black Race and Red Race*

During the year that I spent in Washington, and for some little time before this, there had been considerable agitation in the state of West Virginia over the question of moving the capital of the state from Wheeling to some other central point. As a result of this, the Legislature designated three cities to be voted upon by the citizens of the state as the permanent seat of government. Among these cities was Charleston, only five miles from Malden, my home. At the close of my school year in Washington I was very pleasantly surprised to receive, from a committee of three white people in Charleston, an invitation to canvass the state in the interests of that city. This invitation I accepted, and spent nearly three months in speaking in various parts of the state. Charleston was successful in winning the prize, and is now the permanent seat of government.

The reputation that I made as a speaker during this campaign induced a number of persons to make an earnest effort to get me to enter political life, but I refused, still believing that I could find other service which would prove of more permanent value to my race. Even then I had a strong feeling that what our people most needed was to get a foundation in education, industry, and property, and for this I felt that they could better afford to strive than for political preferment. As for my individual self, it appeared to me to be reasonably certain that I could succeed in political life, but I had a feeling that it would be a rather selfish kind of success—individual success at the cost of failing to do my duty in assisting in laying a foundation for the masses.

At this period in the progress of our race a very large proportion of the young men who went to school or to college did so with the expressed determination to prepare themselves to be great lawyers, or Congressmen, and many of the women planned to become music teachers; but I had a reasonably fixed idea, even at that early period in my life, that there was a need for something to be done to prepare the way for successful lawyers, Congressmen, and music teachers.

I felt that the conditions were a good deal like those of an old coloured man, during the days of slavery, who wanted to learn how to play on the guitar. In his desire to take guitar lessons he applied to one of his young masters to teach him, but the young man, not having much faith in the ability of the slave to master the guitar at his age, sought to discourage him by telling him: "Uncle Jake, I will give you guitar lessons; but, Jake, I will have to charge you three dollars for the first lesson, two dollars for the second lesson, and one dollar for the third lesson. But I will charge you only twenty-five cents for the last lesson."

Uncle Jake answered: "All right, boss, I hires you on dem terms. But, boss! I wants yer to be sure an' give me dat las' lesson first."

Soon after my work in connection with the removal of the capital was finished, I received an invitation which gave me great joy and which at the same time was a very pleasant surprise. This was a letter from General Armstrong, inviting me to return to Hampton at the next Commencement to deliver what was called the "post-graduate address." This was an honour which I had not dreamed of receiving. With much care I prepared the best address that I was capable of. I chose for my subject "The Force That Wins."

As I returned to Hampton for the purpose of delivering this address, I went over much of the same ground—now, however, covered entirely by railroad—that I had traversed nearly six years before, when I first sought entrance into Hampton Institute as a student. Now I was able to ride the whole distance in the train. I was constantly contrasting this with my first journey to Hampton. I think I may say, without seeming egotism, that it is seldom that five years have wrought such a change in the life and aspirations of an individual.

At Hampton I received a warm welcome from teachers and students. I found that during my absence from Hampton the institute each year had been getting closer to the real needs and conditions of our people; that the industrial reaching, as well as that of the academic department, had greatly improved. The plan of the school was not modelled after that of any other institution then in existence, but every improvement was made under the magnificent leadership of General Armstrong solely with the view of meeting and helping the needs of our people as they presented themselves at the time. Too often, it seems to me, in missionary and educational work among underdeveloped races, people yield to the temptation of doing that which was done a hundred years before, or is being done in other communities a thousand miles away. The temptation often is to run each individual through a certain educational mould, regardless of the condition of the subject or the end to be accomplished. This was not so at Hampton Institute.

The address which I delivered on Commencement Day seems to have pleased every one, and many kind and encouraging words were spoken to me regarding it. Soon after my return to my home in West Virginia, where I had planned to continue teaching, I was again surprised to receive a letter from General Armstrong, asking me to return to Hampton partly as a teacher and partly to pursue some supplementary studies. This was in the summer of 1879. Soon after I began my first teaching in West Virginia I had picked out four of the brightest and most promising of my pupils, in addition to my two brothers, to whom I have already referred, and had given them special attention, with the view of having them go to Hampton. They had gone there, and in each case the teachers had found them so well prepared that they entered advanced classes. This fact, it seems, led to my being called back to Hampton as a teacher. One of the young men that I sent to Hampton in this way is now Dr. Samuel E. Courtney, a successful physician in Boston, and a member of the School Board of that city.

About this time the experiment was being tried for the first time, by General Armstrong, of educating Indians at Hampton. Few people then had any confidence in the ability of the Indians to receive education and to profit by it. General Armstrong was anxious to try the experiment systematically on a large scale. He secured from the reservations in the Western states over one hundred wild and for the most part perfectly ignorant Indians, the greater proportion of whom were young men. The special work which the General desired me to do was be a sort of "house father" to the Indian young men—that is, I was to live in the building with them and have the charge of their discipline, clothing, rooms, and so on. This was a very tempting offer, but I had become so much absorbed in my work in West Virginia that I dreaded to give it up. However, I tore myself away from it. I did not know how to refuse to perform any service that General Armstrong desired of me.

On going to Hampton, I took up my residence in a building with about seventy-five Indian youths. I was the only person in the building who was not a member of their race. At first I had a good deal of doubt about my ability to succeed. I knew that the average Indian felt himself above the white man, and, of course, he felt himself far above the Negro, largely on account of the fact of the Negro having submitted to slavery—a thing which the Indian would never do. The Indians, in the Indian Territory, owned a large number of slaves during the days of slavery. Aside from this, there was a general feeling that the attempt to education and civilize the red men at Hampton would be a failure. All this made me proceed very cautiously, for I felt keenly the great responsibility. But I was determined to succeed. It was not long before I had the complete confidence of the Indians, and not only this, but I think I am safe in saying that I had their love and respect. I found that they were about like any other human beings; that they responded to kind treatment and resented ill-treatment. They were continually planning to do something that would add to my happiness and comfort. The things that they disliked most, I think, were to have their long hair cut, to give up wearing their blankets, and to cease smoking; but no white American ever thinks that any other race is wholly civilized until he wears the white man's clothes, eats the white man's food, speaks the white man's language, and professes the white man's religion.

When the difficulty of learning the English language was subtracted, I found that in the matter of learning trades and in mastering academic studies there was little difference between the coloured and Indian students. It was a constant delight to me to note the interest which the coloured students took in trying to help the Indians in every way possible. There were a few of the coloured students who felt that the Indians ought not to be admitted to Hampton, but these were in the minority. Whenever they were asked to do so, the Negro students gladly took the Indians as room-mates, in order that they might teach them to speak English and to acquire civilized habits.

I have often wondered if there was a white institution in this country whose students would have welcomed the incoming of more than a hundred companions of another race in the cordial way that these black students at Hampton welcomed the red ones. How often I have wanted to say to white students that they lift themselves up in proportion as they help to lift others, and the more unfortunate the race, and the lower in the scale of civilization, the more does one raise one's self by giving the assistance.

This reminds me of a conversation which I once had with the Hon. Frederick Douglass. At one time Mr. Douglass was travelling in the state of Pennsylvania, and was forced, on account of his colour, to ride in the baggage-car, in spite of the fact that he had paid the same price for his passage that the other passengers had paid. When some of the white passengers went into the baggage-car to console Mr. Douglass, and one of them said to him: "I am sorry, Mr. Douglass, that you have been degraded in this manner," Mr. Douglass straightened himself up on the box upon which he was sitting, and replied: "They cannot degrade Frederick Douglass. The soul that is within me no man can degrade. I am not the one that is being degraded on account of this treatment, but those who are inflicting it upon me."

In one part of the country, where the law demands the separation of the races on the railroad trains, I saw at one time a rather amusing instance which showed how difficult it sometimes is to know where the black begins and the white ends.

There was a man who was well known in his community as a Negro, but who was so white that even an expert would have hard work to classify him as a black man. This man was riding in the part of the train set aside for the coloured passengers. When the train conductor reached him, he showed at once that he was perplexed. If the man was a Negro, the conductor did not want to send him to the white people's coach; at the same time, if he was a white man, the conductor did not want to insult him by asking him if he was a Negro. The official looked him over carefully, examining his hair, eyes, nose, and hands, but still seemed puzzled. Finally, to solve the difficulty, he stooped over and peeped at the man's feet. When I saw the conductor examining the feet of the man in question, I said to myself, "That will settle it;" and so it did, for the trainman promptly decided that the passenger was a Negro, and let him remain where he was. I congratulated myself that my race was fortunate in not losing one of its members.

My experience has been that the time to test a true gentleman is to observe him when he is in contact with individuals of a race that is less fortunate than his own. This is illustrated in no better way than by observing the conduct of the old-school type of Southern gentleman when he is in contact with his former slaves or their descendants.

An example of what I mean is shown in a story told of George Washington, who, meeting a coloured man in the road once, who politely lifted his hat, lifted his own in return. Some of his white friends who saw the incident criticised Washington for his action. In reply to their criticism George Washington said: "Do you suppose that I am going to permit a poor, ignorant, coloured man to be more polite than I am?"

While I was in charge of the Indian boys at Hampton, I had one or two experiences which illustrate the curious workings of caste in America. One of the Indian boys was taken ill, and it became my duty to take him to Washington, deliver him over to the Secretary of the Interior, and get a receipt for him, in order that he might be returned to his Western reservation. At that time I was rather ignorant of the ways of the world. During my journey to Washington, on a steamboat, when the bell rang for dinner, I was careful to wait and not enter the dining room until after the greater part of the passengers had finished their meal. Then, with my charge, I went to the dining saloon. The man in charge politely informed me that the Indian could be served, but that I could not. I never could understand how he knew just where to draw the colour line, since the Indian and I were of about the same complexion. The steward, however, seemed to be an expert in this manner. I had been directed by the authorities at Hampton to stop at a certain hotel in Washington with my charge, but when I went to this hotel the clerk stated that he would be glad to receive the Indian into the house, but said that he could not accommodate me.

An illustration of something of this same feeling came under my observation afterward. I happened to find myself in a town in which so much excitement and indignation were being expressed that it seemed likely for a time that there would be a lynching. The occasion of the trouble was that a dark-skinned man had stopped at the local hotel. Investigation, however, developed the fact that this individual was a citizen of Morocco, and that while travelling in this country he spoke the English language. As soon as it was learned that he was not an American Negro, all the signs of indignation disappeared. The man who was the innocent cause of the excitement, though, found it prudent after that not to speak English.

At the end of my first year with the Indians there came another opening for me at Hampton, which, as I look back over my life now, seems to have come providentially, to help to prepare me for my work at Tuskegee later. General Armstrong had found out that there was quite a number of young coloured men and women who were intensely in earnest in wishing to get an education, but who were prevented from entering Hampton Institute because they were too poor to be able to pay any portion of the cost of their board, or even to supply themselves with books. He conceived the idea of starting a night-school in connection with the Institute, into which a limited number of the most promising of these young men and women would be received, on condition that they were to work for ten hours during the day, and attend school for two hours at night. They were to be paid something above the cost of their board for their work. The greater part of their earnings was to be reserved in the school's treasury as a fund to be drawn on to pay their board when they had become students in the day-school, after they had spent one or two years in the night-school. In this way they would obtain a start in their books and a knowledge of some trade or industry, in addition to the other far-reaching benefits of the institution.

General Armstrong asked me to take charge of the night-school, and I did so. At the beginning of this school there were about twelve strong, earnest men and women who entered the class. During the day the greater part of the young men worked in the school's sawmill, and the young women worked in the laundry. The work was not easy in either place, but in all my teaching I never taught pupils who gave me much genuine satisfaction as these did. They were good students, and mastered their work thoroughly. They were so much in earnest that only the ringing of the retiring-bell would make them stop studying, and often they would urge me to continue the lessons after the usual hour for going to bed had come.

These students showed so much earnestness, both in their hard work during the day, as well as in their application to their studies at night, that I gave them the name of "The Plucky Class"—a name which soon grew popular and spread throughout the institution. After a student had been in the night-school long enough to prove what was in him, I gave him a printed certificate which read something like this:—

> "This is to certify that James Smith is a member of The Plucky Class of the Hampton Institute, and is in good and regular standing."

The students prized these certificates highly, and they added greatly to the popularity of the night-school. Within a few weeks this department had grown to such an extent that there were about twenty-five students in attendance. I have followed the course of many of these twenty-five men and women ever since then, and they are now holding important and useful positions in nearly every part of the South. The night-school at Hampton, which started with only twelve students, now numbers between three and four hundred, and is one of the permanent and most important features of the institution.

# CHAPTER VII

## *Early Days at Tuskegee*

During the time that I had charge of the Indians and the night-school at Hampton, I pursued some studies myself, under the direction of the instructors there. One of these instructors was the Rev. Dr. H.B. Frissell, the present Principal of the Hampton Institute, General Armstrong's successor.

In May, 1881, near the close of my first year in teaching the night-school, in a way that I had not dared expect, the opportunity opened for me to begin my life-work. One night in the chapel, after the usual chapel exercises were over, General Armstrong referred to the fact that he had received a letter from some gentlemen in Alabama asking him to recommend some one to take charge of what was to be a normal school for the coloured people in the little town of Tuskegee in that state. These gentlemen seemed to take it for granted that no coloured man suitable for the position could be secured, and they were expecting the General to recommend a white man for the place. The next day General Armstrong sent for me to come to his office, and, much to my surprise, asked me if I thought I could fill the position in Alabama. I told him that I would be willing to try. Accordingly, he wrote to the people who had applied to him for the information, that he did not know of any white man to suggest, but if they would be willing to take a coloured man, he had one whom he could recommend. In this letter he gave them my name.

Several days passed before anything more was heard about the matter. Some time afterward, one Sunday evening during the chapel exercises, a messenger came in and handed the general a telegram. At the end of the exercises he read the telegram to the school. In substance, these were its words: "Booker T. Washington will suit us. Send him at once."

There was a great deal of joy expressed among the students and teachers, and I received very hearty congratulations. I began to get ready at once to go to Tuskegee. I went by way of my old home in

West Virginia, where I remained for several days, after which I proceeded to Tuskegee. I found Tuskegee to be a town of about two thousand inhabitants, nearly one-half of whom were coloured. It was in what was known as the Black Belt of the South. In the county in which Tuskegee is situated the coloured people outnumbered the whites by about three to one. In some of the adjoining and near-by counties the proportion was not far from six coloured persons to one white.

I have often been asked to define the term "Black Belt." So far as I can learn, the term was first used to designated a part of the country which was distinguished by the colour of the soil. The part of the country possessing this thick, dark, and naturally rich soil was, of course, the part of the South where the slaves were most profitable, and consequently they were taken there in the largest numbers. Later, and especially since the war, the term seems to be used wholly in a political sense—that is, to designate the counties where the black people outnumber the white.

Before going to Tuskegee I had expected to find there a building and all the necessary apparatus ready for me to begin teaching. To my disappointment, I found nothing of the kind. I did find, though, that which no costly building and apparatus can supply,—hundreds of hungry, earnest souls who wanted to secure knowledge.

Tuskegee seemed an ideal place for the school. It was in the midst of the great bulk of the Negro population, and was rather secluded, being five miles from the main line of railroad, with which it was connected by a short line. During the days of slavery, and since, the town had been a centre for the education of the white people. This was an added advantage, for the reason that I found the white people possessing a degree of culture and education that is not surpassed by many localities. While the coloured people were ignorant, they had not, as a rule, degraded and weakened their bodies by vices such as are common to the lower class of people in the large cities. In general, I found the relations between the two races pleasant. For example, the largest, and I think at that time the only hardware store in the town was owned and operated jointly by a coloured man and a white man. This copartnership continued until the death of the white partner.

I found that about a year previous to my going to Tuskegee some of the coloured people who had heard something of the work of education being done at Hampton had applied to the state Legislature, through their representatives, for a small appropriation to be used in starting a normal school in Tuskegee. This request the Legislature had complied with to the extent of granting an annual appropriation of two thousand dollars. I soon learned, however, that this money could be used only for the payment of the salaries of the instructors, and that there was no provision for securing land, buildings, or apparatus. The task before me did not seem a very encouraging one. It seemed much like making bricks without straw. The coloured people were overjoyed, and were constantly offering their services in any way in which they could be of assistance in getting the school started.

My first task was to find a place in which to open the school. After looking the town over with some care, the most suitable place that could be secured seemed to be a rather dilapidated shanty near the coloured Methodist church, together with the church itself as a sort of assembly-room. Both the church and the shanty were in about as bad condition as was possible. I recall that during the first months of school that I taught in this building it was in such poor repair that, whenever it rained, one of the older students would very kindly leave his lessons and hold an umbrella over me while I heard the recitations of the others. I remember, also, that on more than one occasion my landlady held an umbrella over me while I ate breakfast.

At the time I went to Alabama the coloured people were taking considerable interest in politics, and they were very anxious that I should become one of them politically, in every respect. They seemed to have a little distrust of strangers in this regard. I recall that one man, who seemed to have been designated by the others to look after my political destiny, came to me on several occasions and said, with a good deal of earnestness: "We wants you to be sure to vote jes' like we votes. We can't read de newspapers very much, but we knows how to vote, an' we wants you to vote jes' like we votes." He added: "We watches de white man, and we keeps watching de white man till we finds out which way de white man's gwine to vote; an' when we finds out which way de white man's gwine to vote, den we votes 'xactly de other way. Den we knows we's right."

I am glad to add, however, that at the present time the disposition to vote against the white man merely because he is white is largely disappearing, and the race is learning to vote from principle, for what the voter considers to be for the best interests of both races.

I reached Tuskegee, as I have said, early in June, 1881. The first month I spent in finding accommodations for the school, and in travelling through Alabama, examining into the actual life of the people, especially in the court districts, and in getting the school advertised among the class of people that I wanted to have attend it. The most of my travelling was done over the country roads, with a mule and a cart or a mule and a buggy wagon for conveyance. I ate and slept with the people, in their little cabins. I saw their farms, their schools, their churches. Since, in the case of the most of these visits, there had been no notice given in advance that a stranger was expected, I had the advantage of seeing the real, everyday life of the people.

In the plantation districts I found that, as a rule, the whole family slept in one room, and that in addition to the immediate family there sometimes were relatives, or others not related to the family, who slept in the same room. On more than one occasion I went outside the house to get ready for bed, or to wait until the family had gone to bed. They usually contrived some kind of a place for me to sleep, either on the floor or in a special part of another's bed. Rarely was there any place provided in the cabin where one could bathe even the face and hands, but usually some provision was made for this outside the house, in the yard.

The common diet of the people was fat pork and corn bread. At times I have eaten in cabins where they had only corn bread and "black-eye peas" cooked in plain water. The people seemed to have no other idea than to live on this fat meat and corn bread,—the meat, and the meal of which the bread was made, having been bought at a high price at a store in town, notwithstanding the fact that the land all about the cabin homes could easily have been made to produce nearly every kind of garden vegetable that is raised anywhere in the country. Their one object seemed to be to plant nothing but cotton; and in many cases cotton was planted up to the very door of the cabin.

In these cabin homes I often found sewing-machines which had been bought, or were being bought, on instalments, frequently at a cost of as much as sixty dollars, or showy clocks for which the occupants of the cabins had paid twelve or fourteen dollars. I remember that on one occasion when I went into one of these cabins for dinner, when I sat down to the table for a meal with the four members of the family, I noticed that, while there were five of us at the table, there was but one fork for the five of us to use. Naturally there was an awkward pause on my part. In the opposite corner of that same cabin was an organ for which the people told me they were paying sixty dollars in monthly instalments. One fork, and a sixty-dollar organ!

In most cases the sewing-machine was not used, the clocks were so worthless that they did not keep correct time—and if they had, in nine cases out of ten there would have been no one in the family who could have told the time of day—while the organ, of course, was rarely used for want of a person who could play upon it.

In the case to which I have referred, where the family sat down to the table for the meal at which I was their guest, I could see plainly that this was an awkward and unusual proceeding, and was done in my honour. In most cases, when the family got up in the morning, for example, the wife would put a piece of meat in a frying-pan and put a lump of dough in a "skillet," as they called it. These utensils would be placed on the fire, and in ten or fifteen minutes breakfast would be ready. Frequently the husband would take his bread and meat in his hand and start for the field, eating as he walked. The mother would sit down in a corner and eat her breakfast, perhaps from a plate and perhaps directly from the "skillet" or frying-pan, while the children would eat their portion of the bread and meat while running about the yard. At certain seasons of the year, when meat was scarce, it was rarely that the children who were not old enough or strong enough to work in the fields would have the luxury of meat.

The breakfast over, and with practically no attention given to the house, the whole family would, as a general thing, proceed to the cotton-field. Every child that was large enough to carry a hoe was put to work, and the baby—for usually there was at least one baby—would be laid down at the end of the cotton row, so that its mother could give it a certain amount of attention when she had finished chopping her row. The noon meal and the supper were taken in much the same way as the breakfast.

All the days of the family would be spent after much this same routine, except Saturday and Sunday. On Saturday the whole family would spend at least half a day, and often a whole day, in town. The idea in going to town was, I suppose, to do shopping, but all the shopping that the whole family had money for could have been attended to in ten minutes by one person. Still, the whole family remained in town for most of the day, spending the greater part of the time in standing on the streets, the women, too often, sitting about somewhere smoking or dipping snuff. Sunday was usually spent in going to some big meeting. With few exceptions, I found that the crops were mortgaged in the counties where I went, and that the most of the coloured farmers were in debt. The state had not been able to build schoolhouses in the country districts, and, as a rule, the schools were taught in churches or in log cabins. More than once, while on my journeys, I found that there was no provision made in the house used for school purposes for heating the building during the winter, and consequently a fire had to be built in the yard, and teacher and pupils passed in and out of the house as they got cold or warm. With few exceptions, I found the teachers in these country schools to be miserably poor in preparation for their work, and poor in moral character. The schools were in session from three to five months. There was practically no apparatus in the schoolhouses, except that occasionally there was a rough blackboard. I recall that one day I went into a schoolhouse—or rather into an abandoned log cabin that was being used as a schoolhouse—and found five pupils who were studying a lesson from one book. Two of these, on the front seat, were using the book between them; behind these were two others peeping over the shoulders of the first two, and behind the four was a fifth little fellow who was peeping over the shoulders of all four.

What I have said concerning the character of the schoolhouses and teachers will also apply quite accurately as a description of the church buildings and the ministers.

I met some very interesting characters during my travels. As illustrating the peculiar mental processes of the country people, I remember that I asked one coloured man, who was about sixty years old, to tell me something of his history. He said that he had been born in Virginia, and sold into Alabama in 1845. I asked him how many were sold at the same time. He said, "There were five of us; myself and brother and three mules."

In giving all these descriptions of what I saw during my month of travel in the country around Tuskegee, I wish my readers to keep in mind the fact that there were many encouraging exceptions to the conditions which I have described. I have stated in such plain words what I saw, mainly for the reason that later I want to emphasize the encouraging changes that have taken place in the community, not wholly by the work of the Tuskegee school, but by that of other institutions as well.

# CHAPTER VIII

## *Teaching School in a Stable and a Hen-House*

I confess that what I saw during my month of travel and investigation left me with a very heavy heart. The work to be done in order to lift these people up seemed almost beyond accomplishing. I was only one person, and it seemed to me that the little effort which I could put forth could go such a short distance toward bringing about results. I wondered if I could accomplish anything, and if it were worth while for me to try.

Of one thing I felt more strongly convinced than ever, after spending this month in seeing the actual life of the coloured people, and that was that, in order to lift them up, something must be done more than merely to imitate New England education as it then existed. I saw more clearly than ever the wisdom of the system which General Armstrong had inaugurated at Hampton. To take the children of such people as I had been among for a month, and each day give them a few hours of mere book education, I felt would be almost a waste of time.

After consultation with the citizens of Tuskegee, I set July 4, 1881, as the day for the opening of the school in the little shanty and church which had been secured for its accommodation. The white people, as well as the coloured, were greatly interested in the starting of the new school, and the opening day was looked forward to with much earnest discussion. There were not a few white people in the vicinity of Tuskegee who looked with some disfavour upon the project. They questioned its value to the coloured people, and had a fear that it might result in bringing about trouble between the races. Some had the feeling that in proportion as the Negro received education, in the same proportion would his value decrease as an economic factor in the state. These people feared the result of education would be that the Negroes would leave the farms, and that it would be difficult to secure them for domestic service.

The white people who questioned the wisdom of starting this new school had in their minds pictures of what was called an educated Negro, with a high hat, imitation gold eye-glasses, a showy walking-stick, kid gloves, fancy boots, and what not—in a word, a man who was determined to live by his wits. It was difficult for these people to see how education would produce any other kind of a coloured man.

In the midst of all the difficulties which I encountered in getting the little school started, and since then through a period of nineteen years, there are two men among all the many friends of the school in Tuskegee upon whom I have depended constantly for advice and guidance; and the success of the undertaking is largely due to these men, from whom I have never sought anything in vain. I mention them simply as types. One is a white man and an ex-slaveholder, Mr. George W. Campbell; the other is a black man and an ex-slave, Mr. Lewis Adams. These were the men who wrote to General Armstrong for a teacher.

Mr. Campbell is a merchant and banker, and had had little experience in dealing with matters pertaining to education. Mr. Adams was a mechanic, and had learned the trades of shoemaking, harness-making, and tinsmithing during the days of slavery. He had never been to school a day in his life, but in some way he had learned to read and write while a slave. From the first, these two men saw clearly what my plan of education was, sympathized with me, and supported me in every effort. In the days which were darkest financially for the school, Mr. Campbell was never appealed to when he was not willing to extend all the aid in his power. I do not know two men, one an ex-slaveholder, one an ex-slave, whose advice and judgment I would feel more like following in everything which concerns the life and development of the school at Tuskegee than those of these two men.

I have always felt that Mr. Adams, in a large degree, derived his unusual power of mind from the training given his hands in the process of mastering well three trades during the days of slavery. If one goes to-day into any Southern town, and asks for the leading and most reliable coloured man in the community, I believe that in five cases out of ten he will be directed to a Negro who learned a trade during the days of slavery.

On the morning that the school opened, thirty students reported for admission. I was the only teacher. The students were about equally divided between the sexes. Most of them lived in Macon County, the county in which Tuskegee is situated, and of which it is the county-seat. A great many more students wanted to enter the school, but it had been decided to receive only those who were above fifteen years of age, and who had previously received some education. The greater part of the thirty were public-school teachers, and some of them were nearly forty years of age. With the teachers came some of their former pupils, and when they were examined it was amusing to note that in several cases the pupil entered a higher class than did his former teacher. It was also interesting to note how many big books some of them had studied, and how many high-sounding subjects some of them claimed to have mastered. The bigger the book and the longer the name of the subject, the prouder they felt of their accomplishment. Some had studied Latin, and one or two Greek. This they thought entitled them to special distinction.

In fact, one of the saddest things I saw during the month of travel which I have described was a young man, who had attended some high school, sitting down in a one-room cabin, with grease on his clothing, filth all around him, and weeds in the yard and garden, engaged in studying a French grammar.

The students who came first seemed to be fond of memorizing long and complicated "rules" in grammar and mathematics, but had little thought or knowledge of applying these rules to their everyday affairs of their life. One subject which they liked to talk about, and tell me that they had mastered, in arithmetic, was "banking and discount," but I soon found out that neither they nor almost any one in the neighbourhood in which they had lived had ever had a bank account. In registering the names of the students, I found that almost every one of them had one or more middle initials. When I asked what the "J" stood for, in the name of John J. Jones, it was explained to me that this was a part of his "entitles." Most of the students wanted to get an education because they thought it would enable them to earn more money as school-teachers.

Notwithstanding what I have said about them in these respects, I have never seen a more earnest and willing company of young men and women than these students were. They were all willing to learn the right thing as soon as it was shown them what was right. I was determined to start them off on a solid and thorough foundation, so far as their books were concerned. I soon learned that most of them had the merest smattering of the high-sounding things that they had studied. While they could locate the Desert of Sahara or the capital of China on an artificial globe, I found out that the girls could not locate the proper places for the knives and forks on an actual dinner-table, or the places on which the bread and meat should be set.

I had to summon a good deal of courage to take a student who had been studying cube root and "banking and discount," and explain to him that the wisest thing for him to do first was thoroughly master the multiplication table.

The number of pupils increased each week, until by the end of the first month there were nearly fifty. Many of them, however, said that, as they could remain only for two or three months, they wanted to enter a high class and get a diploma the first year if possible.

At the end of the first six weeks a new and rare face entered the school as a co-teacher. This was Miss Olivia A. Davidson, who later became my wife. Miss Davidson was born in Ohio, and received her preparatory education in the public schools of that state. When little more than a girl, she heard of the need of teachers in the South. She went to the state of Mississippi and began teaching there. Later she taught in the city of Memphis. While teaching in Mississippi, one of her pupils became ill with smallpox. Every one in the community was so frightened that no one would nurse the boy. Miss Davidson closed her school and remained by the bedside of the boy night and day until he recovered. While she was at her Ohio home on her vacation, the worst epidemic of yellow fever broke out in Memphis, Tenn., that perhaps has ever occurred in the South. When she heard of this, she at once telegraphed the Mayor of Memphis, offering her services as a yellow-fever nurse, although she had never had the disease.

Miss Davidon's experience in the South showed her that the people needed something more than mere book-learning. She heard of the Hampton system of education, and decided that this was what she wanted in order to prepare herself for better work in the South. The attention of Mrs. Mary Hemenway, of Boston, was attracted to her rare ability. Through Mrs. Hemenway's kindness and generosity, Miss Davidson, after graduating at Hampton, received an opportunity to complete a two years' course of training at the Massachusetts State Normal School at Framingham.

Before she went to Framingham, some one suggested to Miss Davidson that, since she was so very light in colour, she might find it more comfortable not to be known as a coloured women in this school in Massachusetts. She at once replied that under no circumstances and for no considerations would she consent to deceive any one in regard to her racial identity.

Soon after her graduation from the Framingham institution, Miss Davidson came to Tuskegee, bringing into the school many valuable and fresh ideas as to the best methods of teaching, as well as a rare moral character and a life of unselfishness that I think has seldom been equalled. No single individual did more toward laying the foundations of the Tuskegee Institute so as to insure the successful work that has been done there than Olivia A. Davidson.

Miss Davidson and I began consulting as to the future of the school from the first. The students were making progress in learning books and in developing their minds; but it became apparent at once that, if we were to make any permanent impression upon those who had come to us for training we must do something besides teach them mere books. The students had come from homes where they had had no opportunities for lessons which would teach them how to care for their bodies. With few exceptions, the homes in Tuskegee in which the students boarded were but little improvement upon those from which they had come. We wanted to teach the students how to bathe; how to care for their teeth and clothing. We wanted to teach them what to eat, and how to eat it properly, and how to care for their rooms. Aside from this, we wanted to give them such a practical knowledge of some one industry, together with the spirit of industry, thrift, and economy, that they would be sure of knowing how to make a living after they had left us. We wanted to teach them to study actual things instead of mere books alone.

We found that the most of our students came from the country districts, where agriculture in some form or other was the main dependence of the people. We learned that about eighty-five per cent of the coloured people in the Gulf states depended upon agriculture for their living. Since this was true, we wanted to be careful not to educate our students out of sympathy with agricultural life, so that they would be attracted from the country to the cities, and yield to the temptation of trying to live by their wits. We wanted to give them such an education as would fit a large proportion of them to be teachers, and at the same time cause them to return to the plantation districts and show the people there how to put new energy and new ideas into farming, as well as into the intellectual and moral and religious life of the people.

All these ideas and needs crowded themselves upon us with a seriousness that seemed well-nigh overwhelming. What were we to do? We had only the little old shanty and the abandoned church which the good coloured people of the town of Tuskegee had kindly loaned us for the accommodation of the classes. The number of students was increasing daily. The more we saw of them, and the more we travelled through the country districts, the more we saw that our efforts were reaching, to only a partial degree, the actual needs of the people whom we wanted to lift up through the medium of the students whom we should educate and send out as leaders.

The more we talked with the students, who were then coming to us from several parts of the state, the more we found that the chief ambition among a large proportion of them was to get an education so that they would not have to work any longer with their hands.

This is illustrated by a story told of a coloured man in Alabama, who, one hot day in July, while he was at work in a cotton-field, suddenly stopped, and, looking toward the skies, said: "O Lawd, de cottom am so grassy, de work am so hard, and the sun am so hot dat I b'lieve dis darky am called to preach!"

About three months after the opening of the school, and at the time when we were in the greatest anxiety about our work, there came into market for sale an old and abandoned plantation which was situated about a mile from the town of Tuskegee. The mansion house—or "big house," as it would have been called—which had been occupied by the owners during slavery, had been burned. After making a careful examination of the place, it seemed to be just the location that we wanted in order to make our work effective and permanent.

But how were we to get it? The price asked for it was very little —only five hundred dollars—but we had no money, and we were strangers in the town and had no credit. The owner of the land agreed to let us occupy the place if we could make a payment of two hundred and fifty dollars down, with the understanding that the remaining two hundred and fifty dollars must be paid within a year. Although five hundred dollars was cheap for the land, it was a large sum when one did not have any part of it.

In the midst of the difficulty I summoned a great deal of courage and wrote to my friend General J.F.B. Marshall, the Treasurer of the Hampton Institute, putting the situation before him and beseeching him to lend me the two hundred and fifty dollars on my own personal responsibility. Within a few days a reply came to the effect that he had no authority to lend me the money belonging to the Hampton Institute, but that he would gladly lend me the amount needed from his own personal funds.

I confess that the securing of this money in this way was a great surprise to me, as well as a source of gratification. Up to that time I never had had in my possession so much money as one hundred dollars at a time, and the loan which I had asked General Marshall for seemed a tremendously large sum to me. The fact of my being responsible for the repaying of such a large amount of money weighed very heavily upon me.

I lost no time in getting ready to move the school on to the new farm. At the time we occupied the place there were standing upon it a cabin, formerly used as a dining room, an old kitchen, a stable, and an old hen-house. Within a few weeks we had all of these structures in use. The stable was repaired and used as a recitation-room, and very presently the hen-house was utilized for the same purpose.

I recall that one morning, when I told an old coloured man who lived near, and who sometimes helped me, that our school had grown so large that it would be necessary for us to use the hen-house for school purposes, and that I wanted him to help me give it a thorough cleaning out the next day, he replied, in the most earnest manner: "What you mean, boss? You sholy ain't gwine clean out de hen-house in de *day*-time?"

Nearly all the work of getting the new location ready for school purposes was done by the students after school was over in the afternoon. As soon as we got the cabins in condition to be used, I determined to clear up some land so that we could plant a crop. When I explained my plan to the young men, I noticed that they did not seem to take to it very kindly. It was hard for them to see the connection between clearing land and an education. Besides, many of them had been school-teachers, and they questioned whether or not clearing land would be in keeping with their dignity. In order to relieve them from any embarrassment, each afternoon after school I took my axe and led the way to the woods. When they saw that I was not afraid or ashamed to work, they began to assist with more enthusiasm. We kept at the work each afternoon, until we had cleared about twenty acres and had planted a crop.

In the meantime Miss Davidson was devising plans to repay the loan. Her first effort was made by holding festivals, or "suppers." She made a personal canvass among the white and coloured families in the town of Tuskegee, and got them to agree to give something, like a cake, a chicken, bread, or pies, that could be sold at the festival. Of course the coloured people were glad to give anything that they could spare, but I want to add that Miss Davidson did not apply to a single white family, so far as I now remember, that failed to donate something; and in many ways the white families showed their interest in the school.

Several of these festivals were held, and quite a little sum of money was raised. A canvass was also made among the people of both races for direct gifts of money, and most of those applied to gave small sums. It was often pathetic to note the gifts of the older coloured people, most of whom had spent their best days in slavery. Sometimes they would give five cents, sometimes twenty-five cents. Sometimes the contribution was a quilt, or a quantity of sugarcane. I recall one old coloured women who was about seventy years of age, who came to see me when we were raising money to pay for the farm. She hobbled into the room where I was, leaning on a cane. She was clad in rags; but they were clean. She said: "Mr. Washin'ton, God knows I spent de bes' days of my life in slavery. God knows I's ignorant an' poor; but," she added, "I knows what you an' Miss Davidson is tryin' to do. I knows you is tryin' to make better men an' better women for de coloured race. I ain't got no money, but I wants you to take dese six eggs, what I's been savin' up, an' I wants you to put dese six eggs into the eddication of dese boys an' gals."

Since the work at Tuskegee started, it has been my privilege to receive many gifts for the benefit of the institution, but never any, I think, that touched me so deeply as this one.

# CHAPTER IX

## *Anxious Days and Sleepless Nights*

The coming of Christmas, that first year of our residence in Alabama, gave us an opportunity to get a farther insight into the real life of the people. The first thing that reminded us that Christmas had arrived was the "foreday" visits of scores of children rapping at our doors, asking for "Chris'mus gifts! Chris'mus gifts!" Between the hours of two o'clock and five o'clock in the morning I presume that we must have had a half-hundred such calls. This custom prevails throughout this portion of the South to-day.

During the days of slavery it was a custom quite generally observed throughout all the Southern states to give the coloured people a week of holiday at Christmas, or to allow the holiday to continue as long as the "yule log" lasted. The male members of the race, and often the female members, were expected to get drunk. We found that for a whole week the coloured people in and around Tuskegee dropped work the day before Christmas, and that it was difficult for any one to perform any service from the time they stopped work until after the New Year. Persons who at other times did not use strong drink thought it quite the proper thing to indulge in it rather freely during the Christmas week. There was a widespread hilarity, and a free use of guns, pistols, and gunpowder generally. The sacredness of the season seemed to have been almost wholly lost sight of.

During this first Christmas vacation I went some distance from the town to visit the people on one of the large plantations. In their poverty and ignorance it was pathetic to see their attempts to get joy out of the season that in most parts of the country is so sacred and so dear to the heart. In one cabin I noticed that all that the five children had to remind them of the coming of Christ was a single bunch of firecrackers, which they had divided among them. In another cabin, where there were at least a half-dozen persons, they had only ten cents' worth of ginger-cakes, which had been bought in the store the day before. In another family they had only a few pieces of sugarcane. In still another cabin I found nothing but a new jug of cheap, mean whiskey, which the husband and wife were making free use of, notwithstanding the fact that the husband was one of the local ministers. In a few instances I found that the people had gotten hold of some bright-coloured cards that had been designed for advertising purposes, and were making the most of these. In other homes some member of the family had bought a new pistol. In the majority of cases there was nothing to be seen in the cabin to remind one of the coming of the Saviour, except that the people had ceased work in the fields and were lounging about their homes. At night, during Christmas week, they usually had what they called a "frolic," in some cabin on the plantation. That meant a kind of rough dance, where there was likely to be a good deal of whiskey used, and where there might be some shooting or cutting with razors.

While I was making this Christmas visit I met an old coloured man who was one of the numerous local preachers, who tried to convince me, from the experience Adam had in the Garden of Eden, that God had cursed all labour, and that, therefore, it was a sin for any man to work. For that reason this man sought to do as little work as possible. He seemed at that time to be supremely happy, because he was living, as he expressed it, through one week that was free from sin.

In the school we made a special effort to teach our students the meaning of Christmas, and to give them lessons in its proper observance. In this we have been successful to a degree that makes me feel safe in saying that the season now has a new meaning, not only through all that immediate region, but, in a measure, wherever our graduates have gone.

At the present time one of the most satisfactory features of the Christmas and Thanksgiving season at Tuskegee is the unselfish and beautiful way in which our graduates and students spend their time in administering to the comfort and happiness of others, especially the unfortunate. Not long ago some of our young men spent a holiday in rebuilding a cabin for a helpless coloured women who was about seventy-five years old. At another time I remember that I made it known in chapel, one night, that a very poor student was suffering from cold, because he needed a coat. The next morning two coats were sent to my office for him.

I have referred to the disposition on the part of the white people in the town of Tuskegee and vicinity to help the school. From the first, I resolved to make the school a real part of the community in which it was located. I was determined that no one should have the feeling that it was a foreign institution, dropped down in the midst of the people, for which they had no responsibility and in which they had no interest. I noticed that the very fact that they had been asked to contribute toward the purchase of the land made them begin to feel as if it was going to be their school, to a large degree. I noted that just in proportion as we made the white people feel that the institution was a part of the life of the community, and that, while we wanted to make friends in Boston, for example, we also wanted to make white friends in Tuskegee, and that we wanted to make the school of real service to all the people, their attitude toward the school became favourable.

Perhaps I might add right here, what I hope to demonstrate later, that, so far as I know, the Tuskegee school at the present time has no warmer and more enthusiastic friends anywhere than it has among the white citizens of Tuskegee and throughout the state of Alabama and the entire South. From the first, I have advised our people in the South to make friends in every straightforward, manly way with their next-door neighbour, whether he be a black man or a white man. I have also advised them, where no principle is at stake, to consult the interests of their local communities, and to advise with their friends in regard to their voting.

For several months the work of securing the money with which to pay for the farm went on without ceasing. At the end of three months enough was secured to repay the loan of two hundred and fifty dollars to General Marshall, and within two months more we had secured the entire five hundred dollars and had received a deed of the one hundred acres of land. This gave us a great deal of satisfaction. It was not only a source of satisfaction to secure a permanent location for the school, but it was equally satisfactory to know that the greater part of the money with which it was paid for had been gotten from the white and coloured people in the town of Tuskegee.

The most of this money was obtained by holding festivals and concerts, and from small individual donations.

Our next effort was in the direction of increasing the cultivation of the land, so as to secure some return from it, and at the same time give the students training in agriculture. All the industries at Tuskegee have been started in natural and logical order, growing out of the needs of a community settlement. We began with farming, because we wanted something to eat.

Many of the students, also, were able to remain in school but a few weeks at a time, because they had so little money with which to pay their board. Thus another object which made it desirable to get an industrial system started was in order to make it available as a means of helping the students to earn money enough so that they might be able to remain in school during the nine months' session of the school year.

The first animal that the school came into possession of was an old blind horse given us by one of the white citizens of Tuskegee. Perhaps I may add here that at the present time the school owns over two hundred horses, colts, mules, cows, calves, and oxen, and about seven hundred hogs and pigs, as well as a large number of sheep and goats.

The school was constantly growing in numbers, so much so that, after we had got the farm paid for, the cultivation of the land begun, and the old cabins which we had found on the place somewhat repaired, we turned our attention toward providing a large, substantial building. After having given a good deal of thought to the subject, we finally had the plans drawn for a building that was estimated to cost about six thousand dollars. This seemed to us a tremendous sum, but we knew that the school must go backward or forward, and that our work would mean little unless we could get hold of the students in their home life.

One incident which occurred about this time gave me a great deal of satisfaction as well as surprise. When it became known in the town that we were discussing the plans for a new, large building, a Southern white man who was operating a sawmill not far from Tuskegee came to me and said that he would gladly put all the lumber necessary to erect the building on the grounds, with no other guarantee for payment than my word that it would be paid for when we secured some money. I told the man frankly that at the time we did not have in our hands one dollar of the money needed. Notwithstanding this, he insisted on being allowed to put the lumber on the grounds. After we had secured some portion of the money we permitted him to do this.

Miss Davidson again began the work of securing in various ways small contributions for the new building from the white and coloured people in and near Tuskegee. I think I never saw a community of people so happy over anything as were the coloured people over the prospect of this new building. One day, when we were holding a meeting to secure funds for its erection, an old, antebellum coloured man came a distance of twelve miles and brought in his ox-cart a large hog. When the meeting was in progress, he rose in the midst of the company and said that he had no money which he could give, but he had raised two fine hogs, and that he had brought one of them as a contribution toward the expenses of the building. He closed his announcement by saying: "Any nigger that's got any love for his race, or any respect for himself, will bring a hog to the next meeting." Quite a number of men in the community also volunteered to give several days' work, each, toward the erection of the building.

After we had secured all the help that we could in Tuskegee, Miss Davidson decided to go North for the purpose of securing additional funds. For weeks she visited individuals and spoke in churches and before Sunday schools and other organizations. She found this work quite trying, and often embarrassing. The school was not known, but she was not long in winning her way into the confidence of the best people in the North.

The first gift from any Northern person was received from a New York lady whom Miss Davidson met on the boat that was bringing her North. They fell into a conversation, and the Northern lady became so much interested in the effort being made at Tuskegee that before they parted Miss Davidson was handed a check for fifty dollars. For some time before our marriage, and also after it, Miss

Davidson kept up the work of securing money in the North and in the South by interesting people by personal visits and through correspondence. At the same time she kept in close touch with the work at Tuskegee, as lady principal and classroom teacher. In addition to this, she worked among the older people in and near Tuskegee, and taught a Sunday school class in the town. She was never very strong, but never seemed happy unless she was giving all of her strength to the cause which she loved. Often, at night, after spending the day in going from door to door trying to interest persons in the work at Tuskegee, she would be so exhausted that she could not undress herself. A lady upon whom she called, in Boston, afterward told me that at one time when Miss Davidson called her to see and send up her card the lady was detained a little before she could see Miss Davidson, and when she entered the parlour she found Miss Davidson so exhausted that she had fallen asleep.

While putting up our first building, which was named Porter Hall, after Mr. A.H. Porter, of Brooklyn, N.Y., who gave a generous sum toward its erection, the need for money became acute. I had given one of our creditors a promise that upon a certain day he should be paid four hundred dollars. On the morning of that day we did not have a dollar. The mail arrived at the school at ten o'clock, and in this mail there was a check sent by Miss Davidson for exactly four hundred dollars. I could relate many instances of almost the same character. This four hundred dollars was given by two ladies in Boston. Two years later, when the work at Tuskegee had grown considerably, and when we were in the midst of a season when we were so much in need of money that the future looked doubtful and gloomy, the same two Boston ladies sent us six thousand dollars. Words cannot describe our surprise, or the encouragement that the gift brought to us. Perhaps I might add here that for fourteen years these same friends have sent us six thousand dollars a year.

As soon as the plans were drawn for the new building, the students began digging out the earth where the foundations were to be laid, working after the regular classes were over. They had not fully outgrown the idea that it was hardly the proper thing for them to use their hands, since they had come there, as one of them expressed it, "to be educated, and not to work." Gradually, though, I noted with satisfaction that a sentiment in favour of work was gaining ground. After a few weeks of hard work the foundations were ready, and a day was appointed for the laying of the corner-stone.

When it is considered that the laying of this corner-stone took place in the heart of the South, in the "Black Belt," in the centre of that part of our country that was most devoted to slavery; that at that time slavery had been abolished only about sixteen years; that only sixteen years before no Negro could be taught from books without the teacher receiving the condemnation of the law or of public sentiment—when all this is considered, the scene that was witnessed on that spring day at Tuskegee was a remarkable one. I believe there are few places in the world where it could have taken place.

The principal address was delivered by the Hon. Waddy Thompson, the Superintendent of Education for the county. About the corner-stone were gathered the teachers, the students, their parents and friends, the county officials—who were white—and all the leading white men in that vicinity, together with many of the black men and women whom the same white people but a few years before had held a title to as property. The members of both races were anxious to exercise the privilege of placing under the corner-stone some momento.

Before the building was completed we passed through some very trying seasons. More than once our hearts were made to bleed, as it were, because bills were falling due that we did not have the money to meet. Perhaps no one who has not gone through the experience, month after month, of trying to erect buildings and provide equipment for a school when no one knew where the money was to come from, can properly appreciate the difficulties under which we laboured. During the first years at Tuskegee I recall that night after night I would roll and toss on my bed, without sleep, because of the anxiety and uncertainty which we were in regarding money. I knew that, in a large degree, we were trying an experiment—that of testing whether or not it was possible for Negroes to build up and control the affairs of a large education institution. I knew that if we failed it would injure the whole race. I knew that the presumption was against us. I knew that in the case of white people beginning such an enterprise it would be taken for granted that they were going to succeed, but in our case I felt that people would be surprised if we succeeded. All this made a burden which pressed down on us, sometimes, it seemed, at the rate of a thousand pounds to the square inch.

In all our difficulties and anxieties, however, I never went to a white or a black person in the town of Tuskegee for any assistance that was in their power to render, without being helped according to their means. More than a dozen times, when bills figuring up into the hundreds of dollars were falling due, I applied to the white men of Tuskegee for small loans, often borrowing small amounts from as many as a half-dozen persons, to meet our obligations. One thing I was determined to do from the first, and that was to keep the credit of the school high; and this, I think I can say without boasting, we have done all through these years.

I shall always remember a bit of advice given me by Mr. George W. Campbell, the white man to whom I have referred to as the one who induced General Armstrong to send me to Tuskegee. Soon after I entered upon the work Mr. Campbell said to me, in his fatherly way: "Washington, always remember that credit is capital."

At one time when we were in the greatest distress for money that we ever experienced, I placed the situation frankly before General Armstrong. Without hesitation he gave me his personal check for all the money which he had saved for his own use. This was not the only time that General Armstrong helped Tuskegee in this way. I do not think I have ever made this fact public before.

During the summer of 1882, at the end of the first year's work of the school, I was married to Miss Fannie N. Smith, of Malden, W. Va. We began keeping house in Tuskegee early in the fall. This made a home for our teachers, who now had been increased to four in number. My wife was also a graduate of the Hampton Institute. After earnest and constant work in the interests of the school, together with her housekeeping duties, my wife passed away in May, 1884. One child, Portia M. Washington, was born during our marriage.

From the first, my wife most earnestly devoted her thoughts and time to the work of the school, and was completely one with me in every interest and ambition. She passed away, however, before she had an opportunity of seeing what the school was designed to be.

# CHAPTER X

## *A Harder Task than Making Bricks Without Straw*

From the very beginning, at Tuskegee, I was determined to have the students do not only the agricultural and domestic work, but to have them erect their own buildings. My plan was to have them, while performing this service, taught the latest and best methods of labour, so that the school would not only get the benefit of their efforts, but the students themselves would be taught to see not only utility in labour, but beauty and dignity; would be taught, in fact, how to lift labour up from mere drudgery and toil, and would learn to love work for its own sake. My plan was not to teach them to work in the old way, but to show them how to make the forces of nature—air, water, steam, electricity, horse-power—assist them in their labour.

At first many advised against the experiment of having the buildings erected by the labour of the students, but I was determined to stick to it. I told those who doubted the wisdom of the plan that I knew that our first buildings would not be so comfortable or so complete in their finish as buildings erected by the experienced hands of outside workmen, but that in the teaching of civilization, self-help, and self-reliance, the erection of buildings by the students themselves would more than compensate for any lack of comfort or fine finish.

I further told those who doubted the wisdom of this plan, that the majority of our students came to us in poverty, from the cabins of the cotton, sugar, and rice plantations of the South, and that while I knew it would please the students very much to place them at once in finely constructed buildings, I felt that it would be following out a more natural process of development to teach them how to construct their own buildings. Mistakes I knew would be made, but these mistakes would teach us valuable lessons for the future.

During the now nineteen years' existence of the Tuskegee school, the plan of having the buildings erected by student labour has been adhered to. In this time forty buildings, counting small and large, have been built, and all except four are almost wholly the product of student labour. As an additional result, hundreds of men are now scattered throughout the South who received their knowledge of mechanics while being taught how to erect these buildings. Skill and knowledge are now handed down from one set of students to another in this way, until at the present time a building of any description or size can be constructed wholly by our instructors and students, from the drawing of the plans to the putting in of the electric fixtures, without going off the grounds for a single workman.

Not a few times, when a new student has been led into the temptation of marring the looks of some building by leadpencil marks or by the cuts of a jack-knife, I have heard an old student remind him: "Don't do that. That is our building. I helped put it up."

In the early days of the school I think my most trying experience was in the matter of brickmaking. As soon as we got the farm work reasonably well started, we directed our next efforts toward the industry of making bricks. We needed these for use in connection with the erection of our own buildings; but there was also another reason for establishing this industry. There was no brickyard in the town, and in addition to our own needs there was a demand for bricks in the general market.

I had always sympathized with the "Children of Israel," in their task of "making bricks without straw," but ours was the task of making bricks with no money and no experience.

In the first place, the work was hard and dirty, and it was difficult to get the students to help. When it came to brickmaking, their distaste for manual labour in connection with book education became especially manifest. It was not a pleasant task for one to stand in the mud-pit for hours, with the mud up to his knees. More than one man became disgusted and left the school.

We tried several locations before we opened up a pit that furnished brick clay. I had always supposed that brickmaking was very simple, but I soon found out by bitter experience that it required special skill and knowledge, particularly in the burning of the bricks. After a good deal of effort we moulded about twenty-five thousand bricks, and put them into a kiln to be burned. This kiln turned out to be a failure, because it was not properly constructed or properly burned. We began at once, however, on a second kiln. This, for some reason, also proved a failure. The failure of this kiln made it still more difficult to get the students to take part in the work. Several of the teachers, however, who had been trained in the industries at Hampton, volunteered their services, and in some way we succeeded in getting a third kiln ready for burning. The burning of a kiln required about a week. Toward the latter part of the week, when it seemed as if we were going to have a good many thousand bricks in a few hours, in the middle of the night the kiln fell. For the third time we had failed.

The failure of this last kiln left me without a single dollar with which to make another experiment. Most of the teachers advised the abandoning of the effort to make bricks. In the midst of my troubles I thought of a watch which had come into my possession years before. I took the watch to the city of Montgomery, which was not far distant, and placed it in a pawn-shop. I secured cash upon it to the amount of fifteen dollars, with which to renew the brickmaking experiment. I returned to Tuskegee, and, with the help of the fifteen dollars, rallied our rather demoralized and discouraged forces and began a fourth attempt to make bricks. This time, I am glad to say, we were successful. Before I got hold of any money, the time-limit on my watch had expired, and I have never seen it since; but I have never regretted the loss of it.

Brickmaking has now become such an important industry at the school that last season our students manufactured twelve hundred thousand of first-class bricks, of a quality suitable to be sold in any market. Aside from this, scores of young men have mastered the brickmaking trade—both the making of bricks by hand and by machinery—and are now engaged in this industry in many parts of the South.

The making of these bricks taught me an important lesson in regard to the relations of the two races in the South. Many white people who had had no contact with the school, and perhaps no sympathy with it, came to us to buy bricks because they found out that ours were good bricks. They discovered that we were supplying a real want in the community. The making of these bricks caused many of the white residents of the neighbourhood to begin to feel that the education of the Negro was not making him worthless, but that in educating our students we were adding something to the wealth and comfort of the community. As the people of the neighbourhood came to us to buy bricks, we got acquainted with them; they traded with us and we with them. Our business interests became intermingled. We had something which they wanted; they had something which we wanted. This, in a large measure, helped to lay the foundation for the pleasant relations that have continued to exist between us and the white people in that section, and which now extend throughout the South.

Wherever one of our brickmakers has gone in the South, we find that he has something to contribute to the well-being of the community into which he has gone; something that has made the community feel that, in a degree, it is indebted to him, and perhaps, to a certain extent, dependent upon him. In this way pleasant relations between the races have been simulated.

My experience is that there is something in human nature which always makes an individual recognize and reward merit, no matter under what colour of skin merit is found. I have found, too, that it is the visible, the tangible, that goes a long ways in softening prejudices. The actual sight of a first-class house that a Negro has built is ten times more potent than pages of discussion about a house that he ought to build, or perhaps could build.

The same principle of industrial education has been carried out in the building of our own wagons, carts, and buggies, from the first. We now own and use on our farm and about the school dozens of these vehicles, and every one of them has been built by the hands of the students. Aside from this, we help supply the local market with these vehicles. The supplying of them to the people in the community has had the same effect as the supplying of bricks, and the man who learns at Tuskegee to build and repair wagons and carts is regarded as a benefactor by both races in the community where he goes. The people with whom he lives and works are going to think twice before they part with such a man.

The individual who can do something that the world wants done will, in the end, make his way regardless of race. One man may go into a community prepared to supply the people there with an analysis of Greek sentences. The community may not at the time be prepared for, or feel the need of, Greek analysis, but it may feel its need of bricks and houses and wagons. If the man can supply the need for those, then, it will lead eventually to a demand for the first product, and with the demand will come the ability to appreciate it and to profit by it.

About the time that we succeeded in burning our first kiln of bricks we began facing in an emphasized form the objection of the students to being taught to work. By this time it had gotten to be pretty well advertised throughout the state that every student who came to Tuskegee, no matter what his financial ability might be, must learn some industry. Quite a number of letters came from parents protesting against their children engaging in labour while they were in the school. Other parents came to the school to protest in person. Most of the new students brought a written or a verbal request from their parents to the effect that they wanted their children taught nothing but books. The more books, the larger they were, and the longer the titles printed upon them, the better pleased the students and their parents seemed to be.

I gave little heed to these protests, except that I lost no opportunity to go into as many parts of the state as I could, for the purpose of speaking to the parents, and showing them the value of industrial education. Besides, I talked to the students constantly on the subject. Notwithstanding the unpopularity of industrial work, the school continued to increase in numbers to such an extent that by the middle of the second year there was an attendance of about one hundred and fifty, representing almost all parts of the state of Alabama, and including a few from other states.

In the summer of 1882 Miss Davidson and I both went North and engaged in the work of raising funds for the completion of our new building. On my way North I stopped in New York to try to get a letter of recommendation from an officer of a missionary organization who had become somewhat acquainted with me a few years previous.

This man not only refused to give me the letter, but advised me most earnestly to go back home at once, and not make any attempt to get money, for he was quite sure that I would never get more than enough to pay my travelling expenses. I thanked him for his advice, and proceeded on my journey.

The first place I went to in the North, was Northampton, Mass., where I spent nearly a half-day in looking for a coloured family with whom I could board, never dreaming that any hotel would admit me. I was greatly surprised when I found that I would have no trouble in being accommodated at a hotel.

We were successful in getting money enough so that on Thanksgiving Day of that year we held our first service in the chapel of Porter Hall, although the building was not completed.

In looking about for some one to preach the Thanksgiving sermon, I found one of the rarest men that it has ever been my privilege to know. This was the Rev. Robert C. Bedford, a white man from Wisconsin, who was then pastor of a little coloured Congregational church in Montgomery, Ala. Before going to Montgomery to look for some one to preach this sermon I had never heard of Mr. Bedford. He had never heard of me. He gladly consented to come to Tuskegee and hold the Thanksgiving service. It was the first service of the kind that the coloured people there had ever observed, and what a deep interest they manifested in it! The sight of the new building made it a day of Thanksgiving for them never to be forgotten.

Mr. Bedford consented to become one of the trustees of the school, and in that capacity, and as a worker for it, he has been connected with it for eighteen years. During this time he has borne the school upon his heart night and day, and is never so happy as when he is performing some service, no matter how humble, for it. He completely obliterates himself in everything, and looks only for permission to serve where service is most disagreeable, and where others would not be attracted. In all my relations with him he has seemed to me to approach as nearly to the spirit of the Master as almost any man I ever met.

A little later there came into the service of the school another man, quite young at the time, and fresh from Hampton, without whose service the school never could have become what it is. This was Mr. Warren Logan, who now for seventeen years has been the treasurer of the Institute, and the acting principal during my absence. He has always shown a degree of unselfishness and an amount of business tact, coupled with a clear judgment, that has kept the school in good condition no matter how long I have been absent from it. During all the financial stress through which the school has passed, his patience and faith in our ultimate success have not left him.

As soon as our first building was near enough to completion so that we could occupy a portion of it—which was near the middle of the second year of the school—we opened a boarding department. Students had begun coming from quite a distance, and in such increasing numbers that we felt more and more that we were merely skimming over the surface, in that we were not getting hold of the students in their home life.

We had nothing but the students and their appetites with which to begin a boarding department. No provision had been made in the new building for a kitchen and dining room; but we discovered that by digging out a large amount of earth from under the building we could make a partially lighted basement room that could be used for a kitchen and dining room. Again I called on the students to volunteer for work, this time to assist in digging out the basement. This they did, and in a few weeks we had a place to cook and eat in, although it was very rough and uncomfortable. Any one seeing the place now would never believe that it was once used for a dining room.

The most serious problem, though, was to get the boarding department started off in running order, with nothing to do with in the way of furniture, and with no money with which to buy anything. The merchants in the town would let us have what food we wanted on credit. In fact, in those earlier years I was constantly embarrassed because people seemed to have more faith in me than I had in myself. It was pretty hard to cook, however, without stoves, and awkward to eat without dishes. At first the cooking was done out-of-doors, in the old-fashioned, primitive style, in pots and skillets placed over a fire. Some of the carpenters' benches that had been used in the construction of the building were utilized for tables. As for dishes, there were too few to make it worth while to spend time in describing them.

No one connected with the boarding department seemed to have any idea that meals must be served at certain fixed and regular hours, and this was a source of great worry. Everything was so out of joint and so inconvenient that I feel safe in saying that for the first two weeks something was wrong at every meal. Either the meat was not done or had been burnt, or the salt had been left out of the bread, or the tea had been forgotten.

Early one morning I was standing near the dining-room door listening to the complaints of the students. The complaints that morning were especially emphatic and numerous, because the whole breakfast had been a failure. One of the girls who had failed to get any breakfast came out and went to the well to draw some water to drink and take the place of the breakfast which she had not been able to get. When she reached the well, she found that the rope was broken and that she could get no water. She turned from the well and said, in the most discouraged tone, not knowing that I was where I could hear her, "We can't even get water to drink at this school." I think no one remark ever came so near discouraging me as that one.

At another time, when Mr. Bedford—whom I have already spoken of as one of our trustees, and a devoted friend of the institution—was visiting the school, he was given a bedroom immediately over the dining room. Early in the morning he was awakened by a rather animated discussion between two boys in the dining room below. The discussion was over the question as to whose turn it was to use the coffee-cup that morning. One boy won the case by proving that for three mornings he had not had an opportunity to use the cup at all.

But gradually, with patience and hard work, we brought order out of chaos, just as will be true of any problem if we stick to it with patience and wisdom and earnest effort.

As I look back now over that part of our struggle, I am glad to see that we had it. I am glad that we endured all those discomforts and inconveniences. I am glad that our students had to dig out the place for their kitchen and dining room. I am glad that our first boarding-place was in the dismal, ill-lighted, and damp basement. Had we started in a fine, attractive, convenient room, I fear we would have "lost our heads" and become "stuck up." It means a great deal, I think, to start off on a foundation which one has made for one's self.

When our old students return to Tuskegee now, as they often do, and go into our large, beautiful, well-ventilated, and well-lighted dining room, and see tempting, well-cooked food—largely grown by the students themselves—and see tables, neat tablecloths and napkins, and vases of flowers upon the tables, and hear singing birds, and note that each meal is served exactly upon the minute, with no disorder, and with almost no complaint coming from the hundreds that now fill our dining room, they, too, often say to me that they are glad that we started as we did, and built ourselves up year by year, by a slow and natural process of growth.

# CHAPTER XI

## *Making Their Beds Before They Could Lie On Them*

A little later in the history of the school we had a visit from General J.F.B. Marshall, the Treasurer of the Hampton Institute, who had had faith enough to lend us the first two hundred and fifty dollars with which to make a payment down on the farm. He remained with us a week, and made a careful inspection of everything. He seemed well pleased with our progress, and wrote back interesting and encouraging reports to Hampton. A little later Miss Mary F. Mackie, the teacher who had given me the "sweeping" examination when I entered Hampton, came to see us, and still later General Armstrong himself came.

At the time of the visits of these Hampton friends the number of teachers at Tuskegee had increase considerably, and the most of the new teachers were graduates of the Hampton Institute. We gave our Hampton friends, especially General Armstrong, a cordial welcome. They were all surprised and pleased at the rapid progress that the school had made within so short a time. The coloured people from miles around came to the school to get a look at General Armstrong, about whom they had heard so much. The General was not only welcomed by the members of my own race, but by the Southern white people as well.

This first visit which General Armstrong made to Tuskegee gave me an opportunity to get an insight into his character such as I had not before had. I refer to his interest in the Southern white people. Before this I had had the thought that General Armstrong, having fought the Southern white man, rather cherished a feeling of bitterness toward the white South, and was interested in helping only the coloured man there. But this visit convinced me that I did not know the greatness and the generosity of the man. I soon learned, by his visits to the Southern white people, and from his conversations with them, that he was as anxious about the prosperity and the happiness of the white race as the black. He cherished no bitterness against the South, and was happy when an opportunity offered for manifesting his sympathy. In all my acquaintance with General Armstrong I never heard him speak, in public or in private, a single bitter word against the white man in the South. From his example in this respect I learned the lesson that great men cultivate love, and that only little men cherish a spirit of hatred. I learned that assistance given to the weak makes the one who gives it strong; and that oppression of the unfortunate makes one weak.

It is now long ago that I learned this lesson from General Armstrong, and resolved that I would permit no man, no matter what his colour might be, to narrow and degrade my soul by making me hate him. With God's help, I believe that I have completely rid myself of any ill feeling toward the Southern white man for any wrong that he may have inflicted upon my race. I am made to feel just as happy now when I am rendering service to Southern white men as when the service is rendered to a member of my own race. I pity from the bottom of my heart any individual who is so unfortunate as to get into the habit of holding race prejudice.

The more I consider the subject, the more strongly I am convinced that the most harmful effect of the practice to which the people in certain sections of the South have felt themselves compelled to resort, in order to get rid of the force of the Negroes' ballot, is not wholly in the wrong done to the Negro, but in the permanent injury to the morals of the white man. The wrong to the Negro is temporary, but to the morals of the white man the injury is permanent. I have noted time and time again that when an individual perjures himself in order to break the force of the black man's ballot, he soon learns to practise dishonesty in other relations of life, not only where the Negro is concerned, but equally so where a white man is concerned. The white man who begins by cheating a Negro usually ends by cheating a white man. The white man who begins to break the law by lynching a Negro soon yields to the temptation to lynch a white man. All this, it seems to me, makes it important that the whole Nation lend a hand in trying to lift the burden of ignorance from the South.

Another thing that is becoming more apparent each year in the development of education in the South is the influence of General Armstrong's idea of education; and this not upon the blacks alone, but upon the whites also. At the present time there is almost no Southern state that is not putting forth efforts in the direction of securing industrial education for its white boys and girls, and in most cases it is easy to trace the history of these efforts back to General Armstrong.

Soon after the opening of our humble boarding department students began coming to us in still larger numbers. For weeks we not only had to contend with the difficulty of providing board, with no money, but also with that of providing sleeping accommodations. For this purpose we rented a number of cabins near the school. These cabins were in a dilapidated condition, and during the winter months the students who occupied them necessarily suffered from the cold. We charge the students eight dollars a month—all they were able to pay—for their board. This included, besides board, room, fuel, and washing. We also gave the students credit on their board bills for all the work which they did for the school which was of any value to the institution. The cost of tuition, which was fifty dollars a year for each student, we had to secure then, as now, wherever we could.

This small charge in cash gave us no capital with which to start a boarding department. The weather during the second winter of our work was very cold. We were not able to provide enough bed-clothes to keep the students warm. In fact, for some time we were not able to provide, except in a few cases, bedsteads and mattresses of any kind. During the coldest nights I was so troubled about the discomfort of the students that I could not sleep myself. I recall that on several occasions I went in the middle of the night to the shanties occupied by the young men, for the purpose of confronting them. Often I found some of them sitting huddled around a fire, with the one blanket which we had been able to provide wrapped around them, trying in this way to keep warm. During the whole night some of them did not attempt to lie down. One morning, when the night previous had been unusually cold, I asked those of the students in the chapel who thought that they had been frostbitten during the night to raise their hands. Three hands went up. Notwithstanding these experiences, there was almost no complaining on the part of the students. They knew that we were doing the best that we could for them. They were happy in the privilege of being permitted to enjoy any kind of opportunity that would enable them to improve their condition. They were constantly asking what they might do to lighten the burdens of the teachers.

I have heard it stated more than once, both in the North and in the South, that coloured people would not obey and respect each other when one member of the race is placed in a position of authority over others. In regard to this general belief and these statements, I can say that during the nineteen years of my experience at Tuskegee I never, either by word or act, have been treated with disrespect by any student or officer connected with the institution. On the other hand, I am constantly embarrassed by the many acts of thoughtful kindness. The students do not seem to want to see me carry a large book or a satchel or any kind of a burden through the grounds. In such cases more than one always offers to relieve me. I almost never go out of my office when the rain is falling that some student does not come to my side with an umbrella and ask to be allowed to hold it over me.

While writing upon this subject, it is a pleasure for me to add that in all my contact with the white people of the South I have never received a single personal insult. The white people in and near Tuskegee, to an especial degree, seem to count it as a privilege to show me all the respect within their power, and often go out of their way to do this.

Not very long ago I was making a journey between Dallas (Texas) and Houston. In some way it became known in advance that I was on the train. At nearly every station at which the train stopped, numbers of white people, including in most cases the officials of the town, came aboard and introduced themselves and thanked me heartily for the work that I was trying to do for the South.

On another occasion, when I was making a trip from Augusta, Georgia, to Atlanta, being rather tired from much travel, I rode in a Pullman sleeper. When I went into the car, I found there two ladies from Boston whom I knew well. These good ladies were perfectly ignorant, it seems, of the customs of the South, and in the goodness of their hearts insisted that I take a seat with them in their section. After some hesitation I consented. I had been there but a few minutes when one of them, without my knowledge, ordered supper to be served for the three of us. This embarrassed me still further. The car was full of Southern white men, most of whom had their eyes on our party. When I found that supper had been ordered, I tried to contrive some excuse that would permit me to leave the section, but the ladies insisted that I must eat with them. I finally settled back in my seat with a sigh, and said to myself, "I am in for it now, sure."

To add further to the embarrassment of the situation, soon after the supper was placed on the table one of the ladies remembered that she had in her satchel a special kind of tea which she wished served, and as she said she felt quite sure the porter did not know how to brew it properly, she insisted upon getting up and preparing and serving it herself. At last the meal was over; and it seemed the longest one that I had ever eaten. When we were through, I decided to get myself out of the embarrassing situation and go to the smoking-room, where most of the men were by that time, to see how the land lay. In the meantime, however, it had become known in some way throughout the car who I was. When I went into the smoking-room I was never more surprised in my life than when each man, nearly every one of them a citizen of Georgia, came up and introduced himself to me and thanked me earnestly for the work that I was trying to do for the whole South. This was not flattery, because each one of these individuals knew that he had nothing to gain by trying to flatter me.

From the first I have sought to impress the students with the idea that Tuskegee is not my institution, or that of the officers, but that it is their institution, and that they have as much interest in it as any of the trustees or instructors. I have further sought to have them feel that I am at the institution as their friend and adviser, and not as their overseer. It has been my aim to have them speak with directness and frankness about anything that concerns the life of the school. Two or three times a year I ask the students to write me a letter criticising or making complaints or suggestions about anything connected with the institution. When this is not done, I have them meet me in the chapel for a heart-to-heart talk about the conduct of the school. There are no meetings with our students that I enjoy more than these, and none are more helpful to me in planning for the future. These meetings, it seems to me, enable me to get at the very heart of all that concerns the school. Few things help an individual more than to place responsibility upon him, and to let him know that you trust him. When I have read of labour troubles between employers and employees, I have often thought that many strikes and similar disturbances might be avoided if the employers would cultivate the habit of getting nearer to their employees, of consulting and advising with them, and letting them feel that the interests of the two are the same. Every individual responds to confidence, and this is not more true of any race than of the Negroes. Let them once understand that you are unselfishly interested in them, and you can lead them to any extent.

It was my aim from the first at Tuskegee to not only have the buildings erected by the students themselves, but to have them make their own furniture as far as was possible. I now marvel at the patience of the students while sleeping upon the floor while waiting for some kind of a bedstead to be constructed, or at their sleeping without any kind of a mattress while waiting for something that looked like a mattress to be made.

In the early days we had very few students who had been used to handling carpenters' tools, and the bedsteads made by the students then were very rough and very weak. Not unfrequently when I went into the students' rooms in the morning I would find at least two bedsteads lying about on the floor. The problem of providing mattresses was a difficult one to solve. We finally mastered this, however, by getting some cheap cloth and sewing pieces of this together as to make large bags. These bags we filled with the pine straw—or, as it is sometimes called, pine needles—which we secured from the forests near by. I am glad to say that the industry of mattress-making has grown steadily since then, and has been improved to such an extent that at the present time it is an important branch of the work which is taught systematically to a number of our girls, and that the mattresses that now come out of the mattress-shop at Tuskegee are about as good as those bought in the average store. For some time after the opening of the boarding department we had no chairs in the students' bedrooms or in the dining rooms. Instead of chairs we used stools which the students constructed by nailing together three pieces of rough board. As a rule, the furniture in the students' rooms during the early days of the school consisted of a bed, some stools, and sometimes a rough table made by the students. The plan of having the students make the furniture is still followed, but the number of pieces in a room has been increased, and the workmanship has so improved that little fault can be found with the articles now. One thing that I have always insisted upon at Tuskegee is that everywhere there should be absolute cleanliness. Over and over again the students were reminded in those first years—and are reminded now—that people would excuse us for our poverty, for our lack of comforts and conveniences, but that they would not excuse us for dirt.

Another thing that has been insisted upon at the school is the use of the tooth-brush. "The gospel of the tooth-brush," as General Armstrong used to call it, is part of our creed at Tuskegee. No student is permitted to remain who does not keep and use a tooth-brush. Several times, in recent years, students have come to us who brought with them almost no other article except a tooth-brush. They had heard from the lips of other students about our insisting upon the use of this, and so, to make a good impression, they brought at least a tooth-brush with them. I remember that one morning, not long ago, I went with the lady principal on her usual morning tour of inspection of the girls' rooms. We found one room that contained three girls who had recently arrived at the school. When I asked them if they had tooth-brushes, one of the girls replied, pointing to a brush: "Yes, sir. That is our brush. We bought it together, yesterday." It did not take them long to learn a different lesson.

It has been interesting to note the effect that the use of the tooth-brush has had in bringing about a higher degree of civilization among the students. With few exceptions, I have noticed that, if we can get a student to the point where, when the first or second tooth-brush disappears, he of his own motion buys another, I have not been disappointed in the future of that individual. Absolute cleanliness of the body has been insisted upon from the first. The students have been taught to bathe as regularly as to take their meals. This lesson we began teaching before we had anything in the shape of a bath-house. Most of the students came from plantation districts, and often we had to teach them how to sleep at night; that is, whether between the two sheets—after we got to the point where we could provide them two sheets—or under both of them. Naturally I found it difficult to teach them to sleep between two sheets when we were able to supply but one. The importance of the use of the nightgown received the same attention.

For a long time one of the most difficult tasks was to teach the students that all the buttons were to be kept on their clothes, and that there must be no torn places or grease-spots. This lesson, I am pleased to be able to say, has been so thoroughly learned and so faithfully handed down from year to year by one set of students to another that often at the present time, when the students march out of the chapel in the evening and their dress is inspected, as it is every night, not one button is found to be missing.

# CHAPTER XII

## *Raising Money*

When we opened our boarding department, we provided rooms in the attic of Porter Hall, our first building, for a number of girls. But the number of students, of both sexes, continued to increase. We could find rooms outside the school grounds for many of the young men, but the girls we did not care to expose in this way. Very soon the problem of providing more rooms for the girls, as well as a larger boarding department for all the students, grew serious. As a result, we finally decided to undertake the construction of a still larger building—a building that would contain rooms for the girls and boarding accommodations for all.

After having had a preliminary sketch of the needed building made, we found that it would cost about ten thousand dollars. We had no money whatever with which to begin; still we decided to give the needed building a name. We knew we could name it, even though we were in doubt about our ability to secure the means for its construction. We decided to call the proposed building Alabama Hall, in honour of the state in which we were labouring. Again Miss Davidson began making efforts to enlist the interest and help of the coloured and white people in and near Tuskegee. They responded willingly, in proportion to their means. The students, as in the case of our first building, Porter Hall, began digging out the dirt in order to allow the laying of the foundations.

When we seemed at the end of our resources, so far as securing money was concerned, something occurred which showed the greatness of General Armstrong—something which proved how far he was above the ordinary individual. When we were in the midst of great anxiety as to where and how we were to get funds for the new building, I received a telegram from General Armstrong asking me if I could spend a month travelling with him through the North, and asking me, if I could do so, to come to Hampton at once. Of course I accepted General Armstrong's invitation, and went to Hampton immediately. On arriving there I found that the General had decided to take a quartette of singers through the North, and hold meetings for a month in important cities, at which meetings he and I were to speak. Imagine my surprise when the General told me, further, that these meetings were to be held, not in the interests of Hampton, but in the interests of Tuskegee, and that the Hampton Institute was to be responsible for all the expenses.

Although he never told me so in so many words, I found that General Armstrong took this method of introducing me to the people of the North, as well as for the sake of securing some immediate funds to be used in the erection of Alabama Hall. A weak and narrow man would have reasoned that all the money which came to Tuskegee in this way would be just so much taken from the Hampton Institute; but none of these selfish or short-sighted feelings ever entered the breast of General Armstrong. He was too big to be little, too good to be mean. He knew that the people in the North who gave money gave it for the purpose of helping the whole cause of Negro civilization, and not merely for the advancement of any one school. The General knew, too, that the way to strengthen Hampton was to make it a centre of unselfish power in the working out of the whole Southern problem.

In regard to the addresses which I was to make in the North, I recall just one piece of advice which the General gave me. He said: "Give them an idea for every word." I think it would be hard to improve upon this advice; and it might be made to apply to all public speaking. From that time to the present I have always tried to keep his advice in mind.

Meetings were held in New York, Brooklyn, Boston, Philadelphia, and other large cities, and at all of these meetings General Armstrong pleaded, together with myself, for help, not for Hampton, but for Tuskegee. At these meetings an especial effort was made to secure help for the building of Alabama Hall, as well as to introduce the school to the attention of the general public. In both these respects the meetings proved successful.

After that kindly introduction I began going North alone to secure funds. During the last fifteen years I have been compelled to spend a large proportion of my time away from the school, in an effort to secure money to provide for the growing needs of the institution. In my efforts to get funds I have had some experiences that may be of interest to my readers. Time and time again I have been asked, by people who are trying to secure money for philanthropic purposes, what rule or rules I followed to secure the interest and help of people who were able to contribute money to worthy objects. As far as the science of what is called begging can be reduced to rules, I would say that I have had but two rules. First, always to do my whole duty regarding making our work known to individuals and organizations; and, second, not to worry about the results. This second rule has been the hardest for me to live up to. When bills are on the eve of falling due, with not a dollar in hand with which to meet them, it is pretty difficult to learn not to worry, although I think I am learning more and more each year that all worry simply consumes, and to no purpose, just so much physical and mental strength that might otherwise be given to effective work. After considerable experience in coming into contact with wealthy and noted men, I have observed that those who have accomplished the greatest results are those who "keep under the body"; are those who never grow excited or lose self-control, but are always calm, self-possessed, patient, and polite. I think that President William McKinley is the best example of a man of this class that I have ever seen.

In order to be successful in any kind of undertaking, I think the main thing is for one to grow to the point where he completely forgets himself; that is, to lose himself in a great cause. In proportion as one loses himself in the way, in the same degree does he get the highest happiness out of his work.

My experience in getting money for Tuskegee has taught me to have no patience with those people who are always condemning the rich because they are rich, and because they do not give more to objects of charity. In the first place, those who are guilty of such sweeping criticisms do not know how many people would be made poor, and how much suffering would result, if wealthy people were to part all at once with any large proportion of their wealth in a way to disorganize and cripple great business enterprises. Then very few persons have any idea of the large number of applications for help that rich people are constantly being flooded with. I know wealthy people who receive as much as twenty calls a day for help. More than once when I have gone into the offices of rich men, I have found half a dozen persons waiting to see them, and all come for the same purpose, that of securing money. And all these calls in person, to say nothing of the applications received through the mails. Very few people have any idea of the amount of money given away by persons who never permit their names to be known. I have often heard persons condemned for not giving away money, who, to my own knowledge, were giving away thousands of dollars every year so quietly that the world knew nothing about it.

As an example of this, there are two ladies in New York, whose names rarely appear in print, but who, in a quiet way, have given us the means with which to erect three large and important buildings during the last eight years. Besides the gift of these buildings, they have made other generous donations to the school. And they not only help Tuskegee, but they are constantly seeking opportunities to help other worthy causes.

Although it has been my privilege to be the medium through which a good many hundred thousand dollars have been received for the work at Tuskegee, I have always avoided what the world calls "begging." I often tell people that I have never "begged" any money, and that I am not a "beggar." My experience and observation have convinced me that persistent asking outright for money from the rich does not, as a rule, secure help. I have usually proceeded on the principle that persons who possess sense enough to earn money have sense enough to know how to give it away, and that the mere making known of the facts regarding Tuskegee, and especially the facts regarding the work of the graduates, has been more effective than outright begging. I think that the presentation of facts, on a high, dignified plane, is all the begging that most rich people care for.

While the work of going from door to door and from office to office is hard, disagreeable, and costly in bodily strength, yet it has some compensations. Such work gives one a rare opportunity to study human nature. It also has its compensations in giving one an opportunity to meet some of the best people in the world—to be more correct, I think I should say *the best* people in the world. When one takes a broad survey of the country, he will find that the most useful and influential people in it are those who take the deepest interest in institutions that exist for the purpose of making the world better.

At one time, when I was in Boston, I called at the door of a rather wealthy lady, and was admitted to the vestibule and sent up my card. While I was waiting for an answer, her husband came in, and asked me in the most abrupt manner what I wanted. When I tried to explain the object of my call, he became still more ungentlemanly in his words and manner; and finally grew so excited that I left the house without waiting for a reply from the lady. A few blocks from that house I called to see a gentleman who received me in the most cordial manner. He wrote me his check for a generous sum, and then, before I had had an opportunity to thank him, said: "I am so grateful to you, Mr. Washington, for giving me the opportunity to help a good cause. It is a privilege to have a share in it. We in Boston are constantly indebted to you for doing *our* work." My experience in securing money convinces me that the first type of man is growing more rare all the time, and that the latter type is increasing; that is, that, more and more, rich people are coming to regard men and women who apply to them for help for worthy objects, not as beggars, but as agents for doing their work.

In the city of Boston I have rarely called upon an individual for funds that I have not been thanked for calling, usually before I could get an opportunity to thank the donor for the money. In that city the donors seem to feel, in a large degree, that an honour is being conferred upon them in their being permitted to give. Nowhere else have I met with, in so large a measure, this fine and Christlike spirit as in the city of Boston, although there are many notable instances of it outside that city. I repeat my belief that the world is growing in the direction of giving. I repeat that the main rule by which I have been guided in collecting money is to do my full duty in regard to giving people who have money an opportunity for help.

In the early years of the Tuskegee school I walked the streets or travelled country roads in the North for days and days without receiving a dollar. Often as it happened, when during the week I had been disappointed in not getting a cent from the very individuals from whom I most expected help, and when I was almost broken down and discouraged, that generous help has come from some one who I had had little idea would give at all.

I recall that on one occasion I obtained information that led me to believe that a gentleman who lived about two miles out in the country from Stamford, Conn., might become interest in our efforts at Tuskegee if our conditions and needs were presented to him. On an unusually cold and stormy day I walked the two miles to see him. After some difficulty I succeeded in securing an interview with him. He listened with some degree of interest to what I had to say, but did not give me anything. I could not help having the feeling that, in a measure, the three hours that I had spent in seeing him had been thrown away. Still, I had followed my usual rule of doing my duty. If I had not seen him, I should have felt unhappy over neglect of duty.

Two years after this visit a letter came to Tuskegee from this man, which read like this: "Enclosed I send you a New York draft for ten thousand dollars, to be used in furtherance of your work. I had placed this sum in my will for your school, but deem it wiser to give it to you while I live. I recall with pleasure your visit to me two years ago."

I can hardly imagine any occurrence which could have given me more genuine satisfaction than the receipt of this draft. It was by far the largest single donation which up to that time the school had ever received. It came at a time when an unusually long period had passed since we had received any money. We were in great distress because of lack of funds, and the nervous strain was tremendous. It is difficult for me to think of any situation that is more trying on the nerves than that of conducting a large institution, with heavy obligations to meet, without knowing where the money is to come from to meet these obligations from month to month.

In our case I felt a double responsibility, and this made the anxiety all the more intense. If the institution had been officered by white persons, and had failed, it would have injured the cause of Negro education; but I knew that the failure of our institution, officered by

Negroes, would not only mean the loss of a school, but would cause people, in a large degree, to lose faith in the ability of the entire race. The receipt of this draft for ten thousand dollars, under all these circumstances, partially lifted a burden that had been pressing down upon me for days.

From the beginning of our work to the present I have always had the feeling, and lose no opportunity to impress our teachers with the same idea, that the school will always be supported in proportion as the inside of the institution is kept clean and pure and wholesome.

The first time I ever saw the late Collis P. Huntington, the great railroad man, he gave me two dollars for our school. The last time I saw him, which was a few months before he died, he gave me fifty thousand dollars toward our endowment fund. Between these two gifts there were others of generous proportions which came every year from both Mr. and Mrs. Huntington.

Some people may say that it was Tuskegee's good luck that brought to us this gift of fifty thousand dollars. No, it was not luck. It was hard work. Nothing ever comes to me, that is worth having, except as the result of hard work. When Mr. Huntington gave me the first two dollars, I did not blame him for not giving me more, but made up my mind that I was going to convince him by tangible results that we were worthy of larger gifts. For a dozen years I made a strong effort to convince Mr. Huntington of the value of our work. I noted that just in proportion as the usefulness of the school grew, his donations increased. Never did I meet an individual who took a more kindly and sympathetic interest in our school than did Mr. Huntington. He not only gave money to us, but took time in which to advise me, as a father would a son, about the general conduct of the school.

More than once I have found myself in some pretty tight places while collecting money in the North. The following incident I have never related but once before, for the reason that I feared that people would not believe it. One morning I found myself in Providence, Rhode Island, without a cent of money with which to buy breakfast. In crossing the street to see a lady from whom I hoped to get some money, I found a bright new twenty-five-cent piece in the middle of the street track. I not only had this twenty-five cents for my breakfast, but within a few minutes I had a donation from the lady on whom I had started to call.

At one of our Commencements I was bold enough to invite the Rev. E. Winchester Donald, D.D., rector of Trinity Church, Boston, to preach the Commencement sermon. As we then had no room large enough to accommodate all who would be present, the place of meeting was under a large improvised arbour, built partly of brush and partly of rough boards. Soon after Dr. Donald had begun speaking, the rain came down in torrents, and he had to stop, while some one held an umbrella over him.

The boldness of what I had done never dawned upon me until I saw the picture made by the rector of Trinity Church standing before that large audience under an old umbrella, waiting for the rain to cease so that he could go on with his address.

It was not very long before the rain ceased and Dr. Donald finished his sermon; and an excellent sermon it was, too, in spite of the weather. After he had gone to his room, and had gotten the wet threads of his clothes dry, Dr. Donald ventured the remark that a large chapel at Tuskegee would not be out of place. The next day a letter came from two ladies who were then travelling in Italy, saying that they had decided to give us the money for such a chapel as we needed.

A short time ago we received twenty thousand dollars from Mr. Andrew Carnegie, to be used for the purpose of erecting a new library building. Our first library and reading-room were in a corner of a shanty, and the whole thing occupied a space about five by twelve feet. It required ten years of work before I was able to secure Mr. Carnegie's interest and help. The first time I saw him, ten years ago, he seemed to take but little interest in our school, but I was determined to show him that we were worthy of his help. After ten years of hard work I wrote him a letter reading as follows:

December 15, 1900.

Mr. Andrew Carnegie, 5 W. Fifty-first St., New York.

Dear Sir: Complying with the request which you made of me when I saw you at your residence a few days ago, I now submit in writing an appeal for a library building for our institution.

We have 1100 students, 86 officers and instructors, together with their families, and about 200 coloured people living near the school, all of whom would make use of the library building.

We have over 12,000 books, periodicals, etc., gifts from our friends, but we have no suitable place for them, and we have no suitable reading-room.

Our graduates go to work in every section of the South, and whatever knowledge might be obtained in the library would serve to assist in the elevation of the whole Negro race.

Such a building as we need could be erected for about $20,000. All of the work for the building, such as brickmaking, brick-masonry, carpentry, blacksmithing, etc., would be done by the students. The money which you would give would not only supply the building, but the erection of the building would give a large number of students an opportunity to learn the building trades, and the students would use the money paid to them to keep themselves in school. I do not believe that a similar amount of money often could be made go so far in uplifting a whole race.

If you wish further information, I shall be glad to furnish it.

Yours truly,
Booker T. Washington, Principal.

The next mail brought back the following reply: "I will be very glad to pay the bills for the library building as they are incurred, to the extent of twenty thousand dollars, and I am glad of this opportunity to show the interest I have in your noble work."

I have found that strict business methods go a long way in securing the interest of rich people. It has been my constant aim at Tuskegee to carry out, in our financial and other operations, such business methods as would be approved of by any New York banking house.

I have spoken of several large gifts to the school; but by far the greater proportion of the money that has built up the institution has come in the form of small donations from persons of moderate means. It is upon these small gifts, which carry with them the interest of hundreds of donors, that any philanthropic work must depend largely for its support. In my efforts to get money I have often been surprised at the patience and deep interest of the ministers, who are besieged on every hand and at all hours of the day for help. If no other consideration had convinced me of the value of the Christian life, the Christlike work which the Church of all denominations in America has done during the last thirty-five years for the elevation of the black man would have made me a Christian. In a large degree it has been the pennies, the nickels, and the dimes which have come from the Sunday-schools, the Christian Endeavour societies, and the missionary societies, as well as from the church proper, that have helped to elevate the Negro at so rapid a rate.

This speaking of small gifts reminds me to say that very few Tuskegee graduates fail to send us an annual contribution. These contributions range from twenty-five cents up to ten dollars.

Soon after beginning our third year's work we were surprised to receive money from three special sources, and up to the present time we have continued to receive help from them. First, the State Legislature of Alabama increased its annual appropriation from two thousand dollars to three thousand dollars; I might add that still later it increased this sum to four thousand five hundred dollars a year. The effort to secure this increase was led by the Hon. M.F. Foster, the member of the Legislature from Tuskegee. Second, we received one thousand dollars from the John F. Slater Fund. Our work seemed to please the trustees of this fund, as they soon began increasing their annual grant. This has been added to from time to time until at present we receive eleven thousand dollars annually from the Fund. The other help to which I have referred came in the shape of an allowance from the Peabody Fund. This was at first five hundred dollars, but it has since been increased to fifteen hundred dollars.

The effort to secure help from the Slater and Peabody Funds brought me into contact with two rare men—men who have had much to do in shaping the policy for the education of the Negro. I refer to the Hon. J.L.M. Curry, of Washington, who is the general agent for these two funds, and Mr. Morris K. Jesup, of New York. Dr. Curry is a native of the South, an ex-Confederate soldier, yet I do not believe there is any man in the country who is more deeply interest in the highest welfare of the Negro than Dr. Curry, or one who is more free from race prejudice. He enjoys the unique distinction of possessing to an equal degree the confidence of the black man and the Southern white man. I shall never forget the first time I met him. It was in Richmond, Va., where he was then living. I had heard much about him. When I first went into his presence, trembling because of my youth and inexperience, he took me by the hand so cordially, and spoke such encouraging words, and gave me such helpful advice regarding the proper course to pursue, that I came to know him then, as I have known him ever since, as a high example of one who is constantly and unselfishly at work for the betterment of humanity.

Mr. Morris K. Jesup, the treasurer of the Slater Fund, I refer to because I know of no man of wealth and large and complication business responsibilities who gives not only money but his time and thought to the subject of the proper method of elevating the Negro to the extent that is true of Mr. Jesup. It is very largely through this effort and influence that during the last few years the subject of industrial education has assumed the importance that it has, and been placed on its present footing.

# CHAPTER XIII

## *Two Thousand Miles for a Five-Minute Speech*

Soon after the opening of our boarding department, quite a number of students who evidently were worthy, but who were so poor that they did not have any money to pay even the small charges at the school, began applying for admission. This class was composed of both men and women. It was a great trial to refuse admission to these applicants, and in 1884 we established a night-school to accommodate a few of them.

The night-school was organized on a plan similar to the one which I had helped to establish at Hampton. At first it was composed of about a dozen students. They were admitted to the night-school only when they had no money with which to pay any part of their board in the regular day-school. It was further required that they must work for ten hours during the day at some trade or industry, and study academic branches for two hours during the evening. This was the requirement for the first one or two years of their stay. They were to be paid something above the cost of their board, with the understanding that all of their earnings, except a very small part, were to be reserved in the school's treasury, to be used for paying their board in the regular day-school after they had entered that department. The night-school, started in this manner, has grown until there are at present four hundred and fifty-seven students enrolled in it alone.

There could hardly be a more severe test of a student's worth than this branch of the Institute's worth. It is largely because it furnishes such a good opportunity to test the backbone of a student that I place such high value upon our night-school. Any one who is willing to work ten hours a day at the brick-yard, or in the laundry, through one or two years, in order that he or she may have the privilege of studying academic branches for two hours in the evening, has enough bottom to warrant being further educated.

After the student has left the night-school he enters the day-school, where he takes academic branches four days in a week, and works at his trade two days. Besides this he usually works at his trade during the three summer months. As a rule, after a student has succeeded in going through the night-school test, he finds a way to finish the regular course in industrial and academic training. No student, no matter how much money he may be able to command, is permitted to go through school without doing manual labour. In fact, the industrial work is now as popular as the academic branches. Some of the most successful men and women who have graduated from the institution obtained their start in the night-school.

While a great deal of stress is laid upon the industrial side of the work at Tuskegee, we do not neglect or overlook in any degree the religious and spiritual side. The school is strictly undenominational, but it is thoroughly Christian, and the spiritual training or the students is not neglected. Our preaching service, prayer-meetings, Sunday-school, Christian Endeavour Society, Young Men's Christian Association, and various missionary organizations, testify to this.

In 1885, Miss Olivia Davidson, to whom I have already referred as being largely responsible for the success of the school during its early history, and I were married. During our married life she continued to divide her time and strength between our home and the work for the school. She not only continued to work in the school at Tuskegee, but also kept up her habit of going North to secure funds. In 1889 she died, after four years of happy married life and eight years of hard and happy work for the school. She literally wore herself out in her never ceasing efforts in behalf of the work that she so dearly loved. During our married life there were born to us two bright, beautiful boys, Booker Taliaferro and Ernest Davidson. The older of these, Booker, has already mastered the brick-maker's trade at Tuskegee.

I have often been asked how I began the practice of public speaking. In answer I would say that I never planned to give any large part of my life to speaking in public. I have always had more of an ambition to *do* things than merely to talk *about* doing them. It seems that when I went North with General Armstrong to speak at the series of public meetings to which I have referred, the President of the National Educational Association, the Hon. Thomas W. Bicknell, was present at one of those meetings and heard me speak. A few days afterward he sent me an invitation to deliver an address at the next meeting of the Educational Association. This meeting was to be held in Madison, Wis. I accepted the invitation. This was, in a sense, the beginning of my public-speaking career.

On the evening that I spoke before the Association there must have been not far from four thousand persons present. Without my knowing it, there were a large number of people present from Alabama, and some from the town of Tuskegee. These white people afterward frankly told me that they went to this meeting expecting to hear the South roundly abused, but were pleasantly surprised to find that there was no word of abuse in my address. On the contrary, the South was given credit for all the praiseworthy things that it had done. A white lady who was teacher in a college in Tuskegee wrote back to the local paper that she was gratified, as well as surprised, to note the credit which I gave the white people of Tuskegee for their help in getting the school started. This address at Madison was the first that I had delivered that in any large measure dealt with the general problem of the races. Those who heard it seemed to be pleased with what I said and with the general position that I took.

When I first came to Tuskegee, I determined that I would make it my home, that I would take as much pride in the right actions of the people of the town as any white man could do, and that I would, at the same time, deplore the wrong-doing of the people as much as any white man. I determined never to say anything in a public address in the North that I would not be willing to say in the South. I early learned that it is a hard matter to convert an individual by abusing him, and that this is more often accomplished by giving credit for all the praiseworthy actions performed than by calling attention alone to all the evil done.

While pursuing this policy I have not failed, at the proper time and in the proper manner, to call attention, in no uncertain terms, to the wrongs which any part of the South has been guilty of. I have found that there is a large element in the South that is quick to respond to straightforward, honest criticism of any wrong policy. As a rule, the place to criticise the South, when criticism is necessary, is in the South—not in Boston. A Boston man who came to Alabama to criticise Boston would not effect so much good, I think, as one who had his word of criticism to say in Boston.

In this address at Madison I took the ground that the policy to be pursued with references to the races was, by every honourable means, to bring them together and to encourage the cultivation of friendly relations, instead of doing that which would embitter. I further contended that, in relation to his vote, the Negro should more and more consider the interests of the community in which he lived, rather than seek alone to please some one who lived a thousand miles away from him and from his interests.

In this address I said that the whole future of the Negro rested largely upon the question as to whether or not he should make himself, through his skill, intelligence, and character, of such undeniable value to the community in which he lived that the community could not dispense with his presence. I said that any individual who learned to do something better than anybody else—learned to do a common thing in an uncommon manner—had solved his problem, regardless of the colour of his skin, and that in proportion as the Negro learned to produce what other people wanted and must have, in the same proportion would he be respected.

I spoke of an instance where one of our graduates had produced two hundred and sixty-six bushels of sweet potatoes from an acre of ground, in a community where the average production had been only forty-nine bushels to the acre. He had been able to do this by reason of his knowledge of the chemistry of the soil and by his knowledge of improved methods of agriculture. The white farmers in the neighbourhood respected him, and came to him for ideas regarding the raising of sweet potatoes. These white farmers honoured and respected him because he, by his skill and knowledge, had added something to the wealth and the comfort of the community in which he lived. I explained that my theory of education for the Negro would not, for example, confine him for all time to farm life—to the production of the best and the most sweet potatoes—but that, if he succeeded in this line of industry, he could lay the foundations upon which his children and grandchildren could grow to higher and more important things in life.

Such, in brief, were some of the views I advocated in this first address dealing with the broad question of the relations of the two races, and since that time I have not found any reason for changing my views on any important point.

In my early life I used to cherish a feeling of ill will toward any one who spoke in bitter terms against the Negro, or who advocated measures that tended to oppress the black man or take from him opportunities for growth in the most complete manner. Now, whenever I hear any one advocating measures that are meant to curtail the development of another, I pity the individual who would do this. I know that the one who makes this mistake does so because of his own lack of opportunity for the highest kind of growth. I pity him because I know that he is trying to stop the progress of the world, and because I know that in time the development and the ceaseless advance of humanity will make him ashamed of his weak and narrow position. One might as well try to stop the progress of a mighty railroad train by throwing his body across the track, as to try to stop the growth of the world in the direction of giving mankind more intelligence, more culture, more skill, more liberty, and in the direction of extending more sympathy and more brotherly kindness.

The address which I delivered at Madison, before the National Educational Association, gave me a rather wide introduction in the North, and soon after that opportunities began offering themselves for me to address audiences there.

I was anxious, however, that the way might also be opened for me to speak directly to a representative Southern white audience. A partial opportunity of this kind, one that seemed to me might serve as an entering wedge, presented itself in 1893, when the international meeting of Christian Workers was held at Atlanta, Ga. When this invitation came to me, I had engagements in Boston that seemed to make it impossible for me to speak in Atlanta. Still, after looking over my list of dates and places carefully, I found that I could take a train from Boston that would get me into Atlanta about thirty minutes before my address was to be delivered, and that I could remain in that city before taking another train for Boston. My invitation to speak in Atlanta stipulated that I was to confine my address to five minutes. The question, then, was whether or not I could put enough into a five-minute address to make it worth while for me to make such a trip.

I knew that the audience would be largely composed of the most influential class of white men and women, and that it would be a rare opportunity for me to let them know what we were trying to do at Tuskegee, as well as to speak to them about the relations of the races. So I decided to make the trip. I spoke for five minutes to an audience of two thousand people, composed mostly of Southern and Northern whites. What I said seemed to be received with favour and enthusiasm. The Atlanta papers of the next day commented in friendly terms on my address, and a good deal was said about it in different parts of the country. I felt that I had in some degree accomplished my object—that of getting a hearing from the dominant class of the South.

The demands made upon me for public addresses continued to increase, coming in about equal numbers from my own people and from Northern whites. I gave as much time to these addresses as I could spare from the immediate work at Tuskegee. Most of the addresses in the North were made for the direct purpose of getting funds with which to support the school. Those delivered before the coloured people had for their main object the impressing upon them the importance of industrial and technical education in addition to academic and religious training.

I now come to that one of the incidents in my life which seems to have excited the greatest amount of interest, and which perhaps went farther than anything else in giving me a reputation that in a sense might be called National. I refer to the address which I delivered at the opening of the Atlanta Cotton states and International Exposition, at Atlanta, Ga., September 18, 1895.

So much has been said and written about this incident, and so many questions have been asked me concerning the address, that perhaps I may be excused for taking up the matter with some detail. The five-minute address in Atlanta, which I came from Boston to deliver, was possibly the prime cause for an opportunity being given me to make the second address there. In the spring of 1895 I received a telegram from prominent citizens in Atlanta asking me to accompany a committee from that city to Washington for the purpose of appearing before a committee of Congress in the interest of securing Government help for the Exposition. The committee was composed of about twenty-five of the most prominent and most influential white men of Georgia. All the members of this committee were white men except Bishop Grant, Bishop Gaines, and myself. The Mayor and several other city and state officials spoke before the committee. They were followed by the two coloured bishops. My name was the last on the list of speakers. I had never before appeared before such a committee, nor had I ever delivered any address in the capital of the Nation. I had many misgivings as to what I ought to say, and as to the impression that my address would make. While I cannot recall in detail what I said, I remember that I tried to impress upon the committee, with all the earnestness and plainness of any language that I could command, that if Congress wanted to do something which would assist in ridding the South of the race question and making friends between the two races, it should, in every proper way, encourage the material and intellectual growth of both races. I said that the Atlanta Exposition would present an opportunity for both races to show what advance they had made since freedom, and would at the same time afford encouragement to them to make still greater progress.

I tried to emphasize the fact that while the Negro should not be deprived by unfair means of the franchise, political agitation alone would not save him, and that back of the ballot he must have property, industry, skill, economy, intelligence, and character, and that no race without these elements could permanently succeed. I said that in granting the appropriation Congress could do something that would prove to be of real and lasting value to both races, and that it was the first great opportunity of the kind that had been presented since the close of the Civil War.

I spoke for fifteen or twenty minutes, and was surprised at the close of my address to receive the hearty congratulations of the Georgia committee and of the members of Congress who were present. The Committee was unanimous in making a favourable report, and in a few days the bill passed Congress. With the passing of this bill the success of the Atlanta Exposition was assured.

Soon after this trip to Washington the directors of the Exposition decided that it would be a fitting recognition of the coloured race to erect a large and attractive building which should be devoted wholly to showing the progress of the Negro since freedom. It was further decided to have the building designed and erected wholly by Negro mechanics. This plan was carried out. In design, beauty, and general finish the Negro Building was equal to the others on the grounds.

After it was decided to have a separate Negro exhibit, the question arose as to who should take care of it. The officials of the Exposition were anxious that I should assume this responsibility, but I declined to do so, on the plea that the work at Tuskegee at that time demanded my time and strength. Largely at my suggestion, Mr. I. Garland Penn, of Lynchburg, Va., was selected to be at the head of the Negro department. I gave him all the aid that I could. The Negro exhibit, as a whole, was large and creditable. The two exhibits in this department which attracted the greatest amount of attention were those from the Hampton Institute and the Tuskegee Institute. The people who seemed to be the most surprised, as well as pleased, at what they saw in the Negro Building were the Southern white people.

As the day for the opening of the Exposition drew near, the Board of Directors began preparing the programme for the opening exercises. In the discussion from day to day of the various features of this programme, the question came up as to the advisability of putting a member of the Negro race on for one of the opening addresses, since the Negroes had been asked to take such a prominent part in the Exposition. It was argued, further, that such recognition would mark the good feeling prevailing between the two races. Of course there were those who were opposed to any such recognition of the rights of the Negro, but the Board of Directors, composed of men who represented the best and most progressive element in the South, had their way, and voted to invite a black man to speak on the opening day. The next thing was to decide upon the person who was thus to represent the Negro race. After the question had been canvassed for several days, the directors voted unanimously to ask me to deliver one of the opening-day addresses, and in a few days after that I received the official invitation.

The receiving of this invitation brought to me a sense of responsibility that it would be hard for any one not placed in my position to appreciate. What were my feelings when this invitation came to me? I remembered that I had been a slave; that my early years had been spent in the lowest depths of poverty and ignorance, and that I had had little opportunity to prepare me for such a responsibility as this. It was only a few years before that time that any white man in the audience might have claimed me as his slave; and it was easily possible that some of my former owners might be present to hear me speak.

I knew, too, that this was the first time in the entire history of the Negro that a member of my race had been asked to speak from the same platform with white Southern men and women on any important National occasion. I was asked now to speak to an audience composed of the wealth and culture of the white South, the representatives of my former masters. I knew, too, that while the greater part of my audience would be composed of Southern people, yet there would be present a large number of Northern whites, as well as a great many men and women of my own race.

I was determined to say nothing that I did not feel from the bottom of my heart to be true and right. When the invitation came to me, there was not one word of intimation as to what I should say or as to what I should omit. In this I felt that the Board of Directors had paid a tribute to me. They knew that by one sentence I could have blasted, in a large degree, the success of the Exposition. I was also painfully conscious of the fact that, while I must be true to my own race in my utterances, I had it in my power to make such an ill-timed address as would result in preventing any similar invitation being extended to a black man again for years to come. I was equally determined to be true to the North, as well as to the best element of the white South, in what I had to say.

The papers, North and South, had taken up the discussion of my coming speech, and as the time for it drew near this discussion became more and more widespread. Not a few of the Southern white papers were unfriendly to the idea of my speaking. From my own race I received many suggestions as to what I ought to say. I prepared myself as best I could for the address, but as the eighteenth of September drew nearer, the heavier my heart became, and the more I feared that my effort would prove a failure and a disappointment.

The invitation had come at a time when I was very busy with my school work, as it was the beginning of our school year. After preparing my address, I went through it, as I usually do with those utterances which I consider particularly important, with Mrs. Washington, and she approved of what I intended to say. On the sixteenth of September, the day before I was to start for Atlanta, so many of the Tuskegee teachers expressed a desire to hear my address that I consented to read it to them in a body. When I had done so, and had heard their criticisms and comments, I felt somewhat relieved, since they seemed to think well of what I had to say.

On the morning of September 17, together with Mrs. Washington and my three children, I started for Atlanta. I felt a good deal as I suppose a man feels when he is on his way to the gallows. In passing through the town of Tuskegee I met a white farmer who lived some distance out in the country. In a jesting manner this man said: "Washington, you have spoken before the Northern white people, the Negroes in the South, and to us country white people in the South; but Atlanta, to-morrow, you will have before you the Northern whites, the Southern whites, and the Negroes all together. I am afraid that you have got yourself in a tight place." This farmer diagnosed the situation correctly, but his frank words did not add anything to my comfort.

In the course of the journey from Tuskegee to Atlanta both coloured and white people came to the train to point me out, and discussed with perfect freedom, in my hearings, what was going to take place the next day. We were met by a committee in Atlanta. Almost the first thing that I heard when I got off the train in that city was an expression something like this, from an old coloured man near by: "Dat's de man of my race what's gwine to make a speech at de Exposition to-morrow. I'se sho' gwine to hear him."

Atlanta was literally packed, at the time, with people from all parts of the country, and with representatives of foreign governments, as well as with military and civic organizations. The afternoon papers had forecasts of the next day's proceedings in flaring headlines. All this tended to add to my burden. I did not sleep much that night. The next morning, before day, I went carefully over what I planned to say. I also kneeled down and asked God's blessing upon my effort. Right here, perhaps, I ought to add that I make it a rule never to go before an audience, on any occasion, without asking the blessing of God upon what I want to say.

I always make it a rule to make especial preparation for each separate address. No two audiences are exactly alike. It is my aim to reach and talk to the heart of each individual audience, taking it into my confidence very much as I would a person. When I am speaking to an audience, I care little for how what I am saying is going to sound in the newspapers, or to another audience, or to an individual. At the time, the audience before me absorbs all my sympathy, thought, and energy.

Early in the morning a committee called to escort me to my place in the procession which was to march to the Exposition grounds. In this procession were prominent coloured citizens in carriages, as well as several Negro military organizations. I noted that the Exposition officials seemed to go out of their way to see that all of the coloured people in the procession were properly placed and properly treated. The procession was about three hours in reaching the Exposition grounds, and during all of this time the sun was shining down upon us disagreeably hot. When we reached the grounds, the heat, together with my nervous anxiety, made me feel as if I were about ready to collapse, and to feel that my address was not going to be a success. When I entered the audience-room, I found it packed with humanity from bottom to top, and there were thousands outside who could not get in.

The room was very large, and well suited to public speaking. When I entered the room, there were vigorous cheers from the coloured portion of the audience, and faint cheers from some of the white people. I had been told, while I had been in Atlanta, that while many white people were going to be present to hear me speak, simply out of curiosity, and that others who would be present would be in full sympathy with me, there was a still larger element of the audience which would consist of those who were going to be present for the purpose of hearing me make a fool of myself, or, at least, of hearing me say some foolish thing so that they could say to the officials who had invited me to speak, "I told you so!"

One of the trustees of the Tuskegee Institute, as well as my personal friend, Mr. William H. Baldwin, Jr., was at the time General Manager of the Southern Railroad, and happened to be in Atlanta on that day. He was so nervous about the kind of reception that I would have, and the effect that my speech would produce, that he could not persuade himself to go into the building, but walked back and forth in the grounds outside until the opening exercises were over.

# CHAPTER XIV

## *The Atlanta Exposition Address*

The Atlanta Exposition, at which I had been asked to make an address as a representative of the Negro race, as stated in the last chapter, was opened with a short address from Governor Bullock. After other interesting exercises, including an invocation from Bishop Nelson, of Georgia, a dedicatory ode by Albert Howell, Jr., and addresses by the President of the Exposition and Mrs. Joseph Thompson, the President of the Woman's Board, Governor Bullock introduced me with the words, "We have with us to-day a representative of Negro enterprise and Negro civilization."

When I arose to speak, there was considerable cheering, especially from the coloured people. As I remember it now, the thing that was uppermost in my mind was the desire to say something that would cement the friendship of the races and bring about hearty cooperation between them. So far as my outward surroundings were concerned, the only thing that I recall distinctly now is that when I got up, I saw thousands of eyes looking intently into my face. The following is the address which I delivered:—

MR. PRESIDENT AND GENTLEMEN OF THE BOARD OF DIRECTORS AND CITIZENS.

One-third of the population of the South is of the Negro race. No enterprise seeking the material, civil, or moral welfare of this section can disregard this element of our population and reach the highest success. I but convey to you, Mr. President and Directors, the sentiment of the masses of my race when I say that in no way have the value and manhood of the American Negro been more fittingly and generously recognized than by the managers of this magnificent Exposition at every stage of its progress. It is a recognition that will do more to cement the friendship of the two races than any occurrence since the dawn of our freedom.

Not only this, but the opportunity here afforded will awaken among us a new era of industrial progress. Ignorant and inexperienced, it is not strange that in the first years of our new life we began at the top instead of at the bottom; that a seat in Congress or the state legislature was more sought than real estate or industrial skill; that the political convention or stump speaking had more attractions than starting a dairy farm or truck garden.

A ship lost at sea for many days suddenly sighted a friendly vessel. From the mast of the unfortunate vessel was seen a signal, "Water, water; we die of thirst!" The answer from the friendly vessel at once came back, "Cast down your bucket where you are." A second time the signal, "Water, water; send us water!" ran up from the distressed vessel, and was answered, "Cast down your bucket where you are." And a third and fourth signal for water was answered, "Cast down your bucket where you are." The captain of the distressed vessel, at last heeding the injunction, cast down his bucket, and it came up full of fresh, sparkling water from the mouth of the Amazon River. To those of my race who depend on bettering their condition in a foreign land or who underestimate the importance of cultivating friendly relations with the Southern white man, who is their next-door neighbour, I would say: "Cast down your bucket where you are"—cast it down in making friends in every manly way of the people of all races by whom we are surrounded.

Cast it down in agriculture, mechanics, in commerce, in domestic service, and in the professions. And in this connection it is well to bear in mind that whatever other sins the South may be called to bear, when it comes to business, pure and simple, it is in the South that the Negro is given a man's chance in the commercial world, and in nothing is this Exposition more eloquent than in emphasizing this chance. Our greatest danger is that in the great leap from slavery to freedom we may overlook the fact that the masses of us are to live by the productions of our hands, and fail to keep in mind that we shall prosper in proportion as we learn to dignify and glorify common labour and put brains and skill into the common occupations of life; shall prosper in proportion as we learn to draw the line between the superficial and the substantial, the ornamental gewgaws of life and the useful. No race can prosper till it learns that there is as much dignity in tilling a field as in writing a poem. It is at the bottom of life we must begin, and not at the top. Nor should we permit our grievances to overshadow our opportunities.

To those of the white race who look to the incoming of those of foreign birth and strange tongue and habits of the prosperity of the South, were I permitted I would repeat what I say to my own race: "Cast down your bucket where you are." Cast it down among the eight millions of Negroes whose habits you know, whose fidelity and love you have tested in days when to have proved treacherous meant the ruin of your firesides. Cast down your bucket among these people who have, without strikes and labour wars, tilled your fields, cleared your forests, builded your railroads and cities, and brought forth treasures from the bowels of the earth, and helped make possible this magnificent representation of the progress of the South. Casting down your bucket among my people, helping and encouraging them as you are doing on these grounds, and to education of head, hand, and heart, you will find that they will buy your surplus land, make blossom the waste places in your fields, and run your factories. While doing this, you can be sure in the future, as in the past, that you and your families will be surrounded by the most patient, faithful, law-abiding, and unresentful people that the world has seen. As we have proved our loyalty to you in the past, nursing your children, watching by the sickbed of your mothers and fathers, and often following them with tear-dimmed eyes to their graves, so in the future, in our humble way, we shall stand by you with a devotion that no foreigner can approach, ready to lay down our lives, if need be, in defence of yours, interlacing our industrial, commercial, civil, and religious life with yours in a way that shall make the interests of both races one. In all things that are purely social we can be as separate as the fingers, yet one as the hand in all things essential to mutual progress.

There is no defence or security for any of us except in the highest intelligence and development of all. If anywhere there are efforts tending to curtail the fullest growth of the Negro, let these efforts be turned into stimulating, encouraging, and making him the most useful and intelligent citizen. Effort or means so invested will pay a thousand per cent interest. These efforts will be twice blessed—"blessing him that gives and him that takes."

There is no escape through law of man or God from the inevitable:—

The laws of changeless justice bind
  Oppressor with oppressed;
And close as sin and suffering joined
  We march to fate abreast.

Nearly sixteen millions of hands will aid you in pulling the load upward, or they will pull against you the load downward. We shall constitute one-third and more of the ignorance and crime of the South, or one-third its intelligence and progress; we shall contribute one-third to the business and industrial prosperity of the South, or we shall prove a veritable body of death, stagnating, depressing, retarding every effort to advance the body politic.

Gentlemen of the Exposition, as we present to you our humble effort at an exhibition of our progress, you must not expect overmuch. Starting thirty years ago with ownership here and there in a few quilts and pumpkins and chickens (gathered from miscellaneous sources), remember the path that has led from these to the inventions and production of agricultural implements, buggies, steam-engines, newspapers, books, statuary, carving, paintings, the management of drug-stores and banks, has not been trodden without contact with thorns and thistles. While we take pride in what we exhibit as a result of our independent efforts, we do not for a moment forget that our part in this exhibition would fall far short of your expectations but for the constant help that has come to our education life, not only from the Southern states, but especially from Northern philanthropists, who have made their gifts a constant stream of blessing and encouragement.

The wisest among my race understand that the agitation of questions of social equality is the extremest folly, and that progress in the enjoyment of all the privileges that will come to us must be the result of severe and constant struggle rather than of artificial forcing. No race that has anything to contribute to the markets of the world is long in any degree ostracized. It is important and right that all privileges of the law be ours, but it is vastly more important that we be prepared for the exercises of these privileges. The opportunity to earn a dollar in a factory just now is worth infinitely more than the opportunity to spend a dollar in an opera-house.

In conclusion, may I repeat that nothing in thirty years has given us more hope and encouragement, and drawn us so near to you of the white race, as this opportunity offered by the Exposition; and here bending, as it were, over the altar that represents the results of the struggles of your race and mine, both starting practically empty-handed three decades ago, I pledge that in your effort to work out the great and intricate problem which God has laid at the doors of the South, you shall have at all times the patient, sympathetic help of my race; only let this be constantly in mind, that, while from representations in these buildings of the product of field, of forest, of mine, of factory, letters, and art, much good will come, yet far above and beyond material benefits will be that higher good, that, let us pray God, will come, in a blotting out of sectional differences and racial animosities and suspicions, in a determination to administer absolute justice, in a willing obedience among all classes to the mandates of law. This, this, coupled with our material prosperity, will bring into our beloved South a new heaven and a new earth.

The first thing that I remember, after I had finished speaking, was that Governor Bullock rushed across the platform and took me by the hand, and that others did the same. I received so many and such hearty congratulations that I found it difficult to get out of the building. I did not appreciate to any degree, however, the impression which my address seemed to have made, until the next morning, when I went into the business part of the city. As soon as I was recognized, I was surprised to find myself pointed out and surrounded by a crowd of men who wished to shake hands with me. This was kept up on every street on to which I went, to an extent which embarrassed me so much that I went back to my boarding-place. The next morning I returned to Tuskegee. At the station in Atlanta, and at almost all of the stations at which the train stopped between that city and Tuskegee, I found a crowd of people anxious to shake hands with me.

The papers in all parts of the United States published the address in full, and for months afterward there were complimentary editorial references to it. Mr. Clark Howell, the editor of the Atlanta *Constitution*, telegraphed to a New York paper, among other words, the following, "I do not exaggerate when I say that Professor Booker T. Washington's address yesterday was one of the most notable speeches, both as to character and as to the warmth of its reception, ever delivered to a Southern audience. The address was a revelation. The whole speech is a platform upon which blacks and whites can stand with full justice to each other."

The Boston *Transcript* said editorially: "The speech of Booker T. Washington at the Atlanta Exposition, this week, seems to have dwarfed all the other proceedings and the Exposition itself. The sensation that it has caused in the press has never been equalled."

I very soon began receiving all kinds of propositions from lecture bureaus, and editors of magazines and papers, to take the lecture platform, and to write articles. One lecture bureau offered me fifty thousand dollars, or two hundred dollars a night and expenses, if I would place my services at its disposal for a given period. To all these communications I replied that my life-work was at Tuskegee; and that whenever I spoke it must be in the interests of the Tuskegee school and my race, and that I would enter into no arrangements that seemed to place a mere commercial value upon my services.

Some days after its delivery I sent a copy of my address to the President of the United States, the Hon. Grover Cleveland. I received from him the following autographed reply:—

Gray Gables, Buzzard's Bay, Mass.,
October 6, 1895.

Booker T. Washington, Esq.:

My Dear Sir: I thank you for sending me a copy of your address delivered at the Atlanta Exposition.

I thank you with much enthusiasm for making the address. I have read it with intense interest, and I think the Exposition would be fully justified if it did not do more than furnish the opportunity for its delivery. Your words cannot fail to delight and encourage all who wish well for your race; and if our coloured fellow-citizens do not from your utterances gather new hope and form new determinations to gain every valuable advantage offered them by their citizenship, it will be strange indeed.

Yours very truly,
Grover Cleveland.

Later I met Mr. Cleveland, for the first time, when, as President, he visited the Atlanta Exposition. At the request of myself and others he consented to spend an hour in the Negro Building, for the purpose of inspecting the Negro exhibit and of giving the coloured people in attendance an opportunity to shake hands with him. As soon as I met Mr. Cleveland I became impressed with his simplicity, greatness, and rugged honesty. I have met him many times since then, both at public functions and at his private residence in Princeton, and the more I see of him the more I admire him. When he visited the Negro Building in Atlanta he seemed to give himself up wholly, for that hour, to the coloured people. He seemed to be as careful to shake hands with some old coloured "auntie" clad partially in rags, and to take as much pleasure in doing so, as if he were greeting some millionaire. Many of the coloured people took advantage of the occasion to get him to write his name in a book or on a slip of paper. He was as careful and patient in doing this as if he were putting his signature to some great state document.

Mr. Cleveland has not only shown his friendship for me in many personal ways, but has always consented to do anything I have asked of him for our school. This he has done, whether it was to make a personal donation or to use his influence in securing the donations of others. Judging from my personal acquaintance with Mr. Cleveland, I do not believe that he is conscious of possessing any colour prejudice. He is too great for that. In my contact with people I find that, as a rule, it is only the little, narrow people who live for themselves, who never read good books, who do not travel, who never open up their souls in a way to permit them to come into contact with other souls—with the great outside world. No man whose vision is bounded by colour can come into contact with what is highest and best in the world. In meeting men, in many places, I have found that the happiest people are those who do the most for others; the most miserable are those who do the least. I have also found that few things, if any, are capable of making one so blind and narrow as race prejudice. I often say to our students, in the course of my talks to them on Sunday evenings in the chapel, that the longer I live and the more experience I have of the world, the more I am convinced that, after all, the one thing that is most worth living for—and dying for, if need be—is the opportunity of making some one else more happy and more useful.

The coloured people and the coloured newspapers at first seemed to be greatly pleased with the character of my Atlanta address, as well as with its reception. But after the first burst of enthusiasm began to die away, and the coloured people began reading the speech in cold type, some of them seemed to feel that they had been hypnotized. They seemed to feel that I had been too liberal in my remarks toward the Southern whites, and that I had not spoken out strongly enough for what they termed the "rights" of my race. For a while there was a reaction, so far as a certain element of my own race was concerned, but later these reactionary ones seemed to have been won over to my way of believing and acting.

While speaking of changes in public sentiment, I recall that about ten years after the school at Tuskegee was established, I had an experience that I shall never forget. Dr. Lyman Abbott, then the pastor of Plymouth Church, and also editor of the *Outlook* (then the *Christian Union*), asked me to write a letter for his paper giving my opinion of the exact condition, mental and moral, of the coloured ministers in the South, as based upon my observations. I wrote the letter, giving the exact facts as I conceived them to be. The picture painted was a rather black one—or, since I am black, shall I say "white"? It could not be otherwise with a race but a few years out of slavery, a race which had not had time or opportunity to produce a competent ministry.

What I said soon reached every Negro minister in the country, I think, and the letters of condemnation which I received from them were not few. I think that for a year after the publication of this article every association and every conference or religious body of any kind, of my race, that met, did not fail before adjourning to pass a resolution condemning me, or calling upon me to retract or modify what I had said. Many of these organizations went so far in their resolutions as to advise parents to cease sending their children to Tuskegee. One association even appointed a "missionary" whose duty it was to warn the people against sending their children to Tuskegee. This missionary had a son in the school, and I noticed that, whatever the "missionary" might have said or done with regard to others, he was careful not to take his son away from the institution. Many of the coloured papers, especially those that were the organs of religious bodies, joined in the general chorus of condemnation or demands for retraction.

During the whole time of the excitement, and through all the criticism, I did not utter a word of explanation of retraction. I knew that I was right, and that time and the sober second thought of the people would vindicate me. It was not long before the bishops and other church leaders began to make careful investigation of the conditions of the ministry, and they found out that I was right. In fact, the oldest and most influential bishop in one branch of the Methodist Church said that my words were far too mild. Very soon public sentiment began making itself felt, in demanding a purifying of the ministry. While this is not yet complete by any means, I think I may say, without egotism, and I have been told by many of our most influential ministers, that my words had much to do with starting a demand for the placing of a higher type of men in the pulpit. I have had the satisfaction of having many who once condemned me thank me heartily for my frank words.

The change of the attitude of the Negro ministry, so far as regards myself, is so complete that at the present time I have no warmer friends among any class than I have among the clergymen. The improvement in the character and life of the Negro ministers is one of the most gratifying evidences of the progress of the race. My experience with them, as well as other events in my life, convince me that the thing to do, when one feels sure that he has said or done the right thing, and is condemned, is to stand still and keep quiet. If he is right, time will show it.

In the midst of the discussion which was going on concerning my Atlanta speech, I received the letter which I give below, from Dr. Gilman, the President of Johns Hopkins University, who had been made chairman of the judges of award in connection with the Atlanta Exposition:—

Johns Hopkins University, Baltimore,
President's Office, September 30, 1895.

Dear Mr. Washington: Would it be agreeable to you to be one of the Judges of Award in the Department of Education at Atlanta? If so, I shall be glad to place your name upon the list. A line by telegraph will be welcomed.

Yours very truly,
D.C. Gilman

I think I was even more surprised to receive this invitation than I had been to receive the invitation to speak at the opening of the Exposition. It was to be a part of my duty, as one of the jurors, to pass not only upon the exhibits of the coloured schools, but also upon those of the white schools. I accepted the position, and spent a month in Atlanta in performance of the duties which it entailed. The board of jurors was a large one, consist in all of sixty members. It was about equally divided between Southern white people and Northern white people. Among them were college presidents, leading scientists and men of letters, and specialists in many subjects. When the group of jurors to which I was assigned met for organization, Mr. Thomas Nelson Page, who was one of the number, moved that I be made secretary of that division, and the motion was unanimously adopted. Nearly half of our division were Southern people. In performing my duties in the inspection of the exhibits of white schools I was in every case treated with respect, and at the close of our labours I parted from my associates with regret.

I am often asked to express myself more freely than I do upon the political condition and the political future of my race. These recollections of my experience in Atlanta give me the opportunity to do so briefly. My own belief is, although I have never before said so in so many words, that the time will come when the Negro in the South will be accorded all the political rights which his ability, character, and material possessions entitle him to. I think, though, that the opportunity to freely exercise such political rights will not come in any large degree through outside or artificial forcing, but will be accorded to the Negro by the Southern white people themselves, and that they will protect him in the exercise of those rights. Just as soon as the South gets over the old feeling that it is being forced by "foreigners," or "aliens," to do something which it does not want to do, I believe that the change in the direction that I have indicated is going to begin. In fact, there are indications that it is already beginning in a slight degree.

Let me illustrate my meaning. Suppose that some months before the opening of the Atlanta Exposition there had been a general demand from the press and public platform outside the South that a Negro be given a place on the opening programme, and that a Negro be placed upon the board of jurors of award. Would any such recognition of the race have taken place? I do not think so. The Atlanta officials went as far as they did because they felt it to be a pleasure, as well as a duty, to reward what they considered merit in the Negro race.

Say what we will, there is something in human nature which we cannot blot out, which makes one man, in the end, recognize and reward merit in another, regardless of colour or race.

I believe it is the duty of the Negro—as the greater part of the race is already doing—to deport himself modestly in regard to political claims, depending upon the slow but sure influences that proceed from the possession of property, intelligence, and high character for the full recognition of his political rights. I think that the according of the full exercise of political rights is going to be a matter of natural, slow growth, not an over-night, gourd-vine affair. I do not believe that the Negro should cease voting, for a man cannot learn the exercise of self-government by ceasing to vote, any more than a boy can learn to swim by keeping out of the water, but I do believe that in his voting he should more and more be influenced by those of intelligence and character who are his next-door neighbours.

I know coloured men who, through the encouragement, help, and advice of Southern white people, have accumulated thousands of dollars' worth of property, but who, at the same time, would never think of going to those same persons for advice concerning the casting of their ballots. This, it seems to me, is unwise and unreasonable, and should cease. In saying this I do not mean that the Negro should truckle, or not vote from principle, for the instant he ceases to vote from principle he loses the confidence and respect of the Southern white man even.

I do not believe that any state should make a law that permits an ignorant and poverty-stricken white man to vote, and prevents a black man in the same condition from voting. Such a law is not only unjust, but it will react, as all unjust laws do, in time; for the effect of such a law is to encourage the Negro to secure education and property, and at the same time it encourages the white man to remain in ignorance and poverty. I believe that in time, through the operation of intelligence and friendly race relations, all cheating at the ballot box in the South will cease. It will become apparent that the white man who begins by cheating a Negro out of his ballot soon learns to cheat a white man out of his, and that the man who does this ends his career of dishonesty by the theft of property or by some equally serious crime. In my opinion, the time will come when the South will encourage all of its citizens to vote. It will see that it pays better, from every standpoint, to have healthy, vigorous life than to have that political stagnation which always results when one-half of the population has no share and no interest in the Government.

As a rule, I believe in universal, free suffrage, but I believe that in the South we are confronted with peculiar conditions that justify the protection of the ballot in many of the states, for a while at least, either by an education test, a property test, or by both combined; but whatever tests are required, they should be made to apply with equal and exact justice to both races.

# CHAPTER XV

## *The Secret of Success in Public Speaking*

As to how my address at Atlanta was received by the audience in the Exposition building, I think I prefer to let Mr. James Creelman, the noted war correspondent, tell. Mr. Creelman was present, and telegraphed the following account to the New York World:—

Atlanta, September 18.

While President Cleveland was waiting at Gray Gables to-day, to send the electric spark that started the machinery of the Atlanta Exposition, a Negro Moses stood before a great audience of white people and delivered an oration that marks a new epoch in the history of the South; and a body of Negro troops marched in a procession with the citizen soldiery of Georgia and Louisiana. The whole city is thrilling to-night with a realization of the extraordinary significance of these two unprecedented events. Nothing has happened since Henry Grady's immortal speech before the New England society in New York that indicates so profoundly the spirit of the New South, except, perhaps, the opening of the Exposition itself.

When Professor Booker T. Washington, Principal of an industrial school for coloured people in Tuskegee, Ala., stood on the platform of thes Auditorium, with the sun shining over the heads of his auditors into his eyes, and with his whole face lit up with the fire of prophecy, Clark Howell, the successor of Henry Grady, said to me, "That man's speech is the beginning of a moral revolution in America."

It is the first time that a Negro has made a speech in the South on any important occasion before an audience composed of white men and women. It electrified the audience, and the response was as if it had come from the throat of a whirlwind.

Mrs. Thompson had hardly taken her seat when all eyes were turned on a tall tawny Negro sitting in the front row of the platform. It was Professor Booker T. Washington, President of the Tuskegee (Alabama) Normal and Industrial Institute, who must rank from this time forth as the foremost man of his race in America. Gilmore's Band played the "Star-Spangled Banner," and the audience cheered. The tune changed to "Dixie" and the audience roared with shrill "hi-yis." Again the music changed, this time to "Yankee Doodle," and the clamour lessened.

All this time the eyes of the thousands present looked straight at the Negro orator. A strange thing was to happen. A black man was to speak for his people, with none to interrupt him. As Professor Washington strode to the edge of the stage, the low, descending sun shot fiery rays through the windows into his face. A great shout greeted him. He turned his head to avoid the blinding light, and moved about the platform for relief. Then he turned his wonderful countenance to the sun without a blink of the eyelids, and began to talk.

There was a remarkable figure; tall, bony, straight as a Sioux chief, high forehead, straight nose, heavy jaws, and strong, determined mouth, with big white teeth, piercing eyes, and a commanding manner. The sinews stood out on his bronzed neck, and his muscular right arm swung high in the air, with a lead-pencil grasped in the clinched brown fist. His big feet were planted squarely, with the heels together and the toes turned out. His voice range out clear and true, and he paused impressively as he made each point. Within ten minutes the multitude was in an uproar of enthusiasm—handkerchiefs were waved, canes were flourished, hats were tossed in the air. The fairest women of Georgia stood up and cheered. It was as if the orator had bewitched them.

And when he held his dusky hand high above his head, with the fingers stretched wide apart, and said to the white people of the South on behalf of his race, "In all things that are purely

> social we can be as separate as the fingers, yet one as the hand in all things essential to mutual progress," the great wave of sound dashed itself against the walls, and the whole audience was on its feet in a delirium of applause, and I thought at that moment of the night when Henry Grady stood among the curling wreaths of tobacco-smoke in Delmonico's banquet-hall and said, "I am a Cavalier among Roundheads."
>
> I have heard the great orators of many countries, but not even Gladstone himself could have pleased a cause with more consummate power than did this angular Negro, standing in a nimbus of sunshine, surrounded by the men who once fought to keep his race in bondage. The roar might swell ever so high, but the expression of his earnest face never changed.
>
> A ragged, ebony giant, squatted on the floor in one of the aisles, watched the orator with burning eyes and tremulous face until the supreme burst of applause came, and then the tears ran down his face. Most of the Negroes in the audience were crying, perhaps without knowing just why.
>
> At the close of the speech Governor Bullock rushed across the stage and seized the orator's hand. Another shout greeted this demonstration, and for a few minutes the two men stood facing each other, hand in hand.

So far as I could spare the time from the immediate work at Tuskegee, after my Atlanta address, I accepted some of the invitations to speak in public which came to me, especially those that would take me into territory where I thought it would pay to plead the cause of my race, but I always did this with the understanding that I was to be free to talk about my life-work and the needs of my people. I also had it understood that I was not to speak in the capacity of a professional lecturer, or for mere commercial gain.

In my efforts on the public platform I never have been able to understand why people come to hear me speak. This question I never can rid myself of. Time and time again, as I have stood in the street in front of a building and have seen men and women passing in large numbers into the audience room where I was to speak, I have felt ashamed that I should be the cause of people—as it seemed to me—wasting a valuable hour of their time. Some years ago I was to deliver an address before a literary society in Madison, Wis. An hour before the time set for me to speak, a fierce snow-storm began, and continued for several hours. I made up my mind that there would be no audience, and that I should not have to speak, but, as a matter of duty, I went to the church, and found it packed with people. The surprise gave me a shock that I did not recover from during the whole evening.

People often ask me if I feel nervous before speaking, or else they suggest that, since I speak often, they suppose that I get used to it. In answer to this question I have to say that I always suffer intensely from nervousness before speaking. More than once, just before I was to make an important address, this nervous strain has been so great that I have resolved never again to speak in public. I not only feel nervous before speaking, but after I have finished I usually feel a sense of regret, because it seems to me as if I had left out of my address the main thing and the best thing that I had meant to say.

There is a great compensation, though, for this preliminary nervous suffering, that comes to me after I have been speaking for about ten minutes, and have come to feel that I have really mastered my audience, and that we have gotten into full and complete sympathy with each other. It seems to me that there is rarely such a combination of mental and physical delight in any effort as that which comes to a public speaker when he feels that he has a great audience completely within his control. There is a thread of sympathy and oneness that connects a public speaker with his audience, that is just as strong as though it was something tangible and visible. If in an audience of a thousand people there is one person who is not in sympathy with my views, or is inclined to be doubtful, cold, or critical, I can pick him out. When I have found him I usually go straight at him, and it is a great satisfaction to watch the process of his thawing out. I find that the most effective medicine for such individuals is administered at first in the form of a story, although I never tell an anecdote simply for the sake of telling one. That kind of thing, I think, is empty and hollow, and an audience soon finds it out.

I believe that one always does himself and his audience an injustice when he speaks merely for the sake of speaking. I do not believe that one should speak unless, deep down in his heart, he feels convinced that he has a message to deliver. When one feels, from the bottom of his feet to the top of his head, that he has something to say that is going to help some individual or some cause, then let him say it; and in delivering his message I do not believe that many of the artificial rules of elocution can, under such circumstances, help him very much. Although there are certain things, such as pauses, breathing, and pitch of voice, that are very important, none of these can take the place of soul in an address. When I have an address to deliver, I like to forget all about the rules for the proper use of the English language, and all about rhetoric and that sort of thing, and I like to make the audience forget all about these things, too.

Nothing tends to throw me off my balance so quickly, when I am speaking, as to have some one leave the room. To prevent this, I make up my mind, as a rule, that I will try to make my address so interesting, will try to state so many interesting facts one after another, that no one can leave. The average audience, I have come to believe, wants facts rather than generalities or sermonizing. Most people, I think, are able to draw proper conclusions if they are given the facts in an interesting form on which to base them.

As to the kind of audience that I like best to talk to, I would put at the top of the list an organization of strong, wide-awake, business men, such, for example, as is found in Boston, New York, Chicago, and Buffalo. I have found no other audience so quick to see a point, and so responsive. Within the last few years I have had the privilege of speaking before most of the leading organizations of this kind in the large cities of the United States. The best time to get hold of an organization of business men is after a good dinner, although I think that one of the worst instruments of torture that was ever invented is the custom which makes it necessary for a speaker to sit through a fourteen-course dinner, every minute of the time feeling sure that his speech is going to prove a dismal failure and disappointment.

I rarely take part in one of these long dinners that I do not wish that I could put myself back in the little cabin where I was a slave boy, and again go through the experience there—one that I shall never forget—of getting molasses to eat once a week from the "big house." Our usual diet on the plantation was corn bread and pork, but on Sunday morning my mother was permitted to bring down a little molasses from the "big house" for her three children, and when it was received how I did wish that every day was Sunday! I would get my tin plate and hold it up for the sweet morsel, but I would always shut my eyes while the molasses was being poured out into the plate, with the hope that when I opened them I would be surprised to see how much I had got. When I opened my eyes I would tip the plate in one direction and another, so as to make the molasses spread all over it, in the full belief that there would be more of it and that it would last longer if spread out in this way. So strong are my childish impressions of those Sunday morning feasts that it would be pretty hard for any one to convince me that there is not more molasses on a plate when it is spread all over the plate than when it occupies a little corner—if there is a corner in a plate. At any rate, I have never believed in "cornering" syrup. My share of the syrup was usually about two tablespoonfuls, and those two spoonfuls of molasses were much more enjoyable to me than is a fourteen-course dinner after which I am to speak.

Next to a company of business men, I prefer to speak to an audience of Southern people, of either race, together or taken separately. Their enthusiasm and responsiveness are a constant delight. The "amens" and "dat's de truf" that come spontaneously from the coloured individuals are calculated to spur any speaker on to his best efforts. I think that next in order of preference I would place a college audience. It has been my privilege to deliver addresses at many of our leading colleges, including Harvard, Yale, Williams, Amherst, Fisk University, the University of Pennsylvania, Wellesley, the University of Michigan, Trinity College in North Carolina, and many others.

It has been a matter of deep interest to me to note the number of people who have come to shake hands with me after an address, who say that this is the first time they have ever called a Negro "Mister."

When speaking directly in the interests of the Tuskegee Institute, I usually arrange, some time in advance, a series of meetings in important centres. This takes me before churches, Sunday-schools, Christian Endeavour Societies, and men's and women's clubs. When doing this I sometimes speak before as many as four organizations in a single day.

Three years ago, at the suggestion of Mr. Morris K. Jesup, of New York, and Dr. J.L.M. Curry, the general agent of the fund, the trustees of the John F. Slater Fund voted a sum of money to be used in paying the expenses of Mrs. Washington and myself while holding a series of meetings among the coloured people in the large centres of Negro population, especially in the large cities of the ex-slave-holding states. Each year during the last three years we have devoted some weeks to this work. The plan that we have followed has been for me to speak in the morning to the ministers, teachers, and professional men. In the afternoon Mrs. Washington would speak to the women alone, and in the evening I spoke to a large mass-meeting. In almost every case the meetings have been attended not only by the coloured people in large numbers, but by the white people. In Chattanooga, Tenn., for example, there was present at the mass-meeting an audience of not less than three thousand persons, and I was informed that eight hundred of these were white. I have done no work that I really enjoyed more than this, or that I think has accomplished more good.

These meetings have given Mrs. Washington and myself an opportunity to get first-hand, accurate information as to the real condition of the race, by seeing the people in their homes, their churches, their Sunday-schools, and their places of work, as well as in the prisons and dens of crime. These meetings also gave us an opportunity to see the relations that exist between the races. I never feel so hopeful about the race as I do after being engaged in a series of these meetings. I know that on such occasions there is much that comes to the surface that is superficial and deceptive, but I have had experience enough not to be deceived by mere signs and fleeting enthusiasms. I have taken pains to go to the bottom of things and get facts, in a cold, business-like manner.

I have seen the statement made lately, by one who claims to know what he is talking about, that, taking the whole Negro race into account, ninety per cent of the Negro women are not virtuous. There never was a baser falsehood uttered concerning a race, or a statement made that was less capable of being proved by actual facts.

No one can come into contact with the race for twenty years, as I have done in the heart of the South, without being convinced that the race is constantly making slow but sure progress materially, educationally, and morally. One might take up the life of the worst element in New York City, for example, and prove almost anything he wanted to prove concerning the white man, but all will agree that this is not a fair test.

Early in the year 1897 I received a letter inviting me to deliver an address at the dedication of the Robert Gould Shaw monument in Boston. I accepted the invitation. It is not necessary for me, I am sure, to explain who Robert Gould Shaw was, and what he did. The monument to his memory stands near the head of the Boston Common, facing the State House. It is counted to be the most perfect piece of art of the kind to be found in the country.

The exercises connected with the dedication were held in Music Hall, in Boston, and the great hall was packed from top to bottom with one of the most distinguished audiences that ever assembled in the city. Among those present were more persons representing the famous old anti-slavery element than it is likely will ever be brought together in the country again. The late Hon. Roger Wolcott, then Governor of Massachusetts, was the presiding officer, and on the platform with him were many other officials and hundreds of distinguished men. A report of the meeting which appeared in the Boston *Transcript* will describe it better than any words of mine could do:—

> The core and kernel of yesterday's great noon meeting, in honour of the Brotherhood of Man, in Music Hall, was the superb address of the Negro President of Tuskegee. "Booker T. Washington received his Harvard A.M. last June, the first of his race," said Governor Wolcott, "to receive an honorary degree from the oldest university in the land, and this for the wise leadership of his people." When Mr. Washington rose in the flag-filled, enthusiasm-warmed, patriotic, and glowing atmosphere of Music Hall, people felt keenly

that here was the civic justification of the old abolition spirit of Massachusetts; in his person the proof of her ancient and indomitable faith; in his strong thought and rich oratory, the crown and glory of the old war days of suffering and strife. The scene was full of historic beauty and deep significance. "Cold" Boston was alive with the fire that is always hot in her heart for righteousness and truth. Rows and rows of people who are seldom seen at any public function, whole families of those who are certain to be out of town on a holiday, crowded the place to overflowing. The city was at her birthright fête in the persons of hundreds of her best citizens, men and women whose names and lives stand for the virtues that make for honourable civic pride.

Battle-music had filled the air. Ovation after ovation, applause warm and prolonged, had greeted the officers and friends of Colonel Shaw, the sculptor St. Gaudens, the memorial Committee, the Governor and his staff, and the Negro soldiers of the Fifty-fourth Massachusetts as they came upon the platform or entered the hall. Colonel Henry Lee, of Governor Andrew's old staff, had made a noble, simple presentation speech for the committee, paying tribute to Mr. John M. Forbes, in whose stead he served. Governor Wolcott had made his short, memorable speech, saying, "Fort Wagner marked an epoch in the history of a race, and called it into manhood." Mayor Quincy had received the monument for the city of Boston. The story of Colonel Shaw and his black regiment had been told in gallant words, and then, after the singing of

*Mine eyes have seen the glory*
*Of the coming of the Lord,*

Booker Washington arose. It was, of course, just the moment for him. The multitude, shaken out of its usual symphony-concert calm, quivered with an excitement that was not suppressed. A dozen times it had sprung to its feet to cheer and wave and hurrah, as one person. When this man of culture and voice and power, as well as a dark skin, began, and uttered the names of Stearns and of Andrew, feeling began to mount. You could see

> tears glisten in the eyes of soldiers and civilians. When the orator turned to the coloured soldiers on the platform, to the colour-bearer of Fort Wagner, who smilingly bore still the flag he had never lowered even when wounded, and said, "To you, to the scarred and scattered remnants of the Fifty-fourth, who, with empty sleeve and wanting leg, have honoured this occasion with your presence, to you, your commander is not dead. Though Boston erected no monument and history recorded no story, in you and in the loyal race which you represent, Robert Gould Shaw would have a monument which time could not wear away," then came the climax of the emotion of the day and the hour. It was Roger Wolcott, as well as the Governor of Massachusetts, the individual representative of the people's sympathy as well as the chief magistrate, who had sprung first to his feet and cried, "Three cheers to Booker T. Washington!"

Among those on the platform was Sergeant William H. Carney, of New Bedford, Mass., the brave coloured officer who was the colour-bearer at Fort Wagner and held the American flag. In spite of the fact that a large part of his regiment was killed, he escape, and exclaimed, after the battle was over, "The old flag never touched the ground."

This flag Sergeant Carney held in his hands as he sat on the platform, and when I turned to address the survivors of the coloured regiment who were present, and referred to Sergeant Carney, he rose, as if by instinct, and raised the flag. It has been my privilege to witness a good many satisfactory and rather sensational demonstrations in connection with some of my public addresses, but in dramatic effect I have never seen or experienced anything which equalled this. For a number of minutes the audience seemed to entirely lose control of itself.

In the general rejoicing throughout the country which followed the close of the Spanish-American war, peace celebrations were arranged in several of the large cities. I was asked by President William R. Harper, of the University of Chicago, who was chairman of the committee of invitations for the celebration to be held in the city of Chicago, to deliver one of the addresses at the celebration there. I accepted the invitation, and delivered two addresses there during the Jubilee week. The first of these, and the principal one, was given in the Auditorium, on the evening of Sunday, October 16. This was the largest audience that I have ever addressed, in any part of the country; and besides speaking in the main Auditorium, I also addressed, that same evening, two overflow audiences in other parts of the city.

It was said that there were sixteen thousand persons in the Auditorium, and it seemed to me as if there were as many more on the outside trying to get in. It was impossible for any one to get near the entrance without the aid of a policeman. President William McKinley attended this meeting, as did also the members of his Cabinet, many foreign ministers, and a large number of army and navy officers, many of whom had distinguished themselves in the war which had just closed. The speakers, besides myself, on Sunday evening, were Rabbi Emil G. Hirsch, Father Thomas P. Hodnett, and Dr. John H. Barrows.

The Chicago *Times-Herald*, in describing the meeting, said of my address:—

> He pictured the Negro choosing slavery rather than extinction; recalled Crispus Attucks shedding his blood at the beginning of the American Revolution, that white Americans might be free, while black Americans remained in slavery; rehearsed the conduct of the Negroes with Jackson at New Orleans; drew a vivid and pathetic picture of the Southern slaves protecting and supporting the families of their masters while the latter were fighting to perpetuate black slavery; recounted the bravery of coloured troops at Port Hudson and Forts Wagner and Pillow, and praised the heroism of the black regiments that stormed El Caney and Santiago to give freedom to the enslaved people of Cuba, forgetting, for the time being, the unjust discrimination that law and custom make against them in their own country.
>
> In all of these things, the speaker declared, his race had chosen the better part. And then he made his eloquent appeal to the consciences of the white Americans: "When you have gotten the full story of the heroic conduct of the Negro in the Spanish-American war, have heard it from the lips of Northern

soldier and Southern soldier, from ex-abolitionist and ex-masters, then decide within yourselves whether a race that is thus willing to die for its country should not be given the highest opportunity to live for its country."

The part of the speech which seemed to arouse the wildest and most sensational enthusiasm was that in which I thanked the President for his recognition of the Negro in his appointments during the Spanish-American war. The President was sitting in a box at the right of the stage. When I addressed him I turned toward the box, and as I finished the sentence thanking him for his generosity, the whole audience rose and cheered again and again, waving handkerchiefs and hats and canes, until the President arose in the box and bowed his acknowledgements. At that the enthusiasm broke out again, and the demonstration was almost indescribable.

One portion of my address at Chicago seemed to have been misunderstood by the Southern press, and some of the Southern papers took occasion to criticise me rather strongly. These criticisms continued for several weeks, until I finally received a letter from the editor of the *Age-Herald*, published in Birmingham, Ala., asking me if I would say just what I meant by this part of the address. I replied to him in a letter which seemed to satisfy my critics. In this letter I said that I had made it a rule never to say before a Northern audience anything that I would not say before an audience in the South. I said that I did not think it was necessary for me to go into extended explanations; if my seventeen years of work in the heart of the South had not been explanation enough, I did not see how words could explain. I said that I made the same plea that I had made in my address at Atlanta, for the blotting out of race prejudice in "commercial and civil relations." I said that what is termed social recognition was a question which I never discussed, and then I quoted from my Atlanta address what I had said there in regard to that subject.

In meeting crowds of people at public gatherings, there is one type of individual that I dread. I mean the crank. I have become so accustomed to these people now that I can pick them out at a distance when I see them elbowing their way up to me. The average crank has a long beard, poorly cared for, a lean, narrow face, and wears a black coat. The front of his vest and coat are slick with grease, and his trousers bag at the knees.

In Chicago, after I had spoken at a meeting, I met one of these fellows. They usually have some process for curing all of the ills of the world at once. This Chicago specimen had a patent process by which he said Indian corn could be kept through a period of three or four years, and he felt sure that if the Negro race in the South would, as a whole, adopt his process, it would settle the whole race question. It mattered nothing that I tried to convince him that our present problem was to teach the Negroes how to produce enough corn to last them through one year. Another Chicago crank had a scheme by which he wanted me to join him in an effort to close up all the National banks in the country. If that was done, he felt sure it would put the Negro on his feet.

The number of people who stand ready to consume one's time, to no purpose, is almost countless. At one time I spoke before a large audience in Boston in the evening. The next morning I was awakened by having a card brought to my room, and with it a message that some one was anxious to see me. Thinking that it must be something very important, I dressed hastily and went down. When I reached the hotel office I found a blank and innocent-looking individual waiting for me, who coolly remarked: "I heard you talk at a meeting last night. I rather liked your talk, and so I came in this morning to hear you talk some more."

I am often asked how it is possible for me to superintend the work at Tuskegee and at the same time be so much away from the school. In partial answer to this I would say that I think I have learned, in some degree at least, to disregard the old maxim which says, "Do not get others to do that which you can do yourself." My motto, on the other hand, is, "Do not do that which others can do as well."

One of the most encouraging signs in connection with the Tuskegee school is found in the fact that the organization is so thorough that the daily work of the school is not dependent upon the presence of any one individual. The whole executive force, including instructors and clerks, now numbers eighty-six. This force is so organized and subdivided that the machinery of the school goes on day by day like clockwork. Most of our teachers have been connected with the institutions for a number of years, and are as much interested in it as I am. In my absence, Mr. Warren Logan, the treasurer, who has been at the school seventeen years, is the executive. He is efficiently supported by Mrs. Washington, and by my faithful secretary, Mr. Emmett J. Scott, who handles the bulk of my correspondence and keeps me in daily touch with the life of the school, and who also keeps me informed of whatever takes place in the South that concerns the race. I owe more to his tact, wisdom, and hard work than I can describe.

The main executive work of the school, whether I am at Tuskegee or not, centres in what we call the executive council. This council meets twice a week, and is composed of the nine persons who are at the head of the nine departments of the school. For example: Mrs. B.K. Bruce, the Lady Principal, the widow of the late ex-senator Bruce, is a member of the council, and represents in it all that pertains to the life of the girls at the school. In addition to the executive council there is a financial committee of six, that meets every week and decides upon the expenditures for the week. Once a month, and sometimes oftener, there is a general meeting of all the instructors. Aside from these there are innumerable smaller meetings, such as that of the instructors in the Phelps Hall Bible Training School, or of the instructors in the agricultural department.

In order that I may keep in constant touch with the life of the institution, I have a system of reports so arranged that a record of the school's work reaches me every day of the year, no matter in what part of the country I am. I know by these reports even what students are excused from school, and why they are excused—whether for reasons of ill health or otherwise. Through the medium of these reports I know each day what the income of the school in money is; I know how many gallons of milk and how many pounds of butter come from the dairy; what the bill of fare for the teachers and students is; whether a certain kind of meat was boiled or baked, and whether certain vegetables served in the dining room were bought from a store or procured from our own farm. Human nature I find to be very much the same the world over, and it is sometimes not hard to yield to the temptation to go to a barrel of rice that has come from the store—with the grain all prepared to go in the pot—rather than to take the time and trouble to go to the field and dig and wash one's own sweet potatoes, which might be prepared in a manner to take the place of the rice.

I am often asked how, in the midst of so much work, a large part of which is for the public, I can find time for any rest or recreation, and what kind of recreation or sports I am fond of. This is rather a difficult question to answer. I have a strong feeling that every individual owes it to himself, and to the cause which he is serving, to keep a vigorous, healthy body, with the nerves steady and strong, prepared for great efforts and prepared for disappointments and trying positions. As far as I can, I make it a rule to plan for each day's work—not merely to go through with the same routine of daily duties, but to get rid of the routine work as early in the day as possible, and then to enter upon some new or advance work. I make it a rule to clear my desk every day, before leaving my office, of all correspondence and memoranda, so that on the morrow I can begin a *new* day of work. I make it a rule never to let my work drive me, but to so master it, and keep it in such complete control, and to keep so far ahead of it, that I will be the master instead of the servant. There is a physical and mental and spiritual enjoyment that comes from a consciousness of being the absolute master of one's work, in all its details, that is very satisfactory and inspiring. My experience teachers me that, if one learns to follow this plan, he gets a freshness of body and vigour of mind out of work that goes a long way toward keeping him strong and healthy. I believe that when one can grow to the point where he loves his work, this gives him a kind of strength that is most valuable.

When I begin my work in the morning, I expect to have a successful and pleasant day of it, but at the same time I prepare myself for unpleasant and unexpected hard places. I prepare myself to hear that one of our school buildings is on fire, or has burned, or that some disagreeable accident has occurred, or that some one has abused me in a public address or printed article, for something that I have done or omitted to do, or for something that he had heard that I had said—probably something that I had never thought of saying.

In nineteen years of continuous work I have taken but one vacation. That was two years ago, when some of my friends put the money into my hands and forced Mrs. Washington and myself to spend three months in Europe. I have said that I believe it is the duty of every one to keep his body in good condition. I try to look after the little ills, with the idea that if I take care of the little ills the big ones will not come. When I find myself unable to sleep well, I know that something is wrong. If I find any part of my system the least weak, and not performing its duty, I consult a good physician. The ability to sleep well, at any time and in any place, I find of great advantage. I have so trained myself that I can lie down for a nap of fifteen or twenty minutes, and get up refreshed in body and mind.

I have said that I make it a rule to finish up each day's work before leaving it. There is, perhaps, one exception to this. When I have an unusually difficult question to decide—one that appeals strongly to the emotions—I find it a safe rule to sleep over it for a night, or to wait until I have had an opportunity to talk it over with my wife and friends.

As to my reading; the most time I get for solid reading is when I am on the cars. Newspapers are to me a constant source of delight and recreation. The only trouble is that I read too many of them. Fiction I care little for. Frequently I have to almost force myself to read a novel that is on every one's lips. The kind of reading that I have the greatest fondness for is biography. I like to be sure that I am reading about a real man or a real thing. I think I do not go too far when I say that I have read nearly every book and magazine article that has been written about Abraham Lincoln. In literature he is my patron saint.

Out of the twelve months in a year I suppose that, on an average, I spend six months away from Tuskegee. While my being absent from the school so much unquestionably has its disadvantages, yet there are at the same time some compensations. The change of work brings a certain kind of rest. I enjoy a ride of a long distance on the cars, when I am permitted to ride where I can be comfortable. I get rest on the cars, except when the inevitable individual who seems to be on every train approaches me with the now familiar phrase: "Isn't this Booker Washington? I want to introduce myself to you." Absence from the school enables me to lose sight of the unimportant details of the work, and study it in a broader and more comprehensive manner than I could do on the grounds. This absence also brings me into contact with the best work being done in educational lines, and into contact with the best educators in the land.

But, after all this is said, the time when I get the most solid rest and recreation is when I can be at Tuskegee, and, after our evening meal is over, can sit down, as is our custom, with my wife and Portia and Booker and Davidson, my three children, and read a story, or each take turns in telling a story. To me there is nothing on earth equal to that, although what is nearly equal to it is to go with them for an hour or more, as we like to do on Sunday afternoons, into the woods, where we can live for a while near the heart of nature, where no one can disturb or vex us, surrounded by pure air, the trees, the shrubbery, the flowers, and the sweet fragrance that springs from a hundred plants, enjoying the chirp of the crickets and the songs of the birds. This is solid rest.

My garden, also, what little time I can be at Tuskegee, is another source of rest and enjoyment. Somehow I like, as often as possible, to touch nature, not something that is artificial or an imitation, but the real thing. When I can leave my office in time so that I can spend thirty or forty minutes in spading the ground, in planting seeds, in digging about the plants, I feel that I am coming into contact with something that is giving me strength for the many duties and hard places that await me out in the big world. I pity the man or woman who has never learned to enjoy nature and to get strength and inspiration out of it.

Aside from the large number of fowls and animals kept by the school, I keep individually a number of pigs and fowls of the best grades, and in raising these I take a great deal of pleasure. I think the pig is my favourite animal. Few things are more satisfactory to me than a high-grade Berkshire or Poland China pig.

Games I care little for. I have never seen a game of football. In cards I do not know one card from another. A game of old-fashioned marbles with my two boys, once in a while, is all I care for in this direction. I suppose I would care for games now if I had had any time in my youth to give to them, but that was not possible.

# CHAPTER XVI

## *Europe*

In 1893 I was married to Miss Margaret James Murray, a native of Mississippi, and a graduate of Fisk University, in Nashville, Tenn., who had come to Tuskegee as a teacher several years before, and at the time we were married was filling the position of Lady Principal. Not only is Mrs. Washington completely one with me in the work directly connected with the school, relieving me of many burdens and perplexities, but aside from her work on the school grounds, she carries on a mothers' meeting in the town of Tuskegee, and a plantation work among the women, children, and men who live in a settlement connected with a large plantation about eight miles from Tuskegee. Both the mothers' meeting and the plantation work are carried on, not only with a view to helping those who are directly reached, but also for the purpose of furnishing object-lessons in these two kinds of work that may be followed by our students when they go out into the world for their own life-work.

Aside from these two enterprises, Mrs. Washington is also largely responsible for a woman's club at the school which brings together, twice a month, the women who live on the school grounds and those who live near, for the discussion of some important topic. She is also the President of what is known as the Federation of Southern Coloured Women's Clubs, and is Chairman of the Executive Committee of the National Federation of Coloured Women's Clubs.

Portia, the oldest of my three children, has learned dressmaking. She has unusual ability in instrumental music. Aside from her studies at Tuskegee, she has already begun to teach there.

Booker Taliaferro is my next oldest child. Young as he is, he has already nearly mastered the brickmason's trade. He began working at this trade when he was quite small, dividing his time between this and class work; and he has developed great skill in the trade and a fondness for it. He says that he is going to be an architect and brickmason. One of the most satisfactory letters that I have ever received from any one came to me from Booker, last summer. When I left home for the summer, I told him that he must work at his trade half of each day, and that the other half of the day he could spend as he pleased. When I had been away from home two weeks, I received the following letter from him:

> Tuskegee, Alabama.
>
> My dear Papa: Before you left home you told me to work at my trade half of each day. I like my work so much that I want to work at my trade all day. Besides, I want to earn all the money I can, so that when I go to another school I shall have money to pay my expenses.
>
> Your son,
> Booker.

My youngest child, Earnest Davidson Washington, says that he is going to be a physician. In addition to going to school, where he studies books and has manual training, he regularly spends a portion of his time in the office of our resident physician, and has already learned to do many of the studies which pertain to a doctor's office.

The thing in my life which brings me the keenest regret is that my work in connection with public affairs keeps me for so much of the time away from my family, where, of all places in the world, I delight to be. I always envy the individual whose life-work is so laid that he can spend his evenings at home. I have sometimes thought that people who have this rare privilege do not appreciate it as they should. It is such a rest and relief to get away from crowds of people, and handshaking, and travelling, to get home, even if it be for but a very brief while.

Another thing at Tuskegee out of which I get a great deal of pleasure and satisfaction is in the meeting with our students, and teachers, and their families, in the chapel for devotional exercises every evening at half-past eight, the last thing before retiring for the night. It is an inspiring sight when one stands on the platform there and sees before him eleven or twelve hundred earnest young men and women; and one cannot but feel that it is a privilege to help to guide them to a higher and more useful life.

In the spring of 1899 there came to me what I might describe as almost the greatest surprise of my life. Some good ladies in Boston arranged a public meeting in the interests of Tuskegee, to be held in the Hollis Street Theatre. This meeting was attended by large numbers of the best people of Boston, of both races. Bishop Lawrence presided. In addition to an address made by myself, Mr. Paul Lawrence Dunbar read from his poems, and Dr. W.E.B. Du Bois read an original sketch.

Some of those who attended this meeting noticed that I seemed unusually tired, and some little time after the close of the meeting, one of the ladies who had been interested in it asked me in a casual way if I had ever been to Europe. I replied that I never had. She asked me if I had ever thought of going, and I told her no; that it was something entirely beyond me. This conversation soon passed out of my mind, but a few days afterward I was informed that some friends in Boston, including Mr. Francis J. Garrison, had raised a sum of money sufficient to pay all the expenses of Mrs. Washington and myself during a three or four months' trip to Europe. It was added with emphasis that we *must* go. A year previous to this Mr. Garrison had attempted to get me to promise to go to Europe for a summer's rest, with the understanding that he would be responsible for raising the money among his friends for the expenses of the trip. At that time such a journey seemed so entirely foreign to anything that I should ever be able to undertake that I confess I did not give the matter very serious attention; but later Mr. Garrison joined his efforts to those of the ladies whom I have mentioned, and when their plans were made known to me Mr. Garrison not only had the route mapped out, but had, I believe, selected the steamer upon which we were to sail.

The whole thing was so sudden and so unexpected that I was completely taken off my feet. I had been at work steadily for eighteen years in connection with Tuskegee, and I had never thought of anything else but ending my life in that way. Each day the school seemed to depend upon me more largely for its daily expenses, and I told these Boston friends that, while I thanked them sincerely for their thoughtfulness and generosity, I could not go to Europe, for the reason that the school could not live financially while I was absent. They then informed me that Mr. Henry L. Higginson, and some other good friends who I know do not want their names made public, were then raising a sum of money which would be sufficient to keep the school in operation while I was away. At this point I was compelled to surrender. Every avenue of escape had been closed.

Deep down in my heart the whole thing seemed more like a dream than like reality, and for a long time it was difficult for me to make myself believe that I was actually going to Europe. I had been born and largely reared in the lowest depths of slavery, ignorance, and poverty. In my childhood I had suffered for want of a place to sleep, for lack of food, clothing, and shelter. I had not had the privilege of sitting down to a dining-table until I was quite well grown. Luxuries had always seemed to me to be something meant for white people, not for my race. I had always regarded Europe, and London, and Paris, much as I regarded heaven. And now could it be that I was actually going to Europe? Such thoughts as these were constantly with me.

Two other thoughts troubled me a good deal. I feared that people who heard that Mrs. Washington and I were going to Europe might not know all the circumstances, and might get the idea that we had become, as some might say, "stuck up," and were trying to "show off." I recalled that from my youth I had heard it said that too often, when people of my race reached any degree of success, they were inclined to unduly exalt themselves; to try and ape the wealthy, and in so doing to lose their heads. The fear that people might think this of us haunted me a good deal. Then, too, I could not see how my conscience would permit me to spare the time from my work and be happy. It seemed mean and selfish in me to be taking a vacation while others were at work, and while there was so much that needed to be done. From the time I could remember, I had always been at work, and I did not see how I could spend three or four months in doing nothing. The fact was that I did not know how to take a vacation.

Mrs. Washington had much the same difficulty in getting away, but she was anxious to go because she thought that I needed the rest. There were many important National questions bearing upon the life of the race which were being agitated at that time, and this made it all the harder for us to decide to go. We finally gave our Boston friends our promise that we would go, and then they insisted that the date of our departure be set as soon as possible. So we decided upon May 10. My good friend Mr. Garrison kindly took charge of all the details necessary for the success of the trip, and he, as well as other friends, gave us a great number of letters of introduction to people in France and England, and made other arrangements for our comfort and convenience abroad. Good-bys were said at Tuskegee, and we were in New York May 9, ready to sail the next day. Our daughter Portia, who was then studying in South Framingham, Mass., came to New York to see us off. Mr. Scott, my secretary, came with me to New York, in order that I might clear up the last bit of business before I left. Other friends also came to New York to see us off. Just before we went on board the steamer another pleasant surprise came to us in the form of a letter from two generous ladies, stating that they had decided to give us the money with which to erect a new building to be used in properly housing all our industries for girls at Tuskegee.

We were to sail on the *Friesland*, of the Red Star Line, and a beautiful vessel she was. We went on board just before noon, the hour of sailing. I had never before been on board a large ocean steamer, and the feeling which took possession of me when I found myself there is rather hard to describe. It was a feeling, I think, of awe mingled with delight. We were agreeably surprised to find that the captain, as well as several of the other officers, not only knew who we were, but was expecting us and gave us a pleasant greeting. There were several passengers whom we knew, including Senator Sewell, of New Jersey, and Edward Marshall, the newspaper correspondent. I had just a little fear that we would not be treated civilly by some of the passengers. This fear was based upon what I had heard other people of my race, who had crossed the ocean, say about unpleasant experiences in crossing the ocean in American vessels. But in our case, from the captain down to the most humble servant, we were treated with the greatest kindness. Nor was this kindness confined to those who were connected with the steamer; it was shown by all the passengers also. There were not a few Southern men and women on board, and they were as cordial as those from other parts of the country.

As soon as the last good-bys were said, and the steamer had cut loose from the wharf, the load of care, anxiety, and responsibility which I had carried for eighteen years began to lift itself from my shoulders at the rate, it seemed to me, of a pound a minute. It was the first time in all those years that I had felt, even in a measure, free from care; and my feeling of relief it is hard to describe on paper. Added to this was the delightful anticipation of being in Europe soon. It all seemed more like a dream than like a reality.

Mr. Garrison had thoughtfully arranged to have us have one of the most comfortable rooms on the ship. The second or third day out I began to sleep, and I think that I slept at the rate of fifteen hours a day during the remainder of the ten days' passage. Then it was that I began to understand how tired I really was. These long sleeps I kept up for a month after we landed on the other side. It was such an unusual feeling to wake up in the morning and realize that I had no engagements; did not have to take a train at a certain hour; did not have an appointment to meet some one, or to make an address, at a certain hour. How different all this was from the experiences that I have been through when travelling, when I have sometimes slept in three different beds in a single night!

When Sunday came, the captain invited me to conduct the religious services, but, not being a minister, I declined. The passengers, however, began making requests that I deliver an address to them in the dining-saloon some time during the voyage, and this I consented to do. Senator Sewell presided at this meeting. After ten days of delightful weather, during which I was not seasick for a day, we landed at the interesting old city of Antwerp, in Belgium.

The next day after we landed happened to be one of those numberless holidays which the people of those countries are in the habit of observing. It was a bright, beautiful day. Our room in the hotel faced the main public square, and the sights there—the people coming in from the country with all kinds of beautiful flowers to sell, the women coming in with their dogs drawing large, brightly polished cans filled with milk, the people streaming into the cathedral—filled me with a sense of newness that I had never before experienced.

After spending some time in Antwerp, we were invited to go with a party of a half-dozen persons on a trip through Holland. This party included Edward Marshall and some American artists who had come over on the same steamer with us. We accepted the invitation, and enjoyed the trip greatly. I think it was all the more interesting and instructive because we went for most of the way on one of the slow, old-fashioned canal-boats. This gave us an opportunity of seeing and studying the real life of the people in the country districts. We went in this way as far as Rotterdam, and later went to The Hague, where the Peace Conference was then in session, and where we were kindly received by the American representatives.

The thing that impressed itself most on me in Holland was the thoroughness of the agriculture and the excellence of the Holstein cattle. I never knew, before visiting Holland, how much it was possible for people to get out of a small plot of ground. It seemed to me that absolutely no land was wasted. It was worth a trip to Holland, too, just to get a sight of three or four hundred fine Holstein cows grazing in one of those intensely green fields.

From Holland we went to Belgium, and made a hasty trip through that country, stopping at Brussels, where we visited the battlefield of Waterloo. From Belgium we went direct to Paris, where we found that Mr. Theodore Stanton, the son of Mrs. Elizabeth Cady Stanton, had kindly provided accommodations for us. We had barely got settled in Paris before an invitation came to me from the University Club of Paris to be its guest at a banquet which was soon to be given. The other guests were ex-President Benjamin Harrison and Archbishop Ireland, who were in Paris at the time. The American Ambassador, General Horace Porter, presided at the banquet. My address on this occasion seemed to give satisfaction to those who heard it. General Harrison kindly devoted a large portion of his remarks at dinner to myself and to the influence of the work at Tuskegee on the American race question. After my address at this banquet other invitations came to me, but I declined the most of them, knowing that if I accepted them all, the object of my visit would be defeated. I did, however, consent to deliver an address in the American chapel the following Sunday morning, and at this meeting General Harrison, General Porter, and other distinguished Americans were present.

Later we received a formal call from the American Ambassador, and were invited to attend a reception at his residence. At this reception we met many Americans, among them Justices Fuller and Harlan, of the United States Supreme Court. During our entire stay of a month in Paris, both the American Ambassador and his wife, as well as several other Americans, were very kind to us.

While in Paris we saw a good deal of the now famous American Negro painter, Mr. Henry O. Tanner, whom we had formerly known in America. It was very satisfactory to find how well known Mr. Tanner was in the field of art, and to note the high standing which all classes accorded to him. When we told some Americans that we were going to the Luxembourg Palace to see a painting by an American Negro, it was hard to convince them that a Negro had been thus honoured. I do not believe that they were really convinced of the fact until they saw the picture for themselves. My acquaintance with Mr. Tanner reenforced in my mind the truth which I am constantly trying to impress upon our students at Tuskegee—and on our people throughout the country, as far as I can reach them with my voice—that any man, regardless of colour, will be recognized and rewarded just in proportion as he learns to do something well—learns to do it better than some one else—however humble the thing may be. As I have said, I believe that my race will succeed in proportion as it learns to do a common thing in an uncommon manner; learns to do a thing so thoroughly that no one can improve upon what it has done; learns to make its services of indispensable value. This was the spirit that inspired me in my first effort at Hampton, when I was given the opportunity to sweep and dust that schoolroom. In a degree I felt that my whole future life depended upon the thoroughness with which I cleaned that room, and I was determined to do it so well that no one could find any fault with the job. Few people ever stopped, I found, when looking at his pictures, to inquire whether Mr. Tanner was a Negro painter, a French painter, or a German painter. They simply knew that he was able to produce something which the world wanted—a great painting—and the matter of his colour did not enter into their minds. When a Negro girl learns to cook, to wash dishes, to sew, or write a book, or a Negro boy learns to groom horses, or to grow sweet potatoes, or to produce butter, or to build a house, or to be able to practise medicine, as well or better than some one else, they will be rewarded regardless of race or colour. In the long run, the world is going to have the best, and any difference in race, religion, or previous history will not long keep the world from what it wants.

I think that the whole future of my race hinges on the question as to whether or not it can make itself of such indispensible value that the people in the town and the state where we reside will feel that our presence is necessary to the happiness and well-being of the community. No man who continues to add something to the material, intellectual, and moral well-being of the place in which he lives is long left without proper reward. This is a great human law which cannot be permanently nullified.

The love of pleasure and excitement which seems in a large measure to possess the French people impressed itself upon me. I think they are more noted in this respect than is true of the people of my own race. In point of morality and moral earnestness I do not believe that the French are ahead of my own race in America. Severe competition and the great stress of life have led them to learn to do things more thoroughly and to exercise greater economy; but time, I think, will bring my race to the same point. In the matter of truth and high honour I do not believe that the average Frenchman is ahead of the American Negro; while so far as mercy and kindness to dumb animals go, I believe that my race is far ahead. In fact, when I left France, I had more faith in the future of the black man in America than I had ever possessed.

From Paris we went to London, and reached there early in July, just about the height of the London social season. Parliament was in session, and there was a great deal of gaiety. Mr. Garrison and other friends had provided us with a large number of letters of introduction, and they had also sent letters to other persons in different parts of the United Kingdom, apprising these people of our coming. Very soon after reaching London we were flooded with invitations to attend all manner of social functions, and a great many invitations came to me asking that I deliver public addresses. The most of these invitations I declined, for the reason that I wanted to rest. Neither were we able to accept more than a small proportion of the other invitations. The Rev. Dr. Brooke Herford and Mrs. Herford, whom I had known in Boston, consulted with the American Ambassador, the Hon. Joseph Choate, and arranged for me to speak at a public meeting to be held in Exeter Hall. Mr. Choate kindly consented to preside. The meeting was largely attended. There were many distinguished persons present, among them several members of Parliament, including Mr. James Bryce, who spoke at the meeting. What the American Ambassador said in introducing me, as well as a synopsis of what I said, was widely published in England and in the American papers at the time. Dr. and Mrs. Herford gave Mrs. Washington and myself a reception, at which we had the privilege of meeting some of the best people in England. Throughout our stay in London Ambassador Choate was most kind and attentive to us. At the Ambassador's reception I met, for the first time, Mark Twain.

We were the guests several times of Mrs. T. Fisher Unwin, the daughter of the English statesman, Richard Cobden. It seemed as if both Mr. and Mrs. Unwin could not do enough for our comfort and happiness. Later, for nearly a week, we were the guests of the daughter of John Bright, now Mrs. Clark, of Street, England. Both Mr. and Mrs. Clark, with their daughter, visited us at Tuskegee the next year. In Birmingham, England, we were the guests for several days of Mr. Joseph Sturge, whose father was a great abolitionist and friend of Whittier and Garrison. It was a great privilege to meet throughout England those who had known and honoured the late William Lloyd Garrison, the Hon. Frederick Douglass, and other abolitionists. The English abolitionists with whom we came in contact never seemed to tire of talking about these two Americans. Before going to England I had had no proper conception of the deep interest displayed by the abolitionists of England in the cause of freedom, nor did I realize the amount of substantial help given by them.

In Bristol, England, both Mrs. Washington and I spoke at the Women's Liberal Club. I was also the principal speaker at the Commencement exercises of the Royal College for the Blind. These exercises were held in the Crystal Palace, and the presiding officer was the late Duke of Westminster, who was said to be, I believe, the richest man in England, if not in the world. The Duke, as well as his wife and their daughter, seemed to be pleased with what I said, and thanked me heartily. Through the kindness of Lady Aberdeen, my wife and I were enabled to go with a party of those who were attending the International Congress of Women, then in session in London, to see Queen Victoria, at Windsor Castle, where, afterward, we were all the guests of her Majesty at tea. In our party was Miss Susan B. Anthony, and I was deeply impressed with the fact that one did not often get an opportunity to see, during the same hour, two women so remarkable in different ways as Susan B. Anthony and Queen Victoria.

In the House of Commons, which we visited several times, we met Sir Henry M. Stanley. I talked with him about Africa and its relation to the American Negro, and after my interview with him I became more convinced than ever that there was no hope of the American Negro's improving his condition by emigrating to Africa.

On various occasions Mrs. Washington and I were the guests of Englishmen in their country homes, where, I think, one sees the Englishman at his best. In one thing, at least, I feel sure that the English are ahead of Americans, and that is, that they have learned how to get more out of life. The home life of the English seems to me to be about as perfect as anything can be. Everything moves like clockwork. I was impressed, too, with the deference that the servants show to their "masters" and "mistresses,"—terms which I suppose would not be tolerated in America. The English servant expects, as a rule, to be nothing but a servant, and so he perfects himself in the art to a degree that no class of servants in America has yet reached. In our country the servant expects to become, in a few years, a "master" himself. Which system is preferable? I will not venture an answer.

Another thing that impressed itself upon me throughout England was the high regard that all classes have for law and order, and the ease and thoroughness with which everything is done. The Englishmen, I found, took plenty of time for eating, as for everything else. I am not sure if, in the long run, they do not accomplish as much or more than rushing, nervous Americans do.

My visit to England gave me a higher regard for the nobility than I had had. I had no idea that they were so generally loved and respected by the classes, nor had I any correct conception of how much time and money they spent in works of philanthropy, and how much real heart they put into this work. My impression had been that they merely spent money freely and had a "good time."

It was hard for me to get accustomed to speaking to English audiences. The average Englishman is so serious, and is so tremendously in earnest about everything, that when I told a story that would have made an American audience roar with laughter, the Englishmen simply looked me straight in the face without even cracking a smile.

When the Englishman takes you into his heart and friendship, he binds you there as with cords of steel, and I do not believe that there are many other friendships that are so lasting or so satisfactory. Perhaps I can illustrate this point in no better way than by relating the following incident. Mrs. Washington and I were invited to attend a reception given by the Duke and Duchess of Sutherland, at Stafford House—said to be the finest house in London; I may add that I believe the Duchess of Sutherland is said to be the most beautiful woman in England. There must have been at least three hundred persons at this reception. Twice during the evening the Duchess sought us out for a conversation, and she asked me to write her when we got home, and tell her more about the work at Tuskegee. This I did. When Christmas came we were surprised and delighted to receive her photograph with her autograph on it. The correspondence has continued, and we now feel that in the Duchess of Sutherland we have one of our warmest friends.

After three months in Europe we sailed from Southampton in the steamship *St. Louis*. On this steamer there was a fine library that had been presented to the ship by the citizens of St. Louis, Mo. In this library I found a life of Frederick Douglass, which I began reading. I became especially interested in Mr. Douglass's description of the way he was treated on shipboard during his first or second visit to England. In this description he told how he was not permitted to enter the cabin, but had to confine himself to the deck of the ship. A few minutes after I had finished reading this description I was waited on by a committee of ladies and gentlemen with the request that I deliver an address at a concert which was to begin the following evening. And yet there are people who are bold enough to say that race feeling in America is not growing less intense! At this concert the Hon. Benjamin B. Odell, Jr., the present governor of New York, presided. I was never given a more cordial hearing anywhere. A large proportion of the passengers were Southern people. After the concert some of the passengers proposed that a subscription be raised to help the work at Tuskegee, and the money to support several scholarships was the result.

While we were in Paris I was very pleasantly surprised to receive the following invitation from the citizens of West Virginia and of the city near which I had spent my boyhood days:—

Charleston, W. Va., May 16, 1899.

Professor Booker T. Washington, Paris, France.

Dear Sir: Many of the best citizens of West Virginia have united in liberal expressions of admiration and praise of your worth and work, and desire that on your return from Europe you should favour them with your presence and with the inspiration of your words. We must sincerely indorse this move, and on behalf of the citizens of Charleston extend to your our most cordial invitation to have you come to us, that we may honour you who have done so much by your life and work to honour us.

We are,
Very truly yours,
The Common Council of the City of Charleston,
By W. Herman Smith, Mayor.

This invitation from the City Council of Charleston was accompanied by the following:—

Professor Booker T. Washington, Paris, France.

Dear Sir: We, the citizens of Charleston and West Virginia, desire to express our pride in you and the splendid career that you have thus far accomplished, and ask that we be permitted to show our pride and interest in a substantial way.

Your recent visit to your old home in our midst awoke within us the keenest regret that we were not permitted to hear you and render some substantial aid to your work, before you left for Europe.

In view of the foregoing, we earnestly invite you to share the hospitality of our city upon your return from Europe, and give us the opportunity to hear you and put ourselves in touch with your work in a way that will be most gratifying to yourself, and that we may receive the inspiration of your words and presence.

An early reply to this invitation, with an indication of the time you may reach our city, will greatly oblige,

Yours very respectfully,

The Charleston *Daily Gazette*, The *Daily Mail-Tribune*; G.W. Atkinson, Governor; E.L. Boggs, Secretary to Governor; Wm. M.O. Dawson, Secretary of State; L.M. La Follette, Auditor; J.R. Trotter, Superintendent of Schools; E.W. Wilson, ex-Governor; W.A. MacCorkle, ex-Governor; John Q. Dickinson, President Kanawha Valley Bank; L. Prichard, President Charleston National Bank; Geo. S. Couch, President Kanawha National Bank; Ed. Reid, Cashier Kanawha National Bank; Geo. S. Laidley, Superintendent City Schools; L.E. McWhorter, President Board of Education; Chas. K. Payne, wholesale merchant; and many others.

This invitation, coming as it did from the City Council, the state officers, and all the substantial citizens of both races of the community where I had spent my boyhood, and from which I had gone a few years before, unknown, in poverty and ignorance, in quest of an education, not only surprised me, but almost unmanned me. I could not understand what I had done to deserve it all.

I accepted the invitation, and at the appointed day was met at the railway station at Charleston by a committee headed by ex-Governor W.A. MacCorkle, and composed of men of both races. The public reception was held in the Opera-House at Charleston. The Governor of the state, the Hon. George W. Atkinson, presided, and an address of welcome was made by ex-Governor MacCorkle. A prominent part in the reception was taken by the coloured citizens. The Opera-House was filled with citizens of both races, and among the white people were many for whom I had worked when I was a boy. The next day Governor and Mrs. Atkinson gave me a public reception at the State House, which was attended by all classes.

Not long after this the coloured people in Atlanta, Georgia, gave me a reception at which the Governor of the state presided, and a similar reception was given me in New Orleans, which was presided over by the Mayor of the city. Invitations came from many other places which I was not able to accept.

# CHAPTER XVII
## *Last Words*

Before going to Europe some events came into my life which were great surprises to me. In fact, my whole life has largely been one of surprises. I believe that any man's life will be filled with constant, unexpected encouragements of this kind if he makes up his mind to do his level best each day of his life—that is, tries to make each day reach as nearly as possible the high-water mark of pure, unselfish, useful living. I pity the man, black or white, who has never experienced the joy and satisfaction that come to one by reason of an effort to assist in making some one else more useful and more happy.

Six months before he died, and nearly a year after he had been stricken with paralysis, General Armstrong expressed a wish to visit Tuskegee again before he passed away. Notwithstanding the fact that he had lost the use of his limbs to such an extent that he was practically helpless, his wish was gratified, and he was brought to Tuskegee. The owners of the Tuskegee Railroad, white men living in the town, offered to run a special train, without cost, out of the main station—Chehaw, five miles away—to meet him. He arrived on the school grounds about nine o'clock in the evening. Some one had suggested that we give the General a "pine-knot torchlight reception." This plan was carried out, and the moment that his carriage entered the school grounds he began passing between two lines of lighted and waving "fat pine" wood knots held by over a thousand students and teachers. The whole thing was so novel and surprising that the General was completely overcome with happiness. He remained a guest in my home for nearly two months, and, although almost wholly without the use of voice or limb, he spent nearly every hour in devising ways and means to help the South. Time and time again he said to me, during this visit, that it was not only the duty of the country to assist in elevating the Negro of the South, but the poor white man as well. At the end of his visit I resolved anew to devote myself more earnestly than ever to the cause which was so near his heart. I said that if a man in his condition was willing to think, work, and act, I should not be wanting in furthering in every possible way the wish of his heart.

The death of General Armstrong, a few weeks later, gave me the privilege of getting acquainted with one of the finest, most unselfish, and most attractive men that I have ever come in contact with. I refer to the Rev. Dr. Hollis B. Frissell, now the Principal of the Hampton Institute, and General Armstrong's successor. Under the clear, strong, and almost perfect leadership of Dr. Frissell, Hampton has had a career of prosperity and usefulness that is all that the General could have wished for. It seems to be the constant effort of Dr. Frissell to hide his own great personality behind that of General Armstrong—to make himself of "no reputation" for the sake of the cause.

More than once I have been asked what was the greatest surprise that ever came to me. I have little hesitation in answering that question. It was the following letter, which came to me one Sunday morning when I was sitting on the veranda of my home at Tuskegee, surrounded by my wife and three children:—

Harvard University, Cambridge, May 28, 1896.

President Booker T. Washington,

My Dear Sir: Harvard University desired to confer on you at the approaching Commencement an honorary degree; but it is our custom to confer degrees only on gentlemen who are present. Our Commencement occurs this year on June 24, and your presence would be desirable from about noon till about five o'clock in the afternoon. Would it be possible for you to be in Cambridge on that day?

Believe me, with great regard,
Very truly yours,
Charles W. Eliot.

This was a recognition that had never in the slightest manner entered into my mind, and it was hard for me to realize that I was to be honoured by a degree from the oldest and most renowned university in America. As I sat upon my veranda, with this letter in my hand, tears came into my eyes. My whole former life—my life as a slave on the plantation, my work in the coal-mine, the times when I was without food and clothing, when I made my bed under a sidewalk, my struggles for an education, the trying days I had had at Tuskegee, days when I did not know where to turn for a dollar to continue the work there, the ostracism and sometimes oppression of my race,—all this passed before me and nearly overcame me.

I had never sought or cared for what the world calls fame. I have always looked upon fame as something to be used in accomplishing good. I have often said to my friends that if I can use whatever prominence may have come to me as an instrument with which to do good, I am content to have it. I care for it only as a means to be used for doing good, just as wealth may be used. The more I come into contact with wealthy people, the more I believe that they are growing in the direction of looking upon their money simply as an instrument which God has placed in their hand for doing good with. I never go to the office of Mr. John D. Rockefeller, who more than once has been generous to Tuskegee, without being reminded of this. The close, careful, and minute investigation that he always makes in order to be sure that every dollar that he gives will do the most good—an investigation that is just as searching as if he were investing money in a business enterprise—convinces me that the growth in this direction is most encouraging.

At nine o'clock, on the morning of June 24, I met President Eliot, the Board of Overseers of Harvard University, and the other guests, at the designated place on the university grounds, for the purpose of being escorted to Sanders Theatre, where the Commencement exercises were to be held and degrees conferred. Among others invited to be present for the purpose of receiving a degree at this time were General Nelson A. Miles, Dr. Bell, the inventor of the Bell telephone, Bishop Vincent, and the Rev. Minot J. Savage. We were placed in line immediately behind the President and the Board of Overseers, and directly afterward the Governor of Massachusetts, escorted by the Lancers, arrived and took his place in the line of march by the side of President Eliot. In the line there were also various other officers and professors, clad in cap and gown. In this order we marched to Sanders Theatre, where, after the usual Commencement exercises, came the conferring of the honorary degrees. This, it seems, is always considered the most interesting feature at Harvard. It is not known, until the individuals appear, upon whom the honorary degrees are to be conferred, and those receiving these honours are cheered by the students and others in proportion to their popularity. During the conferring of the degrees excitement and enthusiasm are at the highest pitch.

When my name was called, I rose, and President Eliot, in beautiful and strong English, conferred upon me the degree of Master of Arts. After these exercises were over, those who had received honorary degrees were invited to lunch with the President. After the lunch we were formed in line again, and were escorted by the Marshal of the day, who that year happened to be Bishop William Lawrence, through the grounds, where, at different points, those who had been honoured were called by name and received the Harvard yell. This march ended at Memorial Hall, where the alumni dinner was served. To see over a thousand strong men, representing all that is best in State, Church, business, and education, with the glow and enthusiasm of college loyalty and college pride,—which has, I think, a peculiar Harvard flavour,—is a sight that does not easily fade from memory.

Among the speakers after dinner were President Eliot, Governor Roger Wolcott, General Miles, Dr. Minot J. Savage, the Hon. Henry Cabot Lodge, and myself. When I was called upon, I said, among other things:—

> It would in some measure relieve my embarrassment if I could, even in a slight degree, feel myself worthy of the great honour which you do me to-day. Why you have called me from the Black Belt of the South, from among my humble people, to share in the honours of this occasion, is not for me to explain; and yet it may not be inappropriate for me to suggest that it seems to me that one of the most vital questions that touch our American life is how to bring the strong, wealthy, and learned

into helpful touch with the poorest, most ignorant, and humblest, and at the same time make one appreciate the vitalizing, strengthening influence of the other. How shall we make the mansion on yon Beacon Street feel and see the need of the spirits in the lowliest cabin in Alabama cotton-fields or Louisiana sugar-bottoms? This problem Harvard University is solving, not by bringing itself down, but by bringing the masses up.

If my life in the past has meant anything in the lifting up of my people and the bringing about of better relations between your race and mine, I assure you from this day it will mean doubly more. In the economy of God there is but one standard by which an individual can succeed—there is but one for a race. This country demands that every race shall measure itself by the American standard. By it a race must rise or fall, succeed or fail, and in the last analysis mere sentiment counts for little. During the next half-century and more, my race must continue passing through the severe American crucible. We are to be tested in our patience, our forbearance, our perseverance, our power to endure wrong, to withstand temptations, to economize, to acquire and use skill; in our ability to compete, to succeed in commerce, to disregard the superficial for the real, the appearance for the substance, to be great and yet small, learned and yet simple, high and yet the servant of all.

As this was the first time that a New England university had conferred an honorary degree upon a Negro, it was the occasion of much newspaper comment throughout the country. A correspondent of a New York paper said:—

When the name of Booker T. Washington was called, and he arose to acknowledge and accept, there was such an outburst of applause as greeted no other name except that of the popular soldier patriot, General Miles. The applause was not studied and stiff, sympathetic and condoling; it was enthusiasm and admiration. Every part of the audience from pit to gallery joined in, and a glow covered the cheeks of those around me, proving sincere appreciation of the rising struggle of an ex-slave and the work he has accomplished for his race.

A Boston paper said, editorially:—

In conferring the honorary degree of Master of Arts upon the Principal of Tuskegee Institute, Harvard University has honoured itself as well as the object of this distinction. The work which Professor Booker T. Washington has accomplished for the education, good citizenship, and popular enlightenment in his chosen field of labour in the South entitles him to rank with our national benefactors. The university which can claim him on its list of sons, whether in regular course or *honoris causa*, may be proud.

It has been mentioned that Mr. Washington is the first of his race to receive an honorary degree from a New England university. This, in itself, is a distinction. But the degree was not conferred because Mr. Washington is a coloured man, or because he was born in slavery, but because he has shown, by his work for the elevation of the people of the Black Belt of the South, a genius and a broad humanity which count for greatness in any man, whether his skin be white or black.

Another Boston paper said:—

It is Harvard which, first among New England colleges, confers an honorary degree upon a black man. No one who has followed the history of Tuskegee and its work can fail to admire the courage, persistence, and splendid common sense of Booker T. Washington. Well may Harvard honour the ex-slave, the value of whose services, alike to his race and country, only the future can estimate.

The correspondent of the New York *Times* wrote:—

All the speeches were enthusiastically received, but the coloured man carried off the oratorical honours, and the applause which broke out when he had finished was vociferous and long-continued.

Soon after I began work at Tuskegee I formed a resolution, in the secret of my heart, that I would try to build up a school that would be of so much service to the country that the President of the United States would one day come to see it. This was, I confess, rather a bold resolution, and for a number of years I kept it hidden in my own thoughts, not daring to share it with any one.

In November, 1897, I made the first move in this direction, and that was in securing a visit from a member of President McKinley's Cabinet, the Hon. James Wilson, Secretary of Agriculture. He came to deliver an address at the formal opening of the Slater-Armstrong Agricultural Building, our first large building to be used for the purpose of giving training to our students in agriculture and kindred branches.

In the fall of 1898 I heard that President McKinley was likely to visit Atlanta, Georgia, for the purpose of taking part in the Peace Jubilee exercises to be held there to commemorate the successful close of the Spanish-American war. At this time I had been hard at work, together with our teachers, for eighteen years, trying to build up a school that we thought would be of service to the Nation, and I determined to make a direct effort to secure a visit from the President and his Cabinet. I went to Washington, and I was not long in the city before I found my way to the White House. When I got there I found the waiting rooms full of people, and my heart began to sink, for I feared there would not be much chance of my seeing the President that day, if at all. But, at any rate, I got an opportunity to see Mr. J. Addison Porter, the secretary to the President, and explained to him my mission. Mr. Porter kindly sent my card directly to the President, and in a few minutes word came from Mr. McKinley that he would see me.

How any man can see so many people of all kinds, with all kinds of errands, and do so much hard work, and still keep himself calm, patient, and fresh for each visitor in the way that President McKinley does, I cannot understand. When I saw the President he kindly thanked me for the work which we were doing at Tuskegee for the interests of the country. I then told him, briefly, the object of my visit. I impressed upon him the fact that a visit from the

Chief Executive of the Nation would not only encourage our students and teachers, but would help the entire race. He seemed interested, but did not make a promise to go to Tuskegee, for the reason that his plans about going to Atlanta were not then fully made; but he asked me to call the matter to his attention a few weeks later.

By the middle of the following month the President had definitely decided to attend the Peace Jubilee at Atlanta. I went to Washington again and saw him, with a view of getting him to extend his trip to Tuskegee. On this second visit Mr. Charles W. Hare, a prominent white citizen of Tuskegee, kindly volunteered to accompany me, to reenforce my invitation with one from the white people of Tuskegee and the vicinity.

Just previous to my going to Washington the second time, the country had been excited, and the coloured people greatly depressed, because of several severe race riots which had occurred at different points in the South. As soon as I saw the President, I perceived that his heart was greatly burdened by reason of these race disturbances. Although there were many people waiting to see him, he detained me for some time, discussing the condition and prospects of the race. He remarked several times that he was determined to show his interest and faith in the race, not merely in words, but by acts. When I told him that I thought that at that time scarcely anything would go farther in giving hope and encouragement to the race than the fact that the President of the Nation would be willing to travel one hundred and forty miles out of his way to spend a day at a Negro institution, he seemed deeply impressed.

While I was with the President, a white citizen of Atlanta, a Democrat and an ex-slaveholder, came into the room, and the President asked his opinion as to the wisdom of his going to Tuskegee. Without hesitation the Atlanta man replied that it was the proper thing for him to do. This opinion was re-enforced by that friend of the race, Dr. J.L.M. Curry. The President promised that he would visit our school on the 16th of December.

When it became known that the President was going to visit our school, the white citizens of the town of Tuskegee—a mile distant from the school—were as much pleased as were our students and teachers. The white people of this town, including both men and women, began arranging to decorate the town, and to form themselves into committees for the purpose of cooperating with the officers of our school in order that the distinguished visitor might have a fitting reception. I think I never realized before this how much the white people of Tuskegee and vicinity thought of our institution. During the days when we were preparing for the President's reception, dozens of these people came to me and said that, while they did not want to push themselves into prominence, if there was anything they could do to help, or to relieve me personally, I had but to intimate it and they would be only too glad to assist. In fact, the thing that touched me almost as deeply as the visit of the President itself was the deep pride which all classes of citizens in Alabama seemed to take in our work.

The morning of December 16th brought to the little city of Tuskegee such a crowd as it had never seen before. With the President came Mrs. McKinley and all of the Cabinet officers but one; and most of them brought their wives or some members of their families. Several prominent generals came, including General Shafter and General Joseph Wheeler, who were recently returned from the Spanish-American war. There was also a host of newspaper correspondents. The Alabama Legislature was in session in Montgomery at this time. This body passed a resolution to adjourn for the purpose of visiting Tuskegee. Just before the arrival of the President's party the Legislature arrived, headed by the governor and other state officials.

The citizens of Tuskegee had decorated the town from the station to the school in a generous manner. In order to economize in the matter of time, we arranged to have the whole school pass in review before the President. Each student carried a stalk of sugar-cane with some open bolls of cotton fastened to the end of it. Following the students the work of all departments of the school passed in review, displayed on "floats" drawn by horses, mules, and oxen. On these floats we tried to exhibit not only the present work of the school, but to show the contrasts between the old methods of doing things and the new. As an example, we showed the old method of dairying in contrast with the improved methods, the old methods of tilling the soil in contrast with the new, the old methods of cooking and housekeeping in contrast with the new. These floats consumed an hour and a half of time in passing.

In his address in our large, new chapel, which the students had recently completed, the President said, among other things:—

> To meet you under such pleasant auspices and to have the opportunity of a personal observation of your work is indeed most gratifying. The Tuskegee Normal and Industrial Institute is ideal in its conception, and has already a large and growing reputation in the country, and is not unknown abroad. I congratulate all who are associated in this undertaking for the good work which it is doing in the education of its students to lead lives of honour and usefulness, thus exalting the race for which it was established.
>
> Nowhere, I think, could a more delightful location have been chosen for this unique educational experiment, which has attracted the attention and won the support even of conservative philanthropists in all sections of the country.
>
> To speak of Tuskegee without paying special tribute to Booker T. Washington's genius and perseverance would be impossible. The inception of this noble enterprise was his, and he deserves high credit for it. His was the enthusiasm and enterprise which made its steady progress possible and established in the institution its present high standard of accomplishment. He has won a worthy reputation as one of the great leaders of his race, widely known and much respected at home and abroad as an accomplished educator, a great orator, and a true philanthropist.

The Hon. John D. Long, the Secretary of the Navy, said in part:—

> I cannot make a speech to-day. My heart is too full—full of hope, admiration, and pride for my countrymen of both sections and both colours. I am filled with gratitude and admiration for

> your work, and from this time forward I shall have absolute confidence in your progress and in the solution of the problem in which you are engaged.
>
> The problem, I say, has been solved. A picture has been presented to-day which should be put upon canvas with the pictures of Washington and Lincoln, and transmitted to future time and generations—a picture which the press of the country should spread broadcast over the land, a most dramatic picture, and that picture is this: The President of the United States standing on this platform; on one side the Governor of Alabama, on the other, completing the trinity, a representative of a race only a few years ago in bondage, the coloured President of the Tuskegee Normal and Industrial Institute.
>
> God bless the President under whose majesty such a scene as that is presented to the American people. God bless the state of Alabama, which is showing that it can deal with this problem for itself. God bless the orator, philanthropist, and disciple of the Great Master—who, if he were on earth, would be doing the same work—Booker T. Washington.

Postmaster General Smith closed the address which he made with these words:—

> We have witnessed many spectacles within the last few days. We have seen the magnificent grandeur and the magnificent achievements of one of the great metropolitan cities of the South. We have seen heroes of the war pass by in procession. We have seen floral parades. But I am sure my colleagues will agree with me in saying that we have witnessed no spectacle more impressive and more encouraging, more inspiring for our future, than that which we have witnessed here this morning.

Some days after the President returned to Washington I received the letter which follows:—

Executive Mansion, Washington, Dec. 23, 1899.

Dear Sir: By this mail I take pleasure in sending you engrossed copies of the souvenir of the visit of the President to your institution. These sheets bear the autographs of the President and the members of the Cabinet who accompanied him on the trip. Let me take this opportunity of congratulating you most heartily and sincerely upon the great success of the exercises provided for and entertainment furnished us under your auspices during our visit to Tuskegee. Every feature of the programme was perfectly executed and was viewed or participated in with the heartiest satisfaction by every visitor present. The unique exhibition which you gave of your pupils engaged in their industrial vocations was not only artistic but thoroughly impressive. The tribute paid by the President and his Cabinet to your work was none too high, and forms a most encouraging augury, I think, for the future prosperity of your institution. I cannot close without assuring you that the modesty shown by yourself in the exercises was most favourably commented upon by all the members of our party.

With best wishes for the continued advance of your most useful and patriotic undertaking, kind personal regards, and the compliments of the season, believe me, always,

Very sincerely yours,
John Addison Porter,
Secretary to the President.

To President Booker T. Washington, Tuskegee Normal and Industrial Institute, Tuskegee, Ala.

Twenty years have now passed since I made the first humble effort at Tuskegee, in a broken-down shanty and an old hen-house, without owning a dollar's worth of property, and with but one teacher and thirty students. At the present time the institution owns twenty-three hundred acres of land, one thousand of which are under cultivation each year, entirely by student labour. There are now upon the grounds, counting large and small, sixty-six buildings; and all except four of these have been almost wholly erected by the labour of our students. While the students are at work upon the land and in erecting buildings, they are taught, by competent instructors, the latest methods of agriculture and the trades connected with building.

There are in constant operation at the school, in connection with thorough academic and religious training, thirty industrial departments. All of these teach industries at which our men and women can find immediate employment as soon as they leave the institution. The only difficulty now is that the demand for our graduates from both white and black people in the South is so great that we cannot supply more than one-half the persons for whom applications come to us. Neither have we the buildings nor the money for current expenses to enable us to admit to the school more than one-half the young men and women who apply to us for admission.

In our industrial teaching we keep three things in mind: first, that the student shall be so educated that he shall be enabled to meet conditions as they exist *now*, in the part of the South where he lives—in a word, to be able to do the thing which the world wants done; second, that every student who graduates from the school shall have enough skill, coupled with intelligence and moral character, to enable him to make a living for himself and others; third, to send every graduate out feeling and knowing that labour is dignified and beautiful—to make each one love labour instead of trying to escape it. In addition to the agricultural training which we give to young men, and the training given to our girls in all the usual domestic employments, we now train a number of girls in agriculture each year. These girls are taught gardening, fruit-growing, dairying, bee-culture, and poultry-raising.

While the institution is in no sense denominational, we have a department known as the Phelps Hall Bible Training School, in which a number of students are prepared for the ministry and other forms of Christian work, especially work in the country districts. What is equally important, each one of the students works half of each day at some industry, in order to get skill and the love of work, so that when he goes out from the institution he is prepared to set the people with whom he goes to labour a proper example in the matter of industry.

The value of our property is now over $700,000. If we add to this our endowment fund, which at present is $1,000,000, the value of the total property is now $1,700,000. Aside from the need for more buildings and for money for current expenses, the endowment fund should be increased to at least $3,000,000. The annual current expenses are now about $150,000. The greater part of this I collect each year by going from door to door and from house to house. All of our property is free from mortgage, and is deeded to an undenominational board of trustees who have the control of the institution.

From thirty students the number has grown to fourteen hundred, coming from twenty-seven states and territories, from Africa, Cuba, Puerto Rico, Jamaica, and other foreign countries. In our departments there are one hundred and ten officers and instructors; and if we add the families of our instructors, we have a constant population upon our grounds of not far from seventeen hundred people.

I have often been asked how we keep so large a body of people together, and at the same time keep them out of mischief. There are two answers: that the men and women who come to us for an education are in earnest; and that everybody is kept busy. The following outline of our daily work will testify to this:—

> 5 A.M., rising bell; 5.50 A.M., warning breakfast bell; 6 A.M., breakfast bell; 6.20 A.M., breakfast over; 6.20 to 6.50 A.M., rooms are cleaned; 6.50, work bell; 7.30, morning study hours; 8.20, morning school bell; 8.25, inspection of young men's toilet in ranks; 8.40, devotional exercises in chapel; 8.55, "five minutes with the daily news;" 9 A.M., class work begins; 12, class work closes; 12.15 P.M., dinner; 1 P.M., work bell; 1.30 P.M., class work begins; 3.30 P.M., class work ends; 5.30 P.M., bell to "knock off" work; 6 P.M., supper; 7.10 P.M., evening prayers; 7.30 P.M., evening study hours; 8.45 P.M., evening study hour closes; 9.20 P.M., warning retiring bell; 9.30 P.M., retiring bell.

We try to keep constantly in mind the fact that the worth of the school is to be judged by its graduates. Counting those who have finished the full course, together with those who have taken enough training to enable them to do reasonably good work, we can safely say that at least six thousand men and women from Tuskegee are now at work in different parts of the South; men and women who, by their own example or by direct efforts, are showing the masses of our race how to improve their material, educational, and moral and religious life. What is equally important, they are exhibiting a degree of common sense and self-control which is causing better relations to exist between the races, and is causing the Southern white man to learn to believe in the value of educating the men and women of my race. Aside from this, there is the influence that is constantly being exerted through the mothers' meeting and the plantation work conducted by Mrs. Washington.

Wherever our graduates go, the changes which soon begin to appear in the buying of land, improving homes, saving money, in education, and in high moral characters are remarkable. Whole communities are fast being revolutionized through the instrumentality of these men and women.

Ten years ago I organized at Tuskegee the first Negro Conference. This is an annual gathering which now brings to the school eight or nine hundred representative men and women of the race, who come to spend a day in finding out what the actual industrial, mental, and moral conditions of the people are, and in forming plans for improvement. Out from this central Negro Conference at Tuskegee have grown numerous state and local conferences which are doing the same kind of work. As a result of the influence of these gatherings, one delegate reported at the last annual meeting that ten families in his community had bought and paid for homes. On the day following the annual Negro Conference, there is the "Workers' Conference." This is composed of officers and teachers who are engaged in educational work in the larger institutions in the South. The Negro Conference furnishes a rare opportunity for these workers to study the real condition of the rank and file of the people.

In the summer of 1900, with the assistance of such prominent coloured men as Mr. T. Thomas Fortune, who has always upheld my hands in every effort, I organized the National Negro Business League, which held its first meeting in Boston, and brought together for the first time a large number of the coloured men who are engaged in various lines of trade or business in different parts of the United States. Thirty states were represented at our first meeting. Out of this national meeting grew state and local business leagues.

In addition to looking after the executive side of the work at Tuskegee, and raising the greater part of the money for the support of the school, I cannot seem to escape the duty of answering at least a part of the calls which come to me unsought to address Southern white audiences and audiences of my own race, as well as frequent gatherings in the North. As to how much of my time is spent in this way, the following clipping from a Buffalo (N.Y.) paper will tell. This has reference to an occasion when I spoke before the National Educational Association in that city.

Booker T. Washington, the foremost educator among the coloured people of the world, was a very busy man from the time he arrived in the city the other night from the West and registered at the Iroquois. He had hardly removed the stains of travel when it was time to partake of supper. Then he held a public levee in the parlours of the Iroquois until eight o'clock. During that time he was greeted by over two hundred eminent teachers and educators from all parts of the United States. Shortly after eight o'clock he was driven in a carriage to Music Hall, and in one hour and a half he made two ringing addresses, to as many as five thousand people, on Negro education. Then Mr. Washington was taken in charge by a delegation of coloured citizens, headed by the Rev. Mr. Watkins, and hustled off to a small informal reception, arranged in honour of the visitor by the people of his race.

Nor can I, in addition to making these addresses, escape the duty of calling the attention of the South and of the country in general, through the medium of the press, to matters that pertain to the interests of both races. This, for example, I have done in regard to the evil habit of lynching. When the Louisiana State Constitutional Convention was in session, I wrote an open letter to that body pleading for justice for the race. In all such efforts I have received warm and hearty support from the Southern newspapers, as well as from those in all other parts of the country.

Despite superficial and temporary signs which might lead one to entertain a contrary opinion, there was never a time when I felt more hopeful for the race than I do at the present. The great human law that in the end recognizes and rewards merit is everlasting and universal. The outside world does not know, neither can it appreciate, the struggle that is constantly going on in the hearts of both the Southern white people and their former slaves to free themselves from racial prejudice; and while both races are thus struggling they should have the sympathy, the support, and the forbearance of the rest of the world.

As I write the closing words of this autobiography I find myself—not by design—in the city of Richmond, Virginia: the city which only a few decades ago was the capital of the Southern Confederacy, and where, about twenty-five years ago, because of my poverty I slept night after night under a sidewalk.

This time I am in Richmond as the guest of the coloured people of the city; and came at their request to deliver an address last night to both races in the Academy of Music, the largest and finest audience room in the city. This was the first time that the coloured people had ever been permitted to use this hall. The day before I came, the City Council passed a vote to attend the meeting in a body to hear me speak. The state Legislature, including the House of Delegates and the Senate, also passed a unanimous vote to attend in a body. In the presence of hundreds of coloured people, many distinguished white citizens, the City Council, the state Legislature, and state officials, I delivered my message, which was one of hope and cheer; and from the bottom of my heart I thanked both races for this welcome back to the state that gave me birth.

# THE NARRATIVE OF THE LIFE OF FREDERICK DOUGLASS

FREDERICK
DOUGLASS

**Disclaimer**

Throughout the text, readers may find language and sentiments that appear both offensive and unacceptable. These words were duly reported by the former slave who wrote this book, and was forced to endure such dehumanizing attitudes on a daily basis. To better serve the author's original intentions and to ensure that the full impact of the writing is retained, we have decided to keep the original language in its entirety, though many segments may prove uncomfortable for the modern reader.

This edition published in 2020 by Arcturus Publishing Limited
26/27 Bickels Yard, 151–153 Bermondsey Street,
London SE1 3HA



Cover design: Peter Ridley
Cover illustration: Peter Gray

AD006326US

Printed in the UK

MIX
Paper from responsible sources
FSC
www.fsc.org
FSC® C018072

# Contents

# Introduction

Frederick Douglass was born a slave in Talbot County, Maryland, in 1818. He suffered through a tumultuous childhood, moving from one owner to another. His mother was a slave, but he was never certain of his father's identity, though it is likely that his father was the white master of the place of his birth, a plantation on the Tuckahoe River. By the age of six, he had twice been wrenched away from his family, first from his mother and then from his grandmother, and he was sent to the Wye House plantation.

After the death of Wye House's overseer, Aaron Anthony, life took a turn for the better for Frederick. He was sold to Lucretia Auld, who sent him to serve her brother-in-law Hugh in Baltimore. There, unlike most slaves, he obtained an education. Hugh's wife Sofia taught him to read and Douglass studied by himself, seeking out newspapers, books, and pamphlets whenever he could, convinced that education was the only route out of slavery.

In 1837, he fell in love with a free black woman from Baltimore called Anna Murray. It was all the motivation he needed to seek his escape from servitude. A year later, he managed to flee his masters. Taking the name "Douglass", he dedicated his life to eradicating slavery. It was not long before he published his autobiography, entitled *Narrative of the Life of Frederick Douglass, an American Slave* (1845), which became extraordinarily successful. He edited some of the major black newspapers of the era, including *The North Star* and *Frederick Douglass' Paper*, lectured across the country, and campaigned against slavery. When the Civil War arrived in 1861, Douglass firmly supported the Union because he believed it was fighting a war against slavery. After 1865, Douglass continued to campaign vigorously against the injustices of the Jim Crow laws and segregation, setting the stage for activists like Booker T. Washington.

By the end of the century, he was widely respected in official circles and was appointed as the minister to Haiti by President Benjamin Harrison in 1889. Despite spending most of his life in the north, Douglass never lost his appreciation for Maryland, the place of his birth. In 1895, Douglass died, giving way to a new generation of activists. His radical efforts had inspired countless Americans and revealed the true horrors of slavery to the American public.

# Preface

In the month of August, 1841, I attended an antislavery convention in Nantucket, at which it was my happiness to become acquainted with FREDERICK DOUGLASS, the writer of the following Narrative. He was a stranger to nearly every member of that body; but, having recently made his escape from the southern prison-house of bondage, and feeling his curiosity excited to ascertain the principles and measures of the abolitionists,—of whom he had heard a somewhat vague description while he was a slave,—he was induced to give his attendance, on the occasion alluded to, though at that time a resident in New Bedford.

Fortunate, most fortunate occurrence!—fortunate for the millions of his manacled brethren, yet panting for deliverance from their awful thraldom!—fortunate for the cause of negro emancipation, and of universal liberty!—fortunate for the land of his birth, which he has already done so much to save and bless!—fortunate for a large circle of friends and acquaintances, whose sympathy and affection he has strongly secured by the many sufferings he has endured, by his virtuous traits of character, by his ever-abiding remembrance of those who are in bonds, as being bound with them!—fortunate for the multitudes, in various parts of our republic, whose minds he has enlightened on the subject of slavery, and who have been melted to tears by his pathos, or roused to virtuous indignation by his stirring eloquence against the enslavers of men!—fortunate for himself, as it at once brought him into the field of public usefulness, "gave the world assurance of a MAN," quickened the slumbering energies of his soul, and consecrated him to the great work of breaking the rod of the oppressor, and letting the oppressed go free!

I shall never forget his first speech at the convention—the extraordinary emotion it excited in my own mind—the powerful impression it created upon a crowded auditory, completely taken by surprise—the applause which followed from the beginning to the end of his felicitous remarks. I think I never hated slavery so intensely as at that moment; certainly, my perception of the enormous outrage which is inflicted by it, on the godlike nature of its victims, was rendered far more clear than ever. There stood one, in physical proportion and stature commanding and exact—in intellect richly endowed—in natural eloquence a prodigy—in soul manifestly "created but a little lower than the angels"—yet a slave, ay, a fugitive slave,—trembling for his safety, hardly daring to believe that on the American soil, a single white person could be found who would befriend him at all hazards, for the love of God and humanity! Capable of high attainments as an intellectual and moral being—needing nothing but a comparatively small amount of cultivation to make him an ornament to society and a blessing to his race—by the law of the land, by the voice of the people, by the terms of the slave code, he was only a piece of property, a beast of burden, a chattel personal, nevertheless!

A beloved friend from New Bedford prevailed on Mr. DOUGLASS to address the convention. He came forward to the platform with a hesitancy and embarrassment, necessarily the attendants of a sensitive mind in such a novel position. After apologizing for his ignorance, and reminding the audience that slavery was a poor school for the human intellect and heart, he proceeded to narrate some of the facts in his own history as a slave, and in the course of his speech gave utterance to many noble thoughts and thrilling reflections. As soon as he had taken his seat, filled with hope and admiration, I rose, and declared that PATRICK HENRY, of revolutionary fame, never made a speech more eloquent in the cause of liberty, than the one we had just listened to from the lips of that hunted fugitive. So I believed at that time,—such is my belief now. I reminded the audience of the peril which surrounded this self-emancipated young man at the North,—even in Massachusetts, on the soil of the Pilgrim Fathers, among the descendants of revolutionary sires; and I appealed to them, whether they would ever allow him to be carried back into slavery,—law or no law, constitution or no constitution. The response was unanimous and in thunder-tones—"NO!" "Will you succor and protect him as a brother-man—a resident of the old Bay State?" "YES!" shouted the whole mass, with an energy so startling, that the ruthless tyrants south of Mason and Dixon's line might almost have heard the mighty burst of feeling, and recognized it as the pledge of an invincible determination, on the part of those who gave it, never to betray him that wanders, but to hide the outcast, and firmly to abide the consequences.

It was at once deeply impressed upon my mind, that, if Mr. DOUGLASS could be persuaded to consecrate his time and talents to the promotion of the anti-slavery enterprise, a powerful impetus would be given to it, and a stunning blow at the same time inflicted on northern prejudice against a colored complexion. I therefore endeavored to instil hope and courage into his mind, in order that he might dare to engage in a vocation so anomalous and responsible for a person in his situation; and I was seconded in this effort by warm-hearted friends, especially by the late General Agent of the Massachusetts Anti-Slavery Society, Mr. JOHN A. COLLINS, whose judgment in this instance entirely coincided with my own. At first, he could give no encouragement; with unfeigned diffidence, he expressed his conviction that he was not adequate to the performance of so great a task; the path marked out was wholly an untrodden one; he was sincerely apprehensive that he should do more harm than good. After much deliberation, however, he consented to make a trial; and ever since that period, he has acted as a lecturing agent, under the auspices either of the American or the Massachusetts Anti-Slavery Society. In labors he has been most abundant; and his success in combating prejudice, in gaining proselytes, in agitating the public mind, has far surpassed the most sanguine expectations that were raised at the commencement of his brilliant career. He has borne himself with gentleness and meekness, yet with true manliness of character. As a public speaker, he excels in pathos, wit, comparison, imitation, strength of reasoning, and fluency of language. There is in him that union of head and heart, which is indispensable to an enlightenment of the heads and a winning of the hearts of others. May his strength continue to be equal to his day! May he continue to "grow in grace, and in the knowledge of God," that he may be increasingly serviceable in the cause of bleeding humanity, whether at home or abroad!

It is certainly a very remarkable fact, that one of the most efficient advocates of the slave population, now before the public, is a fugitive slave, in the person of FREDERICK DOUGLASS; and that the free colored population of the United States are as ably represented by one of their own number, in the person of CHARLES LENOX REMOND, whose eloquent appeals have extorted the highest applause of multitudes on both sides of the Atlantic. Let the calumniators of the colored race despise themselves for their baseness and illiberality of spirit, and henceforth cease to talk of the natural inferiority of those who require nothing but time and opportunity to attain to the highest point of human excellence.

It may, perhaps, be fairly questioned, whether any other portion of the population of the earth could have endured the privations, sufferings and horrors of slavery, without having become more degraded in the scale of humanity than the slaves of African descent. Nothing has been left undone to cripple their intellects, darken their minds, debase their moral nature, obliterate all traces of their relationship to mankind; and yet how wonderfully they have sustained the mighty load of a most frightful bondage, under which they have been groaning for centuries! To illustrate the effect of slavery on the white man,—to show that he has no powers of endurance, in such a condition, superior to those of his black brother,—DANIEL O'CONNELL, the distinguished advocate of universal emancipation, and the mightiest champion of prostrate but not conquered Ireland, relates the following anecdote in a speech delivered by him in the Conciliation Hall, Dublin, before the Loyal National Repeal Association, March 31, 1845. "No matter," said Mr. O'CONNELL, "under what specious term it may disguise itself, slavery is still hideous. *It has a natural, an inevitable tendency to brutalize every noble faculty of man.* An American sailor, who was cast away on the shore of Africa, where he was kept in slavery for three years, was, at the expiration of that period, found to be imbruted and stultified—he had lost all reasoning power; and having forgotten his native language, could only utter some savage gibberish between Arabic and English, which nobody could understand, and which even he himself found difficulty in pronouncing. So much for the humanizing influence of THE DOMESTIC INSTITUTION!"

Admitting this to have been an extraordinary case of mental deterioration, it proves at least that the white slave can sink as low in the scale of humanity as the black one.

Mr. DOUGLASS has very properly chosen to write his own Narrative, in his own style, and according to the best of his ability, rather than to employ some one else. It is, therefore, entirely his own production; and, considering how long and dark was the career he had to run as a slave,—how few have been his opportunities to improve his mind since he broke his iron fetters—it is, in my judgment, highly creditable to his head and heart. He who can peruse it without a tearful eye, a heaving breast, an afflicted spirit,—without being filled with an unutterable abhorrence of slavery and all its abettors, and animated with a determination to seek the immediate overthrow of that execrable system,—without trembling for the fate of this country in the hands of a righteous God, who is ever on the side of the oppressed, and whose arm is not shortened that it cannot save,—must have a flinty heart, and be qualified to act the part of a trafficker "in slaves and the souls of men." I am confident that it is essentially true in all its statements; that nothing has been set down in malice, nothing exaggerated, nothing drawn from the imagination; that it comes short of the reality, rather than overstates a single fact in regard to SLAVERY AS IT IS. The experience of FREDERICK DOUGLASS, as a slave, was not a peculiar one; his lot was not especially a hard one; his case may be regarded as a very fair specimen of the treatment of slaves in Maryland, in which State it is conceded that they are better fed and less cruelly treated than in Georgia, Alabama, or Louisiana. Many have suffered incomparably more, while very few on the plantations have suffered less, than himself. Yet how deplorable was his situation! what terrible chastisements were inflicted upon his person! what still more shocking outrages were perpetrated upon his mind! with all his noble powers and sublime aspirations, how like a brute was he treated, even by those professing to have the same mind in them that was in Christ Jesus! to what dreadful liabilities was he continually subjected! how destitute of friendly counsel and aid, even in his greatest extremities! how heavy was the midnight of woe which shrouded in blackness the last ray of hope, and filled the future with terror and gloom! what longings after freedom took possession of his breast, and how his misery augmented, in proportion as he grew reflective and intelligent,—thus demonstrating that a happy slave is an extinct man! how he thought, reasoned, felt, under the lash of the driver, with the chains upon his limbs! what perils he encountered in his endeavors to escape from his horrible doom! and how signal have been his deliverance and preservation in the midst of a nation of pitiless enemies!

This Narrative contains many affecting incidents, many passages of great eloquence and power; but I think the most thrilling one of them all is the description DOUGLASS gives of his feelings, as he stood soliloquizing respecting his fate, and the chances of his one day being a free man, on the banks of the Chesapeake Bay—viewing the receding vessels as they flew with their white wings before the breeze, and apostrophizing them as animated by the living spirit of freedom. Who can read that passage, and be insensible to its pathos and sublimity? Compressed into it is a whole Alexandrian library of thought, feeling, and sentiment—all that can, all that need be urged, in the form of expostulation, entreaty, rebuke, against that crime of crimes,—making man the property of his fellow-man! O, how accursed is that system, which entombs the godlike mind of man, defaces the divine image, reduces those who by creation were crowned with glory and honor to a level with four-footed beasts, and exalts the dealer in human flesh above all that is called God! Why should its existence be prolonged one hour? Is it not evil, only evil, and that continually? What does its presence imply but the absence of all fear of God, all regard for man, on the part of the people of the United States? Heaven speed its eternal overthrow!

So profoundly ignorant of the nature of slavery are many persons, that they are stubbornly incredulous whenever they read or listen to any recital of the cruelties which are daily inflicted on its victims. They do not deny that the slaves are held as property; but that terrible fact seems to convey to their minds no idea of injustice, exposure to outrage, or savage barbarity. Tell them of cruel scourgings, of mutilations and brandings, of scenes of pollution and blood, of the banishment of all light and knowledge, and they affect to be greatly indignant at such enormous exaggerations, such wholesale misstatements, such abominable libels on the character of the southern planters! As if all these direful outrages were not the natural results of slavery! As if it were less cruel to reduce a human being to the condition of a thing, than to give him a severe flagellation, or to deprive him of necessary food and clothing! As if whips, chains, thumb-screws, paddles, bloodhounds, overseers, drivers, patrols, were not all indispensable to keep the slaves down, and to give protection to their ruthless oppressors! As if, when the marriage institution is abolished, concubinage, adultery, and incest, must not necessarily abound; when all the rights of humanity are annihilated, any barrier remains to protect the victim from the fury of the spoiler; when absolute power is assumed over life and liberty, it will not be wielded with destructive sway! Skeptics of this character abound in society. In some few instances, their incredulity arises from a want of reflection; but, generally, it indicates a hatred of the light, a desire to shield slavery from the assaults of its foes, a contempt of the colored race, whether bond or free. Such will try to discredit the shocking tales of slaveholding cruelty which are recorded in this truthful Narrative; but they will labor in vain. Mr. DOUGLASS has frankly disclosed the place of his birth, the names of those who claimed ownership in his body and soul, and the names also of those who committed the crimes which he has alleged against them. His statements, therefore, may easily be disproved, if they are untrue.

In the course of his Narrative, he relates two instances of murderous cruelty,—in one of which a planter deliberately shot a slave belonging to a neighboring plantation, who had unintentionally gotten within his lordly domain in quest of fish; and in the other, an overseer blew out the brains of a slave who had fled to a stream of water to escape a bloody scourging. Mr. DOUGLASS states that in neither of these instances was any thing done by way of legal arrest or judicial investigation. The Baltimore American, of March 17, 1845, relates a similar case of atrocity, perpetrated with similar impunity—as follows:— "*Shooting a Slave.*—We learn, upon the authority of a letter from Charles county, Maryland, received by a gentleman of this city, that a young man, named Matthews, a nephew of General Matthews, and whose father, it is believed, holds an office at Washington, killed one of the slaves upon his father's farm by shooting him. The letter states that young Matthews had been left in charge of the farm; that he gave an order to the servant, which was disobeyed, when he proceeded to the house, *obtained a gun, and, returning, shot the servant.* He immediately, the letter continues, fled to his father's residence, where he still remains unmolested."—Let it never be forgotten, that no slaveholder or overseer can be convicted of any outrage perpetrated on the person of a slave, however diabolical it may be, on the testimony of colored witnesses, whether bond or free. By the slave code, they are adjudged to be as incompetent to testify against a white man, as though they were indeed a part of the brute creation. Hence, there is no legal protection in fact, whatever there may be in form, for the slave population; and any amount of cruelty may be inflicted on them with impunity. Is it possible for the human mind to conceive of a more horrible state of society?

The effect of a religious profession on the conduct of southern masters is vividly described in the following Narrative, and shown to be any thing but salutary. In the nature of the case, it must be in the highest degree pernicious. The testimony of Mr. DOUGLASS, on this point, is sustained by a cloud of witnesses, whose veracity is unimpeachable. "A slaveholder's profession of Christianity is a palpable imposture. He is a felon of the highest grade. He is a man-stealer. It is of no importance what you put in the other scale."

Reader! are you with the man-stealers in sympathy

and purpose, or on the side of their down-trodden victims? If with the former, then are you the foe of God and man. If with the latter, what are you prepared to do and dare in their behalf? Be faithful, be vigilant, be untiring in your efforts to break every yoke, and let the oppressed go free. Come what may—cost what it may—inscribe on the banner which you unfurl to the breeze, as your religious and political motto—"NO COMPROMISE WITH SLAVERY! NO UNION WITH SLAVEHOLDERS!"

WM. LLOYD GARRISON.
BOSTON, *May* 1, 1845.

# Letter From Wendell Phillips, Esq.

BOSTON, *April* 22, 1845.

My Dear Friend:

You remember the old fable of "The Man and the Lion," where the lion complained that he should not be so misrepresented "when the lions write history."

I am glad the time has come when the "lions write history." We have been left long enough to gather character of slavery from the involuntary evidence of the masters. One might, indeed, rest sufficiently satisfied with what, it is evident, must be, in general the results of such a relation, without seeking farther to find whether they have followed in every instance. Indeed, those who stare at the half-peck of corn a week, and love to count the lashes on the slave's back, are seldom the "stuff" out of which reformers and abolitionists are to be made. I remember that, in 1838, many were waiting for the results of the West India experiment, before they could come into our ranks. Those "results" have come long ago; but, alas! few of that number have come with them, as converts. A man must be disposed to judge of emancipation by other tests than whether it has increased the produce of sugar,—and to hate slavery for other reasons because it starves men and whips, women,—before he is ready to lay the first stone of his anti-slavery life.

I was glad to learn, in your story, how early the most neglected of God's children waken to a sense of their rights, and of the injustice done them. Experience is a keen teacher; and long before you had mastered your A B C, or knew where the "white sails" of the Chesapeake were bound, you began, I see, to gauge the wretchedness of the slave, not by his hunger and want, not by his lashes and toil, but by the cruel and blighting death which gathers over his soul.

In connection with this, there is one circumstance which makes your recollections peculiarly valuable, and renders your early insight the more remarkable. You come from that part of the country where we are told slavery appears with its fairest features. Let us hear, then, what it is at its best estate—gaze on its bright side, if it has one; and then imagination may task her powers to add dark lines to the picture, as she travels southward to that (for the colored man) Valley of the Shadow of Death, where the Mississippi sweeps along.

Again, we have known you long, and can put the

most entire confidence in your truth, candor, and sincerity. Every one who has heard you speak has felt, and, I am confident, every one who reads your book will feel, persuaded that you give them a fair specimen of the whole truth. No one-sided portrait,—no wholesale complaints,— but strict justice done, whenever individual kindliness has neutralized, for a moment, the deadly system with which it was strangely allied. You have been with us, too, some years, and can fairly compare the twilight of rights, which your race enjoy at the North, with that "noon of night" under which they labor south of Mason and Dixon's line. Tell us whether, after all, the half-free colored man of Massachusetts is worse off than the pampered slave of the rice swamps!

In reading your life, no one can say that we have unfairly picked out some rare specimens of cruelty. We know that the bitter drops, which even you have drained from the cup, are no incidental aggravations, no individual ills, but such as must mingle always and necessarily in the lot of every slave. They are the essential ingredients, not the occasional results, of the system.

After all, I shall read your book with trembling for you. Some years ago, when you were beginning to tell me your real name and birthplace, you may remember I stopped you, and preferred to remain ignorant of all. With the exception of a vague description, so I continued, till the other day, when you read me your memoirs. I hardly knew, at the time, whether to thank you or not for the sight of them, when I reflected that it was still dangerous, in Massachusetts, for honest men to tell their names! They say the fathers, in 1776, signed the Declaration of Independence with the halter about their necks. You, too, publish your declaration of freedom with danger compassing you around. In all the broad lands which the Constitution of the United States overshadows, there is no single spot,—however narrow or desolate,—where a fugitive slave can plant himself and say, "I am safe." The whole armory of Northern Law has no shield for you. I am free to say that, in your place, I should throw the MS. into the fire.

You, perhaps, may tell your story in safety, endeared as you are to so many warm hearts by rare gifts, and a still rarer devotion of them to the service of others. But it will be owing only to your labors, and the fearless efforts of those who, trampling the laws and Constitution of the country under their feet, are determined that they will "hide the outcast," and that their hearths shall be, spite of the law, an asylum for the oppressed, if, some time or other, the humblest may stand in our streets, and bear witness in safety against the cruelties of which he has been the victim.

Yet it is sad to think, that these very throbbing hearts which welcome your story, and form your best safeguard in telling it, are all beating contrary to the "statute in such case made and provided." Go on, my dear friend, till you, and those who, like you, have been saved, so as by fire, from the dark prison-house, shall stereotype these free, illegal pulses into statutes; and New England, cutting loose from a blood-stained Union, shall glory in being the house of refuge for the oppressed;—till we no longer merely "*hide* the outcast," or make a merit of standing idly by while he is hunted in our midst; but, consecrating anew the soil of the Pilgrims as an asylum for the oppressed, proclaim our *welcome* to the slave so loudly, that the tones shall reach every hut in the Carolinas, and make the broken-hearted bondman leap up at the thought of old Massachusetts.

God speed the day!

Till then, and ever,

Yours truly,

WENDELL PHILLIPS.

FREDERICK DOUGLASS.

# Chapter I

I was born in Tuckahoe, near Hillsborough, and about twelve miles from Easton, in Talbot county, Maryland. I have no accurate knowledge of my age, never having seen any authentic record containing it. By far the larger part of the slaves know as little of their ages as horses know of theirs, and it is the wish of most masters within my knowledge to keep their slaves thus ignorant. I do not remember to have ever met a slave who could tell of his birthday. They seldom come nearer to it than planting-time, harvest-time, cherry-time, spring-time, or fall-time. A want of information concerning my own was a source of unhappiness to me even during childhood. The white children could tell their ages. I could not tell why I ought to be deprived of the same privilege. I was not allowed to make any inquiries of my master concerning it. He deemed all such inquiries on the part of a slave improper and impertinent, and evidence of a restless spirit. The nearest estimate I can give makes me now between twenty-seven and twenty-eight years of age. I come to this, from hearing my master say, some time during 1835, I was about seventeen years old.

My mother was named Harriet Bailey. She was the daughter of Isaac and Betsey Bailey, both colored, and quite dark. My mother was of a darker complexion than either my grandmother or grandfather.

My father was a white man. He was admitted to be such by all I ever heard speak of my parentage. The opinion was also whispered that my master was my father; but of the correctness of this opinion, I know nothing; the means of knowing was withheld from me. My mother and I were separated when I was but an infant—before I knew her as my mother. It is a common custom, in the part of Maryland from which I ran away, to part children from their mothers at a very early age. Frequently, before the child has reached its twelfth month, its mother is taken from it, and hired out on some farm a considerable distance off, and the child is placed under the care of an old woman, too old for field labor. For what this separation is done, I do not know, unless it be to hinder the development of the child's affection toward its mother, and to blunt and destroy the natural affection of the mother for the child. This is the inevitable result.

I never saw my mother, to know her as such, more than four or five times in my life; and each of these times was very short in duration, and at night. She was hired by a Mr. Stewart, who lived about twelve miles from my home. She made her journeys to see me in the night, travelling the whole distance on foot, after the performance of her day's work. She was a field hand, and a whipping is the penalty of not being in the field at sunrise, unless a slave has special permission from his or her master to the contrary—a permission which they seldom get, and one that gives to him that gives it the proud name of being a kind master. I do not recollect of ever seeing my mother by the light of day. She was with me in the night. She would lie down with me, and get me to sleep, but long before I waked she was gone. Very little communication ever took place between us. Death soon ended what little we could have while she lived, and with it her hardships and suffering. She died when I was about seven years old, on one of my master's farms, near Lee's Mill. I was not allowed to be present during her illness, at her death, or burial. She was gone long before I knew any thing about it. Never having enjoyed, to any considerable extent, her soothing presence, her tender and watchful care, I received the tidings of her death with much the same emotions I should have probably felt at the death of a stranger.

Called thus suddenly away, she left me without the slightest intimation of who my father was. The whisper that my master was my father, may or may not be true; and, true or false, it is of but little consequence to my purpose whilst the fact remains, in all its glaring odiousness, that slaveholders have ordained, and by law established, that the children of slave women shall in all cases follow the condition of their mothers; and this is done too obviously to administer to their own lusts, and make a gratification of their wicked desires profitable as well as pleasurable; for by this cunning arrangement, the slaveholder, in cases not a few, sustains to his slaves the double relation of master and father.

I know of such cases; and it is worthy of remark that such slaves invariably suffer greater hardships, and have more to contend with, than others. They are, in the first place, a constant offence to their mistress. She is ever disposed to find fault with them; they can seldom do any thing to please her; she is never better pleased than when she sees them under the lash, especially when she suspects her husband of showing to his mulatto children favors which he withholds from his black slaves. The master is frequently compelled to sell this class of his slaves, out of deference to the feelings of his white wife; and, cruel as the deed may strike any one to be, for a man to sell his own children to human flesh-mongers, it is often the dictate of humanity for him to do so; for, unless he does this, he must not only whip them himself, but must stand by and see one white son tie up his brother, of but few shades darker complexion than himself, and ply the gory lash to his naked back; and if he lisp one word of disapproval, it is set down to his parental partiality, and only makes a bad matter worse, both for himself and the slave whom he would protect and defend.

Every year brings with it multitudes of this class of slaves. It was doubtless in consequence of a knowledge of this fact, that one great statesman of the south predicted the downfall of slavery by the inevitable laws of population. Whether this prophecy is ever fulfilled, or not, it is nevertheless plain that a very different-looking class of people are springing up at the south, and are now held in slavery, from those originally brought to this country from Africa; and if their increase will do no other good, it will do away the force of the argument, that God cursed Ham, and therefore American slavery is right. If the lineal descendants of Ham are alone to be scripturally enslaved, it is certain that slavery at the south must soon become unscriptural; for thousands are ushered into the world, annually, who, like myself, owe their existence to white fathers, and those fathers most frequently their own masters.

I have had two masters. My first master's name was Anthony. I do not remember his first name. He was generally called Captain Anthony—a title which, I presume, he acquired by sailing a craft on the Chesapeake Bay. He was not considered a rich slaveholder. He owned two or three farms, and about thirty slaves. His farms and slaves were under the care of an overseer. The overseer's name was Plummer. Mr. Plummer was a miserable drunkard, a profane swearer, and a savage monster. He always went armed with a cowskin and a heavy cudgel. I have known him to cut and slash the women's heads so horribly, that even master would be enraged at his cruelty, and would threaten to whip him if he did not mind himself. Master, however, was not a humane slaveholder. It required extraordinary barbarity on the part of an overseer to affect him. He was a cruel man, hardened by a long life of slaveholding. He would at times seem to take great pleasure in whipping a slave. I have often been awakened at the dawn of day by the most heart-rending shrieks of an own aunt of mine, whom he used to tie up to a joist, and whip upon her naked back till she was literally covered with blood. No words, no tears, no prayers, from his gory victim, seemed to move his iron heart from its bloody purpose. The louder she screamed, the harder he whipped; and where the blood ran fastest, there he whipped longest. He would whip her to make her scream, and whip her to make her hush; and not until overcome by fatigue, would he cease to swing the blood-clotted cowskin. I remember the first time I ever witnessed this horrible exhibition. I was quite a child, but I well remember it. I never shall forget it whilst I remember any thing. It was the first of a long series of such outrages, of which I was doomed to be a witness and a participant. It struck me with awful force. It was the blood-stained gate, the entrance to the hell of slavery, through which I was about to pass. It was a most terrible spectacle. I wish I could commit to paper the feelings with which I beheld it.

This occurrence took place very soon after I went to live with my old master, and under the following circumstances. Aunt Hester went out one night,—where or for what I do not know,—and happened to be absent when my master desired her presence. He had ordered her not to go out evenings, and warned her that she must never let him catch her in company with a young man, who was paying attention to her, belonging to Colonel Lloyd. The young man's name was Ned Roberts, generally called Lloyd's Ned. Why master was so careful of her, may be safely left to conjecture. She was a woman of noble form, and of graceful proportions, having very few equals, and fewer superiors, in personal appearance, among the colored or white women of our neighborhood.

Aunt Hester had not only disobeyed his orders in going out, but had been found in company with Lloyd's Ned; which circumstance, I found, from what he said while whipping her, was the chief offence. Had he been a man of pure morals himself, he might have been thought interested in protecting the innocence of my aunt; but those who knew him will not suspect him of any such virtue. Before he commenced whipping Aunt Hester, he took her into the kitchen, and stripped her from neck to waist, leaving her neck, shoulders, and back, entirely naked. He then told her to cross her hands, calling her at the same time a d—d b—h. After crossing her hands, he tied them with a strong rope, and led her to a stool under a large hook in the joist, put in for the purpose. He made her get upon the stool, and tied her hands to the hook. She now stood fair for his infernal purpose. Her arms were stretched up at their full length, so that she stood upon the ends of her toes. He then said to her, "Now, you d—d b—h, I'll learn you how to disobey my orders!" and after rolling up his sleeves, be commenced to lay on the heavy cowskin, and soon the warm, red blood (amid heart-rending shrieks from her, and horrid oaths from him) came dripping to the floor. I was so terrified and horror-stricken at the sight, that I hid myself in a closet, and dared not venture out till long after the bloody transaction was over. I expected it would be my turn next. It was all new to me. I had never seen any thing like it before. I had always lived with my grandmother on the outskirts of the plantation, where she was put to raise the children of the younger women. I had therefore been, until now, out of the way of the bloody scenes that often occurred on the plantation.

# Chapter II

My master's family consisted of two sons, Andrew and Richard; one daughter, Lucretia, and her husband, Captain Thomas Auld. They lived in one house, upon the home plantation of Colonel Edward Lloyd. My master was Colonel Lloyd's clerk and superintendent. He was what might be called the overseer of the overseers. I spent two years of childhood on this plantation in my old master's family. It was here that I witnessed the bloody transaction recorded in the first chapter; and as I received my first impressions of slavery on this plantation, I will give some description of it, and of slavery as it there existed. The plantation is about twelve miles north of Easton, in Talbot county, and is situated on the border of Miles River. The principal products raised upon it were tobacco, corn, and wheat. These were raised in great abundance; so that, with the products of this and the other farms belonging to him, he was able to keep in almost constant employment a large sloop, in carrying them to market at Baltimore.

This sloop was named Sally Lloyd, in honor of one of the colonel's daughters. My master's son-in-law, Captain Auld, was master of the vessel; she was otherwise manned by the colonel's own slaves. Their names were Peter, Isaac, Rich, and Jake. These were esteemed very highly by the other slaves, and looked upon as the privileged ones of the plantation; for it was no small affair, in the eyes of the slaves, to be allowed to see Baltimore.

Colonel Lloyd kept from three to four hundred slaves on his home plantation, and owned a large number more on the neighboring farms belonging to him. The names of the farms nearest to the home plantation were Wye Town and New Design. "Wye Town" was under the overseership of a man named Noah Willis. New Design was under the overseership of a Mr. Townsend. The overseers of these, and all the rest of the farms, numbering over twenty, received advice and direction from the managers of the home plantation. This was the great business place. It was the seat of government for the whole twenty farms. All disputes among the overseers were settled here. If a slave was convicted of any high misdemeanor, became unmanageable, or evinced a determination to run away, he was brought immediately here, severely whipped, put on board the sloop, carried to Baltimore, and sold to Austin Woolfolk, or some other slave-trader, as a warning to the slaves remaining.

Here, too, the slaves of all the other farms received their monthly allowance of food, and their yearly clothing. The men and women slaves received, as their monthly allowance of food, eight pounds of pork, or its equivalent in fish, and one bushel of corn meal Their yearly clothing consisted of two coarse linen shirts, one pair of linen trousers, like the shirts, one jacket, one pair of trousers for winter, made of coarse negro cloth, one pair of stockings, and one pair of shoes; the whole of which could not have cost more than seven dollars. The allowance of the slave children was given to their mothers, or the old women having the care of them. The children unable to work in the field had neither shoes, stockings, jackets, nor trousers, given to them; their clothing consisted of two coarse linen shirts per year. When these failed them, they went naked until the next allowance-day. Children from seven to ten years old, of both sexes, almost naked, might be seen at all seasons of the year.

There were no beds given the slaves, unless one coarse blanket be considered such, and none but the men and women had these. This, however, is not considered a very great privation. They find less difficulty from the want of beds, than from the want of time to sleep; for when their day's work in the field is done, the most of them having their washing, mending, and cooking to do, and having few or none of the ordinary facilities for doing either of these, very many of their sleeping hours are consumed in preparing for the field the coming day; and when this is done, old and young, male and female, married and single, drop down side by side, on one common bed,—the cold, damp floor,—each covering himself or herself with their miserable blankets; and here they sleep till they are summoned to the field by the driver's horn. At the sound of this, all must rise, and be off to the field. There must be no halting; every one must be at his or her post; and woe betides them who hear not this morning summons to the field; for if they are not awakened by the sense of hearing, they are by the sense of feeling: no age nor sex finds any favor. Mr. Severe, the overseer, used to stand by the door of the quarter, armed with a large hickory stick and heavy cowskin, ready to whip any one who was so unfortunate as not to hear, or, from any other cause, was prevented from being ready to start for the field at the sound of the horn.

Mr. Severe was rightly named: he was a cruel man. I have seen him whip a woman, causing the blood to run half an hour at the time; and this, too, in the midst of her crying children, pleading for their mother's release. He seemed to take pleasure in manifesting his fiendish barbarity. Added to his cruelty, he was a profane swearer. It was enough to chill the blood and stiffen the hair of an ordinary man to hear him talk. Scarce a sentence escaped him but that was commenced or concluded by some horrid oath. The field was the place to witness his cruelty and profanity. His presence made it both the field of blood and of blasphemy. From the rising till the going down of the sun, he was cursing, raving, cutting, and slashing among the slaves of the field, in the most frightful manner. His career was short.

He died very soon after I went to Colonel Lloyd's; and he died as he lived, uttering, with his dying groans, bitter curses and horrid oaths. His death was regarded by the slaves as the result of a merciful providence.

Mr. Severe's place was filled by a Mr. Hopkins. He was a very different man. He was less cruel, less profane, and made less noise, than Mr. Severe. His course was characterized by no extraordinary demonstrations of cruelty. He whipped, but seemed to take no pleasure in it. He was called by the slaves a good overseer.

The home plantation of Colonel Lloyd wore the appearance of a country village. All the mechanical operations for all the farms were performed here. The shoemaking and mending, the blacksmithing, cartwrighting, coopering, weaving, and grain-grinding, were all performed by the slaves on the home plantation. The whole place wore a business-like aspect very unlike the neighboring farms. The number of houses, too, conspired to give it advantage over the neighboring farms. It was called by the slaves the *Great House Farm*. Few privileges were esteemed higher, by the slaves of the out-farms, than that of being selected to do errands at the Great House Farm. It was associated in their minds with greatness. A representative could not be prouder of his election to a seat in the American Congress, than a slave on one of the out-farms would be of his election to do errands at the Great House Farm. They regarded it as evidence of great confidence reposed in them by their overseers; and it was on this account, as well as a constant desire to be out of the field from under the driver's lash, that they esteemed it a high privilege, one worth careful living for. He was called the smartest and most trusty fellow, who had this honor conferred upon him the most frequently. The competitors for this office sought as diligently to please their overseers, as the office-seekers in the political parties seek to please and deceive the people. The same traits of character might be seen in Colonel Lloyd's slaves, as are seen in the slaves of the political parties.

The slaves selected to go to the Great House Farm, for the monthly allowance for themselves and their fellow-slaves, were peculiarly enthusiastic. While on their way, they would make the dense old woods, for miles around, reverberate with their wild songs, revealing at once the highest joy and the deepest sadness. They would compose and sing as they went along, consulting neither time nor tune. The thought that came up, came out—if not in the word, in the sound; —and as frequently in the one as in the other. They would sometimes sing the most pathetic sentiment in the most rapturous tone, and the most rapturous sentiment in the most pathetic tone. Into all of their songs they would manage to weave something of the Great House Farm. Especially would they do this, when leaving home. They would then sing most exultingly the following words:—

> "I am going away to the Great House Farm!
> O, yea! O, yea! O!"

This they would sing, as a chorus, to words which to many would seem unmeaning jargon, but which, nevertheless, were full of meaning to themselves. I have sometimes thought that the mere hearing of those songs would do more to impress some minds with the horrible character of slavery, than the reading of whole volumes of philosophy on the subject could do.

I did not, when a slave, understand the deep meaning of those rude and apparently incoherent songs. I was myself within the circle; so that I neither saw nor heard as those without might see and hear. They told a tale of woe which was then altogether beyond my feeble comprehension; they were tones loud, long, and deep; they breathed the prayer and complaint of souls boiling over with the bitterest anguish. Every tone was a testimony against slavery, and a prayer to God for deliverance from chains. The hearing of those wild notes always depressed my spirit, and filled me with ineffable sadness. I have frequently found myself in tears while hearing them. The mere recurrence to those songs, even now, afflicts me; and while I am writing these lines, an expression of feeling has already found its way down my cheek. To those songs I trace my first glimmering conception of the dehumanizing character of slavery. I can never get rid of that conception. Those songs still follow me, to deepen my hatred of slavery, and quicken my sympathies for my brethren in bonds. If any one wishes to be impressed with the soul-killing effects of slavery, let him go to Colonel Lloyd's plantation, and, on allowance-day, place himself in the deep pine woods, and there let him, in silence, analyze the sounds that shall pass through the chambers of his soul,—and if he is not thus impressed, it will only be because "there is no flesh in his obdurate heart."

I have often been utterly astonished, since I came to the north, to find persons who could speak of the singing, among slaves, as evidence of their contentment and happiness. It is impossible to conceive of a greater mistake. Slaves sing most when they are most unhappy. The songs of the slave represent the sorrows of his heart; and he is relieved by them, only as an aching heart is relieved by its tears. At least, such is my experience. I have often sung to drown my sorrow, but seldom to express my happiness. Crying for joy, and singing for joy, were alike uncommon to me while in the jaws of slavery. The singing of a man cast away upon a desolate island might be as appropriately considered as evidence of contentment and happiness, as the singing of a slave; the songs of the one and of the other are prompted by the same emotion.

# Chapter III

Colonel Lloyd kept a large and finely cultivated garden, which afforded almost constant employment for four men, besides the chief gardener, (Mr. M'Durmond). This garden was probably the greatest attraction of the place. During the summer months, people came from far and near—from Baltimore, Easton, and Annapolis—to see it. It abounded in fruits of almost every description, from the hardy apple of the north to the delicate orange of the south. This garden was not the least source of trouble on the plantation. Its excellent fruit was quite a temptation to the hungry swarms of boys, as well as the older slaves, belonging to the colonel, few of whom had the virtue or the vice to resist it. Scarcely a day passed, during the summer, but that some slave had to take the lash for stealing fruit. The colonel had to resort to all kinds of stratagems to keep his slaves out of the garden. The last most successful one was that of tarring his fence all around; after which, if a slave was caught with any tar upon his person, it was deemed sufficient proof that he had either been into the garden, or had tried to get in. In either case, he was severely whipped by the chief gardener. This plan worked well; the slaves became as fearful of *tar* as of the lash. They seemed to realize the impossibility of touching tar without being defiled.

The colonel also kept a splendid riding equipage. His stable and carriage-house presented the appearance of some of our large city livery establishments. His horses were of the finest form and noblest blood. His carriage-house contained three splendid coaches, three or four gigs, besides dearborns and barouches of the most fashionable style.

This establishment was under the care of two slaves—old Barney and young Barney—father and son. To attend to this establishment was their sole work. But it was by no means an easy employment; for in nothing was Colonel Lloyd more particular than in the management of his horses. The slightest inattention to these was unpardonable, and was visited upon those, under whose care they were placed, with the severest punishment; no excuse could shield them, if the colonel only suspected any want of attention to his horses—a supposition which he frequently indulged, and one which, of course, made the office of old and young Barney a very trying one. They never knew when they were safe from punishment. They were frequently whipped when least deserving, and escaped whipping when most deserving it. Every thing depended upon the looks of the horses, and the state of Colonel Lloyd's own mind when his horses were brought to him for use. If a horse did not move fast enough, or hold his head high enough, it was owing to some fault of his keepers. It was painful to stand near the stable-door, and hear the various complaints against the keepers when a horse was taken out for use. "This horse has not had proper attention. He has not been sufficiently rubbed and curried, or he has not been properly fed; his food was too wet or too dry; he got it too soon or too late; he was too hot or too cold; he had too much hay, and not enough of grain; or he had too much grain, and not enough of hay; instead of old Barney's attending to the horse, he had very improperly left it to his son." To all these complaints, no matter how unjust, the slave must answer never a word. Colonel Lloyd could not brook any contradiction from a slave. When he spoke, a slave must stand, listen, and tremble; and such was literally the case. I have seen Colonel Lloyd make old Barney, a man between fifty and sixty years of age, uncover his bald head, kneel down upon the cold, damp ground, and receive upon his naked and toil-worn shoulders more than thirty lashes at the time. Colonel Lloyd had three sons—Edward, Murray, and Daniel,—and three sons-in-law, Mr. Winder, Mr. Nicholson, and Mr. Lowndes. All of these lived at the Great House Farm, and enjoyed the luxury of whipping the servants when they pleased, from old Barney down to William Wilkes, the coach-driver. I have seen Winder make one of the house-servants stand off from him a suitable distance to be touched with the end of his whip, and at every stroke raise great ridges upon his back.

To describe the wealth of Colonel Lloyd would be almost equal to describing the riches of Job. He kept from ten to fifteen house-servants. He was said to own a thousand slaves, and I think this estimate quite within the truth. Colonel Lloyd owned so many that he did not know them when he saw them; nor did all the slaves of the out-farms know him. It is reported of him, that, while riding along the road one day, he met a colored man, and addressed him in the usual manner of speaking to colored people on the public highways of the south: "Well, boy, whom do you belong to?" "To Colonel Lloyd," replied the slave. "Well, does the colonel treat you well?" "No, sir," was the ready reply. "What, does he work you too hard?" "Yea, sir." "Well, don't he give you enough to eat?" "Yes, sir, he gives me enough, such as it is."

The colonel, after ascertaining where the slave belonged, rode on; the man also went on about his business, not dreaming that be had been conversing with his master. He thought, said, and heard nothing more of the matter, until two or three weeks afterwards. The poor man was then informed by his overseer that, for having found fault with his master, he was now to be sold to a Georgia trader. He was immediately chained and handcuffed; and thus, without a moment's warning, he was snatched away, and forever sundered, from his family and friends, by a hand more unrelenting than death. This is the penalty of telling the truth, of telling the simple truth, in answer to a series of plain questions.

It is partly in consequence of such facts, that slaves, when inquired of as to their condition and the character of their masters, almost universally say they are contented, and that their masters are kind. The slaveholders have been known to send in spies among their slaves, to ascertain their views and feelings in regard to their condition. The frequency of this has had the effect to establish among the slaves the maxim, that a still tongue makes a wise head. They suppress the truth rather than take the consequences of telling it, and in so doing prove themselves a part of the human family. If they have any thing to say of their masters, it is generally in their masters' favor, especially when speaking to an untried man. I have been frequently asked, when a slave, if I had a kind master, and do not remember ever to have given a negative answer; nor did I, in pursuing this course, consider myself as uttering what was absolutely false; for I always measured the kindness of my master by the standard of kindness set up among slaveholders around us. Moreover, slaves are like other people, and imbibe prejudices quite common to others. They think their own better than that of others. Many, under the influence of this prejudice, think their own masters are better than the masters of other slaves; and this, too, in some cases, when the very reverse is true. Indeed, it is not uncommon for slaves even to fall out and quarrel among themselves about the relative goodness of their masters, each contending for the superior goodness of his own over that of the others. At the very same time, they mutually execrate their masters when viewed separately. It was so on our plantation. When Colonel Lloyd's slaves met the slaves of Jacob Jepson, they seldom parted without a quarrel about their masters; Colonel Lloyd's slaves contending that he was the richest, and Mr. Jepson's slaves that he was the smartest, and most of a man. Colonel Lloyd's slaves would boast his ability to buy and sell Jacob Jepson. Mr. Jepson's slaves would boast his ability to whip Colonel Lloyd. These quarrels would almost always end in a fight between the parties, and those that whipped were supposed to have gained the point at issue. They seemed to think that the greatness of their masters was transferable to themselves. It was considered as being bad enough to be a slave; but to be a poor man's slave was deemed a disgrace indeed!

# Chapter IV

Mr. Hopkins remained but a short time in the office of overseer. Why his career was so short, I do not know, but suppose he lacked the necessary severity to suit Colonel Lloyd. Mr. Hopkins was succeeded by Mr. Austin Gore, a man possessing, in an eminent degree, all those traits of character indispensable to what is called a first-rate overseer. Mr. Gore had served Colonel Lloyd, in the capacity of overseer, upon one of the out-farms, and had shown himself worthy of the high station of overseer upon the home or Great House Farm. Mr. Gore was proud, ambitious, and persevering. He was artful, cruel, and obdurate. He was just the man for such a place, and it was just the place for such a man. It afforded scope for the full exercise of all his powers, and he seemed to be perfectly at home in it. He was one of those who could torture the slightest look, word, or gesture, on the part of the slave, into impudence, and would treat it accordingly. There must be no answering back to him; no explanation was allowed a slave, showing himself to have been wrongfully accused. Mr. Gore acted fully up to the maxim laid down by slaveholders,—"It is better that a dozen slaves suffer under the lash, than that the overseer should be convicted, in the presence of the slaves, of having been at fault." No matter how innocent a slave might be—it availed him nothing, when accused by Mr. Gore of any misdemeanor. To be accused was to be convicted, and to be convicted was to be punished; the one always following the other with immutable certainty. To escape punishment was to escape accusation; and few slaves had the fortune to do either, under the overseership of Mr. Gore. He was just proud enough to demand the most debasing homage of the slave, and quite servile enough to crouch, himself, at the feet of the master. He was ambitious enough to be contented with nothing short of the highest rank of overseers, and persevering enough to reach the height of his ambition. He was cruel enough to inflict the severest punishment, artful enough to descend to the lowest trickery, and obdurate enough to be insensible to the voice of a reproving conscience. He was, of all the overseers, the most dreaded by the slaves. His presence was painful; his eye flashed confusion; and seldom was his sharp, shrill voice heard, without producing horror and trembling in their ranks.

Mr. Gore was a grave man, and, though a young man, he indulged in no jokes, said no funny words, seldom smiled. His words were in perfect keeping with his looks, and his looks were in perfect keeping with his words.

Overseers will sometimes indulge in a witty word, even with the slaves; not so with Mr. Gore. He spoke but to command, and commanded but to be obeyed; he dealt sparingly with his words, and bountifully with his whip, never using the former where the latter would answer as well. When he whipped, he seemed to do so from a sense of duty, and feared no consequences. He did nothing reluctantly, no matter how disagreeable; always at his post, never inconsistent. He never promised but to fulfil. He was, in a word, a man of the most inflexible firmness and stone-like coolness.

His savage barbarity was equalled only by the consummate coolness with which he committed the grossest and most savage deeds upon the slaves under his charge. Mr. Gore once undertook to whip one of Colonel Lloyd's slaves, by the name of Demby. He had given Demby but few stripes, when, to get rid of the scourging, he ran and plunged himself into a creek, and stood there at the depth of his shoulders, refusing to come out. Mr. Gore told him that he would give him three calls, and that, if he did not come out at the third call, he would shoot him. The first call was given. Demby made no response, but stood his ground. The second and third calls were given with the same result. Mr. Gore then, without consultation or deliberation with any one, not even giving Demby an additional call, raised his musket to his face, taking deadly aim at his standing victim, and in an instant poor Demby was no more. His mangled body sank out of sight, and blood and brains marked the water where he had stood.

A thrill of horror flashed through every soul upon the plantation, excepting Mr. Gore. He alone seemed cool and collected. He was asked by Colonel Lloyd and my old master, why he resorted to this extraordinary expedient. His reply was, (as well as I can remember,) that Demby had become unmanageable. He was setting a dangerous example to the other slaves,—one which, if suffered to pass without some such demonstration on his part, would finally lead to the total subversion of all rule and order upon the plantation. He argued that if one slave refused to be corrected, and escaped with his life, the other slaves would soon copy the example; the result of which would be, the freedom of the slaves, and the enslavement of the whites. Mr. Gore's defence was satisfactory. He was continued in his station as overseer upon the home plantation. His fame as an overseer went abroad. His horrid crime was not even submitted to judicial investigation. It was committed in the presence of slaves, and they of course could neither institute a suit, nor testify against him; and thus the guilty perpetrator of one of the bloodiest and most foul murders goes unwhipped of justice, and uncensured by the community in which he lives. Mr. Gore lived in St. Michael's, Talbot county, Maryland, when I left there; and if he is still alive, he very probably lives there now; and if so, he is now, as he was then, as highly esteemed and as much respected as though his guilty soul had not been stained with his brother's blood.

I speak advisedly when I say this,—that killing a slave,

or any colored person, in Talbot county, Maryland, is not treated as a crime, either by the courts or the community. Mr. Thomas Lanman, of St. Michael's, killed two slaves, one of whom he killed with a hatchet, by knocking his brains out. He used to boast of the commission of the awful and bloody deed. I have heard him do so laughingly, saying, among other things, that he was the only benefactor of his country in the company, and that when others would do as much as he had done, we should be relieved of "the d—d niggers."

The wife of Mr. Giles Hick, living but a short distance from where I used to live, murdered my wife's cousin, a young girl between fifteen and sixteen years of age, mangling her person in the most horrible manner, breaking her nose and breastbone with a stick, so that the poor girl expired in a few hours afterward. She was immediately buried, but had not been in her untimely grave but a few hours before she was taken up and examined by the coroner, who decided that she had come to her death by severe beating. The offence for which this girl was thus murdered was this:— She had been set that night to mind Mrs. Hick's baby, and during the night she fell asleep, and the baby cried. She, having lost her rest for several nights previous, did not hear the crying. They were both in the room with Mrs. Hicks. Mrs. Hicks, finding the girl slow to move, jumped from her bed, seized an oak stick of wood by the fireplace, and with it broke the girl's nose and breastbone, and thus ended her life. I will not say that this most horrid murder produced no sensation in the community. It did produce sensation, but not enough to bring the murderess to punishment. There was a warrant issued for her arrest, but it was never served. Thus she escaped not only punishment, but even the pain of being arraigned before a court for her horrid crime.

Whilst I am detailing bloody deeds which took place during my stay on Colonel Lloyd's plantation, I will briefly narrate another, which occurred about the same time as the murder of Demby by Mr. Gore.

Colonel Lloyd's slaves were in the habit of spending a part of their nights and Sundays in fishing for oysters, and in this way made up the deficiency of their scanty allowance. An old man belonging to Colonel Lloyd, while thus engaged, happened to get beyond the limits of Colonel Lloyd's, and on the premises of Mr. Beal Bondly. At this trespass, Mr. Bondly took offence, and with his musket came down to the shore, and blew its deadly contents into the poor old man.

Mr. Bondly came over to see Colonel Lloyd the next day, whether to pay him for his property, or to justify himself in what he had done, I know not. At any rate, this whole fiendish transaction was soon hushed up. There was very little said about it at all, and nothing done. It was a common saying, even among little white boys, that it was worth a half-cent to kill a "nigger," and a half-cent to bury one.

# Chapter V

As to my own treatment while I lived on Colonel Lloyd's plantation, it was very similar to that of the other slave children. I was not old enough to work in the field, and there being little else than field work to do, I had a great deal of leisure time. The most I had to do was to drive up the cows at evening, keep the fowls out of the garden, keep the front yard clean, and run of errands for my old master's daughter, Mrs. Lucretia Auld. The most of my leisure time I spent in helping Master Daniel Lloyd in finding his birds, after he had shot them. My connection with Master Daniel was of some advantage to me. He became quite attached to me, and was a sort of protector of me. He would not allow the older boys to impose upon me, and would divide his cakes with me.

I was seldom whipped by my old master, and suffered little from any thing else than hunger and cold. I suffered much from hunger, but much more from cold. In hottest summer and coldest winter, I was kept almost naked—

no shoes, no stockings, no jacket, no trousers, nothing on but a coarse tow linen shirt, reaching only to my knees. I had no bed. I must have perished with cold, but that, the coldest nights, I used to steal a bag which was used for carrying corn to the mill. I would crawl into this bag, and there sleep on the cold, damp, clay floor, with my head in and feet out. My feet have been so cracked with the frost, that the pen with which I am writing might be laid in the gashes.

We were not regularly allowanced. Our food was coarse corn meal boiled. This was called *mush*. It was put into a large wooden tray or trough, and set down upon the ground. The children were then called, like so many pigs, and like so many pigs they would come and devour the mush; some with oyster-shells, others with pieces of shingle, some with naked hands, and none with spoons. He that ate fastest got most; he that was strongest secured the best place; and few left the trough satisfied.

I was probably between seven and eight years old when I left Colonel Lloyd's plantation. I left it with joy. I shall never forget the ecstasy with which I received the intelligence that my old master (Anthony) had determined to let me go to Baltimore, to live with Mr. Hugh Auld, brother to my old master's son-in-law, Captain Thomas Auld. I received this information about three days before my departure. They were three of the happiest days I ever enjoyed. I spent the most part of all these three days in the creek, washing off the plantation scurf, and preparing myself for my departure.

The pride of appearance which this would indicate was not my own. I spent the time in washing, not so much because I wished to, but because Mrs. Lucretia had told me I must get all the dead skin off my feet and knees before I could go to Baltimore; for the people in Baltimore were very cleanly, and would laugh at me if I looked dirty. Besides, she was going to give me a pair or trousers, which I should not put on unless I got all the dirt off me. The thought of owning a pair of trousers was great indeed! It was almost a sufficient motive, not only to make me take off what would be called by pig-drovers the mange, but the skin itself. I went at it in good earnest, working for the first time with the hope of reward.

The ties that ordinarily bind children to their homes were all suspended in my case. I found no severe trial in my departure. My home was charmless; it was not home to me; on parting from it, I could not feel that I was leaving any thing which I could have enjoyed by staying. My mother was dead, my grandmother lived far off, so that I seldom saw her. I had two sisters and one brother, that lived in the same house with me; but the early separation of us from our mother had well nigh blotted the fact of our relationship from our memories. I looked for home elsewhere, and was confident of finding none which I should relish less than the one which I was leaving. If, however, I found in my new home hardship, hunger, whipping, and nakedness, I had the consolation that I should not have escaped any one of them by staying. Having already had more than a taste of them in the house of my old master, and having endured them there, I very naturally inferred my ability to endure them elsewhere, and especially at Baltimore; for I had something of the feeling about Baltimore that is expressed in the proverb, that "being hanged in England is preferable to dying a natural death in Ireland." I had the strongest desire to see Baltimore. Cousin Tom, though not fluent in speech, had inspired me with that desire by his eloquent description of the place. I could never point out any thing at the Great House, no matter how beautiful or powerful, but that he had seen something at Baltimore far exceeding, both in beauty and strength, the object which I pointed out to him. Even the Great House itself, with all its pictures, was far inferior to many buildings in Baltimore. So strong was my desire, that I thought a gratification of it would fully compensate for whatever loss of comforts I should sustain by the exchange. I left without a regret, and with the highest hopes of future happiness.

We sailed out of Miles River for Baltimore on a Saturday morning. I remember only the day of the week, for at that time I had no knowledge of the days of the month, nor the months of the year. On setting sail, I walked aft, and gave to Colonel Lloyd's plantation what I hoped would be the last look. I then placed myself in the bows of the sloop, and there spent the remainder of the day in looking ahead, interesting myself in what was in the distance rather than in things nearby or behind.

In the afternoon of that day, we reached Annapolis, the capital of the State. We stopped but a few moments so that I had no time to go on shore. It was the first large town that I had ever seen, and though it would look small compared with some of our New England factory villages, I thought it a wonderful place for its size—more imposing even than the Great House Farm!

We arrived at Baltimore early on Sunday morning, landing at Smith's Wharf, not far from Bowley's Wharf. We had on board the sloop a large flock of sheep; and after aiding in driving them to the slaughterhouse of Mr. Curtis on Louden Slater's Hill, I was conducted by Rich, one of the hands belonging on board of the sloop, to my new home in Alliciana Street, near Mr. Gardner's ship-yard, on Fells Point.

Mr. and Mrs. Auld were both at home, and met me at the door with their little son Thomas, to take care of whom I had been given. And here I saw what I had never seen before; it was a white face beaming with the most kindly emotions; it was the face of my new mistress, Sophia Auld. I wish I could describe the rapture that flashed through my soul as I beheld it. It was a new and strange sight to me, brightening up my pathway with the light of happiness. Little Thomas was told, there was his Freddy,—and I was told to take care of little Thomas; and thus I entered upon the duties of my new home with the most cheering prospect ahead.

I look upon my departure from Colonel Lloyd's plantation as one of the most interesting events of my life.

It is possible, and even quite probable, that but for the mere circumstance of being removed from that plantation to Baltimore, I should have to-day, instead of being here seated by my own table, in the enjoyment of freedom and the happiness of home, writing this Narrative, been confined in the galling chains of slavery. Going to live at Baltimore laid the foundation, and opened the gateway, to all my subsequent prosperity. I have ever regarded it as the first plain manifestation of that kind providence which has ever since attended me, and marked my life with so many favors. I regarded the selection of myself as being somewhat remarkable. There were a number of slave children that might have been sent from the plantation to Baltimore. There were those younger, those older, and those of the same age. I was chosen from among them all, and was the first, last, and only choice.

I may be deemed superstitious, and even egotistical, in regarding this event as a special interposition of Divine Providence in my favor. But I should be false to the earliest sentiments of my soul, if I suppressed the opinion. I prefer to be true to myself, even at the hazard of incurring the ridicule of others, rather than to be false, and incur my own abhorrence. From my earliest recollection, I date the entertainment of a deep conviction that slavery would not always be able to hold me within its foul embrace; and in the darkest hours of my career in slavery, this living word of faith and spirit of hope departed not from me, but remained like ministering angels to cheer me through the gloom. This good spirit was from God, and to him I offer thanksgiving and praise.

# Chapter VI

My new mistress proved to be all she appeared when I first met her at the door,—a woman of the kindest heart and finest feelings. She had never had a slave under her control previously to myself, and prior to her marriage she had been dependent upon her own industry for a living. She was by trade a weaver; and by constant application to her business, she had been in a good degree preserved from the blighting and dehumanizing effects of slavery. I was utterly astonished at her goodness. I scarcely knew how to behave towards her. She was entirely unlike any other white woman I had ever seen. I could not approach her as I was accustomed to approach other white ladies. My early instruction was all out of place. The crouching servility, usually so acceptable a quality in a slave, did not answer when manifested toward her. Her favor was not gained by it; she seemed to be disturbed by it. She did not deem it impudent or unmannerly for a slave to look her in the face. The meanest slave was put fully at ease in her presence, and none left without feeling better for having seen her. Her face was made of heavenly smiles, and her voice of tranquil music.

But, alas! this kind heart had but a short time to remain such. The fatal poison of irresponsible power was already in her hands, and soon commenced its infernal work. That cheerful eye, under the influence of slavery, soon became red with rage; that voice, made all of sweet accord, changed to one of harsh and horrid discord; and that angelic face gave place to that of a demon.

Very soon after I went to live with Mr. and Mrs. Auld, she very kindly commenced to teach me the A, B, C. After I had learned this, she assisted me in learning to spell words of three or four letters. Just at this point of my progress, Mr. Auld found out what was going on, and at once forbade Mrs. Auld to instruct me further, telling her, among other things, that it was unlawful, as well as unsafe, to teach a slave to read. To use his own words, further, he said, "If you give a nigger an inch, he will take an ell. A nigger should know nothing but to obey his master—to do as he is told to do. Learning would *spoil* the best nigger in the world. Now," said he, "if you teach that nigger (speaking of myself) how to read, there would be no keeping him. It would forever unfit him to be a slave. He would at once become unmanageable, and of no value to his master. As to himself, it could do him no good, but a great deal of harm. It would make him discontented and unhappy."

These words sank deep into my heart, stirred up sentiments within that lay slumbering, and called into existence an entirely new train of thought. It was a new and special revelation, explaining dark and mysterious things, with which my youthful understanding had struggled, but struggled in vain. I now understood what had been to me a most perplexing difficulty—to wit, the white man's power to enslave the black man. It was a grand achievement, and I prized it highly. From that moment, I understood the pathway from slavery to freedom. It was just what I wanted, and I got it at a time when I the least expected it. Whilst I was saddened by the thought of losing the aid of my kind mistress, I was gladdened by the invaluable instruction which, by the merest accident, I had gained from my master. Though conscious of the difficulty of learning without a teacher, I set out with high hope, and a fixed purpose, at whatever cost of trouble, to learn how to read. The very decided manner with which he spoke, and strove to impress his wife with the evil consequences of giving me instruction, served to convince me that he was deeply sensible of the truths he was uttering. It gave me the best assurance that I might rely with the utmost confidence on the results which, he said, would flow from teaching me to read. What he most dreaded, that I most desired. What he most loved, that I most hated. That which to him was a great evil, to be carefully shunned, was to me a great good, to be diligently sought; and the argument which he so warmly urged, against my learning to read, only served to inspire me with a desire and determination to learn. In learning to read, I owe almost as much to the bitter opposition of my master, as to the kindly aid of my mistress. I acknowledge the benefit of both.

I had resided but a short time in Baltimore before I observed a marked difference, in the treatment of slaves, from that which I had witnessed in the country. A city slave is almost a free man, compared with a slave on the plantation. He is much better fed and clothed, and enjoys privileges altogether unknown to the slave on the plantation. There is a vestige of decency, a sense of shame, that does much to curb and check those outbreaks of atrocious cruelty so commonly enacted upon the plantation. He is a desperate slaveholder, who will shock the humanity of his non-slaveholding neighbors with the cries of his lacerated slave. Few are willing to incur the odium attaching to the reputation of being a cruel master; and above all things, they would not be known as not giving a slave enough to eat. Every city slaveholder is anxious to have it known of him, that he feeds his slaves well; and it is due to them to say, that most of them do give their slaves enough to eat. There are, however, some painful exceptions to this rule. Directly opposite to us, on Philpot Street, lived Mr. Thomas Hamilton. He owned two slaves. Their names were Henrietta and Mary. Henrietta was about twenty-two years of age, Mary was about fourteen; and of all the mangled and emaciated creatures I ever looked upon, these two were the most so. His heart must be harder than stone, that could look upon these unmoved. The head, neck, and shoulders of Mary were literally cut to pieces. I have frequently felt her head, and found it nearly covered with festering sores, caused by the lash of her cruel mistress. I do not know that her master ever whipped her, but I have been an eye-witness to the cruelty of Mrs. Hamilton. I used to be in Mr. Hamilton's house nearly every day. Mrs. Hamilton used to sit in a large chair in the middle of the room, with a heavy cowskin always by her side, and scarce an hour passed during the day but was marked by the blood of one of these slaves. The girls seldom passed her without her saying, "Move faster, you *black gip*!" at the same time giving them a blow with the cowskin over the head or shoulders, often drawing the blood. She would then say, "Take that, you *black gip*!"—continuing, "If you don't move faster, I'll move you!" Added to the cruel lashings to which these slaves were subjected, they were kept nearly half-starved. They seldom knew what it was to eat a full meal. I have seen Mary contending with the pigs for the offal thrown into the street. So much was Mary kicked and cut to pieces, that she was oftener called "*pecked*" than by her name.

# Chapter VII

I lived in Master Hugh's family about seven years. During this time, I succeeded in learning to read and write. In accomplishing this, I was compelled to resort to various stratagems. I had no regular teacher. My mistress, who had kindly commenced to instruct me, had, in compliance with the advice and direction of her husband, not only ceased to instruct, but had set her face against my being instructed by any one else. It is due, however, to my mistress to say of her, that she did not adopt this course of treatment immediately. She at first lacked the depravity indispensable to shutting me up in mental darkness. It was at least necessary for her to have some training in the exercise of irresponsible power, to make her equal to the task of treating me as though I were a brute.

My mistress was, as I have said, a kind and tender-hearted woman; and in the simplicity of her soul she commenced, when I first went to live with her, to treat me as she supposed one human being ought to treat another. In entering upon the duties of a slaveholder, she did not seem to perceive that I sustained to her the relation of a mere chattel, and that for her to treat me as a human being was not only wrong, but dangerously so. Slavery proved as injurious to her as it did to me. When I went there, she was a pious, warm, and tender-hearted woman. There was no sorrow or suffering for which she had not a tear. She had bread for the hungry, clothes for the naked, and comfort for every mourner that came within her reach. Slavery soon proved its ability to divest her of these heavenly qualities. Under its influence, the tender heart became stone, and the lamblike disposition gave way to one of tiger-like fierceness. The first step in her downward course was in her ceasing to instruct me. She now commenced to practise her husband's precepts. She finally became even more violent in her opposition than her husband himself. She was not satisfied with simply doing as well as he had commanded; she seemed anxious to do better. Nothing seemed to make her more angry than to see me with a newspaper. She seemed to think that here lay the danger. I have had her rush at me with a face made all up of fury, and snatch from me a newspaper, in a manner that fully revealed her apprehension. She was an apt woman; and a little experience soon demonstrated, to her satisfaction, that education and slavery were incompatible with each other.

From this time I was most narrowly watched. If I was in a separate room any considerable length of time,

I was sure to be suspected of having a book, and was at once called to give an account of myself. All this, however, was too late. The first step had been taken. Mistress, in teaching me the alphabet, had given me the *inch*, and no precaution could prevent me from taking the *ell*.

The plan which I adopted, and the one by which I was most successful, was that of making friends of all the little white boys whom I met in the street. As many of these as I could, I converted into teachers. With their kindly aid, obtained at different times and in different places, I finally succeeded in learning to read. When I was sent on errands, I always took my book with me, and by going one part of my errand quickly, I found time to get a lesson before my return. I used also to carry bread with me, enough of which was always in the house, and to which I was always welcome; for I was much better off in this regard than many of the poor white children in our neighborhood. This bread I used to bestow upon the hungry little urchins, who, in return, would give me that more valuable bread of knowledge. I am strongly tempted to give the names of two or three of those little boys, as a testimonial of the gratitude and affection I bear them; but prudence forbids;—not that it would injure me, but it might embarrass them; for it is almost an unpardonable offence to teach slaves to read in this Christian country. It is enough to say of the dear little fellows, that they lived on Philpot Street, very near Durgin and Bailey's ship-yard. I used to talk this matter of slavery over with them. I would sometimes say to them, I wished I could be as free as they would be when they got to be men. "You will be free as soon as you are twenty-one, *but I am a slave for life*! Have not I as good a right to be free as you have?" These words used to trouble them; they would express for me the liveliest sympathy, and console me with the hope that something would occur by which I might be free.

I was now about twelve years old, and the thought of being *a slave for life* began to bear heavily upon my heart. Just about this time, I got hold of a book entitled "The Columbian Orator." Every opportunity I got, I used to read this book. Among much of other interesting matter, I found in it a dialogue between a master and his slave. The slave was represented as having run away from his master three times. The dialogue represented the conversation which took place between them, when the slave was retaken the third time. In this dialogue, the whole argument in behalf of slavery was brought forward by the master, all of which was disposed of by the slave. The slave was made to say some very smart as well as impressive things in reply to his master—things which had the desired though unexpected effect; for the conversation resulted in the voluntary emancipation of the slave on the part of the master.

In the same book, I met with one of Sheridan's mighty speeches on and in behalf of Catholic emancipation. These were choice documents to me. I read them over and over again with unabated interest. They gave tongue to interesting thoughts of my own soul, which had frequently flashed through my mind, and died away for want of utterance. The moral which I gained from the dialogue was the power of truth over the conscience of even a slaveholder. What I got from Sheridan was a bold denunciation of slavery, and a powerful vindication of human rights. The reading of these documents enabled me to utter my thoughts, and to meet the arguments brought forward to sustain slavery; but while they relieved me of one difficulty, they brought on another even more painful than the one of which I was relieved. The more I read, the more I was led to abhor and detest my enslavers. I could regard them in no other light than a band of successful robbers, who had left their homes, and gone to Africa, and stolen us from our homes, and in a strange land reduced us to slavery. I loathed them as being the meanest as well as the most wicked of men. As I read and contemplated the subject, behold! that very discontentment which Master Hugh had predicted would follow my learning to read had already come, to torment and sting my soul to unutterable anguish. As I writhed under it, I would at times feel that learning to read had been a curse rather than a blessing. It had given me a view of my wretched condition, without the remedy. It opened my eyes to the horrible pit, but to no ladder upon which to get out. In moments of agony, I envied my fellow-slaves for their stupidity. I have often wished myself a beast. I preferred the condition of the meanest reptile to my own. Any thing, no matter what, to get rid of thinking! It was this everlasting thinking of my condition that tormented me. There was no getting rid of it. It was pressed upon me by every object within sight or hearing, animate or inanimate. The silver trump of freedom had roused my soul to eternal wakefulness. Freedom now appeared, to disappear no more forever. It was heard in every sound, and seen in every thing. It was ever present to torment me with a sense of my wretched condition. I saw nothing without seeing it, I heard nothing without hearing it, and felt nothing without feeling it. It looked from every star, it smiled in every calm, breathed in every wind, and moved in every storm.

I often found myself regretting my own existence, and wishing myself dead; and but for the hope of being free, I have no doubt but that I should have killed myself, or done something for which I should have been killed. While in this state of mind, I was eager to hear any one speak of slavery. I was a ready listener. Every little while, I could hear something about the abolitionists. It was some time before I found what the word meant. It was always used in such connections as to make it an interesting word to me. If a slave ran away and succeeded in getting clear, or if a slave killed his master, set fire to a barn, or did any thing very wrong in the mind of a slaveholder, it was spoken of as the fruit of *abolition*. Hearing the word in this connection very often, I set about learning what it meant. The dictionary afforded me little or no help. I found it was "the act of abolishing;" but then I did not know what was to be abolished. Here I was perplexed. I did not dare to ask any one about its meaning, for I was satisfied that it was something they wanted me to know very little about. After a patient waiting, I got one of our city papers, containing an account of the number of petitions from the north, praying for the abolition of slavery in the District of Columbia, and of the slave trade between the States. From this time I understood the words *abolition* and *abolitionist*, and always drew near when that word was spoken, expecting to bear something of importance to myself and fellow-slaves. The light broke in upon me by degrees. I went one day down on the wharf of Mr. Waters; and seeing two Irishmen unloading a scow of stone, I went, unasked, and helped them. When we had finished, one of them came to me and asked me if I were a slave. I told him I was. He asked, "Are ye a slave for life?" I told him that I was. The good Irishman seemed to be deeply affected by the statement. He said to the other that it was a pity so fine a little fellow as myself should be a slave for life. He said it was a shame to hold me. They both advised me to run away to the north; that I should find friends there, and that I should be free. I pretended not to be interested in what they said, and treated them as if I did not understand them; for I feared they might be treacherous. White men have been known to encourage slaves to escape, and then, to get the reward, catch them and return them to their masters. I was afraid that these seemingly good men might use me so; but I nevertheless remembered their advice, and from that time I resolved to run away. I looked forward to a time at which it would be safe for me to escape. I was too young to think of doing so immediately; besides, I wished to learn how to write, as I might have occasion to write my own pass. I consoled myself with the hope that I should one day find a good chance. Meanwhile, I would learn to write.

The idea as to how I might learn to write was suggested to me by being in Durgin and Bailey's ship-yard, and frequently seeing the ship carpenters, after hewing, and getting a piece of timber ready for use, write on the timber the name of that part of the ship for which it was intended. When a piece of timber was intended for the larboard side, it would be marked thus—"L." When a piece was for the starboard side, it would be marked thus— "S." A piece for the larboard side forward, would be marked thus—"L. F." When a piece was for starboard side forward, it would be marked thus—"S. F." For larboard aft, it would be marked thus—"L. A." For starboard aft, it would be marked thus—"S. A." I soon learned the names of these letters, and for what they were intended when placed upon a piece of timber in the ship-yard. I immediately commenced copying them, and in a short time was able to make the four letters named. After that, when I met with any boy who I knew could write, I would tell him I could write as well as he. The next word would be, "I don't believe you. Let me see you try it." I would then make the letters which I had been so fortunate as to learn, and ask him to beat that. In this way I got a good many lessons in writing, which it is quite possible I should never have gotten in any other way. During this time, my copy-book was the board fence, brick wall, and pavement; my pen and ink was a lump of chalk. With these, I learned mainly how to write. I then commenced and continued copying the Italics in Webster's Spelling Book, until I could make them all without looking on the book. By this time, my little Master Thomas had gone to school, and learned how to write, and had written over a number of copy-books. These had been brought home, and shown to some of our near neighbors, and then laid aside. My mistress used to go to class meeting at the Wilk Street meeting house every Monday afternoon, and leave me to take care of the house. When left thus, I used to spend the time in writing in the spaces left in Master Thomas's copy-book, copying what he had written. I continued to do this until I could write a hand very similar to that of Master Thomas. Thus, after a long, tedious effort for years, I finally succeeded in learning how to write.

# Chapter VIII

In a very short time after I went to live at Baltimore, my old master's youngest son Richard died; and in about three years and six months after his death, my old master, Captain Anthony, died, leaving only his son, Andrew, and daughter, Lucretia, to share his estate. He died while on a visit to see his daughter at Hillsborough. Cut off thus unexpectedly, he left no will as to the disposal of his property. It was therefore necessary to have a valuation of the property, that it might be equally divided between Mrs. Lucretia and Master Andrew. I was immediately sent for, to be valued with the other property. Here again my feelings rose up in detestation of slavery. I had now a new conception of my degraded condition. Prior to this, I had become, if not insensible to my lot, at least partly so. I left Baltimore with a young heart overborne with sadness, and a soul full of apprehension. I took passage with Captain Rowe, in the schooner *Wild Cat*, and, after a sail of about twenty-four hours, I found myself near the place of my birth. I had now been absent from it almost, if not quite, five years. I, however, remembered the place very well. I was only about five years old when I left it, to go and live with my old master on Colonel Lloyd's plantation; so that I was now between ten and eleven years old.

We were all ranked together at the valuation. Men and women, old and young, married and single, were ranked with horses, sheep, and swine. There were horses and men, cattle and women, pigs and children, all holding the same rank in the scale of being, and were all subjected to the same narrow examination. Silvery-headed age and sprightly youth, maids and matrons, had to undergo the same indelicate inspection. At this moment, I saw more clearly than ever the brutalizing effects of slavery upon both slave and slaveholder.

After the valuation, then came the division. I have no language to express the high excitement and deep anxiety which were felt among us poor slaves during this time. Our fate for life was now to be decided. We had no more voice in that decision than the brutes among whom we were ranked. A single word from the white men was enough—against all our wishes, prayers, and entreaties—to sunder forever the dearest friends, dearest kindred, and strongest ties known to human beings. In addition to the pain of separation, there was the horrid dread of falling into the hands of Master Andrew. He was known to us all as being a most cruel wretch,—a common drunkard, who had, by his reckless mismanagement and profligate dissipation already wasted a large portion of his father's property. We all felt that we might as well be sold at once to the Georgia traders, as to pass into his hands; for we knew that that would be our inevitable condition,—a condition held by us all in the utmost horror and dread.

I suffered more anxiety than most of my fellow-slaves. I had known what it was to be kindly treated; they had known nothing of the kind. They had seen little or nothing of the world. They were in very deed men and women of sorrow, and acquainted with grief. Their backs had been made familiar with the bloody lash, so that they had become callous; mine was yet tender; for while at Baltimore I got few whippings, and few slaves could boast of a kinder master and mistress than myself; and the thought of passing out of their hands into those of Master Andrew—a man who, but a few days before, to give me a sample of his bloody disposition, took my little brother by the throat, threw him on the ground, and with the heel of his boot stamped upon his head till the blood gushed from his nose and ears—was well calculated to make me anxious as to my fate. After he had committed this savage outrage upon my brother, he turned to me, and said that was the way he meant to serve me one of these days,—meaning, I suppose, when I came into his possession.

Thanks to a kind Providence, I fell to the portion of Mrs. Lucretia, and was sent immediately back to Baltimore, to live again in the family of Master Hugh. Their joy at my return equalled their sorrow at my departure. It was a glad day to me. I had escaped a fate worse than lion's jaws. I was absent from Baltimore, for the purpose of valuation and division, just about one month, and it seemed to have been six.

Very soon after my return to Baltimore, my mistress, Lucretia, died, leaving her husband and one child, Amanda; and in a very short time after her death, Master Andrew died. Now all the property of my old master, slaves included, was in the hands of strangers,—strangers who had had nothing to do with accumulating it. Not a slave was left free. All remained slaves, from the youngest to the oldest. If any one thing in my experience, more than another, served to deepen my conviction of the infernal character of slavery, and to fill me with unutterable loathing of slaveholders, it was their base ingratitude to my poor old grandmother. She had served my old master faithfully from youth to old age. She had been the source of all his wealth; she had peopled his plantation with slaves; she had become a great grandmother in his service. She had rocked him in infancy, attended him in childhood, served him through life, and at his death wiped from his icy brow the cold death-sweat, and closed his eyes forever. She was nevertheless left a slave—a slave for life—a slave in the hands of strangers; and in their hands she saw her children, her grandchildren, and her great-grand children, divided, like so many sheep, without being gratified with the small privilege of a single word, as to their or her own destiny. And, to cap the climax of their base ingratitude and fiendish barbarity, my grandmother, who was now very old, having outlived my old master and all his children, having seen the beginning and end of all of them, and her present owners finding she was of but little value, her frame already racked with the pains of old age, and complete helplessness fast stealing over her once active limbs, they took her to the woods, built her a little hut, put up a little mud-chimney, and then made her welcome to the privilege of supporting herself there in perfect loneliness; thus virtually turning her out to die! If my poor old grandmother now lives, she lives to suffer in utter loneliness; she lives to remember and mourn over the loss of children, the loss of grandchildren, and the loss of great-grandchildren. They are, in the language of the slave's poet, Whittier,—

"Gone, gone, sold and gone
To the rice swamp dank and lone,
Where the slave-whip ceaseless swings,
Where the noisome insect stings,
Where the fever-demon strews
Poison with the failing dews,
Where the sickly sunbeams glare
Through the hot and misty air:—
Gone, gone, sold and gone
To the rice swamp dank and lone,
From Virginia hills and waters—
Woe is me, my stolen daughters!"

The hearth is desolate. The children, the unconscious children, who once sang and danced in her presence, are gone. She gropes her way, in the darkness of age, for a drink of water. Instead of the voices of her children, she hears by day the moans of the dove, and by night the screams of the hideous owl. All is gloom. The grave is at the door. And now, when weighed down by the pains and aches of old age, when the head inclines to the feet, when the beginning and ending of human existence meet, and helpless infancy and painful old age combine together—at this time, this most needful time, the time for the exercise of that tenderness and affection which children only can exercise towards a declining parent— my poor old grandmother, the devoted mother of twelve children, is left all alone, in yonder little hut, before a few dim embers. She stands—she sits—she staggers—she falls—she groans—she dies—and there are none of her children or grandchildren present, to wipe from her wrinkled brow the cold sweat of death, or to place beneath the sod her fallen remains. Will not a righteous God visit for these things?

In about two years after the death of Mrs. Lucretia, Master Thomas married his second wife. Her name was Rowena Hamilton. She was the eldest daughter of Mr. William Hamilton. Master now lived in St. Michael's. Not long after his marriage, a misunderstanding took place between himself and Master Hugh; and as a means of punishing his brother, he took me from him to live with himself at St. Michael's. Here I underwent another most painful separation. It, however, was not so severe as the one I dreaded at the division of property; for, during this interval, a great change had taken place in Master Hugh and his once kind and affectionate wife. The influence of brandy upon him, and of slavery upon her, had effected a disastrous change in the characters of both; so that, as far as they were concerned, I thought I had little to lose by the change. But it was not to them that I was attached. It was to those little Baltimore boys that I felt the strongest attachment. I had received many good lessons from them, and was still receiving them, and the thought of leaving them was painful indeed. I was leaving, too, without the hope of ever being allowed to return. Master Thomas had said he would never let me return again. The barrier betwixt himself and brother he considered impassable.

I then had to regret that I did not at least make the attempt to carry out my resolution to run away; for the chances of success are tenfold greater from the city than from the country.

I sailed from Baltimore for St. Michael's in the sloop Amanda, Captain Edward Dodson. On my passage, I paid particular attention to the direction which the steamboats took to go to Philadelphia. I found, instead of going down, on reaching North Point they went up the bay, in a north-easterly direction. I deemed this knowledge of the utmost importance. My determination to run away was again revived. I resolved to wait only so long as the offering of a favorable opportunity. When that came, I was determined to be off.

# Chapter IX

I have now reached a period of my life when I can give dates. I left Baltimore, and went to live with Master Thomas Auld, at St. Michael's, in March, 1832. It was now more than seven years since I lived with him in the family of my old master, on Colonel Lloyd's plantation. We of course were now almost entire strangers to each other. He was to me a new master, and I to him a new slave. I was ignorant of his temper and disposition; he was equally so of mine. A very short time, however, brought us into full acquaintance with each other. I was made acquainted with his wife not less than with himself. They were well matched, being equally mean and cruel. I was now, for the first time during a space of more than seven years, made to feel the painful gnawings of hunger—a something which I had not experienced before since I left Colonel Lloyd's plantation. It went hard enough with me then, when I could look back to no period at which I had enjoyed a sufficiency. It was tenfold harder after living in Master Hugh's family, where I had always had enough to eat, and of that which was good. I have said Master Thomas was a mean man. He was so. Not to give a slave enough to eat, is regarded as the most aggravated development of meanness even among slaveholders. The rule is, no matter how coarse the food, only let there be enough of it. This is the theory; and in the part of Maryland from which I came, it is the general practice,—though there are many exceptions. Master Thomas gave us enough of neither coarse nor fine food. There were four slaves of us in the kitchen—my sister Eliza, my aunt Priscilla, Henny, and myself; and we were allowed less than a half of a bushel of corn-meal per week, and very little else, either in the shape of meat or vegetables. It was not enough for us to subsist upon. We were therefore reduced to the wretched necessity of living at the expense of our neighbors. This we did by begging and stealing, whichever came handy in the time of need, the one being considered as legitimate as the other. A great many times have we poor creatures been nearly perishing with hunger, when food in abundance lay mouldering in the safe and smoke-house, and our pious mistress was aware of the fact; and yet that mistress and her husband would kneel every morning, and pray that God would bless them in basket and store!

Bad as all slaveholders are, we seldom meet one destitute of every element of character commanding respect. My master was one of this rare sort. I do not know of one single noble act ever performed by him. The leading trait in his character was meanness; and if there were any other element in his nature, it was made subject to this. He was mean; and, like most other mean men, he lacked the ability to conceal his meanness. Captain Auld was not born a slaveholder. He had been a poor man, master only of a Bay craft. He came into possession of all his slaves by marriage; and of all men, adopted slave-holders are the worst. He was cruel, but cowardly. He commanded without firmness. In the enforcement of his rules, he was at times rigid, and at times lax. At times, he spoke to his slaves with the firmness of Napoleon and the fury of a demon; at other times, he might well be mistaken for an inquirer who had lost his way. He did nothing of himself. He might have passed for a lion, but for his ears. In all things noble which he attempted, his own meanness shone most conspicuous. His airs, words, and actions, were the airs, words, and actions of born slaveholders, and, being assumed, were awkward enough. He was not even a good imitator. He possessed all the disposition to deceive, but wanted the power. Having no resources within himself, he was compelled to be the copyist of many, and being such, he was forever the victim of inconsistency; and of consequence he was an object of contempt, and was held as such even by his slaves. The luxury of having slaves of his own to wait upon him was something new and unprepared for. He was a slaveholder without the ability to hold slaves. He found himself incapable of managing his slaves either by force, fear, or fraud. We seldom called him “master;” we generally called him “Captain Auld,” and were hardly disposed to title him at all. I doubt not that our conduct had much to do with making him appear awkward, and of consequence fretful. Our want of reverence for him must have perplexed him greatly. He wished to have us call him master, but lacked the firmness necessary to command us to do so. His wife used to insist upon our calling him so, but to no purpose. In August, 1832, my master attended a Methodist camp-meeting held in the Bay-side, Talbot county, and there experienced religion. I indulged a faint hope that his conversion would lead him to emancipate his slaves, and that, if he did not do this, it would, at any rate, make him more kind and humane. I was disappointed in both these respects. It neither made him to be humane to his slaves, nor to emancipate them. If it had any effect on his character, it made him more cruel and hateful in all his ways; for I believe him to have been a much worse man after his conversion than before. Prior to his conversion, he relied upon his own depravity to shield and sustain him in his savage barbarity; but after his conversion, he found religious sanction and support for his slaveholding cruelty. He made the greatest pretensions to piety. His house was the house of prayer. He prayed morning, noon, and night. He very soon distinguished himself among his brethren, and was soon made a class-leader and exhorter. His activity in revivals was great, and he proved himself an instrument in the hands of the church in converting many souls. His house was the preachers' home. They used to take great pleasure in coming there to put up; for while he starved us, he stuffed them. We have had three or four preachers there at a time. The names of those who used to come most frequently while I lived there, were Mr. Storks, Mr. Ewery, Mr. Humphry, and Mr. Hickey. I have also seen Mr. George Cookman at our house. We slaves loved Mr. Cookman. We believed him to be a good man. We thought him instrumental in getting Mr. Samuel Harrison, a very rich slaveholder, to emancipate his slaves; and by some means got the impression that he was laboring to effect the emancipation of all the slaves. When he was at our house, we were sure to be called in to prayers. When the others were there, we were sometimes called in and sometimes not. Mr. Cookman took more notice of us than either of the other ministers. He could not come among us without betraying his sympathy for us, and, stupid as we were, we had the sagacity to see it.

While I lived with my master in St. Michael's, there was a white young man, a Mr. Wilson, who proposed to keep a Sabbath school for the instruction of such slaves as might be disposed to learn to read the New Testament. We met but three times, when Mr. West and Mr. Fairbanks, both class-leaders, with many others, came upon us with sticks and other missiles, drove us off, and forbade us to meet again. Thus ended our little Sabbath school in the pious town of St. Michael's.

I have said my master found religious sanction for his

cruelty. As an example, I will state one of many facts going to prove the charge. I have seen him tie up a lame young woman, and whip her with a heavy cowskin upon her naked shoulders, causing the warm red blood to drip; and, in justification of the bloody deed, he would quote this passage of Scripture—"He that knoweth his master's will, and doeth it not, shall be beaten with many stripes."

Master would keep this lacerated young, woman tied up in this horrid situation four or five hours at a time. I have known him to tie her up early in the morning, and whip her before breakfast; leave her, go to his store, return at dinner, and whip her again, cutting her in the places already made raw with his cruel lash. The secret of master's cruelty toward "Henny" is found in the fact of her being almost helpless. When quite a child, she fell into the fire, and burned herself horribly. Her hands were so burnt, that she never got the use of them. She could do very little but bear heavy burdens. She was to master a bill of expense; and as he was a mean man, she was a constant offence to him. He seemed desirous of getting the poor girl out of existence. He gave her away once to his sister; but, being a poor gift, she was not disposed to keep her. Finally, my benevolent master, to use his own words, "set her adrift to take care of herself." Here was a recently-converted man, holding on upon the mother, and at the same time turning out her helpless child, to starve and die! Master Thomas was one of the many pious slaveholders who hold slaves for the very charitable purpose of taking care of them.

My master and myself had quite a number of differences. He found me unsuitable to his purpose. My city life, he said, had had a very pernicious effect upon me. It had almost ruined me for every good purpose, and fitted me for every thing which was bad. One of my greatest faults was that of letting his horse run away, and go down to his father-in-law's farm, which was about five miles from St. Michael's. I would then have to go after it. My reason for this kind of carelessness, or carefulness, was, that I could always get something to eat when I went there. Master William Hamilton, my master's father-in-law, always gave his slaves enough to eat. I never left there hungry, no matter how great the need of my speedy return. Master Thomas at length said he would stand it no longer. I had lived with him nine months, during which time he had given me a number of severe whippings, all to no good purpose. He resolved to put me out, as he said, to be broken; and, for this purpose, he let me for one year to a man named Edward Covey. Mr. Covey was a poor man, a farm-renter. He rented the place upon which he lived, as also the hands with which he tilled it. Mr. Covey had acquired a very high reputation for breaking young slaves, and this reputation was of immense value to him. It enabled him to get his farm tilled with much less expense to himself than he could have had it done without such a reputation. Some slaveholders thought it not much loss to allow Mr. Covey to have their slaves one year, for the sake of the training to which they were subjected, without any other compensation. He could hire young help with great ease, in consequence of this reputation. Added to the natural good qualities of Mr. Covey, he was a professor of religion—a pious soul—a member and a class-leader in the Methodist church. All of this added weight to his reputation as a "nigger-breaker." I was aware of all the facts, having been made acquainted with them by a young man who had lived there. I nevertheless made the change gladly; for I was sure of getting enough to eat, which is not the smallest consideration to a hungry man.

# Chapter X

I left Master Thomas's house, and went to live with Mr. Covey, on the 1st of January, 1833. I was now, for the first time in my life, a field hand. In my new employment, I found myself even more awkward than a country boy appeared to be in a large city. I had been at my new home but one week before Mr. Covey gave me a very severe whipping, cutting my back, causing the blood to run, and raising ridges on my flesh as large as my little finger. The details of this affair are as follows: Mr. Covey sent me, very early in the morning of one of our coldest days in the month of January, to the woods, to get a load of wood. He gave me a team of unbroken oxen. He told me which was the in-hand ox, and which the off-hand one. He then tied the end of a large rope around the horns of the in-hand ox, and gave me the other end of it, and told me, if the oxen started to run, that I must hold on upon the rope. I had never driven oxen before, and of course I was very awkward. I, however, succeeded in getting to the edge of the woods with little difficulty; but I had got a very few rods into the woods, when the oxen took fright, and started full tilt, carrying the cart against trees, and over stumps, in the most frightful manner. I expected every moment that my brains would be dashed out against the trees. After running thus for a considerable distance, they finally upset the cart, dashing it with great force against a tree, and threw themselves into it dense thicket. How I escaped death, I do not know. There I was, entirely alone, in a thick wood, in a place new to me. My cart was upset and shattered, my oxen were entangled among the young trees, and there was none to help me. After a long spell of effort, I succeeded in getting my cart righted, my oxen disentangled, and again yoked to the cart. I now proceeded with my team to the place where I had, the day before, been chopping wood, and loaded my cart pretty heavily, thinking in this way to tame my oxen. I then proceeded on my way home. I had now consumed one half of the day. I got out of the woods safely, and now felt out of danger, I stopped my oxen to open the woods gate; and just as I did so, before I could get hold of my ox-rope, the oxen again started, rushed through the gate, catching it between the wheel and the body of the cart, tearing it to pieces, and coming within a few inches of crushing me against the gate-post. Thus twice, in one short day, I escaped death by the merest chance. On my return, I told Mr. Covey what had happened, and how it happened. He ordered me to return to the woods again immediately. I did so, and he followed on after me. Just as I got into the woods, he came up and told me to stop my cart, and that he would teach me how to trifle away my time, and break gates. He then went to a large gum-tree, and with his axe cut three large switches, and, after trimming them up neatly with his pocket-knife, he ordered me to take off my clothes. I made him no answer, but stood with my clothes on. He repeated his order. I still made him no answer, nor did I move to strip myself. Upon this he rushed at me with the fierceness of a tiger, tore off my clothes, and lashed me till he had worn out his switches, cutting me so savagely as to leave the marks visible for a long time after. This whipping was the first of a number just like it, and for similar offences.

I lived with Mr. Covey one year. During the first six months, of that year, scarce a week passed without his whipping me. I was seldom free from a sore back. My awkwardness was almost always his excuse for whipping me. We were worked fully up to the point of endurance. Long before day we were up, our horses fed, and by the first approach of day we were off to the field with our hoes and ploughing teams. Mr. Covey gave us enough to eat, but scarce time to eat it. We were often less than five minutes taking our meals. We were often in the field from the first approach of day till its last lingering ray had left us; and at saving-fodder time, midnight often caught us in the field binding blades.

Covey would be out with us. The way he used to stand it, was this. He would spend the most of his afternoons in bed. He would then come out fresh in the evening, ready to urge us on with his words, example, and frequently with the whip. Mr. Covey was one of the few slaveholders who could and did work with his hands. He was a hard-working man. He knew by himself just what a man or a boy could do. There was no deceiving him. His work went on in his absence almost as well as in his presence; and he had the faculty of making us feel that he was ever present with us. This he did by surprising us. He seldom approached the spot where we were at work openly, if he could do it secretly. He always aimed at taking us by surprise. Such was his cunning, that we used to call him, among ourselves, "the snake." When we were at work in the cornfield, he would sometimes crawl on his hands and knees to avoid detection, and all at once he would rise nearly in our midst, and scream out, "Ha, ha! Come, come! Dash on, dash on!" This being his mode of attack, it was never safe to stop a single minute. His comings were like a thief in the night. He appeared to us as being ever at hand. He was under every tree, behind every stump, in every bush, and at every window, on the plantation. He would sometimes mount his horse, as if bound to St. Michael's, a distance of seven miles, and in half an hour afterwards you would see him coiled up in the corner of the wood-fence, watching every motion of the slaves. He would, for this purpose, leave his horse tied up in the woods. Again, he would sometimes walk up to us, and give us orders as though he was upon the point of starting on a long journey, turn his back upon us, and make as though he was going to the house to get ready; and, before he would get half way thither, he would turn short and crawl into a fence-corner, or behind some tree, and there watch us till the going down of the sun.

Mr. Covey's *forte* consisted in his power to deceive. His life was devoted to planning and perpetrating the grossest deceptions. Every thing he possessed in the shape of learning or religion, he made conform to his disposition to deceive. He seemed to think himself equal to deceiving the Almighty. He would make a short prayer in the morning, and a long prayer at night; and, strange as it may seem, few men would at times appear more devotional than he. The exercises of his family devotions were always commenced with singing; and, as he was a very poor singer himself, the duty of raising the hymn generally came upon me. He would read his hymn, and nod at me to commence. I would at times do so; at others, I would not. My non-compliance would almost always produce much confusion. To show himself independent of me, he would start and stagger through with his hymn in the most discordant manner. In this state of mind, he prayed with more than ordinary spirit. Poor man! Such was his disposition, and success at deceiving, I do verily believe that he sometimes deceived himself into the solemn belief, that he was a sincere worshipper of the most high God; and this, too, at a time when he may be said to have been guilty of compelling his woman slave to commit the sin of adultery. The facts in the case are these: Mr. Covey was a poor man; he was just commencing in life; he was only able to buy one slave; and, shocking as is the fact, he bought her, as he said, for *a breeder*. This woman was named Caroline. Mr. Covey bought her from Mr. Thomas Lowe, about six miles from St. Michael's. She was a large, able-bodied woman, about twenty years old. She had already given birth to one child, which proved her to be just what he wanted. After buying her, he hired a married man of Mr. Samuel Harrison, to live with him one year; and him he used to fasten up with her every night! The result was, that, at the end of the year, the miserable woman gave birth to twins. At this result Mr. Covey seemed to be highly pleased, both with the man and the wretched woman. Such was his joy, and that of his wife, that nothing they could do for Caroline during her confinement was too good, or too hard, to be done. The children were regarded as being quite an addition to his wealth.

If at any one time of my life more than another, I was made to drink the bitterest dregs of slavery, that time was during the first six months of my stay with Mr. Covey. We were worked in all weathers. It was never too hot or too cold; it could never rain, blow, hail, or snow, too hard for us to work in the field. Work, work, work, was scarcely more the order of the day than of the night. The longest days were too short for him, and the shortest nights too long for him. I was somewhat unmanageable when I first went there, but a few months of this discipline tamed me. Mr. Covey succeeded in breaking me. I was broken in body, soul, and spirit. My natural elasticity was crushed, my intellect languished, the disposition to read departed, the cheerful spark that lingered about my eye died; the dark night of slavery closed in upon me; and behold a man transformed into a brute!

Sunday was my only leisure time. I spent this in a sort of beast-like stupor, between sleep and wake, under some large tree. At times I would rise up, a flash of energetic freedom would dart through my soul, accompanied with a faint beam of hope, that flickered for a moment, and then vanished. I sank down again, mourning over my wretched condition. I was sometimes prompted to take my life, and that of Covey, but was prevented by a combination of hope and fear. My sufferings on this plantation seem now like a dream rather than a stern reality.

Our house stood within a few rods of the Chesapeake Bay, whose broad bosom was ever white with sails from every quarter of the habitable globe. Those beautiful vessels, robed in purest white, so delightful to the eye of freemen, were to me so many shrouded ghosts, to terrify and torment me with thoughts of my wretched condition. I have often, in the deep stillness of a summer's Sabbath, stood all alone upon the lofty banks of that noble bay, and traced, with saddened heart and tearful eye, the countless number of sails moving off to the mighty ocean. The sight of these always affected me powerfully. My thoughts would compel utterance; and there, with no audience but the Almighty, I would pour out my soul's complaint, in my rude way, with an apostrophe to the moving multitude of ships:—

"You are loosed from your moorings, and are free; I am fast in my chains, and am a slave! You move merrily before the gentle gale, and I sadly before the bloody whip! You are freedom's swift-winged angels, that fly round the world; I am confined in bands of iron! O that I were free! O, that I were on one of your gallant decks, and under your protecting wing! Alas! betwixt me and you, the turbid waters roll. Go on, go on. O that I could also go! Could I but swim! If I could fly! O, why was I born a man, of whom to make a brute. The glad ship is gone; she hides in the dim distance. I am left in the hottest hell of unending slavery. O God, save me! God, deliver me! Let me be free! Is there any God? Why am I a slave? I will run away. I will not stand it. Get caught, or get clear, I'll try it. I had as well die with ague as the fever. I have only one life to lose. I had as well be killed running as die standing. Only think of it; one hundred miles straight north, and I am free! Try it? Yes! God helping me, I will. It cannot be that I shall live and die a slave. I will take to the water. This very bay shall yet bear me into freedom. The steamboats steered in a north-east course from North Point. I will do the same; and when I get to the head of the bay, I will turn my canoe adrift, and walk straight through Delaware into

Pennsylvania. When I get there, I shall not be required to have a pass; I can travel without being disturbed. Let but the first opportunity offer, and, come what will, I am off. Meanwhile, I will try to bear up under the yoke. I am not the only slave in the world. Why should I fret? I can bear as much as any of them. Besides, I am but a boy, and all boys are bound to some one. It may be that my misery in slavery will only increase my happiness when I get free. There is a better day coming."

Thus I used to think, and thus I used to speak to myself; goaded almost to madness at one moment, and at the next reconciling myself to my wretched lot.

I have already intimated that my condition was much worse, during the first six months of my stay at Mr. Covey's, than in the last six. The circumstances leading to the change in Mr. Covey's course toward me form an epoch in my humble history. You have seen how a man was made a slave; you shall see how a slave was made a man. On one of the hottest days of the month of August, 1833, Bill Smith, William Hughes, a slave named Eli, and myself, were engaged in fanning wheat. Hughes was clearing the fanned wheat from before the fan, Eli was turning, Smith was feeding, and I was carrying wheat to the fan. The work was simple, requiring strength rather than intellect; yet, to one entirely unused to such work, it came very hard. About three o'clock of that day, I broke down; my strength failed me; I was seized with a violent aching of the head, attended with extreme dizziness; I trembled in every limb. Finding what was coming, I nerved myself up, feeling it would never do to stop work. I stood as long as I could stagger to the hopper with grain. When I could stand no longer, I fell, and felt as held down by an immense weight. The fan of course stopped; every one had his own work to do; and no one could do the work of the other, and have his own go on at the same time.

Mr. Covey was at the house, about one hundred yards from the treading-yard where we were fanning. On hearing the fan stop, he left immediately, and came to the spot where we were. He hastily inquired what the matter was. Bill answered that I was sick, and there was no one to bring wheat to the fan. I had by this time crawled away under the side of the post and rail-fence by which the yard was enclosed, hoping to find relief by getting out of the sun. He then asked where I was. He was told by one of the hands. He came to the spot, and, after looking at me awhile, asked me what was the matter. I told him as well as I could, for I scarce had strength to speak. He then gave me a savage kick in the side, and told me to get up. I tried to do so, but fell back in the attempt. He gave me another kick, and again told me to rise. I again tried, and succeeded in gaining my feet; but, stooping to get the tub with which I was feeding the fan, I again staggered and fell. While down in this situation, Mr. Covey took up the hickory slat with which Hughes had been striking off the half-bushel measure, and with it gave me a heavy blow upon the head, making a large wound, and the blood ran freely; and with this again told me to get up. I made no effort to comply, having now made up my mind to let him do his worst. In a short time after receiving this blow, my head grew better. Mr. Covey had now left me to my fate. At this moment I resolved, for the first time, to go to my master, enter a complaint, and ask his protection. In order to this, I must that afternoon walk seven miles; and this, under the circumstances, was truly a severe undertaking. I was exceedingly feeble; made so as much by the kicks and blows which I received, as by the severe fit of sickness to which I had been subjected. I, however, watched my chance, while Covey was looking in an opposite direction, and started for St. Michael's. I succeeded in getting a considerable distance on my way to the woods, when Covey discovered me, and called after me to come back, threatening what he would do if I did not come. I, disregarded both his calls and his threats, and made my way to the woods as fast as my feeble state would allow; and thinking I might be overhauled by him if I kept the road, I walked through the woods, keeping far enough from the road to avoid detection, and near enough to prevent losing my way. I had not gone far before my little strength again failed me. I could go no farther. I fell down, and lay for a considerable time. The blood was yet oozing from the wound on my head. For a time I thought I should bleed to death; and think now that I should have done so, but that the blood so matted my hair as to stop the wound. After lying there about three quarters of an hour, I nerved myself up again, and started on my way, through bogs and briers, barefooted and bareheaded, tearing my feet sometimes at nearly every step; and after a journey of about seven miles, occupying some five hours to perform it, I arrived at master's store. I then presented an appearance enough to affect any but a heart of iron. From the crown of my head to my feet, I was covered with blood. My hair was all clotted with dust and blood; my shirt was stiff with blood. My legs and feet were torn in sundry places with briers and thorns, and were also covered with blood. I suppose I looked like a man who had escaped a den of wild beasts, and barely escaped them. In this state I appeared before my master, humbly entreating him to interpose his authority for my protection. I told him all the circumstances as well as I could, and it seemed, as I spoke, at times to affect him. He would then walk the floor, and seek to justify Covey by saying he expected I deserved it. He asked me what I wanted. I told him, to let me get a new home; that as sure as I lived with Mr. Covey again, I should live with but to die with him; that Covey would surely kill me; he was in a fair way for it. Master Thomas ridiculed the idea that there was any danger of Mr. Covey's killing me, and said that he knew Mr. Covey; that he was a good man, and that he could not think of taking me from him; that, should he do so, he would lose the whole year's wages; that I belonged to Mr. Covey for one year, and that I must go back to him, come what might; and that I must not trouble him with any more stories, or that he would himself *get hold of me*. After threatening me thus, he gave me a very large dose of salts, telling me that I might remain in St. Michael's that night, (it being quite late,) but that I must be off back to Mr. Covey's early in the morning; and that if I did not, he would *get hold of me*, which meant that he would whip me. I remained all night, and, according to his orders, I started off to Covey's in the morning, (Saturday morning,) wearied in body and broken in spirit. I got no supper that night, or breakfast that morning. I reached Covey's about nine o'clock; and just as I was getting over the fence that divided Mrs. Kemp's fields from ours, out ran Covey with his cowskin, to give me another whipping. Before he could reach me, I succeeded in getting to the cornfield; and as the corn was very high, it afforded me the means of hiding. He seemed very angry, and searched for me a long time. My behavior was altogether unaccountable. He finally gave up the chase, thinking, I suppose, that I must come home for something to eat; he would give himself no further trouble in looking for me. I spent that day mostly in the woods, having the alternative before me,—to go home and be whipped to death, or stay in the woods and be starved to death. That night, I fell in with Sandy Jenkins, a slave with whom I was somewhat acquainted. Sandy had a free wife who lived about four miles from Mr. Covey's; and it being Saturday, he was on his way to see her. I told him my circumstances, and he very kindly invited me to go home with him. I went home with him, and talked this whole matter over, and got his advice as to what course it was best for me to pursue. I found Sandy an old adviser. He told me, with great solemnity, I must go back to Covey; but that before I went, I must go with him into another part of the woods, where there was a certain *root*, which, if I would take some of it with me, carrying it *always on my right side*, would render it impossible for Mr. Covey, or any other white man, to whip me. He said he had carried it for years; and since he had done so, he had never received a blow, and never expected to while he carried it. I at first rejected the idea, that the simple carrying of a root in my pocket would have any such effect as he had said, and was not disposed to take it; but Sandy impressed the necessity with much earnestness, telling me it could do no harm, if it did no good. To please him, I at length took the root, and, according to his direction, carried it upon my right side. This was Sunday morning. I immediately started for home; and upon entering the yard gate, out came Mr. Covey on his way to meeting. He spoke, to me very kindly, bade me drive the pigs from a lot near by, and passed on towards the church. Now, this singular conduct of Mr. Covey really made me begin to think that there was something in the *root* which Sandy, had given me; and had it been on any other day than Sunday, I could have attributed the conduct to no other cause than the influence of that root, and as it was, I was half inclined to think the *root* to be something more than I at first had taken it to be. All went well till Monday morning. On this morning, the virtue of the *root* was fully tested. Long before daylight I was called to go and rub, curry, and feed, the horses. I obeyed, and was glad to obey. But whilst thus engaged, whilst in the act of throwing down some blades from the loft, Mr. Covey entered the stable with a long rope; and just as I was half out of the loft, he caught hold of my legs, and was about tying me. As soon as I found what he was up to, I gave a sudden spring, and as I did so, he holding to my legs, I was brought sprawling on the stable floor. Mr. Covey seemed now to think he had me, and could do what he pleased; but at this moment—from whence came the spirit I don't know—I resolved to fight; and, suiting my action to the resolution, I seized Covey hard by the throat; and, as I did so, I rose. He held onto me, and I to him. My resistance was so entirely unexpected, that Covey seemed taken all aback. He trembled like a leaf. This gave me assurance, and I held him uneasy, causing the blood to run where I touched him with the ends of my fingers. Mr. Covey soon called out to Hughes for help. Hughes came, and, while Covey held me, attempted to tie my right hand. While he was in the act of doing so, I watched my chance, and gave him a heavy kick close under the ribs. This kick fairly sickened Hughes, so that he left me in the hands of Mr. Covey. This kick had the effect of not only weakening Hughes, but Covey also. When he saw Hughes bending over with pain, his courage quailed.

He asked me if I meant to persist in my resistance. I told him I did, come what might; that he had used me like a brute for six months, and that I was determined to be used so no longer. With that, he strove to drag me to a stick that was lying just out of the stable door. He meant to knock me down. But just as he was leaning over to get the stick, I seized him with both hands by his collar, and brought him by a sudden snatch to the ground. By this time, Bill came. Covey called upon him for assistance. Bill wanted to know what he could do. Covey said, "Take hold of him, take hold of him!" Bill said his master hired him out to work, and not to help to whip me; so he left Covey and myself to fight our own battle out. We were at it for nearly two hours. Covey at length let me go, puffing and blowing at a great rate, saying that if I had not resisted, he would not have whipped me half so much. The truth was, that he had not whipped me at all. I considered him as getting entirely the worst end of the bargain; for he had drawn no blood from me, but I had from him. The whole six months afterwards, that I spent with Mr. Covey, he never laid the weight of his finger upon me in anger. He would occasionally say, he didn't want to get hold of me again. "No," thought I, "you need not; for you will come off worse than you did before."

This battle with Mr. Covey was the turning-point in my career as a slave. It rekindled the few expiring embers of freedom, and revived within me a sense of my own manhood. It recalled the departed self-confidence, and inspired me again with a determination to be free. The gratification afforded by the triumph was a full compensation for whatever else might follow, even death itself. He only can understand the deep satisfaction which I experienced, who has himself repelled by force the bloody arm of slavery. I felt as I never felt before. It was a glorious resurrection, from the tomb of slavery, to the heaven of freedom. My long-crushed spirit rose, cowardice departed, bold defiance took its place; and I now resolved that, however long I might remain a slave in form, the day had passed forever when I could be a slave in fact. I did not hesitate to let it be known of me, that the white man who expected to succeed in whipping, must also succeed in killing me.

From this time I was never again what might be called fairly whipped, though I remained a slave four years afterwards. I had several fights, but was never whipped.

It was for a long time a matter of surprise to me why Mr. Covey did not immediately have me taken by the constable to the whipping-post, and there regularly whipped for the crime of raising my hand against a white man in defence of myself. And the only explanation I can now think of does not entirely satisfy me; but such as it is, I will give it. Mr. Covey enjoyed the most unbounded reputation for being a first-rate overseer and negro-breaker. It was of considerable importance to him. That reputation was at stake; and had he sent me—a boy about sixteen years old—to the public whipping-post, his reputation would have been lost; so, to save his reputation, he suffered me to go unpunished.

My term of actual service to Mr. Edward Covey ended on Christmas day, 1833. The days between Christmas and New Year's day are allowed as holidays; and, accordingly, we were not required to perform any labor, more than to feed and take care of the stock. This time we regarded as our own, by the grace of our masters; and we therefore used or abused it nearly as we pleased. Those of us who had families at a distance, were generally allowed to spend the whole six days in their society. This time, however, was spent in various ways. The staid, sober, thinking and industrious ones of our number would employ themselves in making corn-brooms, mats, horse-collars, and baskets; and another class of us would spend the time in hunting opossums, hares, and coons. But by far the larger part engaged in such sports and merriments as playing ball, wrestling, running foot-races, fiddling, dancing, and drinking whisky; and this latter mode of spending the time was by far the most agreeable to the feelings of our masters. A slave who would work during the holidays was considered by our masters as scarcely deserving them. He was regarded as one who rejected the favor of his master. It was deemed a disgrace not to get drunk at Christmas; and he was regarded as lazy indeed, who had not provided himself with the necessary means, during the year, to get whisky enough to last him through Christmas.

From what I know of the effect of these holidays upon the slave, I believe them to be among the most effective means in the hands of the slaveholder in keeping down the spirit of insurrection. Were the slaveholders at once to abandon this practice, I have not the slightest doubt it would lead to an immediate insurrection among the slaves. These holidays serve as conductors, or safety-valves, to carry off the rebellious spirit of enslaved humanity. But for these, the slave would be forced up to the wildest desperation; and woe betide the slaveholder, the day he ventures to remove or hinder the operation of those conductors! I warn him that, in such an event, a spirit will go forth in their midst, more to be dreaded than the most appalling earthquake.

The holidays are part and parcel of the gross fraud, wrong, and inhumanity of slavery. They are professedly a custom established by the benevolence of the slaveholders; but I undertake to say, it is the result of selfishness, and one of the grossest frauds committed upon the down-trodden slave. They do not give the slaves this time because they would not like to have their work during its continuance, but because they know it would be unsafe to deprive them of it. This will be seen by the fact, that the slaveholders like to have their slaves spend those days just in such a manner as to make them as glad of their ending as of their beginning. Their object seems to be, to disgust their slaves with freedom, by plunging them into the lowest depths of dissipation. For instance, the slaveholders not only like to see the slave drink of his own accord, but will adopt various plans to make him drunk. One plan is, to make bets on their slaves, as to who can drink the most whisky without getting drunk; and in this way they succeed in getting whole multitudes to drink to excess. Thus, when the slave asks for virtuous freedom, the cunning slaveholder, knowing his ignorance, cheats him with a dose of vicious dissipation, artfully labelled with the name of liberty. The most of us used to drink it down, and the result was just what might be supposed: many of us were led to think that there was little to choose between liberty and slavery. We felt, and very properly too, that we had almost as well be slaves to man as to rum. So, when the holidays ended, we staggered up from the filth of our wallowing, took a long breath, and marched to the field,—feeling, upon the whole, rather glad to go, from what our master had deceived us into a belief was freedom, back to the arms of slavery.

I have said that this mode of treatment is a part of the whole system of fraud and inhumanity of slavery. It is so. The mode here adopted to disgust the slave with freedom, by allowing him to see only the abuse of it, is carried out in other things. For instance, a slave loves molasses; he steals some. His master, in many cases, goes off to town, and buys a large quantity; he returns, takes his whip, and commands the slave to eat the molasses, until the poor fellow is made sick at the very mention of it. The same mode is sometimes adopted to make the slaves refrain from asking for more food than their regular allowance. A slave runs through his allowance, and applies for more. His master is enraged at him; but, not willing to send him off without food, gives him more than is necessary, and compels him to eat it within a given time. Then, if he complains that he cannot eat it, he is said to be satisfied neither full nor fasting, and is whipped for being hard to please! I have an abundance of such illustrations of the same principle, drawn from my own observation, but think the cases I have cited sufficient. The practice is a very common one.

On the first of January, 1834, I left Mr. Covey, and went to live with Mr. William Freeland, who lived about three miles from St. Michael's. I soon found Mr. Freeland a very different man from Mr. Covey. Though not rich, he was what would be called an educated southern gentleman. Mr. Covey, as I have shown, was a well-trained negro-breaker and slave-driver. The former (slaveholder though he was) seemed to possess some regard for honor, some reverence for justice and some respect for humanity. The latter seemed totally insensible to all such sentiments. Mr. Freeland had many of the faults peculiar to slaveholders, such as being very passionate and fretful; but I must do him the justice to say, that he was exceedingly free from those degrading vices to which Mr. Covey was constantly addicted. The one was open and frank, and we always knew where to find him. The other was a most artful deceiver, and could be understood only by such as were skilful enough to detect his cunningly-devised frauds. Another advantage I gained in my new master was, he made no pretensions to, or profession of, religion; and this, in my opinion, was truly a great advantage. I assert most unhesitatingly, that the religion of the south is a mere covering for the most horrid crimes,—a justifier of the most appalling barbarity,—a sanctifier of the most hateful frauds,—and a dark shelter under, which the darkest, foulest, grossest, and most infernal deeds of slaveholders find the strongest protection. Were I to be again reduced to the chains of slavery, next to that enslavement, I should regard being the slave of a religious master the greatest calamity that could befall me. For of all slaveholders with whom I have ever met, religious slaveholders are the worst. I have ever found them the meanest and basest, the most cruel and cowardly, of all others. It was my unhappy lot not only to belong to a religious slaveholder, but to live in a community of such religionists. Very near Mr. Freeland lived the Rev. Daniel Weeden, and in the same neighborhood lived the Rev. Rigby Hopkins. These were members and ministers in the Reformed Methodist Church. Mr. Weeden owned, among others, a woman slave, whose name I have forgotten. This woman's back, for weeks, was kept literally raw, made so by the lash of this merciless, *religious* wretch. He used to hire hands. His maxim was, "Behave well or behave ill, it is the duty of a master occasionally to whip a slave, to remind him of his master's authority." Such was his theory, and such his practice.

Mr. Hopkins was even worse than Mr. Weeden. His chief boast was his ability to manage slaves. The peculiar, feature of his government was that of whipping slaves in advance of deserving it. He always managed to have one or more of his slaves to whip every Monday morning. He did this to alarm their fears, and strike terror into those who escaped. His plan was to whip for the smallest offences, to prevent the commission of large ones. Mr. Hopkins could always find some excuse for whipping a slave. It would astonish one, unaccustomed to a slaveholding life, to see with what wonderful ease a slaveholder can find things, of which to make occasion to whip a slave.

A mere look, word, or motion,—a mistake, accident, or want of power,—are all matters for which a slave may be whipped at any time. Does a slave look dissatisfied? It is said, he has the devil in him, and it must be whipped out. Does he speak loudly when spoken to by his master? Then he is getting high-minded, and should be taken down a button-hole lower. Does he forget to pull off his hat at the approach of a white person? Then he is wanting in reverence, and should be whipped for it. Does he ever venture to vindicate his conduct, when censured for it? Then he is guilty of impudence,—one of the greatest crimes of which a slave can be guilty. Does he ever venture to suggest a different mode of doing things from that pointed out by his master? He is indeed presumptuous, and getting above himself; and nothing less than a flogging will do for him. Does he, while ploughing, break a plough,—or, while hoeing, break a hoe? It is owing to his carelessness, and for it a slave must always be whipped. Mr. Hopkins could always find something of this sort to justify the use of the lash, and he seldom failed to embrace such opportunities. There was not a man in the whole county, with whom the slaves who had the getting their own home, would not prefer to live, rather than with this Rev. Mr. Hopkins. And yet there was not a man any where round, who, made higher professions of religion, or was more active in revivals,—more attentive to the class, love-feast, prayer and preaching meetings, or more devotional in his family,—that prayed earlier, later, louder, and longer,—than this same reverend slave-driver, Rigby Hopkins.

But to return to Mr. Freeland, and to my experience while in his employment. He, like Mr. Covey, gave us enough to eat; but, unlike Mr. Covey, he also gave us sufficient time to take our meals. He worked us hard, but always between sunrise and sunset. He required a good deal of work to be done, but gave us good tools with which to work. His farm was large, but he employed hands enough to work it, and with ease, compared with many of his neighbors. My treatment, while in his employment, was heavenly, compared with what I experienced at the hands of Mr. Edward Covey.

Mr. Freeland was himself the owner of but two slaves. Their names were Henry Harris and John Harris. The rest of his hands he hired. These consisted of myself, Sandy Jenkins* and Handy Caldwell. Henry and John were quite intelligent, and in a very little while after I went there, I succeeded in creating in them a strong desire to learn how to read. This desire soon sprang up in the others also. They very soon mustered up some old spelling-books, and nothing would do but that I must keep a Sabbath school. I agreed to do so, and accordingly devoted my Sundays to teaching these my loved fellow-slaves how to read. Neither of them knew his letters when I went there. Some of the slaves of the neighboring farms found what was going on, and also availed themselves of this little opportunity to learn to read. It was understood, among all who came, that there must be as little display about it as possible. It was necessary to keep our religious masters at St. Michael's unacquainted with the fact, that, instead of spending the Sabbath in wrestling, boxing, and drinking whisky, we were trying to learn how to read the will of God;

* This is the same man who gave me the roots to prevent my being whipped by Mr. Covey. He was "a clever soul." We used frequently to talk about the fight with Covey, and as often as we did so, he would claim my success as the result of the roots which he gave me. This superstition is very common among the more ignorant slaves. A slave seldom dies but that his death is attributed to trickery.

for they had much rather see us engaged in those degrading sports, than to see us behaving like intellectual, moral, and accountable beings. My blood boils as I think of the bloody manner in which Messrs. Wright Fairbanks and Garrison West, both class-leaders, in connection with many others, rushed in upon us with sticks and stones, and broke up our virtuous little Sabbath school, at St. Michael's—all calling themselves Christians! humble followers of the Lord Jesus Christ! But I am again digressing.

I held my Sabbath school at the house of a free colored man, whose name I deem it imprudent to mention; for should it be known, it might embarrass him greatly, though the crime of holding the school was committed ten years ago. I had at one time over forty scholars, and those of the right sort, ardently desiring to learn. They were of all ages, though mostly men and women. I look back to those Sundays with an amount of pleasure not to be expressed. They were great days to my soul. The work of instructing my dear fellow-slaves was the sweetest engagement with which I was ever blessed. We loved each other, and to leave them at the close of the Sabbath was a severe cross indeed. When I think that these precious souls are to-day shut up in the prison-house of slavery, my feelings overcome me, and I am almost ready to ask, "Does a righteous God govern the universe? and for what does he hold the thunders in his right hand, if not to smite the oppressor, and deliver the spoiled out of the hand of the spoiler?" These dear souls came not to Sabbath school because it was popular to do so, nor did I teach them because it was reputable to be thus engaged. Every moment they spent in that school, they were liable to be taken up, and given thirty-nine lashes. They came because they wished to learn. Their minds had been starved by their cruel masters. They had been shut up in mental darkness. I taught them, because it was the delight of my soul to be doing something that looked like bettering the condition of my race. I kept up my school nearly the whole year I lived with Mr. Freeland; and, beside my Sabbath school, I devoted three evenings in the week, during the winter, to teaching the slaves at home. And I have the happiness to know, that several of those who came to Sabbath school learned how to read; and that one, at least, is now free through my agency.

The year passed off smoothly. It seemed only about half as long as the year which preceded it. I went through it without receiving a single blow. I will give Mr. Freeland the credit of being the best master I ever had, *till I became my own master*. For the ease with which I passed the year, I was, however, somewhat indebted to the society of my fellow-slaves. They were noble souls; they not only possessed loving hearts, but brave ones. We were linked and inter-linked with each other. I loved them with a love stronger than any thing I have experienced since. It is sometimes said that we slaves do not love and confide in each other. In answer to this assertion,

I can say, I never loved any or confided in any people more than my fellow-slaves, and especially those with whom I lived at Mr. Freeland's. I believe we would have died for each other. We never undertook to do any thing, of any importance, without a mutual consultation. We never moved separately. We were one; and as much so by our tempers and dispositions, as by the mutual hardships to which we were necessarily subjected by our condition as slaves.

At the close of the year 1834, Mr. Freeland again hired me of my master, for the year 1835. But, by this time, I began to want to live *upon free land* as well as *with Freeland*; and I was no longer content, therefore, to live with him or any other slaveholder. I began, with the commencement of the year, to prepare myself for a final struggle, which should decide my fate one way or the other. My tendency was upward. I was fast approaching manhood, and year after year had passed, and I was still a slave. These thought roused me—I must do something. I therefore resolved that 1835 should not pass without witnessing an attempt, on my part, to secure my liberty. But I was not willing to cherish this determination alone. My fellow-slaves were dear to me. I was anxious to have them participate with me in this, my life-giving determination. I therefore, though with great prudence, commenced early to ascertain their views and feelings in regard to their condition, and to imbue their minds with thoughts of freedom. I bent myself to devising ways and means for our escape, and meanwhile strove, on all fitting occasions, to impress them with the gross fraud and inhumanity of slavery. I went first to Henry, next to John, then to the others. I found, in them all, warm hearts and noble spirits. They were ready to hear, and ready to act when a feasible plan should be proposed. This was what I wanted. I talked to them of our want of manhood, if we submitted to our enslavement without at least one noble effort to be free. We met often, and consulted frequently, and told our hopes and fears, recounted the difficulties, real and imagined, which we should be called on to meet. At times we were almost disposed to give up, and try to content ourselves with our wretched lot; at others, we were firm and unbending in our determination to go. Whenever we suggested any plan, there was shrinking—the odds were fearful. Our path was beset with the greatest obstacles; and if we succeeded in gaining the end of it, our right to be free was yet questionable—we were yet liable to be returned to bondage. We could see no spot, this side of the ocean, where we could be free. We knew nothing about Canada. Our knowledge of the north did not extend farther than New York; and to go there, and be forever harassed with the frightful liability of being returned to slavery—with the certainty of being treated tenfold worse than before—the thought was truly a horrible one, and one which it was not easy to overcome. The case sometimes stood thus: At every gate through which we were to pass, we saw a watchman—at every ferry a guard—on every bridge a sentinel—and in every wood a patrol. We were hemmed in upon every side. Here were the difficulties, real or imagined—the good to be sought, and the evil to be shunned. On the one hand, there stood slavery, a stern reality, glaring frightfully upon us,—its robes already crimsoned with the blood of millions, and even now feasting itself greedily upon our own flesh. On the other hand, away back in the dim distance, under the flickering light of the north star, behind some craggy hill or snow-covered mountain, stood a doubtful freedom—half frozen—beckoning us to come and share its hospitality. This in itself was sometimes enough to stagger us; but when we permitted ourselves to survey the road, we were frequently appalled. Upon either side we saw grim death, assuming the most horrid shapes. Now it was starvation, causing us to eat our own flesh;—now we were contending with the waves, and were drowned;—now we were overtaken, and torn to pieces by the fangs of the terrible bloodhound. We were stung by scorpions, chased by wild beasts, bitten by snakes, and finally, after having nearly reached the desired spot,—after swimming rivers, encountering wild beasts, sleeping in the woods, suffering hunger and nakedness,—we were overtaken by our pursuers, and, in our resistance, we were shot dead upon the spot! I say, this picture sometimes appalled us, and made us

> "rather bear those ills we had,
> Than fly to others, that we knew not of."

In coming to a fixed determination to run away, we did more than Patrick Henry, when he resolved upon liberty or death. With us it was a doubtful liberty at most, and almost certain death if we failed. For my part, I should prefer death to hopeless bondage.

Sandy, one of our number, gave up the notion, but still encouraged us. Our company then consisted of Henry Harris, John Harris, Henry Bailey, Charles Roberts, and myself. Henry Bailey was my uncle, and belonged to my master. Charles married my aunt: he belonged to my master's father-in-law, Mr. William Hamilton.

The plan we finally concluded upon was, to get a large canoe belonging to Mr. Hamilton, and upon the Saturday night previous to Easter holidays, paddle directly up the Chesapeake Bay. On our arrival at the head of the bay, a distance of seventy or eighty miles from where we lived, it was our purpose to turn our canoe adrift, and follow the guidance of the north star till we got beyond the limits of Maryland. Our reason for taking the water route was, that we were less liable to be suspected as runaways; we hoped to be regarded as fishermen; whereas, if we should take the land route, we should be subjected to interruptions of almost every kind. Any one having a white face, and being so disposed, could stop us, and subject us to examination.

The week before our intended start, I wrote several protections, one for each of us. As well as I can remember, they were in the following words, to wit:—

"THIS is to certify that I, the undersigned, have given the bearer, my servant, full liberty to go to Baltimore, and spend the Easter holidays. Written with mine own hand, &c., 1835.

"WILLIAM HAMILTON,
"Near St. Michael's, in Talbot county, Maryland."

We were not going to Baltimore; but, in going up the bay, we went toward Baltimore, and these protections were only intended to protect us while on the bay.

As the time drew near for our departure, our anxiety became more and more intense. It was truly a matter of life and death with us. The strength of our determination was about to be fully tested. At this time, I was very active in explaining every difficulty, removing every doubt, dispelling every fear, and inspiring all with the firmness indispensable to success in our undertaking; assuring them that half was gained the instant we made the move; we had talked long enough; we were now ready to move; if not now, we never should be; and if we did not intend to move now, we had as well fold our arms, sit down, and acknowledge ourselves fit only to be slaves. This, none of us were prepared to acknowledge. Every man stood firm; and at our last meeting we pledged ourselves afresh, in the most solemn manner, that, at the time appointed, we would certainly start in pursuit of freedom. This was in the middle of the week, at the end of which we were to be off. We went, as usual, to our several fields of labor, but with bosoms highly agitated with thoughts of our truly hazardous undertaking. We tried to conceal our feelings as much as possible; and I think we succeeded very well.

After a painful waiting, the Saturday morning, whose night was to witness our departure, came. I hailed it with joy, bring what of sadness it might. Friday night was a sleepless one for me. I probably felt more anxious than the rest, because I was, by common consent, at the head of the whole affair. The responsibility of success or failure lay heavily upon me. The glory of the one, and the confusion of the other, were alike mine. The first two hours of that morning were such as I never experienced before, and hope never to again. Early in the morning, we went, as usual, to the field. We were spreading manure; and all at once, while thus engaged, I was overwhelmed with an indescribable feeling, in the fulness of which I turned to Sandy, who was near by, and said, "We are betrayed!" "Well," said he, "that thought has this moment struck me." We said no more. I was never more certain of any thing.

The horn was blown as usual, and we went up from the field to the house for breakfast. I went for the form, more than for want of any thing to eat that morning. Just as I got to the house, in looking, out at the lane gate, I saw four white men, with two colored men. The white men were on horseback, and the colored ones were walking behind, as if tied. I watched them a few moments till they got up to our lane gate. Here they halted, and tied the colored men to the gate-post. I was not yet certain as to what the matter was. In a few moments, in rode Mr. Hamilton, with a speed betokening great excitement. He came to the door, and inquired if Master William was in. He was told he was at the barn. Mr. Hamilton, without dismounting, rode up to the barn with extraordinary speed. In a few moments, he and Mr. Freeland returned to the house. By this time, the three constables rode up, and in great haste dismounted, tied their horses, and met Master William and Mr. Hamilton returning from the barn; and after talking awhile, they all walked up to the kitchen door. There was no one in the kitchen but myself and John. Henry and Sandy were up at the barn. Mr. Freeland put his head in at the door, and called me by name, saying, there were some gentlemen at the door who wished to see me. I stepped to the door, and inquired what they wanted. They at once seized me, and, without giving me any satisfaction, tied me—lashing my hands closely together. I insisted upon knowing what the matter was. They at length said, that they had learned I had been in a "scrape," and that I was to be examined before my master; and if their information proved false, I should not be hurt.

In a few moments, they succeeded in tying John. They then turned to Henry, who had by this time returned, and commanded him to cross his hands. "I won't!" said Henry, in a firm tone, indicating his readiness to meet the consequences of his refusal. "Won't you?" said Tom Graham, the constable. "No, I won't!" said Henry, in a still stronger tone. With this, two of the constables pulled out their shining pistols, and swore, by their Creator, that they would make him cross his hands or kill him. Each cocked his pistol, and, with fingers on the trigger, walked up to Henry, saying, at the same time, if he did not cross his hands, they would blow his damned heart out. "Shoot me, shoot me!" said Henry; "you can't kill me but once. Shoot, shoot,—and be damned! *I won't be tied!*" This he said in a tone of loud defiance; and at the same time, with a motion as quick as lightning, he with one single stroke dashed the pistols from the hand of each constable. As he did this, all hands fell upon him, and, after beating him some time, they finally overpowered him, and got him tied.

During the scuffle, I managed, I know not how, to get my pass out, and, without being discovered, put it into the fire. We were all now tied; and just as we were to leave for Easton jail, Betsy Freeland, mother of William Freeland, came to the door with her hands full of biscuits, and divided them between Henry and John. She then delivered herself of a speech, to the following effect:—addressing herself to me, she. said, "*You devil! You yellow devil!* it was you that put it into the heads of Henry and John to run away. But for you, you long-legged mulatto devil! Henry nor John would never have thought of such a thing." I made no reply, and was immediately hurried off towards St. Michael's. Just a moment previous to the scuffle with Henry, Mr. Hamilton suggested the propriety of making a search for the protections which he had understood Frederick had written for himself and the rest. But, just at the moment he was about carrying his proposal into effect, his aid was needed in helping to tie Henry; and the excitement attending the scuffle caused them either to forget, or to deem it unsafe, under the circumstances, to search. So we were not yet convicted of the intention to run away.

When we got about half way to St. Michael's, while the constables having us in charge were looking ahead, Henry inquired of me what he should do with his pass. I told him to eat it with his biscuit, and own nothing; and we passed the word around, "*Own nothing;*" and "*Own nothing!*" said we all. Our confidence in each other was unshaken. We were resolved to succeed or fail together, after the calamity had befallen us as much as before. We were now prepared for any thing. We were to be dragged that morning fifteen miles behind horses, and then to be placed in the Easton jail. When we reached St. Michael's, we underwent a sort of examination. We all denied that we ever intended to run away. We did this more to bring out the evidence against us, than from any hope of getting clear of being sold; for, as I have said, we were ready for that. The fact was, we cared but little where we went, so we went together. Our greatest concern was about separation. We dreaded that more than any thing this side of death. We found the evidence against us to be the testimony of one person; our master would not tell who it was; but we came to a unanimous decision among ourselves as to who their informant was. We were sent off to the jail at Easton. When we got there, we were delivered up to the sheriff, Mr. Joseph Graham, and by him placed in jail. Henry, John, and myself, were placed in one room together—Charles, and Henry Bailey, in another. Their object in separating us was to hinder concert.

We had been in jail scarcely twenty minutes, when a swarm of slave traders, and agents for slave traders, flocked into jail to look at us, and to ascertain if we were for sale. Such a set of beings I never saw before! I felt myself surrounded by so many fiends from perdition. A band of pirates never looked more like their father, the devil. They laughed and grinned over us, saying, "Ah, my boys! we have got you, haven't we?" And after taunting us in various ways, they one by one went into an examination of us, with intent to ascertain our value. They would impudently ask us if we would not like to have them for our masters. We would make them no answer, and leave them to find out as best they could. Then they would curse and swear at us, telling us that they could take the devil out of us in a very little while, if we were only in their hands.

While in jail, we found ourselves in much more comfortable quarters, than we expected when we went there. We did not get much to eat, nor that which was very good; but we had a good clean room, from the windows of which we could see what was going on in the street, which was very much better than though we had been placed in one of the dark, damp cells. Upon the whole, we got along very well, so far as the jail and its keeper were concerned. Immediately after the holidays were over, contrary to all our expectations, Mr. Hamilton and Mr. Freeland came up to Easton, and took Charles, the two Henrys, and John, out of jail, and carried them home, leaving me alone. I regarded this separation as a final one. It caused me more pain than any thing else in the whole transaction. I was ready for any thing rather than separation. I supposed that they had consulted together, and had decided that, as I was the whole cause of the intention of the others to run away, it was hard to make the innocent suffer with the guilty; and that they had, therefore, concluded to take the others home, and sell me, as a warning to the others that remained. It is due to the noble Henry to say, he seemed almost as reluctant at leaving the prison as at leaving home to come to the prison. But we knew we should, in all probability, be separated, if we were sold; and since he was in their hands, he concluded to go peaceably home.

I was now left to my fate. I was all alone, and within the walls of a stone prison. But a few days before, and I was full of hope. I expected to have been safe in a land of freedom; but now I was covered with gloom, sunk down to the utmost despair. I thought the possibility of freedom was gone. I was kept in this way about one week, at the end of which, Captain Auld, my master, to my surprise and utter astonishment, came up, and took me out, with the intention of sending me, with a gentleman of his acquaintance, into Alabama. But, from some cause or other, he did not send me to Alabama, but concluded to send me back to Baltimore, to live again with his brother Hugh, and to learn a trade.

Thus, after an absence of three years and one month, I was once more permitted to return to my old home at Baltimore. My master sent me away, because there existed against me a very great prejudice in the community, and he feared I might be killed.

In a few weeks after I went to Baltimore, Master Hugh hired me to Mr. William Gardner, an extensive ship-builder, on Fell's Point. I was put there to learn how to calk. It, however, proved a very unfavorable place for the accomplishment of this object. Mr. Gardner was engaged that spring in building two large man-of-war brigs, professedly for the Mexican government. The vessels were to be launched in the July of that year, and in failure thereof, Mr. Gardner was to lose a considerable sum; so that when I entered, all was hurry. There was no time to learn any thing. Every man had to do that which he knew how to do. In entering the ship-yard, my orders from Mr. Gardner were, to do whatever the carpenters commanded me to do. This was placing me at the beck and call of about seventy-five men. I was to regard all these as masters. Their word was to be my law. My situation was a most trying one. At times I needed a dozen pair of hands. I was called a dozen ways in the space of a single minute. Three or four voices would strike my ear at the same moment. It was—"Fred., come help me to cant this timber here."—"Fred., come carry this timber yonder."—"Fred., bring that roller here."—"Fred., go get a fresh can of water."—"Fred., come help saw off the end of this timber."—"Fred., go quick, and get the crowbar."—"Fred., hold on the end of this fall."—"Fred., go to the blacksmith's shop, and get a new punch."—"Hurra, Fred.! run and bring me a cold chisel."—"I say, Fred., bear a hand, and get up a fire as quick as lightning under that steam-box."—"Halloo, nigger! come, turn this grindstone."—"Come, come! move, move! and *bowse* this timber forward."—"I say, darky, blast your eyes, why don't you heat up some pitch?"—"Halloo! halloo! halloo!" (Three voices at the same time.) "Come here!—Go there!—Hold on where you are! Damn you, if you move, I'll knock your brains out!"

This was my school for eight months; and I might have remained there longer, but for a most horrid fight I had with four of the white apprentices, in which my left eye was nearly knocked out, and I was horribly mangled in other respects. The facts in the case were these: Until a very little while after I went there, white and black ship-carpenters worked side by side, and no one seemed to see any impropriety in it. All hands seemed to be very well satisfied. Many of the black carpenters were freemen. Things seemed to be going on very well. All at once, the white carpenters knocked off, and said they would not work with free colored workmen. Their reason for this, as alleged, was, that if free colored carpenters were encouraged, they would soon take the trade into their own hands, and poor white men would be thrown out of employment. They therefore felt called upon at once to put a stop to it. And, taking advantage of Mr. Gardner's necessities, they broke off, swearing they would work no longer, unless he would discharge his black carpenters. Now, though this did not extend to me in form, it did reach me in fact. My fellow-apprentices very soon began to feel it degrading to them to work with me. They began to put on airs, and talk about the "niggers" taking the country, saying we all ought to be killed; and, being encouraged by the journeymen, they commenced making my condition as hard as they could, by hectoring me around, and sometimes striking me. I, of course, kept the vow I made after the fight with Mr. Covey, and struck back again, regardless of consequences; and while I kept them from combining, I succeeded very well; for I could whip the whole of them, taking them separately. They, however, at length combined, and came upon me, armed with sticks, stones, and heavy handspikes. One came in front with a half brick. There was one at each side of me, and one behind me. While I was attending to those in front, and on either side, the one behind ran up with the handspike, and struck me a heavy blow upon the head. It stunned me. I fell, and with this they all ran upon me, and fell to beating me with their fists. I let them lay on for a while, gathering strength. In an instant, I gave a sudden surge, and rose to my hands and knees. Just as I did that, one of their number gave me, with his heavy boot, a powerful kick in the left eye. My eyeball seemed to have burst. When they saw my eye closed, and badly swollen, they left me. With this I seized the handspike, and for a time pursued them. But here the carpenters interfered, and I thought I might as well give it up. It was impossible to stand my hand against so many. All this took place in sight of not less than fifty white ship-carpenters, and not one interposed a friendly word; but some cried, "Kill the damned nigger! Kill him! kill him! He struck a white person." I found my only chance for life was in flight. I succeeded in getting away without an additional blow, and barely so; for to strike a white man is death by Lynch law,—and that was the law in Mr. Gardner's ship-yard; nor is there much of any other out of Mr. Gardner's ship-yard.

I went directly home, and told the story of my wrongs to Master Hugh; and I am happy to say of him, irreligious as he was, his conduct was heavenly, compared with that of his brother Thomas under similar circumstances. He listened attentively to my narration of the circumstances leading to the savage outrage, and gave many proofs of his strong indignation at it. The heart of my once overkind mistress was again melted into pity. My puffed-out eye and blood-covered face moved her to tears. She took a chair by me, washed the blood from my face, and, with a mother's tenderness, bound up my head, covering the wounded eye with a lean piece of fresh beef. It was almost compensation for my suffering to witness, once more, a manifestation of kindness from this, my once affectionate old mistress. Master Hugh was very much enraged. He gave expression to his feelings by pouring out curses upon the heads of those who did the deed. As soon as I got a little the better of my bruises, he took me with him to Esquire Watson's, on Bond Street, to see what could be done about the matter. Mr. Watson inquired who saw the assault committed. Master Hugh told him it was done in Mr. Gardner's ship-yard, at midday, where there were a large company of men at work. "As to that," he said, "the deed was done, and there was no question as to who did it." His answer was, he could do nothing in the case, unless some white man would come forward and testify. He could issue no warrant on my word. If I had been killed in the presence of a thousand colored people, their testimony combined would have been insufficient to have arrested one of the murderers. Master Hugh, for once, was compelled to say this state of things was too bad. Of course, it was impossible to get any white man to volunteer his testimony in my behalf, and against the white young men. Even those who may have sympathized with me were not prepared to do this. It required a degree of courage unknown to them to do so; for just at that time, the slightest manifestation of humanity toward a colored person was denounced as abolitionism, and that name subjected its bearer to frightful liabilities. The watchwords of the bloody-minded in that region, and in those days, were, "Damn the abolitionists!" and "Damn the niggers!" There was nothing done, and probably nothing would have been done if I had been killed. Such was, and such remains, the state of things in the Christian city of Baltimore.

Master Hugh, finding he could get no redress, refused to let me go back again to Mr. Gardner. He kept me himself, and his wife dressed my wound till I was again restored to health. He then took me into the ship-yard of which he was foreman, in the employment of Mr. Walter Price. There I was immediately set to calking, and very soon learned the art of using my mallet and irons. In the course of one year from the time I left Mr. Gardner's, I was able to command the highest wages given to the most experienced calkers. I was now of some importance to my master. I was bringing him from six to seven dollars per week. I sometimes brought him nine dollars per week: my wages were a dollar and a half a day. After learning how to calk, I sought my own employment, made my own contracts, and collected the money which I earned. My pathway became much more smooth than before; my condition was now much more comfortable. When I could get no calking to do, I did nothing. During these leisure times, those old notions about freedom would steal over me again. When in Mr. Gardner's employment, I was kept in such a perpetual whirl of excitement, I could think of nothing, scarcely, but my life; and in thinking of my life, I almost forgot my liberty. I have observed this in my experience of slavery, —that whenever my condition was improved, instead of its increasing my contentment, it only increased my desire to be free, and set me to thinking of plans to gain my freedom. I have found that, to make a contented slave, it is necessary to make a thoughtless one. It is necessary to darken his moral and mental vision, and, as far as possible, to annihilate the power of reason. He must be able to detect no inconsistencies in slavery; he must be made to feel that slavery is right; and he can be brought to that only when he ceases to be a man.

I was now getting, as I have said, one dollar and fifty cents per day. I contracted for it; I earned it; it was paid to me; it was rightfully my own; yet, upon each returning Saturday night, I was compelled to deliver every cent of that money to Master Hugh. And why? Not because he earned it,—not because he had any hand in earning it,—not because I owed it to him,—nor because he possessed the slightest shadow of a right to it; but solely because he had the power to compel me to give it up. The right of the grim-visaged pirate upon the high seas is exactly the same.

# Chapter XI

I now come to that part of my life during which I planned, and finally succeeded in making, my escape from slavery. But before narrating any of the peculiar circumstances, I deem it proper to make known my intention not to state all the facts connected with the transaction. My reasons for pursuing this course may be understood from the following: First, were I to give a minute statement of all the facts, it is not only possible, but quite probable, that others would thereby be involved in the most embarrassing difficulties. Secondly, such a statement would most undoubtedly induce greater vigilance on the part of slaveholders than has existed heretofore among them; which would, of course, be the means of guarding a door whereby some dear brother bondman might escape his galling chains. I deeply regret the necessity that impels me to suppress any thing of importance connected with my experience in slavery. It would afford me great pleasure indeed, as well as materially add to the interest of my narrative, were I at liberty to gratify a curiosity, which I know exists in the minds of many, by an accurate statement of all the facts pertaining to my most fortunate escape. But I must deprive myself of this pleasure, and the curious of the gratification which such a statement would afford. I would allow myself to suffer under the greatest imputations which evil-minded men might suggest, rather than exculpate myself, and thereby run the hazard of closing the slightest avenue by which a brother slave might clear himself of the chains and fetters of slavery.

I have never approved of the very public manner in which some of our western friends have conducted what they call the *underground railroad*, but which, I think, by their open declarations, has been made most emphatically the *upperground railroad*. I honor those good men and women for their noble daring, and applaud them for willingly subjecting themselves to bloody persecution, by openly avowing their participation in the escape of slaves. I, however, can see very little good resulting from such a course, either to themselves or the slaves escaping; while, upon the other hand, I see and feel assured that those open declarations are a positive evil to the slaves remaining, who are seeking to escape. They do nothing towards enlightening the slave, whilst they do much towards enlightening the master. They stimulate him to greater watchfulness, and enhance his power to capture his slave. We owe something to the slaves south of the line as well as to those north of it; and in aiding the latter on their way to freedom, we should be careful to do nothing which would be likely to hinder the former from escaping from slavery. I would keep the merciless slaveholder profoundly ignorant of the means of flight adopted by the slave. I would leave him to imagine himself surrounded by myriads of invisible tormentors, ever ready to snatch from his infernal grasp his trembling prey. Let him be left to feel his way in the dark; let darkness commensurate with his crime hover over him; and let him feel that at every step he takes, in pursuit of the flying bondman, he is running the frightful risk of having his hot brains dashed out by an invisible agency. Let us render the tyrant no aid; let us not hold the light by which he can trace the footprints of our flying brother. But enough of this, I will now proceed to the statement of those facts, connected with my escape, for which I am alone responsible, and for which no one can be made to suffer but myself.

In the early part of the year 1838, I became quite restless. I could see no reason why I should, at the end of each week, pour the reward of my toil into the purse of my master. When I carried to him my weekly wages, he would, after counting the money, look me in the face with a robber-like fierceness, and ask, "Is this all?" He was satisfied with nothing less than the last cent. He would, however, when I made him six dollars, sometimes give me six cents, to encourage me. It had the opposite effect. I regarded it as a sort of admission of my right to the whole. The fact that he gave me any part of my wages was proof, to my mind, that he believed me entitled to the whole of them. I always felt worse for having received any thing; for I feared that the giving me a few cents would ease his conscience, and make him feel himself to be a pretty honorable sort of robber. My discontent grew upon me. I was ever on the look-out for means of escape; and, finding no direct means, I determined to try to hire my time, with a view of getting money with which to make my escape. In the spring of 1838, when Master Thomas came to Baltimore to purchase his spring goods, I got an opportunity, and applied to him to allow me to hire my time. He unhesitatingly refused my request, and told me this was another stratagem by which to escape. He told me I could go nowhere but that he could get me; and that, in the event of my running away, he should spare no pains in his efforts to catch me. He exhorted me to content myself, and be obedient. He told me, if I would be happy, I must lay out no plans for the future. He said, if I behaved myself properly, he would take care of me. Indeed, he advised me to complete thoughtlessness of the future, and taught me to depend solely upon him for happiness. He seemed to see fully the pressing necessity of setting aside my intellectual nature, in order to contentment in slavery. But in spite of him, and even in spite of myself, I continued to think, and to think about the injustice of my enslavement, and the means of escape.

About two months after this, I applied to Master Hugh for the privilege of hiring my time. He was not acquainted with the fact that I had applied to Master Thomas, and had been refused. He too, at first, seemed disposed to refuse; but, after some reflection, he granted me the privilege, and proposed the following terms: I was to be allowed all my time, make all contracts with those for whom I worked, and find my own employment; and, in return for this liberty, I was to pay him three dollars at the end of each week; find myself in calking tools, and in board and clothing. My board was two dollars and a half per week. This, with the wear and tear of clothing and calking tools, made my regular expenses about six dollars per week. This amount I was compelled to make up, or relinquish the privilege of hiring my time. Rain or shine, work or no work, at the end of each week the, money must be forthcoming, or I must give up my privilege. This arrangement, it will be perceived, was decidedly in my master's favor. It relieved him of all need of looking after me. His money was sure. He received all the benefits of slaveholding without its evils; while I endured all the evils of a slave, and suffered all the care and anxiety of a freeman. I found it a hard bargain. But, hard as it was, I thought it better than the old mode of getting along. It was a step towards freedom to be allowed to bear the responsibilities of a freeman, and I was determined to hold on upon it. I bent myself to the work of making money. I was ready to work at night as well as day, and by the most untiring perseverance and industry, I made enough to meet my expenses, and lay up a little money every week. I went on thus from May till August. Master Hugh then refused to allow me to hire my time longer. The ground for his refusal was a failure on my part, one Saturday night, to pay him for my week's time. This failure was occasioned by my attending a camp meeting about ten miles from Baltimore. During the week, I had entered into an engagement with a number of young friends to start from Baltimore to the camp ground early Saturday evening; and being detained by my employer, I was unable to get down to Master Hugh's without disappointing the company. I knew that Master Hugh was in no special need of the money that night. I therefore decided to go to camp meeting, and upon my return pay him the three dollars. I staid at the camp meeting one day longer than I intended when I left. But as soon as I returned, I called upon him to pay him what he considered his due. I found him very angry; he could scarce restrain his wrath. He said he had a great mind to give me a severe whipping. He wished to know how I dared go out of the city without asking his permission. I told him I hired my time, and while I paid him the price which he asked for it, I did not know that I was bound to ask him when and where I should go. This reply troubled him; and, after reflecting a few moments, he turned to me, and said I should hire my time no longer; that the next thing he should know of, I would be running away. Upon the same plea, he told me to bring my tools and clothing home forthwith. I did so; but instead of seeking work, as I had been accustomed to do previously to hiring my time, I spent the whole week without the performance of a single stroke of work. I did this in retaliation. Saturday night, he called upon me as usual for my week's wages. I told him I had no wages; I had done no work that week. Here we were upon the point of coming to blows. He raved, and swore his determination to get hold of me. I did not allow myself a single word; but was resolved, if he laid the weight of his hand upon me, it should be blow for blow. He did not strike me, but told me that he would find me in constant employment in future. I thought the matter over during the next day, Sunday, and finally resolved upon the third day of September, as the day upon which I would make a second attempt to secure my freedom. I now had three weeks during which to prepare for my journey. Early on Monday morning, before Master Hugh had time to make any engagement for me, I went out and got employment of Mr. Butler, at his ship-yard near the drawbridge, upon what is called the City Block, thus making it unnecessary for him to seek employment for me. At the end of the week, I brought him between eight and nine dollars. He seemed very well pleased, and asked me why I did not do the same the week before. He little knew what my plans were. My object in working steadily was to remove any suspicion he might entertain of my intent to run away; and in this I succeeded admirably. I suppose he thought I was never better satisfied with my condition than at the very time during which I was planning my escape.

The second week passed, and again I carried him my full wages; and so well pleased was he, that he gave me twenty-five cents, (quite a large sum for a slaveholder to give a slave,) and bade me to make a good use of it. I told him I would.

Things went on without very smoothly indeed, but within there was trouble. It is impossible for me to describe my feelings as the time of my contemplated start drew near. I had a number of warm-hearted friends in Baltimore,—friends that I loved almost as I did my life,—and the thought of being separated from them forever was painful beyond expression. It is my opinion that thousands would escape from slavery, who now remain, but for the strong cords of affection that bind them to their friends. The thought of leaving my friends was decidedly the most painful thought with which I had to contend. The love of them was my tender point, and shook my decision more than all things else. Besides the pain of separation, the dread and apprehension of a failure exceeded what I had experienced at my first attempt. The appalling defeat I then sustained returned to torment me. I felt assured that, if I failed in this attempt, my case would be a hopeless one—it would seal my fate as a slave forever. I could not hope to get off with any thing less than the severest punishment, and being placed beyond the means of escape. It required no very vivid imagination to depict the most frightful scenes through which I should have to pass, in case I failed. The wretchedness of slavery, and the blessedness of freedom, were perpetually before me. It was life and death with me. But I remained firm, and, according to my resolution, on the third day of September, 1838, I left my chains, and succeeded in reaching New York without the slightest interruption of any kind. How I did so,—what means I adopted,—what direction I travelled, and by what mode of conveyance,—I must leave unexplained, for the reasons before mentioned.

I have been frequently asked how I felt when I found myself in a free State. I have never been able to answer the question with any satisfaction to myself. It was a moment of the highest excitement I ever experienced. I suppose I felt as one may imagine the unarmed mariner to feel when he is rescued by a friendly man-of-war from the pursuit of a pirate. In writing to a dear friend, immediately after my arrival at New York, I said I felt like one who had escaped a den of hungry lions. This state of mind, however, very soon subsided; and I was again seized with a feeling of great insecurity and loneliness. I was yet liable to be taken back, and subjected to all the tortures of slavery. This in itself was enough to damp the ardor of my enthusiasm. But the loneliness overcame me. There I was in the midst of thousands, and yet a perfect stranger; without home and without friends, in the midst of thousands of my own brethren—children of a common Father, and yet I dared not to unfold to any one of them my sad condition. I was afraid to speak to any one for fear of speaking to the wrong one, and thereby falling into the hands of money-loving kidnappers, whose business it was to lie in wait for the panting fugitive, as the ferocious beasts of the forest lie in wait for their prey. The motto which I adopted when I started from slavery was this—"Trust no man!" I saw in every white man an enemy, and in almost every colored man cause for distrust. It was a most painful situation; and, to understand it, one must needs experience it, or imagine himself in similar circumstances. Let him be a fugitive slave in a strange land—a land given up to be the hunting-ground for slaveholders—whose inhabitants are legalized kidnappers—where he is every moment subjected to the terrible liability of being seized upon by his fellowmen, as the hideous crocodile seizes upon his prey!—say, let him place himself in my situation—without home or friends—without money or credit—wanting shelter, and no one to give it—wanting bread, and no money to buy it,—and at the same time let him feel that he is pursued by merciless men-hunters, and in total darkness as to what to do, where to go, or where to stay,—perfectly helpless both as to the means of defence and means of escape,—in the midst of plenty, yet suffering the terrible gnawings of hunger,— in the midst of houses, yet having no home,—among fellow-men, yet feeling as if in the midst of wild beasts, whose greediness to swallow up the trembling and half-famished fugitive is only equalled by that with which the monsters of the deep swallow up the helpless fish upon which they subsist,—I say, let him be placed in this most trying situation,—the situation in which I was placed,—then, and not till then, will he fully appreciate the hardships of, and know how to sympathize with, the toil-worn and whip-scarred fugitive slave.

Thank Heaven, I remained but a short time in this distressed situation. I was relieved from it by the humane hand of Mr. DAVID RUGGLES, whose vigilance, kindness, and perseverance, I shall never forget. I am glad of an opportunity to express, as far as words can, the love and gratitude I bear him. Mr. Ruggles is now afflicted with blindness, and is himself in need of the same kind offices which he was once so forward in the performance of toward others. I had been in New York but a few days, when Mr. Ruggles sought me out, and very kindly took me to his boarding-house at the corner of Church and Lespenard Streets. Mr. Ruggles was then very deeply engaged in the memorable *Darg* case, as well as attending to a number of other fugitive slaves, devising ways and means for their successful escape; and, though watched and hemmed in on almost every side, he seemed to be more than a match for his enemies.

Very soon after I went to Mr. Ruggles, he wished to know of me where I wanted to go; as he deemed it unsafe for me to remain in New York. I told him I was a calker, and should like to go where I could get work. I thought of going to Canada; but he decided against it, and in favor of my going to New Bedford, thinking I should be able to get work there at my trade. At this time, Anna*, my intended wife, came on; for I wrote to her immediately after my arrival at New York, (notwithstanding my homeless, houseless, and helpless condition,) informing her of my successful flight, and wishing her to come on forthwith. In a few days after her arrival, Mr. Ruggles called in the Rev. J. W. C. Pennington, who, in the presence of Mr. Ruggles, Mrs. Michaels, and two or three others, performed the marriage ceremony, and gave us a certificate, of which the following is an exact copy:—

"THIS may certify, that I joined together in holy matrimony Frederick Johnson** and Anna Murray, as man and wife, in the presence of Mr. David Ruggles and Mrs. Michaels.

"JAMES W. C. PENNINGTON.

"*New York, Sept.* 15, 1838."

Upon receiving this certificate, and a five-dollar bill from Mr. Ruggles, I shouldered one part of our baggage, and Anna took up the other, and we set out forthwith to take passage on board of the steamboat John W. Richmond for Newport, on our way to New Bedford. Mr. Ruggles gave me a letter to a Mr. Shaw in Newport, and told me, in case my money did not serve me to

* She was free.

** I had changed my name from Frederick *Bailey* to that of *Johnson*.

New Bedford, to stop in Newport and obtain further assistance; but upon our arrival at Newport, we were so anxious to get to a place of safety, that, notwithstanding we lacked the necessary money to pay our fare, we decided to take seats in the stage, and promise to pay when we got to New Bedford. We were encouraged to do this by two excellent gentlemen, residents of New Bedford, whose names I afterward ascertained to be Joseph Ricketson and William C. Taber. They seemed at once to understand our circumstances, and gave us such assurance of their friendliness as put us fully at ease in their presence. It was good indeed to meet with such friends, at such a time. Upon reaching New Bedford, we were directed to the house of Mr. Nathan Johnson, by whom we were kindly received, and hospitably provided for. Both Mr. and Mrs. Johnson took a deep and lively interest in our welfare. They proved themselves quite worthy of the name of abolitionists. When the stage-driver found us unable to pay our fare, he held on upon our baggage as security for the debt. I had but to mention the fact to Mr. Johnson, and he forthwith advanced the money.

We now began to feel a degree of safety, and to prepare ourselves for the duties and responsibilities of a life of freedom. On the morning after our arrival at New Bedford, while at the breakfast-table, the question arose as to what name I should be called by. The name given me by my mother was, "Frederick Augustus Washington Bailey." I, however, had dispensed with the two middle names long before I left Maryland, so that I was generally known by the name of "Frederick Bailey." I started from Baltimore bearing the name of "Stanley." When I got to New York, I again changed my name to "Frederick Johnson," and thought that would be the last change. But when I got to New Bedford, I found it necessary again to change my name. The reason of this necessity was, that there were so many Johnsons in New Bedford, it was already quite difficult to distinguish between them. I gave Mr. Johnson the privilege of choosing me a name, but told him be must not take from me the name of "Frederick." I must hold on to that, to preserve a sense of my identity. Mr. Johnson had just been reading the "Lady of the Lake," and at once suggested that my name be "Douglass." From that time until now I have been called "Frederick Douglass;" and as I am more widely known by that name than by either of the others, I shall continue to use it as my own.

I was quite disappointed at the general appearance of things in New Bedford. The impression which I had received respecting the character and condition of the people of the north, I found to be singularly erroneous, I had very strangely supposed, while in slavery, that few of the comforts, and scarcely any of the luxuries, of life were enjoyed at the north, compared with what were enjoyed by the slaveholders of the south. I probably came to this conclusion from the fact that northern people owned no slaves. I supposed that they were about upon a level with the non-slaveholding population of the south. I knew *they* were exceedingly poor, and I had been accustomed to regard their poverty as the necessary consequence of their being non-slaveholders. I had somehow imbibed the opinion that, in the absence of slaves, there could be no wealth, and very little refinement. And upon coming to the north, I expected to meet with a rough, hard-handed, and uncultivated population, living in the most Spartan-like simplicity, knowing nothing of the ease, luxury, pomp, and grandeur of southern slaveholders. Such being my conjectures, any one acquainted with the appearance of New Bedford may very readily infer how palpably I must have seen my mistake.

In the afternoon of the day when I reached New Bedford, I visited the wharves, to take a view of the shipping. Here I found myself surrounded with the strongest proofs of wealth. Lying at the wharves, and riding in the stream, I saw many ships of the finest model, in the best order, and of the largest size. Upon the right and left, I was walled in by granite warehouses of the widest dimensions, stowed to their utmost capacity with the necessaries and comforts of life. Added to this, almost every body seemed to be at work, but noiselessly so, compared with what I had been accustomed to in Baltimore. There were no loud songs heard from those engaged in loading and unloading ships. I heard no deep oaths or horrid curses on the laborer. I saw no whipping of men; but all seemed to go smoothly on. Every man appeared to understand his work, and went at it with a sober, yet cheerful earnestness, which betokened the deep interest which he felt in what he was doing, as well as a sense of his own dignity as a man. To me this looked exceedingly strange. From the wharves I strolled around and over the town, gazing with wonder and admiration at the splendid churches, beautiful dwellings, and finely-cultivated gardens; evincing an amount of wealth, comfort, taste, and refinement, such as I had never seen in any part of slaveholding Maryland.

Every thing looked clean, new, and beautiful. I saw few or no dilapidated houses, with poverty-stricken inmates; no half-naked children and barefooted women, such as I had been accustomed to see in Hillsborough, Easton, St. Michael's, and Baltimore. The people looked more able, stronger, healthier, and happier, than those of Maryland. I was for once made glad by a view of extreme wealth, without being saddened by seeing extreme poverty. But the most astonishing as well as the most interesting thing to me was the condition of the colored people, a great many of whom, like myself, had escaped thither as a refuge from the hunters of men. I found many, who had not been seven years out of their chains, living in finer houses, and evidently enjoying more of the comforts of life, than the average of slaveholders in Maryland. I will venture to assert that my friend Mr. Nathan Johnson (of whom I can say with a grateful heart, "I was hungry, and he gave me meat; I was thirsty, and he gave me drink; I was a stranger, and he took me in") lived in a neater house; dined at a better table; took, paid for, and read, more newspapers; better understood the moral, religious, and political character of the nation,—than nine tenths of the slaveholders in Talbot county, Maryland. Yet Mr. Johnson was a working man. His hands were hardened by toil, and not his alone, but those also of Mrs. Johnson. I found the colored people much more spirited than I had supposed they would be. I found among them a determination to protect each other from the blood-thirsty kidnapper, at all hazards. Soon after my arrival, I was told of a circumstance which illustrated their spirit. A colored man and a fugitive slave were on unfriendly terms. The former was heard to threaten the latter with informing his master of his whereabouts. Straightway a meeting was called among the colored people, under the stereotyped notice, "Business of importance!" The betrayer was invited to attend. The people came at the appointed hour, and organized the meeting by appointing a very religious old gentleman as president, who, I believe, made a prayer, after which he addressed the meeting as follows: "*Friends, we have got him here, and I would recommend that you young men just take him outside the door, and kill him!*" With this, a number of them bolted at him; but they were intercepted by some more timid than themselves, and the betrayer escaped their vengeance, and has not been seen in New Bedford since. I believe there have been no more such threats, and should there be hereafter, I doubt not that death would be the consequence.

I found employment, the third day after my arrival, in stowing a sloop with a load of oil. It was new, dirty, and hard work for me; but I went at it with a glad heart and a willing hand. I was now my own master. It was a happy moment, the rapture of which can be understood only by those who have been slaves. It was the first work, the reward of which was to be entirely my own. There was no Master Hugh standing ready, the moment I earned the money, to rob me of it. I worked that day with a pleasure I had never before experienced. I was at work for myself and newly-married wife. It was to me the starting-point of a new existence. When I got through with that job, I went in pursuit of a job of calking; but such was the strength of prejudice against color, among the white calkers, that they refused to work with me, and of course I could get no employment.* Finding my trade of no immediate benefit, I threw off my calking habiliments, and prepared myself to do any kind of work I could get to do. Mr. Johnson kindly let me have his wood-horse and saw, and I very soon found myself a plenty of work. There was no work too hard—none too dirty. I was ready to saw wood, shovel coal, carry the hod, sweep the chimney, or roll oil casks,—all of which I did for nearly three years in New Bedford, before I became known to the anti-slavery world.

* I am told that colored persons can now get employment at calking in New Bedford—a result of anti-slavery effort.

In about four months after I went to New Bedford, there came a young man to me, and inquired if I did not wish to take the "Liberator." I told him I did; but, just having made my escape from slavery, I remarked that I was unable to pay for it then. I, however, finally became a subscriber to it. The paper came, and I read it from week to week with such feelings as it would be quite idle for me to attempt to describe. The paper became my meat and my drink. My soul was set all on fire. Its sympathy for my brethren in bonds—its scathing denunciations of slaveholders—its faithful exposures of slavery—and its powerful attacks upon the upholders of the institution—sent a thrill of joy through my soul, such as I had never felt before!

I had not long been a reader of the "Liberator," before I got a pretty correct idea of the principles, measures and spirit of the anti-slavery reform. I took right hold of the cause. I could do but little; but what I could, I did with a joyful heart, and never felt happier than when in an anti-slavery meeting. I seldom had much to say at the meetings, because what I wanted to say was said so much better by others. But, while attending an anti-slavery convention at Nantucket, on the 11th of August, 1841, I felt strongly moved to speak, and was at the same time much urged to do so by Mr. William C. Coffin, a gentleman who had heard me speak in the colored people's meeting at New Bedford. It was a severe cross, and I took it up reluctantly. The truth was, I felt myself a slave, and the idea of speaking to white people weighed me down. I spoke but a few moments, when I felt a degree of freedom, and said what I desired with considerable ease. From that time until now, I have been engaged in pleading the cause of my brethren—with what success, and with what devotion, I leave those acquainted with my labors to decide.

# Appendix

I find, since reading over the foregoing Narrative that I have, in several instances, spoken in such a tone and manner, respecting religion, as may possibly lead those unacquainted with my religious views to suppose me an opponent of all religion. To remove the liability of such misapprehension, I deem it proper to append the following brief explanation. What I have said respecting and against religion, I mean strictly to apply to the *slaveholding religion* of this land, and with no possible reference to Christianity proper; for, between the Christianity of this land, and the Christianity of Christ, I recognize the widest, possible difference—so wide, that to receive the one as good, pure, and holy, is of necessity to reject the other as bad, corrupt, and wicked. To be the friend of the one, is of necessity to be the enemy of the other. I love the pure, peaceable, and impartial Christianity of Christ: I therefore hate the corrupt, slaveholding, women-whipping, cradle-plundering, partial and hypocritical Christianity of this land. Indeed, I can see no reason, but the most deceitful one, for calling the religion of this land Christianity. I look upon it as the climax of all misnomers, the boldest of all frauds, and the grossest of all libels. Never was there a clearer case of "stealing the livery of the court of heaven to serve the devil in." I am filled with unutterable loathing when I contemplate the religious pomp and show, together with the horrible inconsistencies, which every where surround me. We have men-stealers for ministers, women-whippers for missionaries, and cradle-plunderers for church members. The man who wields the blood-clotted cowskin during the week fills the pulpit on Sunday, and claims to be a minister of the meek and lowly Jesus. The man who robs me of my earnings at the end of each week meets me as a class-leader on Sunday morning, to show me the way of life, and the path of salvation. He who sells my sister, for purposes of prostitution, stands forth as the pious advocate of purity. He who proclaims it a religious duty to read the Bible denies me the right of learning to read the name of the God who made me. He who is the religious advocate of marriage robs whole millions of its sacred influence, and leaves them to the ravages of wholesale pollution. The warm defender of the sacredness of the family relation is the same that scatters whole families,— sundering husbands and wives, parents and children, sisters and brothers, leaving the hut vacant, and the hearth desolate. We see the thief preaching against theft, and the adulterer against adultery. We have men sold to build churches, women sold to support the gospel, and babes sold to purchase Bibles for the *poor heathen! all for the glory of God and the good of souls!* The slave auctioneer's bell and the church-going bell chime in with each other, and the bitter cries of the heart-broken slave are drowned in the religious shouts of his pious master. Revivals of religion and revivals in the slave-trade go hand in hand together. The slave prison and the church stand near each other. The clanking of fetters and the rattling of chains in the prison, and the pious psalm and solemn prayer in the church, may be heard at the same time. The dealers in the bodies and souls of men erect their stand in the presence of the pulpit, and they mutually help each other. The dealer gives his blood-stained gold to support the pulpit, and the pulpit, in return, covers his infernal business with the garb of Christianity. Here we have religion and robbery the allies of each other—devils dressed in angels' robes, and hell presenting the semblance of paradise.

"Just God! and these are they,
Who minister at thine altar, God of right!
Men who their hands, with prayer and blessing, lay
On Israel's ark of light.

"What! preach, and kidnap men?
Give thanks, and rob thy own afflicted poor?
alk of thy glorious liberty, and then
Bolt hard the captive's door?

"What! servants of thy own
Merciful Son, who came to seek and save
The homeless and the outcast, fettering down
The tasked and plundered slave!

Pilate and Herod friends!
"Chief priests and rulers, as of old, combine!
Just God and holy! is that church which lends
Strength to the spoiler thine?"

The Christianity of America is a Christianity, of whose votaries it may be as truly said, as it was of the ancient scribes and Pharisees, "They bind heavy burdens, and grievous to be borne, and lay them on men's shoulders, but they themselves will not move them with one of their fingers. All their works they do for to be seen of men.—They love the uppermost rooms at feasts, and the chief seats in the synagogues, ... and to be called of men, Rabbi, Rabbi.—But woe unto you, scribes and Pharisees, hypocrites! for ye shut up the kingdom of heaven against men; for ye neither go in yourselves, neither suffer ye them that are entering to go in. Ye devour widows' houses, and for a pretence make long prayers; therefore ye shall receive the greater damnation. Ye compass sea and land to make one proselyte, and when he is made, ye make him twofold more the child of hell than yourselves.—Woe unto you, scribes and Pharisees, hypocrites! for ye pay tithe of mint, and anise, and cumin, and have omitted the weightier matters of the law, judgment, mercy, and faith; these ought ye to have done, and not to leave the other undone. Ye blind guides! which strain at a gnat, and swallow a camel. Woe unto you, scribes and Pharisees, hypocrites! for ye make clean the outside of the cup and of the platter; but within, they are full of extortion and excess.—Woe unto you, scribes and Pharisees, hypocrites! for ye are like unto whited sepulchres, which indeed appear beautiful outward, but are within full of dead men's bones, and of all uncleanness. Even so ye also outwardly appear righteous unto men, but within ye are full of hypocrisy and iniquity."

Dark and terrible as is this picture, I hold it to be strictly true of the overwhelming mass of professed Christians in America. They strain at a gnat, and swallow a camel. Could any thing be more true of our churches? They would be shocked at the proposition of fellowshipping a *sheep*-stealer; and at the same time they hug to their communion a *man*-stealer, and brand me with being an infidel, if I find fault with them for it. They attend with Pharisaical strictness to the outward forms of religion, and at the same time neglect the weightier matters of the law, judgment, mercy, and faith. They are always ready to sacrifice, but seldom to show mercy. They are they who are represented as professing to love God whom they have not seen, whilst they hate their brother whom they have seen. They love the heathen on the other side of the globe. They can pray for him, pay money to have the Bible put into his hand, and missionaries to instruct him; while they despise and totally neglect the heathen at their own doors.

Such is, very briefly, my view of the religion of this land; and to avoid any misunderstanding, growing out of the use of general terms, I mean, by the religion of this land, that which is revealed in the words, deeds, and actions, of those bodies, north and south, calling themselves Christian churches, and yet in union with slaveholders. It is against religion, as presented by these bodies, that I have felt it my duty to testify.

I conclude these remarks by copying the following portrait of the religion of the south, (which is, by communion and fellowship, the religion of the north,) which I soberly affirm is "true to the life," and without caricature or the slightest exaggeration. It is said to have been drawn, several years before the present anti-slavery agitation began, by a northern Methodist preacher, who, while residing at the south, had an opportunity to see slaveholding morals, manners, and piety, with his own eyes. "Shall I not visit for these things? saith the Lord. Shall not my soul be avenged on such a nation as this?"

# A Parody

"Come, saints and sinners, hear me tell
How pious priests whip Jack and Nell,
And women buy and children sell,
And preach all sinners down to hell,
And sing of heavenly union.

"They'll bleat and baa, dona like goats,
Gorge down black sheep, and strain at motes,
Array their backs in fine black coats,
Then seize their negroes by their throats,
And choke, for heavenly union.

"They'll church you if you sip a dram,
And damn you if you steal a lamb;
Yet rob old Tony, Doll, and Sam,
Of human rights, and bread and ham;
Kidnapper's heavenly union.

"They'll loudly talk of Christ's reward,
And bind his image with a cord,
And scold, and swing the lash abhorred,
And sell their brother in the Lord
To handcuffed heavenly union.

"They'll read and sing a sacred song,
And make a prayer both loud and long,
And teach the right and do the wrong,
Hailing the brother, sister throng,
With words of heavenly union.

"We wonder how such saints can sing,
Or praise the Lord upon the wing,
Who roar, and scold, and whip, and sting,
And to their slaves and mammon cling,
In guilty conscience union.

"They'll raise tobacco, corn, and rye,
And drive, and thieve, and cheat, and lie,
And lay up treasures in the sky,
By making switch and cowskin fly,
In hope of heavenly union.

"They'll crack old Tony on the skull,
And preach and roar like Bashan bull,
Or braying ass, of mischief full,
Then seize old Jacob by the wool,
And pull for heavenly union.

"A roaring, ranting, sleek man-thief,
Who lived on mutton, veal, and beef,
Yet never would afford relief
To needy, sable sons of grief,
Was big with heavenly union.

"'Love not the world,' the preacher said,
And winked his eye, and shook his head;
He seized on Tom, and Dick, and Ned,
Cut short their meat, and clothes, and bread,
Yet still loved heavenly union.

"Another preacher whining spoke
Of One whose heart for sinners broke:
He tied old Nanny to an oak,
And drew the blood at every stroke,
And prayed for heavenly union.

"Two others oped their iron jaws,
And waved their children-stealing paws;
There sat their children in gewgaws;
By stinting negroes' backs and maws,
They kept up heavenly union.

"All good from Jack another takes,
And entertains their flirts and rakes,
Who dress as sleek as glossy snakes,
And cram their mouths with sweetened cakes;
And this goes down for union."

Sincerely and earnestly hoping that this little book may do something toward throwing light on the American slave system, and hastening the glad day of deliverance to the millions of my brethren in bonds—faithfully relying upon the power of truth, love, and justice, for success in my humble efforts—and solemnly pledging my self anew to the sacred cause,—I subscribe myself,

FREDERICK DOUGLASS.
LYNN, *Mass.*, *April* 28, 1845.